THE ROAD TO FRANCE

MW00623587

A Travel Guide for Exploring the Battlefields of Europe

VOLUME I
BY JOHN DUNLAVEY

Volume I – France
Volume II – Belgium, Netherlands and Luxembourg
Volume III – Germany
Volume IV – Austria and Hungary
Volume V – Czech Republic, Slovakia and Poland
Volume VI – Ireland and United Kingdom
Volume VII – Mediterranean (Italy, Greece, Spain, Turkey)

Published in the United States of America
First Edition

Library of Congress Control Number: 2015901155

ISBN-13:978-09860955-0-4
ISBN-10: 0986095508

Cover Design by Anita Jovanovic
Photographs by John R. Dunlavey, except as noted
Maps by John Dunlavey, except:
Maps 19, 20, 21, 22, 23, 24, 25, 26 by Laura Allen, Migito Design
All maps edited by John R. Dunlavey

Front cover photos: L'Ossuaire de Douaumont in Verdun (center). Photo bar, left to right: Roman soldiers, courtesy of Lyon's Musées Gallo-Romans; Stained glass window, Clermont-Ferrand Cathedral; St. Joan of Arc, Paris; Kellerman Statue, Valmy; Char B1, Stonne.

Back cover photos, left to right: Tiger I, Vimoutiers; Vimy Ridge Memorial; American Cemetery, Somme; roadway in Alsace.

For
Louise O'Leary Wilson
1945–2014

"War is an ugly thing, but not the ugliest of things. The decayed and degraded state of moral and patriotic feeling which thinks that nothing is worth war is much worse."
– John Stuart Mill

TABLE OF CONTENTS

LIST OF MAPS

LIST OF PHOTOS

I. INTRODUCTION

Why did I write this book? In part, I had a somewhat self-serving purpose. Alcuin, Charlemagne's biographer, wrote, "The way to live forever is to pass on knowledge"—and we all want to live forever, right?

The real reason I researched and visited these fields and memorials was to honor soldiers, like my dad, who fought for a greater purpose far away from home. This book is a humble effort to remember their sacrifice and to keep the "history" and their honor alive. I hope this book inspires tourists, students, teachers and historians to honor these soldiers' courage and to learn from history that we must keep the peace while also having the courage to defeat evil when necessary.

The inspiration to write this book first came to me during a trip I took to Europe with my dad in 2007. We saw the locations of Operation Market Garden and the Battle of the Bulge, as well as Normandy and the Hürtgen Forest. I have always loved history, especially military history, and always enjoyed taking trips with family and friends—even when we're hungry, tired and lost! During the 2007 trip, I was fascinated by a personal tour we received from a wild Dutchman named Ron Von Rijt. Some friends of ours had put us in touch with Ron for a two-day tour of the Battle of the Hürtgen Forest and the northern section of the Battle of the Bulge. I was amazed by the terrain and the small memorials and humbled by the courage and sacrifice that manifested there. I was captivated by the fact that the Dutchman had dedicated a large portion of his life to honoring American and German soldiers. In fact, he had signed up to take care of three American graves in one of the American cemeteries in Holland, and had also built a memorial in downtown Schmidt, Germany.

While touring the Hürtgen Forest, no matter how well Ron explained the battle, I had a difficult time understanding our location relative to the overall battle movements. The experience made me reflect upon how great it would be to have a written guide that would help me better understand the Battle of Hürtgen Forest. After the trip, I started a short write-up. Then I began thinking about all the other major battles in Europe. The list kept growing! I was fortunate to have a job in Germany and was able to travel easily from there. I organized my trips so that I could see historic sites, but the highlights weren't just battlefields. I also enjoyed meeting great people, eating great food, seeing beautiful landscapes and letting myself be surprised.

Please also look for these books:

VOLUME II – Belgium, Netherlands and Luxembourg

VOLUME III – Germany

VOLUME IV – Austria and Hungary

VOLUME V – Czech Republic, Slovakia and Poland

VOLUME VI – Ireland and United Kingdom

VOLUME VII – Mediterranean (Italy, Greece, Spain, Turkey)

II. HOW TO USE THIS BOOK AND TIPS FOR TRAVEL

This book is arranged chronologically, starting with the Roman Battle of Alesia in 52 BC and concluding with the World War II Battle of Alsace. For each battle, I provide a description of related events and locations to visit, including GPS coordinates. These "Places to See" also appear on the corresponding maps. Use these to map out your trip and create your own itinerary based on your location. (You'll discover that many sites are quite close to each other.)

OVERALL EUROPE — MAP 1

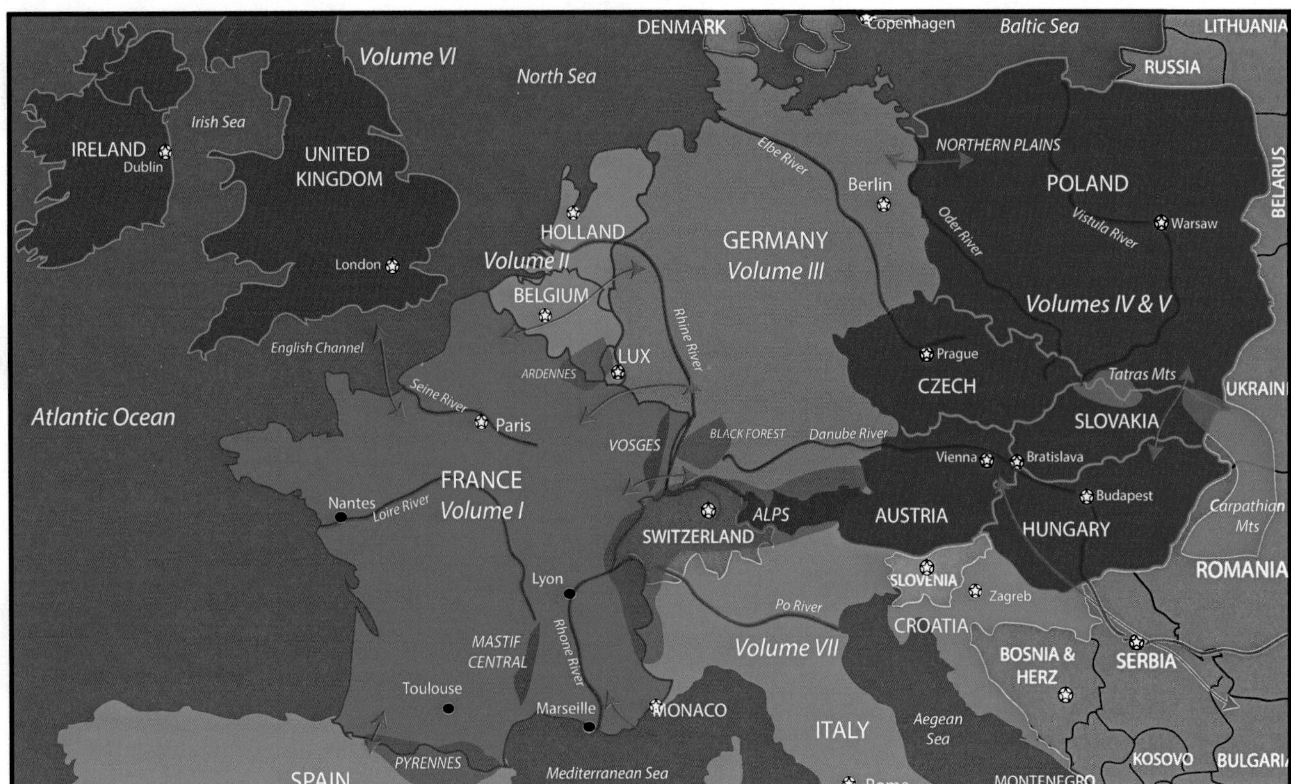

DENMARK
Copenhagen
Baltic Sea
LITHUANIA
Volume VI
North Sea
RUSSIA
Irish Sea
IRELAND
Dublin
UNITED KINGDOM
Elbe River
NORTHERN PLAINS
BELARUS
Berlin
POLAND
Oder River
Vistula River
Warsaw
HOLLAND
Volume II
GERMANY
Volume III
London
BELGIUM
Rhine River
Volumes IV & V
English Channel
LUX
Prague
ARDENNES
CZECH
Tatras Mts
Seine River
Paris
SLOVAKIA
Atlantic Ocean
VOSGES
BLACK FOREST
Danube River
Vienna
Bratislava
FRANCE
Budapest
Nantes
Loire River
Volume I
ALPS
AUSTRIA
HUNGARY
Carpathian Mts
SWITZERLAND
ROMANIA
Lyon
SLOVENIA
Zagreb
Po River
CROATIA
MASTIF CENTRAL
Rhone River
Volume VII
BOSNIA & HERZ
SERBIA
Toulouse
Marseille
MONACO
ITALY
Aegean Sea
PYRENNES
KOSOVO
SPAIN
Mediterranean Sea
Rome
MONTENEGRO

OVERALL EUROPE: The purpose of this map is to briefly highlight the significant terrain and the corresponding traditional invasion routes (shown with red arrows). My series of books are organized by country and within the countries are summaries and maps for each battle. For example, the next map, Map 2 is the Summary of France. It highlights the major battles and places to visit. Then within France are summaries of battles with a supporting map and geo coordinates of places to see related to the battle or topic.

FRANCE SUMMARY – SIGNIFICANT BATTLES AND CAMPAIGNS

MAP 2

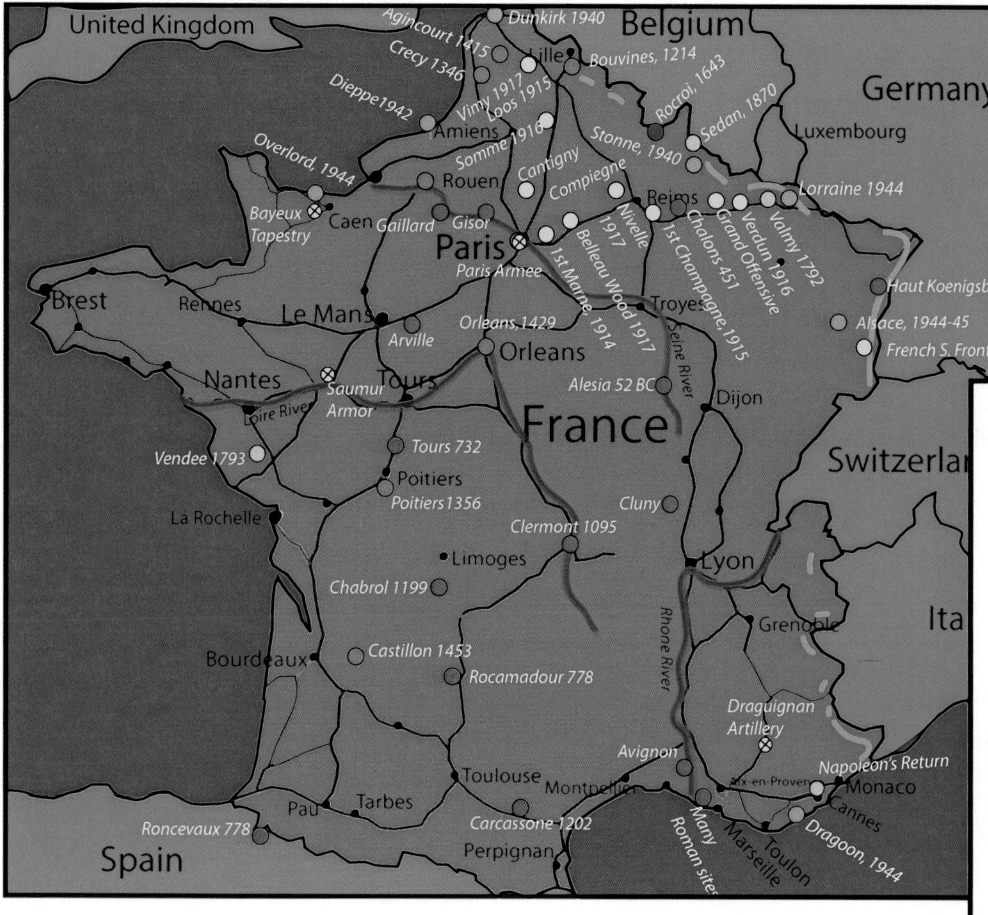
United Kingdom
Belgium
Germany
Luxembourg
Switzerland
Italy
Spain
France
Monaco
Agincourt 1415
Dunkirk 1940
Crecy 1346
Lille
Bouvines, 1214
Dieppe1942
Vimy 1917
Loos 1915
Rocroi, 1643
Sedan, 1870
Amiens
Somme 1916
Stonne, 1940
Overlord, 1944
Rouen
Cantigny
Compiegne
Reims
Lorraine 1944
Bayeux Tapestry
Caen
Gaillard
Gisor
Paris
Paris Armee
Nivelle 1917
1st Champagne,1915
Chalons 451
Grand Offensive
Verdun 1916
Valmy 1792
1st Marne, 1914
Belleau Wood 1917
Troyes
Seine River
Haut Koenigsburg
Alsace, 1944-45
French S. Front
Brest
Rennes
Le Mans
Arville
Orleans,1429
Orleans
Nantes
Saumur Armor
Tours
Loire River
Alesia 52 BC
Dijon
Vendee 1793
Tours 732
Poitiers
Poitiers1356
Cluny
La Rochelle
Clermont 1095
Limoges
Lyon
Chabrol 1199
Rhone River
Grenoble
Bourdeaux
Castillon 1453
Rocamadour 778
Draguignan Artillery
Avignon
Napoleon's Return
Toulouse
Montpelier
Aix-en-Provence
Cannes
Pau
Tarbes
Carcassone 1202
Roncevaux 778
Perpignan
Many Roman sites
Marseille
Toulon
Dragoon, 1944

This map provides the overview of the locations in France to visit. Next, drill down to the location in the book to find the summary of the battle and map. Then each summary has the geo coordinates and information on what to see in that area.

- Roman Period
- Dark Ages (Tours & Roland)
- Crusader Period
- Middle Ages & 100 Years' War
- 30 Years' War
- French Revolution, Napoleon & Franco Prussian War
- World War I
- World War II
- Maginot Line
- ⊗ Multi-Year (Museum)

KEY

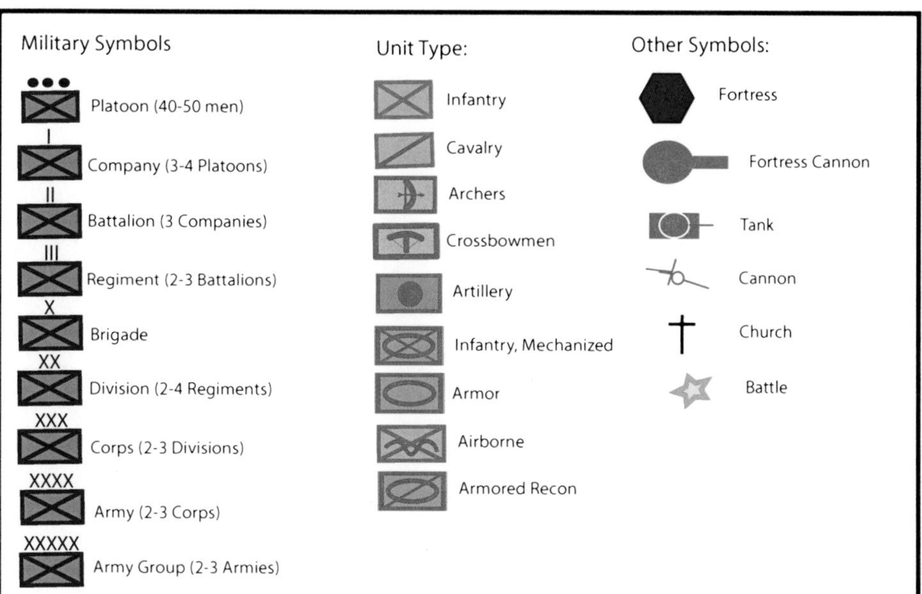
Military Symbols
Platoon (40-50 men)
Company (3-4 Platoons)
Battalion (3 Companies)
Regiment (2-3 Battalions)
Brigade
Division (2-4 Regiments)
Corps (2-3 Divisions)
Army (2-3 Corps)
Army Group (2-3 Armies)
Unit Type:
Infantry
Cavalry
Archers
Crossbowmen
Artillery
Infantry, Mechanized
Armor
Airborne
Armored Recon
Other Symbols:
Fortress
Fortress Cannon
Tank
Cannon
Church
Battle

TRAVEL TIPS

TRANSPORTATION:

ADDRESS VS. GPS COORDINATES: This book does not use addresses because, based on personal experience, I've found that addresses do not match up well. (Plus, many of the places I included might not have addresses!) For this reason, I use GPS coordinates only. The GPS coordinates and maps are based on WGS84 datum. I provide two types of coordinates:

GPS COORDINATE FORMAT

Latitude	Longitude
N 50 06.814	E 8 40.742

DECIMAL AND DEGREES FORMAT

Latitude	Longitude
50.113568	8.679037

Both are for the same location. The majority of rental car and personal GPS systems use one of these two formats.

As an added benefit, the GPS coordinates show how close many of these places are to typical tourist locations. For example, you may be in Paris at the Louvre and find that an American cemetery is just 20 minutes away, or a memorial to the last Templar Commander is only steps from Notre Dame Cathedral.

COMPASS AND MAP: Although you have a GPS, I suggest that you buy a European road map and take a compass with you. Many roads are under construction and navigation can be stressful, so a hard-copy map is very helpful. Also, having a compass when you are on the battlefield will help you pinpoint your direction.

ARRIVAL CITY: I lived in Frankfurt for three years and learned that, because of the volume of airlines arriving daily, good prices are usually available from the USA to Frankfurt. Using Frankfurt as a hub is also a good idea because you'll easily be able to drive, take the train or connect to other flights. Kayak.com is a great tool to find the best prices. (And, FYI, Lufthansa has the best service!)

AIR TRAVEL IN EUROPE: This is a great option, as flights are competitively priced in comparison to trains. However, the planes don't arrive downtown! Kayak.com is a great resource for this as well. An example for comparison: The trip from Frankfurt to Prague is eight hours by train, five hours driving, or a 45-minute flight.

NOTE ON FRANKFURT-HAHN: Surprise! This airport is two hours from Frankfurt. Yes, Ryan Air flies in and out of Hahn, which is great, but you must take a two-hour bus trip to get there at a cost of 15 euros one way. Ryan Air is a great deal, but the inconvenience can outweigh the cost savings. Typically the airports are two hours from where you really want to be, but if you are on a budget, you can get great last-minute deals.

TRAINS: I personally love taking trains, and Europe has some of the most breathtaking countryside in the world. The downside is that trains can be expensive if you don't book ahead. The Deutsche Bahn (DB) has a great website that includes an English language option. Always reserve a seat for an additional 5 euros. For France, you can book via http://en.voyages-sncf.com/en/, or for all of Europe, raileurope.com.

RENTAL CARS: Insurance is one of the most expensive aspects of renting a car. Check with your credit card company or insurance company, as they might cover rental insurance, thereby saving you a lot of money. Keep in mind that most rental cars are standard transmission. Also, in Germany many are diesel. The major rental companies are Hertz, Avis and Sixt.

SPEED LIMITS and Safety: There are cameras everywhere, especially in small towns, so take it slow. In Germany some areas of the Autobahn do not have speed limits; however, others do because of congestion and construction. In France the speed limit is 130 kilometers per hour; it's about the same in other countries. Keep in mind that you should pass only on the left and get to the right when you are done passing. Europe does not typically maintain the same standards regarding snow plows as do the United States or Canada. Also, construction areas can be very tight for passing vehicles.

FUEL: It is expensive. You will pay about 8 to 10 dollars per gallon, or 1.55 euros per liter. Fill up when you can, as you might encounter difficulty finding a fueling station in more rural parts of the country. Typically you pump your gas, then walk inside to pay; there are no credit card machines at the pumps. As a courtesy, you should park your vehicle in a designated area once you have finished fueling, then go back inside for snacks and to use the restroom.

BORDERS: There is no border control; just be sure to slow down by the empty customs booths when you cross into a different country. Beware: The French do sometimes signal cars to the side for questions.

VINENTS: These are toll stickers for your window that you must purchase to drive in Austria, the Czech Republic, Slovakia, Hungary and Poland. They typically cost about 10 euros for three to five days of driving.

TOLLS: As of 2014, the only country with tolls was France. Tolls are used for upkeep and maintenance, and are reflected in the country's nice roads and less-congested highways. You can use a credit card at toll booths only if the card has a chip inside it; otherwise, you need cash.

MONEY AND PAPERS, PLEASE:

CASH/CREDIT CARDS: Credit cards are becoming more popular in Europe, but plan on paying cash at restaurants and small bed and breakfasts (B&Bs).

ATMS: ATMs are the best way to get cash. Be sure to let your bank know that you will be traveling so that your card does not get flagged for fraud (and, consequently, your account does not get frozen). Your bank may charge you a transaction fee when you withdraw cash, but the rate will be better than that at any money exchange.

PASSPORT: You will need a passport, and hotels will ask for it.

VISAS: You will not need any visas to travel in France.

SLEEP, FOOD AND COMMUNICATION:

HOTELS AND B&BS: There are many good hotels and B&Bs, but also some bad ones. I highly recommend using Trip Advisor to find the best price range for your accommodation needs. Be sure to follow up with an email to confirm your bookings. Note that breakfast at hotels may be expensive (20 euros or so). You can opt out of this by asking the hotel or B&B to not include breakfast during your stay. In the next section, I include a list of recommended hotels and B&Bs.

FOOD AND DRINK: See the next section for information about typical French foods. Note: When tipping, you can round up. For example, if the bill is 23 euros, you can pay 25 euros. However, in theory, you should tip 8 to 10 percent.

CELL PHONES: Before your trip, contact your cell phone company to ask for international service, which might include a roaming charge (about 5 dollars per month). When making phone calls, find a place with free Wi-Fi and use a web service like Skype to call people. Buying a "throwaway" phone with cards is an option, but such phones don't always work in certain countries and the cards run out quickly. Therefore, I suggest that you use your own phone.

INTERNET: Many pubs, coffee shops and chains like Starbucks and McDonalds have free Wi-Fi. Just buy a drink...I prefer a Guinness in an Irish pub with my laptop!

POWER AND PLUGS: The power in Europe is 220v 50h, as opposed to 110v 60h in the United States. Most laptops and cell phones can use either. Check your charger, which will typically say 110 to 230v and 50 to 60h. While you probably won't need a power converter, you will need a plug adapter. Europe uses a two-prong plug, which you can buy on Amazon for 3 dollars. France's outlets are a little different from those in the rest of Europe, but the illustrated adapter will work there as well.

TRANSPORTATION AND REFERENCES

The following are photos in reference to the travel guidance.

Left to Right: A main highway in France, typically well maintained and top speeds of 130 KPH. Middle photo is an example of the tight construction on highways, this example is from Germany. Far right, Europe does not always have the same response or kind of snow plows that we are used to in America, prepare and plan accordingly.

CE-336-SV
Eaux et Forets
CHEMIN PRIVÉ

An example of a toll booth in southern France, be ready to use some change or cash. The US credit cards do not always work because we do not have a chip in our cards. The middle photo, a good reminder that throughout Europe theft is an issue and something you want to always take precautions for. And apparently there are some dangerous squirrels in Europe too!

The Iron Harvest: Around World War I battlefields the farmers continue to plow up shells and remains from World War I. Be careful and respectful if you venture near fields. This shell was next to a Loos Memorial.

Power and Plugs: The photos to the left are examples of the standard Europe Continent format. The above photo is an example of the simple adapter you can buy for $3 on Amazon.

III. FOOD, DRINK AND PLACES TO STAY

Some of my favorite things to do in Europe are eat, drink and sleep! Following is brief information about available food, as well as suggestions on where to stay. If you are driving, I recommend that you research parking in advance, as spots can be scarce in some places. As a general rule, avoid hotels near train stations, as such neighborhoods are usually questionable.

PLACES TO STAY:

Following is a list of places to stay in cities and strategic locations throughout France. The pricing in Europe varies considerably depending on the time of year. I suggest that you verify prices and further investigate these recommendations on websites such as Trip Advisor or Booking.com. The numbers correspond to Map 2b ("Places to Stay in France").

1. **BRITTANY, MONT SAINT-MICHEL:** Auberge Saint-Pierre. This hotel is located on the Mont Saint-Michel rock. The hotel parking is in a separate location. Please visit the website to ensure that you will be comfortable parking and walking to the hotel.
   www.auberge-saint-pierre.fr/uk/index.php

   Grande Rue, 50170 Le Mont Saint-Michel
   Tel: +33 2 33 60 14 03
   Coordinates: N 48 38.177 W 1 30.601 (48.636283, -1.510017)

2. **BRITTANY, PONTORSON:** Hotel Montgomery Best Western. Pontorson was a key objective of General George S. Patton's Third Army as it assembled in Brittany in 1944. The town is directly south of Mont Saint-Michel, 40 km east of St. Malo and 20 km west of Avranches.
   www.hotel-montgomery.com/en.php

   13 Rue Couesnon, Pontorson
   Tel: +33 2 33 60 00 09
   Coordinates: N 48 33.177 W 1 30.685 (48.552948, -1.511412)

FOOD AND DRINK

As I write this I am starving and very thirsty. Left to Right: Beef Carpaccio, fries and a beer for lunch near St. Raphael. Next photo, I was taking a break with a beautiful view of the Roman Aqueduct, Pont du Gard. Finally, always a good and cheap meal, the kabab.

In southwest France a typical dish is the Cassoulet, a hearty white bean, duck and sausage stew, gets even better with red wine and fresh bread. Center photo I was sitting admiring the Chartres Cathedral and had an excellent French Onion Soup, fresh bread and a crisp cold coca cola. Oh man! The photo right, fresh mussels, fries and beer in Normandy, sooo good.

While I was in Arles, for one of my meals I resorted to the traditional French menu. First an appetizer of pate, toast, jam and salad and the house red wine. It was served with fresh bread and bottle of tap water, which in most countries they do not provide you water and bread for free, France does. For my main dish I chose the steak and fries, always a good choice. Finishing a meal with an espresso is always helpful to get you to the next site or enough energy to get you back to your room!

While traveling in Europe and on a budget, I highly recommend getting lunch or snacks at a local grocery store. It is especially helpful on a day you are driving to another location. I typically would buy a fresh baguette, some salami, fresh cheese, bag of chips, some bottles of water and something sweet. In total you can spend about 20 euros to cover 4 people for lunch.

3. **PORT-EN-BESSIN:** Hotel Mecure, Omaha Beach. This hotel and restaurant is located on a cul-de-sac on the shore overlooking Omaha Beach and Port-en-Bessin. It is a great location to start your exploration of Normandy and perhaps play a round of golf.
   www.hotel-omaha-beach.com/

   Chemin du Colombier, 14520 Port-en-Bessin
   Tel: +22 2 31 22 44 44
   Coordinates: N 49 20.486 W 0 46.117 (49.341433, -0.768617)

4. **CAEN:** Best Western Le Dauphin. Staying in Caen is convenient for visiting the Canadian and British landing areas.
   www.best-western-le-dauphin.h-rez.com

   29 Rue Gemare, FR-14000 Caen
   Tel: 1-866-332-3590 (from U.S.)
   Coordinates: N 49 11.072 W 0 21.894 (49.184533, -0.3649)

5. **FALAISE:** Chambres d'hôtes La Villageoise. This beautiful B&B is near Trun and the epicenter of the Falaise Pocket battles.
   www.normandie-chambre-charme-lavillageoise.com/

   66 Rue de la Republique, 61160 Trun
   Tel: +33 6 79 49 49 64
   Coordinates: N 48 50.644 E 0 01.877 (48.844067, 0.031283)

6. **FALAISE:** Cottage in Les Loges Saulces. In a quiet and beautiful area of Normandy, this cottage is a great location for exploring the Falaise battles.
   www.ownersdirect.co.uk/accommodation/p8146151#location

7. **SOMME, ALBERT:** Best Western Royal Picardie. Although the hotel is located outside of Albert, it is very convenient and allows for easy exploration of all the Somme locations.
   www.royalpicardie.com/en/

   138 Avenue du Général Leclerc, 80300 Albert
   Tel: +33 3 22 75 37 00
   Coordinates: N 49 59.904 E 2 38.095 (49.9984, 2.634917)

8. **CALAIS:** Metropol Hotel. The Metropol is conveniently located near the train station and World War II museum.
   www.metropolhotel.com

   45 Quai du Rhin, Calais
   Tel: +33 3 21 97 54 00
   Coordinates: N 50 57.213 E 1 50.919 (50.953549, 1.848656)

9. **DIEPPE:** Hotel La Presidence. This hotel is on the beach, close to all the memorials and bunker remains.
www.hotel-la-presidence.com

1 Boulevard de Verdun, 76200 Dieppe
Tel: +33 2 35 84 31 31
Coordinates: N 49 55.527 E 1 04.269 (49.925446, 1.071152)

10. **ROUEN:** La Boulangerie Hotel. This hotel is a great place to stay in downtown Rouen.
www.laboulangerie.fr/

59, Rue Saint-Nicaise, 76000 Rouen
Tel: +33 6 12 94 53 15
Coordinates: N 49 26.709 E 1 06.201 (49.44515, 1.10335)

11. **ROUEN:** Ibis Rouen Champ de Mars. This nice, affordable hotel offers parking and is a 10-minute walk from the main attractions.
www.ibis.com/

12 Avenue Aristide Briand, FR-76000 Rouen
Tel: +33 2 35 08 12 11
Coordinates: N 49 26.140 E 1 06.229 (49.435667, 1.103817)

12. **SAUMUR:** La Croix de la Voulte. One of the best places I've stayed. A beautiful Château B&B with easy access to the Saumur tank museum!
www.lacroixdelavoulte.com/

476 Rue de Boumois, 49400 Saumur
Tel: +33 2 41 38 46 66
Coordinates: N 47 17.693 W 0 06.404 (47.294883, -0.106733)

13. **PARIS:** Hotel Louvre Sainte Anne. Located within walking distance of the Louvre and Opera House, this hotel is also conveniently located near a secure public parking garage.
www.paris-hotel-louvre.com/

32, Rue Sainte-Anne, 75001 Paris
Tel: +33 1 40 20 02 35
Coordinates: N 48 51.999 E 2 20.147 (48.86665, 2.335783)

14. **PARIS AIRPORT:** Charles de Gaulle Best Western Hotel. Modern, convenient and affordable. If you are flying into Paris and too tired to start your driving journey, or are just ending your road trip, this is a good place to stay for a night.
www.bestwestern-pariscdgairport.com/fr/index.php

1 Allée du Verger, 95700 Roissy-en-France

Tel: +33 1 34 29 30 00
Coordinates: N 49 00.199 E 2 31.237 (49.003317, 2.520617)

15. **CHÂTEAU THIERRY:** Champagne B&B. This B&B is a fantastic place to stay. It is owned by American expatriates who are very knowledgeable about the area and places to visit. Halfway between Paris and Reims, it is very convenient for seeing the area's World War I battle sites.
www.marneweb.com/

    1 Rue des Vaches, 02850 Reuilly-Sauvigny
    Tel: +33 6 13 24 46 16
    Coordinates: N 49 03.486 E 3 33.393 (49.0581, 3.55655)

16. **REIMS:** Maison d'hotes Les Telliers. Located in the city center near the cathedral, this B&B is affordable and convenient. However, you must coordinate parking with the hotel.
www.telliers.fr/

    18 Rue des Telliers, 51100 Reims
    Tel: +33 9 53 79 80 74
    Coordinates: N 49 15.397 E 4 01.752 (49.256617, 4.0292)

17. **REIMS:** Le Clos du Mont d'Hor. Located outside Reims, this is a beautiful place to stay among the vineyards and the champagne!
www.mhchampagne.com/en/

    8 Rue du Mont d'Hor, 51220 Saint-Thierry
    Tel: +33 3 26 03 12 42
    Coordinates: N 49 18.334 E 3 58.291 (49.305567, 3.971517)

18. **SEDAN:** Hotellerie Le Château Fort. This hotel is located inside the very impressive castle of Sedan. When you arrive at the castle, to enter the hotel you will have to drive through the main gate and park on the right.
www.Chateaufort-sedan.fr/en/

    Porte des Princes, 08200 Sedan
    Tel: +33 3 24 26 11 00
    Coordinates: N 49 42.131 E 4 56.971 (49.702183, 4.949517)

19. **VERDUN:** Hostellerie du Coq Hardi. This hotel is located in the small downtown of Verdun and is convenient for exploring the area.
www.coq-hardi.com/

    8 Avenue de la Victoire, 55100 Verdun
    Tel: +33 3 29 86 36 36
    Coordinates: N 49 09.673 E 5 23.142 (49.161216, 5.385693)

20. **METZ:** Les Chambres de l'Ile B&B. Located downtown within walking distance of the cathedral, this hotel is also close to many locations of interest.
www.bnbmetz.com/

15 Rue de l'Horticulture, 57050 Longeville-lès-Metz
Tel: +33 6 13 23 28 33
Coordinates: N 49 06.863 E 6 09.432 (49.114389, 6.157192)

21. **ZELLENBERG:** Le Schlossberg. The town of Zellenberg is a convenient location for visiting the Alsace Plain, between Colmar and Selestat. This area has many great B&Bs and hotels. Le Schlossberg is a very welcoming, quiet and clean B&B with updated amenities.
www.leschlossberg.com/en/

59a Rue Fontaine, 68340 Zellenberg
Tel: +33 3 89 47 93 85
Coordinates: N 48 10.080 E 7 19.133 (48.168, 7.318883)

22. **SAINT-DIÉ:** Hotel-Restaurant Le Regal. Located outside Saint-Dié, this hotel has an excellent restaurant, but retains a rustic atmosphere. A great spot from which to explore the Vosges Mountains.
www.leregal.fr/

189 Rue d'Épinal, 88100 Saint-Dié
Tel: +33 3 29 56 61 41
Coordinates: N 48 16.533 E 6 54.051 (48.27555, 6.90085)

23. **GÉRARDMER:** Hotel des Bains. Gérardmer is a beautiful Vosges town next to a lake with many tourist attractions and activities for summer and winter escapes. The hotel itself is beautiful, casual and traditional.
www.hotel-des-bains-gerardmer.com/

16 Boulevard Adolphe Garnier, 88400 Gérardmer
Tel: +33 3 29 63 08 19
Coordinates: N 48 04.233 E 6 52.290 (48.07055, 6.8715)

24. **VOSGES:** Lavelime du Houx Cottage. This cottage/B&B is owned by Sylvie and Herve Claudon, who provide a warm welcome to all visitors. The Claudons are avid historians who offer day tours of World War II battle sites near the Vosges Mountains, specifically those in which the 442nd Regiment and the 36th Infantry Division took part. They don't have a dedicated website at this time, but use the following website for bookings.
www.homeaway.co.uk/p593293a#map

sh-claudon-houx@wanadu.fr
Tel: +33 6 84 67 19 60
Coordinates: N 48 08.338 E 6 41.880 (48.138967, 6.698)

25. DIJON: La Cour Berbisey. Located in downtown Dijon within walking distance of shopping venues and attractions, this B&B also offers parking.
www.lacourberbisey.fr/en/

31 Rue Berbisey, 21000 Dijon
Tel: +33 3 45 83 12 38
Coordinates: N 47 19.088 E 5 02.206 (47.318126, 5.036771)

26. BEAUNE: Château de Challanges. Another of my favorite places. Beaune itself is in the center of Burgundy and is beautiful (plus it has a Sherman tank!). The Château is an excellent place to stay for its beauty, comfort and location.
www.chateaudechallanges.com/uk/index.php

Rue Templiers, 21200 Beaune
Tel: +33 3 80 26 32 62
Coordinates: N 47 00.487 E 4 52.047 (47.008125, 4.867458)

27. LYON: Mercure Lyon La Part Dieu. Locations in the Mercure chain vary in terms of quality; however, this particular hotel is excellent for its location and comfort.
www.hotel-mercure-lyon.com/

50 Rue de la Villette, 69003 Lyon
Tel: +33 4 72 68 25 20
Coordinates: N 45 45.582 E 4 51.692 (45.7597, 4.861533)

28. GRENOBLE: Splendid Hotel. A great location in downtown Grenoble, with parking!
http://www.splendid-hotel.com/en/

22 Rue Thiers, 38000 Grenoble
Tel: +33 4 76 46 33 12
Coordinates: N 45 11.212 E 5 43.252 (45.186866, 5.720862)

29. MONTELIMAR/MIRMANDE: Le Capital. Set in the small and beautiful village of Mirmande, this hotel sits on one of the town's highest points.
www.lacapitelle.com/en.html

Le Rempart, 26270 Mirmande
Tel: +33 4 75 63 02 72
Coordinates: N 44 41.957 E 4 50.147 (44.699283, 4.835783)

30. ARLES: Hotel Du Musée. Arles is a scenic waterside community that Van Gogh captured in many of his paintings. Once a Roman town, it has retained its charm and beauty.
www.hoteldumusee.com/

11 Rue du Grand Prieuré, 13200 Arles
Tel: +33 4 90 93 88 88
Coordinates: N 43 40.748 E 4 37.65 (43.679133, 4.6275)

31. AIX EN PROVENCE: Hotel de L'Arbois Best Western. This hotel is not in downtown Aix, but is very modern and conveniently located.
www.bestwestern.fr

97 Rue du Docteur Albert Aynaud, 13100 Aix-en-Provence
Tel: +33 4 42 58 59 60
Coordinates: N 43 29.401 E 5 21.112 (43.490017, 5.351867)

32. NICE: Hotel Massena. Located in the center of Nice, this is a modern and convenient hotel.
www.hotel-massena-nice.com/

58 Rue Gioffredo, 06000 Nice
Tel: +33 4 92 47 88 88
Coordinates: N 43 41.915 E 7 16.259 (43.698583, 7.270983)

33. SAINT-RAPHAËL: Hotel du Soleil. This is a fantastic place to stay in Saint-Raphaël and along the Riviera. Ask to borrow a bike! The water is only a 15-minute walk or a 5-minute bike ride away.
www.hotel-dusoleil.com/

47 Boulevard Domaine du Soleil, 83700 Saint-Raphaël
Tel: +33 4 94 83 10 00
Coordinates: N 43 25.300 E 6 46.945 (43.421667, 6.782417)

34. CARCASSONNE: La Posada del Castillo. Located within walking distance of the walled fortress town of Carcassonne, this hotel is a wonderful place to stay.
www.laposadadelcastillo.com/

60 Rue de la Barbacane, 11000 Carcassonne
Tel: +33 4 68 71 65 50
Coordinates: N 43 12.411 E 2 21.672 (43.20685, 2.3612)

35. **LOURDES:** Domaine de Merete. Just outside of Lourdes and convenient for visiting the Pyrenees.
http://www.domaine-de-merete.com/

28 Avenue Jean Prat, 65100 Lourdes
Tel: +33 6 89 44 13 75
Coordinates: N 43 06.591 W 0 04.086 (43.109850, -0.068107)

36. **ROCAMADOUR:** Le Troubadour. Located just outside Rocamadour, Le Troubadour is a pleasant and quiet countryside hotel with modern amenities.
http://www.hotel-troubadour.com/

Belveyre, 46500 Rocamadour
Tel: +33 5 65 33 70 27
Coordinates: N 44 48.738 E 1 37.942 (44.812295, 1.632364)

37. **LIMOGES:** Domaine de Faugeras. Originally a 1700s château, this hotel is just outside of Limoges, which is a good stopping point between Lyon and Bordeaux or Poitiers.
http://www.castelfaugeras.fr/

Allée de Faugeras, 87100 Limoges
Tel: +33 5 55 34 66 22
Coordinates: N 45 51.145 E 1 17.353 (45.852421, 1.289218)

38. **BORDEAUX:** La Maison du Lierre. In a great location in Bordeaux, La Maison du Lierre is small, convenient and affordable.
http://www.hotel-maisondulierre-bordeaux.com/

57 Rue Huguerie, 33000 Bordeaux
Tel: +33 5 56 51 92 71
Coordinates: N 44 50.666 W 0 34.865 (44.844431, -0.581077)

39. **39. COGNAC:** Château de L'Yeuse. Located north of Bordeaux and outside Cognac in a quiet and beautiful setting.
www.yeuse.fr

65 Rue de Bellevue, 16100 Cognac
Tel: +33 5 45 36 82 60
Coordinates: N 45 41.212 W 0 17.414 (45.686873, -0.290231)

40. **POITIERS:** Les Cours du Clain. This B&B is located just south of the city center, among quiet and serene fields.
www.lescoursduclain-poitiers.com/

117 Chemin de la Grotte Calvin, 86000 Poitiers
Tel: +33 6 10 16 09 55
Coordinates: N 46 33.761 E 0 19.360 (46.562690, 0.322660)

41. **ORLÉANS:** Hôtel de L'Abeille. Located within the old city limits, this affordable hotel is a great jumping-off point for exploring Orléans.
http://www.hoteldelabeille.com/

64 Rue d'Alsace Lorraine, 45000 Orléans
Tel: +33 2 38 53 54 87
Coordinates: N 47 54.338 E 1 54.304 (47.905639, 1.905067)

PLACES TO STAY

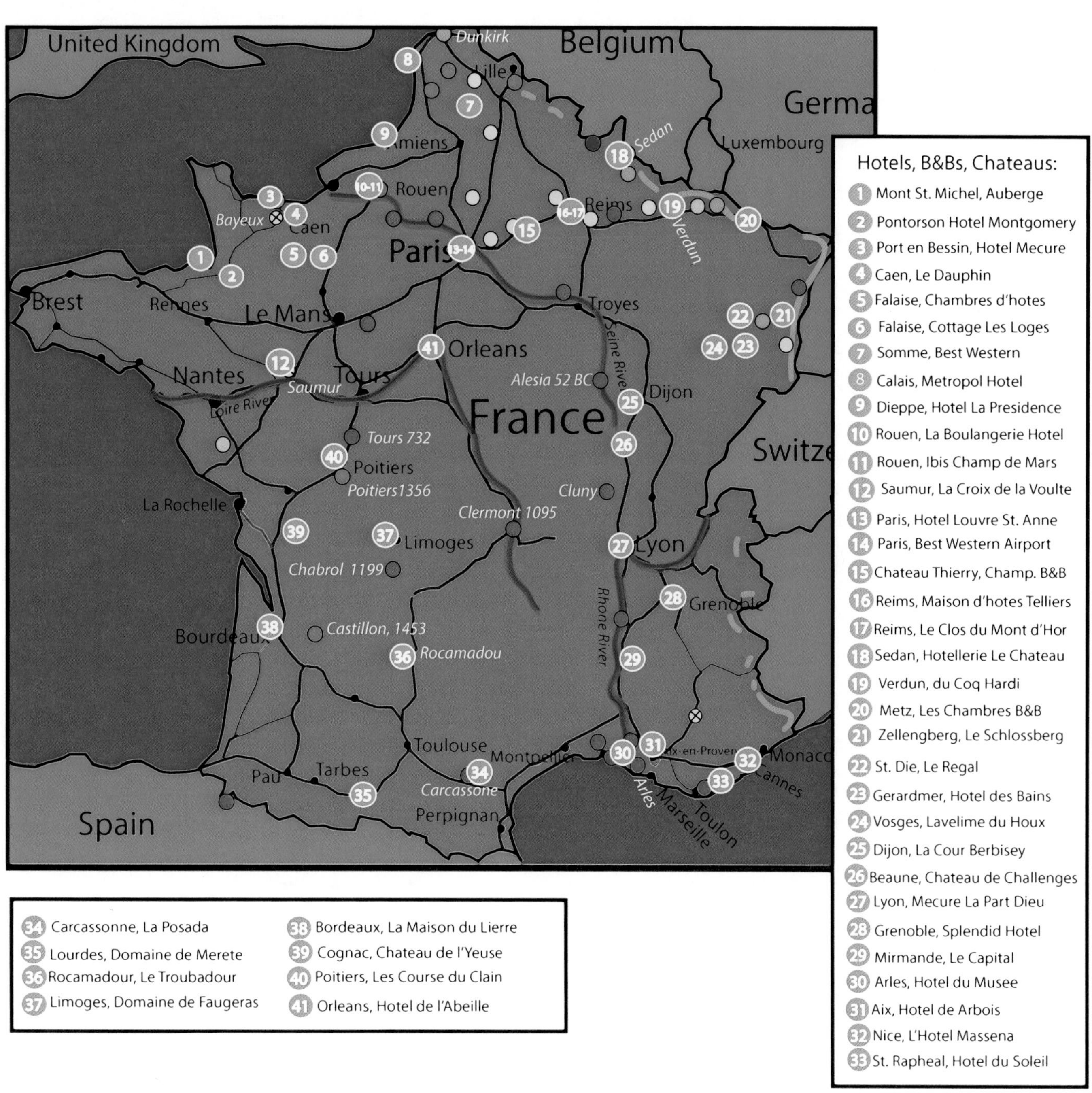
United Kingdom
Belgium
Germa
Luxembourg
Dunkirk
Lille
Amiens
Sedan
Rouen
Bayeux
Caen
Reims
Verdun
Paris
Brest
Rennes
Le Mans
Troyes
Orleans
Nantes
Saumur
Tours
Loire River
Seine River
Alesia 52 BC
Dijon
France
Switz
Tours 732
Poitiers
Poitiers1356
Cluny
La Rochelle
Clermont 1095
Limoges
Lyon
Chabrol 1199
Rhone River
Grenoble
Bourdeaux
Castillon, 1453
Rocamadou
Toulouse
Montpellier
Aix-en-Proven
Monaco
Cannes
Pau
Tarbes
Carcassone
Perpignan
Arles
Marseille
Toulon
Spain
Hotels, B&Bs, Chateaus:
1 Mont St. Michel, Auberge
2 Pontorson Hotel Montgomery
3 Port en Bessin, Hotel Mecure
4 Caen, Le Dauphin
5 Falaise, Chambres d'hotes
6 Falaise, Cottage Les Loges
7 Somme, Best Western
8 Calais, Metropol Hotel
9 Dieppe, Hotel La Presidence
10 Rouen, La Boulangerie Hotel
11 Rouen, Ibis Champ de Mars
12 Saumur, La Croix de la Voulte
13 Paris, Hotel Louvre St. Anne
14 Paris, Best Western Airport
15 Chateau Thierry, Champ. B&B
16 Reims, Maison d'hotes Telliers
17 Reims, Le Clos du Mont d'Hor
18 Sedan, Hotellerie Le Chateau
19 Verdun, du Coq Hardi
20 Metz, Les Chambres B&B
21 Zellengberg, Le Schlossberg
22 St. Die, Le Regal
23 Gerardmer, Hotel des Bains
24 Vosges, Lavelime du Houx
25 Dijon, La Cour Berbisey
26 Beaune, Chateau de Challenges
27 Lyon, Mecure La Part Dieu
28 Grenoble, Splendid Hotel
29 Mirmande, Le Capital
30 Arles, Hotel du Musee
31 Aix, Hotel de Arbois
32 Nice, L'Hotel Massena
33 St. Rapheal, Hotel du Soleil
34 Carcassonne, La Posada
35 Lourdes, Domaine de Merete
36 Rocamadour, Le Troubadour
37 Limoges, Domaine de Faugeras
38 Bordeaux, La Maison du Lierre
39 Cognac, Chateau de l'Yeuse
40 Poitiers, Les Course du Clain
41 Orleans, Hotel de l'Abeille

—Chapter 1—

THE ROMAN PERIOD, 52 BC–476 AD

This chapter highlights the Roman influence in France, beginning with the conclusive Battle of Alesia, where Julius Caesar conquered the Gauls.

BATTLE OF ALESIA

September 52 BC

"Veni, Vidi, Vici."
– Julius Caesar

SUMMARY: The Battle of Alesia was the last great Roman-Gallic battle; during this encounter, the Romans defeated the Gauls. In 52 BC, after 10 years of Roman occupation, the Gallic tribes revolted and killed all the Romans in what is now Orléans. Upon hearing the news, Julius Caesar left his winter camp in Southern Gaul to crush the insurgency. The uprising was led by the recently elected king of the Gauls, Vercingetorix from the Averni tribe, who united the Gauls in an attempt to free Gaul (France) from Roman occupation. However, shortly after the revolt, Julius Caesar arrived and besieged Vercingetorix at Gergovia, where Vercingetorix had taken refuge. As the siege progressed, Caesar's vulnerable supply lines came under attack. Fearing a trap, Caesar retreated, marking his first defeat in battle.

CAESAR returned to his main base and winter quarters to prepare for the next campaign. To bolster his forces, he hired German horsemen as his cavalry, a decision that fostered greater mobility, better scouting and the ability to protect supply lines if he was forced to conduct another siege. As the next campaign began in the summer of 52 BC, Vercingetorix and his force of 80,000 men moved to one of the Gallic hill forts, Alesia, to regroup after being harassed and chased by the Romans. In an incredible engineering feat, Caesar built a 16-kilometer wall and ditch around the fort, trapping the Gauls inside. The Romans then built another ring to defend against any Gallic relieving forces. Amazingly, the "double siege ring" was built in approximately three to four weeks, amid constant harassment from the Gauls.

As supplies ran low, some of the Gallic cavalry broke out of the ring and left to rally a relief force. Within a few days, 100,000 Gauls arrived to attack the Romans from outside the fort while the 80,000 trapped Gauls attacked from inside. After five days of fierce battle, the Gauls surrendered, with tragic losses. Although the Gauls greatly outnumbered the Romans, their ill-equipped forces were no match for the disciplined and well-armed Roman soldiers. It is said that Vercingetorix rode out his horse to Caesar and surrendered himself. He was then chained and taken to Rome for parade. The remaining rebel Gauls were either enslaved or executed.

OUTCOME: Julius Caesar defeated the Gauls in what would become the last great Gallic battle. As a result, what we know as France today became a Roman republic for the next 500 years. After the battle, Caesar returned to Rome, with Vercingetorix in chains, for his triumvirate procession (in other words, a 20-day party). Eight years later, on the "Ides of March" in 44 BC, Caesar was assassinated, an act that sparked a civil war in the Roman Empire.

WHAT WAS IT ABOUT? The Gauls were fighting for freedom from Roman rule, which included taxation and enslavement.

WHO? 80,000 Gauls under the command of Vercingetorix were besieged in Alesia. Outside the area was a relief force of approximately 100,000 men. The Romans, under the command of Caesar, numbered 60,000. In the end, the Gauls suffered 50,000 casualties; the Romans suffered 12,000.

WHEN? September 52 BC (some documents suggest August)

WHY AT ALESIA? Vercingetorix was on the run from the Roman legions and Germanic mercenaries. Alesia was chosen because it was a strong fort for the Gauls and a good spot to regroup shortly before winter. Caesar recognized his opportunity to starve the warriors into submission.

TECHNOLOGY/TACTICS: The Romans built a massive ring fort around Alesia and a second ring fort around themselves for protection from outside relief efforts. The ring fort contained several defenses: a field of "stimuli," or wood blocks with iron hooks; covered pits filled with fire-hardened stakes called "lilies"; two trenches bristling with sharpened wooden stakes called "grave stones"; and a palisade with towers. Incredibly, the Romans built all of these defenses within a month. Tactically, Caesar was able to forge an alliance with Germanic tribes that would benefit from the Gallic defeat. In addition, the Germanic tribes provided Caesar's forces with much-needed cavalry to provide reconnaissance efforts and protect supply lines and flanks. Although Vercingetorix's forces outnumbered the Romans, the Romans were successful due to their superior discipline, training and materiel. The Romans could line up in strong formations, protected by their shields, armor and helmets, and had well-made spears and swords. The Gauls had large numbers, but essentially no armor. They also had weak weapons and possibly some captured materiel. However, the Gallic warriors were recognized for their fierce courage in battle.

QUOTES: "Vercingetorix, after putting on his most beautiful armor and decorating his horse, rode out through the gates. Caesar was sitting down and Vercingetorix, after riding round him in a circle, leaped down from his horse, stripped off his armor and sat at Caesar's feet silent and motionless, until he was taken away under arrest to be kept in custody for the triumph." – Plutarch

"Cry 'Havoc!' and let slip the dogs of war." – William Shakespeare, Julius Caesar

"Veni, Vidi, Vici." ("I came, I saw, I conquered.") – Julius Caesar

PLACES TO SEE (REFERENCE MAP 3):

1. **STATUE OF VERCINGETORIX:** Located at what is believed to be the top of the mound where the Gauls lay under siege is a large statue of Vercingetorix built by Napoleon III. (Some believe the statue looks a lot like Napoleon III, albeit with long hair and a beard!)
   N 47 32.329 E 4 29.530 (47.538817, 4.492167)

2. **MUSÉE ALESIA:** Just up the road from the statue is a small but excellent museum with original artifacts, Roman ruins and an explanation of the battle.
   N 47 32.332 E 4 29.923 (47.538867, 4.498717)

3. **MUSÉE PARC ALÉSIA:** An outstanding new museum and park dedicated to the battle, the Musée Parc Alésia includes reproductions of the Romans' defensive fortifications. (Very impressive!) It is located just outside of town.
   N 47 32.169 E 4 28.133 (47.53615, 4.468883)

BATTLE OF ALESIA SEPTEMBER 52 B.C.

MAP 3

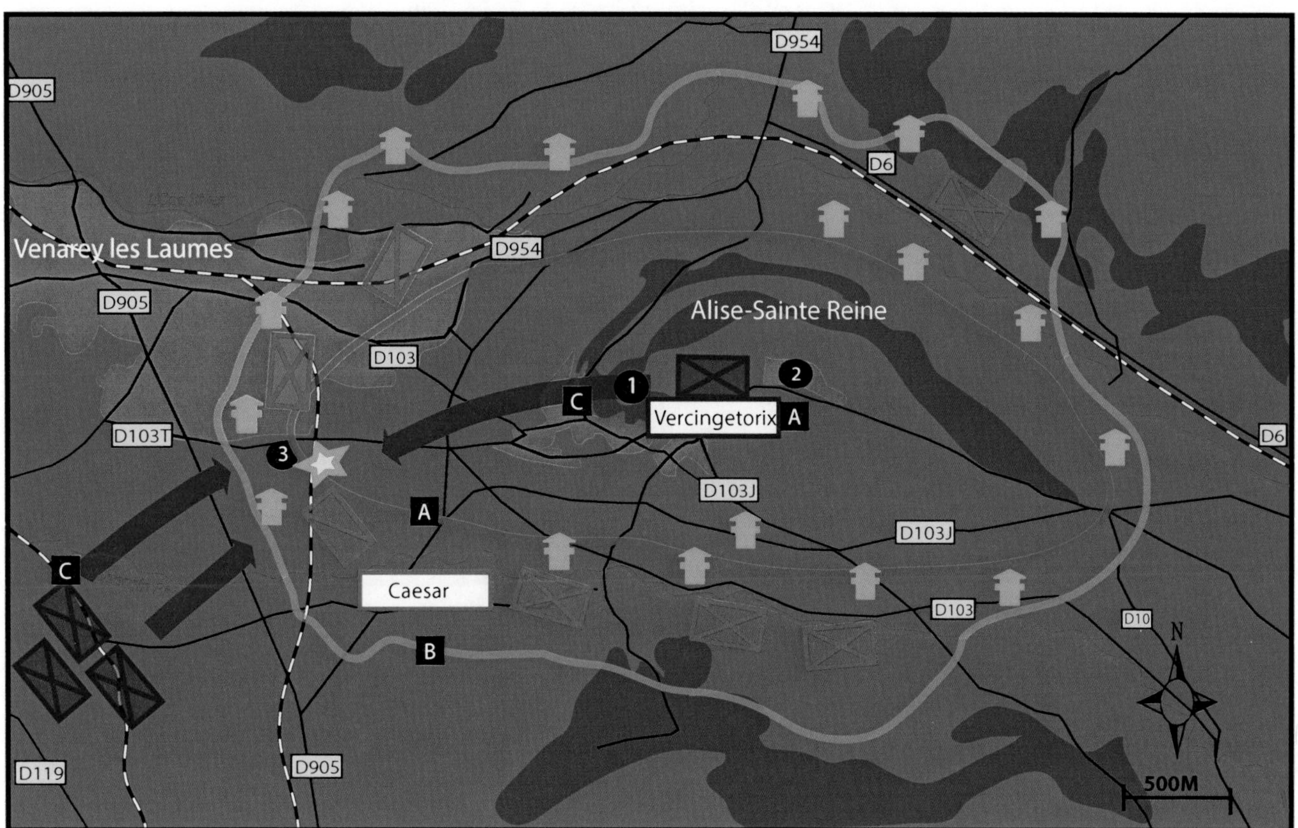
D905
D954
D6
Venarey les Laumes
D905
D954
Alise-Sainte Reine
D103
1
2
C
Vercingetorix
A
D103T
3
D103J
A
D103J
C
Caesar
D103
D10
B
N
D119
D905
D6
500M

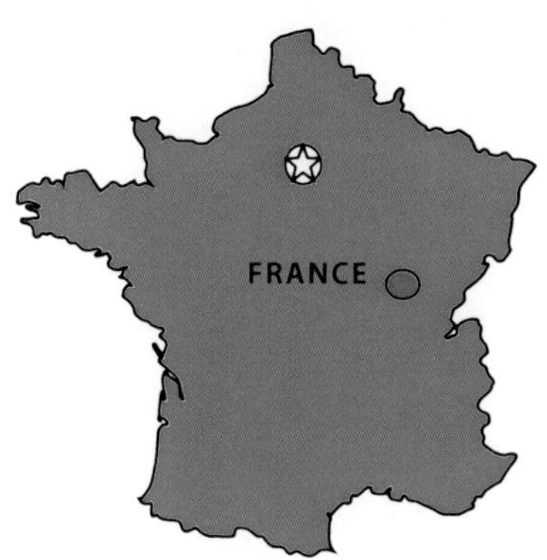
FRANCE

Movements:
A. In early September, Vercingetorix and some of his men retreated into the hill fort of Alesia. Within a week the Romans surrounded him and built a siege wall to trap them.
B. Romans built the 2nd wall toprotect themselves against the rebel forces on the outside.
C. The besieged forces attacked in unison with some 100,000 forces from the outside but were defeated. Soon after Vercingetorix surrendered.

Places to See:
1 Vercingetorix Statue
2 Museum Alesia
3 Alesia Museum and Park

Outerwall (Circumvallation)
Inner wall (Contravallation)
Towers built by Romans

BATTLE OF CHALONS SUR MARNE

September 20, 451 AD

"The Scourge of God"

SUMMARY: The years 434 AD through 451 AD were a rough time for Europe, as Attila the Hun rampaged throughout the continent with a horde of warriors. After turning away from the gates of Constantinople because the Eastern Roman Emperor had paid him off, Attila allegedly received a letter from the Western Emperor's sister, Honoria, asking him to save her because she had had an affair with a servant. Attila used this as an excuse to stage a major offensive. He wanted to obtain Honoria for his wife and the Western Roman Empire as his dowry.

Attila began by attacking Germania and Gaul before working his way down to Rome. In 451 AD, with an army of 300,000, he destroyed Metz, Reims, Koln, Worms and Trier. Luckily, the city of Paris was saved by Genevieve (later St. Genevieve), an extraordinary 30-year-old who addressed the women of Paris thusly: "Let the men flee if they want to, if they are incapable of fighting. We women will pray so hard that God will surely hear our prayers!" The prayers worked and Attila did not attack. Unfortunately for Orléans, Attila stopped there next. In response, the Bishop of Orléans notified Flavius Aetius, the Roman commander, and helped negotiate a pact with King Theodoric I of the Visigoths to align forces that would meet Attila. The fact that King Theodoric I came to the aid of the Romans was ironic, as he was the son of the Visigoth King Aleric, who, 40 years earlier, in 410 AD, had sacked Rome.

At first contact, Flavius and Theodoric disrupted Attila from his siege of Orléans. Upon seeing that his forces were in danger, Attila withdrew east toward Metz to the Cataluanian Plains outside Reims, which was ideal terrain for his horsemen. There, the two armies faced each other. The allies faced east with the Romans on the left flank. The Alans—indigenous to the Caucasus Mountains and whose allegiance was suspect—were in the middle, while the Visigoths, with their cavalry and foot soldiers, were on the right flank. The Huns faced west, with their allies, the Vandals and Ostrogoths, on their flanks. At the start of the battle, the Romans moved to the high ground of a sloped hill, which made the Huns turn their flank slightly. Then the Visigoths saw an opportunity and attacked the Huns' left flank. During the attack, the Visigoth King Theodoric was killed by a spear. However, instead of dispersing, his soldiers rallied under Theodoric's son. At the same moment, the Alans in the middle held up against the Huns' main attack. Seeing that the battle was lost, Attila retreated to his wagon train, where he set up a perimeter of defense. Assuming the worst and wanting to avoid being taken alive, Attila prepared a funeral pyre with all of his treasure, horse saddles and wives ready to burn. However, the Romans and Visigoths did not make a strong attempt to finish the battle. As a result, Attila and his remaining army withdrew the next day and crossed back over the Rhine River, never to return. It is thought that Flavius neglected to pursue Attila so that Flavius could avoid either a possible loss or great victory. Either result could have made his allies, the Visigoths, too powerful. As the historian Edward Gibbon stated, Attila's "retreat across the Rhine confessed the last victory which was achieved in the name of the Western Roman Empire."

OUTCOME: Attila had been prevented from conquering Western Europe, but in 452 he attacked Italy, causing town after town to fall. Attila reached the Mincio River, just north of Rome, where he was met by Pope Leo I. No one knows exactly what was said, but Attila pledged peace and agreed to retreat across the Danube. He later attempted a light attack on Gaul that was defeated, and made some empty threats against Constantinople. That same year, while celebrating his marriage to a new wife, Attila passed out and suffocated on his own blood, either because he had consumed too much alcohol or because he had been poisoned. The Roman commander Flavius Aetius eventually became the Western Roman Emperor, but was betrayed and assassinated by another Roman within two years of defeating Attila.

WHAT WAS IT ABOUT? The destruction of the Roman Empire. Technically, it was also over a woman!

WHO? The Huns are believed to have originated east of the Volga River in the Russian Steppe. They were famous for their mounted men with bows, lassos and spears. Exact numbers are unknown, but it is estimated that 50,000 Romans and Visigoths fought in this battle against 70,000 Huns and their allies. Casualties are also unknown, but the Huns must have suffered greatly to retreat and cross back over the Rhine.

WHEN? September 20, 451 AD (some sources say June 20)

WHY AT CHALONS? The location was chosen because of its flat terrain, where Attila thought he could best employ his cavalry tactics. (The battle is also known as the Battle of the Cataluanian Plains, Maurica or Campus Mauriacus.)

TECHNOLOGY/TACTICS: The Romans' ability to gain the slight high ground on the flank of the Huns seemed to have made the Huns shift their frontal assault and turn their flank, creating an opportunity for the Visigoths to break through the Hun line.

INCIDENTAL FACTS: Attila had been in contact with the Romans for many years; in fact, many Huns served in the Roman Empire during the previous decades, when they had been in contact on the frontier. Attila was educated and spoke Latin. He was once a hostage in Rome.

QUOTES: "The Scourge of God" – a monk, describing Attila

"He was a man born to shake the races of the world, a terror to all lands, who in some way or other frightened everyone by the dread report noised abroad about him, for he was haughty in his carriage, casting his eyes about him on all sides so that the proud man's power was to be seen in the very movements of his body. A lover of war, he was personally restrained in action, most impressive in counsel, gracious to suppliants, and generous to those to whom he had once given his trust. He was short of stature with a broad chest, massive head, and small eyes. His beard was thin and sprinkled with grey, his nose flat, and his complexion swarthy, showing thus the signs of his origins." – Imperial Envoy Pricus, De legationibus Romanorum ad gentes

PLACES TO SEE (REFERENCE MAP 4):

1. **CELTIC FORTRESS:** There is only a marker for the Celtic circular fortress where it is believed Attila made his camp. Currently it is a camping ground. When I went, it consisted of an open circular field and visible earthen walls. **N 49 02.941 E 4 29.626 (49.049017, 4.493767)**

BATTLE OF CHALONS, SEPTEMBER 20, 451 AD

MAP 4

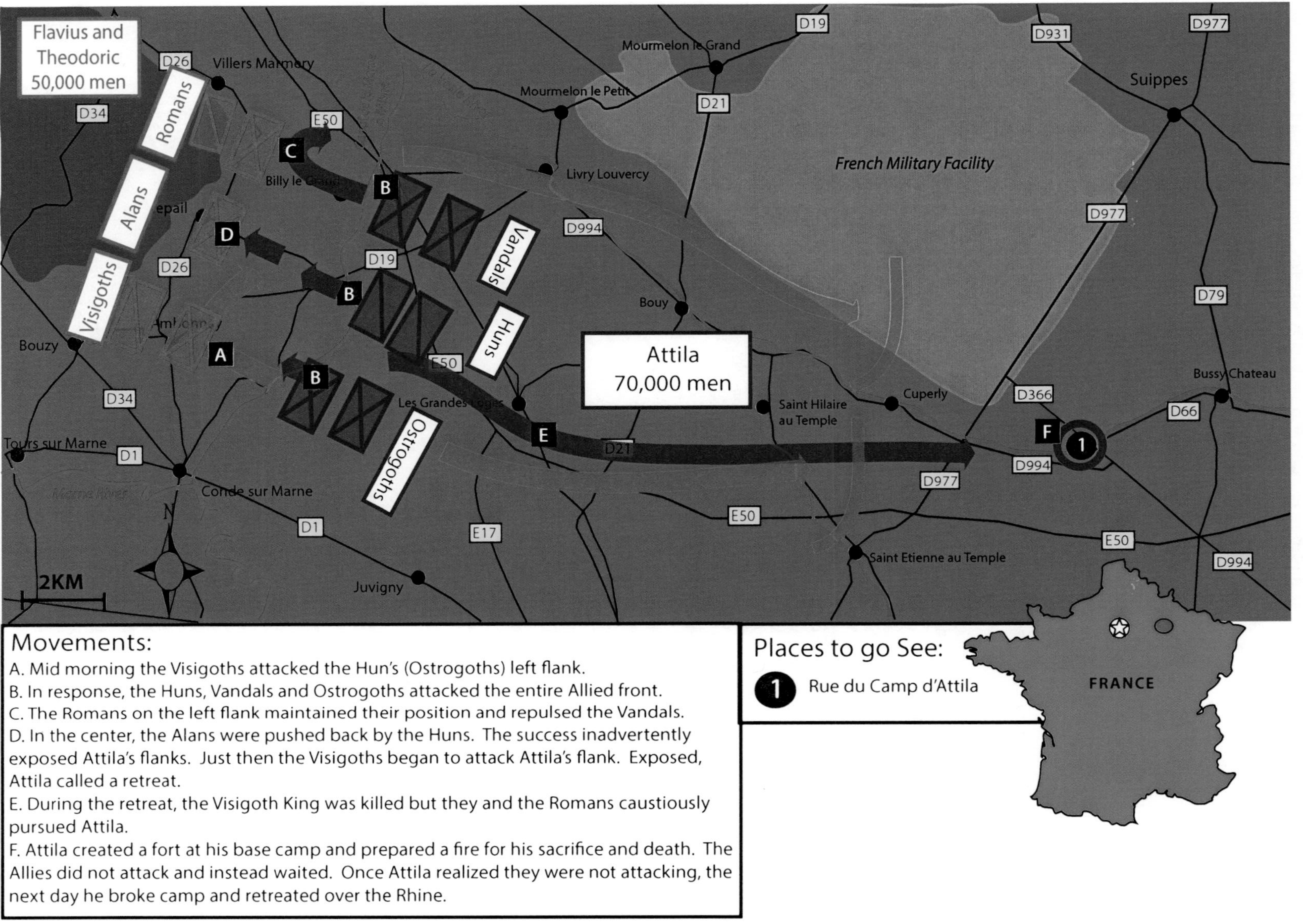
Flavius and Theodoric 50,000 men
Romans
Alans
Visigoths
Attila 70,000 men
Vandals
Huns
Ostrogoths
French Military Facility
Villers Marmery
Mourmelon le Grand
Mourmelon le Petit
Livry Louvercy
Suippes
Billy le Grand
Bouy
Bouzy
Tours sur Marne
Conde sur Marne
Juvigny
Les Grandes Loges
Saint Hilaire au Temple
Cuperly
Bussy Chateau
Saint Etienne au Temple
D26
D34
E50
D19
D994
D21
D931
D977
D79
D366
D66
D1
E17
2KM
FRANCE
A
B
C
D
E
F
Places to go See:
1 Rue du Camp d'Attila
Movements:
A. Mid morning the Visigoths attacked the Hun's (Ostrogoths) left flank.
B. In response, the Huns, Vandals and Ostrogoths attacked the entire Allied front.
C. The Romans on the left flank maintained their position and repulsed the Vandals.
D. In the center, the Alans were pushed back by the Huns. The success inadvertently exposed Attila's flanks. Just then the Visigoths began to attack Attila's flank. Exposed, Attila called a retreat.
E. During the retreat, the Visigoth King was killed but they and the Romans caustiously pursued Attila.
F. Attila created a fort at his base camp and prepared a fire for his sacrifice and death. The Allies did not attack and instead waited. Once Attila realized they were not attacking, the next day he broke camp and retreated over the Rhine.

OTHER ROMAN SITES IN FRANCE

The following are major locations in France related to the Romans. Please note that France contains many other Roman ruins, but too many to list! Out of the following, I recommend Pont du Gard, Arles, Lyon and Nîmes.

PLACES to see (Reference Map 5):

1. **BATTLE OF ARGENTORATUM:** This battle occurred outside Strasbourg in 357 AD. Emperor Julian defeated the Alamanni and their commander Chnodomar. The battle is significant because the victory re-established the Rhine fortifications and forced the Germans out of Gaul once more.
    A. **MUSEUM OF ARCHAEOLOGY, STRASBOURG**: N 48 34.867 E 7 45.133 (48.581117, 7.752217)

2. **AUTUN, BURGUNDY:** Located near the site of the Battle of Alesia, this is another beautiful French town in Burgundy and the location where George S. Patton's Third Army and Alexander Patch's Seventh Army linked up during World War II (see Champagne Campaign).
    A. **PORTE SAINT-ANDRE (GATE, PART OF THE ROMAN WALL)**: N 46 57.464 E 4 18.362 (46.957733, 4.306033)

    B. **ROMAN THEATRE AUTUN:** N 46 57.158 E 4 18.576 (46.952633, 4.3096)

3. **LYON:** Lyon is a beautiful city. Just above the old town are an impressive museum and the remains of two theaters, used for present-day concerts and performances.
    A. **THÉÂTRES ROMAINS DE FOURVIÈRE (ROMAN THEATERS)**: N 45 45.630 E 4 49.196 (45.7605, 4.819933)

    B. **MUSEUM OF LYON:** The museum is very well done, with a nice display of artifacts and good descriptions. Right next to the theater.

4. **VIENNE (JUST SOUTH OF LYON):** An impressive, well-preserved temple, public park and amphitheater used for concerts. The Musée Archeologique, located just across the river from Vienne, contains beautiful, famous mosaics.
    A. **TEMPLE OF AUGUSTE ET LIVIE**: N 45 31.523 E 4 52.458 (45.525383, 4.8743)

    B. **VIENNE BATHS AND GARDEN OF CYBELE:** N 45 31.486 E 4 52.565 (45.524767, 4.876083)

    C. **AMPHITHEATER (LOCATED ON THE HILL ABOVE THE GARDEN AND TEMPLE):** N 45 31.479 E 4 52.692 (45.52465, 4.8782)

D. **SAINT-ROMAIN-EN-GAL MUSÉE ARCHEOLOGIQUE:** N 45 31.749 E 4 52.244 (45.529148, 4.870731)

5. **ORANGE:** Orange has two of the greatest Roman monuments in Europe, the Roman Theater and the Triumphal Arch. The theater's back wall is still standing, which distinguishes it from all other similar monuments. The Musée d'Orange is small, but very interesting.
   A. **ROMAN THEATER**: N 44 08.152 E 4 48.519 (44.135867, 4.80865)

   B. **TRIUMPHAL ARCH:** N 44 08.531 E 4 48.285 (44.142183, 4.80475)

   C. **MUSÉE D'ORANGE:** Across from the theater

6. **PONT DU GARD:** Near Remoulins in southern France is the famous Roman aqueduct, which is a must-see! There is a large park with plenty of space to relax and enjoy the view. It is an amazing structure.
   N 43 56.805 E 4 32.158 (43.94675, 4.535967)

7. **NÎMES:** Nîmes is a great city for architecture, including the founding Roman buildings. The Arena of Nîmes is still in use and is probably the best-preserved amphitheater in Europe after the Roman Colosseum. Nîmes also contains one of the best-preserved Roman temples, the Maison Carrée. A new Roman Museum opened in September 2014.
   A. **AMPHITHEATRE ROMAIN**: N 43 50.090 E 4 21.584 (43.834833, 4.359733)

   B. **MAISON CARRÉE:** N 43 50.261 E 4 21.388 (43.837683, 4.356467)

   C. **ROMAN MUSEUM:** Across from the amphitheater

8. **ARLES:** Arles is a small, beautiful town in southern France. Its ruins are excellent, and the town is a great place to stay as well as easy to explore. The well-preserved Arles Amphitheater is now used for bullfights. Les Alyscamps was a Roman cemetery that was in use through the Middle Ages. Tombs line the pathway to the old chapel. The artist Vincent van Gogh lived here for a few years (including some time spent in a mental hospital) and created many of his famous works here.
   A. **MUSÉE DE L'ARLES ANTIQUE (MUSEUM OF ANCIENT ARLES)**: N 43 40.356 E 4 36.986 (43.6726, 4.616433)

   B. **ARLES AMPHITHEATER:** N 43 40.669 E 4 37.851 (43.677817, 4.63085)

   C. **LES ALYSCAMPS:** N 43 40.363 E 4 38.049 (43.67271, 4.634157)

9. **FREJUS:** Frejus contains a small semicircular Roman theater and a large amphitheater just outside of the old town center, both of which are used for concerts. The remains of an aqueduct are also worth a visit if you don't get to

Pont du Gard.

A. **ROMAN THEATER**: N 43 26.066 E 6 43.723 (43.434433, 6.728717)

B. **AQUEDUCT:** N 43 26.249 E 6 44.490 (43.437483, 6.7415)

C. **ROMAN AMPHITHEATER:** N 43 26.219 E 6 44.327 (43.436983, 6.738783)

10. **TOURS:** St. Martin lived from 316 to 397 AD. He was born in Hungary to a Roman cavalry officer. When he was 10 he became a Christian against his parents' wishes. Martin had to join the Roman army and was stationed in Gaul. Before a battle near Worms, Germany, he stated that he was "a soldier of Christ" and that he couldn't fight. He was imprisoned and stated that he would go in front of the soldiers without weapons. The enemy sued for peace prior to the next battle. Martin was then released from military service. He went on to convert people in Italy, found monasteries and become Bishop of Tours. As bishop, he was a humble and peaceful man who worked to convert the pagans in Gaul. Throughout France you can see many statues or paintings venerating him. The images depict St. Martin as a Roman soldier giving half his cloak to a beggar; they reference the fact that, when he was 18, Martin had given half his cloak to a beggar outside of Amiens and then had a dream of Jesus. St. Martin is the patron saint of soldiers, and his feast day is November 11.
Basilica of St. Martin: N 47 23.552 E 0 40.973 (47.392529, 0.682891)

11. **REIMS:** Porte Mars, the widest triumphal arch in the Roman world, still stands tall within walking distance of the incredible Reims Cathedral. The arch was built in the third century AD and great kings passed through its gates until the mid-1500s.
Porte Mars: N 49 15.639 E 4 01.796 (49.260657, 4.029933)

OTHER ROMAN SITES OF FRANCE

MAP 5

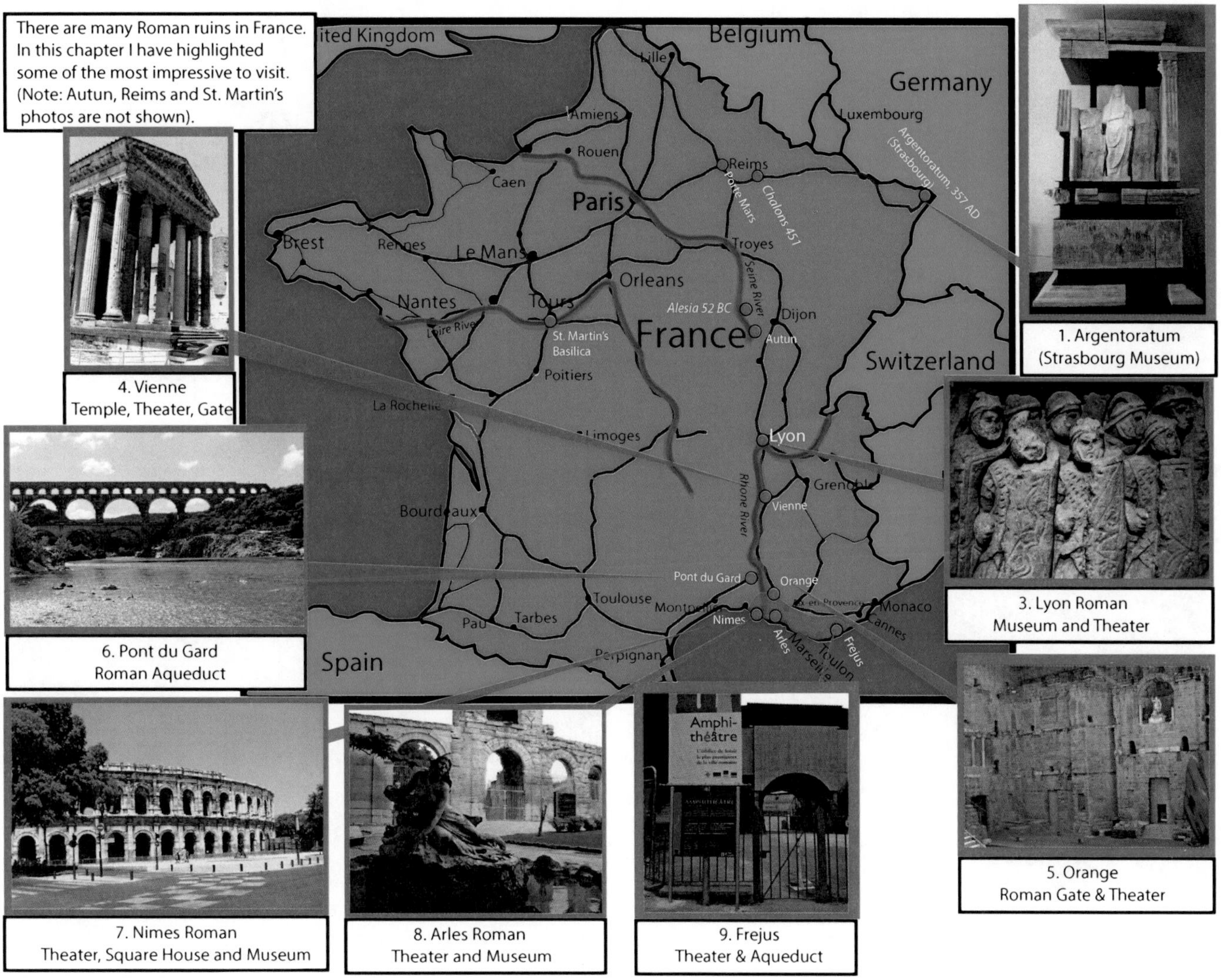

There are many Roman ruins in France. In this chapter I have highlighted some of the most impressive to visit. (Note: Autun, Reims and St. Martin's photos are not shown).

1. Argentoratum (Strasbourg Museum)

3. Lyon Roman Museum and Theater

4. Vienne Temple, Theater, Gate

5. Orange Roman Gate & Theater

6. Pont du Gard Roman Aqueduct

7. Nimes Roman Theater, Square House and Museum

8. Arles Roman Theater and Museum

9. Frejus Theater & Aqueduct

Vercingetorix Throws down his Arms at the feet of Julius Caesar by Lionel Noel Royer, 1899

Vercingetorix Statue on Alesia hill top.

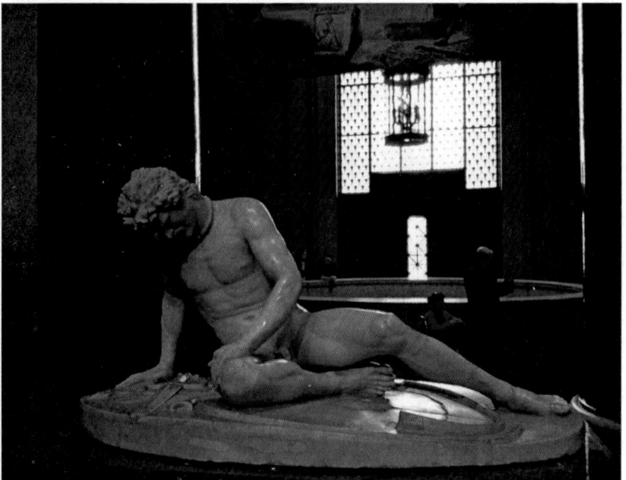

The Dying Gaul, on tour at the Smithsonian.

Battle of Chalons, this location is called "Camp Attila" an old Celtic ring fort which some historians suggest as Attila's camp.

D 103
ALISE-
STE REINE

On the road to Alesia, you can see why the Gauls chose this location as a fort. The natural hill top rises steeply from the surrounding fields.

Arles Theatre, still used for bull fighting and concerts. Arles, is one my favorite places to visit. Small and beautiful, Van Gogh stayed here for a few years.

In the Lyon Museum, it is amazing to see what the Romans artisans could produce. Next to the museum is the Basilica of Notre Dame Fourviere overlooking the old town and city. In old town, you can sit down to have a great local meal..with some wine & bread of course!

Arles had a wonderful feel to it. The restaurants, hotels with the inner courts and the fresh market, photo lower right. Below left is one of the many locations marked with Van Gogh paintings and the views that inspired him.

HOTEL

FELSGOLD

The Roman Aqueduct, Pont du Gard is an amazing site to see. The parking area is only about 1 KM away and a nice walk to the heritage site. Plus a great place to sit and have a beer!

–Chapter 2–

THE DARK AGES, 476 AD–800 AD

After the fall of the Roman Empire, a period of "darkness" descended upon Western Europe. The period was considered dark because the more civilized and centralized Roman systems had fallen apart, leaving many tribes fighting for supremacy. In that struggle, the Catholic Church offered a light and hope in the darkness by providing a basic bureaucracy, collection of knowledge and community organization. France was a starting point for the rebirth of a more civilized Europe, as it played roles in everything from stopping the Muslim invasion in 732 to the ascendancy of Charlemagne.

BATTLE OF TOURS (BATTLE OF POITIERS)

October 10, 732 AD

"With Christ's help he overturned their tents, and hastened to battle to grind them small in slaughter."
– Fouracre, Continuations of Fredegar

SUMMARY: The Battle of Tours saved Christian Europe north of the Pyrenees from invading Muslim forces. After the fall of the Roman Empire, Europe was in disarray. Forces from the east had invaded and Islamic forces were attacking from the south. The Islamic prophet Mohammed had died in 632 AD, but his forces continued their conquest of surrounding lands. In 711 AD, 10,000 Muslims, made up of Arabs, Turks and Berbers from North Africa, crossed from North Africa to Southern Spain, crushing the Visigoths who had been living there since the fall of Rome. Within 20 years, the Muslims would control most of Spain and hold parts of southern France and Aquitaine as well.

In approximately 720 AD, the last of the Visigoths were destroyed in their fort of Carcassonne. Prince Eude of Aquitaine defeated the Muslim raiders and stopped their forces from advancing. However, in May 732 AD, Muslim forces under the command of Abdul Rahman attacked southern France again and defeated Prince Eude outside his capital of Bordeaux. Prince Eude and his remaining men fled north to Paris to alert and seek an alliance with the prince's former enemy, Charles "The Hammer" Martel, the King of the Franks.

In the meantime, Abdul Rahman sent advance forces north and a diversionary force to the east along the Rhone Valley. Rahman and his main force, an estimated 50,000 soldiers, including the Berber families, sacked the Saint-Hilaire church, located outside the walls of Poitiers. They continued ransacking the countryside and headed toward Tours and the riches of St. Martin's Church in late September/early October. In response, Charles Martel quickly assembled a large force, including Prince Eude's men, at Orléans and advanced down past Tours. Charles surprised the Muslim forces before they reached St. Martin's, then continued down toward Poitiers and crossed the river Vienne on October 18. It is believed that he set up his camp and defensive position at Vieux Poitiers and the old Roman theater.

Under Charles, the Franks maintained the first standing professional army in Europe since the Romans. They numbered approximately 20,000 and were well armed, armored and disciplined. Charles positioned his men with the river Clain on his right flank; he kept a forest on his left and rear for protection. It was cold, but Charles and his men were prepared for the weather, in contrast to the Muslims, who wore lighter cotton clothing. After eight days, the Muslims attacked, charging down the hill. The fighting was reported to be extremely fierce, and victory appeared to be within the Muslims' grasp due to their sheer numbers. However, Prince Eude took his cavalry on the left flank and attacked the Muslims' camp. Confused and fearful of losing their treasure, the Muslims retreated to protect their pillaged gold and their families. Abdul Rahman tried to stop the retreat, but was killed during the fighting.

That night, the fighting broke off. Charles took time to rest and regroup his men for an all-out assault in the morning. However, before the break of dawn the Muslim camp dispersed, leaderless and with heavy casualties. One group retreated to the east down the Rhone Valley, pillaging their way back to Narbonne. The second, larger force retreated directly south past Bordeaux, and were chased and largely destroyed by Prince Eude.

OUTCOME: Charles Martel saved Western Christianity and Europe from Islam. Paul Akers, in his editorial about Charles Martel, stated that those who value Christian life and freedom "might spare a minute ... every October to say a silent 'thank you' to a gang of half-savage Germans (Franks) and especially to their leader, Charles 'The Hammer' Martel." What also "saved" Europe was disagreement within the Muslim ranks. After the Muslim loss, the Berbers revolted and their power slowly declined. They lost their hold on Narbonne in 759 AD. Charles and the Franks continued their attempt to consolidate their holdings and victories, slowly gaining territory in Burgundy and Aquitaine. Total control and universal allegiance was finally achieved under Charles's son Pepin and grandson Charlemagne.

WHAT WAS IT ABOUT? For the Muslims, it was about religious conquest for land and wealth. For the Franks, it was about the protection of Christianity and the thwarting of Muslim invaders. The conflict was also an opportunity for the Franks to exploit additional lands in Aquitaine.

WHO? The battle pitted 20,000 Merovingian Franks against 50,000 Muslim Arabs and Berbers (Umayyad Caliphate). The Muslim leader Abdul Rahman was killed in the battle. The leader of the Franks, Charles Martel, led a very successful life after the battle by taking steps to unite Western Europe under his rule. He died in 741 AD and is entombed in Saint Denis Basilica in Paris. His grandson was the famous Charlemagne, who became the Holy Roman Emperor and spread education and Christianity throughout Europe.

WHEN? October 10, 732 AD

WHY AT TOURS? Rahman was on his way to pillage the riches of Tours. Charles departed Tours to meet Rahman, who was leaving Poitiers. They met in the middle. Charles picked a spot with a river to his side, a forest and elevation for protection, and tactical advantage.

TECHNOLOGY/TACTICS: The Franks under Charles Martel were professional, well trained and disciplined. They constituted the first standing army in Europe since the Romans over 200 years earlier. The Christian forces also included men from Aquitaine under Prince Eude, who still had strong Roman influence. The Aquitaine forces included some light cavalry for flanking and skirmishing. As a tactic, Charles employed a triangle phalanx-style combat, which worked well against the Muslim cavalry. The Franks used the terrain, such as the trees, to disguise the size of their force and to protect the flanks so that any cavalry charges would be broken up. For armor and weapons, the Franks used "throwing axes," spears, swords, chain mail, wooden shields and leather tunics.

The Arab Muslims were primarily cavalry using lances, bows and arrows, and swords. The Arabs were well organized and were actually paid and issued armor, chain mail and weapons upon joining the military force. On the other hand, the Muslim Berbers from North Africa were largely unorganized and lightly armed, with little to no armor. The Berbers also slowed down the march because they had brought along their herds and families. In terms of tactics, the Muslims were known to charge and feint retreat. During this battle, the Christians stayed firm and disciplined and were therefore able to overcome the Muslims.

It is believed that the Muslim invaders used the stirrup, which was not well known in Europe at that time. After the battle, Charles Martel and his forces added the stirrup to their saddles, enabling riders to wear more armor and fight with their swords in more balanced positions. Thus, some believe, the heavy cavalry "knight" was born.

Roman historian Procopius said about the Franks: "Each man carried a sword and shield and an axe. Now the iron head of this weapon was thick and exceedingly sharp on both sides while the wooden handle was very short. And they are accustomed always to throw these axes at one signal in the first charge and thus shatter the shields of the enemy and kill the men." Note: The French axe arrived in the New World 800 years later; it was from French traders that American Indians learned the practice of "scalping" with tomahawks.

QUOTE: "And in the shock of the battle the men of the North seemed like a sea that cannot be moved. Firmly they stood, one close to another, forming as it were a bulwark of ice; and with great blows of their swords they hewed down the Arabs. Drawn up in a band around their chief, the people of the Austrasians carried all before them. Their tireless hands drove their swords down to the breasts of the foe." – The Mozarabic Chronicle of 754 AD

PLACES TO SEE (REFERENCE MAP 6):

1. **BATTLEFIELD OVERVIEW:** The information monument is located in Vouneuil-sur-Vienne, in the approximate location of the Muslim camp and the site where the Muslim leader was killed. This location overlooks the battlefield and offers a very well-done description of the battle and sequence.
   N 46 44.064 E 000 30.054 (46.7344, 0.5009)

2. **ROMAN THEATER RUINS, VIEUX-POITIERS:** It is believed that this was the location of the Christian camp. It was likely a substantial building in 732 AD, and both the best defensive position and the best place to stop any attempts to cross the Vienne. The site contains a museum and information plaques.
   N 46 45.713 E 0 30.777 (46.761883, 0.51295)

3. **ÉGLISE SAINT-HILAIRE-LE-GRAND (CHURCH OF SAINT HILARY THE GREAT):** Originally outside the fortified walls of Poitiers, the church was sacked by the Muslims prior to the battle. It is now located within the suburbs of Poitiers.
   N 46 34.644 E 0 19.939 (46.5774, 0.332317)

4. **ST. MARTIN'S CHURCH, TOURS:** The next target of the Muslim raiders, this church was one of the richest in the area. It was saved by the Franks.
   N 47 23.591 E 0 40.970 (47.393183, 0.682833)

5. **TOMB OF CHARLES MARTEL, BASILICA OF ST. DENIS (OUTSIDE PARIS):** St. Denis is the patron saint of France. The basilica is one of the oldest and most beautiful cathedrals in the country.
   N 48 56.133 E 2 21.583 (48.93555, 2.359717)

6. **ST. REMIGIUS MUSEUM AND CLOVIS STATUE:** The museum has a room containing information about local military history, but the majority of it is dedicated to St. Remigius, the founder of Reims. He is especially important because he converted the King of the Franks, Clovis, to Christianity in 496 AD. Clovis, like Constantine, ruled as a warrior and a Catholic, spreading both his rule and his religion. Next to the museum, outside of St. Remigius Church, is a statue depicting the baptism of Clovis I.
   N 49 14.590 E 4 02.422 (49.243162, 4.040362)

BATTLE OF TOURS/POITIERS OCTOBER 10, 732 AD

MAP 6

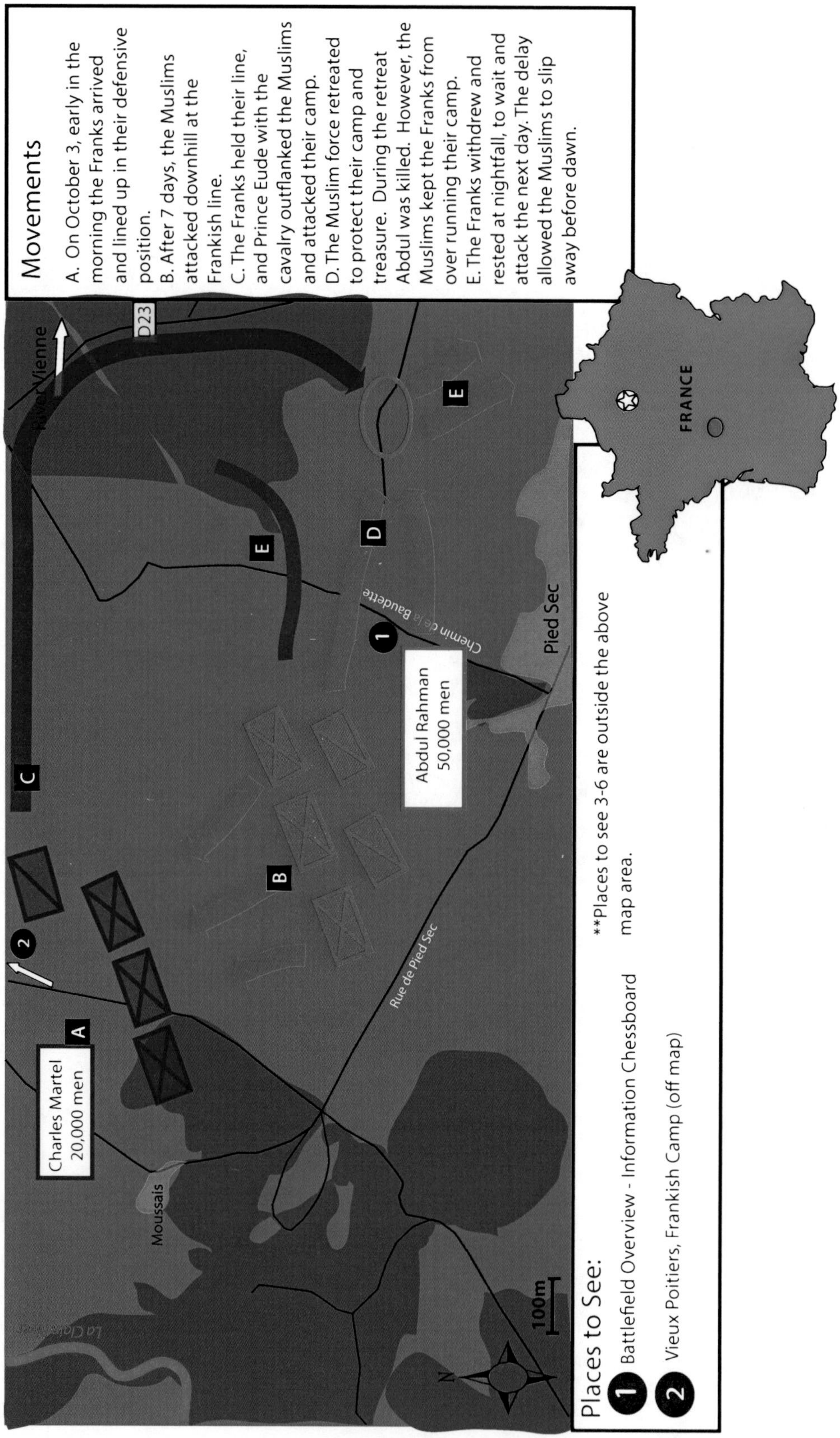

Movements

A. On October 3, early in the morning the Franks arrived and lined up in their defensive position.
B. After 7 days, the Muslims attacked downhill at the Frankish line.
C. The Franks held their line, and Prince Eude with the cavalry outflanked the Muslims and attacked their camp.
D. The Muslim force retreated to protect their camp and treasure. During the retreat Abdul was killed. However, the Muslims kept the Franks from over running their camp.
E. The Franks withdrew and rested at nightfall, to wait and attack the next day. The delay allowed the Muslims to slip away before dawn.

Charles Martel
20,000 men

Abdul Rahman
50,000 men

Moussais

River Vienne

D23

Rue de Pied Sec

Chemin de la Baudette

Pied Sec

100m

N

FRANCE

Places to See:

1. Battlefield Overview - Information Chessboard
2. Vieux Poitiers, Frankish Camp (off map)

**Places to see 3-6 are outside the above map area.

Bataille de Poitiers by Paul Steuben, 1837. A romantics view of the triumph of Charles the Hammer over Abdul Rahaman.

Battle of Poitiers/Tours information park. Just outside of the town Pied Sec is the information board overlooking the battlefield from the Arab positions.

In Reims, a statue of St. Remigius baptizing Clovis the first Frankish King. Clovis was baptized in 493 AD and unified the various Frankish tribes.

The photograph was taken looking above one of the orientation tables at the information park for the Battle of Tours.

Another photograph of the information board and facing north from the location/line of the Muslim Forces facing the position of the Franks. The Frankish line would have been at the far edge of the brown field.

THE SONG OF ROLAND

778 AD

Charlemagne's Captain Roland dies in battle against the Muslims

"God give you strength! Hold the Field, let us not be beaten!"
– The Song of Roland

SUMMARY: The Song of Roland is a legend blended with fact that describes the heroic death of Roland, a great captain in Charlemagne's army. I highlight this legend because it provides historical context to the era of Charlemagne, who held great influence over all of Europe. In 777 AD, the Moorish ruler, Suleiman of Barcelona from the Abassid Dynasty, visited Charlemagne and asked for his protection from the Umayyad Dynasty, which Suleiman had recently ousted from Barcelona. At that time Charlemagne was only 36 but had defeated the Saxons, overthrown the Lombards, captured Aquitaine and become the Holy Roman Emperor. Charlemagne agreed to help Suleiman and took the opportunity to cross the Pyrenees the following year. In 778 AD, after Easter, Charlemagne crossed the Pyrenees with the goal of capturing the city of Saragossa and killing Rahman, the Umayyad ruler. Little documentation about the campaign exists, suggesting that it did not go well. In fact, Charlemagne's army began its return to France in late July 778 AD before the end of the campaign season, indicating that something did, in fact, go wrong.

The chronicles do not mention any fighting in the Pyrenees until about 25 years later, after Charlemagne's reign. It is recorded that the Basques (actually Christians) had attacked Charlemagne's rear guard and captured treasure while the Franks traveled through the pass called Roncesvalles. Einhard, Charlemagne's biographer, stated, "In the battle Einhard the royal seneschal, Anselm the Count of the Palace and Hrouldland [Roland], the warden of the Breton Marches were killed, with very many others." The legend of Roland was born. The legend gained popularity because the ambush took place on the route that monks and pilgrims traveled to Santiago de Compostella. In fact, even 12th-century pilgrim guides contained a variant of the legend. The poem tells the story of Roland, Charlemagne's captain, who volunteered to escort the rear guard as it returned to France after the Franks negotiated a truce with Marsilla, the King of Saragossa. Roland's stepfather, Ganelon, who arranged the truce, betrayed Roland and set up an ambush for the Saracens. During the ambush, Roland's ego got the best of him. Though heavily outnumbered he did not blow his horn for help; rather, he charged the enemy. Not until it was too late—after his comrades, like the fierce-fighting Archbishop Turin and the wise and moderate Olivier, had died—did Roland blow the horn. Apparently he blew it too hard because his temples burst and he died a martyr's death! The legend continued when Charlemagne arrived shortly afterward and pushed the Saracens into the Elbe River. Then, while he buried the dead, Charlemagne was attacked by the Emir of Babylon, whom he defeated. As a result of the victory the Franks easily captured the city of Saragossa. Finally, the Franks returned to Aix en Providence and Roland's stepfather Ganelon stood trial. The decision of his guilt was left up to two men at arms who fought each other. Ganelon was proven guilty by divine intervention. (In other words, the weak guy who fought for Roland defeated the big guy fighting for Ganelon's innocence.) Ganelon was quickly torn apart and 30 of his unlucky relatives were hanged for good measure.

PLACES TO SEE (REFERENCE MAP 7):

1. **ROCAMADOUR:** Rocamadour is a very beautiful town. It's built on the face of a cliff and contains lots of shops and restaurants. Here you can see Roland's sword, "Durendal," which is implanted in the rock face above the chapel. The legend says that after he could not destroy it, he hid it under his body. The sword is said to come from Hector of Troy, but is also said to contain relics from St. Peter, St. Basil, St. Denis and the Blessed Mother Mary.
   N 44 48.017 E 1 37.117 (44.800283, 1.618617)

2. **RONCESVALLES, SPAIN (RONCEVAUX PASS):** This is along the pilgrim route of St. James and is said to be the location of the Battle of Roncevaux Pass, where Roland died. A chapel contains several relics allegedly associated with Roland. It is a great place to visit and is on the way to Santiago de Compostela, the first stop after the Pyrenees into Spain. There is also a stone monument to the battle and a statue of Roland.
   N 43 00.548 W 1 19.17 (43.009133, -1.3195)

3. **LA BRECHE DE ROLAND:** This is a natural break in the mountain, 40 meters wide and 100 meters high, said to have formed when Roland struck the ground in an attempt to break his sword so that it wouldn't fall into the hands of the Saracens.
   N 42 41.450 W 0 02.017 (42.690833, -0.033617)

4. **LOURDES:** In 1858, the Virgin Mary appeared here to Bernadette Soubirous. The location has become a major pilgrimage site for Catholics from throughout the world. It is a very special place to visit and very close to the other locations.
   N 43 05.845 W 0 03.455 (43.097417, -0.057581)

5. **BLAYE:** According to tradition, Roland, Olivier and Turpin were buried in the Church of St. Romain of Blaye. Unfortunately, only the ruins of the church remain, in the shadow of the UNESCO Citadel.
   N 45 07.840 W 0 39.820 (45.130663, -0.663667)

6. **CHARTRES CATHEDRAL:** This beautiful and impressive cathedral just west of Paris contains stained glass windows that tell the story of Roland. **N 48 26.836 E 1 29.229 (48.447261, 1.487142)**

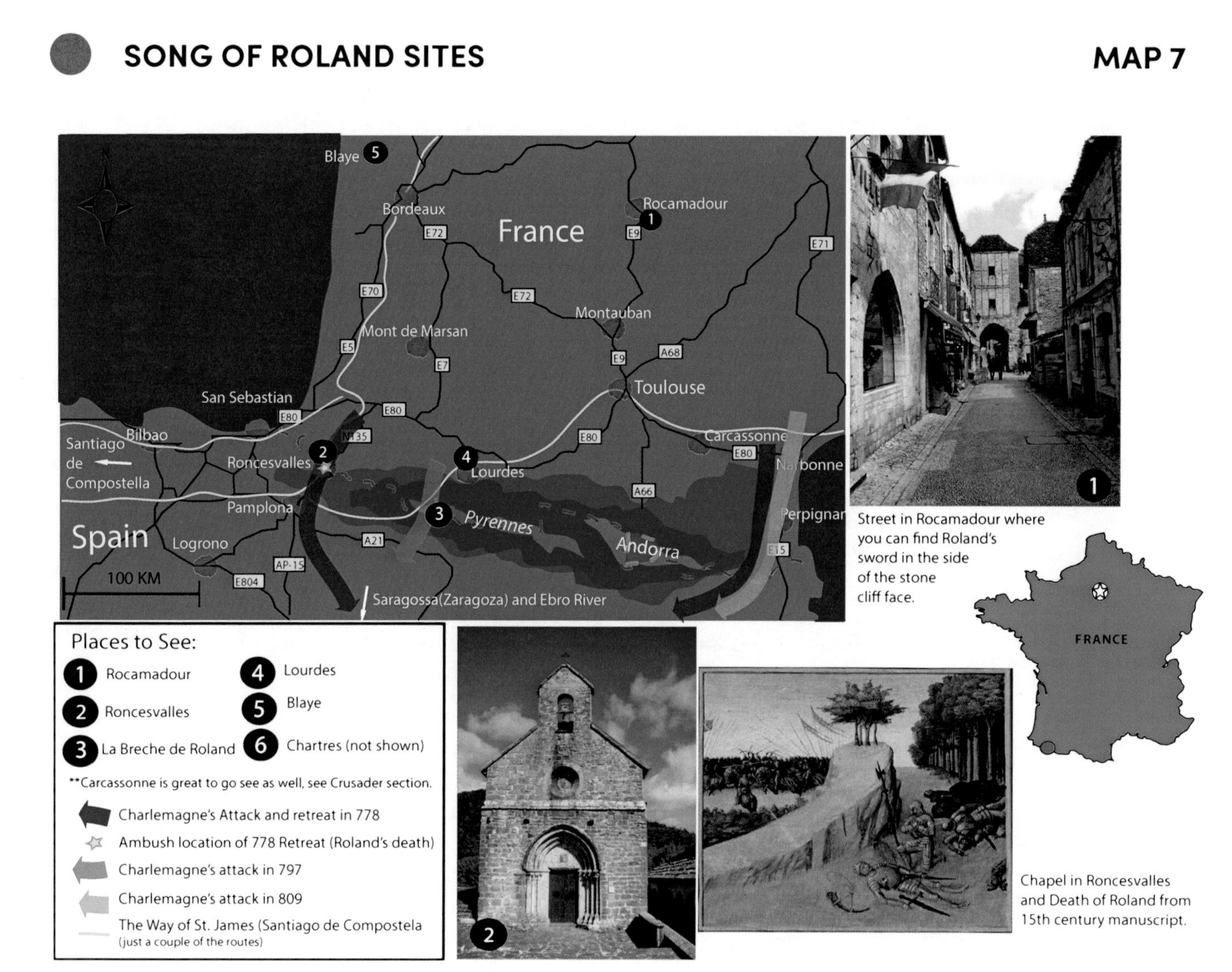
SONG OF ROLAND SITES
MAP 7
Blaye 5
Bordeaux
France
Rocamadour 1
E72
E9
E71
E70
Mont de Marsan
Montauban
E5
E7
E9
A68
Toulouse
San Sebastian
E80
Santiago de Compostella
Bilbao
Roncesvalles 2
4 Lourdes
Carcassonne
Narbonne
Pamplona
3 Pyrennes
Andorra
Perpignan
Spain
Logrono
A21
A66
AP-15
E804
E15
100 KM
Saragossa(Zaragoza) and Ebro River
Places to See:
1 Rocamadour
2 Roncesvalles
3 La Breche de Roland
4 Lourdes
5 Blaye
6 Chartres (not shown)
**Carcassonne is great to go see as well, see Crusader section.
Charlemagne's Attack and retreat in 778
Ambush location of 778 Retreat (Roland's death)
Charlemagne's attack in 797
Charlemagne's attack in 809
The Way of St. James (Santiago de Compostela (just a couple of the routes)
FRANCE

1 Street in Rocamadour where you can find Roland's sword in the side of the stone cliff face.

2 Chapel in Roncesvalles and Death of Roland from 15th century manuscript.

–Chapter 3–

THE CRUSADER PERIOD, 1095–1312

In 1095 France was again a catalyst for change in Western Europe. That year, in Clermont, Pope Urban II called upon Christians to join a crusade to defend the Byzantine Empire from encroaching Muslim hordes and to protect the Christian pilgrims on their way to Jerusalem. His speech initiated two centuries of warfare that brought about the recapture of Jerusalem, introduction of Military Orders and the unfortunate sacking of Constantinople. To note, the Crusades are sometimes seen as the Christians initiating a battle for land that was not theirs and the Muslims as victims. What I want to highlight with the timeline is that the Crusades were a reaction to the Muslim invasion and capture of Christian lands. We must be reminded that Christianity although far from perfect was in Jerusalem well before the Muslims who eventually invaded, captured and destroyed Jewish and Christian centers of worship. One can argue the Crusades were a required effort to protect Christian lands and people. The Crusades also created opportunities for the sharing of knowledge between cultures and fostered advances in technology. This chapter highlights many of the Crusade-related locations within France, including those pertaining to the famed Knights Templar. The following is a brief timeline for reference:

614-28	The Jewish people of Jerusalem revolt against the Byzantines.
620	The Prophet Mohammed makes his "night journey" to Jerusalem.
637	Jerusalem falls to Caliph Umar the Great, Umayyad Dynasty, from Damascus.
750	Riots occur in Jerusalem; the Abbasid Dynasty from Baghdad begins its rule.
799	Charlemagne's ambassadors restore churches and access for Christians.
878	Ahmad ibn Tulun from Egypt conquers Jerusalem.
904	The Abbasids regain control of Jerusalem.
969	The Fatimid Caliphate from Cairo emerges and takes control of Jerusalem.
1009	The Fatimid Caliphate orders the destruction of all synagogues and churches.
1030	The Byzantines negotiate a treaty with the Fatimid Caliphate to rebuild churches and synagogues.
1054	The Great Christian Schism - churches in Jerusalem fall under the Greek Orthodox.
1071	The Battle of Manzikert - Seljuk Turks, in a major victory, defeat the Byzantine army.
1073	The Seljuks capture Jerusalem.
1077	Jerusalem revolts; the Seljuk leader massacres the population.
1095	Pope Urban proclaims the First Crusade.
1096-99	**FIRST CRUSADE –** The Peasants' Crusade of 20,000; peasants and low-ranking nobles led by Peter the Hermit rampage through Europe and are slaughtered by the Turks. The 3,000 survivors join the Princes' Crusade, which includes an estimated 50,000 Crusaders (7,000 knights) and is very successful.
1098	The city of Edessa is taken by Baldwin of Boulogne and Antioch.
1099	The Princes' Crusade captures Jerusalem with Godfrey of Bouillon as ruler.
1118-28	Military orders (the Templars and Hospitallers) are established.
1146	Nur al-Din unites Muslim Syria and reintroduces the idea of Jihad.
1147-49	**SECOND CRUSADE –** Louis VII of France and Emperor Conrad III do not accomplish anything.

1169	Saladin becomes vizier of Egypt, ruling on behalf of Nur al-Din.
1174	Nur al-Din dies suddenly and Saladin becomes the ruler of Damascus and Egypt.
1187	Battle of Hattin – Saladin defeats the King Guy Crusaders in a foolhardy battle and recaptures Jerusalem.
1187-92	**THIRD CRUSADE –** Led by Emperor Frederick Barbarossa (who drowns in Cilicia, Turkey in 1190), King Richard the Lionheart and King Philip Augustus of France.
1191	Richard and Philip capture Acre and Richard defeats Saladin at the Battle of Arsuf.
1192	Richard fails to take Jerusalem, but negotiates access for Christians.
1193	Saladin dies in Damascus.
1202-04	**FOURTH CRUSADE –** Crusaders attack the Yugoslav city of Zara, then invade and sack Constantinople.
1209-55	A Crusade begins against the Albiegensian "heretics" in southern France.
1212	A Crusade in Spain achieves victory at the Battle of Las Navas de Tolosa.
1212	The disastrous Children's Crusade terminates in Italy.
1218-21	**FIFTH CRUSADE –** An attack against Egypt ends in failure.
1229	Teutonic Knights begin a "perpetual" Prussian Crusade.
1228-29	**SIXTH CRUSADE –** Excommunicated Emperor Frederick II retakes Jerusalem without a fight.
1241	A Crusade occurs against the Mongol invasion of Hungary and Poland.
1244	Jerusalem loses to the Muslims (again).
1248-54	**SEVENTH CRUSADE –** King Louis IX of France captures Damietta in Egypt, but is captured himself. Only after a large ransom is paid is he released.
1258	The Mongols sack Baghdad.
1260	The Mamluks (a military caste primarily from the Balkans and Turkey) defeat the Mongols at Ain Jalut; Baybars becomes sultan of Egypt.
1268	Antioch falls to the Mamluks.
1270	**EIGHTH CRUSADE –** The Eighth Crusade fails after King Louis IX of France dies of illness in Tunisia.
1289	The Mamluks capture Tripoli.
1291	The Mamluks conquer Acre, ending Christian settlements in the Levant.

CRUSADER SITES

1095–1312

"In hoc signo vinces"
(In this sign you will conquer.) – Templar motto

SUMMARY: The following sites have a connection to the Crusades, beginning with the cathedral where the Pope initiated the Crusades in 1095, and ending with the demise of the Knights Templar on Friday the 13th in October 1307. (Reference Map 8)

1. **NOTRE DAME CATHEDRAL, CLERMONT-FERRAND, NOVEMBER 28, 1095:** On a cold November day, Pope Urban II called on all Christians to come to the aid of Jerusalem, which had recently been sacked by the Muslims; to defend Christian pilgrims, who were being robbed and murdered on their way to Jerusalem; and to defend Constantinople from the encroaching Muslim forces. The Byzantines had recently suffered a major defeat during which they were greatly weakened and now stood alone on the edge of Christian Europe. The speech was said to be so inspiring that many Christians immediately set out on the long, dangerous journey that became the First Crusade. Per Robert the Monk, Urban was quoted as saying: "I, or rather the Lord, beseech you as Christ's heralds to publish this everywhere and to persuade all people of whatever rank, foot-soldiers and knights, poor and rich, to carry aid promptly to those Christians and to destroy that vile race from the lands of our friends. I say this to those who are present, it is meant also for those who are absent. Moreover, Christ commands it." This is an impressive cathedral with a large statue of Urban II in front, and the town is a nice place to visit. It is worth half a day to see.
   N 45 46.725 E 3 05.152 (45.77875, 3.085867)

KNIGHTS TEMPLAR (1119–1312)

The legendary Knights Templar had a brief but very powerful existence. At their inception, the First Crusade was completed and the Christians held Jerusalem (captured in 1099) and other major Levant cities. The Knights were formed by Hugues de Payns, a relative of a count in Champagne, who went to the Levant and made his home in Jerusalem in 1114. Some time later, Hugues took the vows of poverty, chastity and obedience to the Patriarch of Jerusalem and started the "Poor Knights of Christ and of the Temple of Solomon." Their duty was "to guard ways and paths from bandits for the salvation of pilgrims." As the first "Grand Master," Hugues was given a mosque—which at that time was believed to be Solomon's Temple—to house his men and horses. For the first few years, recruitment was difficult, so in 1128 Hugues and six of his brothers went on a "propaganda" tour.

They traveled throughout Europe, gaining wealth through land grants, gold and silver, and enlisting recruits. Most importantly, the Church defined its Rule of Order at the Council of Troyes in 1129. After this tour, the Knights Templar grew in popularity, power and wealth.

Hugues died in 1136 and was succeeded by Robert de Craon. In 1139, the Pope officially brought the Knights Templar under the protection and responsibility of the Holy See. They earned a prestigious reputation in heroic battles, along with the Hospitallers of St. John of Jerusalem and the Teutonic Knights. The Templar Knights always fought first and retreated last; their courage and discipline were unquestionable. However, the Templar Knights also experienced some major defeats, such as the Battle of Hattin in 1187 when almost all the Knights Templar, except for the Grand Master from Jerusalem, were killed (many after torture) because of poor decisions and pride. That defeat allowed Saladin to capture Jerusalem. The Knights built fortifications throughout the Levant as well as throughout France and its ports. Their wealth began to surpass counts and they even provided loans to the king of France.

After years of growing power and wealth, jealously developed among landowners and the King of France. In 1291, Acre, the last Crusader outpost, fell. With Acre gone, the purpose of the Templar Knights came into question: "If they aren't protecting pilgrims, then what are they doing?" At this time, the Templars were 15,000 men strong, including 1,500 knights, and maintained castles at geographically strategic locations. The Templars were seen as the Pope's Army, and thus were a threat to the King of France, Philip IV, especially after 1302, when Boniface VIII published a papal bull stating that the Pope was supreme over all men, kings included. On September 17, 1307, using reports of obscene practices and worship among the Knights as an excuse, Phillip issued a secret order to arrest all the Knights in France and seize their property. Over the objections of Pope Clement V, who had moved the papacy to Avignon, Philip conducted "interrogations," which quickly produced confessions. Of the 130 Knights in Paris, 38 died during the interrogations.

Unable to protect the Templars and vulnerable to French military forces, Clement V issued a papal bull to arrest all the Knights across Europe, but with the caveat that if they were found not guilty, they would get their property back! On August 12, 1308, the Church set up an investigative commission and in May of 1310, 54 Knights were burned at the stake. On March 22, 1312, a papal bull was issued abolishing the Order of the Temple and on May 2 their property was transferred to the Hospitaller Knights. Finally, on March 18, 1314, the last Grand Master, Jacques de Molay, was burned at the stake in Paris.

The following sites are related to the Templars in France:

2. **COMMANDERIE D'ARVILLE AND KNIGHTS TEMPLAR MUSEUM:** In 1128, the Templar Knights settled in Arville on a woody estate of 2,500 acres granted to them by Geoffroy III, lord of Mondoubleau. The Commanderie became a farming and recruitment center, a training base for Knights waiting

to depart for the Holy Land, and a place of worship. Only 20 minutes off the main highway, this is considered the best-preserved and most informative Templar site in France. It has a great museum, and you can explore the buildings, garden, chapel, pigeon barn, blacksmith shop, etc.
N 48 03.823 E 0 56.879 (48.063717, 0.947983)

3. **GISOR CASTLE (CHÂTEAU DE GISOR):** In 1307, the Templar Knights were falsely accused by King Phillip IV of heresy. On October 13, 1307, the king secretly had all the Templar Knights arrested, including the Grand Master, Jacques de Molay. Gisor Castle, not a Templar property, was used to imprison the captives. It is believed that the carvings on the walls were made by Templar prisoners. The castle is now part of a beautiful open park that includes well-kept ruins. In the 1930s, the caretaker reported that he had discovered a secret chapel with gold underneath the castle. To this day, his claim has not been verified. Well worth a quick stop.
N 49 16.788 E 1 46.383 (49.2798, 1.77305)

4. **CHAPELLE DES TEMPLIERS, METZ:** This is the only remains of a Templar commanderie in the area of Metz. The fact that it has survived is amazing. The paintings on the ceilings and the building's unusual shape are unique. Metz is an underrated city well worth visiting. The cathedral, with its Chagall stained glass windows, is especially amazing. (Also note the World War II forts and battlefields to visit just outside of town.)
N 49 06.867 E 6 10.183 (49.11445, 6.169717)

5. **MUSEUM OF TEMPLARS, PAYNS, NEAR DIJON:** Payns is the hometown of the founder of the Knights Templar, Hugues de Payns. In 1999, the remains of the Payns Commanderie were found. In Payns is a small museum that contains original artifacts.
N 48 22.986 E 3 58.507 (48.383107, 3.975122)

6. **PONT NEUF PLAQUE, PARIS:** A small plaque marks the spot where Jacque de Molay, the last Grand Master, was burned at the stake on March 18, 1314. Phillip IV, King of France, used trumped-up charges of heresy to have all the Knights Templar arrested on Friday October 13, 1307. He did this because he was intimidated by the Order's power and jealous of its wealth and land. Furthermore, he was in serious default on his debt to the Order and under threat of losing his kingdom. As a result, Pope Clement V, who was intimidated by King Phillip, disbanded the Order in 1312. Legend says that de Molay placed a curse on the king and the Pope when he stated at the stake that they would be before God's judgment within one year. Both "lived" up to the curse. That same year the Pope died of stomach problems, while the king died a few months later in a hunting accident. The plaque is just off the Pont Neuf bridge, down the stairs at the tip of the island.
N 48 51.413 E 2 20.456 (48.856883, 2.340933)

7. **MUSEUM OF THE ARMY, PARIS:** The museum has an excellent collection of armor, swords, etc. It is a must-see.
N 48 51.485 E 2 18.707 (48.858083, 2.311783)

8. **PALACE OF THE POPES, AVIGNON:** From 1309 to 1373, the Popes resided in Avignon. In 1305, Clement V, a Frenchman, was elected Pope and never bothered to move to Rome. In 1309, he moved his office staff from Rome to join him in Avignon, which became the residence for seven Popes after him. It was Clement V who, under pressure from the king, initiated the investigation and eventual demise of the Templars. The palace is very impressive. I highly suggest getting the audio guide and buying tickets online ahead of time. It is very popular and near many of the Roman sites. The coordinates provided are for a parking garage under the palace.
N 43 57.168 E 4 48.352 (43.9528, 4.805867)

THE DEATH OF KING RICHARD I, 1199

King Richard the Lionheart was killed by a simple soldier's arrow in 1199. Throughout the previous two years, he had returned from the Crusades, survived Austrian imprisonment, and defeated his cousin, King Phillip of France. He then began to exact his revenge on Phillip's weak "allies" in France. While the English attacked the castle at Châlus-Chabrol, Richard, in typical fashion, failed to heed danger and was hit in the arm by Peter Basil, a crossbowman. (Ironically, the crossbow was Richard's favorite weapon.) During an "operation," a doctor/butcher removed the wood from Richard's arm, then cut again to remove the metal tip. Before long, gangrene set in. Richard's men took the castle shortly afterward and Richard ordered all the defenders hanged except for Peter, whom he confronted, forgave and provided with 100 shillings, stating, "Live on, by my bounty behold the light of day. Let the vanquished learn by my example." On April 6, 1199, King Richard died. As an interesting side note, Richard's entrails are in the castle chapel; his heart is in Rouen Cathedral and his body is south of Saumur at Fontevraud Abbey. Note: In the next hundred years, England would fight France again for this territory.

The following are sites related to Richard:

9. **CHÂTEAU DE CHÂLUS-CHABROL:** The castle is in ruins and fenced off, but available for tour by contacting the town's mayor or the visitor center. One of the community's streets is named for Peter Basil, the man who killed the king.
N 45 39.323 E 0 58.708 (45.655378, 0.978462)

10. **ROUEN CATHEDRAL:** In addition to being the repository of King Richard's heart, the cathedral is beautiful and was used by Claude Monet for a famous series of paintings.
N 49 26.389 E 1 05.719 (49.439817, 1.095317)

11. **FONTEVRAUD ABBEY:** Located just west of Orléans, the abbey contains the traditional tomb of King Richard. The village of Fontevraud-l'Abbaye is very beautiful and close to the Saumur Tank Museum and Amboise, the location of Leonardo Da Vinci's tomb.
N 47 10.883 E 0 03.100 (47.181383, 0.051667)

12. **CHÂTEAU GAILLARD:** In 1196, King Richard the Lionheart, after his return from the Crusades, constructed Château Gaillard to protect Normandy from his cousin, Phillip II of France. It sits on the natural high ground and provides excellent views of the Seine River and the valley below; such features helped King Richard prevent invasions, as well as maintain the ability to launch an attack. In 1204, Phillip captured it after a very long siege. It displays significant advancements in castle design, such as the first use of "murder holes" on the outer walls. It is a great place to visit and very close to Rouen and Gisor.
N 49 14.317 E 1 24.133 (49.238617, 1.402217)

OTHER SITES:

13. **HAUT KOENIGSBURG:** In 1114, the Swabian Emperor Frederick of Hohenstaufen built the first Teutonic Knight castle here. It was destroyed in 1462, rebuilt by the Habsburgs, and then destroyed again by Swedish troops during the Thirty Years' War in 1633. After Germany conquered the Alsace region during the Franco-Prussian War, Kaiser Wilhelm II commissioned the reconstruction of the castle, which was completed in the early 1900s. In 1918 the French took it back after World War I. It is now a very popular site to visit in Alsace, just south of Strasbourg, and well worth a visit.
N 48 14.955 E 7 20.644 (48.24925, 7.344067)

14. **ABBEY CLUNY:** Founded in 910 AD as part of the St. Benedictine Order, this was the most powerful abbey in Western Europe. The monks organized societal rules and the abbey served as a cornerstone of medieval life, holding communities together, defining the code of knights, and preserving education and art. In 1790, the abbey was sacked during the French Revolution and never recovered. Although it is now in ruins, an excellent walking tour is available. The museum at the site contains artifacts and also shows a 3D film.
N 46 26.138 E 4 39.477 (46.435633, 4.65795)

15. **CASTLE CARCASSONNE:** During the Albigensian Crusades from 1209-1255, which were waged against the Cathars in southern France, this castle was a Cathar stronghold. The Cathars were a benign Catholic sect that protested against the corrupt Church but were seen as heretics. It is during this crusade against the Cathars that a papal legate Arnaud Amalric told the knights attacking a Cathar town, "Kill them all, God will know his own." The castle, which was rebuilt in the 1800s, is extremely well maintained, with shops, a museum and restaurants throughout the grounds.
N 43 12.389 E 2 21.987 (43.206491, 2.366455)

CRUSADER SITES IN FRANCE

MAP 8

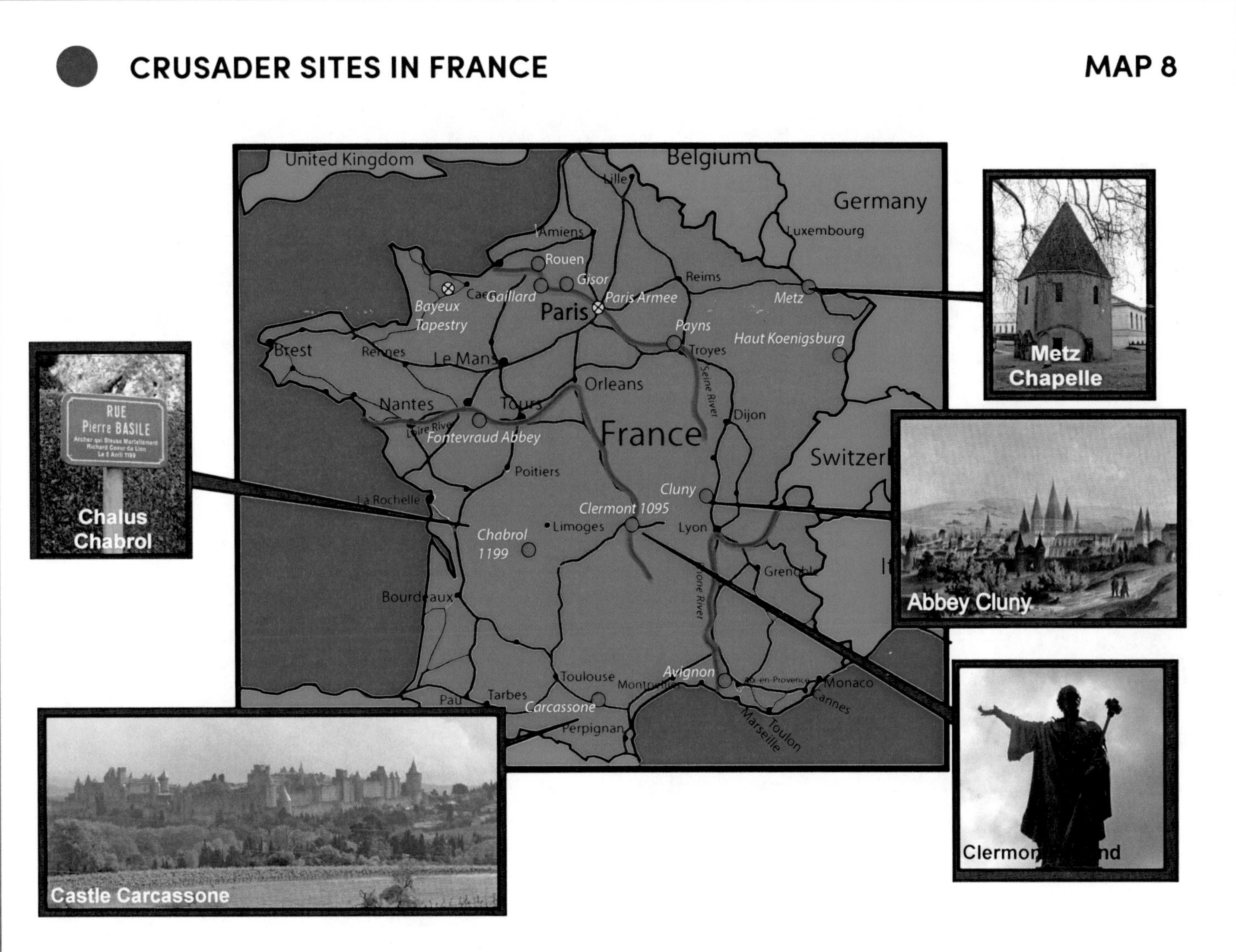
United Kingdom
Belgium
Germany
Lille
Luxembourg
Amiens
Rouen
Gisor
Gaillard
Reims
Metz
Bayeux
Tapestry
Paris
Paris Armee
Payns
Troyes
Haut Koenigsburg
Brest
Rennes
Le Mans
Orleans
Nantes
Tours
Fontevraud Abbey
France
Seine River
Dijon
Switzer
Poitiers
La Rochelle
Cluny
Clermont 1095
Lyon
Chabrol
1199
Limoges
Grenoble
Bourdeaux
Toulouse
Avignon
Monaco
Cannes
Pau
Tarbes
Carcassone
Perpignan
Marseille
Toulon
Metz
Chapelle
RUE
Pierre BASILE
Chalus
Chabrol
Abbey Cluny
Castle Carcassone

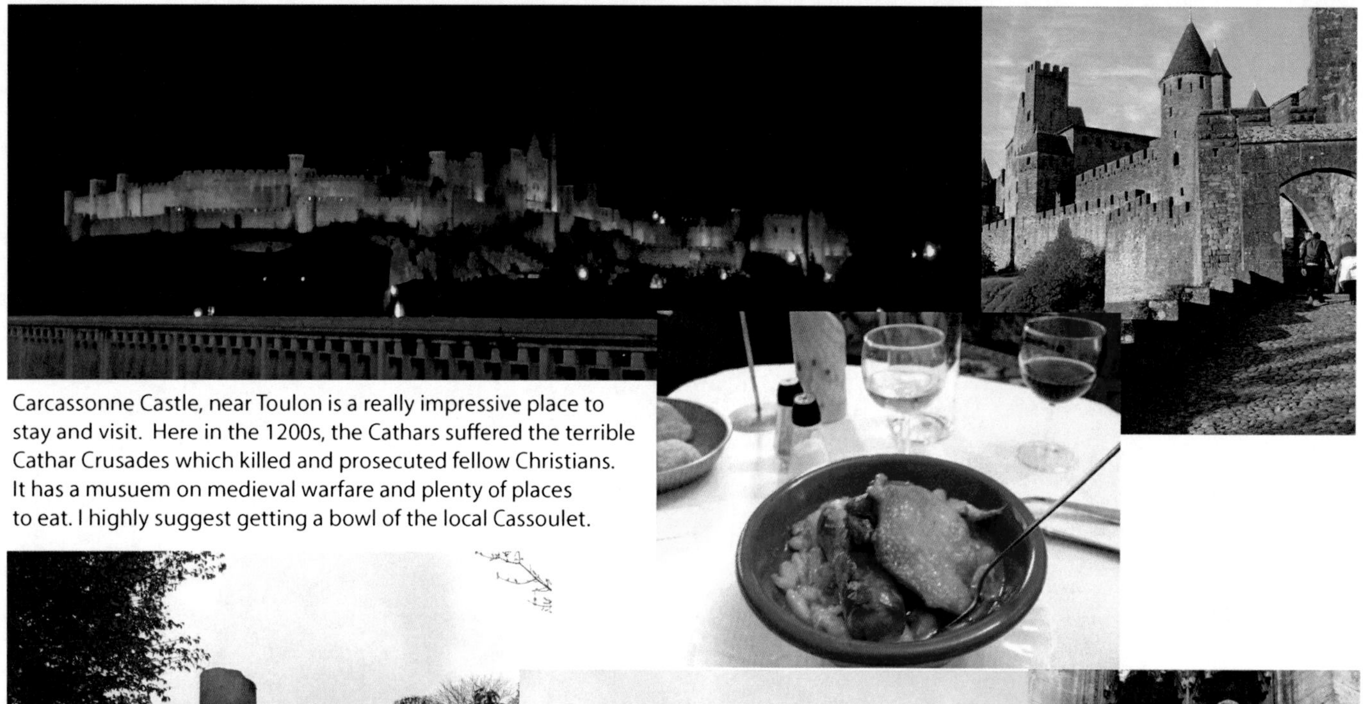

Carcassonne Castle, near Toulon is a really impressive place to stay and visit. Here in the 1200s, the Cathars suffered the terrible Cathar Crusades which killed and prosecuted fellow Christians. It has a musuem on medieval warfare and plenty of places to eat. I highly suggest getting a bowl of the local Cassoulet.

A King's death, in 1199 Richard the Lionheart was killed attacking this castle by the crossbow of Peter Basil. Now you can visit the remains of the castle which houses a small musuem. Peter who was paid and pardoned by King Richard has a street named after him next to the Castle.

North of Paris, in the Rouen Cathedral, is King Richard's tomb. (photo right). Rouen is a wonderful small city to visit for St. Joan of Arc and the beautiful Cathedral which Monet painted in a series of paintings in the shifting sun rays during winter, rain and sun.

les Andelys
Château Gaillard
par Richard Coeur de Lion,
by Richard The Lion Heart,

Just south of Rouen, is Chateau Gaillard built by King Richard to control the trade on the Seine River to - from Normandy. His cousin King Phillip II captured the castle in 1204. A great stop for 2-3 hours.

Castle Gisor is located just south of Chateau Gaillard on the way to Paris in a small park within its old walls. It was not a Templar castle, however it was used to imprison the Templar Knights in 1307 when they were arrested.

Above, the Knights Templar seal. To the right is where it all started, in Clermont Ferrand, west of Lyon. There you can see the statue of Pope Urban II outside the Cathedral which has beautiful stained glass windows and impressive architecture.

In southern France, near the Roman Aqueduct Pont du Gard, is the impressive Avignon Palace and Cathedral. There you can take a self guided listening tour to learn about the French Popes who moved the Papacy to Avignon from 1309 to 1373. It i s always a beautiful opportunity to stop in the many French Churches to rest, give thanks and light a candle.

Commanderie d'Arville, located between Saumur and Paris, is one of the best preserved Knights Templar training centers. (if not the best) There you can take a tour of the museum that provides scenes from the Knights' history and walk around outside to see the various buildings of the Commanderie, the forge, pigeon building, chapel, fish pond, kitchen and more.

Haupt Koenigsburg, located in beautiful Alsace just north of Colmar. The picture to the left you can see the castle on the the far right hill. The Vosges Mountain range flows into the Alsace plain full of vineyards and picturesque villages to visit.

Alsace Region, is truly a great place to spend a few days or more! The local food and wine is excellent. Plus it has many places to visit related to WW2. See the Alsace Campaign in this book to explore more. The photos here are of the towns Riquewihr and Ribeauville.

–Chapter 4–

THE MIDDLE AGES AND THE 100 YEARS' WAR, 1000–1500

As Europe grew out of the Dark Ages and into the Middle Ages, it acquired more complex civilizations and experienced the expansion of learned people and organizations. However, its population continued to fight over hereditary rights. In particular, a battle persisted among the intertwined families of England and France. In this chapter I discuss the major battles of that time period. The following is a brief timeline for reference; also reference Map 10 for a summary of locations related to the 100 Years' War:

1214	The Battle of Bouvines occurs, during which King John's French exploits are defeated.
1215	Magna Carta – The barons force King John to concede additional power.
1259	The Treaty of Paris between Henry III of England and Louis IX of France acknowledges the loss of most of the Angevin Empire. Henry III retains the Duchy of Aquitaine as a vassal of Louis IX.
1328	Charles IV of France dies leaving only daughters. His sister, Isabella of France, now the effective ruler of England, claims the French throne for her son, Edward III of England, who is Charles' closest living male relative. The French nobility favors Philip VI, the closest in the unbroken male line.
1330	Edward III is crowned King of England.
1346	The English defeat the French during the Battle of Crécy.
1347	The English capture Calais.
1348	The Black Death arrives in Europe.
1356	During the Battle of Poitiers, the English again defeat the French.
1360	In the Treaty of Bretigny, Edward III renounces his claim to the French throne. In return he receives the suzerainty of Aquitaine. As a result, the Black Prince becomes the Duke of Aquitaine.
1415	During the Battle of Agincourt, the English defeat the French again.
1417	The English capture Caen.
1420	Henry V and Charles VI sign the Treaty of Troyes, which stipulates that Henry marry Charles' daughter. Henry V dies of dysentery in 1422; Charles VI dies the same year. Henry VI, not even a year old, is crowned King of France and England, though Charles VI's son continues the war.
1429	St. Joan of Arc breaks the siege of Orléans. She escorts the Dauphin to Reims so that he can be crowned King of France.
1430	The Burgundians capture St. Joan of Arc and sell her to the English, who execute her as a heretic.
1450	The French defeat the English during the Battle of Formigny.
1453	The French defeat the English during the Battle of Castillon, considered the end of the 100 Years' War. The English are too busy with the War of the Roses to continue fighting in France. However, the English hold Calais until 1558 and the English king retains the title "King of France" until 1801!

100 YEARS' WAR SUMMARY

MAP 10

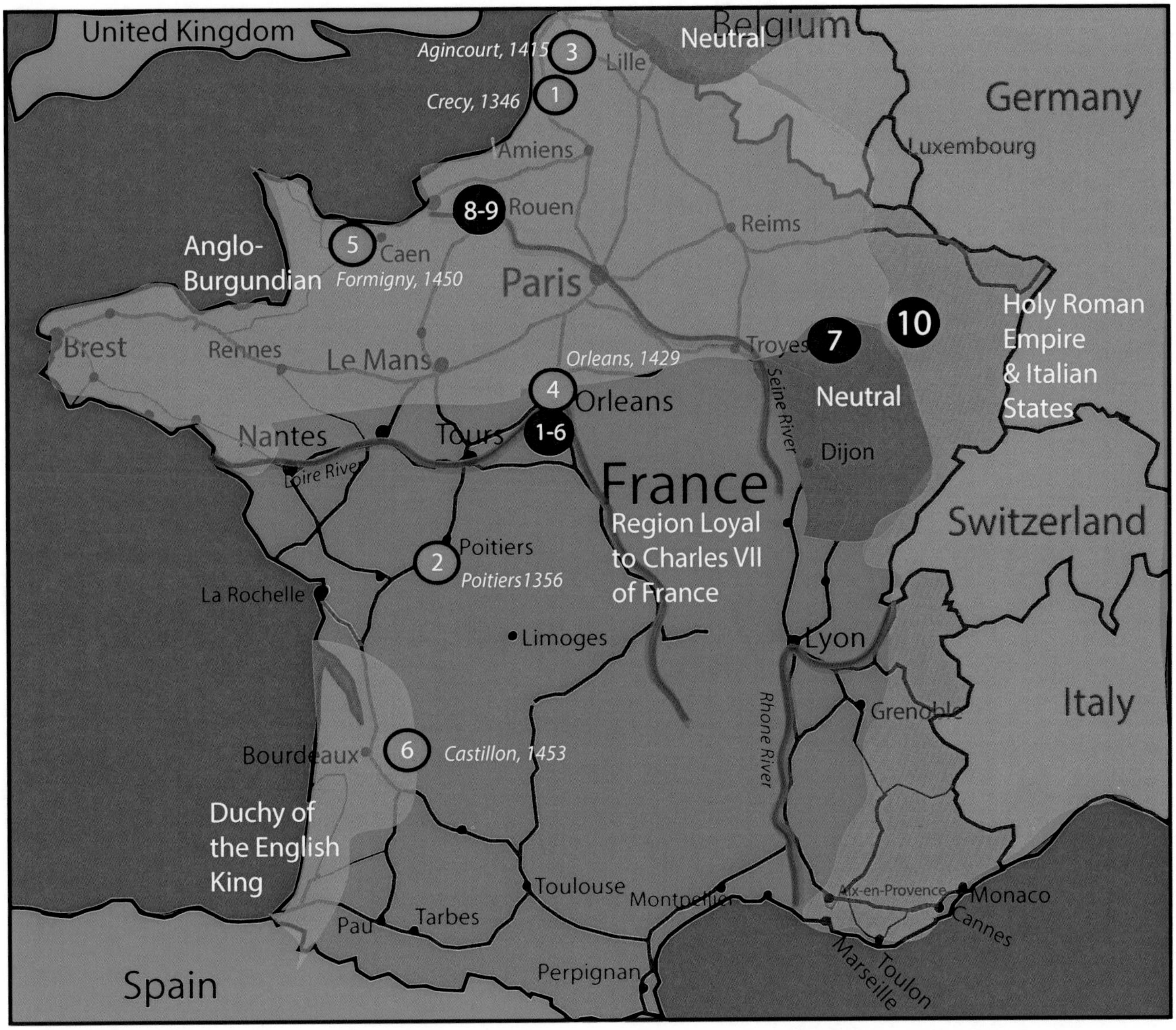

United Kingdom
Agincourt, 1415
Crecy, 1346
Lille
Neutral
Belgium
Germany
Luxembourg
Amiens
Rouen
Reims
Anglo-Burgundian
Caen
Formigny, 1450
Paris
Holy Roman Empire & Italian States
Brest
Rennes
Le Mans
Orleans, 1429
Troyes
Orleans
Neutral
Seine River
Nantes
Tours
Dijon
Loire River
France
Region Loyal to Charles VII of France
Switzerland
Poitiers
Poitiers1356
La Rochelle
Limoges
Lyon
Italy
Grenoble
Rhone River
Bourdeaux
Castillon, 1453
Duchy of the English King
Toulouse
Montpellier
Aix-en-Provence
Monaco
Cannes
Pau
Tarbes
Marseille
Toulon
Spain
Perpignan

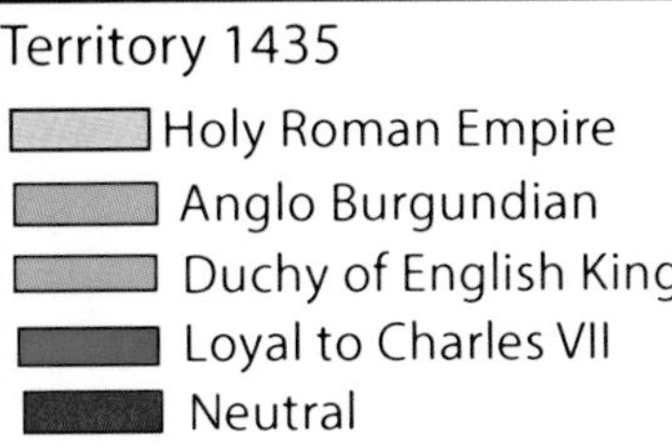
Territory 1435
Holy Roman Empire
Anglo Burgundian
Duchy of English King
Loyal to Charles VII
Neutral

Major Battles
1 Battle of Crecy, 1346
2 Battle of Poitiers 1356
3 Battle of Agincourt, 1415
4 Battle of Orleans, 1429
5 Battle of Formigny, 1450
6 Battle of Castillon, 1453

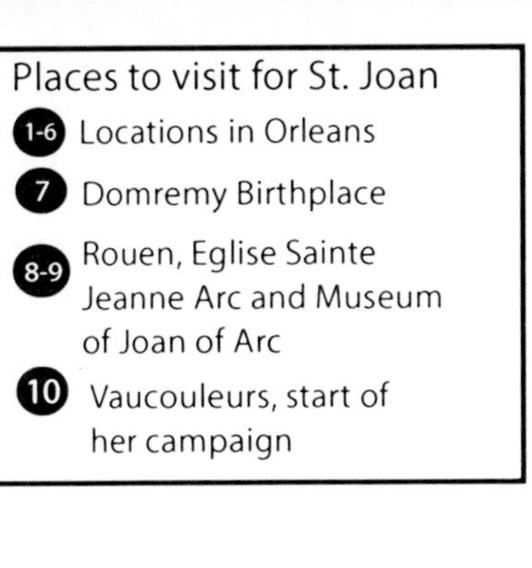
Places to visit for St. Joan
1-6 Locations in Orleans
7 Domremy Birthplace
8-9 Rouen, Eglise Sainte Jeanne Arc and Museum of Joan of Arc
10 Vaucouleurs, start of her campaign

BATTLE OF BOUVINES

July 27, 1214

"Lord I am but a man, but I am king. Thine is to guard the king. Thou wilt lose nothing thereby. "Wherever Thou would go I will follow Thee." – King Philip II

SUMMARY: In the spring of 1214, King John of England invaded southern France with his army; his goal was to regain land lost in previous years. At the same time, King John's allies attacked in the north to destroy the French King Philip II (later known as Philip Augustus). King Philip II was on a campaign to unify France under his rule. He wanted to conquer Normandy and Brittany in the north while sending his son to defeat King John in the south. In the north King Philip II and his 15,000 men marched away from King John's allied forces, commanded by King John's nephew, the Holy Roman Emperor Otto IV. Otto had approximately 25,000 men under his command and was in hot pursuit of the French forces strung out along the old Roman Road to Bouvines. While under pursuit, the French sent their engineers ahead to widen and reinforce the bridge over the Marcq River, a move that would expedite their retreat. However, by mid-morning, one of Philip's commanders from the Knights Hospitallers advised him that Otto's forces were gaining ground in an attempt to attack his rearguard. Shortly afterward, the French rearguard fought Otto's vanguard and successfully held up against Otto's advance. In the meantime, Philip ordered his infantry to cross back over the river and form a defensive line. The French lined up in three sections, each with two formations. In the right and left flanks a formation of infantry backed the cavalry. The infantry was at the front of the center section, backed by the heavy cavalry. Otto arrived believing that he could pounce on a straggling and retreating force. Instead he found a fully formed French defensive line with approximately 4,000 cavalry and knights and 11,000 infantry. The French defensive line forced Otto to hold and set his own men for pitched battle so that he could avoid encirclement. Otto lined up in a formation similar to the French, with a total of 25,000 infantry and knights. Flemish commander Ferrand led the left flank, Emperor Otto and his German cavalry and infantry composed the center, and the right flank consisted of English and Bolognese troops. The process of arranging these formations took approximately an hour. Then, at about noon, with the sun behind them, 300 French cavalry charged from the right flank into the Flemish position on Otto's left. The mounted knights clashed with sword and axe. Next, the pikemen from Germany and the Netherlands attacked the French center, breaking deep into the line. Shortly afterward, the French center broke. The French king was knocked off his horse, but French knights rushed to his aid. As the Allied forces attacked deeper into the French center, they turned their right flank slightly. The maneuver was enough for the French left flank to smash into the English right flank, destroy the heavy cavalry and capture their commander, the Earl of Salisbury. As Otto's right flank collapsed, the French attacked his center. Within a short period Otto was fighting for his life and knocked from his horse. The French quickly descended on the Emperor, but his imperial guard courageously defended him and gave him a horse to escape the battle. The conflict was over after only three hours.

OUTCOME: As a result, King Philip saved his throne and united more of France by capturing Brittany and Normandy. In addition, he gained lands in Flanders, as France had defeated the Flemish Commander Ferrand. Emperor Otto IV was removed from the throne, and another Emperor, Frederick II Hohenstaufen, was elected. King John of England was extremely weakened by his defeat France. Because of his reduced power and influence, King John signed the Magna Carta in 1215.

WHAT WAS IT OVER? Flanders wanted to gain back some of the land it had lost to France; the English also wanted to defeat the French. For the French, it was a battle to save their throne.

WHO? The French forces consisted of 11,000 foot soldiers and 4,000 cavalry under the command of King Philip Augustus. The Allied forces consisted of French, Flemish, German and English troops, approximately 25,000 men in total. They were under the command of the Holy Roman Emperor Otto IV, the nephew of King John of England. Approximately 1,000 French troops were killed; it is estimated that more than 1,000 Allied troops were killed and 9,000 captured.

WHEN? Sunday, July 27, 1214. The fact that this battle took place on a Sunday is significant, as it flouted the laws of war and chivalry, but the Germans had already been excommunicated.

WHY AT BOUVINES? The French commander realized that he needed to stand and fight before his troops were overwhelmed crossing the river. Some also believe that he had found the perfect flat terrain for his cavalry to wage battle.

TECHNOLOGY/TACTICS: Both sides wielded the same type of equipment, swords, chain mail, pikes, crossbows, war hammers and axes. However, Otto IV had been excommunicated, so that is why he lost! In reality, Otto had a discipline issue with his men, as his troops spoke different languages and maintained different cultures. Discipline broke down when the Flemish did not wait for all their forces to catch up and form a line before they engaged the French. The French also had an advantage in the form of more cavalry and the fact that their defensive position came as a surprise to Otto and his forces. Both sides used the cavalry as a hammer to the infantry, breaking lines and creating panic (which occurred early on in the Allied Flemish ranks). To stunt the cavalry charges as best they could, both sides also used pikemen, who wielded long poles, or "pikes," with a spike for the horse, a hook to pull the knight off the horse, and an axe edge to smash into the knight.

QUOTE: "Lord I am but a man, but I am king. Thine is to guard the king. Thou wilt lose nothing thereby. Wherever Thou would go I will follow Thee." – King Philip Augustus

PLACES TO SEE (REFERENCE MAP 9):

***Please note that, based on my research, I have the battle formations fighting perpendicular to the Roman Road and the French backs to the river. Other sources believe that the forces were parallel to the road and that the French right flank was next to the river. Either way, the battle definitely took place around the Roman Road and east of Bouvines and the river.*

1. **ROMAN ROAD, "CHEMIN DE BOUVINES E TOURNAI":** This geo coordinate is on the old Roman Road, believed to be the retreat route for King Philip's army. It is also believed to be the center point of his army and of the battle; the king faced east from this approximate location.
   N 50 34.818 E 3 12.171 (50.5803, 3.20285)

2. **CHAPELLE AUX AUBRES:** This location on the old Roman Road is the approximate site where Otto IV set up his center formations.
   N 50 34.775 E 3 13.182 (50.579583, 3.2197)

3. **BOUVINE CHURCH, "ST. PIERRE CHURCH":** In this church are beautiful 19th-century stained glass windows depicting the battle. Nearby is the spring in which King Philip is said to have quenched his thirst before the battle and after prayer.
   N 50 34.740 E 3 11.209 (50.579, 3.186817)

4. **OBELISK MEMORIAL FOR THE BATTLE:** At this location is a stone obelisk commemorating the battle. It's next to a memorial for World Wars I and II.
   N 50 34.706 E 3 11.310 (50.578433, 3.1885)

5. **BRIDGE OVER THE RIVER LA MARQUE:** The river has been engineered since 1214, but its current location is only approximately near its original location. At this site, part of the French Army crossed the river before the king recalled them to face Otto.
   N 50 34.764 E 3 10.922 (50.5794, 3.182033)

BATTLE OF BOUVINES JULY 27, 1214

MAP 9

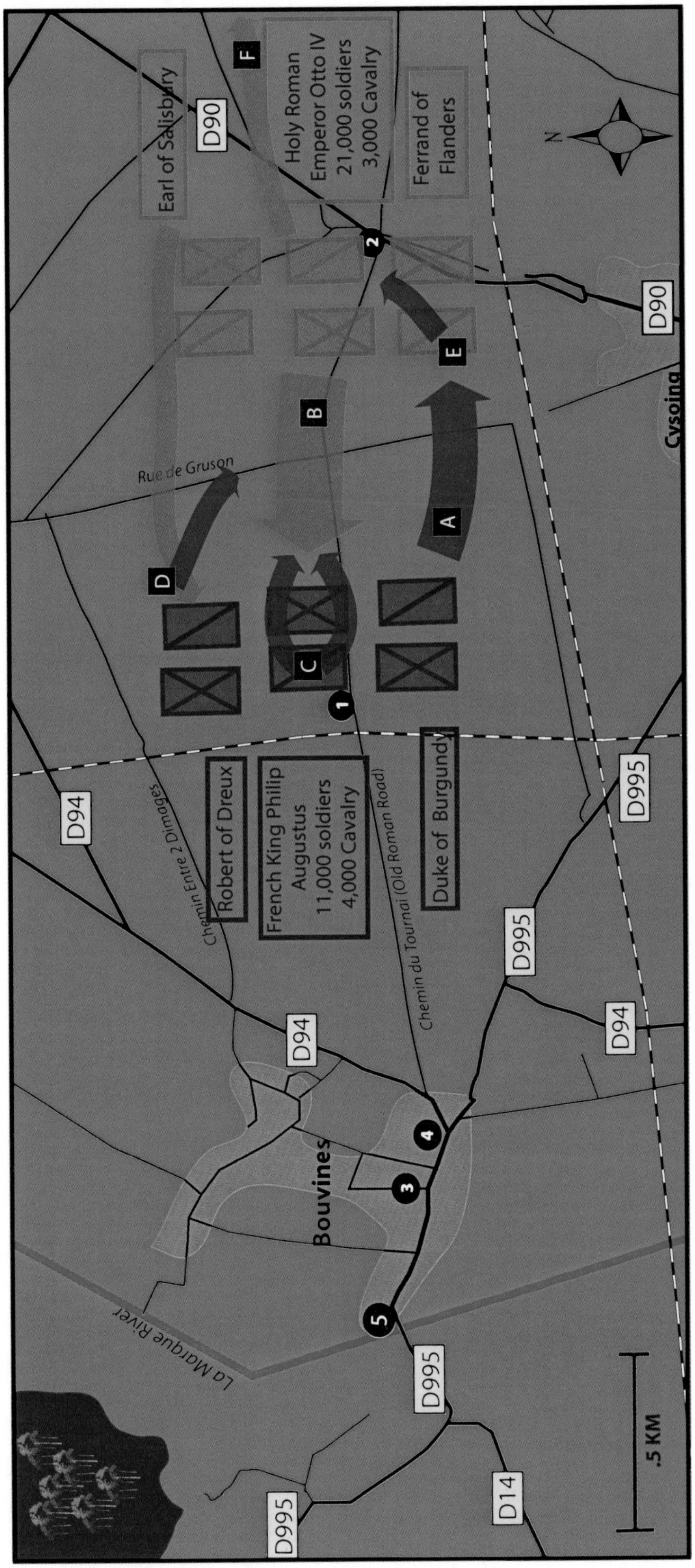

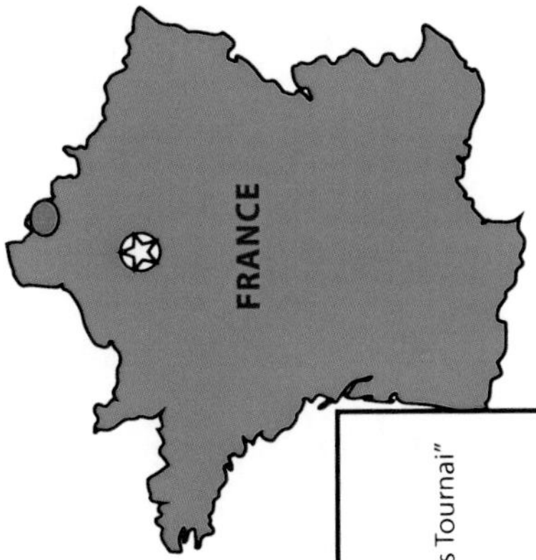

Earl of Salisbury
Holy Roman Emperor Otto IV
21,000 soldiers
3,000 Cavalry
Ferrand of Flanders
Robert of Dreux
French King Philip Augustus
11,000 soldiers
4,000 Cavalry
Duke of Burgundy
Chemin Entre 2 Dimages
Chemin du Tournai (Old Roman Road)
Rue de Gruson
La Marque River
Bouvines
Cysoing
D94
D90
D995
D14
.5 KM
N
FRANCE

Movements:

A. After some skirmishing, at approximately noon, 300 French Knights charged the Flemish Cavalry.
B. Next Otto ordered the powerful pikemen to charge the French center and they broke through the French line.
C. Then the King of France, charged into the battle to bolster his center. In the attack he was unhorsed but saved by his Knights.
D. On the French left, Dreux was reeling back but they unhorsed & captured Salisbury. As a result the Emperor's right flank dissolved in a panic.
E. Finally, the French defeated the Flemish cavalry on the right flank.
F. Next Emperor Otto was surrounded and unhorsed. His knights defended him and he barely escaped with some of his remaining knights.

Places to See:

1. Roman Road: "Chemin de Bouvines Tournai"
2. Chapelle Aux Aubres
3. Bouvine Church, "St. Pierre Church"
4. Obelisk memorial for the battle
5. Today's bridge over the river is close to the location to where it was in 1214.

BATTLE OF CRÉCY

August 26, 1346 – 100 Years' War

"Let the boy earn his spurs." – King Edward III

SUMMARY: The Battle of Crécy was one of the most important conflicts of the 100 Years' War (1337–1453). The 100 Years' War began when the French king died in 1328. Edward III of England decided to claim the French throne because his mother was the French king's sister. However, under French law inheritance followed through male relatives, not female relatives. At this time the British still had land in Ponthieu, near Crécy, and in southwest France, in Aquitaine (the same area where King Richard had been killed 150 years earlier). At the beginning of the 100 Years' War, the new French king had a stronger navy than the English did and began to attack the English wool and wine trade. Within a few years England defeated the French at sea and began to invade Normandy. The French King Philip VI left Paris to meet this threat. The English, outnumbered three to one, retreated across the Somme River toward Flanders, then turned at Crécy to face the French. King Edward III, along with his son, Edward the Prince of Wales, set up a defensive line of pits and trenches. On the left flank they positioned 3,000 longbow archers and 1,000 foot soldiers; on the right flank next to Crécy the 16-year-old Prince of Wales commanded 3,000 additional archers, 1,000 Welsh infantry and 1,000 men at arms. In the center rear/reserve, King Edward positioned 2,000 archers and 700 knights. After 18 hours of chasing the English, the French finally caught up to them. The French were less organized and disciplined than the English were because the French forces contained soldiers of various nationalities and from various principalities. This disorganization and lack of discipline meant that the French attacked before they were ready. For example, when some of the French nobility spotted the English on the hill at approximately 1800 hours, their vanity took over. They wanted to charge the English and King Philip was unable to stop them. The king wanted to rest and wait until the next day but now forced to battle he ordered 6,000 Genoese crossbow mercenaries forward in an attempt to "loosen up" the English lines before the knights charged. With the sun in their eyes and on the heels of an 18-hour march, the Genoese moved forward. Light rain affected the rope on their crossbows, causing the bolts to fall short. The English answered immediately with their longbows. It was stated that they shot "60,000 arrows in 60 seconds" at the Genoese crossbow men. The Genoese mercenaries were defenseless and began to retreat, but were blocked by the line of French knights. Upon seeing their retreat, King Philip ordered his knights to "kill me those scoundrels" (Jean Froissart's Chronicles). While slaying their allies, the knights were pummeled by English arrows. Next, the French knights, with all their bravery, charged the English 15 times without success. Blind John, King of Bohemia, a French Ally wanted to fight and thus was tied between two of his knights so that he could charge the English. However, he was cut down during the battle. At one point the

French managed to get close to the King of England and the prince. In fact, the prince was knocked down. When the king was asked if knights should be sent to the prince's aid, Edward replied, "Let the boy win his spurs." By the end of the day the Prince of Wales (later called the Black Prince because of his dark armor) had won his spurs. The French were beaten back and the king had to retreat with what was left of his forces. The French were destroyed; 10,000 of their forces were killed, including 1,200 irreplaceable knights. By contrast, only 500 English were killed. As a sign of respect for the old blind noble King John, the Black Prince took the ostrich feathers from King John's helmet and made them part of his crest. To this day, Wales's crest includes ostrich feathers.

OUTCOME: England and France fought for another 100 years. The English kept Calais until 1558. The battle inspired efforts to unify France with the goal of defeating a common enemy. It also marked the end of "classic chivalry." No longer did princes fight on horseback or face capture and ransom. Instead, a single arrow could fell a great knight. Just two years later, in 1348, the Black Death hit Europe, killing over one-third of the population.

WHAT WAS IT OVER? French land and inheritance. In addition, trading rights (such as England's ability to send wool to Flanders/Holland and wine from their land in southwest France) were threatened.

WHO? King Edward III of England led a force of 12,000 men, while King Philip IV of France led an estimated 30,000 men. French and Genoese casualties are estimated to have numbered between 10,000 and 30,000. The most likely figure is 10,000, including 11 princes, 1,200 knights and an archbishop. The English lost about 500 men. Among the French dead were such important nobles as:

- Charles II, Count of Alençon, Philip VI's brother

- John I (The Blind) King of Bohemia and Count of Luxemburg

- Louis I, Count of Flanders

- Rudolph, Duke of Lorraine

WHEN? August 21, 1346

WHY AT CRÉCY? It was a defensible position. After crossing the Somme at Crécy, King Edward turned and faced the French. If he needed to retreat, he had Flanders at his rear for refuge.

TECHNOLOGY/TACTICS: The English used the longbow—which outperformed the crossbow in terms of rapid fire and range—to defeat the French heavy cavalry. Use of the longbow required as much as three years of training (as compared to the crossbow, which required little training), but the longbow was much more effective than the crossbow and less expensive than heavily armored knights. The English also had four cannons, thereby instituting the weapon's first use in

Western European battle (though the cannons did not significantly affect the conflict's results). Note: Raising an army was expensive, but the king could call upon his men to deliver troops according to the value of each man's land. For example, if one's land was worth 100 shillings, he had to provide an archer, a value of ten pounds, a light soldier and land valued at 20 pounds a man at arms. However, the more the king asked of his people in terms of taxes, the more land, positions and power he had to grant.

Quote: "Let the boy win his spurs" – King Edward III

PLACES TO SEE (REFERENCE MAP 11):

1. **MOULIN EDOUARD III:** This is a three-story observation tower located on Rue Principale between Crécy en Ponthieu and Wadicourt. It provides a view of the battlefield from King Edward's perspective.
   N 50 15.382 E 1 53.234 (50.256367, 1.887233)

2. **CROIX DE BOHEME:** At this location, the site where King John the Blind died, sits an old stone cross dedicated to his memory. It is located on D56 east of Crécy en Ponthieu.
   N 50 14.626 E 1 54.641 (50.243774, 1.910679)

3. **JOHN THE BLIND MONUMENT, CRÉCY:** Crécy has a nice little downtown. If you visit, this is one of the things you'll see.
   N 50 15.159 E 1 52.952 (50.25265, 1.882533)

4. **STATUE OF THE BURGHERS, CALAIS:** In the city center across from the mayor's house sits a sculpture of six burghers. French sculptor Auguste Rodin completed it in the 1880s. After King Edward III won at Crécy, he made a siege of Calais, the closest port to England. The French king couldn't lift the siege and after almost a year, in August 1347, the city of Calais surrendered. King Edward III required that six town leaders/burghers surrender themselves with nooses around their necks; in return, he would spare the rest of the civilians. At the last moment, King Edward's wife pleaded for the burghers' lives and release. King Edward III relented and freed them. However, he exiled all the inhabitants of Calais and replaced them with English settlers and supporters. As a result, Calais was the last French town to remain in English possession; the French finally recaptured it in 1558.
   N 50 57.137 E 1 51.211 (50.952289, 1.853514)

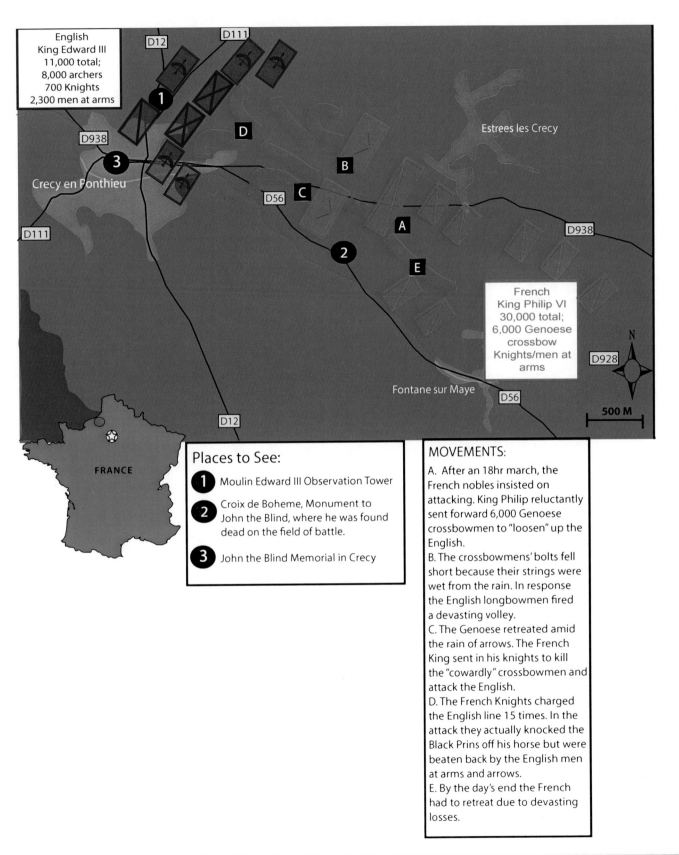

BATTLE OF CRECY, AUGUST 26, 1346

MAP 11

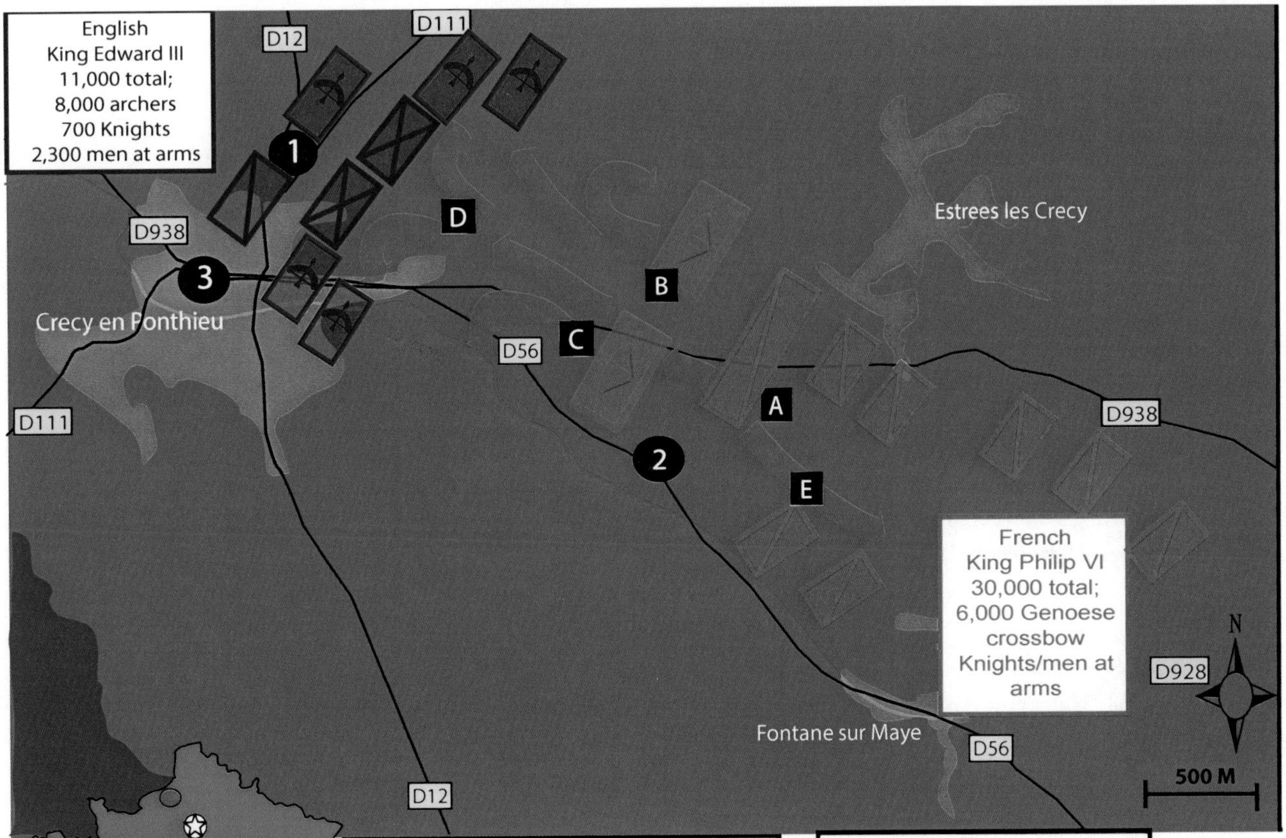

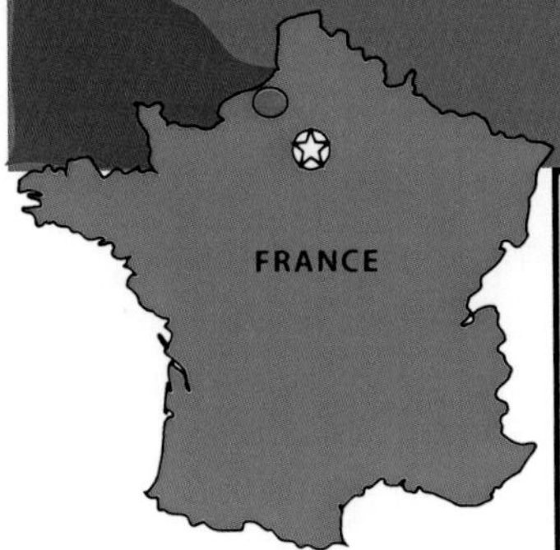

English
King Edward III
11,000 total;
8,000 archers
700 Knights
2,300 men at arms

D12
D111
D938
D56
D928
Crecy en Ponthieu
Estrees les Crecy
Fontane sur Maye
A
B
C
D
E
N
500 M
FRANCE

French
King Philip VI
30,000 total;
6,000 Genoese
crossbow
Knights/men at
arms

Places to See:

1. Moulin Edward III Observation Tower
2. Croix de Boheme, Monument to John the Blind, where he was found dead on the field of battle.
3. John the Blind Memorial in Crecy

MOVEMENTS:

A. After an 18hr march, the French nobles insisted on attacking. King Philip reluctantly sent forward 6,000 Genoese crossbowmen to "loosen" up the English.

B. The crossbowmens' bolts fell short because their strings were wet from the rain. In response the English longbowmen fired a devasting volley.

C. The Genoese retreated amid the rain of arrows. The French King sent in his knights to kill the "cowardly" crossbowmen and attack the English.

D. The French Knights charged the English line 15 times. In the attack they actually knocked the Black Prins off his horse but were beaten back by the English men at arms and arrows.

E. By the day's end the French had to retreat due to devasting losses.

BATTLE OF POITIERS

September 19, 1356 – 100 Years' War

(Known to the French as the Battle of Maupertius)

"From that time on all went wrong with the Kingdom and the state was undone." – Friar Jean de Venette

---

SUMMARY: The Battle of Poitiers (or Maupertius) was the second great victory for the English in the 100 Years' War. The battle ended with the capture of the French king. Since 1348, all of Europe had been experiencing the Black Plague; as of 1356 both England and France were still recovering from the devastation it wreaked, as well as from the expenses of war. Crops and supplies for daily living were scarce, and even more so for war. Despite this fact, in 1350, King John II attempted to reform his French army and fortify his cities as much as possible. In 1355, King Edward II launched three chevauchée (or raids) to destroy French land and turn the inhabitants against their king. During the first raid King Edward II attacked in Calais; then, the Duke of Lancaster attacked in Normandy, while the Prince of Wales attacked from Bordeaux. The first two raids failed, but the Prince of Wales's attack succeeded. In October 1355, Edward, the Prince of Wales (the previously mentioned Black Prince) advanced from his base in Aquitaine, near Bordeaux. His first attack involved a 1,100-kilometer round-trip journey to Narbonne, which he couldn't take, though he did succeed in pillaging and burning more than 500 villages! In response, the French king mobilized his army and alliances. As the Black Prince wintered in Bordeaux, the French retook more than 300 towns and castles. In the summer, the English were at it again; by August 8, the Black Prince and his men had turned to Tours on the Loire River with plans to take the city, then travel north to Orléans. The Black Prince's troops failed to defeat the French forces in Tours and were prevented by the French from crossing the Loire River. The Black Prince attempted to solicit help from the Duke of Lancaster, who was in Normandy, but the French were also blocking the Duke on the Loire. Then the Black Prince received word that the French king was on the move. The French King John II (or John "the Good") led a force of approximately 11,000 from Chartres to destroy the Black Prince and his force of 6,000. The Black Prince retreated south from Montlouis to St. Maure, was blocked at La Haye (Descartes), Chatellerault, then hid in the woods to shadow the French. The king of France surprised the English by the speed with which he not only blocked them at La Haye but also overtook them and passed his flank across the English front. As in modern warfare, both sides sent out scouts to find and make contact with the enemy. The English were low in supplies, food and especially water, and the Black Prince knew they were too slow to outrun the French. He had to fight. Just past Poitiers, the Black Prince consulted the monks of Nouialle Abbey, located on the Miosson River. The monks suggested that he use the Nouialle Woods as a defensive position on the north side of the Miosson. On September 18, the Black Prince set up his forces with the river on his left flank (to the south), the forest on his rear (to the east) and a hedgerow in front of him. He dug a ditch on his right flank. The Black Prince's forces contained 2,000 archers, 1,000 infantry and 3,000 men at arms. The English aligned longbowmen with the Earl of Salisbury on the right flank. The Black Prince positioned his troops in the center and sent longbowmen to the Earl of Warwick on the left flank with instructions to cover the baggage train's movement. The French king maintained forces of approximately 8,000 men at arms and 3,000 infantry in battle formation. Early in the morning of September 19, the French unfurled their banners and dismounted most of their cavalry, as their scouts had seen a strong defensive position. However, the king retained a few hundred heavily armored chargers for shock effect if needed. The French king aligned his army with a mounted force under the command of Marshal Clermont on the left flank, three "divisions" in the center (from front to rear, Dauphin Charles, Duc d'Orléans and King John II) and Marshal Audrehem with more cavalry and crossbowmen in the right flank. The battle started with Marshal Audrehem, as he saw the English baggage train withdrawing south over the river. The French attack failed because it was funneled by the hedgerows and the terrain, making the troops easy targets for English archers using deadly longbows to attack the flanks of heavily armored knights and horses. Next, on the left flank, Marshal Clermont charged and, with the help of his dismounted men at arms, almost broke through the hedges. However, again the hedgerow prevented the French from breaking through and allowed the English longbowmen on the right flank to fire into the French flanks, with devastating effect. Next the Dauphin's dismounted knights and men at arms attacked the English center and right. They broke through the hedgerow and viciously fought hand to hand for over two hours. With no success in sight, the Dauphin withdrew and his father, the king, ordered him to retreat. The Duc d'Orléans, the king's other son, departed the field of battle after his brother. Following that departure, the remaining troops consisted of King John II, his division and the crossbowmen. King John's men were well rested, but now outnumbered. With great courage (or too much pride), King John II advanced on the English with his crossbowmen in front. The English were shocked to discover that they were facing another attack. They feared defeat because they were exhausted in both strength and arrows. King John II broke through the English line, but the Black Prince sent his reserve under the command of Captal de Buch around the back/left flank of the French king. The English nearly surrounded the French, forcing them to retreat. All formations broke and the English captured King John II and his son, Phillip.

OUTCOME: The English slaughtered whatever retreating French troops weren't worth a ransom. King Edward II gave 2,000 gold coins and a life pension to the squire to whom the King of France had surrendered. The Battle of Poitiers was another English victory that severely weakened the French crown and left the country in chaos until the instatement of a new king. In 1358, the king's son was finally installed as the protector regent. Fighting against the English continued and a siege of Paris was lifted. In 1360, both sides signed a peace treaty, but this was more like a "truce" meant to pause combat for only a short time. Until 1801, the English maintained a claim to the French thrown by virtue of the fact that they had defeated and captured the French king in the Battle of Poitiers.

WHAT WAS IT OVER? French land and inheritance.

WHO? The combatants were the English crown, commanded by the Black Prince with 6,000 men, and the French crown, commanded by King John II (also known as John the Good or King Jean II) with 11,000 men. The English suffered minimal casualties (fewer than 200). The French suffered the capture of their king and 2,000 additional men, as well as 2,500 men either killed or wounded in action.

WHEN? September 19, 1356

WHY AT POITIERS? The battle took place at Poitiers because the English held the land of Aquitaine with the capital of Bordeaux. From Bordeaux, the Black Prince attacked the French countryside in an effort to destroy crops and the French people's morale (as well as to erode their support of the French crown).

TECHNOLOGY AND TACTICS: The technology and tactics used in this battle were essentially the same as those employed in Crécy and the Battle of Agincourt. It is important to note that the French tried to adjust their tactics because of their devastating loss to the English at Crécy. Therefore, they dismounted their men to avoid slaughter by longbow. In addition, both sides used intelligence and scouts to gather information about the enemy's positions and whereabouts. The English found a good position for defense, but desperately needed food and water, as well as fodder for their horses. Just like today's militaries, when preparing for battle outside of their terrain the English had to gather materiel and supplies. Before departing from England they scoured the land for 1,000 horses, 2,000 sheaves, 1,000 bows and 400 extra bow strings. However, the English had a difficult time maintaining their supplies, especially arrows and horses. This created an ideal situation for the French, but the latter sealed their fate when they attacked the English instead of surrounding them and forcing surrender.

In terms of equipment, both sides had the same type of armor. Most of the men at arms and knights wore chain mail, leather-padded tunics and steel-plated armor. In addition, most wore the Italian-made bascinet "dogface" helmet. They used such weapons as battle axes (which the French king wielded), swords, spears, daggers, maces, morning stars and lances. The English used longbows, while the French used crossbows. As I stated previously, the longbow was more effective than the crossbow in terms of range, impact and speed. The longbow was so valued that the English banned the export of bows and forbade bowmen from travelling outside the country without a royal-issued license.

QUOTE: "It was agreed that we should take our way, flanking them, in such a manner that if they wished for battle or to draw towards us, in a place not very much to our disadvantage, we should be the first ... the enemy was discomfited, and the king was taken, and his son; and a great number of other great people were both taken and slain." – The Black Prince to the English people

PLACES TO SEE (REFERENCE MAP 12):

1. **MEMORIAL AND EXPLANATION OF BATTLE:** This location contains a memorial and a map explaining the battle formations. Much of the area has been developed, but the forest and river are still there, as well as some of the battlefields. The French don't exactly celebrate this battle, as it was an English victory!
   N 46 30.668 E 0 24.146 (46.511133, 0.402433)

2. **ABBEY NOUAILLE:** The Black Prince stopped here and received advice from the monks, who urged him to use the almost-impenetrable woods of Nouaille for protection. The bridge where the king's baggage train and men crossed back and forth is nearby (Gué de L'Homme Ford).
   N 46 30.648 E 0 24.797 (46.5108, 0.413283)

3. **GROTTES DU PRINCES NOIR AND GUÉ DE RUSSON FORD:** This was one of the French escape routes and the approximate location where the English captured the King of France, on the Champ D'Alexandre. Currently the site contains a field and a farm dirt track. (The coordinates provide only an approximate location for the grotto and ford.)
   N 46 30.745 E 0 23.702 (46.512417, 0.395033)

4. **CHÂTEAU TOUFOU:** This is an example, not far from the battle on the Vienne River, of a protected castle that the Black Prince couldn't capture because of its strong walls. Today it sports a few upgrades and additions, but you can still see the remnants of walls that would have stopped the English raiders.
   N 46 36.968 E 0 35.397 (46.616133, 0.58995)

BATTLE OF POITIERS SEPTEMBER 19, 1356

MAP 12

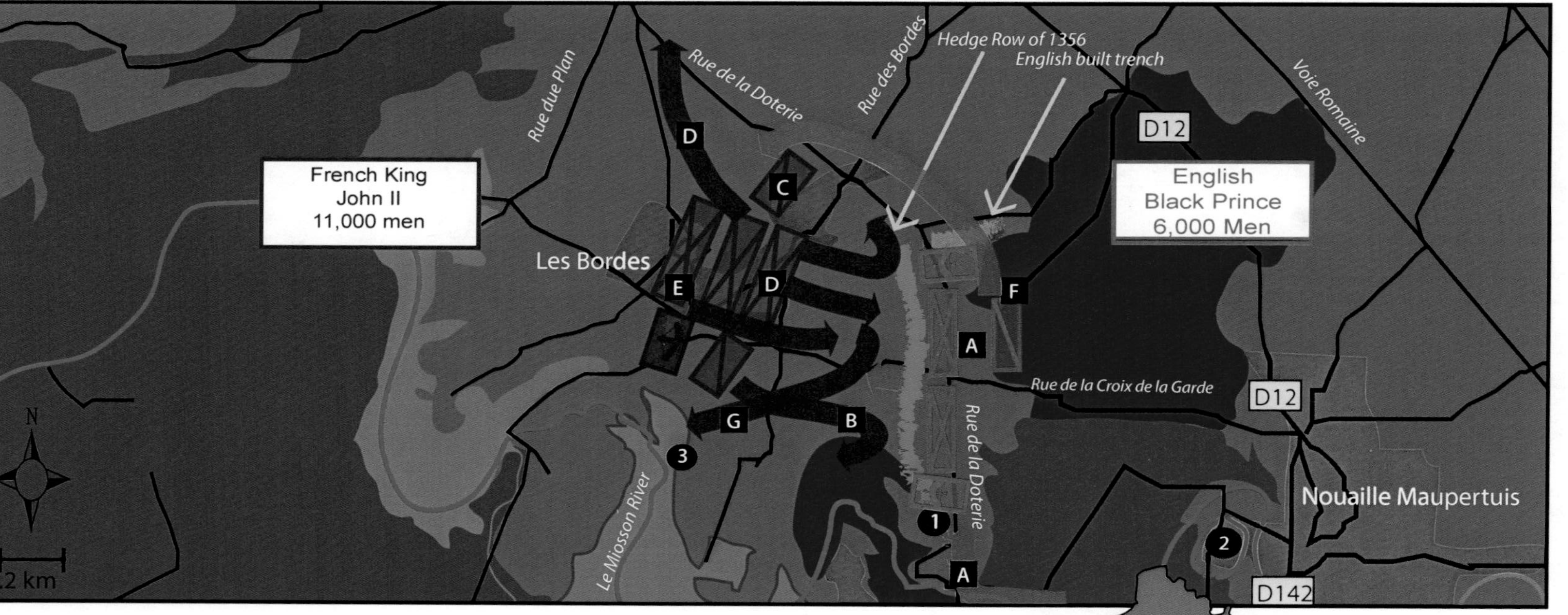
French King
John II
11,000 men
English
Black Prince
6,000 Men
Les Bordes
Nouaille Maupertuis
Rue due Plan
Rue de la Doterie
Rue des Bordes
Hedge Row of 1356
English built trench
Voie Romaine
D12
Rue de la Croix de la Garde
D142
Le Miosson River
A
B
C
D
E
F
G
1
2
3
N
.2 km
FRANCE

MOVEMENTS:

A. September 19, the English dug in behind a large hedge row and they dug a trench to protect their right flank. On their left the English baggage train was still arriving.

B. The French knights under Audrehem, charged the "easy target" of the baggage train but were unsuccessful after vollies of English arrows hit them in the flanks.

C. Next the French left flank under Clermount attacked the English right flank but they too were unable to breakthrough the thick hedge row and were hit hard by the English arrows.

D. Then the Dauphin charged on foot with his men at arms and began to break the English center but had to fall back. He & the Duc d'Orleans were ordered by the King to leave the battlefield.

E. Then after a volley of bolts from his crossbowmen, the King of France charged the English center and began to break through the English line.

F. But the Black Prince sent his reserve under Captel de Buch around the French flank which forced the French to begin a fighting retreat.

G. Surrounded, exhausted and out numbered, the French King surrendered.

Places to See:

1. Memorial Park and Battle Info Board
2. Abbey Nouaille
3. Grottos du Princes Noir
4. Chateau Toufou (NE of battle) / not on map

BATTLE OF AGINCOURT

October 25, 1415 – 100 Years' War

"We few, we happy few, we band of brothers."
– Shakespeare, Henry V

SUMMARY: At Agincourt in 1415, the outnumbered English, armed with deadly longbows, defeated the French knights (again). Since Crécy, the English had lost battles and land in France. Henry V proposed a marriage between himself and the French king's daughter, Catherine, along with recognition of all English claims in France. The French King Charles VI answered with a resounding "NO!" In response, Henry declared war. In August 1415, he landed in Normandy with 11,000 men. Within a month, after a long siege of Harfleur, he had lost half his men to dysentery. Henry decided to retreat toward Calais and cross back to England. The French army maneuvered and blocked his path at Agincourt. On October 25 (St. Crispin's Day), the armies faced one another. The English had approximately 5,000 archers and 900 men at arms against 25,000 French soldiers, archers and mounted knights. The field of battle was narrow, with trees on both sides resting about 1,000 meters apart. A recently plowed muddy field stood in the middle. The English had no reserves; Henry set his archers on the flanks and his men at arms, including himself, in the middle. The French, led by Charles de Albert, the Constable of France, set up three lines. The first two lines consisted of dismounted men at arms and cavalry on the wings, while the third line contained cavalry. Both sides faced off for five hours, waiting for the opponent to weaken its defensive position. Henry knew that as every minute passed his men's bodies weakened from dysentery, the cold and the rain. He decided to move his archers farther ahead, creating a missed opportunity for the French to attack the newly vulnerable troops. After the archers set up within 250 meters of the French, they released a volley. The French cavalry attacked with 1,600 heavily armored charging men and horses coming from the left and 800 from the right. The assault was full frontal, as the trees on both sides made a flanking attack impossible. French arrogance proved decisive once again as their troops attacked the English men at arms in the disabling mud instead of going after the archers, who were not worthy opponents and worth little in ransom. The French crowded and crushed their own men at arms in the middle and, in the heavy armor and mud, could not maneuver. The French killed Henry's two "doubles," but early in the battle the English had taken 2,000 prisoners. This fact proved significant when, after a French attack almost broke the English line, Henry made the ghastly decision to execute all the prisoners because of the threat to his rearguard. In the end, the French retreated and suffered a resounding defeat, again thanks to the English longbow and France's own incompetence. The English lost approximately 450 men while the French lost 10,000 to 12,000.

OUTCOME: Henry V went on to campaign through northern France and won Normandy by 1419. In 1420, King Charles recognized Henry's claim and handed over his daughter, Catherine of Valois, for marriage. Unfortunately, Henry died of dysentery on August 31, 1422. If he had survived another two months he could have been king of both France and England.

WHAT WAS IT OVER? French land and inheritance. And, again, a woman!

WHO? The English forces were under the command of King Henry V and numbered 5,900 men. The French King Charles VI commanded approximately 25,000 soldiers. The English suffered only 450 casualties, while the French suffered 10,000 to 12,000 deaths.

WHEN? St. Crispin's Day, October 25, 1415

WHY AT AGINCOURT? Henry was retreating to Calais when the French cut him off at Agincourt.

TECHNOLOGY/TACTICS: Approaching the end of days for the mounted knight, the French used heavy armor against the lightly armored English longbow archers and men at arms. The longbow pierced the knights' armor, while the terrain created great difficulty for the French knights and men at arms, who were forced to walk or ride through heavy mud for 300 meters. The English men at arms wore lighter armor, such as leather tunics and short-sleeved chain mail. The longbowmen were equipped with bows and arrows and protected themselves with wooden stakes they had placed in front of their positions to thwart the cavalry. After they shot all their arrows, the longbowmen joined the battle with axes, short swords and daggers.

Quote: From Shakespeare's Henry V:

> *"Then will he strip his sleeve and show his scars,*
> *And say, 'These wounds I had on Crispin's day.'*
> *Old men forget: yet all shall be forgot,*
> *But he'll remember with advantages*
> *What feats he did that day.*
>
> *And Crispin Crispian shall ne'er go by,*
> *From this day to the ending of the world,*
> *But we in it shall be remembered;*
> *We few, we happy few, we band of brothers;*
> *For he to-day that sheds his blood with me*
> *Shall be my brother; be he ne'er so vile*
> *This day shall gentle his condition:*
> *And gentlemen in England, now a-bed*
> *Shall think themselves accursed they were not here,*
> *And hold their manhoods cheap whiles any speaks*
> *That fought with us upon Saint Crispin's day."*

PLACES TO SEE (REFERENCE MAP 13):

1. **BATTLEFIELD TABLE OF ORIENTATION AND MONUMENT:** This is located at the end of the battlefield, near the site of the English lines.
   N 50 27.250 E 2 09.075 (50.454169, 2.151249)

2. **MUSEUM (CENTRE HISTORIQUE MEDIEVAL):** Just inside town is a small but well-done museum dedicated to the battle. It includes equipment displays and provides explanations of the politics surrounding the battle as well as information about the battle itself.
   N 50 27.809 E 2 07.661 (50.463483, 2.127683)

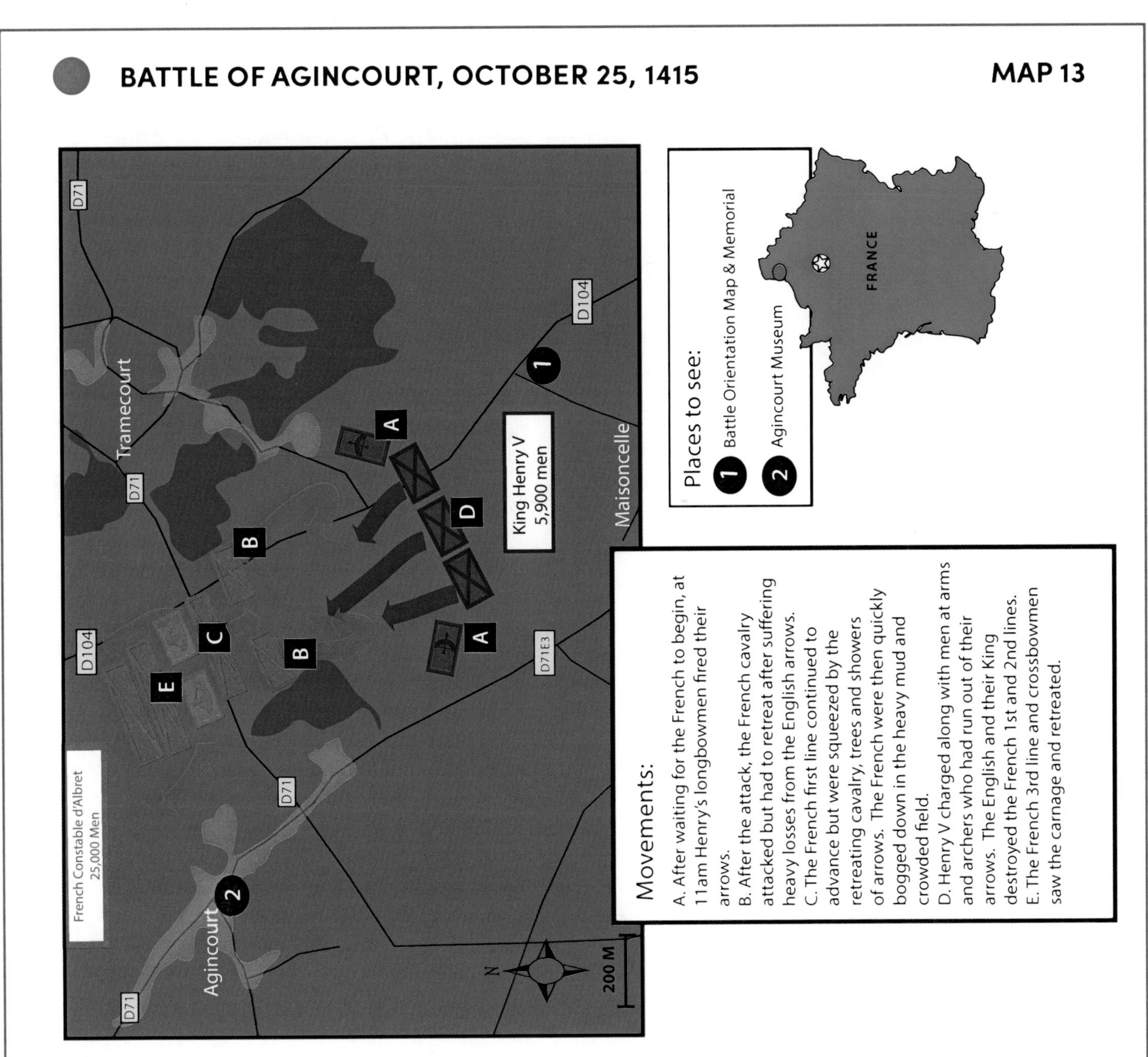
BATTLE OF AGINCOURT, OCTOBER 25, 1415
MAP 13
D71
D104
Tramecourt
Maisoncelle
Agincourt
D71E3
King Henry V
5,900 men
French Constable d'Albret
25,000 Men
A
B
C
D
E
1
2
N
200 M
Places to see:
1 Battle Orientation Map & Memorial
2 Agincourt Museum
FRANCE
Movements:
A. After waiting for the French to begin, at 11am Henry's longbowmen fired their arrows.
B. After the attack, the French cavalry attacked but had to retreat after suffering heavy losses from the English arrows.
C. The French first line continued to advance but were squeezed by the retreating cavalry, trees and showers of arrows. The French were then quickly bogged down in the heavy mud and crowded field.
D. Henry V charged along with men at arms and archers who had run out of their arrows. The English and their King destroyed the French 1st and 2nd lines.
E. The French 3rd line and crossbowmen saw the carnage and retreated.

SIEGE OF ORLÉANS

1429 – 100 Years' War

"I am not afraid...I was born to do this...advance boldly and fear nothing." – St. Joan of Arc

---

SUMMARY: The English defeat at Orléans was the turning point for the French in the 100 Years' War. The French had not won a major battle since the early 1400s and Orléans in central France was one of their last outposts. The common assumption was that when Orléans fell, the English would win all of France. The Siege of Orléans began on October 12, 1428. The English troops consisted of approximately 5,000 soldiers who surrounded the city at various strongholds in the northwest, east and south across the river. However, the north contained only a loose defensive string of English; consequently, the French could use this area to transport supplies for the city's approximately 4,000 French soldiers and 4,000 armed citizens. That same year, a 17-year-old illiterate farmer's daughter accompanied her uncle to a meeting with a French commander. The young woman told the commander that, through visions, her counsel (St. Michael) had told her that she should lead a French army to Orléans. The French commander initially dismissed her, but then recanted and called her back. He knew that French legend stated that France would one day be saved by a woman from Lorraine. The girl, Joan of Arc, was taken to see the king of France, who refused to meet with her until clergy had tested and examined her. The clergy questioned her for over a month and were amazed at her knowledge and eloquence. The king met with her and was convinced. He gave her a "battle" (battalion) consisting of approximately 700 soldiers who would march to Orléans and lift the siege. Joan arrived in Orléans via riverboat on April 28, 1429, bearing supplies and troops with her. After a small celebration in Orléans, she sent two letters to the English asking them to leave. The English refused. At that point, on May 5, Joan of Arc rallied her soldiers and charged out of Orléans, attacking the English-held Fort Saint-Jean-le-Blanc. After a few minutes Joan captured it with no casualties. Then, against all odds, she attacked the walled monastery of Saint Augustine. After fighting from morning to night, the French defeated the English and captured the monastery. That night, Joan had a vision that she would be wounded in her next battle. The following day, May 7, she prepared to take the main fort, Tourelles, outside Orléans. There, against the wishes of the other French commanders, she led the attack. She received a wound in her shoulder and was taken off the battlefield to cheers from the English. However, Joan had suffered only a flesh wound from an arrow; she pulled it out, prayed and returned to battle. Her return struck fear in the English and rallied the fledging French attack; soon afterward the French took Tourelles. After that, the English lifted the siege, as the city could now receive supplies from the south with no issue. The conflict was the first major victory for the French in over 20 years. The following day, the remaining English troops assumed a battle formation and the French followed suit, but Joan protested because it was a Sunday and she felt that fighting would be inappropriate. As a result, the English left and the Siege of Orléans ended.

OUTCOME: The Battle of Orléans was the turning point for the French, who went on to reclaim Paris and Reims. After these victories, St. Joan called for the Dauphin to be crowned King Charles VII in Reims. For the next year Joan continued fighting, but her forces dwindled because the shrewd and ungrateful king started pulling his support and funding. The Burgundians eventually captured Joan during battle and sold her to the English for 10,000 gold coins. She was tortured, raped and falsely condemned as a heretic. On May 30, 1431, Joan of Arc was burned at the stake in Rouen. She was 19. The executioner received orders to scatter her ashes so that they couldn't be venerated. It is stated that the executioner could not burn her heart and had to throw it in the river along with her ashes. In 1920, the Catholic church canonized Joan. The English never fully recovered from the losses St. Joan of Arc had inflicted on them, and the French slowly regained their land, leading to the end of the 100 Years' War in 1453.

WHAT WAS IT OVER? English rights to land in France and trade of goods.

WHO? At the Battle of Orléans, the English commander John Talbot, Earl of Shrewsbury, controlled a force of 5,000 men versus the French Joan of Arc, who commanded 700 men plus the 4,000 men under siege. John Talbot died in 1453 at the Battle of Castillon, near Bordeaux, which was the last battle of the 100 Years' War. Joan of Arc succeeded at additional battles but was ultimately betrayed by the French, turned over to the English and burned at the stake.

WHEN? April 28 through May 8, 1429 (the siege started October 12, 1428)

WHY AT ORLÉANS? It was the last major French stronghold in central France.

TECHNOLOGY/TACTICS: During the siege, the English used cannons with minimal success. They also used their old standby, the longbow. The French started to use cannons, frontal assaults, fire barges and some "higher" powers to oust the English.

QUOTES: "Of the love or hatred God has for the English, I know nothing, but I do know that they will all be thrown out of France, except those who die there." - Joan of Arc

"Hope in God. If you have good hope and faith in Him, you shall be delivered from your enemies." - Joan of Arc

"Be gone, or I will make you go." - Joan of Arc to the English on her approach to Orléans

"Oh Jeanne, without sepulcher without portrait, Who knew that the tomb of Heroes is the Heart of the Living" - André Malraux (French minister of cultural affairs in the 1960s); this quote is on the church in Rouen dedicated to St. Joan.

Christine de Pisan: Considered one of Europe's first female "professional" writers, Christine de Pisan wrote a poem about Joan of Arc in 1429 and called it the "The Song of Joan." Unfortunately, Christine died at age 31, just after completing her work. The following are excerpts from the epic poem.

And you, the King of France, King Charles,
The seventh of that noble name,
Who fought a mighty war before
Good fortune came at all to you:
Do, now, observe your dignity
Exalted by the Maid, who bent
Your enemies beneath your flag
In record time (that's something new!)

And people thought that it would be
Impossible indeed for you
To ever have your country back,
For it was nearly lost; but now,
It's clearly yours; no matter who
Has done you wrong, it's yours once more,
And through the clever Maid who did
Her part therein -- thanks be to God!

You, Joan, were born propitiously;
May He be blessed who gave you life!
Young maid who was ordained of God,
In you the Holy Spirit poured
His ample grace (in whom there was
And is divine munificence),
Refusing none of your requests.
Who'll grant reward enough to you?

When I reflect upon your state,
The youthful maiden that you are,
To whom God gives the force and strength
To be the champion and the one
To suckle France upon her milk
Of peace, the sweetest nourishment,
To overthrow the rebel host:
The wonder passes Nature's work!

But as for us, we've never heard
About a marvel quite so great,
For all the heroes who have lived
In history can't measure up
In bravery against the Maid,

Who strives to rout our enemies.
It's God does that, who's guiding her
Whose courage passes that of men.

And Esther, Judith, Deborah,
Those ladies of enormous worth,
Through them it was that God restored
His people, who were sorely pressed;
Of many others I have learned,
Courageous ladies, valiant all,
Through whom God worked his miracles.
But through the Maid He's done much more.

PLACES TO SEE RELATED TO ST. JOAN OF ARC (REFERENCE MAP 14 FOR THE BATTLE OF ORLÉANS AND MAP 10 FOR THE SUMMARY):

1. **PLACE DU MARTROI:** This is a good starting point for Orléans; it is an equestrian statue of St. Joan.
   N 47 54.146 E 1 54.230 (47.902433, 1.903833)

2. **MAISON DE JEANNE D'ARC:** St. Joan stayed here frequently; it was part of the western wall and home to the city's treasurer. Now it contains a museum dedicated to St. Joan. The original house was destroyed during World War II and has since been rebuilt.
   N 47 54.054 E 1 54.159 (47.9009, 1.90265)

3. **MUSÉE HISTORIQUE ARCHÉOLOGIQUE:** This museum recounts Orléans history and includes artifacts from the period of St. Joan.
   N 47 54.038 E 1 54.320 (47.900633, 1.905333)

4. **(AND 5) FORT DE TOURELLES AND BASTILLE DES AUGUSTINS:** These locations, situated across the street from each other, mark two significant victories for St. Joan. First, on May 6, St. Joan attacked Bastille des Augustins against the current military commanders' advice. This forced the British to retreat into Fort Tourelles. The next day the French attacked the formidable Fort de Tourelles. That night, after being wounded and returning to battle, St. Joan defeated the English, forcing them to withdraw the following morning. Another statue of Joan is located at Bastille des Augustins at N 47 53.681 E 1 54.361. Directly across the street is a monument and a river view marking the entrance to Fort de Tourelles.
   N 47 53.693 E 1 54.353 (47.894883, 1.905883)

6. **TOUR BLANCHE:** This is the last remaining tower of the old wall, dating from the time of battle.
   N 47 53.934 E 1 54.790 (47.8989, 1.913167)

7. **MUSEUM AND BIRTHPLACE OF JOAN OF ARC, DOMREMY LA PUCELLE (NEAR METZ):** In this small town is the original home of St. Joan of Arc. It is a small but nice stop. Most of the information is in French, but the museum next to the house contains a great display providing the story of her life.
   N 48 26.508 E 5 40.464 (48.4418, 5.6744)

8. **ÉGLISE SAINTE-JEANNE D'ARC, ROUEN:** This church was built to commemorate the location where St. Joan was burned at the stake. It is a very beautiful but modern church and park. Overall, Rouen is an excellent town to visit. Its ever-changing weather served as inspiration to Impressionist painters. (For example, Monet painted the cathedral in Rouen as part of his "Cathedrals" series.
   N 49 26.567 E 1 05.314 (49.442783, 1.088567)

9. **MUSEUM OF JOAN OF ARC, ROUEN:** Across from the church is a wax museum dedicated to St. Joan of Arc.
   N 49 26.567 E 1 05.265 (49.442783, 1.08775)

10. **ROBERT DE BAUDRICOURT'S FORTRESS, VAUCOULEURS:** At this location, St. Joan of Arc started her quest. In 1428, she and her uncle sought assistance from Baudricourt because Joan had been hearing voices that told her she needed to do so. Joan met with Baudricourt twice and was sent away. However, during her third visit, after predicting an event (though accounts of this occurrence vary), Baudricourt believed Joan and agreed to help her. He gave Joan some men at arms and credence to visit the king.
    N 48 36.115 E 5 39.836 (48.601917, 5.663933)

OTHER 100 YEARS' WAR LOCATIONS:

BATTLE OF FORMIGNY, APRIL 15, 1450: The Battle of Formigny was a decisive French victory over the British that occurred near the end of the 100 Years' War. In 1449, the French broke the truce of the Treaty of Tours, which had been signed in 1444. They quickly recaptured several sites in Normandy. In response, in the spring of 1450, the English gathered a small army of 5,000 men. The French and English met on the road between Carentan and Bayeux, outside the town of Formigny. The forces clashed for three hours until the English defensive position had to move when a French force arrived from the south. Soon after several charges, the English forces were smashed and their commander captured. In total, the English suffered 3,500 casualties, while 900 men were captured. The French suffered 1,000 casualties. As a result of the French victory, the English had no significant forces left in Normandy with the exception of those in Calais. Locations related to this battle include:

11. **MEMORIAL STATUE:** A beautiful statue in the main intersection of Formigny.
    N 49 19.982 W 0 54.025 (49.333035, -0.900421)

12. **STONE MARKER:** A stone marker and engraving mark the battlefield. The

French forces were to the west of this location and the British to the east.
N 49 20.095 W 0 54.707 (49.334911, -0.911786)

13. **CHAPEL:** A small chapel commemorating the victory was built in 1486 next to the little stream against which the English forces were pinned.
N 49 20.056 W 0 54.493 (49.334271, -0.908224)

BATTLE OF CASTILLON, JULY 17, 1453: The Battle of Castillon was a major French victory and ended the 100 Years' War against the English. As a result of the loss, the English lost all their possessions in France with the exception of Calais and the Channel Islands. In 1451, the French captured Bordeaux, a jewel of the English possessions. After much lobbying by the English subjects in Bordeaux, King Henry VI sent a force of 3,000 men under the command of John Talbot, a cunning and successful 70-year-old commander. On October 27, 1452, the English quickly recaptured Bordeaux. In response, King Charles VII of France, who was surprised by the landing in the west, took his time and refitted his army throughout the winter so that he would be prepared for battle in the spring. In the spring the French laid siege to an English garrison in Castillon. Reluctantly, Talbot attacked the French and attempted to lift the siege. The French had built an excellent defensive position around their 300 guns, with palisades, earth and dirt berms on three sides. The Lidoire River sat on the fourth side. On July 16, Talbot arrived ahead of his main force, with 500 men at arms and 800 archers. He quickly overtook and destroyed a small force of French archers in Castillon. Talbot then decided to attack the main French force, believing that the clouds of dirt he saw were from their retreat. However, the clouds came from the movement of camp followers before the battle. Outnumbered, Talbot reiterated his order to attack. The French artillery decimated his men; the English forces who arrived late continued to attack as well. After an hour of battle, the Duke of Brittany charged the English flank with 1,000 cavalry. The English were finished (including Talbot and his son, who were killed). In total, the English suffered 4,000 casualties, while the French suffered only 100. As a result of the battle, the French recaptured Bordeaux, while the English lost all their possessions in France except for Calais and the Channel Islands. The Battle of Castellon is considered the end of the 100 Years' War.

PLACES TO SEE RELATED TO THE BATTLE OF CASTILLON:

14. **MONUMENT TO JOHN TALBOT:** At one point, this location housed a chapel erected in the memory of John Talbot; the chapel was destroyed during the French Revolution. Now all that remains are an information board, a pillar dedicated to St. Mary and a plaque commemorating John Talbot. Talbot and the English came from Castillon, west of the monument, then faced the French, who were positioned directly north about 400 meters from the monument. The back of the French position was the small La Lidoire River. The Breton cavalry came from the hills behind them and smashed into the British western flank.
N 44 51.078 W 0 01.147 (44.851298,-0.01912)

BATTLE OF ORLEANS APRIL 28 - MAY 8, 1429 — MAP 14

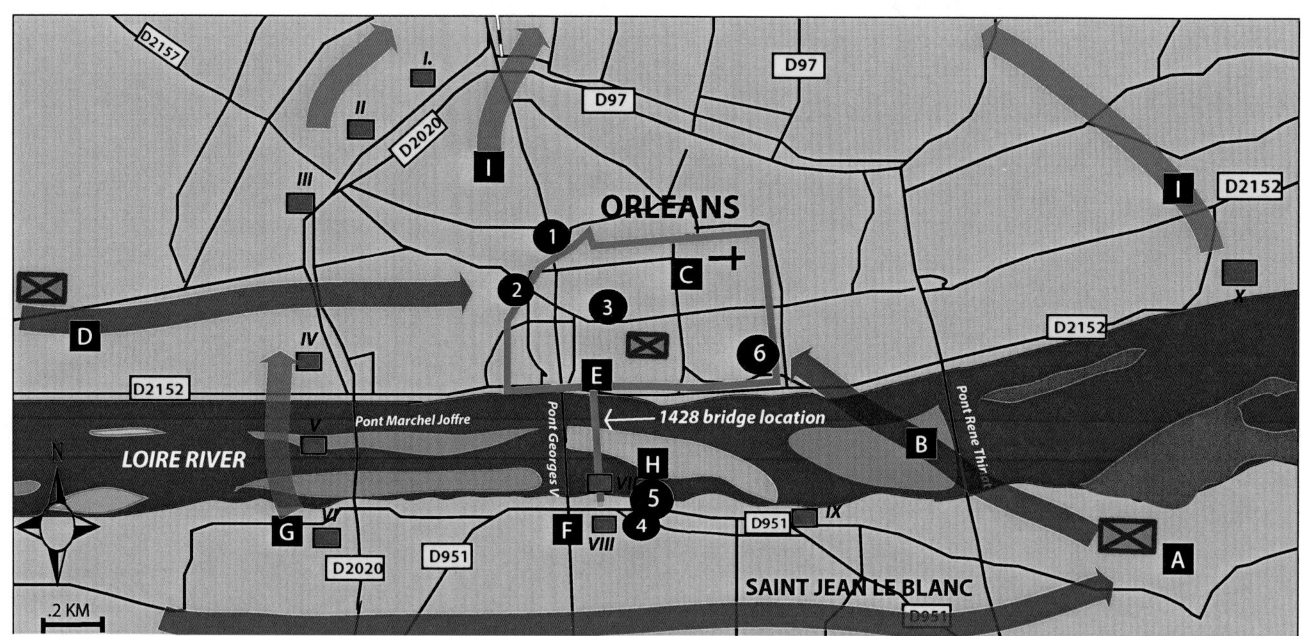
D2157
D2020
D97
D97
D2152
D2152
D2152
ORLEANS
LOIRE RIVER
Pont Marchel Joffre
Pont Georges V
1428 bridge location
D2020
D951
D951
D951
SAINT JEAN LE BLANC
.2 KM

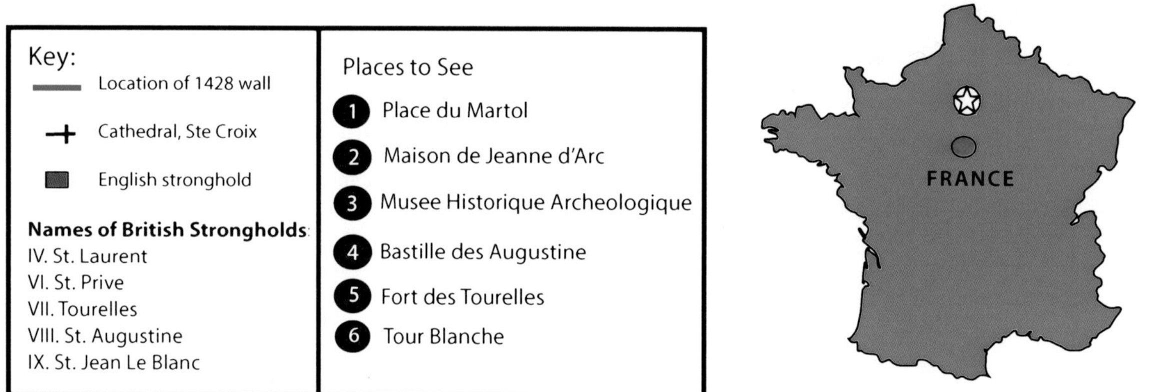
Key:
Location of 1428 wall
Cathedral, Ste Croix
English stronghold
Names of British Strongholds:
IV. St. Laurent
VI. St. Prive
VII. Tourelles
VIII. St. Augustine
IX. St. Jean Le Blanc
Places to See
1 Place du Martol
2 Maison de Jeanne d'Arc
3 Musee Historique Archeologique
4 Bastille des Augustine
5 Fort des Tourelles
6 Tour Blanche
FRANCE

Movements:

A. April 29, St. Joan arrived with supplies and soldiers.
B. St. Joan & 200 men crossed the river with supplies.
C. Inside Orleans, she was celebrated with a parade, food and pay was distributed.
D. French reinforcements arrived into the city but were not challenged by the English.
E. May 6, after the English refused two peace offers from St. Joan, the French crossed the bridge to assualt the English strongholds. The English commander Gladsdale burned down outpost St. Jean le Blanc to consolidate his forces.
F. Nightfall on May 6, St. Joan and the French captured Bastille des Augustine.
G. Commander Glasdale ordered the St. Prive outpost to evacuate to the north.
H. May 7, St. Joan and the French captured Les Tourelles. Commander Glasdale and others died while trying to cross the bridge over the river.
I. May 8, Orleans was liberated and the British siege was lifted. The British retreated to the north.

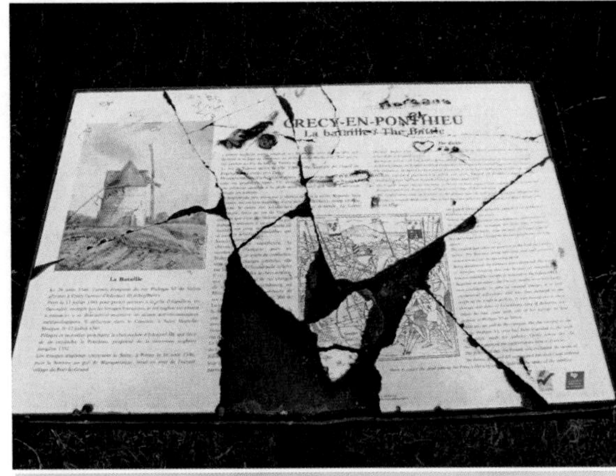
CRECY-EN-PONTHIEU
La bataille - The Battle
La Bataille

The Battle of Crecy, has a tower with a battlefield overview from the position of the English. Unfortunately it has been damaged by vandalism. Above is the ground view of the battlefield looking from King Edward III's view point. The photo to the left is from the French view point looking up to the tower.

AZINCOURT
P

The Battle of Agincourt, is commemorated with an excellent museum in the town(photo left). Just minutes away from the museum is the battle marker and orientation table, photo below left. The photo below right is the view point from the battle marker looking across the field from King Henry V's position towards the French.

St. Joan of Arc changed the course of the war to remove the English from France. Above left is the house of her childhood, in Doremy near Metz. Next to it is a research center and museum. I also included photos of the beautiful countryside and above right the statue of St. Joan in Reims Cathedral.

Rouens has a beautiful Church and Prayer Garden at the location of where she was burned at the stake. (left center) Across from it in the old town of Rouen is a wax museum dedicated to the life of St.Joan. Far left, Rouen is in Normandy which many of the Impressionist painters embraced the changing weather that created different shades of light and colors. Monet, one of those painters created many works of art near Rouen, including his series of the Rouen Cathedral. Photo on the far left is the alter for St. Joan and one of the many grotesques carved in the Cathedral. And finally, a famous statue of St. Joan in Paris. (also there is a copy of the statue in Philidelphia, PA)

JESVS
MARIA

—Chapter 5—

THE 30 YEARS' WAR, 1600s

The 1500s saw the emergence of religious conflict in Europe between the many Protestant sects and the Catholic Church. These battles culminated in the 30 Years' War, a devastating conflict that engulfed the entire continent. It was said to be a religious war, but in reality was about the desire for old territorial claims, trade rights and power. For example, France, a Catholic country, aligned itself with the Protestants of England, Sweden, Germany and the Netherlands to capture the Catholic Habsburg imperial territory bordering France. The war left Europe, especially Germany, devastated. It is estimated that eight million soldiers and civilians died during the conflict. In this chapter, I highlight only one major 30 Years' War battle that took place in France—the Battle of Rocroi. The following is a brief timeline for reference. Note that France was a latecomer to the 30 Years' War, but was constantly stoking the fires and prodding others to fight.

1618	Protestants in Prague revolt against harsh Catholic imperial rulings to impede further Protestant expansions. The Protestants elect Frederick V, Elector of Palatinate, to be the King of Bohemia; unfortunately, the Holy Roman Emperor was also King of Bohemia.
1620	During the Battle of White Mountain, Imperial forces defeat the Protestants outside of Prague.
1620	Spain occupies the Palatinate (across the Rhine from France).
1622	The Duke of Bavaria is made the Elector of Palatinate by the emperor.
1624	Minister Richelieu of France unites Sweden, England, Denmark and France against the emperor.
1625	The Danes invade northern Germany. (France promises only to provide funding.) Sweden does not invade Germany as planned, but invades Poland instead.
1626	The Imperialists badly defeat the Danish king.
1627	The harvest in Germany fails, leading to widespread famine.
1628	The Emperor announces the Edict of Restitution, which returns all property to the Catholics per 1535 agreements; it inflames tensions and brings Sweden into the war.
1630	King Gustavus of Sweden lands in northern Germany.
1631	During the Battle of Breitenfeld, the Swedes defeat the Imperialists and capture Erfurt, Wurzburg and Frankfurt.
1632	During the Battle of Lützen, the Swedes and Imperialists fight again. This time, the King of Sweden is killed in battle, leading to an inconclusive Swedish victory.
1634	Albrecht von Wallenstein, an Imperial mercenary commander, is assassinated by Imperial order due to his disobedience.
1634	During the Battle of Nordlingen, the Imperialists defeat the Protestants in southern Germany; as a result, Imperial territory is connected from Austria to the Palatinate.
1635	France and Sweden sign the Treaty of Compiegne, thereby declaring war on Spain.
1635	Spain invades Lorraine with limited success. In response, France attacks Namur and Italy with a mercenary army.
1638	During the Battle of Wittstock, the Protestants once again defeat the Imperialists in northern Germany.
1643	During the Battle of Rocroi, France defeats the Spanish invading from the Netherlands.
1644-48	During the Congress of Westphalia, European leaders negotiate to end the war, even while battles continue.

BATTLE OF ROCROI

May 19, 1643 – 30 Years' War

"Spain is a canker that eats and eats the whole body or it attacks."
– Cardinal Richelieu, 1633

SUMMARY: The French victory over the Spanish at Rocroi during the 30 Years' War set the stage for the French military system to dominate Europe. The 30 Years' War started in 1618 and lasted until 1648. It began when tensions over control of Holy Roman Empire lands turned to violence between Catholics and Protestants in the various German principalities (i.e., Bohemia/Czech). Eventually, many Europeans, from the Ottomans to the Swedes, were involved. In 1635, the French declared war on the Spanish Hapsburgs so that they (the French) could check the Spanish Crown's influence. At this point in history, the Spanish were a strong force, with newfound wealth from the "new world." They held territory on three sides of France, specifically in parts of Germany, the Netherlands and traditional Spain. In those days, the armies had started to change from small principality forces with mercenaries to larger national forces that were organized and equipped with gunpowder, weapons and full-time soldiers. These armies strained economies because they needed funds, arms and food. Heavy cavalry was no longer the dominant force, as it was checked by "squares" of musketeers for offensive action and by pikemen for defense. On May 19, 1643, at Rocroi, the Spanish "invaded" from the Netherlands with 19,000 men and 8,000 cavalry. The French, under the command of 21-year-old Duc d'Enghein, faced the Spanish with 23,000 men. Each side's formations were similar to those of the other except for the fact that the Spanish used their traditional tercios, which were squares of musketeers and pikemen tightly packed together. For over 100 years, these formations had been extremely successful. The French set up a new linear formation that allowed for more firepower and mobility. At the start of the battle, the French attacked and were checked by the Spanish. Then the cavalry on the French right routed the Spanish cavalry and attacked the Spanish center's flank. This, in turn, created havoc. The French cavalry encircled the Spanish infantry, but couldn't break through the tough Spanish squares. In response, the French turned their cannon on the squares and blew them apart. The Spanish suffered 15,000 casualties (8,000 dead), while the French suffered approximately 4,000. Mobile artillery became a significant tactical weapon, making the capture or elimination of an opponent's cannon critical to victory.

OUTCOME: As a result of the battle, a new era of tactics was born. The internationally used Spanish Square was defeated, and more linear line tactics became "fashionable." The Netherlands gained its freedom from the Spanish. Within five years, the Peace of Westphalia ended the 30 Years' War; all of Europe had been devastated. In addition, King Louis XIV grew up and played a dominant role in Europe. He used his newfound power to attempt an establishment of control over the Rhineland territory, such as in Alsace and the Ruhr.

WHAT WAS IT OVER? The French checked the expansion and power of the Spanish crown. Ironically, two Catholic countries were fighting in a war that had begun as a conflict between Protestants and Catholics.

WHO? Duc d'Enghein was the French general representing King Louis XIV (the Sun King), who was only 5 years old at the time. Duc d'Enghein commanded approximately 17,000 infantry, 6,000 cavalry and 14 cannon. His Spanish opponent was Francisco de Melo, who commanded 19,000 infantry, 8,000 cavalry and 18 cannon.

WHEN? May 19, 1643

WHY AT ROCROI? This was the site where the Spanish crossed into France from the Spanish Netherlands to lay siege on the fortified town of Rocroi. Enghein heard the news and rushed to attack before Spanish reinforcements could reach the battle.

TECHNOLOGY/TACTICS: Both the French and the Spanish maintained similar technology, with musketeers, pikemen and cannon. At this time, to survive, the armies depended on combined arms, discipline, organization and logistics. The pikemen stopped the cavalry and protected the musketeers. The musketeers used a "matchlock," which was heavy and required a rest to fire. Consequently, the musketeers would fire, then rotate back to reload. All the soldiers carried swords and were lightly armored (if at all). The cavalry was now generally used for shock charges, flanking, foraging and scouting. Soon the mercenary armies were replaced by national militaries, military academies, formal training and better logistics. As stated previously, the French modified the Spanish Square so that it provided more firepower in a linear formation as well as afforded greater mobility.

QUOTE: "The dismal course of the conflict, dragging on from one decade to the next and from one deadlock to the next, seems to me an object lesson on the dangers and disasters which can arise when men of narrow hearts and little minds are in high places." – C. V. Wedgwood, 1956 (historian of the 30 Years' War)

PLACES TO SEE (REFERENCE MAP 15):

1. **ROCROI MUSEUM AND FORTIFICATIONS:** This is at the entrance of the Rocroi fortification's east gates.
   N 49 55.564 E 4 31.351 (49.926067, 4.522517)

2. **ROCROI BATTLE LOCATION STELLE (MONUMENT):** This is located on a small dirt road about 6.4 kilometers southwest of town off Chemin de Rouge Fontaine. The battle took place at this location.
   N 49 54.346 E 4 30.302 (49.905767, 4.505033)

3. **VAUBAN MUSEUM, NEUF-BRISACH:** The town/fort of Neuf-Brisach was built by Sébastien Le Prestre de Vauban, a reknowned builder of defenses and forts including Rocroi. His engineering and designs are impressive sites and are located throughout France. Unfortunately, the museum in Neuf-Brisach is not very impressive, but the town itself is worth the trip. It is located near many WWII locations around Colmar.
N 48 00.956 E 7 31.562 (48.015933, 7.526033)

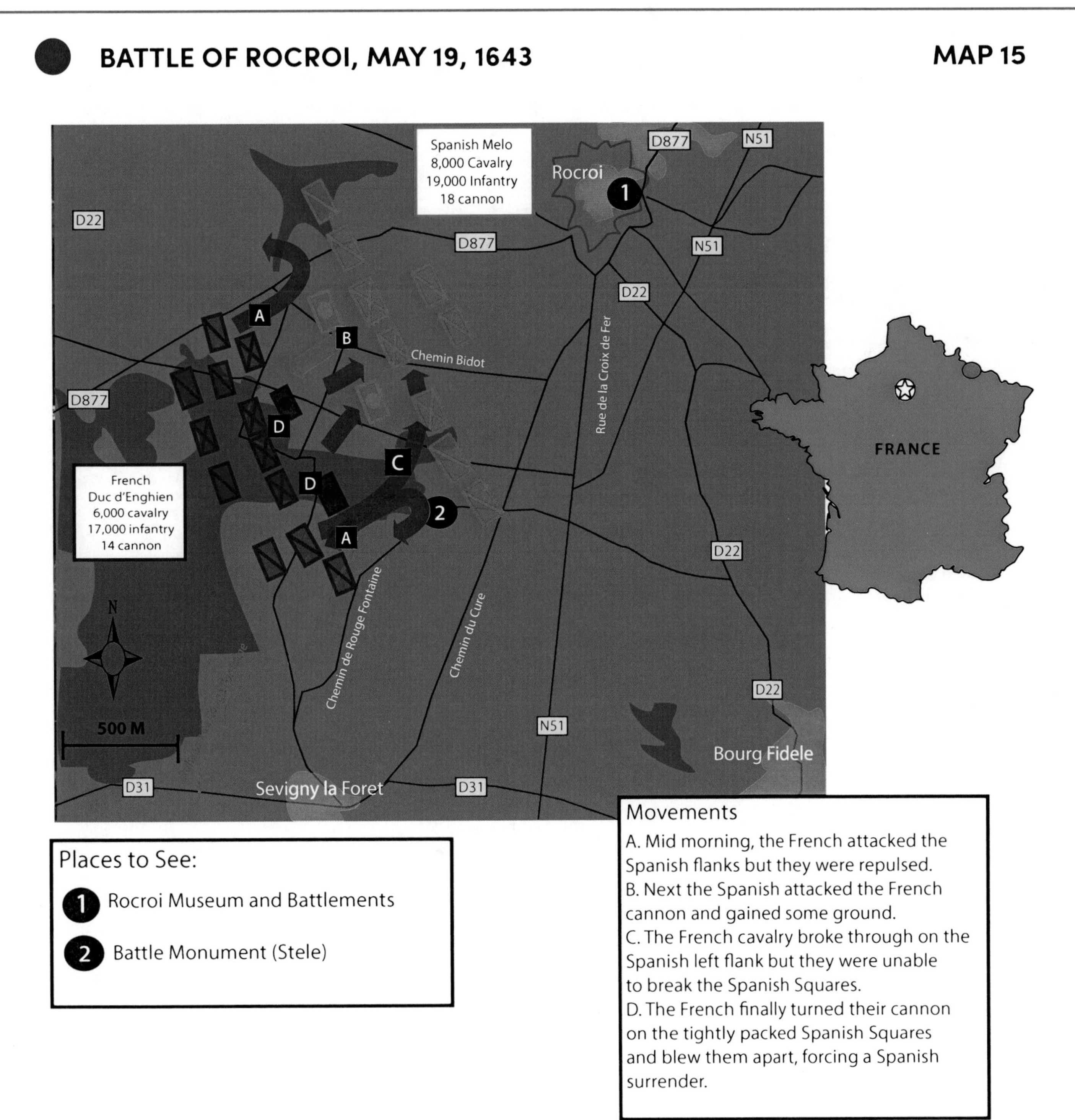
BATTLE OF ROCROI, MAY 19, 1643
MAP 15
Spanish Melo
8,000 Cavalry
19,000 Infantry
18 cannon
Rocroi
D877
N51
D22
Chemin Bidot
Rue de la Croix de Fer
French
Duc d'Enghien
6,000 cavalry
17,000 infantry
14 cannon
Chemin de Rouge Fontaine
Chemin du Cure
FRANCE
500 M
Sevigny la Foret
D31
Bourg Fidele
Places to See:
1 Rocroi Museum and Battlements
2 Battle Monument (Stele)
Movements
A. Mid morning, the French attacked the Spanish flanks but they were repulsed.
B. Next the Spanish attacked the French cannon and gained some ground.
C. The French cavalry broke through on the Spanish left flank but they were unable to break the Spanish Squares.
D. The French finally turned their cannon on the tightly packed Spanish Squares and blew them apart, forcing a Spanish surrender.

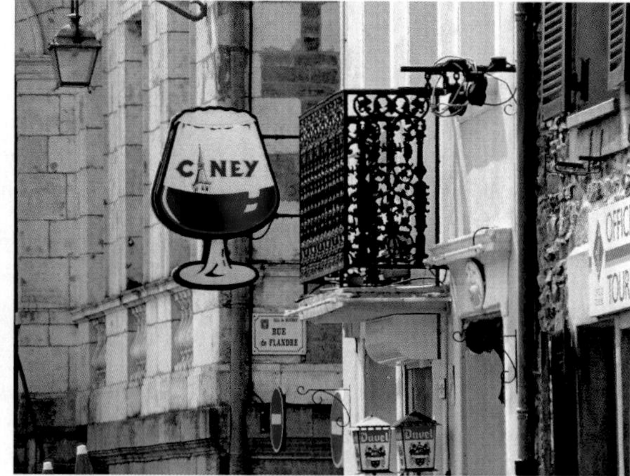
CANEY

Rocroi, is still in its star fortress formation for the most part. You can walk around the entire town to explore the fortress walls, such as the photo above. The actual Battle of Rocroi in 1643 was fought just south of the town. Inside the town, you can visit a nice cafe in the main square for a nice meal and glass of wine!

In the town of Rocroi, is the museum about the battle which has dioramas and equipment to view.

Above is an engraving from an unknown author/artist that illustrates the many steps to load, aim and fire a matchlock weapon that was used during the 30 Years' War. The men were typically surrounded in a "Spanish Square" by pikemen to defend against the cavalry. Then they would fire and rotate to the back of the line. The matchlocks weighed over 20lbs, shot a .75 caliber round smooth bore which lacked range and accuracy.

–Chapter 6–

REVOLUTION, NAPOLEON AND FRANCO-PRUSSIAN WAR, 1775–1900

England had developed a parliament since the 1200s and by the 1700s the parliament shared significant power with the King. In comparison, France resisted gradual advancements in government and the sharing of power. After the 30 Years' War, the country went to the other extreme in the form of an all-powerful Sun King, Louis XIV. Fast forward another 75 years, the French crown's rigid behavior and lack of embracing civil rights resulted in a violent revolution that deposed the crown and Europe descended into the Napoleon Wars. France's identity crisis continued throughout the 1800s. Following is a brief timeline of this period for your reference:

1775

The Bread Riots occur and unrest prevails.

1789

May: France is bankrupt and the king calls an assembly of the Third Estates.
July: The populace sacks monasteries and the homes of the rich.
July 14: The Bastille is stormed; Lafayette is appointed commander on July 15.
August: The Rights of Man is created
September 11: Louis XVI vetoes the decree.
October: Versailles is stormed.

1790

February: Monastic vows and orders are suppressed.
May 19: The Nobility class is abolished.
July 12: An oath to the state (the Civil Constitution of the Clergy) is created.

1791

February 28: During the Day of Daggers, Lafayette orders the arrest of 400 armed aristocrats.
April: The king and queen receive travel restrictions.
June 20-25: The Flight to Varrenes takes place.
August: Louis accepts the constitution.

1792

January: The food riots occur.
March 20: The guillotine is first used.
April: War is declared with Austria.
August: The Tuileries Palace is stormed.
August: Lafayette escapes from arrest to Belgium but is imprisoned by the Austrians.
August: King Louis XVI is imprisoned.
September 3: The Austrians capture Verdun and vow to protect King Louis XVI.
September 20: During the Battle of Valmy, the French defeat the Austrians.
September 21: The First French Republic is declared.
November: The king's correspondence with the Austrians is discovered.
December: The king goes on trial for treason and is found guilty.

1793

January 23: The king is executed as Louis Capet.
March: A rebellion occurs against the revolution. Maximilien Robespierre becomes the leader of the Jacobine Political Club.
March: The Jacobines become the "public safety committee."
June: The Jacobines arrest their political club rival members, the Girondists.
June 24: The constitution is ratified.

July: Louis XVII, aged 10 is given to a cobbler family.

July 13: Jean Paul Marat, a Jacobine leader, is killed by a Girondist.

September 5: The Reign of Terror begins.

October 10: The constitution is put on hold

October 16: Queen Marie Antoinette is executed.

October 21: Priests are outlawed and Notre Dame becomes a center for the "cult of reason."

October 31: Twenty-one Girondists are executed.

December 23: Six thousand Royalist prisoners of war from the Vendée are executed.

1794

January: "Vendée Revenged" the Republican campaign agains the Vendée rebels is launched.

Mass killings of the elite and educated occur.

June: The French beat the Austrians in the Netherlands.

July 27: Robespierre is arrested and executed, ending the Reign of Terror.

1795

The constitution is ratifi¬ed.

October 5: With 5,000 soldiers, Napoleon defeats a 25,000-man Royalist attack on Paris.

October 26: The National Convention is dissolved.

November: The Executive Directory takes control.

1796

March: The Vendée Revenge Campaign ends with an estimated 117,000 to 500,000 massacred.

May 10: During the Battle of Lodi, General Napoleon defeats the Austrians.

1797

France takes control of northern Italy.

1798

February: The Roman Republic is proclaimed and the French take control of the central Papal States.

April: The Helvetian Republic is proclaimed; the French invade Swiss territories and create a republic.

July: During the Battle of Pyramids, Napoleon defeats the Mamluks of Egypt.

August: During the Battle of the Nile, Nelson defeats the French Navy and ends the chances of a French Middle East conquest.

1799

June: Russia defeats France in Trebia, Italy.

August: Napoleon leaves Egypt.

October 9: Napoleon arrives back in France.

November 9: The Executive Directory is dissolved and Napoleon creates the French Consulate.

1800

June 24: During the Battle of Marengo, Napoleon solidifies his power after defeating the Austrian-led Coalition.

1802

A new constitution is adopted and Napoleon is confirmed as the First Consul for life.

1804

Napoleon crowns himself Emperor (including over Italy) and posts family members in leadership positions.

1805

October 19: During the Battle of Ulm, Napoleon defeats the Austrians.

October 21: During the Battle of Trafalgar, the British defeat the French Navy.

December 2: During the Battle of Austerlitz, Napoleon defeats the Russians and Austrians.

1806

October 14: During the Battle of Jena and Auerstadt, Napoleon defeats the Prussians.

1807

February 8: During the Battle of Eylau in Poland, the French defeat the Russians.

June 14: During the Battle of Friedland, the French defeat the Russians.

1808

The Spanish rise up and the Peninsula War begins.

1809

July: During the Battle of Wagram, Napoleon defeats the Austrians.

1812

September: Napoleon arrives in a vacant and torched Moscow.

October–December: The Great French Retreat from Russia takes place.

1813

October 16-19: During the Battle of Leipzig, Napoleon is defeated and begins a fighting retreat to France.

1814

March 7: The Battle of Craonne marks Napoleon's last victory outside Reims.

March 30-31: During the Battle of Paris, Napoleon is defeated and abdicates. Louis XVIII is restored to the throne.

May: Napoleon is exiled to Elba, off the coast of Italy.

1815

February 20: Napoleon escapes Elba and arrives in Paris by March 20.

June 18: During the Battle of Waterloo, Napoleon is defeated and King Louis XVIII is restored to the throne.

October 16: Napoleon is exiled to St. Helena off the coast of Africa, where he dies on May 5, 1821.

1830

During the Revolution of 1830, Charles X is replaced by the July Monarchy of King Louis-Philippe.

1848

The Revolution of 1848 occurs, ending the "July Monarchy" and establishing the Second Republic.

1851

Louis Napoleon stages a coup d'état and is crowned Emperor Napoleon III.

1870

July 2: The Spanish accept Prince Leopold for the King of Spain.

July 19: France declares war on Prussia.

July 28: Napoleon III arrives in Metz to take command of the French Rhine Army.

August 2: French corps cross into Germany.

August 4: During the Battle of Wissembourg, the Germans defeat French defenders.

August 5: The Battle of Spicheren marks a German victory that forces the French to retreat to Metz.

August 6: During the Battle of Woerth (or Reichshoffen or Froeschwiller), the French are defeated.

August 16: During the Battle of Mars-la-Tour, the Prussians defeat the French again.

August 18: During the Battle of Gravelotte, the Prussians win a strategic victory that is also considered a French tactical victory.

September 1: During the Battle of Sedan, Napoleon III is surrounded; he surrenders on September 2.

September 4: A coup d'état occurs against Napoleon III. The Third Republic is proclaimed, calls for more recruits and renews the declaration of war.

September 4: The Siege of Metz begins. (It ends October 23 with the surrender of French troops.)

September 19: The Siege of Paris begins.

November 9: During the Battle of Coulmiers, the French are defeated by the Prussians.

December 4: The Prussians defeat the French at Le Mans.

1871

January 18: Germany is united and an Empire declared.

January 28: An armistice is signed between France and Germany. Germany receives Lorraine and Alsace.

February 17: The Germans stage a victory parade in Paris.

March 18–May: The Commune of Paris is created and fiercely revolts against the Armistice and the French government.

May 10: The Treaty of Frankfurt ends the war between France and Germany. Germany receives Alsace and Lorraine, and France has to pay a war indemnity of five billion gold francs. Germany occupies France until 1873, when the amount is paid in full.

FRENCH REVOLUTION AND NAPOLEONIC ERA

"Louis must die, so that the country may live!" – Maximilien de Robespierre

---

FRENCH REVOLUTION: Thanks to increased debt, food riots, crop famine and an out-of-touch king, France spiraled into revolution and violence for almost 10 years. In May 1789, the Estate General was held for the first time since 1616. The Estate General was a meeting that discussed the status of the nation and addressed such issues as France's severe debt and food shortages. The Estate General included three Estates—Clergy (the First Estate), Nobles (the Second Estate) and Common People (the Third Estate). On June 17, the Third Estate rebelled against the voting rules, declaring a National Assembly. By June 27, King Louis XVI had ordered the First and Second Estates to join the Third Estate in pursuit of peaceful compromises. However, in July the people began to riot and sack monasteries and homes of aristocrats. The middle class formed a National Guard on July 13 under the command of the American Revolution hero, the Marquis de Lafayatte. On July 14, 1789, the French citizens stormed the Bastille in Paris. Throughout 1789 and 1790, the king, National Assembly and people continued negotiations, but the radicals took over. For example, in 1790 the monastic vows and orders were suppressed. Then, in July, the clergy were forced to take an oath to the state (and not to God). In April, the royal couple's travel was restricted. On June 21, 1791, the king and queen tried to escape Paris and reach a Royalist stronghold, but were caught in Varrenes and forced to return. Their capture greatly undermined the king's power and created an impression that he was involved in a foreign conspiracy. In August, the king attempted to pacify the Republicans by accepting the constitution. However, in January 1792 food riots occurred, and in April France invaded Austrian Netherlands (Belgium). In a manifesto, the Austrian Duke of Brunswick stated that if the Republicans hurt the king, he, the Duke of Brunswick, would destroy Paris. As news of the manifesto reached Paris, the Radicals seized the opportunity to malign King Louis XVI as a traitor for collaborating with Austria. On August 10, the French radicals stormed the Tuileries Palace and massacred the Swiss Guard that had been protecting the king and queen. The radicals decided to arrest Lafayette, who a year before had been a hero of the Revolution. He barely escaped to Belgium, but was held as an Austrian prisoner for five years. The Austrians, under the command of the Duke of Brunswick, then invaded France and captured Verdun in early September. The French stopped the Duke's advance at the Battle of Valmy on September 20 (see below) and, as a result, declared the First Republic on September 21. Soon French rebels found documents further indicating that the king had been corresponding with foreigners; consequently, the rebels charged him with treason. On December 3, 1792, the king went on trial and was found guilty. During the trial, the Jacobin radical revolutionary leader Maximilien Robespierre said, "Louis must die, so that the country may live." The king was executed by guillotine as a commoner, Louis Capet, on January 23, 1793. Throughout the following year, the revolution escalated between the moderate Girondists and the radical Jacobins. The Jacobins took more power as the "Public Safety Committee," and on September 5 began what would become known as the Reign of Terror. During this time, the revolutionaries put the constitution on hold, executed the queen on October 16, placed 10-year-old Louis XVII in solitary confinement and passed the Anti-Clerical Law, which outlawed priests. The Cathedral of Notre Dame became a center for the "Cult of Reason," and many more were murdered. On July 27, 1794, the moderates finally arrested and overthrew the ringleader, Robespierre, thereby ending the Reign of Terror. Robespierre was the last to be guillotined. Progress was made in 1795 when the constitution was ratified. However, the violence continued when Royalists attacked Paris with 25,000 men. Napoleon Bonaparte, at that time a young commander, defeated them with 5,000 men, 50 cannons and a "whiff of grapeshot." The National Assembly was dissolved and an Executive Directory took control. From 1796 through 1799, France engaged in battles in Italy, Switzerland and Egypt. On October 9, 1799, Napoleon left Egypt and arrived in France. Now a general, he led a coup and took power from the Directory. He created the French Consulate on November 9, 1799.

NAPOLEONIC WARS: The Napoleonic Wars were a series of battles fought by Allied coalitions against Napoleon's French Empire from 1803–1815. After the French Revolution and the Executive Directory period, Napoleon seized power on November 9, 1799. In response to Napoleon's aggressive forces, the Allies formed coalitions throughout the war. The following is a description of the Battle of Valmy, which took place in 1792. The battle secured the French Revolution and led to the executions of the king and queen. Following that are summaries of the Napoleonic War coalitions.

BATTLE OF VALMY

September 20, 1792 – The French Revolution

"Vive la Nation." – General François Christophe Kellermann

SUMMARY: The Battle of Valmy ensured the survival of the French Revolution and the death of the absolute monarchy. After the violence and revolution escalated, in August 1792 King Louis XVI and his Austrian wife, Queen Marie Antoinette, were forced from the Tuileries Palace and put under house arrest. The Prussians and the Austrians, who were allies of the French Crown, threatened to destroy Paris if the king and queen were hurt. After the king's and queen's arrest, the Prussians responded in the fall of 1792 by invading France so that they could place the French monarchy back into power. After successfully taking the forts Longwy and Verdun, the Prussians turned toward Paris with an army of 34,000 men and 58 cannon. The Prussians were a well-organized and intimidating foe; an additional 45,000 Austrians protected the Prussian flanks. In response, Charles Dumouriez, commander of the 36,000-man French army, positioned his 16,000 men at Sainte-Menehould. One of his officers, General François Christophe Kellerman, was positioned on the windmill-topped heights of Valmy, east of Reims, with 20,000 men. Kellerman had the tactical high ground, but oversaw a mostly volunteer army, while a swamp/bog behind him blocked any attempt at retreat. The Prussian Duke of Brunswick saw Kellerman's situation and decided to attack at 1000 hours. He expected the French to dissolve as they had done during previous encounters. However, the wet ground, fog and newly accurate French artillery (Gribeauval cannons) held back the Prussians. During the battle, Kellerman rallied his men with a cry of "Vive la Nation!" As a result of two failed attacks on the French line, the Prussian commander decided by 1600 hours to disengage and end the battle. The French suffered 300 casualties, while the Prussians suffered only 184 casualties.

OUTCOME: The battle cemented the National movement and opened the doors to Napoleon. The Prussians' decision to withdraw and enter their winter quarters seemed to be a simple matter of waiting until spring to fight again. However, they missed their opportunity to defeat the French Revolution. On the other hand, the French celebrated the battle as a great victory. The following day, September 21, the French monarchy was abolished and the French Republic proclaimed. The movement led to the conviction and execution of the king and queen. Shortly afterward, the Reign of Terror began, spreading the revolution throughout the country in the form of portable guillotines. Then, outside forces threatened France. In response, the French military was organized and went on the offensive. During that time, Napoleon rose through the ranks and drew Europe into almost 20 years of warfare.

WHAT WAS IT OVER? The Prussians attacked France to place King Louis XVI back on the throne after his removal and house arrest.

WHO? The French were led by General Kellerman, who controlled a force of 36,000 troops and 40 cannons. In comparison, the Prussians were led by the Duke of Brunswick, with 34,000 troops and 58 cannons.

WHEN? September 20, 1792

WHY AT VALMY? The Prussians had just conquered the fortress at Verdun and were advancing toward Paris. The French north and center armies set up their defenses at Valmy in an attempt to block the Prussian advance to Paris.

TECHNOLOGY/TACTICS: Both armies maintained similar technology, though the French had advanced artillery. Their new design, the Gribeauval cannon, was light, uniformly produced and accurate. It also had interchangeable parts. The French artillery effectively deterred the compact Prussian formations. In addition, high ground and weather boosted France's ability to defend its position.

QUOTE: The German writer Johann Wolfgang von Goethe was at the battle and said this to his comrades: "From this place, and from this day forth begins a new era in the history of the world, and you can all say that you were present at its birth."

PLACES TO SEE (REFERENCE MAP 16):

1. **BATTLEFIELD MEMORIAL AND INFORMATION BOARDS:** The memorial is located at Kellerman's position. It includes a rebuilt windmill and a statue of Kellerman waving his hat to encourage his troops. It overlooks the fields where the Prussians advanced in their attempt to dislodge the French.
   N 49 04.767 E 4 45.980 (49.07945, 4.766333)

2. **PLACE DE LA BASTILLE, PARIS, JULY 14, 1789:** French commoners had been fighting the Royals since June. By July, the revolution had hit the streets of Paris, as the king had not implemented a constitution for the people. The Bastille was a prison and held only seven prisoners (including one of the vocal revolutionaries) at the time. Soon a large crowd of about 600 people gathered. After a few shots, the crowd stormed the Bastille, causing the garrison to surrender. It was later dismantled, and only stone foundations remain. In the middle is the July Column commemorating France's freedom. Note that Lafayette gave George Washington the key to the Bastille in the 1790s.
   N 48 51.190 E 2 22.147 (48.853167, 2.369118)

3. **FLIGHT TO VARRENES:** On June 21, 1791, King Louis XVI and Queen Marie Antoinette were captured only 30 kilometers from the safety of the Royalist stronghold, the fortress Montmedy. They were attempting to escape the revolution and mount a royalist resurgence. Due to the king's indecision, they did not leave Paris until approximately 0230 on June 21. They disguised them-

selves as a party, with a Russian baroness played by their son's actual baroness. The king was disguised as her butler. Their carriages arrived in the sleepy town of Varrenes at 2300 hours to exchange horses – a relay of sorts to finish their ride. However, the king hesitated and stopped when the horses were not at the town's edge. (They had been put away for the night.) As the group waited 35 minutes, they were overtaken by two Republicans (including a postman) who had recognized the king and his retinue at a previous relay station. The Republicans raced into town and began gathering a roadblock. The disguised king and his two carriages continued into town with false passports. The checkpoint, not knowing the travelers' true identities, told the king and his retinue that the roads were unsafe and convinced them to take refuge in his house. Meanwhile, a road block prevented royalist cavalry that had been sent to meet the king from coming into town. By 0500, Republican soldiers from nearby towns surrounded the king. Four thousand National Guardsmen escorted him and the queen back to Paris. Based on his attempt to leave Paris, as well as his communications with foreign powers, the king was later convicted of treason and executed. Varrenes is a nice town with seven boards that explain the events of that evening. It's only 20 minutes off the main highway. Also in Varrenes is the impressive Pennsylvania World War I monument, as well as a World Wars museum.
Location of parking and sign: N 49 13.612 E 5 2.005 (49.226867, 5.033417)

4. **MARTYRS OF COMPIEGNE, REIGN OF TERROR, PARIS:** During the Reign of Terror, which lasted from September 5, 1793 through July 28, 1794, 16 members of the Carmelite Monastery were executed on July 17. They were guillotined because they would not obey the Civil Constitution of the Clergy, which the revolutionary government had created. They were arrested and condemned as traitors. During their execution in Paris, they renewed their vows and sang the song, "Veni Creator Spiritus." They are buried, along with 1,306 victims of the Reign of Terror, in the Picpus Cemetery in Paris. The cemetery is only minutes from the Place du Nation where the guillotine was set up.
   Cemetery coordinates: N 48 50.633 E 2 24.017 (48.843889, 2.400278)

5. **CARNAVALET MUSEUM, PARIS:** Also known as the Paris City History Museum, this site houses a wide range of artifacts, including those pertaining to Marie Antoinette, as well as paintings.
   N 48 51.444 E 2 21.728 (48.8574, 2.36214)

6. **PLACE DE LA CONCORDE (PLACE DE LA REVOLUTION), PARIS:** At this location the French tore down the statue of Louis XV and set up the guillotine. This is where the king and queen were executed. Now it's home to an Egyptian obelisk.
   N 48 52.140 E 2 18.609 (48.868992, 2.310151)

7. **HISTORIAL DE LA VENDÉE AND MEMORIAL VENDÉE:** In the area known as the Vendée in western France just south of the Loire River, tradi-

tional Catholic citizens revolted against the French Revolution. This episode in France's history is still heatly debated and not even taught in most French schools. The citizens saw the draconian changes in the Revolution as a threat against their Catholic traditions and way of life. At the start in 1793, the people were successful in forcing the National Guard out of their land and won several battles. However, in 1794 the Committee of Public Safety in Paris ordered 12 columns of soldiers to "pacify" the region. It was called the Vendée-Vengé, the Vendée Revenged. The government forces slaughtered the people of the region, some say it was a genocide. By the time the systematic killing of men, women and children ended in 1796, it is estimated between 100,000 to 600,000 were slaughtered. At this location is a memorial for a town that was destroyed and the historical museum with a section on the Vendée War.
N 46 50.812 W 1 28.885 (46.846865, -1.481416)

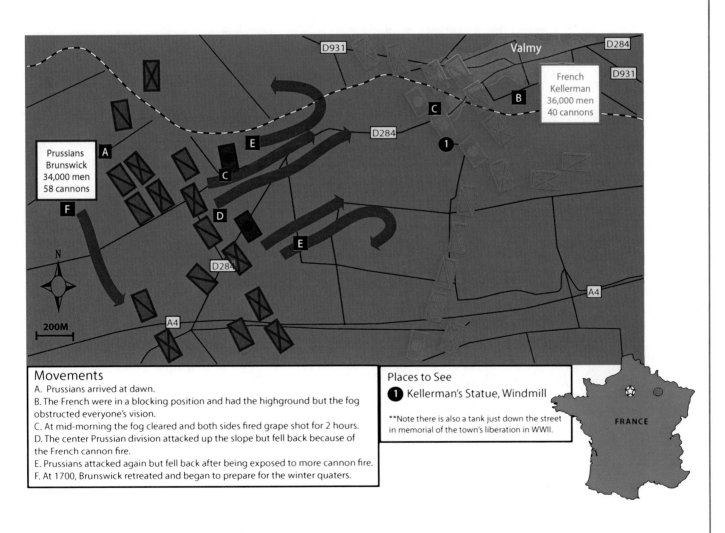

BATTLE OF VALMY, SEPTEMBER 20, 1792

MAP 16

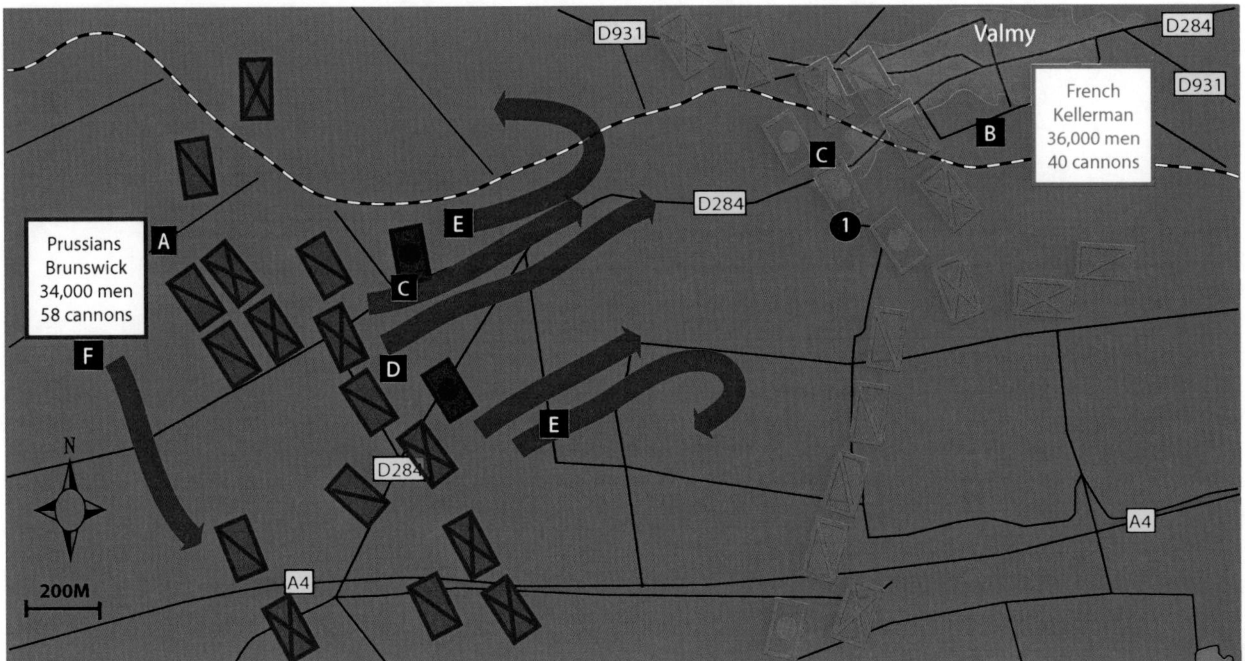

Valmy

French
Kellerman
36,000 men
40 cannons

Prussians
Brunswick
34,000 men
58 cannons

D931 D284 A4 200M N FRANCE

Movements
A. Prussians arrived at dawn.
B. The French were in a blocking position and had the highground but the fog obstructed everyone's vision.
C. At mid-morning the fog cleared and both sides fired grape shot for 2 hours.
D. The center Prussian division attacked up the slope but fell back because of the French cannon fire.
E. Prussians attacked again but fell back after being exposed to more cannon fire.
F. At 1700, Brunswick retreated and began to prepare for the winter quaters.

Places to See
1 Kellerman's Statue, Windmill

**Note there is also a tank just down the street in memorial of the town's liberation in WWII.

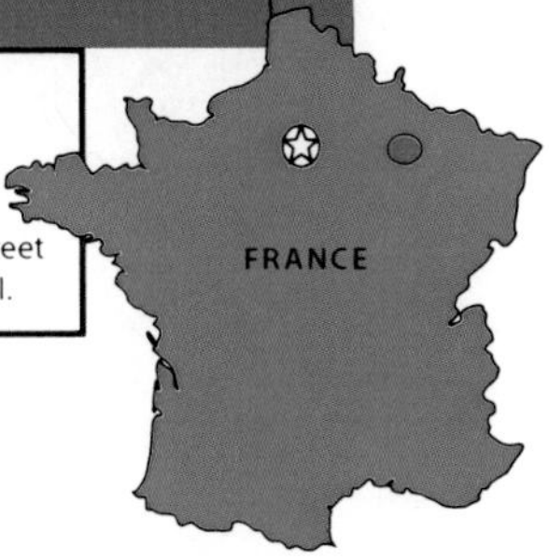

NAPOLEONIC ERA:

Summary of Coalitions

FIRST COALITION, 1792-1797: The First Coalition consisted of Austria, Prussia, England, the kingdom of Sardinia and the kingdom of Naples before Napoleon took over France. The French defeated the coalition using massive conscription and military reforms, emerging triumphant in such conflicts as the Battle of Valmy in 1792, during which they turned back the Prussians. The French also conquered the Netherlands, Belgium, the Pyrenees and the west bank of the Rhine, while Napoleon won in Italy. When Spain signed for peace with the French, France could focus its three armies on Germany and Vienna. Consequently, the Austrians sued for peace and signed a treaty.

SECOND COALITION, 1798-1802: The Second Coalition was formed by the Austrians, Russians and British to resolve treaty-related disputes stemming from the first coalition. It was also a response to France's aggressive behavior. Major events included:

A. The French took control of Switzerland.

B. Napoleon attacked and removed the Hospitaller Knights from Malta. (The czar of Russia was their honorary head.)

C. Napoleon was defeated in Egypt but returned to take control of France. In 1800, Napoleon took command of the army in Italy and drove the Austrians back into the Alps. The Austrians signed a treaty recognizing French control up to the Rhine, the Netherlands and Italy. Russia, which had early success in northern Italy, withdrew from the coalition over a dispute with England, which insisted on the right to inspect every vessel at sea.

THIRD COALITION, 1803-1806: The Third Coalition of Russia, Austria, Portugal and England began as another attempt to defeat Napoleon. England had never really been at peace with France because it had faced the threat of French invasion until the famous Battle of Trafalgar, during which Horatio Nelson destroyed the Franco-Spanish fleet in October 1805. The other members formed the coalition in the summer of 1805 when Napoleon crowned himself King of Italy and Germany. This provocative move led to the Battle of Ulm, during which Napoleon's forces defeated and captured an entire Austrian army. Next, the French followed the retreating Austrians to the gates of Vienna. Napoleon's major force gathered north of Vienna near the Czech town of Brno, where they defeated the Russian and Austrian forces at the Battle of Austerlitz. That victory ostensibly ended the Holy Roman Empire, and the French occupied Vienna. The Russian army was allowed to return home and the French main army camped in southern Germany, boosting the threat to Prussia.

FOURTH COALITION, 1806-1807: The Fourth Coalition was created to protect Prussia from the advancing French. The Prussians and Russians mobilized and the main Prussian army gathered in Saxony. Napoleon advanced on Saxony before the Russian army could meet up with the Prussians. He then defeated the Prussians at the Battle of Jena-Auerstadt. Next he captured Berlin, then turned toward the east and defeated the Russians at the Battle of Friedland in 1807. With most of Europe under his control, Napoleon sent his army into Spain (his current ally) and began the Peninsula War.

FIFTH COALITION, APRIL 10, 1809–OCTOBER 14, 1809: The Fifth Coalition was another attempt by Austria to drive out the French. However, Austria had little help, as the British were engaged in the Peninsula War, the Prussians had declined to assist because they were still hurting from the 1806 loss, and the Russians were at war with Sweden and England. After various conflicts in the Danube Valley, the French beat the Austrians in the Battle of Wagram. As a result, Austria broke up further, losing one-fifth of its population to other rulers. (Poland received Galicia, Bavaria received Salzburg, France took Adriatic ports, etc.) Also on display was the declining quality of the French forces, whose veterans of Jena and Austerlitz were being replaced by conscripts and foreigners. The sheer size of the armies and the length of the war gave Napoleon problems in terms of managing quality and maintaining tactical superiority.

SIXTH COALITION, 1812-1814: The Sixth Coalition consisted of Russia, Britain, Portugal, Sweden, Austria, Spain and Prussia. It began with the French invasion and defeat in Russia, continued with the defeat of Napoleon at Leipzig and ended with the occupation of France and Napoleon's exile to the island of Elba.

SEVENTH COALITION, MARCH 20–JULY 8, 1815: The Seventh Coalition was formed as a result of Napoleon's escape from exile in Elba and the fact that he reassumed power in Paris. It was bad timing on Napoleon's part because the major nations (England, Austria, Prussia and Russia) were meeting at the Congress of Vienna and quickly agreed to each place 150,000 men in the field to stop Napoleon once and for all. Soon afterward, Napoleon was defeated at Waterloo, then was exiled to St. Helena off the western coast of Africa. The French monarchy was reinstated on July 8, 1815.

OTHER NAPOLEON-ERA LOCATIONS

FOLLOWING IS A LIST OF OTHER LOCATIONS RELATED TO THE ERA OF NAPOLEON (REFERENCE MAP 17):

1. **PARIS ARMY MUSEUM AND NAPOLEON'S TOMB (MUSÉE DE L'ARMÉE AND PLACE DES INVALIDES):** The Paris Army Museum is an outstanding place to learn about all eras of military history, but is especially a must-see for information about Napoleon. The museum has a well-done section about Napoleonic-era weapons and uniforms, and even has Napoleon's stuffed horse. On the other side of the museum is Place des Invalides, the location of Napoleon's tomb. **N 48 51.498 E 2 18.771 (48.8583, 2.31285)**

2. **ARC DE TRIOMPHE DE L'ÉTOILE, PARIS:** Commissioned in 1806 to commemorate Napoleon's victories, the Arc de Triomphe was finished in 1836. Also at this site is the French Tomb of the Unknown Soldier.
N 48 52.426 E 2 17.701 (48.873759, 2.295015)

3. **ARC DE TRIOMPHE CARROUSEL, PARIS:** Built from 1806 to 1808 at the gate of the Tuileries Palace, the carrousel commemorates Napoleon's victories from the previous year. The horses are copies of those at the top of St. Mark's Basilica in Venice, which themselves were captured from Constantinople in 1204.
N 48 51.703 E 2 19.975 (48.861722, 2.332919)

4. **BATTLE OF CRAONNE, MARCH 7, 1814:** This is the scene of Napoleon's last victory, when he defeated the Prussians and Russians. Currently a lone statue of Napoleon overlooks the battlefield. The site is very close to a popular World War I museum.
N 49 26.399 E 3 45.881 (49.439983, 3.764683)

5. **NAPOLEON TRAIL:** This is the route Napoleon took in March 1815 when he escaped from Elba and landed at Corsica. He and 1,000 men traveled from Elba to Golfe-Juan east of Cannes to Grenoble. Today, it is a beautiful 325-kilometer (eight-hour) drive passing through beautiful towns such as Grasse, Digne and, ultimately, Grenoble. Following are some of the main points, but please visit www.route-napoleon.com for detailed information.
ROUTE: D6285 to D235 to D6085, then Route National 85 (N85) all the way to Grenoble.

A. Golfe-Juan, Memorial to the "Return of Napoleon," just east of Cannes:
N 43 33.966 E 7 04.504 (43.5661, 7.075067)

B. Grasse, the home of perfume:
N 43 39.604 E 6 55.623 (43.660067, 6.92705)

C. Digne-les-Bains, the lavender capital, entering the mountains:
N 44 05.464 E 6 13.891 (44.091067, 6.231517)

D. N85 pull-off, Golden Eagle for the route, just south of the arrondissement of Gap:
N 44 31.085 E 6 03.128 (44.518083, 6.052133)

E. Saint Firmin:
N 44 46.890 E 6 01.686 (44.7815, 6.0281)

F. Laffrey, Napoleon statue overlooking the lake and mountains:
N 45 01.233 E 5 46.555 (45.02055, 5.775917)

G. Grenoble, capital of the Alps:
N 45 11.603 E 5 43.705 (45.193383, 5.728417)

REVOLUTION & NAPOLEON ERA SUMMARY 1789 – 1815 MAP 17

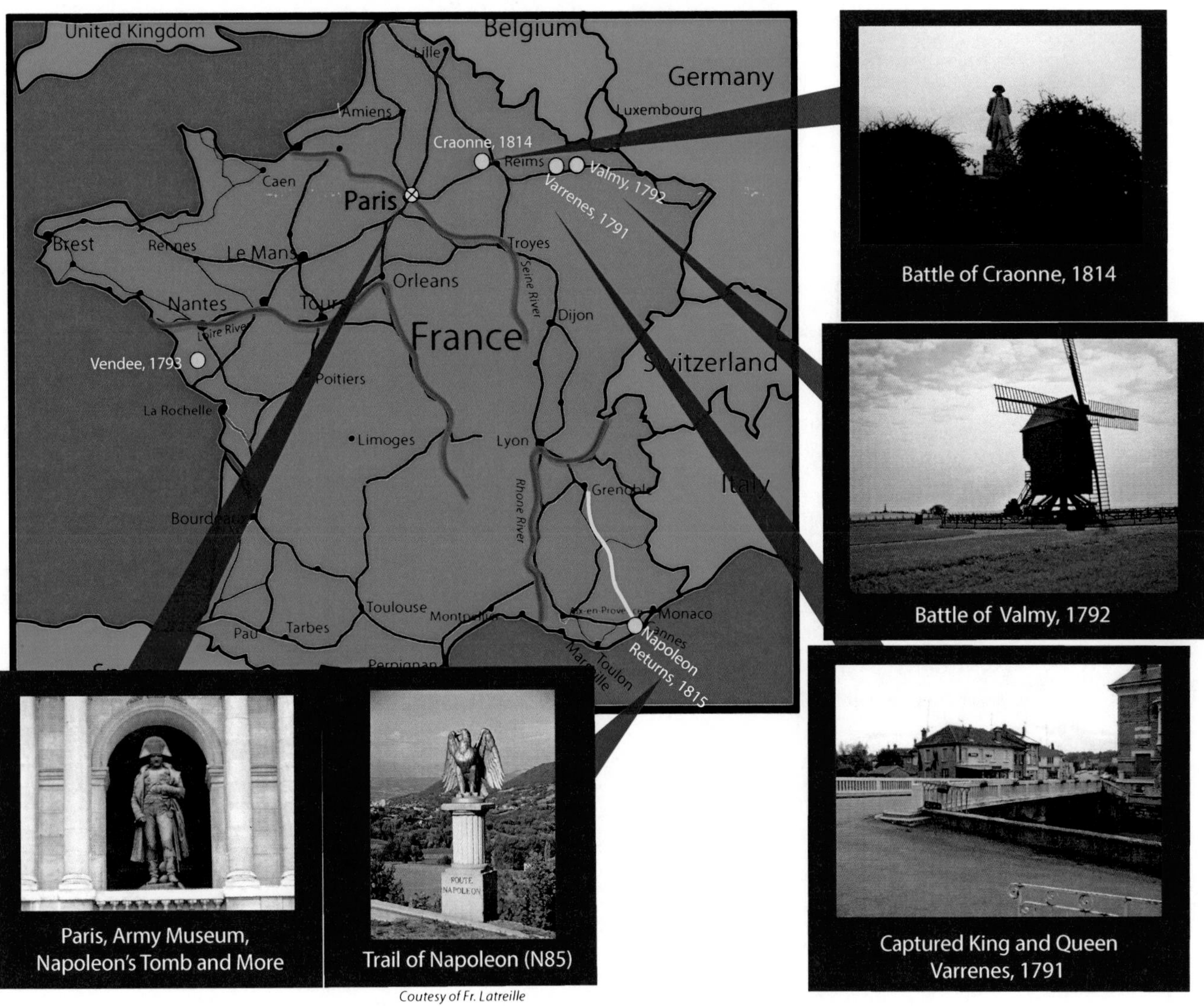
United Kingdom
Belgium
Lille
Germany
Amiens
Luxembourg
Craonne, 1814
Reims
Valmy, 1792
Varrenes, 1791
Caen
Paris
Brest
Le Mans
Troyes
Orleans
Nantes
Seine River
Dijon
France
Vendee, 1793
Switzerland
Poitiers
La Rochelle
Limoges
Lyon
Italy
Rhone River
Toulouse
Monaco
Tarbes
Pau
Napoleon Returns, 1815
Toulon
ROUTE NAPOLEON

Battle of Craonne, 1814

Battle of Valmy, 1792

Paris, Army Museum, Napoleon's Tomb and More

Trail of Napoleon (N85)

Coutesy of Fr. Latreille

Captured King and Queen Varrenes, 1791

BATTLE OF SEDAN

September 1, 1870 – Franco-Prussian War

"Now we have them in the mouse trap."
– Helmuth von Moltke

SUMMARY: The Battle of Sedan ended the Second French Empire and resulted in the unification of Germany. A month before the Battle of Sedan and victories against the French, the Prussians were on the march farther into France toward the fortress at Metz. In an attempt to block the siege, Marshall Patrice de McMahon and Emperor Napoleon III approached Metz with 120,000 men and 564 cannon. On August 30, the Prussian commander Helmuth von Moltke quickly defeated the French at Beaumont. The French retreated to Sedan to resupply and rest. Moltke, with 200,000 men and 774 guns at his disposal, split his forces into three groups. The first group detained the French in Sedan, the second raced ahead to cut off France's retreat route, and the third blocked the river crossing. The French were encircled. To break the encirclement, Napoleon ordered his forces to attack at La Monecelle, but the counterattack collapsed under the weight of concentrated Prussian artillery fire and the arrival of fresh Prussian reinforcements. On the other side of Sedan, the French cavalry courageously charged three times, trying to break the encirclement at Floing, but to no avail. The next day, Emperor Napoleon surrendered his sword and his remaining army of 104,000 soldiers to the Prussians.

OUTCOME: The Second French Empire collapsed and Napoleon III was sent to England in exile. The French Third Republic began and renewed fighting until the Prussians besieged Paris from September through January. After several failed breakout attempts, the French ultimately surrendered on January 28, 1871. As a result of the Prussian commanders' successes, Germany was unified on January 18, 1871 as the German empire. With this unification, as well as the defeat of the French, Germany became the dominant military force in Europe. It maintained a professional army, logistics, railways and telegraphs. After the armistice with France, Chancellor Otto von Bismarck held a celebration parade in Paris. In May, the Treaty of Frankfurt was signed, ending the war. France ceded control of Alsace and Lorraine to Germany and paid 5 billion gold francs. Per the armistice, the Germans occupied France until 1873, at which point France finished its payments. Bismarck also honored the armistice by sending trains of food for the French people. The fact that the German Empire occupied Alsace-Lorraine served as a major obstacle to the forging of long-term peace between France and Germany, as the French were determined to regain their territory. The power shifts, threats and anger boiled over in 1914, leading the world into war.

WHAT WAS IT OVER? In addition to the regular tension between the German-speaking states and France, a possibility existed that the Hohenzollern family would inherit the crown of Spain. Facing the threat of Prussian control on two sides, the French declared war on July 19, 1870. The Prussian confederation received support from the southern German states to defend "Germany."

WHO? The French were led by Marshal Patrice de MacMahon and Emperor Napoleon III, who commanded 120,000 men and 564 guns; they suffered 17,000 casualties and the capture of 104,000 men. The Prussians and their allies were led by General Helmuth von Moltke and Chancellor Otto Von Bismarck, who commanded 200,000 men and 774 cannons; they suffered 8,500 casualties.

WHEN? September 1, 1870

WHY AT SEDAN? The French were attempting to lift the siege at Metz. On their way, they lost a small engagement and retreated to Sedan for resupply and rest. Moltke saw the opportunity for a trap and, with lightning tactics, blocked the retreat and trapped the French.

TECHNOLOGY/TACTICS: The Prussian military's organization, tactics and technology were greatly superior to those of the French. The Germans maintained one of the densest railroad networks in the world and utilized telegraph systems, which boosted mobility, logistics and communication among the fighters. In addition, the Germans relied on the tactic of quick encirclement (seen later during World War II). Germany's Krupp breech-loading artillery pieces were much better than France's muzzle-loading brass cannons. The siege of Paris is also notable for the fact that it marked the first use of anti-aircraft artillery; Krupp built artillery specifically to shoot down the hot air balloons that the French used as lookouts and couriers during the siege. In addition, smokeless gunpowder was used, making the battlefield clearer for troops; this, in turn, led to more casualties and, eventually, a change to duller-colored uniforms. Smokeless powder also made weapons more accurate, while automatic weapons fostered efficiency. Other weapons were lighter for easier handling. With these innovations, Germany set the standard for European armies and the doctrine for warfare. Shortly afterward, as the tensions that sparked World War I began, a number of countries would be defending themselves against the "new" German threat.

QUOTES: "What our sword has won in half a year our sword must guard for half a century." – Field Marshal Helmuth von Moltke

Bismarck quotes:

"The great questions of the time will not be resolved by speeches and majority decisions – that was the great mistake of 1848 and 1849 – but by iron and blood."

"Laws are like sausages, it is better not to see them being made."

"I am bored, all of the great things have been done."

"The Americans have contrived to be surrounded on two sides by weak neighbors and on two sides – by fish!"

"God has a special providence for fools, drunks and the United States of America."

PLACES TO SEE (REFERENCE MAP 18):

1. **SEDAN CASTLE/CHÂTEAU FORT DE SEDAN:** This is at the center of town, which also contains various markers, such as the memorial at the Floing cemetery. Sedan Castle has a section dedicated to the battle, including a panoramic painting. The castle also offers a nice hotel that's a great place to stay on your way through the area.
   N 49 42.082 E 4 56.912 (49.701367, 4.948533)

2. **LAST CARTRIDGE HOUSE:** This is a museum dedicated to the battle; it's 10 minutes from the castle.
   N 49 40.922 E 4 58.496 (49.682033, 4.974933)

3. **OSSUAIRE FRANCO-ALLEMAND:** At this location is a monument to—and burial ground for—more than 2,000 French and German soldiers who died during the Battle of Sedan. It is located just down the street from the museum.
   N 49 40.728 E 4 58.428 (49.6788, 4.9738)

4. **MARFEE HEIGHTS AND CEMETERIES:** The German World War I cemetery sits at this location. Just off the road is an information board about the Battle of Sedan. During the battle, the Prussian IV Corps artillery stood at this ridge, which offers a great view of Sedan and the battlefield.
   N 49 39.820 E 4 55.720 (49.663667, 4.928667)

5. **CALVAIRE D'ILLY:** In northeast Sedan, this is the area where the French cavalry tried to break out after three failed charges through the German line. Here you'll find a few small crosses and an information board.
   N 49 43.797 E 4 57.876 (49.72995 4.9646)

6. **CROIX DE MACMAHON:** At this location is a cross marking the site where General MacMahon was wounded on the morning of September 1.
   N 49 41.312 E 4 58.788 (49.688533, 4.9798)

RELATED:

7. **PARIS COMMUNE, MONTMARTRE:** After the armistice, Paris's working class rose up in pursuit of education, women's rights and maintenance of the republic. For eight weeks, the rebels held to their cause. However, some rebel elements became more radicalized, imprisoning and executing those – such as captured army generals and clergy – opposed to their "cause." In May 1871, the rebellion ended in bloody fighting. Between 10,000 and 20,000 rebels were killed, many of them executed by the French army. The Commune held the high ground, called Montmartre, for most of the period. As a monument

for peace, The Basilica of the Sacre Coeur was built near the site where the Commune maintained cannons and defensive positions.
N 48 53.171 E 2 20.588 (48.886188, 2.343127)

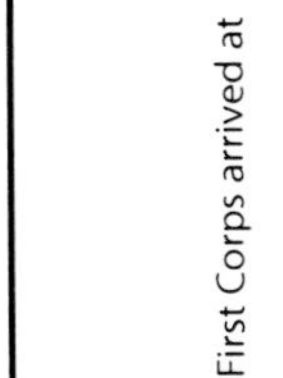

BATTLE OF SEDAN SEPTEMBER 1, 1870

MAP 18

MOVEMENTS:
A. September 1, Bavarian First Corps arrived at Bazeilles.

B. By Dawn, Sept 1, the IX and V Corps arrived at Vrigne-au Bois cutting the escape route and by 0600 they arrived at Floing north of Sedan completing the encirclement.

C. French counterattacked with cavalry to try and breakout. But the attack failed.

D. French retreated to the fortress by 1400.

E. Napoleon III, surrendered by 1630 to stop further bloodshed.

Places to See:
1. Sedan Castle/Chateau Fort de Sedan
2. Last Cartridge House Museum
3. Oussuaire Franco-Allemand
4. Marfee Heights
5. Calvaire d'Illy
6. Cross de MacMahon

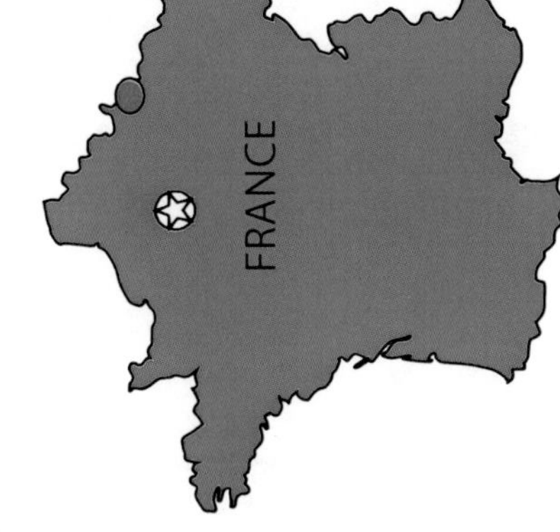
FRANCE

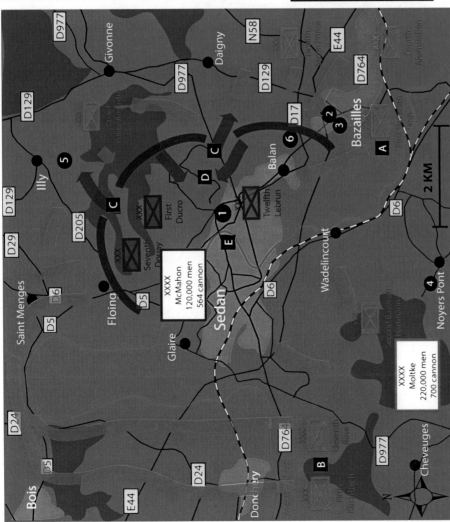

Sedan Castle, is the centerpiece in Sedan. The Castle includes a hotel, theatre and a great museum.

Sedan Castle, largely intact was an important location during the Franco-Prussian War but also during the World Wars. Sedan is historically a logistics/trade center and for WWI was a main rail hub for the Germans.

In the Sedan Castle, they have a large room dedicated to the 1870 Battle of Sedan, to include a panoramic painting and artifacts.

In Sedan there are several locations for monuments and memorials. One of the top sites to visit is the Last Cartridge House Museum. The building was one of the areas of intense fighting around Sedan.

Chapter 7

WORLD WAR I, 1914–1918

The war to end all wars was a tragic and terrible conflict that involved new technologies for death and destruction, and that resulted in never-before-seen numbers of casualties. Further, it left behind a broken world that fostered the rise of such radicals as Francisco Franco, Benito Mussolini, Joseph Stalin and Adolf Hitler. World War I ended with 22,477,000 military casualties for the Allies and 16,403,000 casualties for the Central Powers. This chapter highlights eight major battles of World War I, as well as dozens of museums, cemeteries and memorials. France has a wealth of locations to visit, learn about and honor. The following is a timeline for your reference. (Also reference Map 19.)

1914

June 28: Archduke Franz Ferdinand of Austria and his wife Sophie, Duchess of Hohenberg are assassinated by Serbian nationalist Gavrilo Princip in response to the fact that the Austro-Hungarian Empire had annexed Bosnia and Herzegovina earlier that year.

July 28: Austria declares war on Serbia. Russia, as an ally of Serbia, mobilizes to declare war on Austria; it also calls on the French to mobilize. On August 1, 1914, Germany declares war on Russia because Germany is an ally of Austria.

August 3: Germany declares war on France and attacks France through neutral Belgium.

August 4: England and Canada declare war on Germany because Germany does not withdraw from Belgium.

August 23-30: During the Battle of Tannenberg, Russia invades Germany and Germany crushes the Russian First Army.

September: During the Battle of Masurian Lakes, the Germans partially destroy the Russian Second Army.

September 5-10: The First Battle of the Marne ends in French victory and halts the German advance.

September 14: During the First Battle of Aisne, troops on both sides begin to construct trenches.

October 14–November 22: The First Battle of Ypres ends with no decisive victory.

October 29: Turkey enters the war on Germany's side.

1915

January 1–March 30: The first Allied offensive in Artois and Champagne ends with no decisive results.

January 19: The first German zeppelin air raid on England takes place.

April 22–May 5: During the Second Battle of Ypres, the Germans use poison gas for the first time.

April 23–August: The British attack Turkey at the Dardanelles and Gallipoli.

May 7: A German U-boat sinks the British ship Lusitania, which has 128 Americans on board.

May 23: Italy enters the war on the side of the Allies.

June 29: Italy launches an unsuccessful attack against Austro-Hungary at Isonzo; there will be a total of 12 attacks throughout the war.

September 22–November 6: During the Second Battle of Champagne, the Allied offensive ends with 145,000 casualties and no terrain gained.

1916

February 22–December 18: The Germans launch a surprise attack at Verdun, which becomes the longest battle of the war. It lasts seven months, leads to 700,000 casualties and results in the gain of no territory.

March 9: Pancho Villa raids Columbus, New Mexico.

April 24: The Irish Republican Easter Rebellion begins; it is a battle against British occupation.

May 19: Britain and France conclude the Sykes-Picot agreement to divide the Ottoman Empire after the war.

May 31–June 1: The Battle of Jutland ends without a clear victor. It is the biggest naval battle in history.

July 1–November 13: During the Battle of the Somme, England suffers 60,000 casualties on the first day of fighting.

September 15: Tanks are first used by the British in the Somme Offensive.

1917

February 24: The Zimmerman Note is discovered and passed on to the United States; the telegram details a German request that Mexico attack the United States.

March 11: British troops take Baghdad from the Ottoman Turks.

April 16–May 9: The French Nivelle Offense, which includes the Second Battle of Aisne and the Third Battle of Champagne, ends in a French defeat. Only 500 yards are gained in exchange for 250,000 casualties.

April 10–12: The Canadians gallantly take Vimy Ridge as part of the British diversionary Arras attack.

June 4: The United States declares war on Germany.

June 7–14: The Battle of Messines begins. It is a British offensive and prelude to the Third Battle of Ypres (known as Passchendaele). In this battle, the British detonate 19 mines under the German line.

July 6: T.E. Lawrence (Lawrence of Arabia) leads the Arabs and captures Aquaba from the Ottoman Turks.

July 16–November 6: The Third Battle of Ypres (Passchendaele) takes place. It is a British offensive that reaches Passchendaele, Belgium and that proves to be strategically inconclusive, with approximately 250,000 casualties on both sides.

November 2: The British government releases the Balfour Declaration, committing to the establishment of a Jewish state and a postwar plan to divide most of the Middle East and Africa.

November 7: Bolsheviks overthrow the Russian government and install Communist rule under Vladimir Lenin (after the Germans help move Lenin back from exile into Russia).

December 3: The German/Russian armistice is signed.

December 9: The British take Jerusalem from the Turks.

1918

March 21: The German Spring Ludendorff Offensives begin and include five major attacks:

Battle of Picardy, against the British, March 21
Battle of Lys, against the British, April 9
Third Battle of Aisne, against the French, May 27
Battle of Metz, against the French, June 6
Second Battle of the Marne, against the French and Americans, July 15

May 27: The United States wins its first major action at the Battle of Cantigny.

June 1-26: During the Battle of Belleau Wood, U.S. Marines earn the nickname "Devil Dogs" and stop the Germans.

August 8: During the Amiens Offensive, Allied forces counterattack and force the Germans back to the Hindenburg Line.

September 26–November 11: The Meuse-Argonne Offensive, the final offensive of the war, breaks through the Hindenburg Line on September 27 in the north and again in the center. From the center, the Allies reach Sedan.

November 11, 1918: Fighting ceases at the 11th hour on the 11th day of the 11th month of 1918.

WW1 FRENCH SUMMARY MAP

MAP 19

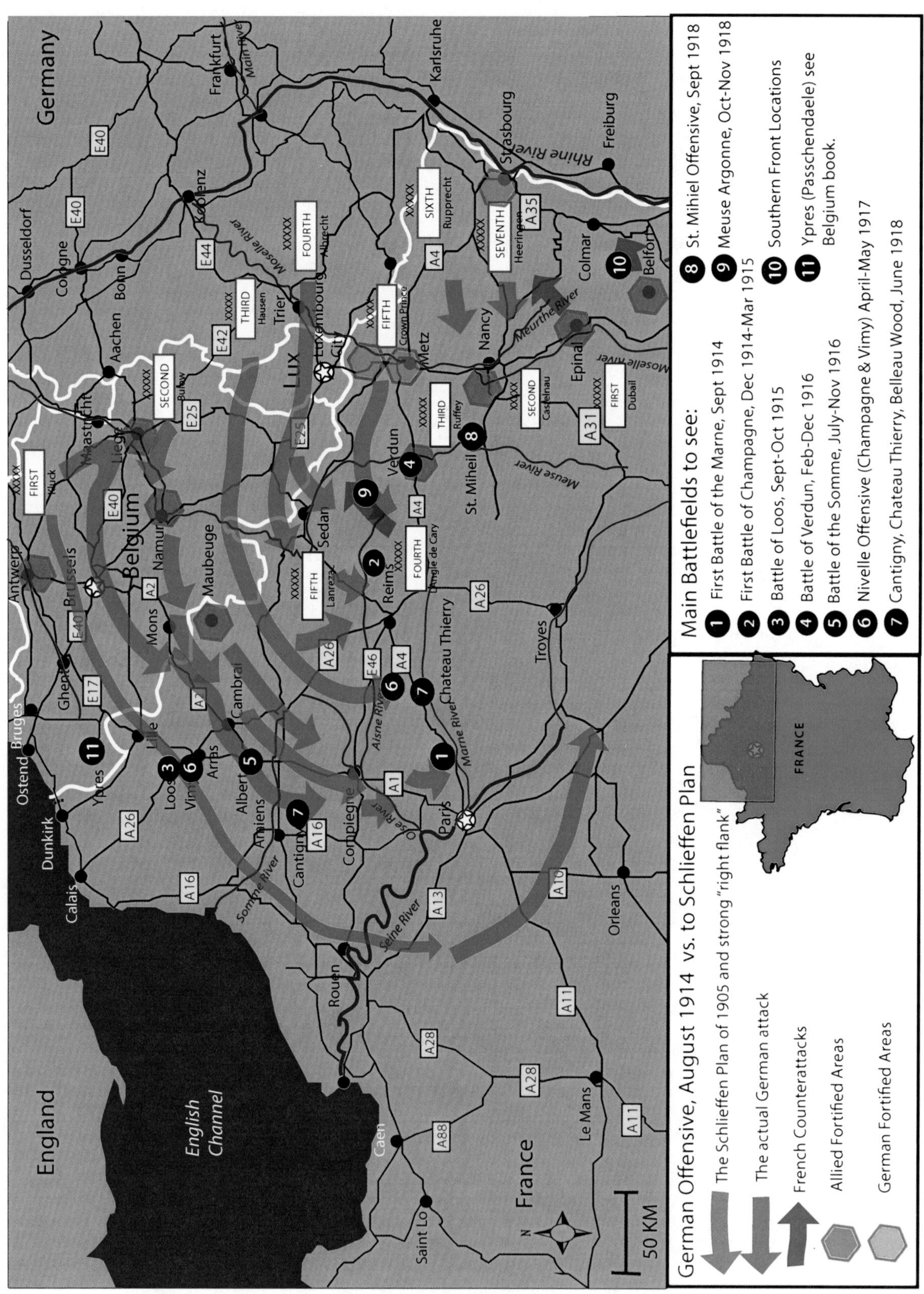

Main Battlefields to see:
1 First Battle of the Marne, Sept 1914
2 First Battle of Champagne, Dec 1914-Mar 1915
3 Battle of Loos, Sept-Oct 1915
4 Battle of Verdun, Feb-Dec 1916
5 Battle of the Somme, July-Nov 1916
6 Nivelle Offensive (Champagne & Vimy) April-May 1917
7 Cantigny, Chateau Thierry, Belleau Wood, June 1918
8 St. Mihiel Offensive, Sept 1918
9 Meuse Argonne, Oct-Nov 1918
10 Southern Front Locations
11 Ypres (Passchendaele) see Belgium book.
German Offensive, August 1914 vs. to Schlieffen Plan
The Schlieffen Plan of 1905 and strong "right flank"
The actual German attack
French Counterattacks
Allied Fortified Areas
German Fortified Areas
FRANCE
England
English Channel
France
Germany
Belgium
Lux
50 KM
N
Saint Lo
Caen
Le Mans
Rouen
Orleans
Paris
Troyes
Calais
Dunkirk
Ostend
Bruges
Ypres
Ghent
Antwerp
Brussels
Lille
Loos
Vimy
Arras
Albert
Amiens
Cantigny
Compiegne
Cambrai
Mons
Maubeuge
Namur
Liege
Maastricht
Aachen
Cologne
Bonn
Dusseldorf
Koblenz
Frankfurt
Karlsruhe
Strasbourg
Freiburg
Colmar
Belfort
Epinal
Nancy
Metz
Trier
Luxembourg City
Sedan
Reims
Verdun
St. Mihiel
Chateau Thierry
Somme River
Seine River
Oise River
Aisne River
Marne River
Meuse River
Moselle River
Meurthe River
Rhine River
Main River
FIRST Kluck
SECOND Bulow
THIRD Hausen
FOURTH Albrecht
FIFTH Crown Prince
SIXTH Rupprecht
SEVENTH Heeringen
FIFTH Lanrezac
FOURTH Langle de Cary
THIRD Ruffey
SECOND Castelnau
FIRST Dubail
XXXXX
E40
E17
E25
E42
E44
E46
A1
A2
A4
A10
A11
A13
A16
A26
A28
A31
A35
A88

FIRST BATTLE OF THE MARNE

September 5-12, 1914

"Miracle on the Marne"

SUMMARY: After a month of German victories, the French Army and British Expeditionary Force stopped the Germans at the Marne River; this victory is known as the "Miracle on the Marne." Since the war's onset, the Germans had been defeating the French, who were in a disorganized retreat to Paris. On September 4, the German First and Second Armies were within 64 kilometers of Paris. Instead of driving on into Paris, they turned to envelop the Allied armies, thereby exposing the German right flank to French forces in and around Paris. The French Commander in Chief, Joseph Joffre, recognized the opportunity for a counterattack. On September 5, on a 300-kilometer front, the French regrouped and attacked along the Marne River with 1,071,000 men against Germany's 1,485,000-man-strong force. At that moment, the German First Army commander recognized the counterattack and wheeled right to meet the initial threat—the French Sixth Army—on the German First Army's right flank. In doing so, he created a 48-kilometer gap between the First Army and the Second Army. The Allies realized the situation and attacked the gap. By September 9, the Allies had come close to encircling some of Germany's armies. On hearing the news, the German commander, Helmuth von Moltke, nephew of the 19th-century German commander of the same name, had a nervous breakdown and his subordinates called an all-out retreat to the Aisne River, 64 kilometers north. The Germans dug in at the Aisne River and trench warfare began.

OUTCOME: The German Schlieffen Plan was stopped and Paris was saved. In addition, a stalemate was created and trench warfare initiated. The casualties were immense; man had applied his industrial wisdom to the destruction of man.

WHO? The Allied force was helmed by the French commander in chief, Joseph Joffre, with 1,000,000 men at his disposal. The English commander, John French, controlled 70,000 men. (Yes, the British commander's last name was French!) Their casualties amounted to 263,000 men. In comparison, the German force of 1,485,000 men, commanded by Moltke and Alexander von Kluck, suffered 220,000 casualties. Note: The Germans would have had three more infantry corps in the battle, but they had to stem a Russian breakthrough in Poland/Prussia. However, the Germans quickly turned their losses in the east to an astounding success at the Battle of Tannenberg.

WHEN? September 5-12, 1914

TECHNOLOGY/TACTICS: The Germans used the Schlieffen Plan to great success until they changed their tactics to stop the advance on Paris. This move allowed the French to reorganize and counterattack. The French used "Parisian cabs" to send 6,000 re-enforcement troops to meet the German threat. The French also used opportunity and aggression to turn the battle to their favor. World War I saw the use of new weapons of warfare, including machine guns, breach-loading cannons, shrapnel rounds, poison gas, smokeless ammunition, barbed wire, airplanes, zeppelins, U-boats, battleships and tanks. It was murderous warfare in proportions never before seen.

QUOTES: "At the point of engaging in a battle on which the fate of the country depends, it is important to remind everyone that it is no longer a time for looking back. Every effort must be made to attack and push back the enemy. A troop that can advance no further must, at all costs, defend the captured ground and face getting killed rather than retreat. In the current circumstances, no failure will be tolerated." - Joseph Joffre

"It is an honor to make such sacrifice for our Allies." - Grand Duke Nicholai, chief of staff of the Russian army after Russia's loss in Tannenberg. Nicolai was speaking about the movement of three German infantry corps from the Western Front to the Eastern Front, suggesting he would have won and France would have lost if the Germans did not shift the infantry to the east.

"Your Majesty, we have lost the war." - Moltke to the Kaiser

"The best form of defense is attack." - Karl von Clausewitz

"My center is giving way, my right is retreating, situation excellent, I am attacking." - Ferdinand Foch

PLACES TO SEE (REFERENCE MAP 20):

1. **MEMORIAL DES BATAILLES DE LA MARNE, DORMANS:** This is a very beautiful chapel at the south side of the Marne, overlooking the site where the Germans and French clashed. It is located at what had been the French force's right flank.
   N 49 04.302 E 3 38.764 (49.0717, 3.646067)

2. **NATIONAL MONUMENT OF THE MARNE VICTORY, MONDEMENT-MONTGIVOUX:** Located at the Battle of the Marshes of Saint-Gond, a decisive point of the Battle of the Marne, this is a 33-meter monolithic monument with information panels and a small museum nearby. It was at the center of the French forces facing north. At this location they held their ground against overwhelming odds.
   N 48 47.193 E 3 46.511 (48.78655, 3.775183)

3. **MARNE MUSEUM AND AMERICAN MEMORIAL TO FRENCH COMBATANTS OF THE MARNE, "HOPELESS VICTORY":** This is an American-built memorial located at the site where the French stopped the Germans. It is just outside Meaux. The Meaux Museum next to the monument opened in 2012. It is well done, with a nice flow, open displays and equipment you won't see elsewhere. The museum also provides information about the Franco-Prussian War, which shifted Europe's power bases and alliances, and, consequently, set up the continent for World War I.
   Marne Museum: N 48 58.248 E 2 54.176 (48.9708, 2.902933)

   American monument: Next to the museum; just park at the museum and walk over.

4. **BRITISH MONUMENT AND MEMORIAL TO THE DEFENSE OF THE MARNE, CONDETZ:** The British Expeditionary Force pulled back along with the French to hold ground. Condetz contains a monument to the British forces who died there.
   N 48 56.586 E 003 7.454 (48.9431, 3.124233)

****Note: Nearby and covered in the section "America Goes to War" is the Château American Memorial and Belleau Woods Cemetery and Memorial*

1ST BATTLE OF THE MARNE SEPTEMBER 5–12, 1914

MAP 20

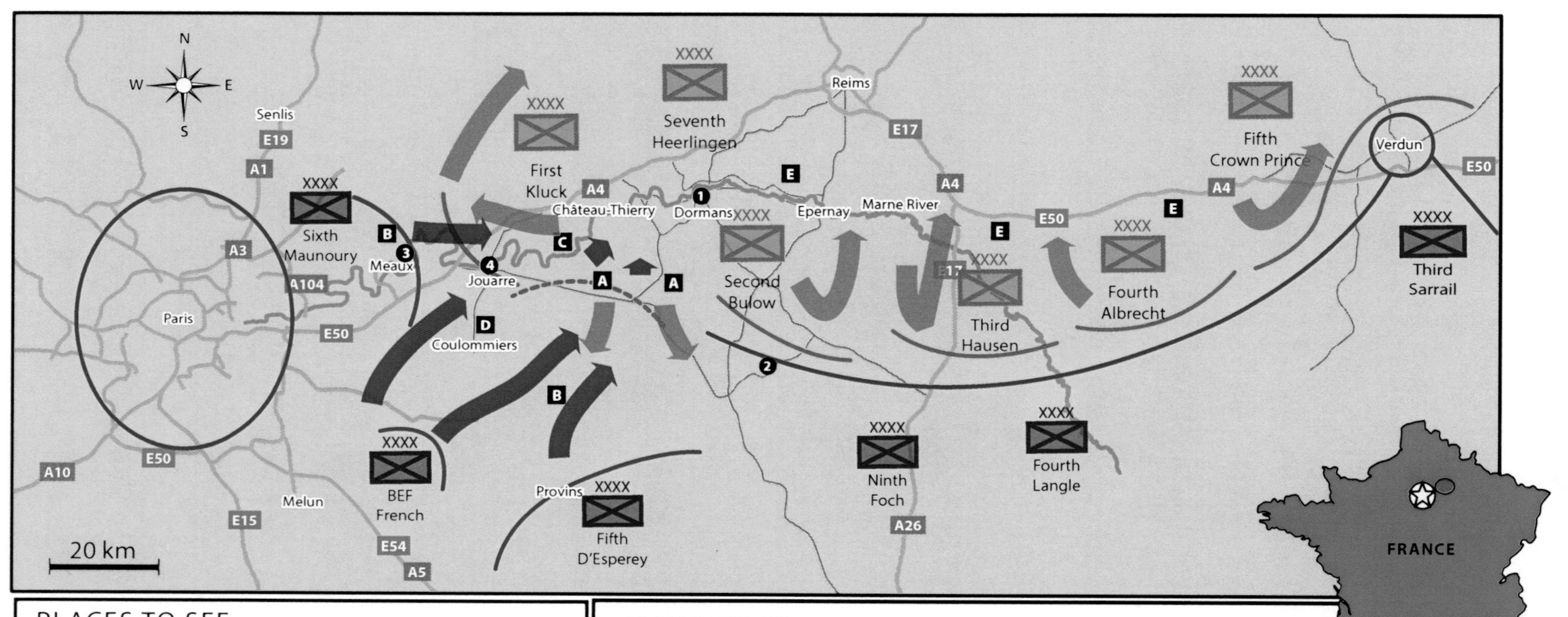
N
W
E
S
Senlis
E19
A1
A3
Paris
A104
E50
A10
E15
Melun
E54
A5
XXXX
Sixth
Maunoury
B
Meaux
3
XXXX
First
Kluck
A4
Château-Thierry
C
4
Jouarre
D
Coulommiers
A
A
B
XXXX
BEF
French
Provins
XXXX
Fifth
D'Esperey
XXXX
Seventh
Heerlingen
1
Dormans
XXXX
Second
Bulow
2
E
Epernay
Reims
E17
A4
Marne River
E
E17
XXXX
Third
Hausen
XXXX
Ninth
Foch
A26
XXXX
Fourth
Langle
E50
E
XXXX
Fourth
Albrecht
A4
XXXX
Fifth
Crown Prince
Verdun
E50
XXXX
Third
Sarrail
FRANCE
20 km

PLACES TO SEE

1. Memorial des Batailles de la Marne
2. National Monument of the Marne Victory
3. Marne Museum and American Memorial to French Combatants of the Marne, "Hopeless Victory"
4. British Monument and Memorial to the defense of the Marne

MOVEMENTS

A. By September 5, the Germans began advancing on Paris but instead of staying on target to envelope Paris, they turned south to envelope the French Armies.

B. In response on September 5, the French and British counterattacked, and hit the German First Army in the right flank.

C. German First Army wheeled right to meet the threat but the move exposed a 30 mile gap between the First and Second Armies.

D. French and BEF attacked through the gap and threatened encircling the Germans.

E. The German Command ordered a retreat to avoid a total loss. The Germans set up their new defensive line on the Aisne River.

DORMANS
1914-1918

Dormans, a beautiful chapel was built in memory of the sacrifices that took place during WW I. It overlooks the fields where the Germans and French clashed just south of the Marne River.

National Monument to the Marne victory. It is 33 meters high and overlooks the battlefield below. It is located at the center of the French defense during the September 1914.

In Condetz, just west of the Marne Victory Monument is a memorial to the British who defended along side the French during the Marne Victory of 1914.

Chateau Thierry, the powerful American memorial overlooks the Marne River at the location the American Forces, 3rd ID "Rock on the Marne" and 2nd ID pushed the Germans back in June 1918.

Left is an example of a beautiful and now peaceful field. This one was near the Marne Victory monument. And of course in another field some of the French cows. They sound like *Meaauuu* vs. Mooo.

"Hopeless Victory", this statue was donated to the French by America in memorial to their defense against the Germans in 1914. It is located next to the new Marne Museum, in Meaux, just outside Paris.

FIRST BATTLE OF CHAMPAGNE

December 20, 1914–March 17, 1915

SECOND BATTLE OF CHAMPAGNE

September 22–October 6, 1915

"Our experience has proved that one can carry the whole defensive system in a single bound." – Joseph Joffre

---

SUMMARY: After the "Miracle on the Marne," both sides began to settle into defensive positions. The French Commander Joffre wanted a decisive battle to end the war within weeks. His plan was to stage a major offensive that would attack the northern and southern edges of the Sayon Salient, which was held by the German Third Army. Joffre believed that an overwhelming force would break the German lines and envelop them. Initially, the French attacked in the south, in Champagne at Perthes and Noyon. Then the British attacked in the north at Givenchy, near Nieuport, Belgium. The Germans' defensive line repulsed most of the attacks and fighting continued until March, when the French attack was called off. The French gained only three kilometers at the cost of 90,000 casualties. The Germans suffered approximately the same number of casualties.

On September 22, 1915, Commander Joffre, convinced that the Germans were still weak and spread thin, decided to attack once again in what became the Second Battle of Champagne. The British attacked in the north, instigating the Battle of Loos. This time, Joffre gathered artillery en masse and for three days bombarded the German lines in the Champagne region. Then the infantry attacked. The effort was successful at first, gaining 3 kilometers, but then German reinforcements arrived and pushed the French back. The result was tremendous losses for the French, with little area gained and a year wasted. The Germans were able to strengthen their positions and weaken the French forces.

OUTCOME: The Germans held their ground and defeated the Allied offensive. In the Second Battle of Champagne, the French pulled artillery from the Verdun region for their bombardment and offensive. The Germans took note of Verdun's weakened state and realized that the French had suffered many casualties. Consequently, the Germans began planning a February 1916 attack on Verdun with the goal of bleeding France white.

WHO? The British, French and Germans. The Allies lost 90,000 men in the first battle and more than 145,000 men in the second battle. The Germans suffered 90,000 casualties in the first battle and approximately 72,500 in the second battle. It was an astonishing amount of casualties for battles that lasted a total of five months.

WHEN? The First Battle lasted from December 20, 1914 through March 17, 1915. The Second Battle lasted from September 22 through October 6, 1915.

WHY AT THESE LOCATIONS? The French believed that the Champagne Salient was the weakest point in the German lines.

TECHNOLOGY/TACTICS: Technology was ahead of tactics. The Germans built up and supplemented their defenses through the use of machine guns, barbed wire (devil's rope) and mines. The French were still developing tactics, as evidenced by the fact that they used a massive artillery bombardment during the Second Battle in an effort to "open up" the German lines.

QUOTE: "Blood is the price of victory." – Karl von Clausewitz

PLACES TO SEE (REFERENCE MAP 21):

1. **FORT DE LA POMPELLE:** This is a fort outside of Reims from where the French fought. It held its own throughout the war and has the battle scars to prove it. It is a very excellent exhibit and tour, with easy access from the main highway.
   N 49 13.072 E 4 07.750 (49.217867, 4.129167)

2. **MONUMENT OSSUAIRE DE LA FERME DE NAVARIN:** Off the main highway sits a memorial that commemorates 10,000 warriors who died while fighting for France's freedom, most of them during the Battle of Champagne. Its location was the epicenter of the front. Three statues of soldiers advancing to the battle top the pyramid-shaped tomb. One of the statues has the features of Quentin Roosevelt, the son of Theodore Roosevelt, who died on July 14, 1917 in Cambrai. The monument is located at the intersection of D220 and D977; only 300 meters north is a German pillbox.
   N 49 13.115 E 4 32.542 (49.218585, 4.542364)

3. **MUSEUM, MARNE 14-18, SUIPPES:** Located just south of the Navarin Memorial is a newly renovated museum with excellent displays, interactive trenches and new interpretations.
   N 49 07.944 E 4 31.924 (49.1324, 4.532067)

4. **FRENCH CEMETERY, SUIPPES:** Located here is a very large French cemetery with approximately 4,000 graves. It sits on the northeast corner of the town of Suippes and shares land with a mass grave containing 5,539 German soldiers.
N 49 07.964 E 4 32.105 (49.132733, 4.535083)

5. **FRENCH CEMETERY, JONCHERY-SUR-SUIPPE:** Also located next to the Suippe River is another major French cemetery, which contains the remains of more than 7,000 soldiers.
N 49 09.153 E 4 28.720 (49.152545, 4.478661)

6. **FRENCH AND GERMAN CEMETERIES, SOUAIN PERTHES LES HURLUS:** Incredibly, a French and German cemetery lay next to each other. The French cemetery, La Crouee, contains 30,732 graves, while the German cemetery contains 13,000 graves.
N 49 11.243 E 4 32.261 (49.18738, 4.537675)

7. **RUSSIAN CEMETERY AND MEMORIALS, SAINT-HILAIRE-LE-GRAND:** This cemetery contains the graves of more than 900 Russian soldiers who fell while fighting for France during World War I.
N 49 09.492 E 4 23.999 (49.158204, 4.399975)

8. **FRENCH, POLISH AND GERMAN CEMETERY, AUBERIVE:** At this location sits another French cemetery next to a German cemetery. The French cemetery contains the graves of 6,424 men who perished during World War I. The German cemetery contains the graves of 5,359 soldiers.
N 49 11.587 E 4 22.084 (49.193119, 4.368062)

****Also nearby is the American memorial Sommepy, just north of the town of Sommepy. I cover it in the in the "Grand Offensive" section.*

2ND BATTLE OF CHAMPAGNE, SEPT. 22–OCT. 6, 1915

MAP 21

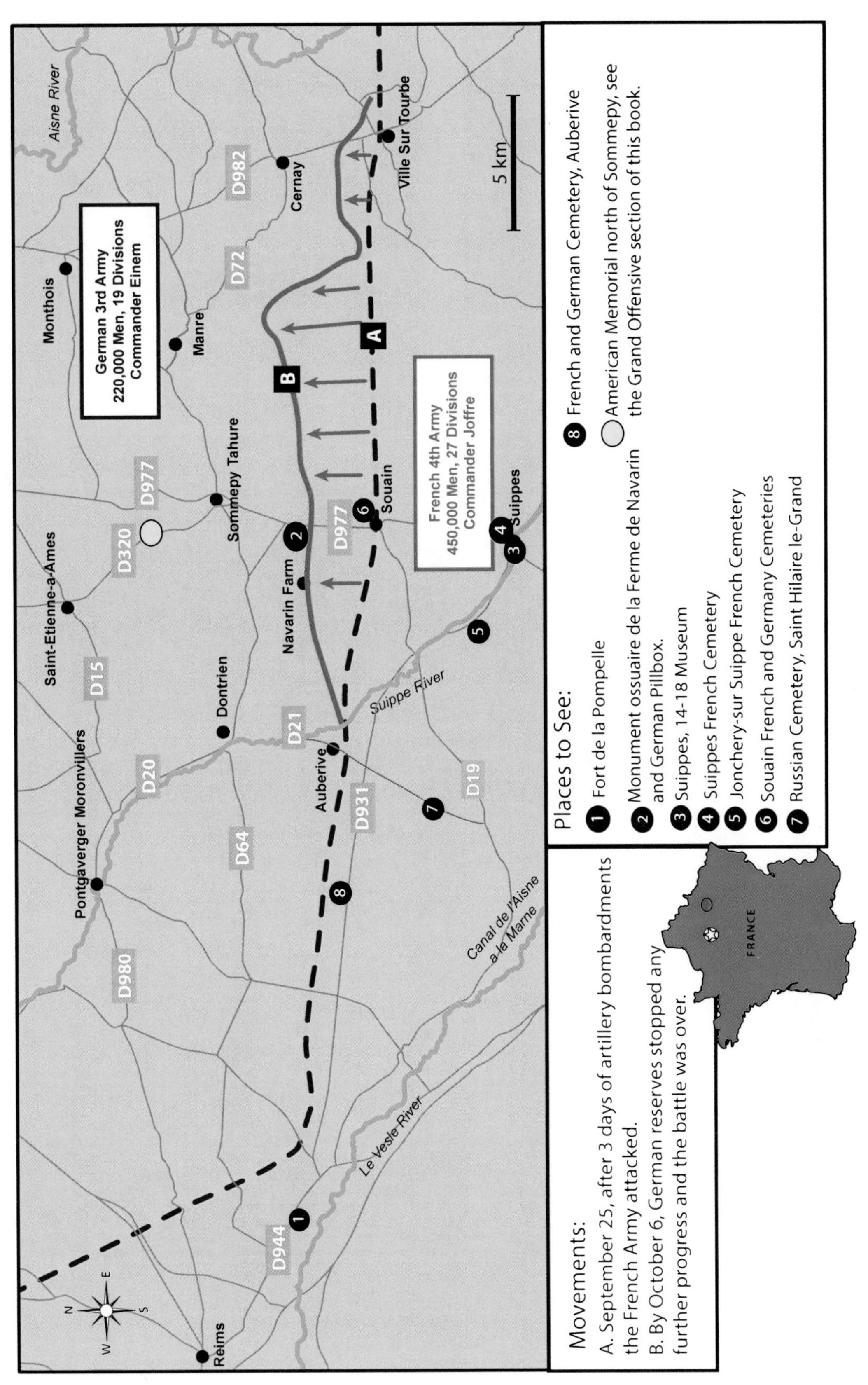
Aisne River
German 3rd Army
220,000 Men, 19 Divisions
Commander Einem
Monthois
Manre
Cernay
Ville Sur Tourbe
5 km
D982
D72
A
B
French 4th Army
450,000 Men, 27 Divisions
Commander Joffre
Sommepy Tahure
Souain
Suippes
Navarin Farm
Saint-Etienne-a-Arnes
D977
D320
D15
Dontrien
Suippe River
D21
Auberive
D931
D19
Pontgaverger Moronvillers
D20
D64
D980
Canal de l'Aisne a la Marne
Le Vesle River
D944
Reims
N
E
S
W
FRANCE
Places to See:
1 Fort de la Pompelle
2 Monument ossuaire de la Ferme de Navarin and German Pillbox.
3 Suippes, 14-18 Museum
4 Suippes French Cemetery
5 Jonchery-sur Suippe French Cemetery
6 Souain French and Germany Cemeteries
7 Russian Cemetery, Saint Hilaire le-Grand
8 French and German Cemetery, Auberive
American Memorial north of Sommepy, see the Grand Offensive section of this book.
Movements:
A. September 25, after 3 days of artillery bombardments the French Army attacked.
B. By October 6, German reserves stopped any further progress and the battle was over.

Fort de la Pompelle, outside of Reims, was the cornerstone preventing the Germans from taking the city. The fort took a severe beating during the entire war—and it shows—but the defenders courageously held their ground.

During World War I, the Germans shelled Reims and used the cathedral as a target to range their guns. It was badly damaged but since has been rebuilt close to its original beauty.

The cathedral contains many beautiful stained-glass windows, including one (above left) of men crushing grapes for the champagne this area is famous for.. The center photo is the Angel of Victory in a city square and the photo to the right is the Smiling Angel, a famous Gothic sculpture (created in the 1220s) know for an optimistic outlook. The angel is smiling for the Annunciation.

La Ferme de Navarino, near Sommepy Tahure, is a memorial and ossuary for 10,000 soldiers who perished in the fields of Champagne. The soldier on the right was carved with the features of Quentin Roosevelt who was shot down on July 14,1918.

Above, Reims Cathedral getting shelled by the Germans, during World War I another terrible casualty of the war.
Collier's New Photography History of the World's War, (1919)

BATTLE OF LOOS

September 25–October 14, 1915

"Known unto God"
- Kipling

SUMMARY: The Battle of Loos was one of Britain's first major attacks. The British had recently brought in their new recruits/conscripts to form what was known as Kitchener's Army, named after Lord Herbert Kitchener, the secretary of defense. The Germans had settled into a defensive position, and recent assaults by the Allies had failed. In the Battle of Loos, the British wanted to attack north of Lens and the French south to oust the Germans from the French mining center. The French Commander Joffre also staged a large offensive in Champagne to break through two portions of the German lines. He believed that two major attacks would finally crack the German defense. At Loos, the British objective was to assault the German lines and penetrate over two lines of defense, nearly 7 kilometers. At 0550 on September 25, after a four-day artillery bombardment, the British opened more than 5,000 cylinders of chlorine gas. Unfortunately, the wind was erratic; the British forces panicked, stalling the attack and, in some cases, forcing the British to travel through their own gas. However, despite such setbacks, in some areas the British gallantly fought their way through German lines (such as when they captured the significant trench defensive complex known as Hohenzollern Redoubt). During the battle, British Sergeant Frank Edwards kicked a football ahead of himself and the Irish Rifles to encourage the men. In many areas, German interlocking machine gunfire annihilated entire units. The next day, two new divisions tried attacking over the flat terrain; they too were met by intact barbed wire and withering German machine gunfire at 1,500 meters. After a lull in fighting, the British lost their momentum and the Germans recaptured Hohenzollern Redoubt. After one more unsuccessful attempt in October, with bad weather setting in, the British called off the attack.

OUTCOME: Although the British New Army received praise for its bravery, the staff was hammered for its poor planning and incompetence. The commander of the British Expeditionary Forces, Sir John French, was removed shortly afterward. The Germans maintained their lines and strengthened their defenses.

WHO? The British attacked with six divisions against an unknown number of Germans. The British suffered more than 50,000 casualties (15,800 killed in action), while the Germans suffered more than 25,000 casualties (1,837 killed in action) in just three weeks of fighting.

WHEN? September 25–October 14, 1915

WHY AT THIS LOCATION? The British believed this was a weak point in the German defense and wanted to kick the Germans out of the French mining centers.

TECHNOLOGY/TACTICS: The British used few new tactics. They relied on the predictable pre-bombardment to destroy German gun emplacements and break up barbed wire. They also used chlorine gas for the first time, albeit unsuccessfully. At this time, gas was used not with artillery shells but with canisters that relied on the wind to blow the gas over the battlefield. One can imagine how unreliable such a system was. The Germans used very effective interlocking fields of fire to cover flank attacks and direct advances. They also built effective trenches using concrete and strong points for protection, defense and morale.

QUOTES: Rudyard Kipling lost his son in this battle; 18-year-old Jack Kipling was considered missing in action until his grave was found in 1992. His gravestone reads, "A Lieutenant of the Great War Irish Guards"; tests were performed to confirm the identification.

Rudyard Kipling coined the epitaph of British unknown soldiers: "Known unto God."

"If any ask us why we died ... Tell them 'Because our fathers lied.'" – Kipling

Have You News of my Boy Jack?

By Rudyard Kipling

"Have you news of my boy Jack?"
Not this tide.
"When d'you think that he'll come back?"
Not with this wind blowing, and this tide.

"Has anyone else had word of him?"
Not this tide.
For what is sunk will hardly swim,
Not with this wind blowing, and this tide.

"Oh, dear, what comfort can I find?"
None this tide,
Nor any tide,
Except he did not shame his kind -
Not even with that wind blowing, and that tide.

Then hold your head up all the more,
This tide,
And every tide;
Because he was the son you bore,
And gave to that wind blowing and that tide.

PLACES TO SEE (REFERENCE MAP 22):

1. **DUD CORNER CEMETERY:** This cemetery and memorial are located on what was a German strongpoint called the Lens Road Redoubt. The Scottish 15th Division captured it during the Battle of Loos. It contains the graves of 1,784 British soldiers and 28 Canadian soldiers. The memorial at the back contains the names of 20,584 men who died while fighting in the Battle of Loos (1915) and the Battle of Bethune (1918).
   N 50 27.633 E 2 46.284 (50.46055, 2.7714)

2. **ST. MARY'S ADVANCED DRESSING STATION CEMETERY:** A beautiful path leads to this cemetery, located in the middle of a field. It holds the graves of 218 soldiers, including Jack Kipling, the son of Rudyard Kipling. His grave was located in 1992 and bore the descriptor "Unknown Irish Lieutenant." The younger Kipling died during the Battle of Loos and his gravestone is located at Plot VII. D. 2. Also at this location are two additional small but beautiful British cemeteries. The smallest is called "Ninth Avenue Cemetery," while the other, just beyond it, does not have a name that I can recall.
   N 50 29.137 E 2 47.35 (50.485617, 2.789167)

3. **HOHENZOLLERN REDOUBT:** This was the German strong point in the fields; at the beginning of a small dirt road is a memorial commemorating the 46th Division. The following geo coordinates take you to the German line's strong point. (Explore it at your own risk!)
   N 50 29.849 E 2 46.620 (50.497483, 2.777)

4. **FROMELLES MUSEUM, "ASSOCIATION POUR LE SOUVENIR DE LA BATAILLE DE FROMELLES":** This museum is well done and located on the second floor of the town hall. Just be aware of the opening times.
   N 50 36.349 E 2 51.226 (50.605817, 2.853767)

5. **FROMELLES MEMORIAL PARK:** At this location a farmer donated his land to the Australians who fought there during the Battle of Fromelles, July 19-20, 1916. Also here is the famous "Cobbers" statue that depicts Sergeant Simon Frazer rescuing an unknown comrade.
   N 50 37.078 E 2 50.130 (50.617967, 2.8355)

BATTLE OF LOOS SEPTEMBER 25 TO OCTOBER 14, 1915 — MAP 22

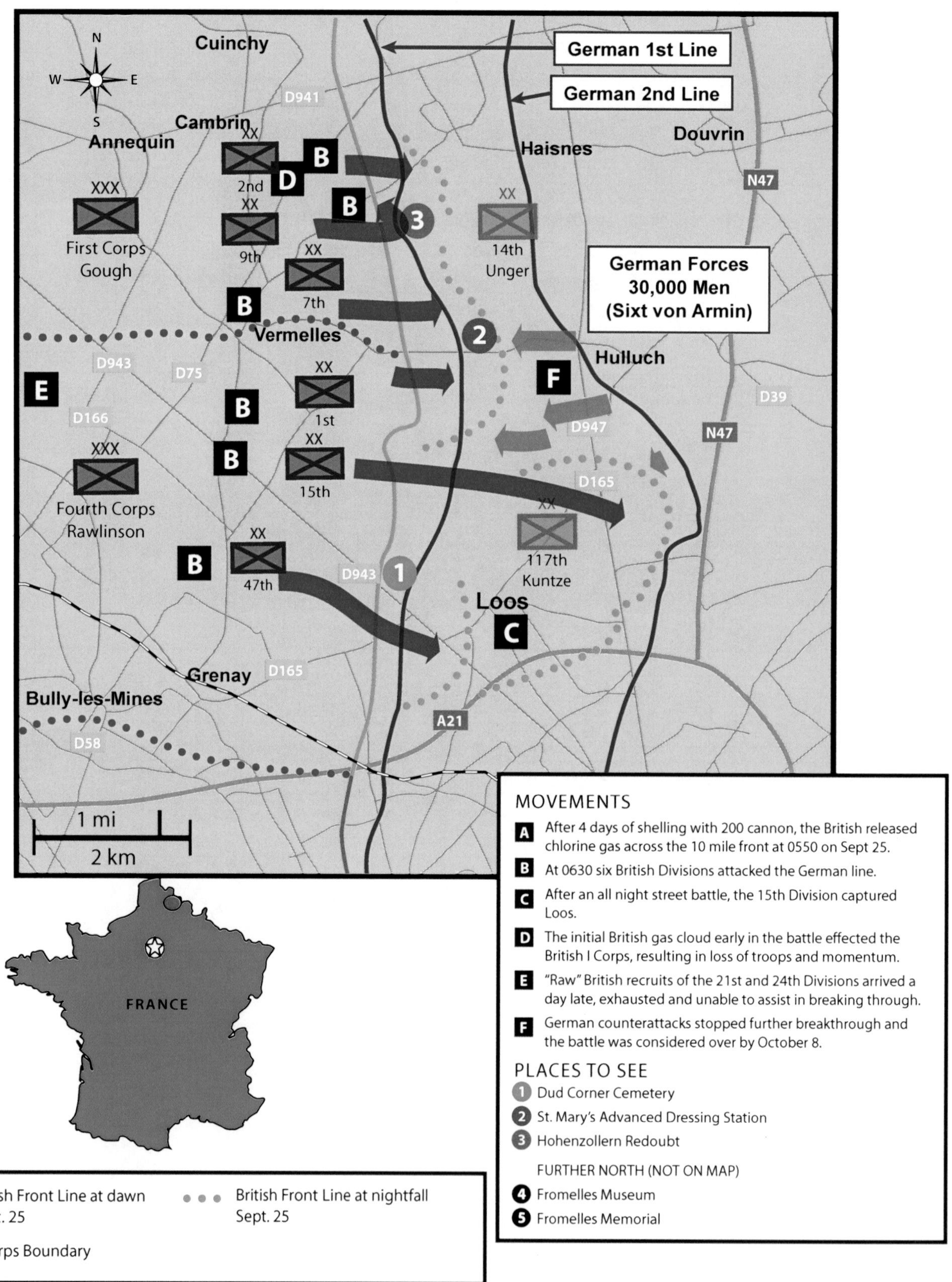
N
W
E
S
Cuinchy
Cambrin
Annequin
German 1st Line
German 2nd Line
Haisnes
Douvrin
D941
N47
XXX
First Corps
Gough
XX
2nd
XX
9th
XX
7th
B
D
B
3
XX
14th
Unger
German Forces
30,000 Men
(Sixt von Armin)
B
Vermelles
2
Hulluch
D943
D75
E
D166
B
XX
1st
F
D947
D39
N47
XXX
Fourth Corps
Rawlinson
B
XX
15th
D165
XX
117th
Kuntze
B
XX
47th
D943
1
Loos
C
Grenay
D165
Bully-les-Mines
D58
A21
1 mi
2 km
FRANCE
MOVEMENTS
A After 4 days of shelling with 200 cannon, the British released chlorine gas across the 10 mile front at 0550 on Sept 25.
B At 0630 six British Divisions attacked the German line.
C After an all night street battle, the 15th Division captured Loos.
D The initial British gas cloud early in the battle effected the British I Corps, resulting in loss of troops and momentum.
E "Raw" British recruits of the 21st and 24th Divisions arrived a day late, exhausted and unable to assist in breaking through.
F German counterattacks stopped further breakthrough and the battle was considered over by October 8.
PLACES TO SEE
1 Dud Corner Cemetery
2 St. Mary's Advanced Dressing Station
3 Hohenzollern Redoubt
FURTHER NORTH (NOT ON MAP)
4 Fromelles Museum
5 Fromelles Memorial
British Front Line at dawn Sept. 25
British Front Line at nightfall Sept. 25
Corps Boundary

These two photos were taken during the Battle of Loos. They show the chemical attacks occuring and the British soldiers advancing through the clouds. *Imperial War Museum*

Dud Corner Cemetery, this photo was taken from the front of the cemetery towards the mine slag mounds. At this location was a German strong point taken by the 15th Scottish.

St. Mary's Advanced Dressing Station, is located in the middle of a serene and peaceful field. A beautifully manicured path leads you to the cemetery, where 218 soldiers are buried.

The above photo was taken from another small cemetery just south of St. Mary's ADS looking back at the small "Ninth Avenue Cemetery and St. Mary's ADS just beyond with the trees.

Center photo, is of John "Jack" Kipling, the son of Rudyard Kipling. Jack was killed in action during the Battle of Loos and his grave above center, finally confirmed in 1992. The grave is located in St. Mary's ADS.

BATTLE OF VERDUN

February 21–December 18, 1916

"They shall not pass."("Ils ne passeront pas.")
- General Robert Nivelle

SUMMARY: The Battle of Verdun lasted 300 days, cost 300,000 lives and led to the wounding of 400,000 men, all within the space of 10 square kilometers—and with no land gained. It is considered one of history's most horrific battles and was essentially a war within the Great War. At 0715 on February 21, after a seven-day delay because of weather, 1,400 German cannons and mortars opened fire on Verdun. Approximately 1,000,000 rounds were used in the 10-hour opening bombardment. The next day, the Germans gained 5 kilometers, up to the town of Flabas. On February 24, the French XXX Corps fell back to its second line of defense and the XX Corps showed up just in time to bolster the defense. The Germans pressed on and took Beaumont, then attacked Fort Douaumont, the largest fort in the Verdun defense. It had been built to accommodate 480 men and four cannon turrets, but at the time of the battle held 68 men and maintained one operational retractable cannon turret. At 1630 on February 25, 14 officers and 79 soldiers of the German 24th took Fort Douaumont. To slow the German advance, the French counterattacked at Douaumont; their ranks included then-Captain Charles de Gaulle, who was captured. The counterattacks worked and allowed 90,000 additional Frenchmen to arrive at the site of battle.

By March 2, the Germans had been delayed but had also advanced too fast. They had not allowed their artillery to move up and provide covering fire; instead, they suffered a pounding at the hands of the French artillery. The Germans managed to take the town of Douaumont, but four of their regiments were devastated. At this point, the attack slowed. On May 22, the French commander, Robert Nivelle, unsuccessfully attacked Douaumont with three divisions and 300 supporting guns. On June 2, the Germans countered and captured the top levels of Fort Vaux with 10,000 men. For five more days the Germans slugged it out door-to-door in the caverns of Fort Vaux until the French garrison surrendered because it had no water or food.

The battle's next major phase arrived in July, when the Germans, with 60,000 men, took Thiemont and obliterated the town of Fleury. Their next obstacle to Verdun was Fort Souville. On July 10, the Germans used 60,000 shells of diphosgene gas (or "Green Cross Gas"), though to little effect, as the French had recently upgraded their gas masks. On July 12, the Germans unleashed a 300,000-shell barrage on Fort Souville and advanced through the machine gun fire and artillery. Only about 100 Germans made it to the top of the fort and caught a glimpse of Verdun from above before they were forced to retreat from the intense French artillery pouring down on them. This was considered the "high point" of the French defense and the farthest that the Germans advanced. On July 1, the Somme offensive began; it helped relieve the attack on Verdun and forced the Germans to move men and artillery in an attempt to defend their northern sector from a breakthrough. At this point, the Germans replaced Commander Erich von Falkenhayn with Paul von Hindenburg.

The final major event at Verdun was the French attack on Fort Douaumont in October. For six days, the French pounded the fort with 530,000 75mm shells and 100,000 155mm shells. To thwart the German machine guns, the French used a "creeping" artillery barrage that advanced ahead of the soldiers. They also brought to bear the 400mm rail guns located 13 kilometers away; six rounds were said to have penetrated the fort. On October 24, with the loss of 100,000 men, the French retook the remains of Fort Douaumont. Shortly afterward, on November 2, the French rolled up Fort Vaux and the Germans retreated. Finally, by December 15, the French had pushed back the Germans to the lines they had maintained in February.

OUTCOME: The result was devastating losses in men and equipment on both sides, all for no ground gained. At Verdun, the French trucks, with their flexibility and speed, were said to have beaten the German logistic rail lines. Because of the trucks and the fact that they had surprised the Germans, the French were able to respond quickly and pour munitions and soldiers into the area. The Germans were close to a breakthrough toward the middle of June, but when the British attacked in the Somme, Falkenhayn was forced to stop sending munitions and replacement divisions to the Verdun area. It proved to be a huge victory for the French, one from which the Germans would never fully recover. Falkenhayn's failure opened the door for Hindenburg and Erich Ludendorff to take control of the war. Also, as a result of the "success" of the Verdun forts, the French decided to build the Maginot Line after World War I.

WHO? The French commanders were Phillipe Pétain and Robert Nivelle, who initially led only 30,000 soldiers. They faced 150,000 men commanded by General Falkenhayn and Crown Prince Wilhelm, head of the Fifth Army. Over an area of 10 square kilometers and spanning 300 days, the French suffered 400,000 casualties (including 163,000 deaths). The Germans suffered more than 300,000 casualties, with 140,000 killed. To this day, people notice a lack of birds in the area; legend says that so much death and destruction took place in Verdun, birds no longer live there.

WHEN? February 21–December 18, 1916

WHY AT VERDUN? Verdun had 18 major forts surrounding it; after Liege and Namur in Belgium fell to German siege cannons, the French concluded that these forts were not worth fully arming. As a result, throughout 1915 the French streamlined their garrisons, stocking them with only 300 guns, limited ammunition and a minimal number of men. The Germans saw this reduction of men and arms as an opportunity to take the "heart of France." Verdun was an imposing obstacle for the Germans and, since the age of the Romans, had been home to a major fort guarding the northern approach to the fields of Champagne. A year earlier, the Germans had been unable to break through at Ypres; now they saw an opportunity to attack a location from which the French would not retreat. In addition, Verdun's capture would open the road to Paris. The Germans believed that the French could not sustain their defense because only a single road existed for logistic support. Verdun was on its own.

TECHNOLOGY/TACTICS: The Germans adjusted their tactics and used Storm Troopers (Stosstruppen) for the first time. During previous battles they had relied on long artillery barrages followed by all-out troop assaults across wide fronts. The Storm Troopers attacked after a short barrage of artillery and filtered through weak points. Typically, they were heavily armed with grenades, machine pistols, pistols and clubs. In addition, Verdun was the first battle during which the Germans used flamethrower teams to burn through strong points, with devastating results. The French strongly believed in artillery as a deciding factor, hence Pétain's quote, "firepower kills" ("le feu tue"). The French were correct, as artillery accounted for 70 percent of the casualties. The French fired more than 24 million rounds throughout the battle, while the Germans fired more than 21 million rounds.

QUOTE: "They shall not pass."("Ils ne passeront pas.") – General Nivelle

PLACES TO SEE (THESE ARE SOME OF THE TOP SITES; MANY MORE EXIST.) (REFERENCE MAP 23):

1. **MÉMORIAL DE VERDUN/FLEURY AND DOUAUMONT MUSEUM:** This is the area's best museum dedicated to the Battle of Verdun. It sits on the site of the Fleury train station.
   N 49 11.691 E 5 26.013 (49.19485, 5.43355)

2. **FLEURY VILLAGE CHAPEL AND NINE DESTROYED VILLAGES:** The town of Fleury once sat on this location. The town was at the center of battle and changed hands 16 times. It was one of nine villages that were destroyed in the battle and never rebuilt. The other villages were Haumont, Beaumont, Louvremont, Ornes, Bezonvaux, Douaumont, Vaux and Cumieres. Chapels were built in each of the destroyed villages to honor and memorialize the soldiers who died (and who, in many case, are buried) there. It's a haunting experience to walk the paths, see the remaining foundations and realize that you can identify trenches and craters better than you can a town.
   A. **FLEURY**: N 49 11.866 E 5 25.689 (49.197767, 5.42815)
   B. **HAUMONT:** N 49 16.341 E 5 21.094 (49.272358, 5.351572)
   C. **BEAUMONT:** N 49 15.521 E 5 24.361 (49.258687, 5.406009)
   D. **LOUVREMONT:** N 49 14.285 E 5 23.918 (49.238082, 5.398638)

E. **ORNES:** N 49 15.141 E 5 28.167 (49.252350, 5.469453)

F. **BEZONVAUX:** N 49 14.201 E 5 28.080 (49.236684, 5.468001)

G. **DOUAUMONT:** N 49 13.185 E 5 25.909 (49.219756, 5.431812)

H. **VAUX:** N 49 12.348 E 5 28.204 (49.205793, 5.470068)

I. **CUMIERES:** N 49 13.888 E 5 16.828 (49.231465, 5.280465)

3. **DOUAUMONT OSSUARY AND NATIONAL CEMETERY:** This is a powerful memorial and cemetery that houses a small museum. It is the burial place of 15,000 French soldiers, and also holds the bones (which you can see through ground-level windows) of more than 130,000 French and German soldiers who fought in the battle. The Ossuary is a must-see when visiting Verdun.
N 49 12.479 E 5 25.438 (49.207983, 5.423967)

4. **BAYONET TRENCH:** This memorial honors French soldiers of the 137th Infantry Regiment who were buried alive by German artillery on June 23, 1916. Legend says that several of the soldiers stood at the ready with their bayonets up. Hence, the memorial features rifles with bayonets sticking out. Unfortunately, vandals have broken much of what remains of the rifles.
N 49 12.805 E 5 25.519 (49.213417, 5.425317)

5. **FORT DOUAUMONT:** The largest and highest fort in the area of Verdun, Douaumont offers a tour during which you can walk around and on top of the fort to see the field of fire, destruction and armaments. Douaumont was the first major fort taken by the Germans without a fight. Like many forts, the French had left it unoccupied because they believed the German 420mm howitzers would destroy them, as the Germans had done to Belgian forts in 1914. On May 8, the Germans tried to heat coffee inside the fort. This created a fire storm when flame thrower fuel caught fire and ignited artillery and grenades; 679 German soldiers died in the incident. The dead were walled off in one of the fort casements and remain there to this day. On October 24, 1916, the French recaptured the fort through the use of three divisions. The recapture of Fort Douaumont marked the beginning of the end of the Battle of Verdun.
N 49 12.984 E 5 26.394 (49.2164, 5.4399)

6. **FORT SOUVILLE:** Another impressive fort with a short tour. You can climb to the top and explore the battle's immensity and destruction.
N 49 11.327 E 5 26.526 (49.188783, 5.4421)

7. **FORT VAUX:** The third major fort to explore around Verdun.
N 49 11.985 E 5 28.190 (49.19975, 5.469833)

8. **DOWNTOWN VERDUN:** Here you'll find many monuments, fortification remains, a river walk and nice cafés and restaurants.
Parking coordinates: N 49 09.821 E 5 23.177 (49.163683, 5.386283)

9. **COLONEL DRIANT'S COMMAND POST AND TOMB AT CAURES WOOD:** At this location Colonel Émile Driant and his 1,200 men held off the German main assault, delaying it for about 24 hours. Driant was killed while rescuing a soldier as his troops withdrew. Only 118 of his men survived.
N 49 16.430 E 5 24.276 (49.273833, 5.4046)

10. **MORT HOMME MONUMENT TO THE 69TH DIVISION:** This is a memorial to the defenders who fought against the major German attack on March 6. The Germans took the hill after a month of fighting.
N 49 13.687 E 5 15.067 (49.228117, 5.251117)

BATTLE OF VERDUN – FEBRUARY 21 TO DECEMBER 18, 1916 MAP 23

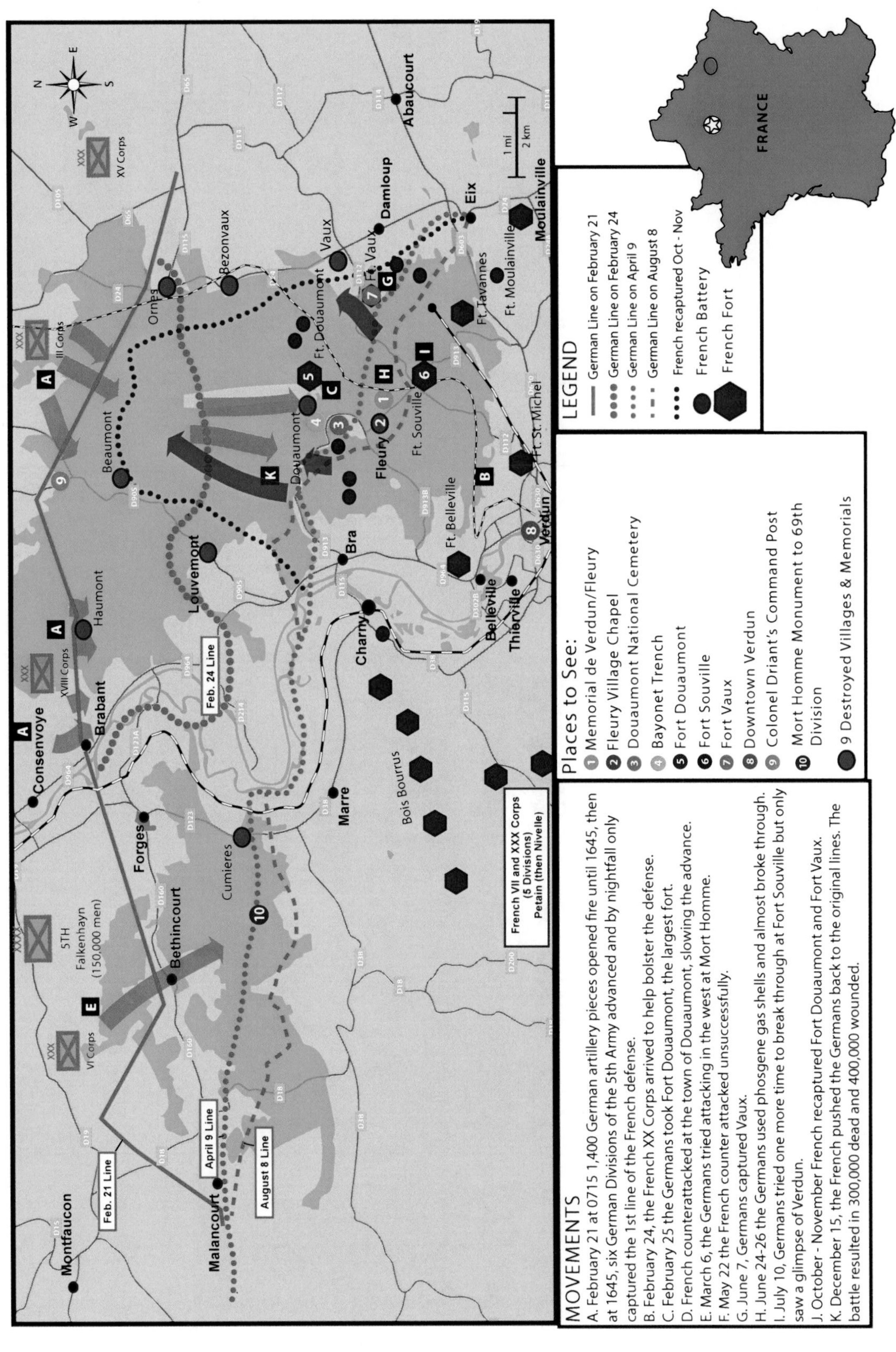
Montfaucon
Feb. 21 Line
VI Corps
E
5TH
Falkenhayn
(150,000 men)
Consenvoye
A
XVIII Corps
Brabant
Haumont
III Corps
Beaumont
XV Corps
Forges
Bethincourt
Malancourt
April 9 Line
August 8 Line
Cumieres
Louvemont
Feb. 24 Line
Ornes
Bezonvaux
K
Douaumont
Ft. Douaumont
Vaux
Marre
Charny
Bra
Fleury
Ft. Vaux
Damloup
Abaucourt
Bois Bourrus
Ft. Souville
Ft. Belleville
Eix
Ft. Tavannes
Ft. Moulainville
Moulainville
Belleville
Thierville
Verdun
Ft. St. Michel
French VII and XXX Corps
(5 Divisions)
Petain (then Nivelle)
1 mi
2 km
MOVEMENTS
A. February 21 at 0715 1,400 German artillery pieces opened fire until 1645, then at 1645, six German Divisions of the 5th Army advanced and by nightfall only captured the 1st line of the French defense.
B. February 24, the French XX Corps arrived to help bolster the defense.
C. February 25 the Germans took Fort Douaumont, the largest fort.
D. French counterattacked at the town of Douaumont, slowing the advance.
E. March 6, the Germans tried attacking in the west at Mort Homme.
F. May 22 the French counter attacked unsuccessfully.
G. June 7, Germans captured Vaux.
H. June 24-26 the Germans used phosgene gas shells and almost broke through.
I. July 10, Germans tried one more time to break through at Fort Souville but only saw a glimpse of Verdun.
J. October - November French recaptured Fort Douaumont and Fort Vaux.
K. December 15, the French pushed the Germans back to the original lines. The battle resulted in 300,000 dead and 400,000 wounded.
Places to See:
1 Memorial de Verdun/Fleury
2 Fleury Village Chapel
3 Douaumont National Cemetery
4 Bayonet Trench
5 Fort Douaumont
6 Fort Souville
7 Fort Vaux
8 Downtown Verdun
9 Colonel Driant's Command Post
10 Mort Homme Monument to 69th Division
9 Destroyed Villages & Memorials
LEGEND
German Line on February 21
German Line on February 24
German Line on April 9
German Line on August 8
French recaptured Oct - Nov
French Battery
French Fort
FRANCE

Battle of Verdun ended after 300 days with 300,000 dead and 400,000 wounded. Above left is a photo of a French soldier getting hit by fire. Center top, the misery and reality of war. Many soldiers were buried in the trenches and just spilled out after the rain or artillery fire.

The Battle of Verdun saw the wide useof flame throwers, like the one above being used by the Germans. These terrible weapons were successful creating fear but also top targets for marksmen. The photo to the left is a shot of German soldiers observing an attack on Fort Vaux.

The photos to the right are of the remains of Fort Vaux. The first photo is of the main entrace. The photo to the far right is the top of Fort Vaux.

The center photo show Fort Douamont at the begining of the battle. The lower photo speaks for itself. The fort was the largest of the forts around Verdun. On February 25, the Germans captured the fort without much of a fight because it was not fully occupied by the French. The French believed the forts had been made obsolete by the German 420mm guns which destroyed the Belgian forts in 1914.

A LA FRANCE IMMORTELLE
A LA GLORIEUSE VILLE
DE VERDUN
LA HOLLANDE AMIE

Verdun, downtown has many monuments including the beautiful walk way to the monument of victory flanked by two 75mm cannons. The photo to the right is a statue provided by Holland in memory of the French warriors, it depicts a winged Valkyrie carrying up a killed soldier to the heavens, to live forever.

Located in the memorial and Ossuary of Douaumont, they brought the human face to the war with photos of soldiers who survived the war. A very moving and incredible memorial. In the front of the tower are 15,000 French graves and inside the Ossuary are the remains of 130,000 French and German soldiers found throughout the battlefield but not identified.

FLEURY-devant-DOUAUMONT

The Trench of Bayonets, near Douaumont.

Fleury, craters and chapel in the background. And a black and white photo of Fleury before the battle.

BATTLE OF THE SOMME

July 1–November 21, 1916

"The infantry would only have to walk over to take possession." - British Commander Rawlinson

---

SUMMARY: On the first day of the Battle of the Somme, British forces suffered the greatest number of casualties ever recorded on a single day of fighting—a devastating 60,000. In December 1915, the British and French had drawn up plans to attack the Germans in the Somme region. The Germans upset these plans when they attacked Verdun in February 1916. As a result, the British forces took the lead in planning and providing the majority of the forces for conflict in the Somme. They initiated the attack on June 24 with an eight-day artillery bombardment, firing more than 1,000,000 rounds at the German first, second and third lines. At 0720 on July 1, the British detonated a 40,000-pound mine under German positions at Hawthorne Ridge; they followed this by detonating 16 other mines at 0728. The Allies followed with an attack on a 30-kilometer front with 280,000 men (13 British divisions and 11 French divisions) against 10 German divisions. Their goal was the town of Bapaume, 19 kilometers from their starting point of Albert. The old Roman Road was the axis point of the attack, with British forces to the north of the road and French forces to the south. The British believed that after the bombardment they could "walk" to the German trenches, but instead they were slaughtered. (For example, of the Newfoundland Regiment's 801 men, 500 were killed instantly.) The Irish of the 34th Division were wiped out less than 2 kilometers from the German lines. The Germans had adapted their tactics and had a "defense in depth." Since 1914, they had been largely unmolested, a fact that gave them time to create strong trenches and bunkers for machine guns and artillery. In addition, the British artillery did not pave a path through the German barbed wire as the British commanders assumed it would. The British artillery did little besides warn the Germans of an upcoming attack. The French, on the other hand, possessed more accurate artillery and adjusted their infantry tactics so that they were more like those of the German Storm Troopers, creating small, high-firepower groups that effectively exploited weak spots in the German defenses. The French achieved all their first-day objectives in the south, while the British suffered the worst losses in history. Out of the 60,000 British casualties that day, 19,240 were dead, 35,493 were wounded, 2,152 were missing and 500 had been taken prisoner. The British met none of their objectives. To add to the horror, most of the casualties came from the same communities, as a man's hometown determined the unit in which he served. The losses devastated entire towns and villages.

On July 14, the British adjusted their tactics and implemented a short creeping barrage, attacking at 0325 with four divisions on a 6,000-yard front and achieving their objectives at Bazentin Ridge. Next, the Fourth Army tried to take Pozières three times, but failed. The Anzacs (Australians and New Zealanders) took it on August 8 and held off German counterattacks. This was the Anzacs' high point; like the Canadians at Vimy Ridge, they "became a nation on that day." The British took Guillemont on September 3 and the Irish 16th Division took Ginchy on September 9. Finally, the French and British linked up their forces again in a straight line, but at a tremendous cost to the British sector—1,000 yards gained at a cost of 82,000 casualties.

On September 15, the next major phase of the battle began at Flers-Courcelette. This is remembered as the first time tanks were used in battle. The British brought out their new secret weapon. Forty-nine tanks were delivered; 32 made it to the line while only 21 made it into battle outside Pozières. The tanks were notoriously unreliable, but did have some "shock and awe" effect on the German lines. With four divisions and the tanks' help, the British captured Flers and, finally, High Wood.

On September 26, the final phase began. Field Marshal Douglas Haig convinced himself that a breakthrough was imminent. Marshal Ferdinand Foch wanted the British to keep up the pressure because the French were on the offensive in Verdun. Consequently, Haig threw in Hubert Gough's reserve army and on the first day the 18th Division gallantly took the German fortress, Thiepval. Next, Haig moved forward with an attack north of Thiepval (later called the Battle of Ancre Heights), where Scottish Highlanders took Beaumont Hamel. The "Glasgow Boys Brigade" took the Frankfurt trench on November 18. However, they surrendered on November 21 with only 45 survivors. This marked the end of the Battle of the Somme; the British lost 420,000 men for a gain of 3 kilometers.

OUTCOME: The result was inconclusive. The Germans withdrew to the stronger Hindenburg Line, but historians argue that without Somme, the Germans would have remained at full strength. The Battle of the Somme cost the Germans a number of veterans whom they would never recover, but it also did the same thing to the Allies. The British learned that they needed to change their tactics, but suffered greatly for that education.

WHO? The British were commanded by General Haig and numbered 13 divisions. The French, commanded by General Foch, numbered 11 divisions. The two sides outnumbered the forces led by German commanders Max von Gallwitz and Fritz von Below, who initially controlled only 11 divisions. The Allies suffered 623,907 casualties, of which 146,431 were killed. They also lost 100 tanks and 782 aircraft. The Germans suffered 595,294 casualties, with 164,055 killed in action. On average, the Allies suffered approximately 1,000 killed in action per day.

WHEN? July 1, 1916–November 21, 1916

WHY AT THE SOMME? The British favored offenses in the Somme region because it was close to their supply routes via the English Channel. They planned to cut off the German U-boat threats supported from the Belgian coast. In addition, they wanted to relieve the pressure on Verdun.

TECHNOLOGY/TACTICS: To repulse the British forces, the Germans used defense in-depth, multiple lines, fortified strong points and mobile reserves. The British, in turn, developed tanks and introduced them to battle. Tanks were impervious to rifles and most of that era's machine guns, but were unreliable, slow (3 kilometers per hour), hot and susceptible to artillery. The tankers started wearing chain mail masks to protect their faces from spalling (i.e., fragments of steel shooting off inside the tank due to impacts on the outside). The French were more successful because they had adjusted their tactics to resemble those of the German Storm Troopers; consequently, they had small bands of heavily armed troops to exploit weak points in defense lines.

QUOTE: A German officer, Friedrich Steinbrecher, stated, "Somme. The whole history of the world cannot contain a more ghastly word."

ALAN SEEGER: One of the first Americans killed in action, Seeger lived in France and volunteered to fight for the country he loved, joining the French Foreign Legion. He wrote the following poem shortly before he died during the Battle of the Somme on July 4, 1916:

Rendezvous with Death

I have a rendezvous with Death
At some disputed barricade,
When Spring comes back with rustling shade
And apple-blossoms fill the air-
I have a rendezvous with Death
When Spring brings back blue days and fair.

PLACES TO SEE (REFERENCE MAP 24):

The area contains many memorials and cemeteries. A good starting point is the museum in Albert. Get a nice B&B and take two or three days to visit. Following are the highlights, listed from north to south:

1. **FRANKFURT TRENCH CEMETERY:** This is where the Glasgow Boys Brigade held out from November 18–21; only 45 survived. The Glasgow defeat marked the end of the Somme Offensive. One hundred and fifty soldiers are buried in this cemetery.
   N 50 5.289 E 2 39.893 (50.08815, 2.664883)

2. **BRITISH MUNICH TRENCH CEMETERY (NEAR FRANKFURT):** At this location, approximately 20 Commonwealth soldiers are buried. The Munich Trench was near this site; the British captured it in 1917.
   N 50 05.261 E 2 40.024 (50.087683, 2.667067)

3. **BEAUMONT-HAMEL NEWFOUNDLAND MEMORIAL:** This is another "must-see." It's a Canadian monument with preserved trenches, craters, barbed wire and a welcome center. The location was part of the initial attack of July 1, 1916. Of the 801 soldiers who attacked, only 68 emerged unscathed. Note that at the time of battle Newfoundland did not consider itself part of Canada. The soldiers' families bought the battlefield so that they could preserve the hallowed ground. The war lasted another two years after the battle, so many of the remains were never recovered.
   N 50 04.430 E 2 38.917 (50.073833, 2.648617)

4. **ULSTER TOWER, THIEPVAL:** This is a monument to the Northern Irish 36th Division, which, from Thiepval Wood, charged the Germans. They were the only soldiers north of the Bapaume road to pierce the German lines. Within two hours, they had penetrated five German lines, but after about 15 hours they had to retreat to their original positions because no one on their flanks had gained ground!
   N 50 03.658 E 2 40.799 (50.060967, 2.679983)

5. **THIEPVAL MONUMENT FRANCO, BRITISH MEMORIAL AND VISITORS CENTER:** This is the largest British memorial in the world. It contains the names of more than 72,000 missing troops who have no grave. This area was captured on September 27, 1916, but was lost in the 1918 Spring Offensive.
   N 50 03.026 E 2 41.237 (50.050433, 2.687283)

6. **GUEUDECOURT (NEWFOUNDLAND) MEMORIAL:** This marks the farthest point taken in the Somme Offensive.
   N 50 03.901 E 2 51.229 (50.065017, 2.853817)

7. **POZIÈRES MEMORIAL:** This memorial, where a windmill once stood, marks the center of the struggle for Pozières. In August 1916, three Australian divisions were thrown against the Germans to capture the Pozières high ground. In the course of 19 attacks over 45 days, they lost more than 23,000 men. Across the street is a monument commemorating the first use of the tank, which took place a month later.
   N 50 02.698 E 2 44.168 (50.044965, 2.736130)

8. **TANK MONUMENT:** This site marks the first use of the tank in September 1916.
   N 50 2.650 E 2 44.198 (50.044167, 2.736633)

9a. **TOMMY'S PUB, POZIÈRES:** The food here is okay, but the pub contains a great collection of photos and artifacts.
   N 50 02.305 E 2 43.486 (50.038417, 2.724767)

9b. BRITISH CEMETERY, POZIÈRES: At this location, on the western edge of Pozières, is another Commonwealth cemetery. It holds the graves of 1,378 soldiers and commemorates the names of more than 14,000 soldiers who have no known grave.
N 50 02.028 E 2 42.927 (50.033796, 2.715444)

10. MOUQUET FARM (CENTRAL BASTION IN THE GERMAN LINE ON POZIÈRES RIDGE): At this site is a stone that contains a plaque describing the battle. The site was the center of the British second objective (after Thiepval).
N 50 02.968 E 2 42.483 (50.049467, 2.70805)

11. DELVILLE WOOD SOUTH AFRICAN MEMORIAL AND MUSEUM, LONGUEVAL: The South African Brigade attached to the 9th Scottish Division attacked the woods at dawn on July 15. After days of continual fighting and artillery strikes (more than 300 rounds per minute), only 143 men of the 3,150 originally in the brigade left the line. Across the street is the Commonwealth Cemetery of Delville Woods.
N 50 01.467 E 2 48.760 (50.02445, 2.812667)

12. MAMETZ WOOD MEMORIAL (WELSH 38TH DIVISION RED DRAGON): At this location, two divisions attacked Mametz Wood; one of them was the 38th Welsh. They were repulsed, but a second attack featuring bitter, two-day, hand-to-hand combat forced the Germans to retreat. The attack left the Welsh division with 4,000 casualties; some blame them for the first offensive's failure, as they took too long to capture the stronghold.
N 50 00.830 E 2 45.381 (50.013833, 2.75635)

13. PIPER'S MEMORIAL: This is a statue dedicated to the pipers who played during attacks in the Somme.
N 50 01.572 E 2 48.209 (50.0262, 2.803483)

14. LE GRAND MINE OF LOCHNAGAR: At 0728 on July 1, 1916, this and 16 other mines exploded (in Le Grand Mine's case, thanks to 60,000 pounds of ammonal). Debris was thrown 4,000 feet into the air, but the Allies couldn't take advantage of the gap that appeared.
N 50 00.933 E 2 41.833 (50.01555, 2.697217)

15. MUSÉE DES ABRIS SOMME 1916, ALBERT: This is one of the best museums dedicated to World War I. It's located below the church and a must-see. You should start your trip with a visit here.
N 50 00.252 E 2 38.918 (50.0042, 2.648633)

FARTHER EAST:

16. BATTLE OF CAMBRAI: In Flesouieres is a British female tank, D51, "Deborah," which was found buried in the village.
N 50 07.381 E 3 07.134 (50.123010, 3.118907)

17. **AMERICAN CEMETERY OF THE SOMME:** This is a memorial and cemetery that holds the graves of 1,844 soldiers who fought during the September 1918 Great Offensive. It is another very impressive cemetery, just outside the town of Boney.
N 49 59.126 E 3 12.958 (49.985433, 3.215967)

18. **BELLICOURT AMERICAN MONUMENT:** On September 29 at 0530, the 27th and 30th American Infantry Divisions attacked this location and breached the 1,000-yard-deep Hindenburg Line through the use of machine guns, mines, barbed wire, artillery and three trench lines. The monument is built over the canal that was directly west of the German line.
N 49 58.508 E 3 13.956 (49.975133, 3.2326)

BATTLE OF THE SOMME – JULY 1 TO NOVEMBER 19, 1916

MAP 24

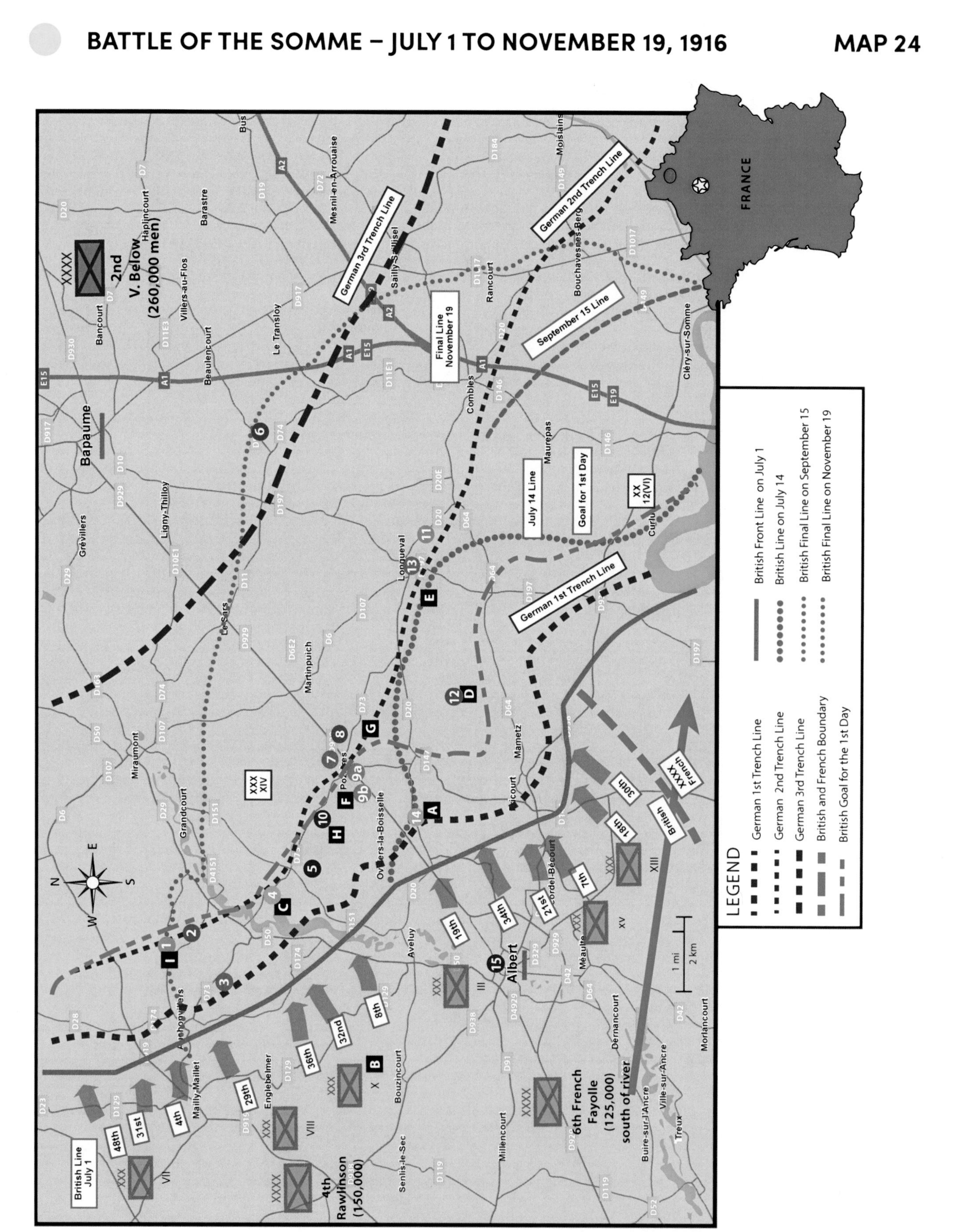

FRANCE
LEGEND
German 1st Trench Line
German 2nd Trench Line
German 3rd Trench Line
British and French Boundary
British Goal for the 1st Day
British Front Line on July 1
British Line on July 14
British Final Line on September 15
British Final Line on November 19
German 3rd Trench Line
German 2nd Trench Line
German 1st Trench Line
Final Line November 19
September 15 Line
July 14 Line
Goal for 1st Day
British Line July 1
2nd
V. Below
(260,000 men)
4th
Rawlinson
(150,000)
6th French
Fayolle
(125,000)
south of river
British
French
Bapaume
Albert
1 mi
2 km

BATTLE OF THE SOMME – JULY 1 TO NOVEMBER 19, 1916

MAP 24

PLACES TO SEE

1. Frankfurt Trench Cemetery
2. Munich Trench Cemetery
3. Beaumont-Hamel Newfoundland Memorial
4. Ulster Tower, Thiepval
5. Thiepval Monument Franco-British
6. Gueudecourt Memorial
7. Pozieres Memorial
8. Tank Monument
9a. Tommy's Pub
9b. British Cemetery Pozieres
10. Mouquet Farm
11. Longueval-Delville Wood Memorial
12. Mametz Wood Memorial
13. Piper's Memorial
14. Le Grand Mine of Lochnagar
15. Musee des Abris Somme 1916, Albert

Further East:

16. Battle of Cambrai
17. American Cemetery of the Somme
18. Bellicourt American Monument

MOVEMENTS

A. After an 8 day artillery barrage of 1,000,000 rounds; July 1 at 0728 the British detonated 17 mines, under the German Lines, including what is now known as the Lochnagar Crater.

B. At 0730 over 60,000 British soldiers attacked German lines and late morning another 40,000 were sent into the fray.

C. By the end of the first day the 36th Irish Division was the only one to breach the German line, in total the British suffered over 60,000 casualties in one day.

D. July 11, the Welsh finally captured Mametz woods after suffering 4,000 casualties.

E. July 14-15, the British and South Africans attacked at night with 20,000 men and gained ground around Longueval and Delville Wood.

F. August 4, the Austrialians captured the windmill at Pozieres but after 45 days of battle they suffered over 25,000 casualties for less than 2 miles.

G. September 15, the British secret weapon was introduced with success, 18 tanks were used in war for the first time and created a small breakthrough near Pozieres.

H. September 26-27, with the help of 3 tanks, Thiepval was finally captured.

I. November 13-18, one more final attack was attempted in the north, the 51st Highlanders caputured Beaumont Hamel and Frankfurt Trench but later surrendered marking the end of the Somme Offensive.

Left to Right: One of the connecting roads headed from the Frankfurt Trench towards Beaumont-Hamel. The poppies were coming out in full bloom and the bright yellow rapeseed seen to the left which is used as cooking oil, biodiesel and animal feed. In the center is the monument to the bag pipers and to the right, Delville Wood Cemetery and Memorial for the South Africans.

Above, and center photo, the Thiepval Memorial. It is a memorial to over 72,000 names of those with no known grave.

Top and Right: Photos of the Germans firing the MG 08 and notice the better design in the trenches, above right. In comparison note the basic design for the British and the weary faces after battle.

Above, Ulster Tower to commemorate the 36th Irish Division who pierced the German line on the first day of the Somme but had to retreat after 15 hours because no one else was there to cover their flanks.

Left: Gueudecourt Newfoundland Memorial, a monument to the furthest advance of the battle of the Somme, which took place in October 1916.

TO OUR DEAR SON

Above, British Commonwealth Cemetery Pozieres at sunset.

After the war, loved ones from England traveled to France to find the graves of their family; the terrible truth.

The left side are clips from real film footage of British soldiers attacking during the Battle of the Somme. The second photo is gut wrenching to see the soldier look back at the camera for possibly one last time. It appears he was hit as he went over. The courage it took to attack is incredible. On the right are photos of the Germans in the attack. The Germans began using tactics to employ storm troopers, soldiers with grenades and typically submachine guns to bring more fire power. They attacked weak points and bypassed the strong points to create havoc in the rear areas and a break through.

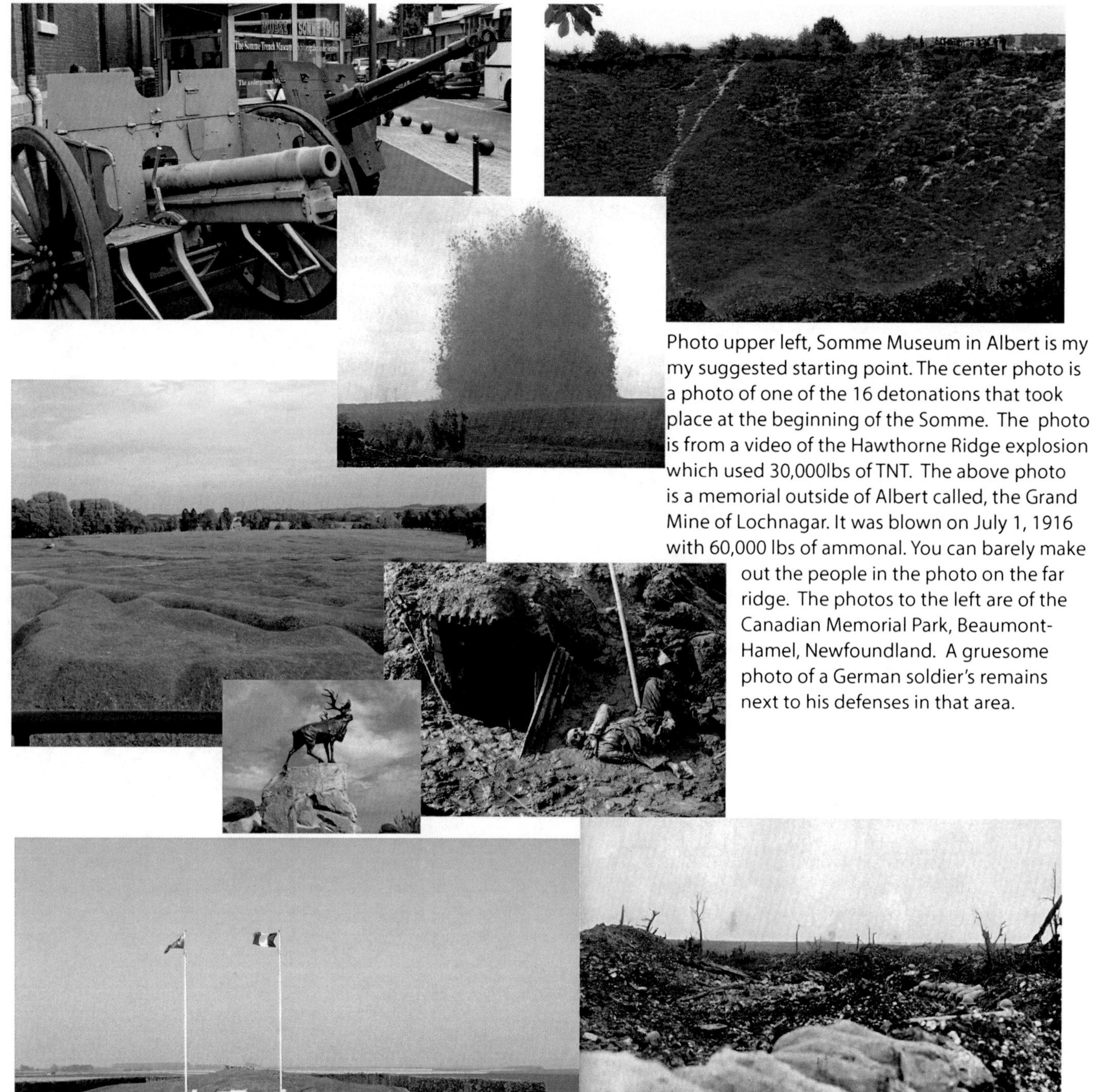

Photo upper left, Somme Museum in Albert is my my suggested starting point. The center photo is a photo of one of the 16 detonations that took place at the beginning of the Somme. The photo is from a video of the Hawthorne Ridge explosion which used 30,000lbs of TNT. The above photo is a memorial outside of Albert called, the Grand Mine of Lochnagar. It was blown on July 1, 1916 with 60,000 lbs of ammonal. You can barely make out the people in the photo on the far ridge. The photos to the left are of the Canadian Memorial Park, Beaumont-Hamel, Newfoundland. A gruesome photo of a German soldier's remains next to his defenses in that area.

Upper left is the memorial outside Pozieres where 3 Austrialian Divisions attacked 19 times over the land you see above in the black and white photo of Pozieres fields. On the bottom left is Mouquet Farm today which was a German stronghold, facing towards Pozieres. To the right a British MK Itank, first used in the Somme.

NIVELLE OFFENSIVE, AISNE, CHAMPAGNE

April 16–May 16, 1917

BATTLE OF VIMY RIDGE

April 9-12, 1917

"In those few minutes I witnessed the birth of a nation."
– Brigadier General A.E. Ross

SUMMARY: The Battle of Verdun officially ended in mid-December and the new French commander, Robert Nivelle, assumed control. He drew up plans for the Allies' Spring Offensive, which became known as the Nivelle Offensive. His plan was to have the British and Commonwealth forces create a diversionary attack in the north at Arras and Vimy. Next, the French would attack with 1,200,000 men and 7,000 cannon on an 80-kilometer front with the goal of making a major breakthrough on Chemin des Dames Ridge. Nivelle believed that the maneuver would end the war within 48 hours and lead to only 10,000 casualties. However, the result was far from Nivelle's predictions. On March 20, the British and Canadians initiated an intense barrage on a 38-kilometer front at Vimy Ridge east of Arras. They fired more than 2,680,000 rounds, including gas shells, for the last 10 hours before zero hour on April 9. The British and the Commonwealth, which consisted of 27 divisions, were up against seven divisions of Germans on the line and 27 more in reserve. In this case, the artillery bombardment proved effective against the Germans because it occurred over a long period of time, disrupting ration supplies, destroying trenches and barbed-wire defenses, and, in the case of gas, killing many pack animals (consequently ensuring that the Germans would encounter difficulty moving their artillery units). On April 9 at 0530, in combination with the "creeping" artillery barrage, darkness and heavy snow, the Allies took the front two German lines. By 1300 on the first day at Vimy Ridge, Canada's four divisions, fighting together for the first time, took the majority of the ridge from three German divisions. The Canadians' success stemmed from extensive training, thorough planning and specific objectives for each platoon, enabling them to continue fighting even if their officers were killed. In addition, the four previous months saw 55 trench raids that harassed the Germans and gathered intelligence.

The Canadians were heavily armed with 80 machine guns for every brigade and a Lewis gun for every platoon. On the attack's second day, they captured the town of Thélus. On the third day, they captured Givenchy en Gohelle. On the German side, Commander Alexander von Falkenhausen was blamed after the battle because he had not applied the German doctrine of "elastic defense." As a result, the German forces were overwhelmed in static positions, while the reserve forces were too far away to counterattack.

On April 20, shortly after the Battles of Arras and Vimy Ridge began, the French opened up their offensive in the south. The conflict started with a massive military bombardment, followed by an attack of infantry and tanks. The Germans were ready for the French because of gathered intelligence and French delays. The Germans prepared their defenses in depth and placed 100 MG08 machine guns every 1,000 meters. The French initially used tanks and men to overwhelm the first German lines, but the Germans responded with pre-measured artillery and destroyed the French soldiers. The French had a minimal gain of approximately 3.2 kilometers. However, throughout the initial five days the French suffered 120,000 casualties, 40,000 of them on the first day alone. They also lost 140 tanks. Nivelle still believed they could break through, and on May 5 a final assault occurred along the German lines, with little gain. As a result, French citizens grew angry and soldiers began to mutiny. In one sector, the French 2nd Division showed up drunk with no rifles. After 21 days of fighting, on May 9 the offensive that was supposed to end the war in 48 hours was itself over.

OUTCOME: Overall, the Nivelle Offensive was a failure, although the British and Canadian sectors achieved some gains, such as Vimy Ridge. As a result, Nivelle was sacked as commander and replaced by a less aggressive Phillipe Pétain. The failure of the battle led to widespread French mutinies that the French suppressed with executions. The Germans sacked Falkenhausen because he had not followed German defense doctrine in the Arras salient, thereby enabling the Canadian and British gains. After the success of Vimy Ridge, it was said that a "nation was born" because Canada had fought heroically on its own and had emerged victorious.

WHO? The French had 1,200,000 men under Nivelle and suffered 270,000 casualties and the loss of 140 tanks. The Germans under Fritz von Below maintained a force of approximately 480,000 soldiers against the French and suffered approximately 140,000 casualties. Against the British and Canadians the Germans had 400,000 men under Falkenhausen and suffered about 120,000 casualties. The British under Douglas Haig had about 350,000 men and suffered 147,656 casualties. The Canadians had a force of 170,000 men under Julian Byng and suffered 11,004 casualties (including 3,598 killed in action) while taking Vimy Ridge.

WHEN? Arras and Vimy Ridge took place April 9-12, 1917, and the Nivelle Offensive took place in Champagne from April 20–May 9, 1917.

WHY AT ARRAS AND CHAMPAGNE? The British attacked at Arras because it was close to their supply routes and an area in which they could sustain their forces. The French attacked in Champagne again because Nivelle believed the Germans would weaken after they moved their forces to counter the British diversionary offensive in Arras.

TECHNOLOGY/TACTICS: Again, the Germans failed to effectively use in the north "elastic defense" or "defense in depth," which required a light defense in the first line and several hardened lines farther back. Artillery and reserves in the back waited to provide support when needed. In addition, the Germans typically placed their artillery on the back side of ridges so that they would be difficult to attack. At this time, the Germans had started producing more than 14,000 machine guns a month, including the lighter version of the MG08. The Allies were using tanks, including the French Char Schneider tank, to little effect. Furthermore, the British used mines and tunnels, primarily built by New Zealanders, to move supplies, provide housing and enable surprise attacks on the German lines. In terms of artillery, the British used "creeping" barrages that fired at set distances to maintain a length of 100 meters ahead of the advancing forces (and thereby keeping the Germans in their bunkers instead of on their machine guns). The Allies found that their artillery was more successful in this battle because they could use "instantaneous fuses" (which exploded at the lightest touch) against barbed wire.

QUOTES: "In those few minutes I witnessed the birth of a nation." – Canadian commander Brigadier General A.E. Ross

Song of Craonne (chorus)

"Adieu life, adieu love
Adieu all the women
It's all over, it's for good
This ghastly war
At Craonne on the plateau
We had to lose our hides
Because we are condemned
We are the sacrificed."

PLACES TO SEE (REFERENCE MAPS 25 AND 26):

THE NIVELLE OFFENSIVE IN CHAMPAGNE:

1. **NATIONAL MONUMENT TO TANKS:** Unfortunately, the monument uses post-World-War tanks to mark the spot where the French first used tanks. Still, it offers great information boards. Think of it this way: modern tanks are better than no tanks at all!
   N 49 24.782 E 3 53.266 (49.413033, 3.887767)

2. **VIEUX CRAONNE:** The town of Craonne was totally destroyed during the battle. It is an important stop from which to appreciate the battle, as well as to see the craters and remains of the town.
   N 49 26.728 E 3 47.385 (49.445467, 3.78975)

3. **PLATEAU CALIFORNIA:** This is where German positions overlooked the fields that the French crossed. It's an excellent place to see terrain, trenches and craters.
N 49 26.688 E 3 46.5862 (49.4448, 3.776433)

4. **LA CAVERNE DU DRAGON, "DRAGONS LAIR," CHEMIN DES DAMES:** This is an underground museum at the base of the ridge where the French counterattacked the Germans. You can see the museum only by tour, so plan your visit in advance.
N 49 26.510 E 3 43.943 (49.441833, 3.732383)

5. **CERNY-EN-LAONNOIS MEMORIAL CHAPEL AND FRENCH AND GERMAN CEMETERIES:** A chapel is located here at the main crossroads. Across the road are cemeteries for the German and French fallen.
N 49 26.578 E 3 39.999 (49.442967, 3.66665)

6. **FORT DE LA MALMAISON, GERMAN CEMETERY:** This contains the graves of more than 11,000 Germans who died during World War II. It was a French fort that was decommissioned prior to World War I. The Germans still used it as a strong point in the defensive line during the Chemin Dames offensives. The French captured it after a battle that lasted from October 23-27, 1917. During that battle, the French captured more than 11,000 Germans. This led to the capture of Chemin Dames Ridge, but at a cost of 10,000 French casualties.
N 49 27.565 E 3 31.415 (49.459417, 3.523583)

7. **BASQUE MONUMENT:** This is a monument to the men of the 36th Division, most from the Pyrenees, in honor of their sacrifice in the Battle of Plateau California.
N 49 25.805 E 3 45.583 (49.430083, 3.759717)

8. **FRENCH NATIONAL CEMETERY, CRAONELLE:** Laid out on the slope that the French fought up during the battle, this cemetery contains the remains of 3,936 combatants, including 24 British graves.
N 49 25.885 E 3 46.391 (49.431417, 3.773183)

THE BATTLES OF VIMY RIDGE AND ARRAS:

9. **MEMORIAL AND MUSÉE DE NOTRE DAME DE LORETTE, SAINT-NAZAIRE:** This holds the remains of more than 44,000 soldiers. It was the high ground fought over during the Battles of Arras and Loos and is just 15 minutes from Vimy Ridge. It is an incredible memorial.
Location of the chapel and museum: N 50 24.057 E 2 43.145 (50.40095, 2.719083)

10. **VIMY RIDGE MEMORIAL AND PARK (INCLUDES GRANGE TUNNEL AND TRENCHES):** If not the best memorial, this is certainly one of the top-five memorials/parks to see in Europe.
    A. **MONUMENT PARKING LOT**: N 50 22.765 E 2 46.417 (50.379417, 2.773617)

    B. **WELCOME CENTER, GRANGE TUNNEL AND TRENCHES:** N 50 22.340 E 2 46.249 (50.372333, 2.770817)

11. **LICHFIELD CRATER:** The Canadians used this crater as a mass grave for the remains of approximately 60 Canadian soldiers killed from April 9-10, 1917. **N 50 21.571 E 2 46.638 (50.359517, 2.7773)**

12. **GERMAN CEMETERY ARRAS:** This German cemetery is the largest in France, with more than 44,000 graves.
    N 50 20.530 E 2 45.251 (50.342167, 2.754183)

NIVELLE OFFENSIVE – 2ND BATTLE OF AISNE, APR. 16 – MAY 16 1917 MAP 25

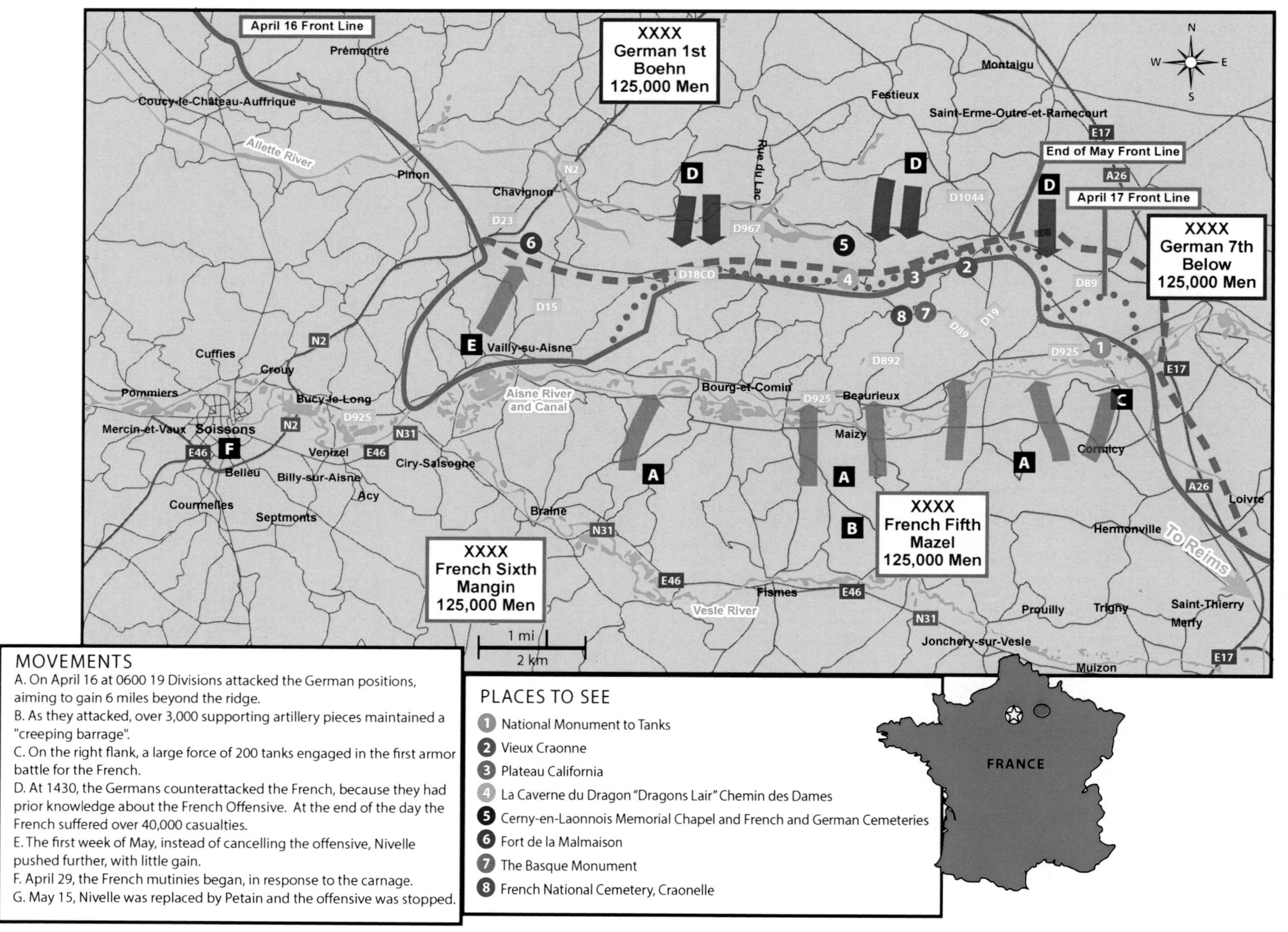
April 16 Front Line
XXXX German 1st Boehn 125,000 Men
End of May Front Line
April 17 Front Line
XXXX German 7th Below 125,000 Men
XXXX French Fifth Mazel 125,000 Men
XXXX French Sixth Mangin 125,000 Men
To Reims
Allette River
Aisne River and Canal
Vesle River
1 mi
2 km
FRANCE
MOVEMENTS
A. On April 16 at 0600 19 Divisions attacked the German positions, aiming to gain 6 miles beyond the ridge.
B. As they attacked, over 3,000 supporting artillery pieces maintained a "creeping barrage".
C. On the right flank, a large force of 200 tanks engaged in the first armor battle for the French.
D. At 1430, the Germans counterattacked the French, because they had prior knowledge about the French Offensive. At the end of the day the French suffered over 40,000 casualties.
E. The first week of May, instead of cancelling the offensive, Nivelle pushed further, with little gain.
F. April 29, the French mutinies began, in response to the carnage.
G. May 15, Nivelle was replaced by Petain and the offensive was stopped.
PLACES TO SEE
1 National Monument to Tanks
2 Vieux Craonne
3 Plateau California
4 La Caverne du Dragon "Dragons Lair" Chemin des Dames
5 Cerny-en-Laonnois Memorial Chapel and French and German Cemeteries
6 Fort de la Malmaison
7 The Basque Monument
8 French National Cemetery, Craonelle

NIVELLE OFFENSIVE: VIMY RIDGE APRIL 9 – 12, 1917

MAP 26

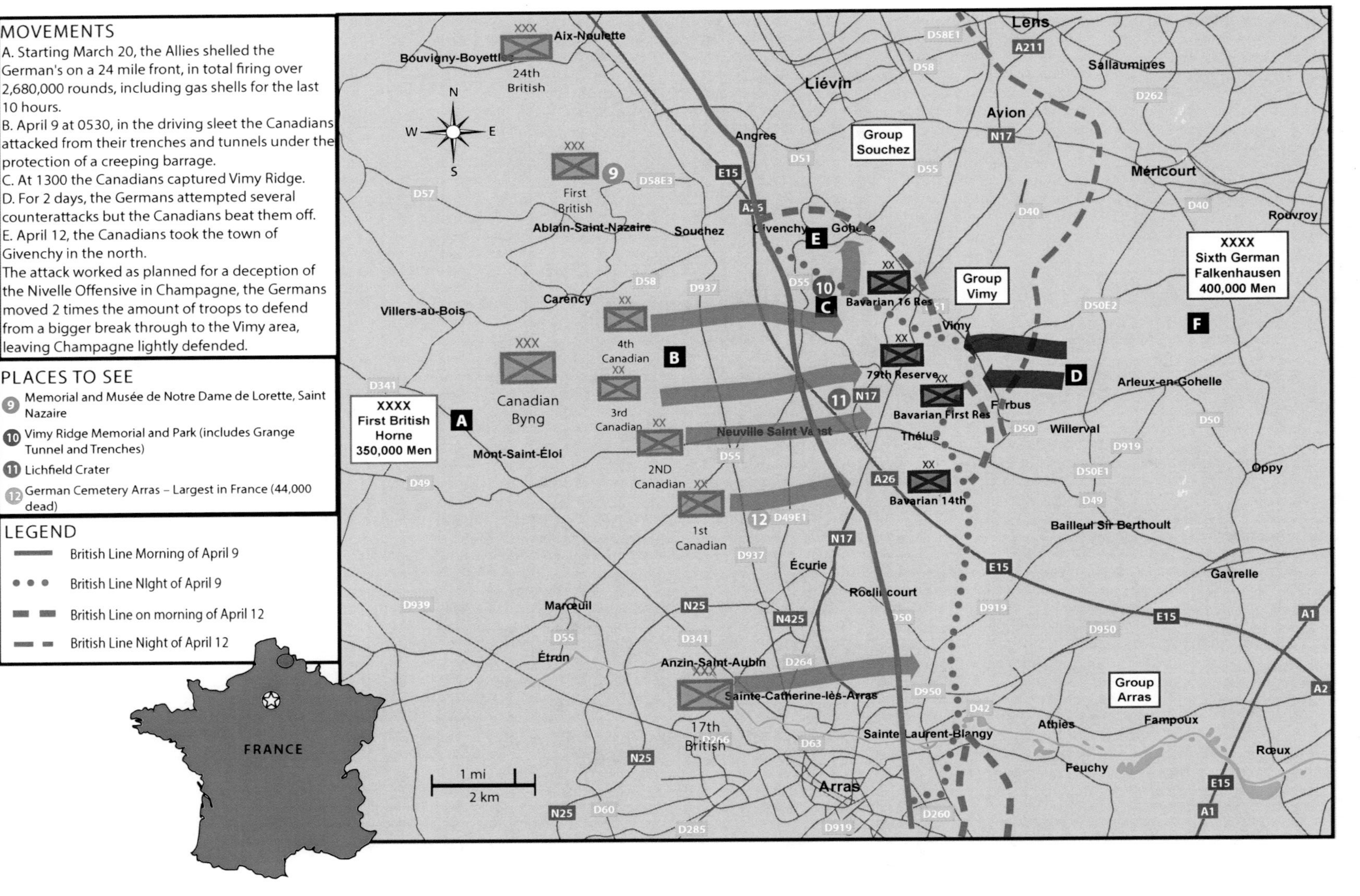
MOVEMENTS
A. Starting March 20, the Allies shelled the German's on a 24 mile front, in total firing over 2,680,000 rounds, including gas shells for the last 10 hours.
B. April 9 at 0530, in the driving sleet the Canadians attacked from their trenches and tunnels under the protection of a creeping barrage.
C. At 1300 the Canadians captured Vimy Ridge.
D. For 2 days, the Germans attempted several counterattacks but the Canadians beat them off.
E. April 12, the Canadians took the town of Givenchy in the north.
The attack worked as planned for a deception of the Nivelle Offensive in Champagne, the Germans moved 2 times the amount of troops to defend from a bigger break through to the Vimy area, leaving Champagne lightly defended.
PLACES TO SEE
9 Memorial and Musée de Notre Dame de Lorette, Saint Nazaire
10 Vimy Ridge Memorial and Park (includes Grange Tunnel and Trenches)
11 Lichfield Crater
12 German Cemetery Arras – Largest in France (44,000 dead)
LEGEND
British Line Morning of April 9
British Line NIght of April 9
British Line on morning of April 12
British Line Night of April 12
XXXX
First British
Horne
350,000 Men
XXXX
Sixth German
Falkenhausen
400,000 Men
XXX
Canadian
Byng
XXX
24th
British
XXX
First
British
XX
4th
Canadian
XX
3rd
Canadian
XX
2ND
Canadian
XX
1st
Canadian
XXX
17th
British
XX
Bavarian 16 Res
XX
79th Reserve
XX
Bavarian First Res
XX
Bavarian 14th
Group
Souchez
Group
Vimy
Group
Arras
Lens
Liévin
Avion
Sallaumines
Méricourt
Rouvroy
Oppy
Arleux-en-Gohelle
Willerval
Farbus
Vimy
Thélus
Bailleul Sir Berthoult
Gavrelle
Fampoux
Rœux
Athies
Feuchy
Sainte Laurent-Blangy
Arras
Sainte-Catherine-lès-Arras
Anzin-Saint-Aubin
Roclincourt
Écurie
Neuville Saint Vaast
Givenchy
Angres
Souchez
Ablain-Saint-Nazaire
Carency
Villers-au-Bois
Mont-Saint-Éloi
Aix-Noulette
Bouvigny-Boyeffles
Marœuil
Étrun
FRANCE
1 mi
2 km
N
E
S
W

VIMY

To the left, the entrance to Vimy Ridge. And above the other side of the monument. In the distance you can see the slag heaps of Loos.

Above, some of the trenches that have been well preserved by the Canadian museum and welcome center. Vimy Ridge was one of my favorite locations to visit. The photo below is of Canadian machine gunners preparing their positions on Vimy Ridge.

Above photo is of the Memorial and Museum, Notre Dame de Lorette, St. Nazaire. Located on the ridge not far from Vimy and Loos it is an exceptional and beautiful memorial to the sacrifices of French soldiers who fought in this area throughout World War I. Over 44,000 soldiers are buried there.

Just northwest of Reims is the French National Tank monument to honor the location where the French tanks were first used in battle. The upper left photo, Schneider tank was used but to little effect. In all, they committed 128 tanks and 118 were lost. The middle photo is of one of the armored vehicles at the memorial, which has Cold War tanks only.

One of the many crosses in the Champagne countryside.

Craonne, what is left of it. The small town on the ridge, was destroyed during the battle. All that remains is some ruins, to include the front steps to the Church.

Plateau California is a great stop on the tour of the battle. This photo is from the German perspective looking out over the fields of the French advance.

An artists memorial to the sacrifices of the Nivelle Offensive.

Left photo, entrance to the excellent underground museum, Dragon's Lair. Center photo is the Cerny en Laonnois Chapel with the French Cemetery located across the street from it.

Further along the line is Fort Malmaison which now has a German cemetery there with the majority of burials for World War II. However the French built fort was used by the Germans as a strongpoint in their defensive line during WW I. The French had over 10,000 casualties in a 3 day operation to capture the fort. To the right, a photo of the Chemin Dames ridge being shelled during the battle.

AMERICA GOES TO WAR

BATTLE OF CANTIGNY

May 28, 1918

BATTLE OF BELLEAU WOOD

June 3-26, 1918

BATTLE OF CHÂTEAU THIERRY

June 3, 1918

SECOND BATTLE OF THE MARNE

July 18–August 6, 1918

"Teufel Hunden" ("Devil Dogs")

SUMMARY: After the Americans declared war on Germany on June 4, 1917, the American Expeditionary Force arrived in France within 30 days. Progress slowed because the American commander, "Black Jack" Pershing, insisted that the American forces be well trained before they went to Europe and that they fight as separate units. (The latter preference stood in opposition to the European wish that the Americans serve as individual replacements for European armies.) By June 1918, more than 1,000,000 American troops were in Europe. The United States relied on French equipment, such as artillery and tanks, to subsidize its efforts. After additional training in France, the U.S. 1st Division entered the defensive line in November 1917 near Nancy. Then, in December, the Russians surrendered. As a result, 50 German divisions freed up. In the spring of 1918, the Germans launched five attacks, collectively known as the Spring Offensives. The German command wanted to quickly give everything it had in an effort to force England out of the war and to reach an armistice before America was at full force. The German Spring Offensives achieved some success; they destroyed the British Fifth Army in the north and reached Château Thierry, only 50 kilometers from Paris, by May 27. However, the U.S. forces rushed into the line to stop the Germans in the French sectors near Château Thierry. Following are three famous battles during which the U.S. forces proved their worth.

MAY 28, 1918 – BATTLE OF CANTIGNY: The Battle of Cantigny marked the first attack by an American division in World War I. The battle was a success, as it led to the capture of the town of Cantigny and represented a turning point against the German 1918 Spring Offensives. The 1st Division, 28th Regiment took 45 minutes to capture Cantigny from the Germans. They used a combined arms attack: first a two-hour artillery barrage followed by support from French aircraft and 12 French tanks. At that point, the United States suffered fierce German counterattacks, but repulsed them all. The American regiment, which contained 3,564 men, suffered 1,067 casualties, including 199 killed in action. The German casualties were not recorded. As a result of their success, the Allies continued with a counteroffensive that gained back land lost during the German Spring Offensives. The 1st Division remained in the line for 71 days and suffered an astounding 5,200 casualties.

JUNE 3, 1918 – BATTLE OF CHÂTEAU THIERRY: After the May 27 offensive, the Germans were only 50 kilometers from Paris. The French petitioned the Americans to provide immediate support. Pershing sent his only available operational units, the 2nd and 3rd Infantry Divisions. The 3rd Division set up a blocking position on the southern bank of the Marne at Château Thierry while the 2nd Division, with a brigade of regular infantry, a machine gun battalion and a brigade of Marines, took up positions west of Château Thierry. On June 3, the American 3rd Division, "the Rock of the Marne," halted the Germans at Château Thierry, knocking them back over the Marne River. After this success, the Americans were given the task of clearing Belleau Wood of Germans. (See below for information about that conflict.) The second major action at Château Thierry occurred on July 18 after the Germans began their fifth and last major offensive on July 15; it resulted in minimal gains.

JULY 18–AUGUST 6, 1918 – SECOND BATTLE OF THE MARNE: After the July 15 German attack (the Fifth Offensive), the French Commander Ferdinand Foch planned a surprise counterattack, the Allies' first major offensive in a year. His plan was to cut off the German salient centered on Soissons. On July 18 at 0445 hours, five American divisions and the Sixth and Tenth French Armies attacked on a 40-kilometer front, catching the Germans off guard. The Americans captured their objective, Hill 204, and took Montair by 1030. One American soldier, Sergeant J.F. Brown, and 12 of his fellow soldiers held out in pocketed positions and returned with battle plans and 155 prisoners. This was a turning point for the Allies. They continued to push the Germans back until August 6, when the Germans retreated to their launching point of the Spring Offensives. The losses were devastating for both sides. The French suffered 95,000 casualties, the British 13,000 and the Americans 12,000. The Germans suffered 168,000 casualties.

JUNE 3-26, 1918 – BATTLE OF BELLEAU WOOD: After the success of Château Thierry on June 3, the United States was given the task of clearing Belleau Wood of Germans. The match up consisted of approximately two U.S. divisions with one brigade of Marines against five German divisions. After Château Thierry fell to the Americans, the Germans moved into the cover of Belleau Wood. The Germans attacked shortly afterward and the French asked the Marine brigade commander, James Harbord, to retreat. He ignored the request and said, "Hold where we stand." With courage and patience, the Americans dug in and held against the German assaults. The French asked again for a retreat and Captain Lloyd Williams of the 2nd Battalion/5th Marines famously said, "Retreat? Hell, we just got here!" After repelling several assaults, the Allies attacked on June 6 at 0345. The French were on the Americans' left flank when the Marines attacked Hill 142. The Americans had failed to properly scout and did not know that a German regiment had built machine gun nests throughout their attack zone. Despite the bad reconnaissance, the Americans captured the hill; however, the battalion suffered 325 enlisted casualties as well as the deaths of nine officers. Next, the 3rd Battalion/5th Marines and 3rd Battalion/6th Marines advanced into Belleau Wood, crossing a wheat field under devastating machine gun fire. A two-time Medal of Honor recipient, Dan Daly, encouraged his men by saying, "Come on, you sons of bitches, do you want to live forever?" Next, heavy hand-to-hand combat ensued and the Marines suffered their worst casualties in a day—31 officers and 1,056 enlisted men. On June 9, the U.S. and French artillery barrage destroyed the woods. The Germans responded with artillery and many rounds of mustard gas. Eventually, after six attacks through interlocking bands of machine gun fire with rifles, bayonets, clubs and fists, the Marines pushed the Germans out of Belleau Wood. On June 26, the report stated, "Woods now U.S. Marine Corps entirely." The action in Belleau Wood earned the Marines the nickname "Teufel Hunden" or "Devil Dogs" from the Germans. The Americans emerged from Belleau Wood with 7,966 wounded and 1,811 killed. The Germans suffered unknown casualties.

OUTCOME: The entrance of the Americans into the war, starting at Cantigny, began to reverse Germany's success. By August 6, the Germans were retreating to their previous lines of defense and had cancelled future planned offenses.

TECHNOLOGY/TACTICS: Combined arms began to improve greatly, resulting in increased movement and gains in land. Overall, the change in tactics sped up the war's conclusion. The Allies succeeded in using tanks with infantry support to take hardened positions. Also, soldiers carried automatic weapons. American soldiers used the "trench gun" (or 12-gauge shotgun). The Germans wanted the gun outlawed because it was so destructive but, somehow, seemed to think that chemical gas was okay.

QUOTES: "The deadliest weapon is a Marine and his rifle." – General Pershing

"We have Americans opposite us who are terribly reckless fellows." – German private

"Vigorous, self-confident and remarkable marksmen." – German report about the Americans

"Retreat? Hell we just got here!" – Captain Williams to the French

"Come on, you sons of bitches, do you want to live forever?" – Dan Daly

PLACES TO SEE (REFERENCE MAPS 27–30):

THE BATTLE OF CANTIGNY:

1. **CANTIGNY MEMORIAL, AMERICA'S FIRST VICTORY:** The Americans' first battle caused almost 1,000 casualties. It was a turning point for the Allies and boosted America's hope for success in World War I.
   N 49 39.793 E 2 29.456 (49.663217, 2.490933)

2. **CANTIGNY 1ST INFANTRY DIVISION MEMORIAL:** This is located just outside town.
   N 49 39.558 E 2 30.085 (49.6593, 2.501417)

3. **U.S. 4TH DIVISION OBELISK ROAD TO SOISSONS:** N 49 18.642 E 3 38.840 (49.3107, 3.647333)

4. **AMIENS CATHEDRAL, PLAQUE TO U.S. SACRIFICES, 6TH REGIMENT, ENGINEERS:** On one of the pillars to the right of the altar in the magnificent Cathedral of Amiens is an engraving that memorializes U.S. soldiers who defended Amiens in March 1918. The cathedral itself is incredible to see. These coordinates are for the parking lot behind the cathedral.
   N 49 53.638 E 2 18.177 (49.893961, 2.302955)

THE BATTLE OF BELLEAU WOOD:

1. **AISNE-MARNE AMERICAN CEMETERY AND BELLEAU WOOD MEMORIAL:** A very impressive cemetery and monument to the 2,288 men who died in the regional fighting. The chapel also contains the names of 1,060 men who have no known grave.
   N 49 04.680E 3 17.496 (49.078, 3.2916)

2. **STONE HUNTING LODGE AT BELLEAU WOOD (GERMAN BATTALION HEADQUARTERS):** Just above the cemetery are the ruins of the old German battalion headquarters; you can still see foxholes and trenches. From this position, the Marines attacked from the west. A hike into the woods reveals many trenches, barbed wire, foxholes and craters.
N 49 04.610 E 3 17.454 (49.076833, 3.2909)

3. **MARINE MONUMENT OF BELLEAU WOOD:** This is just a little farther past the hunting lodge above the cemetery. Artillery pieces from the battle are on display, as are plaques placed by various Marine units that have visited the site.
N 49 04.420 E 3 17.438 (49.073667, 3.290633)

4. **HILL 142:** Located just west of the cemetery, this hill was a bastion of the German defense. On June 6, the Marine 5th Regiment crossed a field of poppies under machine gun fire and charged the hill. The Marines fought fiercely and won the day.
N 49 04.402 E 3 15.575 (49.073367, 3.259583)

5. **GERMAN CEMETERY BELLEAU:** The cemetery holds 8,630 German dead and a mass grave of more than 4,000 Germans. It is located between Hill 142 and the American Cemetery.
N 49 04.974 E 3 17.013 (49.0829, 3.28355)

6. **AMERICAN 26TH DIVISION MEMORIAL CHAPEL:** After July 15, the 26th Infantry Division took over this sector of the front and launched its counterattack. Located just across the street from the cemetery is a chapel rebuilt by veterans of the 26th Division. The interior contains memorials to various men and units, and also includes beautiful stained-glass windows. If the chapel is closed, ask the cemetery's keeper, who has a key.
N 49 04.903 E 3 17.601 (49.081717, 3.29335)

7. **BULLDOG FOUNTAIN, CHÂTEAU STABLES:** This is a famous fountain quenched the thirsts of Army and Marine warriors after the fierce fighting for Belleau Wood. Water was scarce and this fountain gave them much-needed hydration. The fountain had always had a bulldog but it played to the nickname the Marines had just received as Devil Dogs. Since the end of WWI it has become part of the pilgrimage for the Marines. Legend says that it lengthens the lives of the Marines who drink from it.
N 49 05.019 E 3 17.475 (49.08365, 3.29125)

THE BATTLE OF CHÂTEAU THIERRY AND THE SECOND BATTLE OF THE MARNE:

8. **CHÂTEAU THIERRY AMERICAN MONUMENT:** A very impressive monument to the American victory above the town of Château Thierry overlooking the Marne River. It is in a beautiful location and was built to commemorate the defensive actions of the Americans who stopped the Germans at this site.
N 49 02.528 E 3 22.286 (49.042133, 3.371433)

9. **OISE-AISNE AMERICAN CEMETERY AND MEMORIAL:** A quiet and beautiful monument and cemetery that holds the graves of 6,012 American soldiers. The cemetery is located in the center of an American advance into the German front line. It also contains the graves of 90 American soldiers who were dishonorably discharged, then executed for rape or murder during World War II.
   N 49 12.138 E 3 32.935 (49.2023, 3.548917)

10. **FRENCH MONUMENT, LANDOWSKI'S FANTOMES, BUTTE DE CHALMONT:** A haunting memorial to the battle that took place in the fields. Its phantom statues represent ghosts rising from the battlefield. They include a young recruit, a sapper, a machine gunner, a grenadier, a colonel, an infantry soldier, an aviator and a martyr, all escaping from the tomb. The location provides a great panorama of the battlefield where the Allies launched their attacks to recapture ground from July 15 through early August, 1918.
    N 49 12.850 E 3 24.548 (49.214167, 3.409133)

11. **MEMORIAL DES BATAILLES DE LA MARNE (DORMANS):** This is a very beautiful chapel at the south side of the Marne, overlooking the site where the Germans and French clashed. It is located at the right flank of the French forces.
    N 49 04.302 E 3 38.764 (49.0717, 3.646067)

12. **BRITISH MEMORIAL, SOISSONS:** This memorial is dedicated to the 3,887 British soldiers who died in the area during the German Spring Offensive.
    N 49 22.867 E 3 19.747 (49.381117, 3.329117)

13. **FRENCH MEMORIAL, SOISSONS:** Near the British memorial and the cathedral, this memorial commemorates the many French who died in the region.
    N 49 22.858 E 3 19.627 (49.380967, 3.327117)

SUMMARY GERMAN SPRING OFFENSIVES 1918

MAP 27

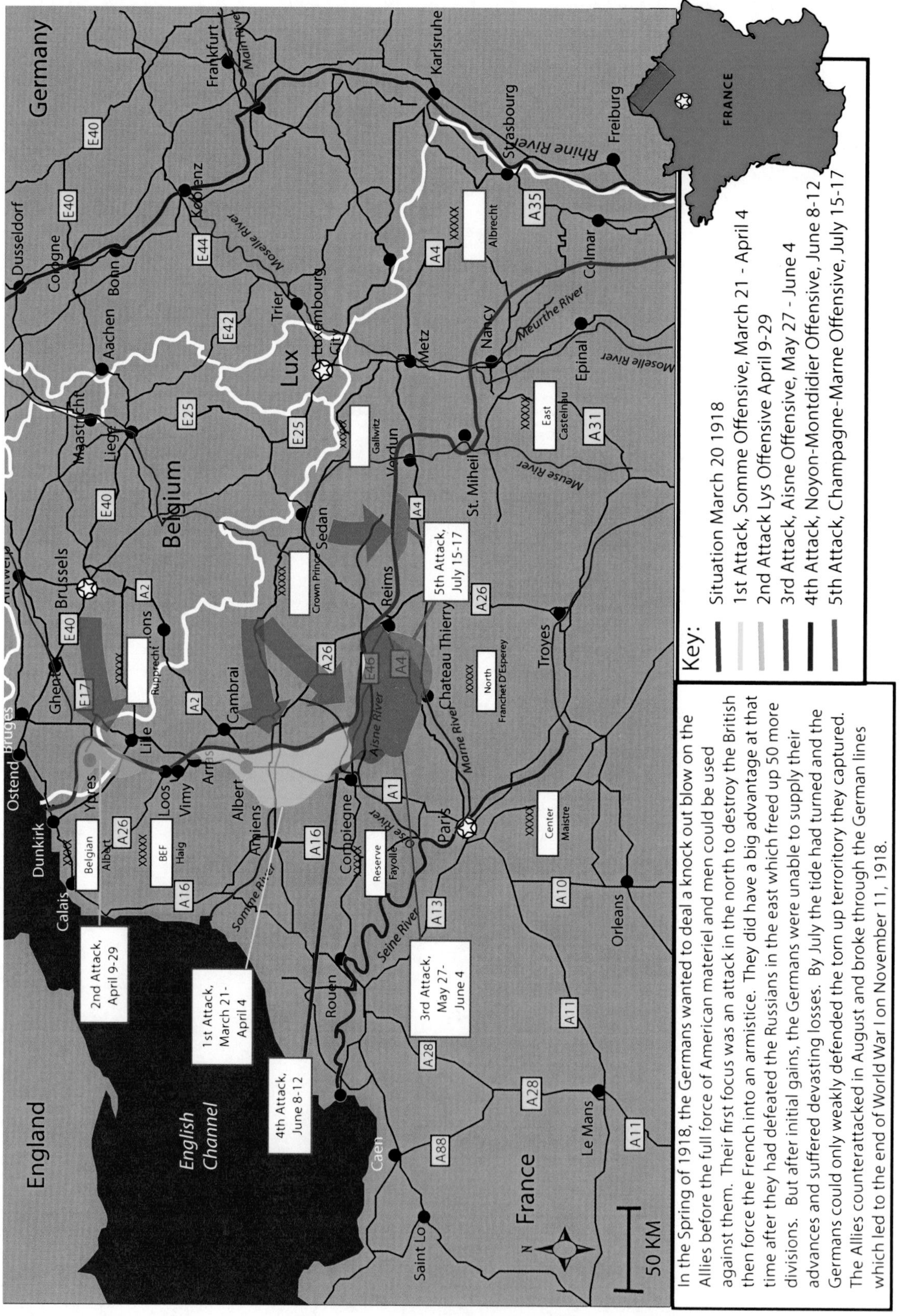
Key:
Situation March 20 1918
1st Attack, Somme Offensive, March 21 - April 4
2nd Attack Lys Offensive April 9-29
3rd Attack, Aisne Offensive, May 27 - June 4
4th Attack, Noyon-Montdidier Offensive, June 8-12
5th Attack, Champagne-Marne Offensive, July 15-17
In the Spring of 1918, the Germans wanted to deal a knock out blow on the Allies before the full force of American materiel and men could be used against them. Their first focus was an attack in the north to destroy the British then force the French into an armistice. They did have a big advantage at that time after they had defeated the Russians in the east which freed up 50 more divisions. But after initial gains, the Germans were unable to supply their advances and suffered devasting losses. By July the tide had turned and the Germans could only weakly defended the torn up terroritory they captured. The Allies counterattacked in August and broke through the German lines which led to the end of World War I on November 11, 1918.
2nd Attack, April 9-29
1st Attack, March 21-April 4
4th Attack, June 8-12
3rd Attack, May 27-June 4
5th Attack, July 15-17
England
English Channel
France
Germany
Belgium
Lux
FRANCE
50 KM
N
Belgian
Albert
BEF
Haig
Rupprecht
Crown Prince
Gallwitz
Albrecht
East
Castelnau
North
Franchet D'Esperey
Center
Maistre
Reserve
Fayolle
Calais
Dunkirk
Ostend
Bruges
Ghent
Brussels
Ypres
Lille
Loos
Vimy
Arras
Albert
Amiens
Cambrai
Compiegne
Rouen
Caen
Saint Lo
Le Mans
Orleans
Paris
Troyes
Chateau Thierry
Reims
Sedan
Verdun
St. Mihiel
Metz
Nancy
Epinal
Colmar
Strasbourg
Freiburg
Karlsruhe
Frankfurt
Koblenz
Bonn
Cologne
Dusseldorf
Aachen
Maastricht
Liege
Trier
Luxembourg City
Somme River
Seine River
Oise River
Aisne River
Marne River
Meuse River
Moselle River
Meurthe River
Rhine River
Main River
E40
E17
E25
E42
E44
E46
A1
A2
A4
A10
A11
A13
A16
A26
A28
A31
A35
A88

BATTLE OF CANTIGNY, MAY 28, 1918

MAP 28

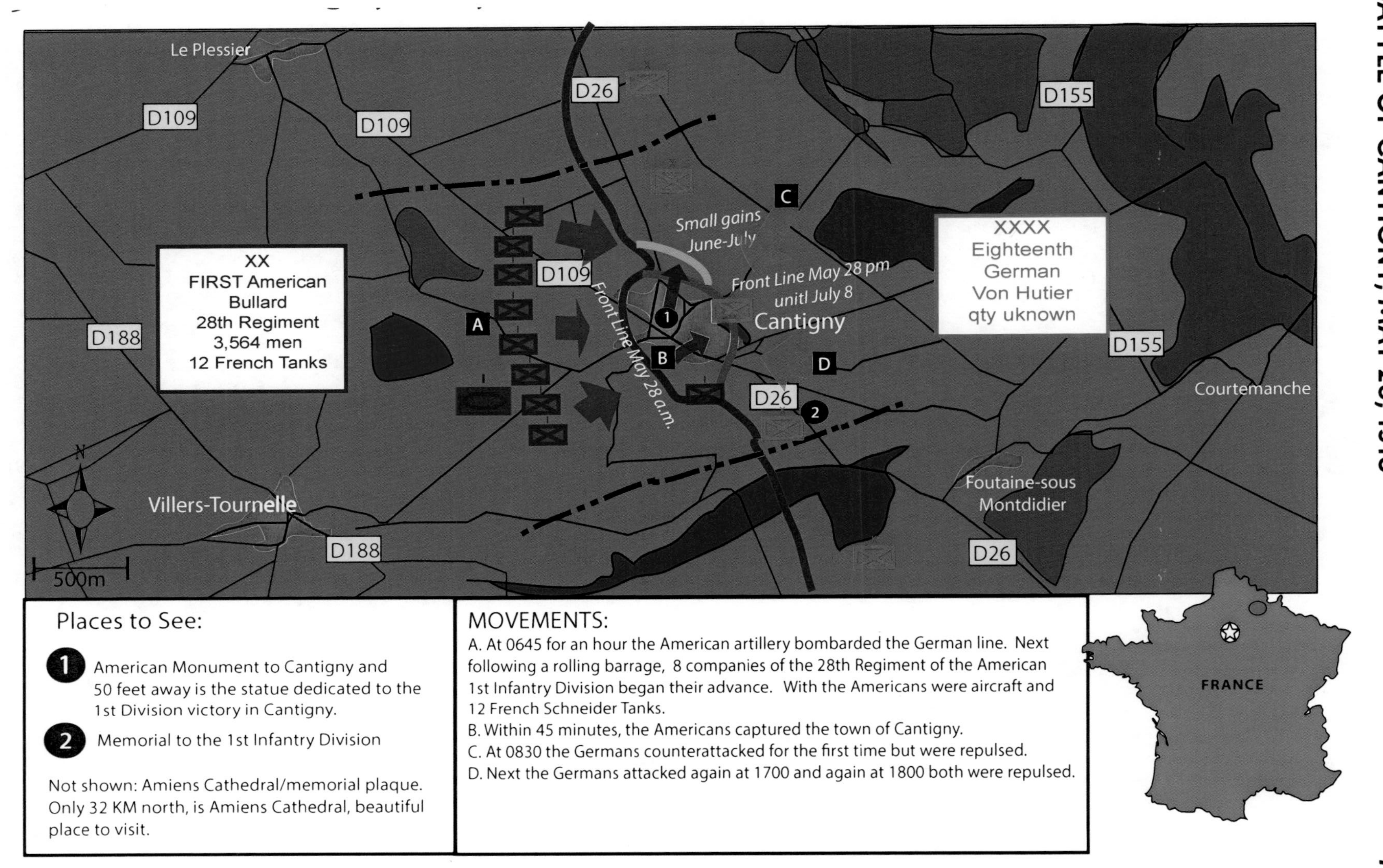
Le Plessier
D109
D109
D26
D155
XX
FIRST American
Bullard
28th Regiment
3,564 men
12 French Tanks
D188
D109
A
Small gains
June-July
C
Front Line May 28 pm
unitl July 8
Cantigny
XXXX
Eighteenth
German
Von Hutier
qty uknown
Front Line May 28 a.m.
1
B
D
D155
D26
2
Courtemanche
N
Villers-Tournelle
Foutaine-sous
Montdidier
D188
D26
500m
FRANCE
Places to See:
1 American Monument to Cantigny and 50 feet away is the statue dedicated to the 1st Division victory in Cantigny.
2 Memorial to the 1st Infantry Division
Not shown: Amiens Cathedral/memorial plaque. Only 32 KM north, is Amiens Cathedral, beautiful place to visit.
MOVEMENTS:
A. At 0645 for an hour the American artillery bombarded the German line. Next following a rolling barrage, 8 companies of the 28th Regiment of the American 1st Infantry Division began their advance. With the Americans were aircraft and 12 French Schneider Tanks.
B. Within 45 minutes, the Americans captured the town of Cantigny.
C. At 0830 the Germans counterattacked for the first time but were repulsed.
D. Next the Germans attacked again at 1700 and again at 1800 both were repulsed.

BATTLE OF BELLEAU WOOD, JUNE 3 – JUNE 25, 1918

MAP 29

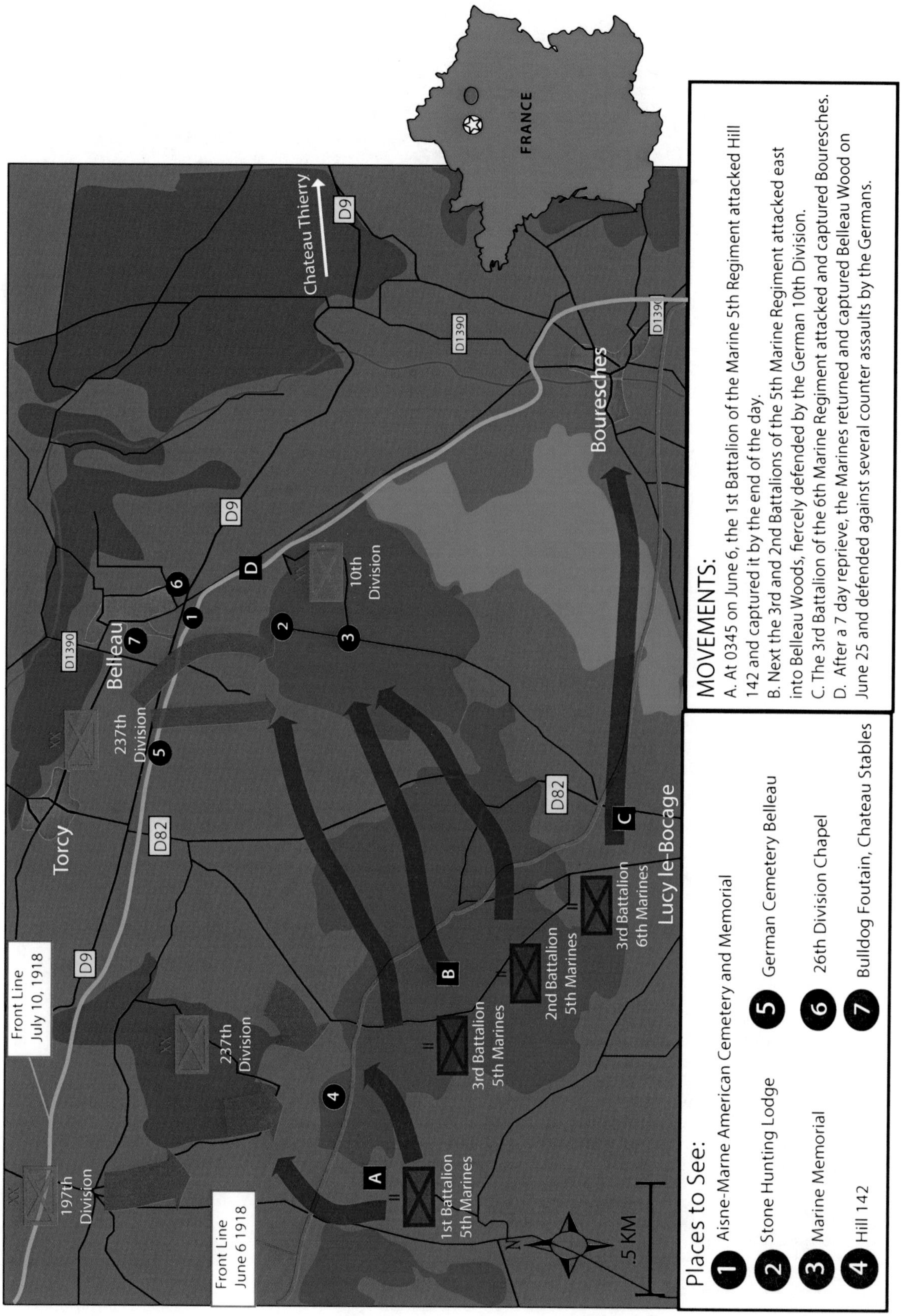

FRANCE
Chateau Thierry
D9
D1390
D1390
Bouresches
D9
D
10th Division
6
1
2
3
7
D1390
Belleau
237th Division
5
Torcy
D82
D82
C
Lucy le-Bocage
3rd Battalion 6th Marines
2nd Battalion 5th Marines
B
3rd Battalion 5th Marines
Front Line July 10, 1918
D9
237th Division
4
A
1st Battalion 5th Marines
197th Division
Front Line June 6 1918
N
.5 KM

MOVEMENTS:

A. At 0345 on June 6, the 1st Battalion of the Marine 5th Regiment attacked Hill 142 and captured it by the end of the day.

B. Next the 3rd and 2nd Battalions of the 5th Marine Regiment attacked east into Belleau Woods, fiercely defended by the German 10th Division.

C. The 3rd Battalion of the 6th Marine Regiment attacked and captured Bouresches.

D. After a 7 day reprieve, the Marines returned and captured Belleau Wood on June 25 and defended against several counter assaults by the Germans.

Places to See:

1. Aisne-Marne American Cemetery and Memorial
2. Stone Hunting Lodge
3. Marine Memorial
4. Hill 142
5. German Cemetery Belleau
6. 26th Division Chapel
7. Bulldog Foutain, Chateau Stables

SECOND BATTLE OF THE MARNE, JULY 18–AUGUST 6, 1918 — MAP 30

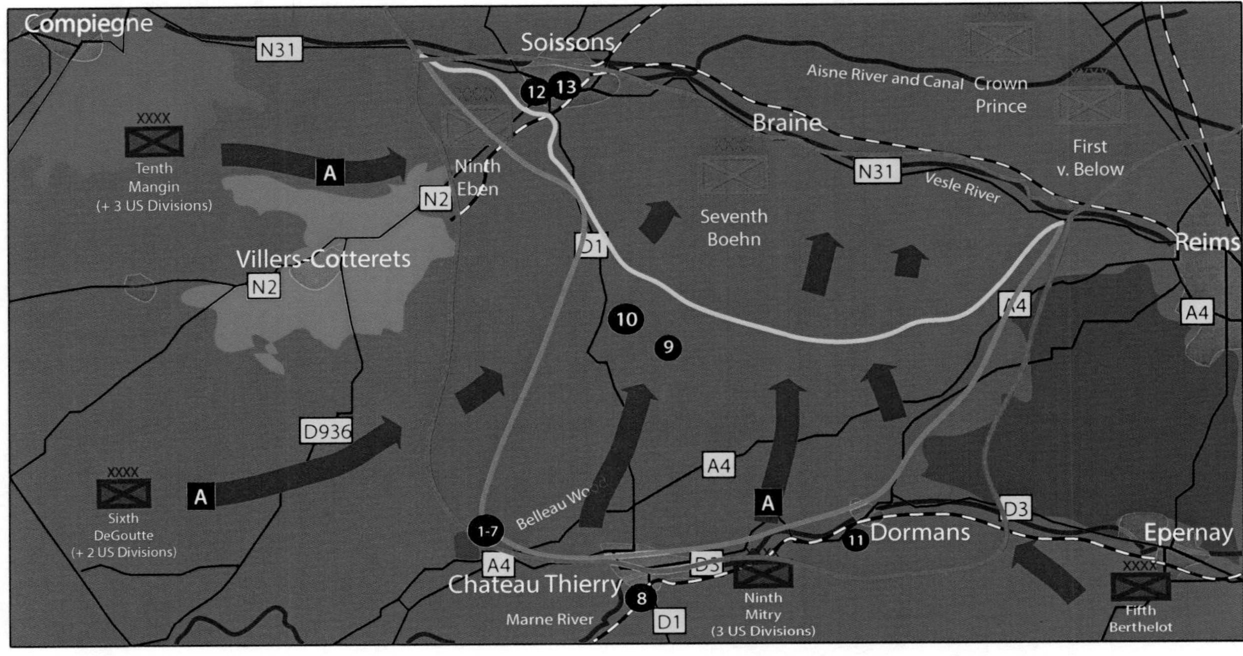
Compiegne
N31
Soissons
12
13
Aisne River and Canal
Crown Prince
Braine
First v. Below
N31
Vesle River
Reims
XXXX
Tenth
Mangin
(+ 3 US Divisions)
A
Ninth
Eben
N2
D1
Seventh
Boehn
Villers-Cotterets
N2
10
9
A4
A4
D936
XXXX
Sixth
DeGoutte
(+ 2 US Divisions)
A
A4
A
D3
1-7
Belleau Wo
Dormans
11
Epernay
A4
Chateau Thierry
D3
8
Ninth
Mitry
(3 US Divisions)
XXXX
Fifth
Berthelot
Marne River
D1

8

9

10

Places to See:

- **1-7** Belleau Wood Places to See. (Map 29)
- **8** American Monument Chateau Thierry
- **9** Oise Aisne American Cemetery
- **10** Butte de Chalmont - The Phantoms
- **11** Dormans Chapel and Memorial
- **12** British Memorial to Soissons Battle
- **13** French Memorial to Soissons Battle

Note: Locations in Compiegne (see next section), also locations in Reims and Nivelle Offensive (see Map25)

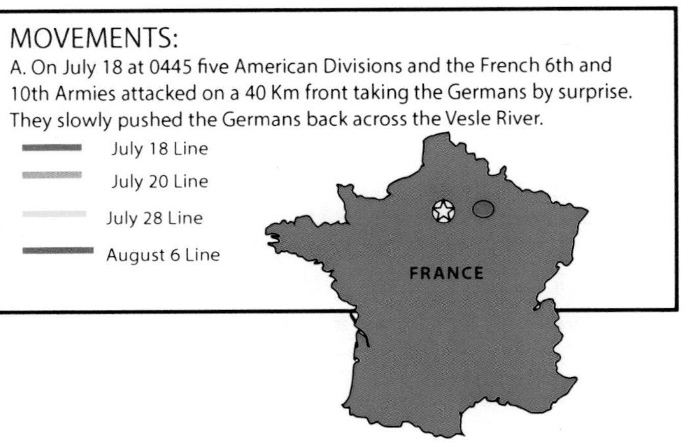
MOVEMENTS:
A. On July 18 at 0445 five American Divisions and the French 6th and 10th Armies attacked on a 40 Km front taking the Germans by surprise. They slowly pushed the Germans back across the Vesle River.
July 18 Line
July 20 Line
July 28 Line
August 6 Line
FRANCE

Far left is the Cantigny memorial to the American soldier. Also in Cantigny, is the ABMC Memorial to the Battle of Cantigny only 50 yards from the Doughboy statue. Below center is the Amiens Cathedral, a breathtaking Cathedral with amazing detail, to include a Gothic era uncle giving nuggies! Amiens was a goal of the German spring offenses.

Above is the Butte de Chalmont, Landowski Phantoms. He started the project in 1919 and unveiled it in 1935. It is located in the middle of the fields in which the Allies launched their July to early August 1918 counter offensive to recapture lost terroritory. Above right is a view of the field that many Allied soldiers heroically crossed to defeat the Germans.

Oise Aisne American Cemetery, located only 23 KM NE of Chateau Thierry in a very rural but beautiful area.

Dormans, has a beautiful chapel and memorial dedicated to the French soldiers who stopped the German advance. This view is from the front door looking towards the Marne River.

Chateau Thierry, a view from the American Monument overlooking the Marne River below.

You will see many of the farms on your drive through the fields. To right, laborers are picking grapes.

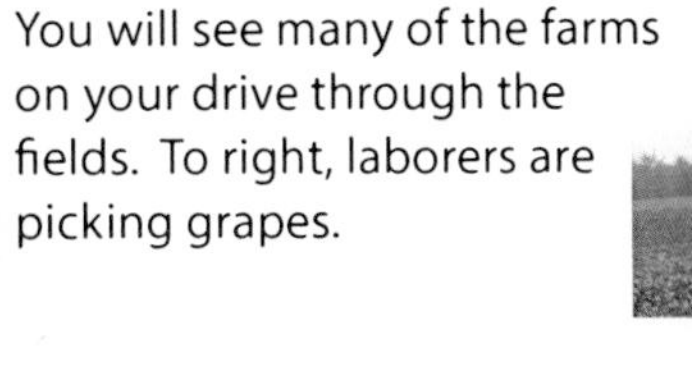

To the left, I believe it was a sugar beet combine. The sugar beet was actualy first exploited by Napoleon after the British embargo blocked sugar cane shipments.

Belleau Wood Marine Memorial surrounded by captured equipment. In the woods you can explore and see the many fox holes and trench remains.

Belleau Wood American Cemetery. A very impressive cemetery located just outside of Chateau Thierry. Behind the chapel are the remains of the German Battalion HQ, "The Stone Hunting Lodge" and the Marine Memorial.

100 DAYS OFFENSIVE

August 8–November 11, 1918

Grand Offensive in France

"Black Day of the German Army"
- Erich Ludendorff

SUMMARY: By the end of July, five major German offenses in 1918 had failed to make a decisive breakthrough. In response, the Supreme Allied Commander, Foch, coordinated a final offensive, which became known as the "Grand Offensive," to breech the Hindenburg Line. Before the "Grand Offensive" took place, three smaller battles occurred—the Battle of Amiens, the Second Battle of the Somme and the Saint-Mihiel Offensive. Following are quick summaries of each major attack during the final months of the Great War.

AUGUST 8-11, 1918, AMIENS OFFENSIVE: The Battle of Amiens punched a 13-kilometer hole in the German line and marked a turning point in the war, as the spent German Army was on the defensive throughout the remainder of it. Shortly after the Germans' last offensive in July, the Allies quickly regrouped and the British planned a surprise attack. The Allies armed themselves with 1,389 cannon, 10 divisions (containing 150,000 men), 550 tanks and 1,900 aircraft. The British attacked north of the Somme River, the Australians south of the river; the Canadians were south of the Australians and the French were south of the Canadians. Surprise was the key to success; the Allies kept communication to a minimum, didn't use a pre-bombardment and moved troops only at night. At 0420 on August 8, the Allies attacked with perfectly timed artillery, advancing 8 kilometers. The Allies suffered 22,200 casualties; the Germans suffered 24,000 casualties and another 50,000 captured. Ludendorff called it the "Black Day of the German Army." The Germans retreated to the Hindenburg Line with few chances of success because they had suffered significant casualties and their morale was destroyed. The Allies had to halt the advance because they had outpaced the artillery and had only six tanks battle-ready.

AUGUST 21–SEPTEMBER 2, 1918, SECOND BATTLE OF THE SOMME: After the success of the Battle of Amiens, the British, Americans, Canadians and Australians attacked the German lines farther north at Albert on August 21. They recaptured Albert on August 22, and by August 29 Bapaume fell. The Australians earned additional distinction on August 31 when they crossed the Somme River and broke through German lines. Then the Canadians gallantly defeated the Germans at the Battle of Canal du Nord, after which the Germans withdrew to the Hindenburg Line, their starting point in the Spring Offensive. Germany had lost all of its gains.

SEPTEMBER 12-18, 1918, SAINT-MIHIEL OFFENSIVE: The Allies planned a large-scale attack, "The Grand Offensive." Before they launched this attack, they drew up plans for the U.S. First Army to attack the Saint-Mihiel salient in an effort to protect the flank of the upcoming offensive through the Argonne Forest. This was the first battle the Americans would fight under their own command. They were up against a well-fortified German sector with tunnels and defenses that had been built in a quiet area throughout the previous four years. The Americans attacked with nine divisions, as well as five French divisions, artillery, aircraft and tanks. They relied heavily upon the French and British for equipment. The Germans had grown complacent and began withdrawing forces to bolster their lines for the upcoming Grand Offensive. The Americans met all their objectives and shocked the Germans with their skill and success. In the middle of the battlefield sits an impressive American memorial, Montsec, jutting out of the flat fields.

SEPTEMBER 26–NOVEMBER 11, 1918, THE GRAND OFFENSIVE: The Allied Supreme Commander, Ferdinand Foch, planned three main thrusts into the German defenses. He meant to disperse any counterattacks and to have all three thrusts converge on Liege, Belgium. The three main battles were:

1. **SEPTEMBER 29, 1918, BATTLE OF ST. QUENTIN CANAL:** The Battle of St. Quentin Canal marked the first point where the Hindenburg Line broke. Consequently, it destroyed all hope for a German victory. Against 13 German divisions, the Allies—with 14 divisions made up of Australians, Americans and British troops—broke a 17-kilometer hole in the Hindenburg Line by October 2. On September 29, the Americans were the first to attack with some tank support; the Australians quickly followed, pushing through the defenses. On October 2, the Australians and British reached the Beaurevoir Line (the third line of defense of the Hindenburg Line). By October 10, the Allies had captured the surrounding hills and cleared that portion of the Hindenburg Line.

2. **SEPTEMBER 26, 1918, MEUSE ARGONNE OFFENSIVE:** This was the largest commitment of the American Expeditionary Force during the war and one of the bloodiest battles in U.S. military history. On September 26, the combination of 550,000 American and French soldiers with 2,780 cannon, 380 tanks and 840 aircraft attacked north and northwest of Verdun; their objective was the German supply hub of Sedan. The Germans blocked the way to Sedan with 190,000 soldiers in heavily fortified trench lines. The Americans initially had little success, but eventually captured Montfaucon by September 29, even after the Germans sent seven additional divisions to repulse the Americans. The Germans made some gains but were repelled by the Americans, including future President Harry Truman, then-Colonel Douglas MacArthur and future founder of the Office of Strategic Services General William Donovan. The French, west of the Americans, had gained 14.5 kilometers in the open terrain, compared to the Americans, who had gained only about 3 kilometers.

   The second phase of the Meuse Argonne Offensive began on October 4; it led to several famous citations for the Americans. The Lost Battalion of the 77th

Division received five Medals of Honor, including one for Major Charles White Whittlesey after his battalion advanced too far ahead of the units on their flanks into the Argonne Forest on October 2. After advancing through the German lines and believing that the French were still on their flanks, 554 men found themselves outnumbered and surrounded for six days behind German lines. After fighting off several German attacks, the battalion numbered only 194 when rescue forces arrived. Shortly after this, the Americans launched another attack, at Romagne, where they finally broke through the German Hindenburg Line on October 14. By the end of October, the American Expeditionary Forces had moved approximately 18 kilometers and cleared the Germans out of the difficult terrain of the Argonne Forest. A second famous citation during this battle was the Medal of Honor received by Sergeant Alvin C. York. On October 8, during a patrol along the Decauville rail line in Chatel-Chéhéry, Sergeant York killed 28 Germans, took 132 prisoners and silenced 32 machine guns. York later stated, "A higher power than man power guided and watched over me and told me what to do."

After the second phase, on November 1, the French and Americans reorganized, refreshed and attacked again. The Americans captured the German fort of Buzancy, allowing the French to cross the Aisne and enter Sedan on November 6. Next, the Americans captured the surrounding hills. In this final battle the Americans suffered 117,000 casualties, the French 70,000 and the Germans 90,000.

3. **SEPTEMBER 28, 1918, FIFTH BATTLE OF YPRES:** I will cover this battle in my book about conflicts in Belgium; the Fifth Battle of Ypres was part of the Grand Offensive to dilute German counterattacks and overwhelm their defenses.

OUTCOME: On "the 11th hour of the 11th day of the 11th month," a cease fire was in place after the signing of the armistice in a rail car in Compiègne. The war ended with the Allies suffering 22,477,500 casualties and the Central Powers 16,403,000. The world was in disarray and deeply wounded. Shortly after the war, the following occurred: the Spanish Flu spread, killing millions; a generation found itself displaced; food sources were destroyed; Communism was on the rise; colonies revolted; the Great Depression was just around the corner; and nationalism was on fire. The Treaty of Versailles had treated Germany unfairly, and Adolf Hitler stepped forward to "save" the country and seek revenge. Eastern Europe was fighting the Reds, Japan was invading China, the Ottoman Empire was in steep decline and America was on the rise as a new Super Power.

WHO? From August 8 to November 11, the Allies suffered the following casualties: France, 531,000; Britain, 411,636; and America, 127,000. The Germans suffered 785,733 casualties and the following captured: 188,700 by the British powers, 139,000 by the French, 44,142 by the Americans and 14,500 by the Belgians.

WHY AT ALL THOSE LOCATIONS? Commander Foch attacked on a broad front, taking advantage of the fact that Germany had to reorganize itself after its five major offenses. The Germans couldn't repel the newly arrived American forces or the reallocated British forces that had come from the Middle East and Italy.

TECHNOLOGY/TACTICS: Tactically, mobile warfare was re-invented through the use of improved tanks to break the stalemate and overrun the strong German defenses. Automatic weapons became more widespread and mobile. (For example, the American Browning Automatic Rifle was first used en masse during the Meuse Argonne Offensive.) This increase in firepower and mobility was evidenced in a larger scale during World War II.

QUOTES: "The First World War was a tragic and unnecessary conflict." - John Keegan

"A great war leaves the country with three armies—an army of cripples, an army of mourners and an army of thieves." - German Proverb

"Patriotism ruins history." - Johann Wolfgang von Goethe

PLACES TO SEE (REFERENCE MAPS 31–34):

THE SECOND SOMME OFFENSIVE AND THE BATTLE OF ST. QUENTIN:

1. **BELLICOURT AMERICAN MONUMENT (OVER THE CANAL):** This commemorates the 90,000 American troops who fought with the British in this sector to capture the Hindenburg Line. The monument is on top of the canal and is part of the Hindenburg Line, which the Allies broke in September 1918.
   N 49 58.499 E 3 13.891 (49.974983, 3.231517)

2. **AMERICAN CEMETERY OF THE SOMME (BONY):** In the farmlands of Picardy not far from the Bellicourt Monument is a cemetery that holds 1,844 American graves. It's located on the site of a strong German position on the Hindenburg Line, one broken by the Allied forces.
   N 49 59.126 E 3 12.958 (49.985433, 3.215967)

3. **RIQUEVAL FARM BRIDGE:** The 6th Battalion North Staffordshire Regiment captured this all-important bridge across the canal. On the east side of the bridge is a partially destroyed pillbox.
   N 49 56.392 E 3 14.523 (49.939867, 3.24205)

4. **BELLICOURT BRITISH CEMETERY:** On the western edge of town is a British cemetery for soldiers who were killed in action (not necessarily during the battle) in this area.
   N 49 57.678 E 3 13.727 (49.9613, 3.228783)

5. **LA BARAQUE BRITISH CEMETERY:** Just south of this small cemetery is a memorial to the 46th British Division, which fought in the battle for St. Quentin.
   N 49 55.666 E 3 14.985 (49.927767, 3.24975)

6. **AUSTRALIAN 4TH DIVISION MONUMENT:** This memorial is on a dirt farm road and serves as a remembrance of the Australians who fought in this sector.
N 49 55.837 E 3 13.604 (49.930617, 3.226733)

7. **FRENCH ST. QUENTIN WAR MEMORIALS NEXT TO THE CANAL:** In St. Quentin is a large memorial to both the French and the battles they waged to capture this sector from the Germans.
N 49 50.498 E 3 17.882 (49.841633, 3.298033)

7a. **AUSTRALIAN NATIONAL MEMORIAL, VILLERS BRETONNEUX:** At this location is a large memorial and cemetery dedicated to the soldiers who fought and died defending and stopping the Germans from reaching Amiens during the Spring Offensive.
N 49 53.175 E 2 30.495 (49.88625, 2.50825)

7b. **AUSTRALIAN MEMORIAL PARK, LE HAMEL:** This location is a memorial to the Australian launching-off point for the Second Battle of the Somme, which ended with "Der Schwarze Tag" (The Black Day) for the Germans on August 8, 1918.
N 49 53.993 E 2 34.887 (49.899883, 2.58145)

THE SAINTE-MIHIEL OFFENSIVE:

8. **AMERICAN CEMETERY, SAINTE-MIHIEL:** This location holds the graves of more than 4,000 soldiers who died in the Sainte-Mihiel offensive.
N 48 57.275 E 5 51.099 (48.954583, 5.85165)

9. **AMERICAN MONTSEC MEMORIAL:** Nineteen kilometers southwest of the Sainte-Mihiel Cemetery is an impressive American memorial on top of the dominating hill Montsec. The Americans captured the hill after intense artillery fire and a smokescreen.
N 48 53.403 E 5 42.809 (48.89005, 5.713483)

10. **1ST DIVISION MEMORIAL, VIGNUELLES:** This is a memorial commemorating the 1st Division; it's in the approximate location where the 26th Division and 1st Division linked up.
N 48 58.708 E 5 42.909 (48.978467, 5.71515)

11. **LES ESPARGES FRENCH CEMETERY, MEMORIALS, TRENCHES AND BUNKERS:** At this location is the French Cemetery du Trottoir, with 2,960 burials and 85 unknown soldiers. The immediate area contains walking paths to other sites and memorials, including well-preserved German trenches, mine craters and concrete bunkers. Another memorial to note is the monument to the 106th and 132nd French units. Take the path of the Monument du Coc, which runs through the woods and past trenches and bunkers. This coordinate will take you to the middle of the hill; from this location, you can follow the signs and paths.
N 49 03.843 E 5 36.593 (49.06405, 5.609883)

12. **GERMAN CEMETERY, THIAUMONT:** This cemetery is located near the American Sainte-Mihiel Cemetery; more than 8,700 Germans are buried here, plus an additional 2,900 in a mass grave.
N 48 56.754 E 5 52.649 (48.9459, 5.877483)

13. **CROIX DES CARMES, TRENCH LINE/BUNKERS AND FEY:** Located in the woods at the battle's frontlines is a cross that commemorates the fallen. The site includes information boards, while trench lines and shell craters cover the area. Also nearby are the ruins of Fey, a community that, like many towns along the frontline, was utterly destroyed and never rebuilt.
N 48 54.981 E 5 59.331 (48.91635, 5.98885)

14. **GERMAN BUNKER:** At this site sits a German bunker that watched over the road (now D3).
N 48 55.753 E 5 54.102 (48.929217, 5.9017)

15. **REMENAUVILLE CHAPEL:** Just off D3 near the bunker is a rebuilt chapel, all that remains of a town of 130 people.
N 48 54.562 E 5 55.768 (48.909367, 5.929467)

THE CHAMPAGNE OFFENSIVE:

16. **SOMMEPY TOWER MEMORIAL:** During the battles of late September and early October, the Americans fought desperately to capture and hold ground against German counterattacks. At this location is an information board about the poem "I Have a Rendezvous with Death" by Alan Seeger, who volunteered for and served in the French Foreign Legion. He was killed during the Battle of the Somme on July 4, 1916.
N 49 17.040E 4 32.064 (49.284, 4.5344)

17. **MONUMENT OSSUAIRE DE LA FERME DE NAVARIN (BATTLE OF CHAMPAGNE):** At this location is the burial site of 10,000 French soldiers who fought in the Champagne campaigns; it's only minutes from the Sommepy Tower.
N 49 13.117 E 4 32.535 (49.218624, 4.542257)

18. **GERMAN BLOCKHOUSE:** One of the remaining German bunkers in the area, just yards from Navarin.
N 49 13.327 E 4 32.653 (49.222117, 4.544217)

19. **FRENCH CEMETERY MONT DE LA GARDE AND GERMAN MARNE CEMETERY:** Located just south of Navarin are a very large French cemetery and a German cemetery, which sit side by side.
N 49 11.243 E 4 32.259 (49.187383, 4.53765)

***For more locations, see the First and Second Battle of Artois and Champagne.*

THE MEUSE ARGONNE OFFENSIVE:

20. **LOST BATTALION MONUMENT:** This is located on Apremont-Binarville Road, which contains an Argonne Forest marker. Just down the hill and into the forest are the remains of foxholes and trenches. A German cemetery is also nearby.
    N 49 15.072 E 4 54.831 (49.2512, 4.91385)

21. **LOST BATTALION MEMORIAL:** Another memorial to the Lost Battalion just farther up the road.
    N 49 15.054 E 4 54.380 (49.2509, 4.906333)

22. **AMERICAN MEUSE ARGONNE CEMETERY:** This is an extremely impressive memorial located in the hills where the Americans experienced some of the most intense combat of the battle. The strongest section of the Hindenburg Line ran behind the cemetery's chapel. Despite intense artillery bombardment and machine gun fire, the U.S. 5th Division captured the ridge on October 14. The cemetery is the largest American cemetery in Europe, containing 14,246 graves.
    N 49 20.046 E 5 05.459 (49.3341, 5.090983)

23. **MONTFAUCON AMERICAN MONUMENT:** At this location the Germans built a strong fortress on the remains of an old abbey. The 200-foot-high American monument sits at the center of fighting next to the abbey ruins. You can climb the steps to see the entire battle area.
    N 49 16.333 E 5 08.500 (49.272217, 5.141667)

24. **ROMAGNE 14-18 MUSEUM:** This is a small, privately owned museum that offers a café. It's located just outside the Meuse Argonne Cemetery and is definitely worth a stop.
    N 49 19.930 E 5 05.051 (49.332167, 5.084183)

25. **SERGEANT YORK HISTORIC TRAIL:** The first sign for this trail is at the intersection of Rue des Goulets and D4 in Chatel-Chéhéry. It is a beautiful path built by the French and Americans, and offers explanation boards that trace Sergeant York's feats of heroism.
    N 49 17.008 E 4 57.248 (49.283467, 4.954133)

26. **MISSOURI MONUMENT:** Most of the 35th Division was from Missouri or Kansas. This is a beautiful memorial to their sacrifices.
    N 49 13.491 E 5 03.368 (49.22485, 5.056133)

27. **PENNSYLVANIA MONUMENT, VARRENES:** This is a very impressive monument to the battles fought by Pennsylvania divisions.
    N 49 13.539 E 5 01.944 (49.22565, 5.0324)

28. **MUSÉE ARGONNE, VARRENES:** This museum is small but very well done. It contains materiel and displays about both World Wars.
    N 49 13.495 E 5 1.893 (49.224917, 5.03155)

29. **CÔTE DE CHÂTILLON:** A ridge and town captured on October 17 by the 84th Brigade of the 42nd Division commanded by Brigadier General Douglas MacArthur. The regimental commander, Lieutenant Colonel "Wild Bill" Donovan, received the Medal of Honor for his bravery during the assault. The woods contain the remains of trenches and bunkers. This GPS coordinate is for a small parking spot off D123.
N 49 19.768 E 5 02.906 (49.329467, 5.048433)

30. **GERMAN CEMETERY, ROMAGNE:** One of many German cemeteries in the region, situated in a beautiful setting under tall trees and with well-kept memorials.
N 49 20.055 E 5 04.940 (49.33425, 5.082333)

31. **VAUQUOIS MONUMENTS AND CRATERS:** A very impressive park where the French fought the Germans in 1915 and the Americans faced the Germans in 1918.
N 49 12.245 E 5 04.081 (49.204083, 5.068017)

32. **HQ CROWN PRINCE:** These woods contain the remains of German bunkers, hardened buildings and trench lines. They were captured by the 77th Infantry Division on September 28.
N 49 12.846 E 4 59.507 (49.2141, 4.991783)

OTHER LOCATIONS RELATED TO THE END OF WORLD WAR I:

33. **ARMISTICE LOCATION, RETHONDES CLAIRIÈRE DE L' ARMISTICE, COMPIEGNE:** This is the location where the Armistice was signed. It contains a monument and small museum, as well as a replica of the railcar in which the signing took place. Hitler later took the railcar and the Germans blew it up in 1945.
N 49 25.633 E 2 54.383 (49.427217, 2.906383)

34. **CAMP ROYALLIEU INTERNMENT CAMP, COMPIÈGNE:** Located here are the remaining buildings of—and a memorial to—a 25-barrack camp used in the deportation of more than 45,000 people, including prisoners of war and political internees, to concentration camps outside France. The memorial and museum contain artifacts, documents and stories about the people who suffered in the camp.
N 49 24.170 E 2 48.486 (49.402833, 2.8081)

35. **PARIS AMERICAN CEMETERY WORLD WAR I, SURESNES CEMETERY:** Located on the west side of Paris, this cemetery contains the graves of more than 1,500 men who died in World War I and more than 20 men who died in World War II.
N 48 52.315 E 2 13.124 (48.871917, 2.218733)

100 DAYS OFFENSIVE – AUGUST 8 – NOVEMBER 11, 1918

MAP 31

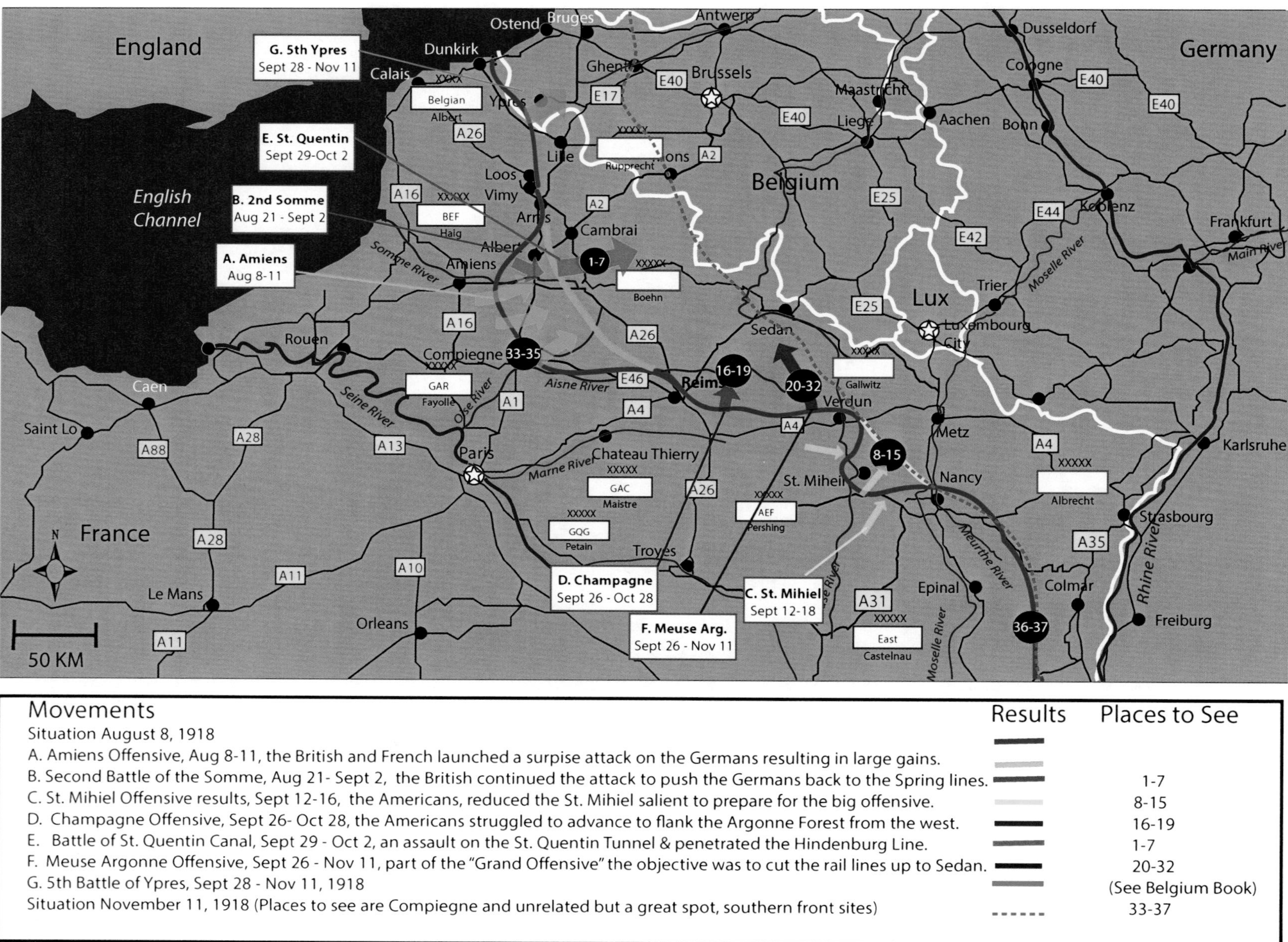
England
English Channel
France
Belgium
Lux
Germany
G. 5th Ypres
Sept 28 - Nov 11
E. St. Quentin
Sept 29-Oct 2
B. 2nd Somme
Aug 21 - Sept 2
A. Amiens
Aug 8-11
D. Champagne
Sept 26 - Oct 28
F. Meuse Arg.
Sept 26 - Nov 11
C. St. Mihiel
Sept 12-18
Belgian
Albert
BEF
Haig
Rupprecht
Boehn
GAR
Fayolle
GAC
Maistre
GQG
Petain
AEF
Pershing
Gallwitz
Albrecht
East
Castelnau
1-7
8-15
16-19
20-32
33-35
36-37
Ostend
Bruges
Antwerp
Dunkirk
Calais
Ypres
Ghent
Brussels
Lille
Loos
Vimy
Arras
Cambrai
Albert
Amiens
Rouen
Caen
Saint Lo
Le Mans
Orleans
Compiegne
Paris
Reims
Sedan
Verdun
Chateau Thierry
St. Mihiel
Troyes
Metz
Nancy
Epinal
Colmar
Strasbourg
Freiburg
Karlsruhe
Frankfurt
Koblenz
Trier
Luxembourg City
Maastricht
Liege
Aachen
Bonn
Cologne
Dusseldorf
Somme River
Seine River
Oise River
Aisne River
Marne River
Meurthe River
Moselle River
Rhine River
Main River
50 KM
Movements
Situation August 8, 1918
A. Amiens Offensive, Aug 8-11, the British and French launched a surpise attack on the Germans resulting in large gains.
B. Second Battle of the Somme, Aug 21- Sept 2, the British continued the attack to push the Germans back to the Spring lines.
C. St. Mihiel Offensive results, Sept 12-16, the Americans, reduced the St. Mihiel salient to prepare for the big offensive.
D. Champagne Offensive, Sept 26- Oct 28, the Americans struggled to advance to flank the Argonne Forest from the west.
E. Battle of St. Quentin Canal, Sept 29 - Oct 2, an assault on the St. Quentin Tunnel & penetrated the Hindenburg Line.
F. Meuse Argonne Offensive, Sept 26 - Nov 11, part of the "Grand Offensive" the objective was to cut the rail lines up to Sedan.
G. 5th Battle of Ypres, Sept 28 - Nov 11, 1918
Situation November 11, 1918 (Places to see are Compiegne and unrelated but a great spot, southern front sites)
Results
Places to See
1-7
8-15
16-19
1-7
20-32
(See Belgium Book)
33-37

BATTLE OF ST. QUENTIN CANAL, SEPT. 29 – OCT. 2, 1918

MAP 32

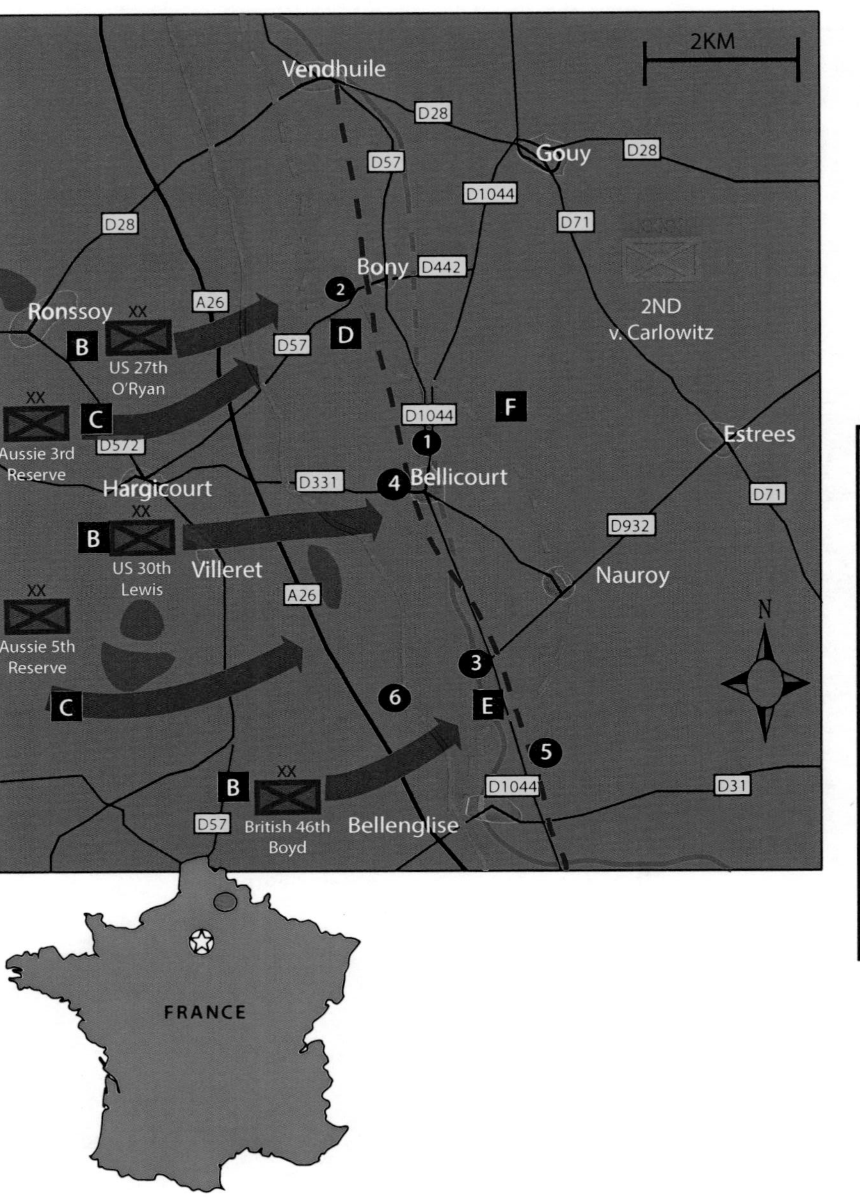
2KM
Vendhuile
D28
Gouy
D57
D1044
D71
D28
Bony
D442
2ND
v. Carlowitz
Ronssoy
A26
B
US 27th
O'Ryan
D57
D
C
Aussie 3rd
Reserve
D572
D1044
F
1
Estrees
Hargicourt
D331
4
Bellicourt
D71
B
US 30th
Lewis
Villeret
D932
Nauroy
A26
Aussie 5th
Reserve
N
3
C
6
E
5
B
D1044
D31
D57
British 46th
Boyd
Bellenglise
FRANCE

Places to See:

1. American Memorial Bellicourt
2. American Cemetery Somme (Bony)
3. Riqueval Farm Bridge
4. Bellicourt British Cemetery
5. La Baraque British Cemetery
6. Australian 4th Division Monument
7. St. Quentin French Memorial (not on map)

MOVEMENTS:

A. Sept 26-27 Allies fired 1,650 cannons with HE and mustard gas. And units fought for some better positioning/small skirmishes.

B. Sept 29 at 0555 in fog the 3 forward divisions attacked.

C. Australian 5th and 3rd Divisions entered behind the American 30th and 27th Divisions because the Germans came out of the tunnels behind the Americans. The US 27th was starting to be decimated.

D. By noon, the Americans and Aussies captured some strong points such as "the Knoll" in the area of the current Cemetery in Bony. Bony was cleared by September 30.

E. In the south, the 46th crossed the canal by 0830.

F. By the end of October 2, the 4th Army had penetrated 6,000 yards into the Hindenburg Line at a width of 10,000 yards.

Allied Line September 29

Allied Line September 30

Hindenburg Line Main Defenses

ST. MIHIEL OFFENSIVE, SEPTEMBER 12–16, 1918

MAP 33

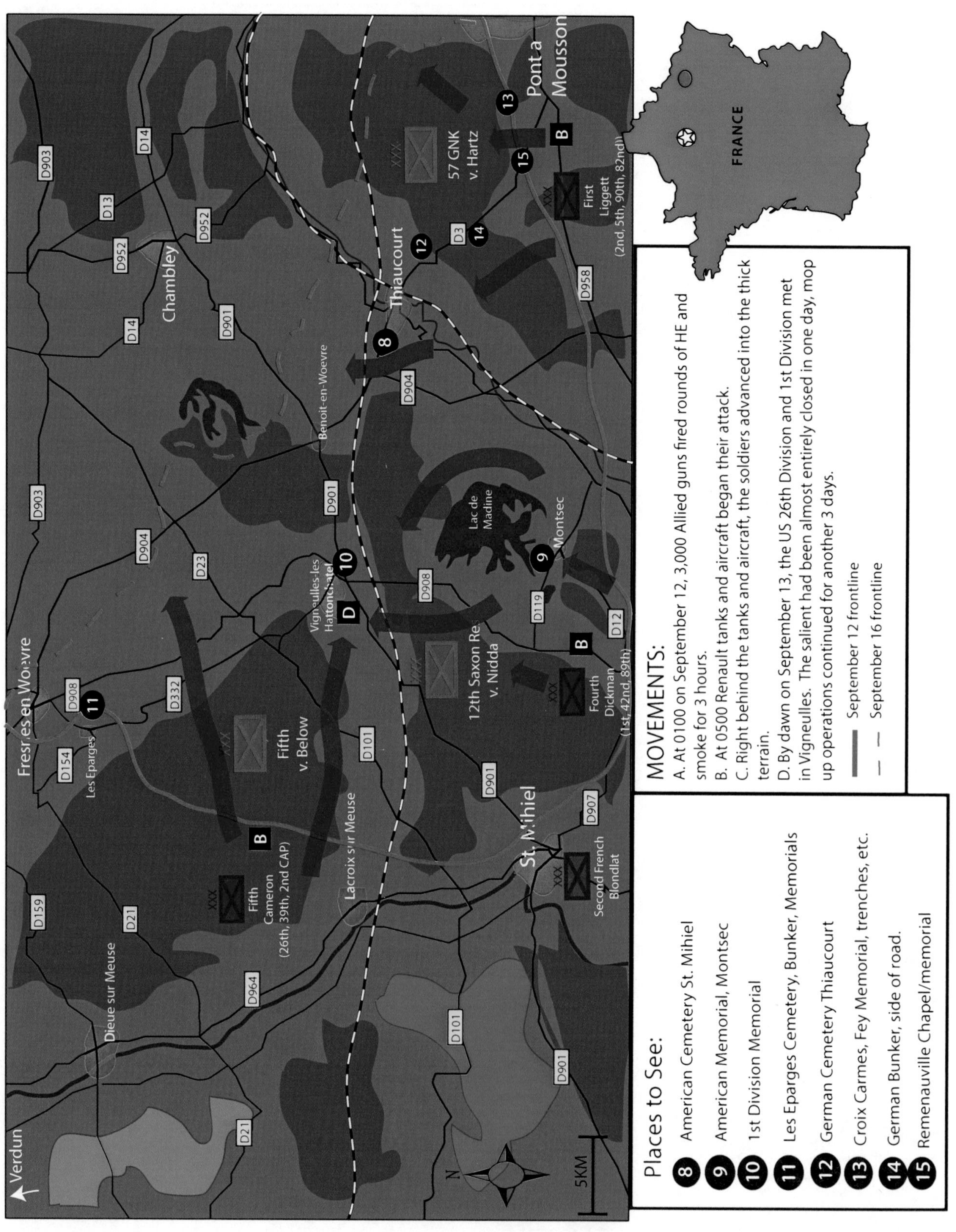
Verdun
Fresnes en Woevre
Les Eparges
Dieue sur Meuse
Chambley
Benoit-en-Woevre
Vigneulles-les Hattonchatel
Lacroix sur Meuse
Thiaucourt
St. Mihiel
Lac de Madine
Montsec
Pont a Mousson
D159
D154
D908
D903
D13
D952
D14
D21
D904
D332
D23
D901
D964
D101
D908
D904
D3
D119
D907
D12
D958
Fifth Cameron (26th, 39th, 2nd CAP)
Fifth v. Below
12th Saxon Re v. Nidda
57 GNK v. Hartz
Fourth Dickman (1st, 42nd, 89th)
Second French Blondlat
First Liggett (2nd, 5th, 90th, 82nd)
XXX
5KM
N
FRANCE
Places to See:
8 American Cemetery St. Mihiel
9 American Memorial, Montsec
10 1st Division Memorial
11 Les Eparges Cemetery, Bunker, Memorials
12 German Cemetery Thiaucourt
13 Croix Carmes, Fey Memorial, trenches, etc.
14 German Bunker, side of road.
15 Remenauville Chapel/memorial
MOVEMENTS:
A. At 0100 on September 12, 3,000 Allied guns fired rounds of HE and smoke for 3 hours.
B. At 0500 Renault tanks and aircraft began their attack.
C. Right behind the tanks and aircraft, the soldiers advanced into the thick terrain.
D. By dawn on September 13, the US 26th Division and 1st Division met in Vigneulles. The salient had been almost entirely closed in one day, mop up operations continued for another 3 days.
September 12 frontline
September 16 frontline

MEUSE – ARGONNE OFFENSIVE, SEPT. 26 – NOV. 11, 1918 MAP 34

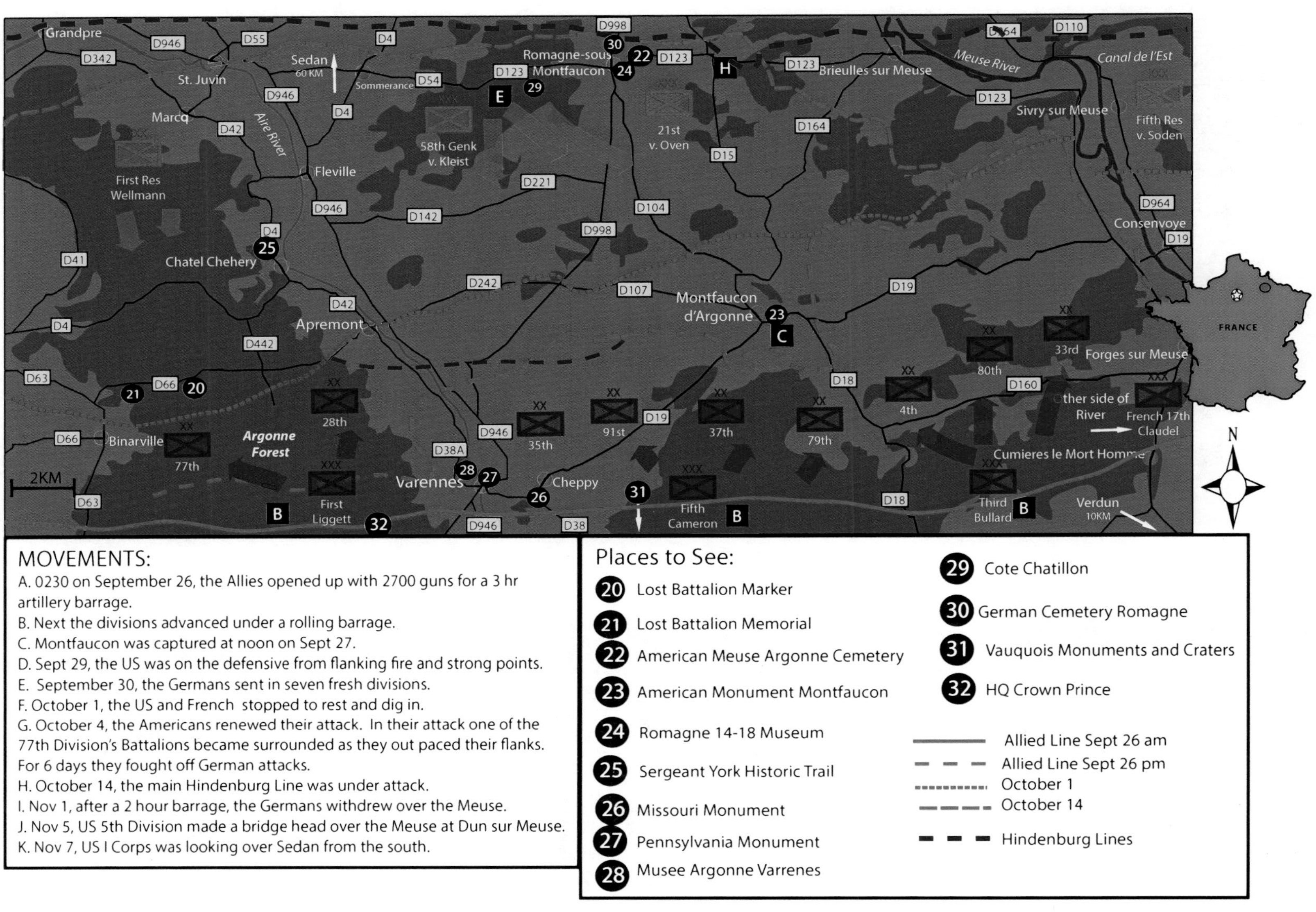
Grandpre
St. Juvin
Marcq
First Res
Wellmann
Sedan
60 KM
Sommerance
Aire River
Fleville
58th Genk
v. Kleist
Chatel Chehery
Apremont
Binarville
Argonne
Forest
77th
28th
First
Liggett
Varennes
Cheppy
35th
91st
37th
79th
4th
80th
33rd
Fifth
Cameron
Third
Bullard
Romagne-sous
Montfaucon
21st
v. Oven
Brieulles sur Meuse
Meuse River
Canal de l'Est
Sivry sur Meuse
Fifth Res
v. Soden
Consenvoye
Montfaucon
d'Argonne
Forges sur Meuse
ther side of
River
French 17th
Claudel
Cumieres le Mort Homme
Verdun
10KM
FRANCE
N
2KM
D342
D946
D55
D4
D998
D123
D54
D42
D41
D63
D66
D442
D142
D221
D242
D107
D104
D15
D164
D19
D18
D160
D964
D110
D38A
D38
MOVEMENTS:
A. 0230 on September 26, the Allies opened up with 2700 guns for a 3 hr artillery barrage.
B. Next the divisions advanced under a rolling barrage.
C. Montfaucon was captured at noon on Sept 27.
D. Sept 29, the US was on the defensive from flanking fire and strong points.
E. September 30, the Germans sent in seven fresh divisions.
F. October 1, the US and French stopped to rest and dig in.
G. October 4, the Americans renewed their attack. In their attack one of the 77th Division's Battalions became surrounded as they out paced their flanks. For 6 days they fought off German attacks.
H. October 14, the main Hindenburg Line was under attack.
I. Nov 1, after a 2 hour barrage, the Germans withdrew over the Meuse.
J. Nov 5, US 5th Division made a bridge head over the Meuse at Dun sur Meuse.
K. Nov 7, US I Corps was looking over Sedan from the south.
Places to See:
20 Lost Battalion Marker
21 Lost Battalion Memorial
22 American Meuse Argonne Cemetery
23 American Monument Montfaucon
24 Romagne 14-18 Museum
25 Sergeant York Historic Trail
26 Missouri Monument
27 Pennsylvania Monument
28 Musee Argonne Varrenes
29 Cote Chatillon
30 German Cemetery Romagne
31 Vauquois Monuments and Craters
32 HQ Crown Prince
Allied Line Sept 26 am
Allied Line Sept 26 pm
October 1
October 14
Hindenburg Lines

The Somme American Cemetery is east of the major British battlefield sites near the village of Bony.

The Bellicourt American Monument is built over a canal. It commemorates the American success in breaking the Hindenburg Line in 1918.

Left: St. Mihiel Cemetery is located south of Metz and marks the sacrifices of the American soldiers who fought during the St. Mihiel Offensive of September 1918. In the surrounding area are many memorials to the battle.

Below: The impressive American Montsec memorial dominates the surrounding fields and is a must see. Below right is a photo of the German cemetery in Thiaucourt only a few miles from the American memorial.

Far left is the Sommepy American memorial. It has a great view of the battle-field. It also still has the remains of trenches and barriers.The next photo is of the memorial in Varrenes, for the divisions of Penn-sylvannia that fought during World War I. It is located at the front line of the Meuse Argonne Offensive of 1918. Next door is a Military Museum and in the town are the information boards about King Louis XVI's "Flight to Varrenes".

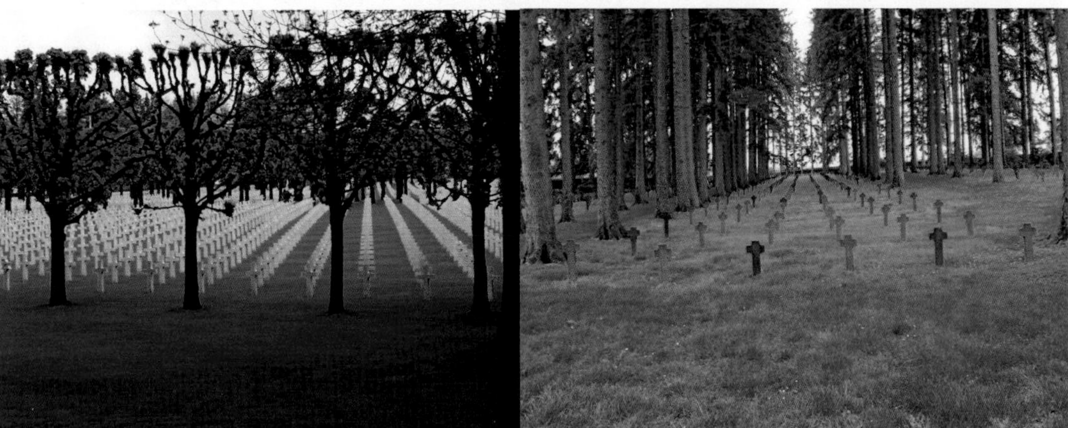

The Meuse Argonne American Cemetery is the largest American Cemetery in Europe. It is located on the strongest portion of the Hindenburg Line which was captured in October 1918. In the same town is a small German cemetery and also a cafe/ museum, *Romagne 14-18*. It is an excellent stop for a lunch break, artifacts and information.

LOST
BATTALION

Far left, only 6KM south of the Argonne Cemetery is the Montfaucon American Monument. It was built over the ruins of the battle for a strong German position, located next to an abbey. It is an amazing view to climb to the top. To the west is the memorial to the Lost Battalion located off D66.

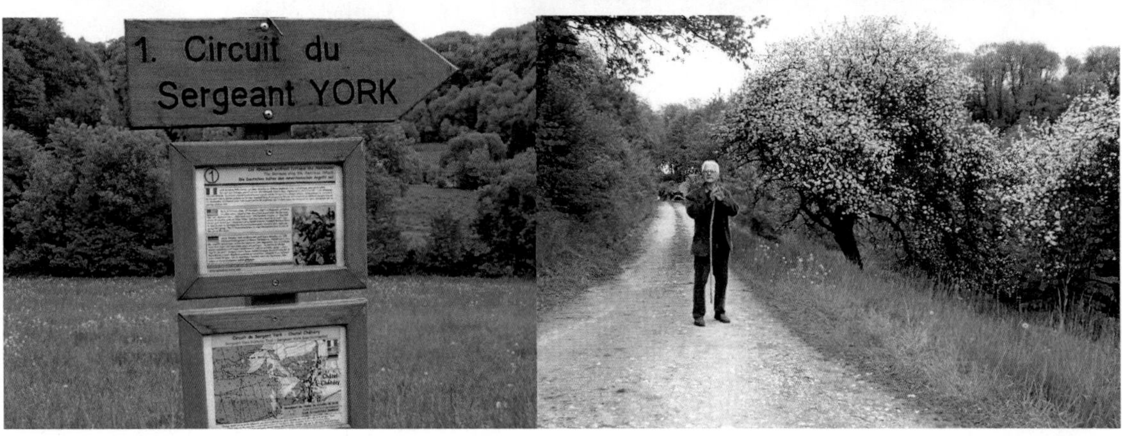
1. Circuit du
Sergeant YORK

In Chatel Chehery, French and American volunteers built a trail to retrace the heroism of Sergeant York. It is not a long or difficult hike but it is very well done. We also had the pleasure of meeting the mayor of the town who showed us the start of the trail.

FRENCH SOUTHERN FRONT

1914-1918

SUMMARY: In the south, the French and Germans fought along difficult terrain and made few gains. This area contains two major sites related to World War I. In 2012, I enjoyed seeing the Musée Mémorial du Linge. It is very well done and features a totally different terrain from other World War I battles. As I took in the trenches, rocks and slope, I marveled at how men had fought in these mountainous conditions. That year, Viel Armand was under construction, but one could explore the woods not far from the trail, finding trenches and taking in amazing views of the Alsace Plain.

PLACES TO SEE (REFERENCE MAP 19):

36. **MUSÉE MÉMORIAL DU LINGE:** This site includes a very well done museum and trenches to walk among. The Linge is one of the best museums and sites dedicated to World War I. It also includes German and French cemeteries. The location is very unique, and the experience of comparing this front to other World War I battle sites is fascinating.
    N 48 05.002 E 7 08.398 (48.083367, 7.139967)

37. **VIEIL ARMAND BATTLES OF WORLD WAR I, HARTMANNSWILLERKOPF:** This site includes opportunities for hiking, as well as trenches, a museum and cemeteries. It offers an incredible view of the Alsace Plain. The Germans and French fought over the mountaintop during World War I. The museum and cemetery were under construction until 2015, but before then you could still hike to the high point and explore the stone trenches and bunkers.
    N 47 51.524 E 7 08.958 (47.858733, 7.1493)

American Cemetery Suresnes is located just west of Paris. A great view, on a clear day.

In Compiegne, is the above memorial with a sword through the German Eagle, a mild suggestion on the result of WW1!

Above, is the museum and memorial park in Compiegne which was the location of the surrender of the Germans in WW1 to France but also the surrender of the French to the Germans in WW2, at the request of Hitler. (the original car was blown up by the SS in WW2).

In the Alsace/Southern Front, the French have several memorials and cemeteries as monuments to their sacrifices during WW1. To include the above photo of Hartmannswillerkopf. A very beautiful setting.

One of my favorite places to visit was the museum and memorial in the Vosges Mountains, *Musee Memorial du Linge*. It is really well done and an incredible battlefield that is seldom thought of for WW1. However, it played a very important role stopping any German advances in the south and Alsace sector. The location is excellent and a favorite location to visit for wine, food, hiking, WW1 and WW2 sites.

Chapter 8

WORLD WAR II, 1939–1945

World War I and World War II are sometimes considered the "Second 30 Years' War" because the combined experience of World War I, the Treaty of Versailles and a series of European civil wars created a tinderbox just waiting to catch fire. World War II was a blaze that ran across Europe. Adolf Hitler struck the match and initial weak Allied leadership helped the fire spread.

World War II ended with more than 50 million deaths, both civilian and military. In terms of military deaths, the Allies suffered more than 16 million, while the Axis suffered more than 8 million. This chapter provides information about nine battles and campaigns. Normandy is very well known, but I hope this chapter provides insight into other, lesser known but just-as-significant locations, such as Lorraine and Alsace. Following is a brief timeline of the European Theater during World War II; also reference Map 35.

1939:

September 1: Germany invades Poland.

September 3: England and France declare war on Germany.

September 17: The Soviet Union invades Poland from the east.

November 30: Soviet forces attack Finland.

1940:

April 9: Germany invades Norway.

May 10: Germany invades the Netherlands, Belgium, Luxembourg and France.

May 15: The Battle of Stonne takes place.

May 26: The evacuation of Dunkirk takes place.

June 22: France surrenders to Germany and Italy.

July 10–October 30: The Battle of Britain takes place.

July 21: Russia occupies Latvia, Lithuania and Estonia.

September 13: Italy invades Egypt.

November 1: Italy attacks Greece.

November 20: Hungary and Romania join the Axis powers.

1941:

March: Bulgaria and Yugoslavia join the Axis powers.

March 5: British troops land in Greece.

March 24: Erwin Rommel and the Afrika Korps attack the British.

April 23: Greece surrenders to Germany after Italy fails to advance.

May 20: Germany invades Crete.

June 22: Germany invades the Soviet Union.

October 20: Germany is within sight of Moscow, but fails to capture it.

December 7: Japan attacks Pearl Harbor and America declares war on Japan.

December 10: Germany and Italy declare war on America.

1942:

January: Germany inflicts stronger air attacks on Malta.

June 20: Rommel captures Tobruk.

August 19: The Battle of Dieppe results in a failed attack.

August 23: The Battle of Stalingrad begins.

October 23: During the Battle of El Alamein, British forces defeat the Germans and force Rommel to retreat to Libya and Tunisia.

November 8: During Operation Torch, the Americans land in Algeria and Morocco.

1943:

January: During the Casablanca Conference, Franklin D. Roosevelt demands "unconditional" surrender; some say this move causes additional deaths.

February 2: The Germans surrender at Stalingrad.

May 13: The Afrika Korps surrender in Tunisia, ending the Axis power in Africa.

July 5: The Battle of Kursk, a major German offensive in Russia, is defeated.

July 10–August 17: The Allies invade and capture Sicily.

July 25: Bennito Mussolini is ousted and taken prisoner.
September 3: The Allies invade the Italian mainland.
September 9: Italy surrenders to the Allies. (Germany occupies Rome and takes charge of defense.)
November 28: During the Tehran Conference, Franklin D. Roosevelt, Joseph Stalin and Winston Churchill meet for the first time.

1944:

January–May: The Battle for Montecassino takes place.
January 22: The Allies land at Anzio.
January 27: The Soviets end the 900-day siege of Leningrad.
June 4: Rome is liberated.
June 6: Operation Overlord, D-Day
June 9: The Soviets attempt another attack on Finland.
August 1: The Warsaw Uprising begins.
August 14: Operation Dragoon lands in Southern France.
August 25: Paris is liberated.
September 11: The Allies cross into Germany near Aachen and begin the Battle of Hürtgen Forest.
September: Lorraine Campaign battles begin at Nancy, Arracourt and Metz.
September: Alsace Campaign battles begin in the Vosges.
September 17: Operation Market Garden in Holland ends in failure.
September 24: The Soviets enter Czechoslovakia.
October 2: The Warsaw Uprising ends in failure.
October 14: Athens is liberated.
October 20: The first German city, Aachen, is captured.
November 22: Metz surrenders to the Americans.
November 23: Strasbourg is liberated by American and French forces.
December 16: Germany attacks the Americans in Ardennes initiating the Battle of the Bulge.
December 31: Operation Nordwind, a German counteroffensive in Alsace, ends in failure.

1945:

January 12: The Soviet Vistula-Oder Offensive takes place.
January 17: The Soviets capture Warsaw.
January 28: The Battle of the Bulge ends in Allied victory.
February 9: The Colmar Pocket is liberated and the remaining Germans are pushed over the Rhine River.
February 4: During the Yalta Conference, Roosevelt, Churchill and Stalin meet to set the foundations of post-war Europe.
February 8: Operation Veritable, Field Marshal Bernard Montgomery's effort to clear the Germans from the west side of the Rhine River, begins.
March 7: The Americans capture an intact bridge over the Rhine River at Remagen.
March 23: Operation Plunder, Montgomery's Rhine River crossing, begins.
April 12: Roosevelt dies and Harry Truman becomes President of the United States.
April 16: The Soviets begin their attack on Berlin.
April 25: The Americans and Soviets meet on the Elbe River. The Soviets reach Berlin the same day.
April 30: Hitler commits suicide.
May 2: Berlin surrenders to the Soviets; the Germans surrender in Italy.
May 7: The United States accepts Germany's unconditional surrender in Reims.

WORLD WAR 2 SUMMARY

MAP 35

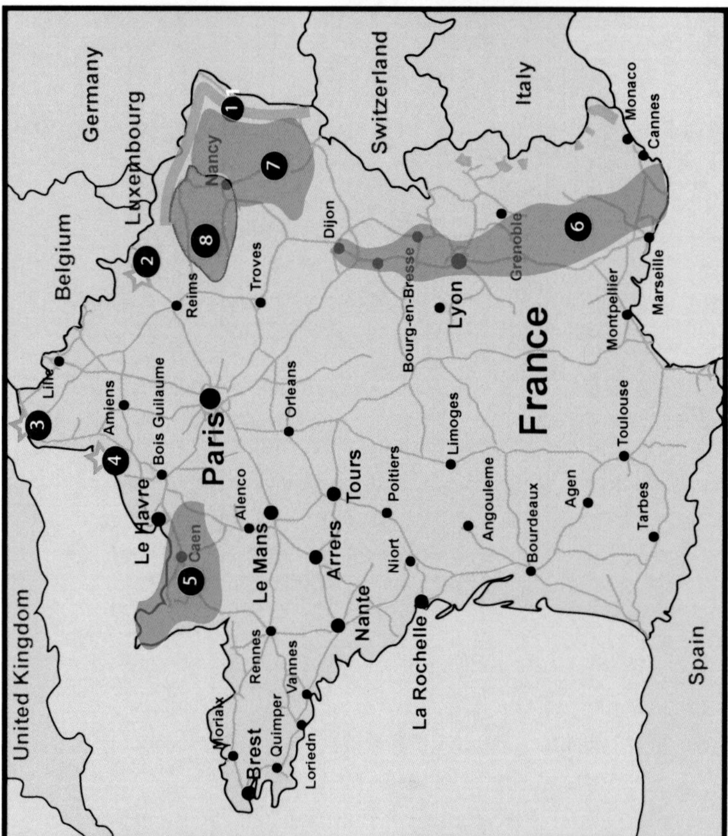
United Kingdom
Belgium
Germany
Luxembourg
Switzerland
Italy
Spain
France
Lille
Amiens
Bois Guillaume
Le Havre
Caen
Reims
Troyes
Nancy
Dijon
Paris
Orleans
Alenco
Le Mans
Tours
Arrers
Nante
Rennes
Vannes
Quimper
Moriax
Brest
Loriedn
Poitiers
Niort
La Rochelle
Limoges
Angouleme
Bourdeaux
Agen
Tarbes
Toulouse
Montpellier
Marseille
Lyon
Bourg-en-Bresse
Grenoble
Cannes
Monaco

1 Maginot Line Sites

2 Battle of Stonne, May 15 1940

3 Dunkirk, May 28 1940

4 Dieppe, August 19 1942

5 Operation Overlord June 6 1944
Atlantic Wall, Mortain & Falaise

6 Operation Dragoon August 14, 1944
Toulon, Montilemar & Link up

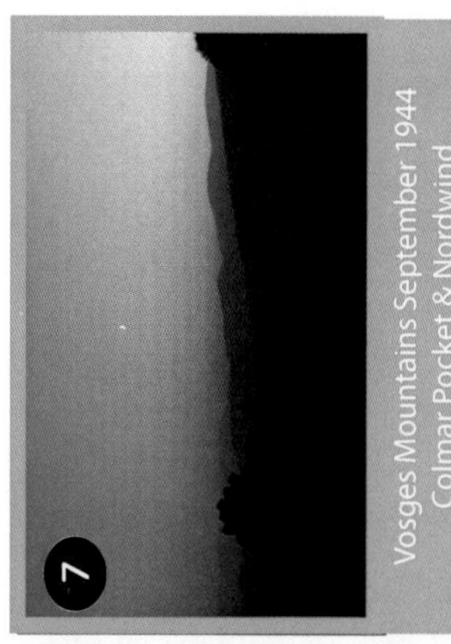
7 Vosges Mountains September 1944
Colmar Pocket & Nordwind

8 Lorraine Campaign September 1944
Metz, Arracourt & West Wall

MAGINOT LINE

1939–1945

"No way through for anyone"
– Maginot line motto

SUMMARY: Contrary to popular belief, the Maginot Line defenders surrendered only after the armistice was signed on June 22, 1940 after fighting since May 10 of that year. The line saw battle twice, once against the Germans and once against the Americans. On May 10, 1940, during Operation Case Yellow, the Germans successfully traveled around the Maginot Line in two main thrusts—one through Belgium and another through the Ardennes Forest, with seven armor divisions past Sedan. In a swift motorized and combined arms attack, the German commanders defeated the better-equipped, numerically superior but poorly commanded French and British forces.

After World War I, the French had decided to build the fortified line. It was to serve several purposes:

1. Avoid surprise and give the French army time to mobilize for a counterattack.

2. Save manpower. (The French population was 40 million, compared to Germany's 70 million.)

3. Protect the industrial areas of Lorraine and Alsace (railroad, steel, coal, ore, etc.).

4. Provide bases for counter-offenses.

5. Channel the Germans through either Belgium or Switzerland.

The Maginot Line was strongest in the south from Metz to Lauter. It protected industrial areas and was intended as an integrated force with reserves and movements available where needed. However, upon the German attack, the French command pulled forces and artillery from these areas. The French did not expect an attack through the Ardennes, which flushed the main forces out to Dunkirk and into the Channel.

The second battle took place in 1944 and 1945 when the Germans defended fortresses, such as Metz, against the Americans. The Americans did what the Germans didn't; they captured major forts by assault. See the chapter on the Lorraine Campaign for additional information.

TECHNOLOGY/TACTICS: The Maginot Line was an amazing structure for its time. It was strongest in the south and consisted of different types of defenses. The line sat approximately 15 kilometers from the German border and was not thin, but rather a defense in depth. It was about 20 kilometers deep. The line consisted of forts (ouvrages), large forts (gros ouvrages) such as Metz and small forts (petits ouvrages). The main large forts contained 75mm and 135mm cannons and housed 500 to 1,000 men. The small forts each housed a company of about 100 to 200 men and were armed primarily with machine guns, mortars and 47mm anti-tank guns. These forts were about 15 kilometers apart and were separated by "casements," each of which included one or two cupolas with a 47mm cannon or machine guns and staffed by 20 men. Barbed wire and tank obstacles such as metal posts and ditches sat between the casements and forts. Because the line had to sustain men and weapons, it required command posts, power plants, water plants, ventilation systems, quarters, kitchens, train systems, workshops and ammunition bunkers. The Maginot Line's main features, which you can still see today, are:

A. Forts (ouvrages) as previously described – 22 large and 36 small

B. Casements (casements d'intervalles) – 311

C. Observatories (observatorires) and infantry shelters (abris) for artillery – 78 shelters and 14 observatories

D. Obstacle Belts—anti-tank ditches, metal stakes and barbed wire

E. Field Fortifications—local defense blockhouses, small bunkers for depth – 4,000 built

QUOTES: "If you entrench yourself behind strong fortifications, you compel the enemy to seek a solution elsewhere." – Karl von Clausewitz

"Fortifications are monuments to man's stupidity." – General George S. Patton

PLACES TO SEE (REFERENCE MAP 36):

1. **FORTRESS HACKENBURG:** This is a gros ouvrage and one of the largest forts. It's well set up for tourists. I'm a fan of M10 tanks and I appreciated the fact that one sits out front as a memorial to the American liberation of the fort and Metz in 1944.
   www.maginot-hackenburg.com
   N 49 20.461 E 6 21.948 (49.341017, 6.3658)

2. **FORT DU FERMONT:** Another gros ouvrage in a well-established location.
   www.ligne-maginot-fort-de-fermont.asso.fr
   N 49 26.964 E 5 39.890 (49.449401, 5.664831)

3. **FORT ROCHONVILLERS:** This is a gros ouvrage located outside the town of Rochonvillers. You can see other bunkers in the surrounding area. This

location has a "wow" factor and is well worth a look. I recommend starting at letter "d" below, as the other locations are under French military "control." In theory, you can still hike around the sites to gain an appreciation of their size. The following are listed from west to east in location:

A. **COMBAT BLOCKS**: The location still retains its impressive turrets and bunkers. You also have the opportunity to hike the area and observe the fields of fire. The following GPS coordinates are for the entrance to the woods, which contain six combat positions. N 49 23.938 E 6 02.058 (49.398967, 6.0343)

B. **BLOCK 9:** Between the two large blocks/casements rests this fighting position and turrets. They are connected underground. N 49 24.337 E 6 03.370 (49.405617, 6.056167)

C. **AMMUNITION ENTRY POINT AND HOUSING BUNKERS:** N 49 24.076 E 6 03.211 (49.401267, 6.053517)

D. **CASEMENT DU GRAND LOT:** N 49 24.398 E 6 03.686 (49.406633, 6.061433)

4. **FORT SCHOENENBURG:** This is located in Alsace and is a very popular gros ouvrage. It is one of the largest in the Maginot Line.
www.lignemaginot.com
N 48 57.982 E 7 54.733 (48.966367, 7.912217)

5. **FORTRESS METZ:** Technically, this is off limits. It's a dangerous area because it was never fully cleared, but it's still a sight to see. See the Lorraine Campaign, Metz section for details of all the forts around the city.

6. **SIMSERHOF BITCHE MAGINOT LINE:** This was the site of a major battle from December 1944 through January 1945.
N 49 03.537 E 7 22.298 (49.058955, 7.371626)

7. **CASEMENT ESCHE:** This very impressive small "outpost/casement" is only five minutes from Hatten. The casement features a Sherman tank on top of it. Inside, you can see artifacts relating to the large tank battle that took place in this area in January 1945.
N 48 53.536 E 7 59.430 (48.892267, 7.9905)

8a. **HATTEN FORT AND MUSEUM:** The site offers a very large collection of vehicles and equipment, including Cold War aircraft. It's very well done and near the highway. It focuses primarily on the Battle of Hatten, which took place in January 1945.
N 48 53.972 E 7 58.154 (48.899533 7.969233)

8b. **MARCKOLSHEIM MUSEUM, SHERMAN AND HALFTRACK:** This third-line casement of the Maginot Line saw intense fighting in mid-June 1940. The interior has been refurbished and contains many exhibits relating to equip-

ment and militaria. On the outside is a halftrack, armored car, cannons and a Sherman tank.
N 48 09.507 E 7 33.354 (48.15845, 7.5559)

PLACES TO SEE, THE ALPS:

9. **FORT SAINT-ROCH:** Overlooking the town of Sospel, northeast of Nice, is a medium-sized ouvrage. The site contains a museum associated with the fort, but you can also hike around and see the outside of the bunkers.
N 43 52.472 E 7 26.552 (43.874533, 7.442533)

10. **FORT DE SAINTE-AGNES:** This fort defended the coastal road from the Italian invasion of 1940. It is just east of Nice and was under the control of the French military until 1990. It offers a beautiful view and the town itself is impressive.
N 43 47.961 E 7 27.736 (43.79935, 7.462267)

MAGINOT LINE AND INVASION OF FRANCE MAY 10, 1940 MAP 36

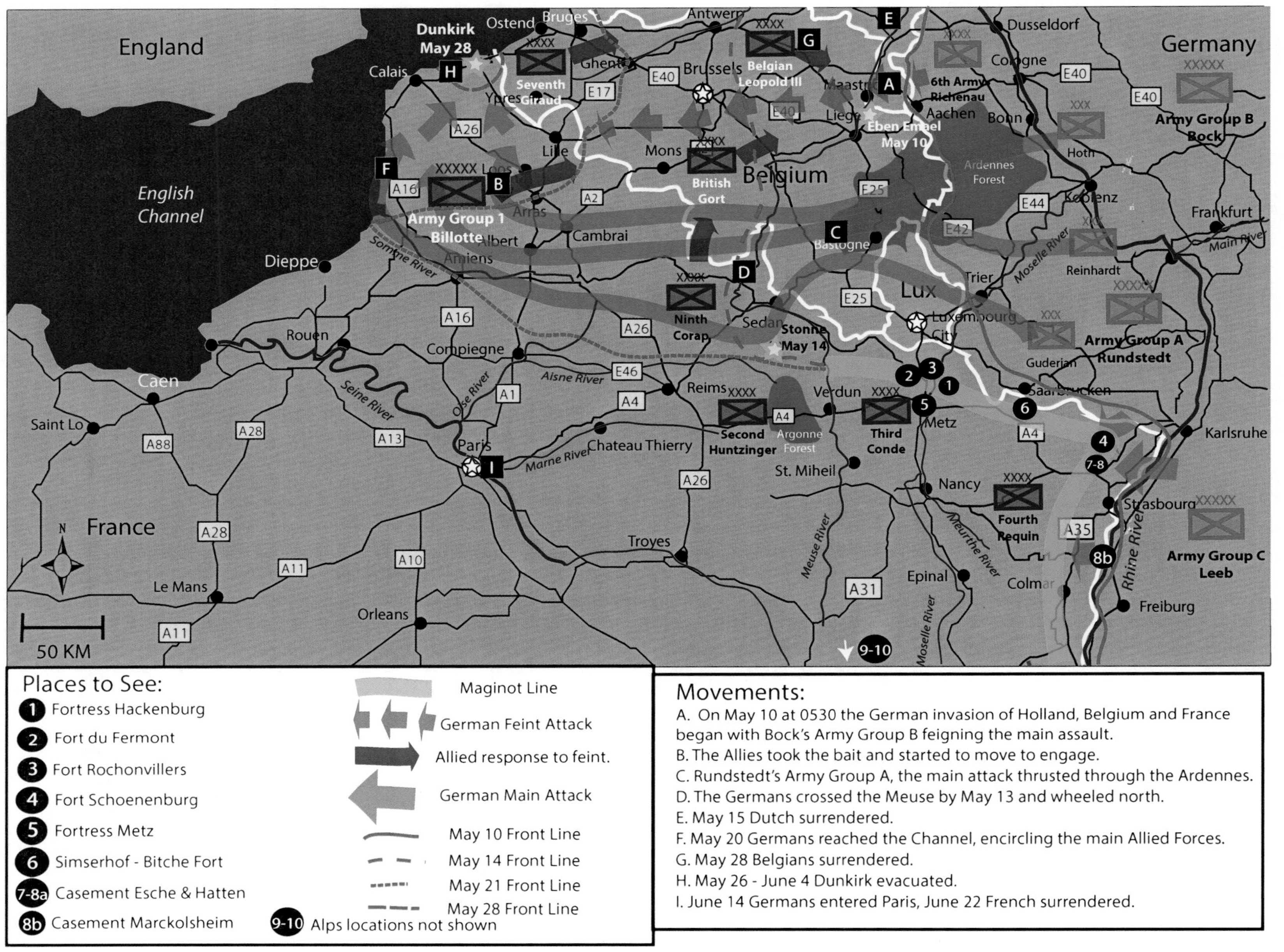
England
English Channel
France
Germany
Belgium
Lux
50 KM
Dunkirk May 28
Army Group B Bock
Army Group A Rundstedt
Army Group C Leeb
Army Group 1 Billotte
Seventh Giraud
British Gort
Belgian Leopold III
Ninth Corap
Second Huntzinger
Third Conde
Fourth Requin
6th Army Richenau
Eben Emael May 10
Stonne May 14
Ardennes Forest
Argonne Forest
Paris
Brussels
Luxembourg City
Places to See:
1 Fortress Hackenburg
2 Fort du Fermont
3 Fort Rochonvillers
4 Fort Schoenenburg
5 Fortress Metz
6 Simserhof - Bitche Fort
7-8a Casement Esche & Hatten
8b Casement Marckolsheim
9-10 Alps locations not shown
Maginot Line
German Feint Attack
Allied response to feint.
German Main Attack
May 10 Front Line
May 14 Front Line
May 21 Front Line
May 28 Front Line
Movements:
A. On May 10 at 0530 the German invasion of Holland, Belgium and France began with Bock's Army Group B feigning the main assault.
B. The Allies took the bait and started to move to engage.
C. Rundstedt's Army Group A, the main attack thrusted through the Ardennes.
D. The Germans crossed the Meuse by May 13 and wheeled north.
E. May 15 Dutch surrendered.
F. May 20 Germans reached the Channel, encircling the main Allied Forces.
G. May 28 Belgians surrendered.
H. May 26 - June 4 Dunkirk evacuated.
I. June 14 Germans entered Paris, June 22 French surrendered.

Fort Schoenenburg, far left the outer fields and forts have some spectacular views and fields of fire! The backside is where the main entrance is. Plan your trip via the website to ensure you make it in time for the tours.

Fort Driant, on the west side of the Metz defensive circle is a great but dangerous place to hike. The remains are hidden but so could be some old mines and unexploded ordnance.

OUVRAGE A 19
HACKENBERG

Just north of Metz, is Fort Hackenburg which is one the largest of the Maginot Line and it also has specific times for visits and tours. On the road up to the entrance you are greeted by a M10 Tank Destroyer "Wolverine". Even if you do not go into the fort you can hike around the area and see the various bunkers. Beware of the bull who is guarding the main fort! Out front of the fort/museum is a memorial to the US forces who liberated the fort in September 1944.

The town of Bitche, contained a strong portion of the Maginot Line, which the US Forces had a difficult time fighting through during the winter of 1944. The photo to the right shows the entrance to the very impressive Simserhof Museum. Far right is the town of Bitche with the great Citadel over-looking the town.

Further south is the museum Casement Esche, outside the town of Hatten. A fierce tank battle took place in January 1945. One of my favorite places to stop. The far right photo is one of the fields across from the Hatten Fort and Museum. It is an open air museum with a excellent collection of vehicles, aircraft, artillery and tanks. To include tanks you can drive! It also has a museum in the Maginot Line and buildings with more artifacts and material from the area battles. Note, the 240mm artillery piece, these are rare to come by.

Near the Rhine River is the Maginot Line Fort and Museum, Marc-kolsheim. It is also managed by local volunteers. It is really well done and includes a Armored Car, Half-track and Sherman tank outside.

BATTLE OF STONNE

May 15-17, 1940

"Verdun of 1940"

SUMMARY: The Germans consider the Battle of Stonne to be the "Verdun of 1940" because the town exchanged hands 17 times in three days. It was a major collision involving German armor, which started an attack, and French armor, which prepared for a counterattack. On May 10, the Germans initiated plan "Fall Gelb" (Case Yellow) and invaded France through Belgium and the Netherlands. The Allies knew about the German plan to attack through Belgium (similar to the Schlieffen Plan during World War I), but didn't know about the Germans' plan to attack through the Belgium Ardennes Forest with seven Panzer divisions. The forest had only four main roads, as well as difficult terrain and a heavy blanket of trees. The German General Erich von Manstein, in coordination with General Heinz Guderian, decided to use a spearhead containing the seven Panzer divisions to quickly thrust through the Ardennes and into Belgium, then cross the Meuse River at Sedan and drive deep into France. The Allies had built up their forces at the French and Belgian borders north of the Maginot Line and the Ardennes Forest. When the Germans attacked through Belgium, the Allies counterattacked into that country. Next, the German motorized and armor divisions attacked through the Ardennes and wheeled north to encircle the Allies in the north. The encirclement forced the Allies to retreat to Dunkirk. General Guderian disobeyed orders and was directly responsible for the success of that plan. He had been directed to dig in after capturing Sedan, but instead sent two armor divisions west toward the channel to achieve the encirclement, then sent another south through the town of Stonne to feint an attack on the back of the Maginot Line. At Stonne, the French were regrouping and preparing themselves for another counterattack into Sedan on May 15. However, on May 15 the Germans attacked the town. Over the next three days the two sides slugged it out, house for house. One very notable hero was the French Char B1 tank commander, Captain Pierre Bilotte. He entered the town with his platoon of seven tanks, without infantry support, and took out two Panzer IVs, 11 Panzer IIIs and two Pak 36s on the main street. His tank suffered 140 hits without penetration. After destroying the German tanks, Bilotte left the town because he had little support. The French reoccupied the town shortly after the attack, but the Germans recaptured it the next day. Eventually the Germans received reinforcements; meanwhile, the French were worn down because they had no reinforcements and because Luftwaffe attacks had cut off their supply lines.

OUTCOME: The Germans continued their invasion of France. On June 22, by Hitler's choice, the French signed the armistice in Compiegne in the same railway car in which the Germans had been forced to surrender on November 11, 1918. The railway car had been removed from a museum so that it could be used!

WHAT WAS IT OVER? In October 1939, after Germany invaded Poland, Hitler asked for a peace treaty with Britain and France. Both refused. As a result, Hitler sped up his plans for the invasion of France.

WHO? The Battle of Stonne was a clash between the Germans and the French. General Guderian ("Hurrying Heinz") commanded three divisions (the 1st, 2nd and 10th Panzer Divisions as well as the Grossdeutschland regiment) with as many as 380 armored tanks/vehicles in the area. The Germans faced the French Commander of the 2nd Army, Charles Huntziger, at Stonne with two divisions and more than 200 armored tanks at his disposal. The Allies in the battle for France maintained 144 divisions, 3,383 tanks and 2,935 aircraft. They suffered 360,000 casualties; including prisoners, 2,292,000 men were out of the fight by June 22. The Germans committed 140 divisions, 2,445 tanks and 5,638 aircraft; they suffered 160,000 casualties.

WHEN? May 15-17, 1940

WHY AT STONNE? It was a strategic location, a plateau where the German Army could turn west or south into France. Also from Stonne, the French could hit the flank of the German advance through France.

TECHNOLOGY/TACTICS: Contrary to popular belief, the French had more and better tanks than the Germans did. However, the French had bad leadership. The French possessed the Char B1, a tank with a 75mm cannon in the haul and a 47mm cannon in the turret; it also had heavy armor. In addition, the French had a faster Hotchkiss H39 tank, which itself had a 40mm cannon in the turret. These tanks had mechanical problems, but overall they outgunned—and maintained better armor than—the Germans. However, France did not use a combination of infantry and tanks as well as the Germans did. The Germans used the Panzer I, II, III and IV in the conflict. The Panzer IV was the only tank with a cannon of similar caliber to the Char B1. The Germans used infantry support with their tanks and also employed Stuka dive bombers to attack the French supply chain and defensive positions. Both sides used artillery to provide support before entering the town, and both sides had anti-tank mobile cannons, such as the Pak 37mm or the French 25mm anti-tank gun. Tactically, General Guderian was relentless in maintaining contact with the retreating French. He applied pressure to keep the French from organizing, counterattacking and creating a stalemate. He was considered an expert on the use of armored forces and the application of Blitzkrieg (lighting war).

QUOTE: The Kriegstagebuch (journal) of the Grossdeutschland regiment indicates that "the name of Stonne entered in the history of the regiment with blood." In the understatement of the year, Guderian, responding to his commanders' request that he slow down, stated that he was on a "reconnaissance in force."

PLACES TO SEE (REFERENCE MAP 37):

1. **AMX TANK AT THE EDGE OF STONNE:** At the edge of town, this tank marks the main route into Stonne next to the hill Pain de Sucre. It offers a great view for taking in the transition of terrain from the Ardennes to the open plains.

At the foot of this butte you can also see the remains of French trenches used during the defense of Stonne in 1940. The tank is not from World War II, but, rather, was used after the war. (It's still a tank, though, and great to see!)
N 49 32.965 E 4 55.920 (49.549417, 4.932)

2. **CHAR B1 TANK IN STONNE AND DESCRIPTION BOARD:** The Char B1 is one of many French tanks that took part in the Battle of Stonne. The Char B1 had a 47mm cannon in its turret and a 75mm cannon in its hull. During this time in the war, most German tanks and anti-tank guns couldn't penetrate the Char B1's armor. Just across the street is a church that contains several plaques as well as a French 25mm anti-tank cannon.
N 49 33.026 E 4 55.491 (49.550433, 4.92485)

3. **STONNE MEMORIAL TO TANK CREW:** Just outside of Stonne is a unique stone memorial to a tank crew that was killed at this location during the Battle of Stonne.
N 49 32.951 E 4 55.396 (49.549183, 4.923267)

4. **MEMORIAL TO FRENCH AND GERMAN SOLDIERS:** Just southwest of Stonne on D30 is a memorial placed by the French to remember soldiers on both sides of this battle.
N 49 32.505 E 4 54.622 (49.54175, 4.910367)

5. **HIKING TRAIL AND MEMORIAL TO 1940, LES GRAND ARMOISES:** This is a great hiking trail just south of Stonne off D30. The trail is well marked and follows a route that includes a command post for two French regiments, a crashed Stuka site, a Messerschmitt engine and the ravine of death where fierce fighting took place. The geo coordinates indicate the start of the path.
N 49 31.945 E 4 53.552 (49.532417, 4.892533)

6. **INFORMATION BOARD, D977/D230A INTERSECTION:** Another stop along the Historic Circuit, at the intersection of D977 and D230A, the road from Les Grand Armoises to the northwest. After this memorial, turn left on D977 toward Tannay.
N 49 33.347 E 4 51.656 (49.555789, 4.860927)

7. **D977 INFORMATION BOARD AND MEMORIAL:** This is an additional stop on the Historic Circuit on D977. Before Tannay are a memorial stone and plaque to the French forces who fought at this location.
N 49 32.833 E 4 51.067 (49.547221, 4.851112)

8. **MEMORIAL AND INFORMATION BOARD, TANNAY:** Part of the Historic Circuit; next to the church is an information board about the events that took place in this town during the Battle of Stonne.
N 49 31.559 E 4 50.022 (49.525983, 4.833697)

9. **30/D977 INTERSECTION MEMORIAL, TANNAY:** This location is part of the Historic Circuit and features a brick and stone memorial to the French

soldiers who fought in this area during the Battle of Stonne. After this, turn back east toward Sy.
N 49 31.154 E 4 49.464 (49.519231, 4.824398)

10. **D30 MEMORIAL AND INFORMATION BOARD, SY:** Located just outside Sy is another memorial to the French fighters in the area.
N 49 31.452 E 4 51.936 (49.524193, 4.865599)

11. **75MM CANNON AND ARTILLERY MEMORIAL, SY:** Located farther south of Stonne is a memorial in front of the church in the town of Sy. The memorial commemorates the French soldiers who fought against the German invasion in May 1940, lending their support to the Battle of Stonne.
N 49 30.941 E 4 52.130 (49.532417, 4.892533)

12. **MEMORIAL AND INFORMATION BOARD, OCHES:** At the church overlooking the town of Oches is a memorial to the French who fought in this area. Stonne is directly to the north.
N 49 30.348 E 4 55.748 (49.505795, 4.929127)

13. **FERME DE LA POLKA, SAINT-PIERREMONT:** Up this small farm road is another information board across from a farm house. It offers a great view and is a great bike ride.
N 49 30.439 E 4 57.638 (49.507309, 4.960633)

14. **SOMMAUTHE MEMORIAL:** North of the small town of Sommauthe on D6 is another memorial on the Historic Circuit.
N 49 29.932 E 4 59.154 (49.498861, 4.985896)

15. **LA BESACE MEMORIAL AND INFORMATION BOARD:** Just south of the town of La Besace is an information board.
N 49 32.640 E 4 58.415 (49.544005, 4.973577)

BEYOND STONNE:

16. **MOURMELON-LE-GRAND, TANK EXHIBIT (CLOSE TO REIMS):** This exhibit includes a few French and American tanks. It's close to Reims and was also the 1944 resting place for divisions like the 101st, which left here for Bastogne in the Battle of the Bulge.
N 49 07.752 E 4 22.934 (49.1292, 4.382233)

17. **BATTLE OF MONTCORNET:** At 0400 on May 17, 1940, the French 4th Armored Division, commanded by Colonel Charles De Gaulle, counterattacked the Germans at the town of Montcornet. The French captured the town and pushed the Germans out. However, the Germans attacked in the afternoon with Luftwaffe support and forced the French to retreat. The French lost 23 tanks and the Germans suffered approximately 100 casualties. The town maintains an AMX Cold-War-era light tank as a memorial to the battle.
N 49 41.665 E 4 00.656 (49.694415, 4.01094)

BATTLE OF STONNE, MAY 15–17 1940

MAP 37

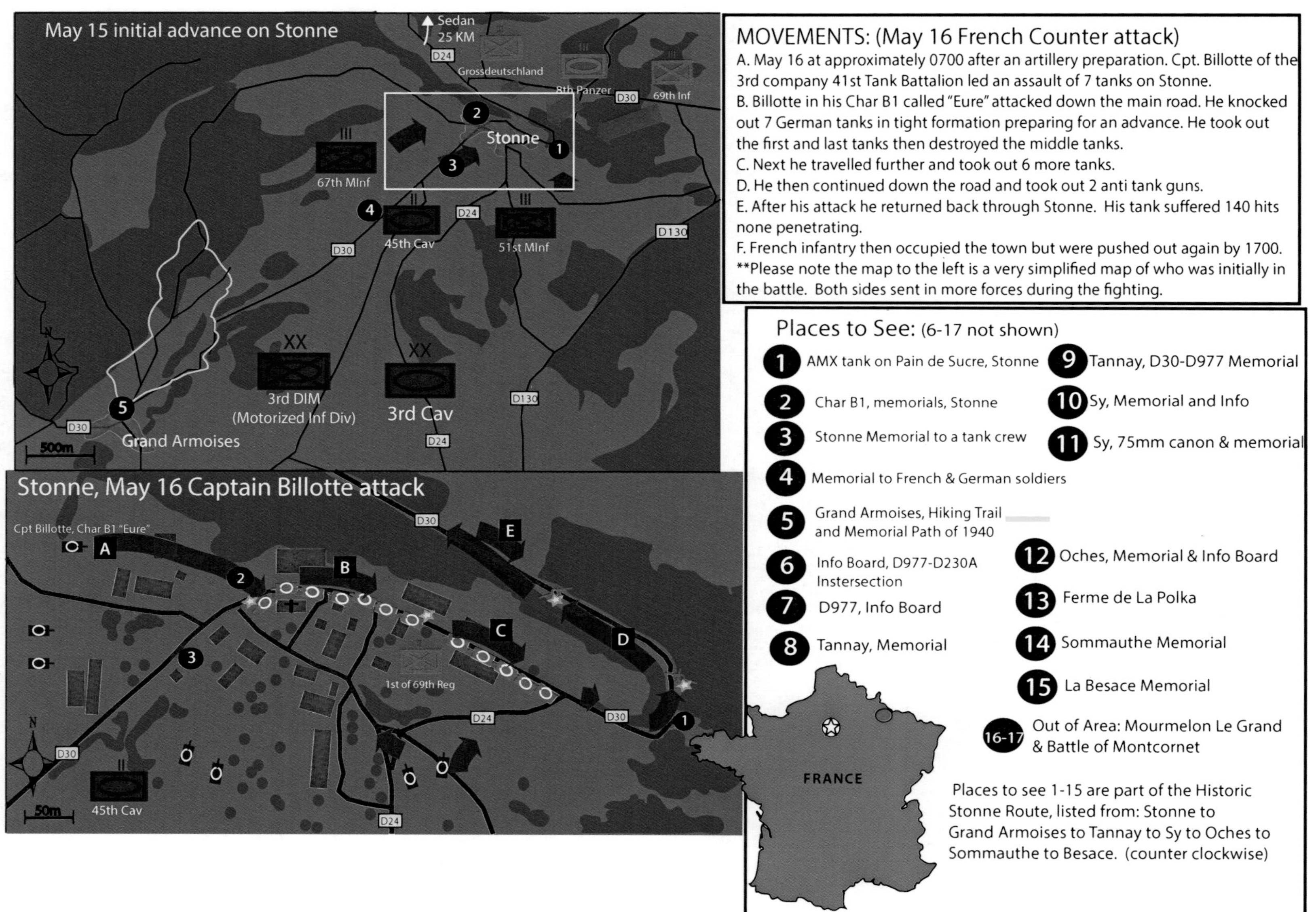
May 15 initial advance on Stonne
Sedan 25 KM
D24
Grossdeutschland
8th Panzer
D30
69th Inf
Stonne
67th MInf
45th Cav
51st MInf
D130
3rd DIM (Motorized Inf Div)
3rd Cav
Grand Armoises
500m
Stonne, May 16 Captain Billotte attack
Cpt Billotte, Char B1 "Eure"
A
B
C
D
E
1st of 69th Reg
45th Cav
50m
MOVEMENTS: (May 16 French Counter attack)
A. May 16 at approximately 0700 after an artillery preparation. Cpt. Billotte of the 3rd company 41st Tank Battalion led an assault of 7 tanks on Stonne.
B. Billotte in his Char B1 called "Eure" attacked down the main road. He knocked out 7 German tanks in tight formation preparing for an advance. He took out the first and last tanks then destroyed the middle tanks.
C. Next he travelled further and took out 6 more tanks.
D. He then continued down the road and took out 2 anti tank guns.
E. After his attack he returned back through Stonne. His tank suffered 140 hits none penetrating.
F. French infantry then occupied the town but were pushed out again by 1700.
**Please note the map to the left is a very simplified map of who was initially in the battle. Both sides sent in more forces during the fighting.
Places to See: (6-17 not shown)
1 AMX tank on Pain de Sucre, Stonne
2 Char B1, memorials, Stonne
3 Stonne Memorial to a tank crew
4 Memorial to French & German soldiers
5 Grand Armoises, Hiking Trail and Memorial Path of 1940
6 Info Board, D977-D230A Instersection
7 D977, Info Board
8 Tannay, Memorial
9 Tannay, D30-D977 Memorial
10 Sy, Memorial and Info
11 Sy, 75mm canon & memorial
12 Oches, Memorial & Info Board
13 Ferme de La Polka
14 Sommauthe Memorial
15 La Besace Memorial
16-17 Out of Area: Mourmelon Le Grand & Battle of Montcornet
FRANCE
Places to see 1-15 are part of the Historic Stonne Route, listed from: Stonne to Grand Armoises to Tannay to Sy to Oches to Sommauthe to Besace. (counter clockwise)

TOULAL

Just south of Sedan in the small town of Stonne are memorials to the sharpe tank battle that took place there in May 1940. Far left is the French Char B1 which was a better tank than anything the Germans had in 1940. It had very effective armor and weapons; a 75mm hull cannon and a 47mm cannon in the turret. The top right photo is a memorial at the edge of town overlooking fields that the Germans came across to capture the plateau of Stonne. At the foot of the memorial is a AMX tank which is a cold war era tank.

Far left middle, is a Bundesarchive photo of a Pz III with a 75mm cannon, the best the Germans could field. It was destroyed during the battle of Stonne. Below the photo, is the approach road to Stonne littered with the tanks.

To the left, the rebuilt church of Stonne, with a 25mm cannon out front. Across from the church is the Char B1 tank and a memorial to the fighting.

Driving through the country side is a great experience, the small roads take you along many farm lands that include the cows and sheep in the fields. However, I would fuel up before leaving Sedan, there are only very small places to fuel up.

BATTLE OF DUNKIRK

May 26–June 4, 1940

"Wars are not won by evacuation."
– Winston Churchill

SUMMARY: On May 10, 1940, the Germans attacked through Belgium, the Netherlands and the Ardennes. The French 1st Army and British Expeditionary Force, approximately 400,000 men in total, counterattacked into Belgium to meet the Germans. What the Allies did not expect was a German breakthrough in the Ardennes; seven Panzer divisions forced the Allies to turn their flank. By May 25, German forces were pushing the Allies to the coast. After several attempted counterattacks, the decision was made to retreat to Dunkirk, set up a perimeter defense and attempt an evacuation (called Operation Dynamo). The Allies had hoped to evacuate at least 45,000 men. The King of England called on the country for a week of prayer, hoping for a miracle. The prayers were answered; the action was considered one of Hitler's biggest mistakes. On May 24, he ordered a three-day halt of all German forces so that they could regroup, solidify their gains and turn their attention to Southern France. Hitler believed that the overconfident Hermann Göring and his Luftwaffe would stop the evacuation. General Gerd von Rundstedt was flabbergasted; he was stopped 16 kilometers from Dunkirk, days away from capturing the remaining British Expeditionary Forces and the French 1st Army. As a result, the British Expeditionary Forces and the French organized their defenses and "the miracle at Dunkirk" occurred. More than 338,000 men were evacuated to fight another day. It was a huge psychological boost but came at a great cost, as the Allies lost thousands of pieces of equipment, while the Luftwaffe sank more than 200 ships. As Churchill warned in a speech on June 4 (he had been elected Prime Minister on May 10), "Wars are not won by evacuation." He knew that the Allies had to re-group, re-arm and fight on. Also on June 4, Churchill gave his famous "We shall fight on the beaches" speech that re-invigorated traditionally stoic English hearts. On June 2, the last of the British were evacuated and two French divisions were left as the rearguard. They surrendered after bitter fighting on June 4.

OUTCOME: As a result of the miracle, the British still had an army. Therefore, they maintained hope that they could win, and didn't need to accept peace terms with the Germans. Had Hitler allowed his generals to destroy the British Expeditionary Forces, they very well may have captured Britain. Shortly after Dunkirk, the Germans activated "Fall Rot" (Case Red)—the invasion of France—and headed south. They entered Paris on June 14; by June 22 the French had signed the armistice agreement.

WHAT WAS IT OVER? The Germans wanted world domination and payback for the Treaty of Versailles.

WHO? The Germans fought against the British, Belgians and French. The Germans maintained more than 800,000 soldiers and trapped 400,000 Allies at Dunkirk. The Germans suffered approximately 52,000 casualties, while the Allies suffered 60,000. In total, 338,000 Allies escaped.

WHEN? May 24–June 4, 1940

WHY AT DUNKIRK? The British Expeditionary Forces, Belgian forces and French 1st Army were fighting in the north on the left flank of the Maginot Line to the coast because they had advanced into Belgium when the German attack started. The Germans surprised the French and the British Expeditionary Forces by breaking through the Ardennes and turning north, trapping the British Expeditionary Forces and the French against Dunkirk. After several attempts to break out, and after the Belgians surrendered on May 28, the Allies had to evacuate.

TECHNOLOGY/TACTICS: The Germans used combined arms tactics—air power, infantry, artillery and armor—to encircle the enemy and destroy them. They did not have better equipment than the Allies, but they had better leadership, faster movements and more aggression. The British Expeditionary Forces and the French lacked a coherent defense and coordinated counterattacks. During the evacuation, the British Royal Air Force fought bravely and provided cover for more than 700 ships ranging in size from 15-foot civilian trawlers to British Navy destroyers. At that time, the British used primarily the Hurricane and Blenheim Beaufighters, which were up against Stuka dive bombers, JU-88 bombers and BF 109 fighters.

QUOTE: Part of Churchill's June 4 speech:

"I have, myself, full confidence that if all do their duty, if nothing is neglected, and if the best arrangements are made, as they are being made, we shall prove ourselves once more able to defend our Island home, to ride out the storm of war, and to outlive the menace of tyranny, if necessary for years, if necessary alone.

Even though large parts of Europe and many old and famous States have fallen or may fall into the grip of the Gestapo and all the odious apparatus of Nazi rule, we shall not flag or fail. We shall go on to the end, we shall fight in France, we shall fight on the seas and oceans, we shall fight with growing confidence and growing strength in the air, we shall defend our Island, whatever the cost may be, we shall fight on the beaches, we shall fight on the landing grounds, we shall fight in the fields and in the streets, we shall fight in the hills; we shall never surrender, and if, which I do not for a moment believe, this Island or a large part of it were subjugated and starving, then our Empire beyond the seas, armed and guarded by the British Fleet, would carry on the struggle, until, in God's good time, the New World, with all its power and might, steps forth to the rescue and the liberation of the Old."

PLACES TO SEE (REFERENCE MAP 38):

1. **BRITISH CEMETERY AND MEMORIAL:** Located on the inland ridge of the defensive line of the British.
   N 51 01.833 E 2 23.380 (51.03055, 2.389667)

2. **EVACUATION MONUMENT ALONG THE SHORE:** During de Gaulle's leadership, the French harbored some resentment that the British had "left" them to face the Germans. This memorial depicts the matters as being not entirely significant; it's a minor memorial to such a large endeavor and "miracle."
   N 51 02.883 E 2 22.888 (51.04805, 2.381467)

3. **MEMORIAL DU SOUVENIR À DUNKERQUE MUSEUM, BASTION 32:** Part of a 19th-century French fortification, this was the location of the French command during the evacuation's last days. Now it houses 12 rooms that contain various artifacts, maps, etc. Unfortunately it is open only from May through September.
   N 51 02.759 E 2 22.872 (51.045983, 2.3812)

BATTLE OF DUNKIRK, MAY 26 – JUNE 4 1940

MAP 38

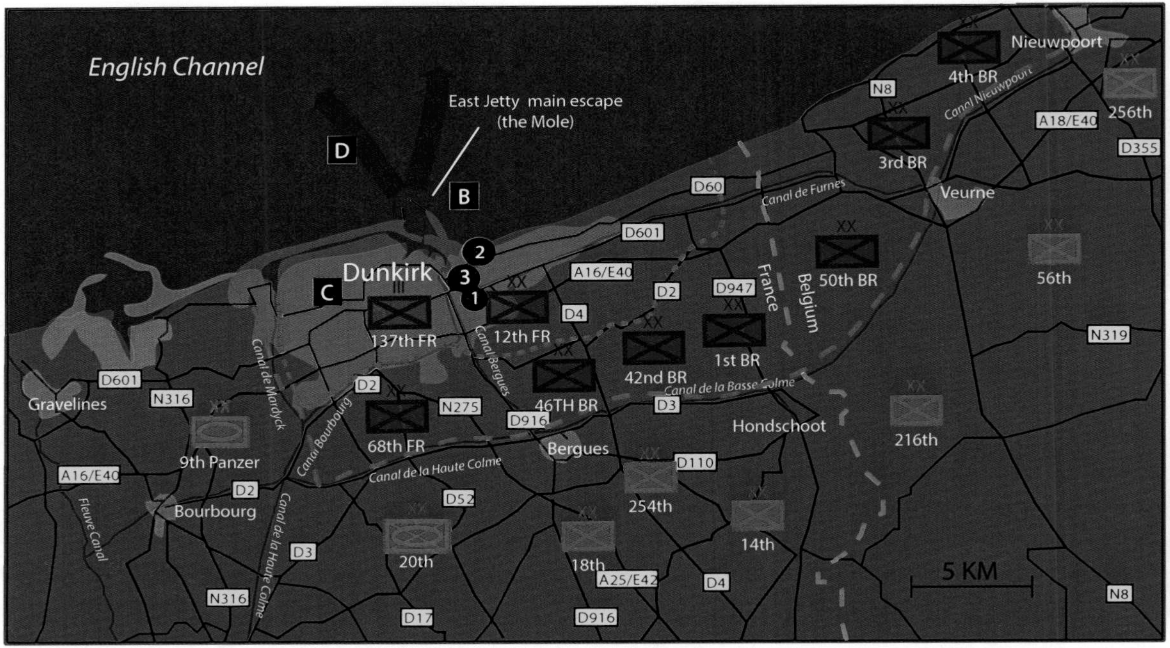
English Channel
East Jetty main escape (the Mole)
D
B
C
Dunkirk
1
2
3
137th FR
12th FR
46TH BR
42nd BR
1st BR
50th BR
3rd BR
4th BR
Nieuwpoort
256th
56th
216th
14th
254th
18th
20th
68th FR
9th Panzer
Gravelines
Bourbourg
Bergues
Hondschoot
Veurne
France
Belgium
Canal de Furnes
Canal Nieuwpoort
Canal de la Basse Colme
Canal de la Haute Colme
Canal Bergues
Canal Bourbourg
Canal de Mardyck
Fleuve Canal
N8
A18/E40
D355
N319
D60
D601
A16/E40
D2
D947
D4
D3
N275
D916
D110
D52
A25/E42
D17
D3
N316
5 KM

The evacuation at Dunkirk harbor. (NARA)

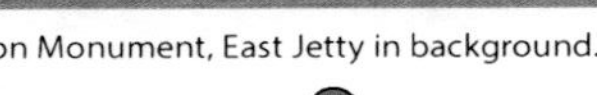
Evacuation Monument, East Jetty in background.

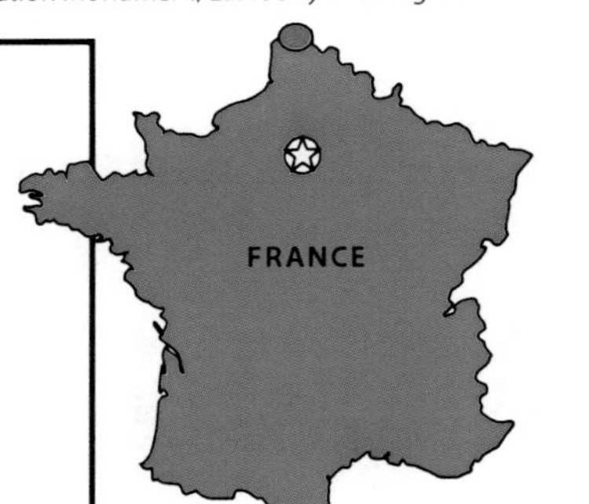
FRANCE

MOVEMENTS:

A. After a May 19 decision that there was no possibility of defeating the German encirclement, the Allies began to plan for an evacuation.
B. On May 26 at 1500 the British initiated Operation Dynamo.
C. May 26-27, the Luftwaffe began intense bombing of the port, including using incendiary bombs to set Dunkirk on fire.
D. May 27, over 20,000 British soldiers were evacuated from Dunkirk.
E. May 31, an all time high, over 68,000 British were evacuated.
F. June 2, the last of the British departed.
G. June 4 at 0345 over 50,000 French were evacuated.
H. June 4 at 0820, the French surrendered Dunkirk to the Germans.

Places to See:

1. British Cemetery and Memorial
2. Evacuation Monument on Shore
3. Museum and Memorial du Souvenir

— — May 30 defensive perimeter
- - - - June 2 defensive perimeter

***Note, to the east is Ostend which has impressive Atlantic Wall remains/museum. Plus also to the west is Calais with more to see for the Atlantic Wall.

BATTLE OF DIEPPE

August 19, 1942

"He will not do it like this a second time."
– Gerd von Rundstedt

SUMMARY: In August 1942, because of recent losses, the Allies were under pressure to achieve a victory. For example, in North Africa the British retreated from Tobruk, while in Russia the Germans conquered Sevastopol. In response, the British General Louis Mountbatten, updating an earlier operation that had been cancelled, designed Operation Jubilee. Its target was the German-controlled port of Dieppe on the French coast. The objective of the Allied force of approximately 6,000 soldiers, mostly Canadian, was to seize and hold the port for a few days. While at the port, they would take out a radar tower, destroy coastal defenses, capture prisoners and gather intelligence. Early in the morning of August 19, 240 ships were on their way to the French coast. First, British commandos landed on the left flank at 0500 to neutralize three each 170mm cannons and four each 105mm cannons poised to destroy any landing at Dieppe. However, only 18 of the commandos reached the battery position. As a result, they couldn't destroy the cannons; instead, they could only shoot at the battery so that the Germans couldn't fully man it. The right flank saw the only success at Dieppe; there, the British commandos, with 50 American Rangers, destroyed the gun battery. Next, Canadian regiments tried landing on the flank beaches, which had received the code names "Blue Beach" (Puys Beach on the left) and "Green Beach" (Pourville Beach on the right). The regiment at Blue Beach took heavy mortar and machine gun fire upon landing. They couldn't create a beachhead and were pinned down by 60 Germans; at day's end, only 30 had escaped. The two regiments on Green Beach had somewhat better success until they reached the River Scie. Then, they were pushed back; only 341 escaped. Thirty minutes after the Blue and Green Beach landings, the main Canadian force landed in the center. Of the 58 tanks committed to the battle, only 27 made it ashore; of those, 15 reached the pebbled beach only to be taken out by withering fire and tank obstacles. At 0700, after bad communication and assessments, the reserve regiment was mistakenly sent to shore and peppered the entire way by the German defense; only 125 of those men would return to England. At 1050, the truth of the situation became apparent and a general retreat was sounded.

OUTCOME: The battle was a complete failure. It resulted in 70 percent casualties and achieved no objectives. However, the information gained from Dieppe would save thousands of lives during Operation Torch in Africa and Operation Overlord in Normandy. Also, the British developed "Hobart's Funnies," which were Churchill and Sherman tanks featuring modifications that overcame German and natural defenses in future landings.

WHAT WAS IT OVER? Pressure to attack the continent, achieve success against the Germans and relieve pressure on the Russian front.

WHO? The Allied forces were made up of 4,963 Canadians, 1,005 British, 15 French, and 50 U.S. Rangers. The Allies committed more than 240 ships, 1,000 aircraft sorties and 58 tanks. The Germans had only to commit the local defense force of approximately 1,500 men and 200 aircraft. The Allies suffered 3,886 casualties. In addition, all their tanks were destroyed, as were 33 landing craft. A destroyer was sunk and 106 aircraft were shot down. The Germans suffered 591 casualties and lost 48 aircraft.

WHEN? August 19, 1942

WHY AT DIEPPE? The Allies wanted to capture a port; compared to other major ports, Dieppe appeared to be weakly defended.

TECHNOLOGY/TACTICS: The British and Canadians introduced the Churchill tank, three of which had flame throwers for use against defensive positions. In terms of aircraft, they used the Spitfire V, which had reached its range limit upon arriving at Dieppe and could spend only a minimal amount of time over the target. The Germans had at their disposal tank obstacles, mines, geography, barbed wire, mortar fire and machine guns. They didn't have to commit any reserves in defense.

QUOTE: "Just as the defending force has gathered valuable experience from... Dieppe, so has the assaulting force...He will not do it like this a second time." – Field Marshal Gerd von Rundstedt

PLACES TO SEE (REFERENCE MAP 39):

1a. ORANGE I, SAINT MARQUERITE MEMORIAL TO NO. 4 BRITISH COMMANDOS: On the right flank (the western edge of battle) is a small memorial stone with an etching of the raid. This location marks the westernmost landing spot of the No. 4 British Commandos on August 19. Attached to them were 50 American Rangers from the 1st Ranger Battalion. Their mission was to land in two locations and destroy the coastal battery, "Hess," containing six each 150mm cannons. Then, as planned, they departed at 0730. It was the only success of Operation Jubilee.
N 49 54.475 E 0 56.097 (49.907917, 0.93495)

1b. ORANGE II, VASTERVIVAL: At this location, some of the No. 4 Commandos landed and attacked upwards through an opening in the cliffs to begin their attack on Battery Hess. There is no memorial here, but the site is worth seeing as a means of appreciating the danger imposed by the terrain, which was covered with barbed wire, mines and machine gun fire.
N 49 55.145 E 0 58.371 (49.919083, 0.97285)

2. BATTERY HESS, MEMORIAL TO NO. 4 COMMANDOS: At this location was "Battery Hess" with six each 150mm cannons. Only this bunker remains;

it contains a memorial to the soldiers. The No. 4 Commandos destroyed the battery, with one lucky shot of a small mortar round hitting the ammunition bunker. The British were in the edge of the woods to the north of town.
N 49 54.499 E 0 58.464 (49.908317, 0.9744)

3. **GREEN BEACH, POURVILLE, MEMORIAL TO THE CAMERON HIGHLANDERS OF CANADA AND THE SOUTH SASKATCHEWAN REGIMENT:** In the small town of Pourville, the westernmost edge of the assault on Dieppe, is a memorial to the forces who landed here. From it you can see how the cliffs and surrounding terrain greatly benefited the Germans. The landings at Green Beach were not that successful due to the intense fire.
N 49 54.983 E 1 01.680 (49.916383, 1.028)

4. **GREEN BEACH, POURVILLE, MEMORIAL BRIDGE PLAQUE TO LIEUTENANT COLONEL C.C. MERRITT:** Merritt was commander of the South Saskatchewan Regiment. At this location, half of Merritt's men were pinned down on the wrong side of the river. Merritt charged the bridge, said, "Come on over, there's nothing to it!" and led his men to attain their objectives. He personally took out several pillboxes and German positions. By the end of the battle Merritt had been wounded and taken prisoner on the beach along with 88 others from his unit.
N 49 55.042 E 1 01.942 (49.917367, 1.032367)

5. **GREEN BEACH, MEMORIAL PARK IN CHURCH LOT, POURVILLE:** At this location is a small park dedicated to the Canadians who fought and died for Dieppe.
N 49 54.964 E 1 01.759 (49.916067, 1.029317)

6. **MUSÉE-MEMORIAL 19 AOÛT 1942:** This is a great little museum and memorial to the battle. It houses before-and-after photographs (many never before seen), an explanatory movie and plenty of artifacts.
N 49 55.512 E 1 04.339 (49.9252, 1.072317)

7. **CHÂTEAU DIEPPE:** This provides a great view of the beachfront overlooking White Beach. This location housed three each 75mm cannons and two each anti-tank cannons. The château was also the battle headquarters of the 2nd Battalion of the 571st Regiment.
N 49 55.392 E 1 04.280 (49.9232, 1.071333)

8. **WHITE BEACH, ROYAL HAMILTON LIGHT INFANTRY MEMORIAL:** On the western edge of the beach, the Hamilton Light Infantry landed with limited success. This site marks an area of White/Red Beach.
N 49 55.671 E 1 04.435 (49.92785, 1.073917)

9. **1ST RANGER BATTALION PLAQUE:** On the boardwalk Rotunde building is a plaque commemorating the 50 American Rangers from the 1st Ranger Battalion who fought with the British commandos to secure the right flank; three of the Rangers were killed in action. They were the first Americans to

die for the liberation of France. In addition, several other plaques commemorate various units of the battle.
N 49 55.597 E 1 04.213 (49.926624, 1.070217)

10. **SQUARE DU CANADA:** Beneath the château (next to a good parking lot and the beach) is Square du Canada. It memorializes the long friendship between France and Canada as evidenced during the battles of World War I, the Dieppe Raid and the liberation in September 1944.
N 49 55.533 E 1 04.228 (49.925546, 1.070464)

11. **RED BEACH, ESSEX SCOTTISH REGIMENT MEMORIAL:** At this location is a memorial to the Essex Scottish Regiment that landed here. Of the 553 men from the battalion, only 52 returned to England that day. As an interesting side note, the monument was built in such a way that every year at 1300 on August 19 the sun shines through a maple leaf onto another maple leaf on the walkway.
N 49 55.836 E 1 04.769 (49.9306, 1.079483)

12. **RED BEACH, FUSILIERS MONT ROYAL REGIMENT MEMORIAL:** A memorial to the fusiliers who landed at this location on the flank of the Essex Regiment. From here you can comprehend how difficult the landing terrain would have been to navigate for the tanks and infantry. This is the area where many of the tanks landed and became stuck in the pebbles.
N 49 55.765 E 1 04.623 (49.929417, 1.07705)

13. **BLUE BEACH, PUY MEMORIAL ROYAL REGIMENT OF CANADA:** At this location, the Royal Regiment landed with the objective of destroying the artillery and anti-aircraft batteries on the eastern flank of Dieppe. The movement was a disaster for the 556 who landed. The smoke screen had dispersed and they arrived in daylight; in addition, the Germans had them flanked. Within four hours, 200 had been killed in action, while another 264 were taken prisoner.
N 49 56.272 E 1 06.583 (49.937867, 1.109717)

14. **YELLOW BEACH, MEMORIAL IN PETIT BERNEVAL TO THE NO. 3 COMMANDOS:** At this location is a stone memorial at the exit of "Yellow Beach." The attack here was not successful because of heavy machine gun fire and the arrival of reinforcements.
N 49 58.075 E 1 11.806 (49.967917, 1.196767)

15. **YELLOW BEACH, REMAINS OF A GERMAN BUNKER:** At this location is a small pathway leading to the remains of a German bunker overlooking the beaches.
N 49 57.736 E 1 10.948 (49.962267, 1.182467)

16. **CANADIAN CEMETERY, DIEPPE:** In this small cemetery, 948 Canadians were laid to rest; 783 were from the Battle of Dieppe.
N 49 53.750 E 1 04.067 (49.895833, 1.067783)

BATTLE OF DIEPPE, AUGUST 19, 1942

MAP 39

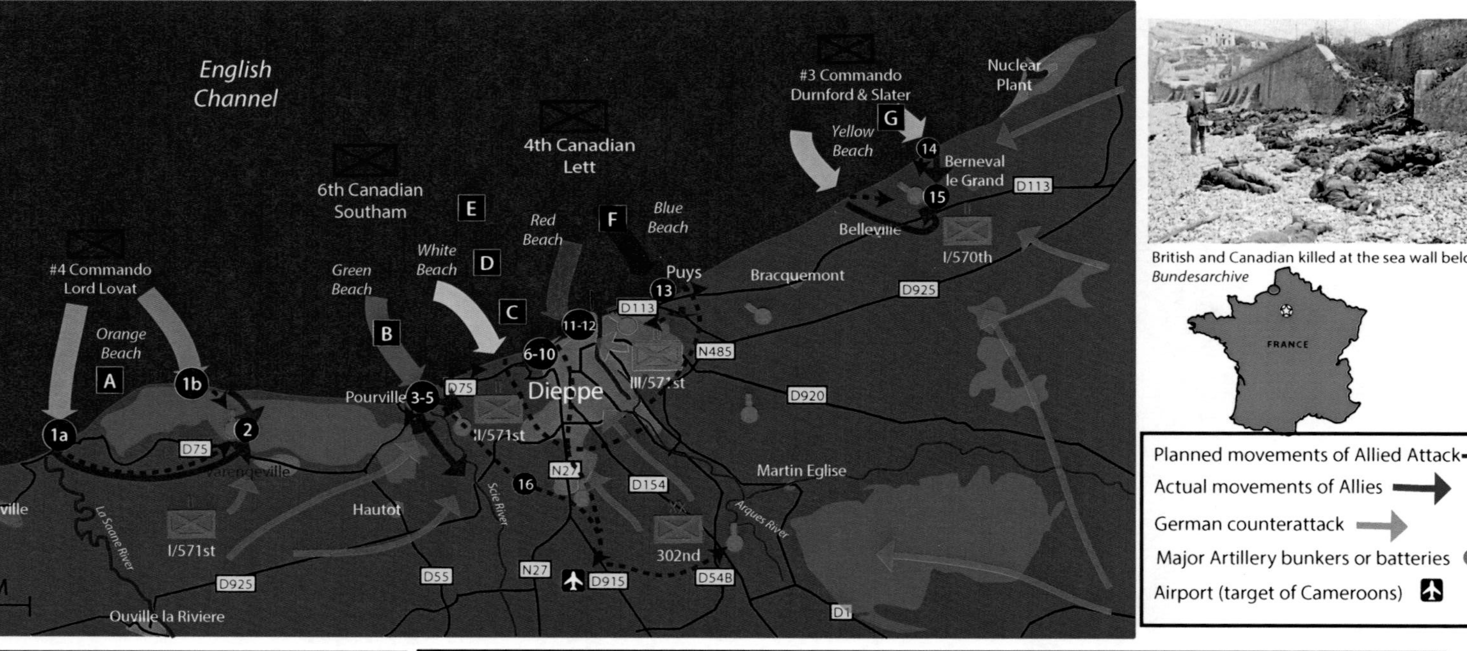
English Channel
#4 Commando Lord Lovat
Orange Beach
A
1a
1b
2
6th Canadian Southam
Green Beach
B
White Beach
D
E
C
4th Canadian Lett
Red Beach
F
Blue Beach
#3 Commando Durnford & Slater
Yellow Beach
G
14
15
Berneval le Grand
Nuclear Plant
Belleville
I/570th
Bracquemont
Puys
13
11-12
6-10
Dieppe
III/571st
II/571st
Pourville
3-5
16
Scie River
Hautot
Quiberville
La Saane River
I/571st
302nd
Martin Eglise
Arques River
Ouville la Riviere
2 KM
D75
D925
D55
N27
D915
D54B
D1
D154
N485
D920
D113
N27

British and Canadian killed at the sea wall below Puy.
Bundesarchive

Planned movements of Allied Attack
Actual movements of Allies
German counterattack
Major Artillery bunkers or batteries
Airport (target of Cameroons)

Places to See:

- 1-2 Orange Beach, Battery Hess(2)
- 3-5 Green Beach, Pourville Memorials
- 6-10 Museum, Chateau, White Beach Memorials, Ranger plaque and Square du Canada.
- 11-12 Red Beach Memorials (Essex and Fusiliers)
- 13 Blue Beach Memorial (Royal Regiment)
- 14 Yellow Beach Memorial (No 3 Commandos)
- 15 Yellow Beach Bunker Remains
- 16 Canadian Memorial and Cemetery

MOVEMENTS: (by beach west to east)

A. Orange Beach, at 0450 the No 4 Commandos and 50 US Rangers climbed the cliffs and successfully destroyed the Gun Battery Hess, by 0730 they departed the beach as planned.

B. Green Beach, the Saskatchewan Regiment and Cameron Highlanders landed at 0520 but on the wrong side of the River Scie, they tried fighting their way through Pourville with bravery but little success, suffering 70% casualties.

C. White & Red Beaches, the main force of Essex and Hamilton Regiments landed at 0530 after 4 destroyers pounded the coast and Hurricanes bombed the defenses. Under a smoke screen they advanced but were stuck at the seawall. Their attack was supposed to take place with the Churchill tanks but they were late in landing.

D. White & Red, 29 tanks landed at Red and White but it was too late, 12 were stuck in the shingle/pebble beach, 2 sank and the remainder could not get into the town because of the German defenses, they bravely returned to the beach to fight on.

E. White & Red, mistakenly the commander sent in the reserve forces at 0700, only to be shot up on approach.

F. Blue Beach, at Puy the Royal Regiment was decimated, of the 556 that landed 200 were KIA and 264 POWs.

G. Yellow Beach, on their approach at 0348 the Commandos came under fire by a patrol, landed and they were only able to snipe at the Gun Battery to harass the Germans from firing accurately on the landing craft and beaches.

8. At 1100, a retreat was called. The withdrawl under fierce flanking fire continued until 1400.

ATLANTIC WALL AND VENGEANCE WEAPONS

SUMMARY: Following are locations for the Atlantic Wall and Vengeance Weapons (V1, V2 and V3). I believe these are the best locations to see well-preserved remains of the Atlantic Wall, and the best museums for the Vengeance Weapons. The Atlantic Wall maintained a series of varying designs from Norway to the Spanish/French border, a distance of over 1,400 kilometers. I am also including sites in northern France that relate to the V1 and V2 weapons, as well as to the lesser-known V3 weapon. This area sits between Dunkirk and Dieppe and is a great place to visit. Many of the farms and parks still hold bunker remains. (The Germans built an amazing number of bunkers.) Hopefully you will be able to see the Cliffs of Dover when you visit!

V1: The V1 (Vergeltungswaffee) was developed by the Luftwaffe as a means of shooting down aircraft. However, Hitler, in his wisdom, wanted to fire the rockets at Allied ground targets. The first V1 was fired on June 13, 1944. By the end of the war more than 9,500 had been fired. The V1 launches killed more than 6,000 people and injured more than 18,000 (primarily in London). The weapon could send an 850-kilogram warhead at a speed of 400 miles per hour and an altitude of 2,000 to 3,000 feet. The Allies could shoot down the flying bomb or nudge it with a wing tip to take it off course. At 400 miles per hour, the weapon almost achieved the top speed of the Spitfire.

V2: The V2 was built by the Wehrmacht at the same Baltic facility, Peenemunde, where the Luftwaffe built the V1. (See the Germany book for information about the museum there). The V2 was first fired in September 1944. By war's end, more than 3,000 had been fired. It traveled at 3,580 miles per hour at an altitude of 55 miles, and had a range of 320 kilometers and a warhead of 1,000 kilograms. It was significantly more deadly than other weapons because no way existed to stop it. It is believed that the 500 V2s that hit London killed more than 2,500 people and wounded more than 6,000.

V3: The V3, called the Hochdruckpumpe (high-pressure pump), had a very unique design. The construction of this location contained three batteries of five 150mm barrels that were in a fixed position on a 45-degree angle pointing at London. The Germans' plan was to fire 500 rounds per hour at the city. The cannons were buried in a massive bunker system that would use perfectly timed explosions to move the shells fast enough to affect London. The battery was never fully operational and ultimately was unsuccessful.

PLACES TO SEE (REFERENCE MAP 40):

1. **MUSEUM (MUSÉE ATLANTIQUE), BATTERIE TODT:** This is a very fascinating museum, built in one of the largest bunkers on the Atlantic Wall. It's set back from the sea in Casement No. 1 of Batterie Todt. Batterie Todt contained four each 380mm naval guns originally made for the Bismarck and Tirpitz. The casement was used to fire at targets in southern England, and also saw limited action during the invasion of Normandy. You can find other casements to the southwest via the road and hiking trail on the coast. The museum features one of the only remaining rail guns. (The other is in Aberdeen Proving Ground in Maryland).
   N 50 50.657 E 001 36.045 (50.844283, 1.60075)

2. **GROSSER KURFAST BATTERY:** This battery is located just off Route Florignzelle. It contained four 280mm cannons surrounded by many bunkers for ammunition, defense and the use of anti-aircraft weapons. The remains lay in fields just off the road. The following geo coordinates take you to the intersection, where you can park nearby. Go straight for a few hundred feet. You'll see remains there, or you can take a right down the path to see additional remains.
   N 50 51.823 E 1 35.680 (50.863717, 1.594667)

3. **GRAND SITE DES DEUX CAPS, CAP GRIS NEZ:** This is a park that contains bunkers along the shore. It's here where some of the strongest German defenses were created. (The site was the shortest distance to the English shore.) On a clear day you can see the White Cliffs of Dover. This site is only two minutes from Batterie Todt.
   N 50 52.151 E 1 35.193 (50.869183, 1.58655)

4. **BATTERY LINDEMAN:** This battery was named after the captain of the sunk Bismarck. The battery housed three massive 406mm cannons. During the war, the battery fired more than 2,200 rounds into England. The battery survived many bombings, but a British railway cannon from across the channel eventually damaged one bunker. A second was damaged during a bombing raid and the third was finally put out of action by the Canadians in September 1944. In the 1980s, the battery area was used to hold backfill during construction of the Chunnel. Today, you can hike and see plenty of bomb craters and bunker remains. Park at the art museum, then go for a hike behind it to the east, where the bunker remains are located.
   N 50 55.339 E 1 43.280 (50.922317, 1.721333)

Musée Memoire 1939–1945 (Musée de la Guerre de Calais): This is a small museum in the central park of Calais. It used to be a German naval bunker.

N 50 57.104 E 1 51.011 (50.951733, 1.850183)

5. **HISTORIQUE DE LA SECONDE GUERRE MONDIALE (AMBLETUESE):** This museum covers the entire war. It contains a few artillery pieces, a Sherman tank and newly developed displays.
   N 50 48.780 E 1 36.376 (50.813, 1.606267)

6. **V3 SITE (LONDON GUN) FORTRESS OF MIMOYECQUES:** This is the location where the Germans began installing the V3. It is also home to a monument commemorating John F. Kennedy's older brother Joseph, who died during a bombing raid on the site.
   N 50 51.067 E 1 45.484 (50.851117, 1.758067)

7. **V2 SITE, LA COUPOLE/THE DOME WIZERNES (NEAR SAINT-OMER):** This is a very well done museum in the former V2 launch preparation building. It covers the German invasion, occupation, retreat and "secret weapons" campaign.
   N 50 42.343 E 2 14.437 (50.705717, 2.240617)

8. **V2 SITE, LE BLOCKHAUS D'ÉPERLECQUES:** Another excellent museum. The Germans built the bunker installation in 1943. It was the first place where V2s were launched and is located just north of Wizernes.
   N 50 49.623 E 2 10.931 (50.82705, 2.182183)

****See the Belgium Guide for information about the Atlantic Wall Museum. It is one of the best museums to visit and is located just northeast of Dunkirk.*

ATLANTIC WALL AND VENGEANCE WEAPONS

MAP 40

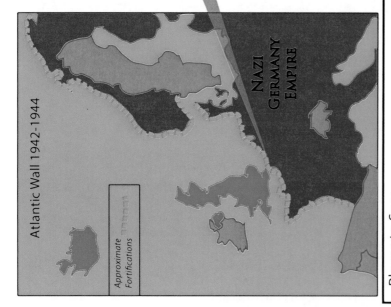

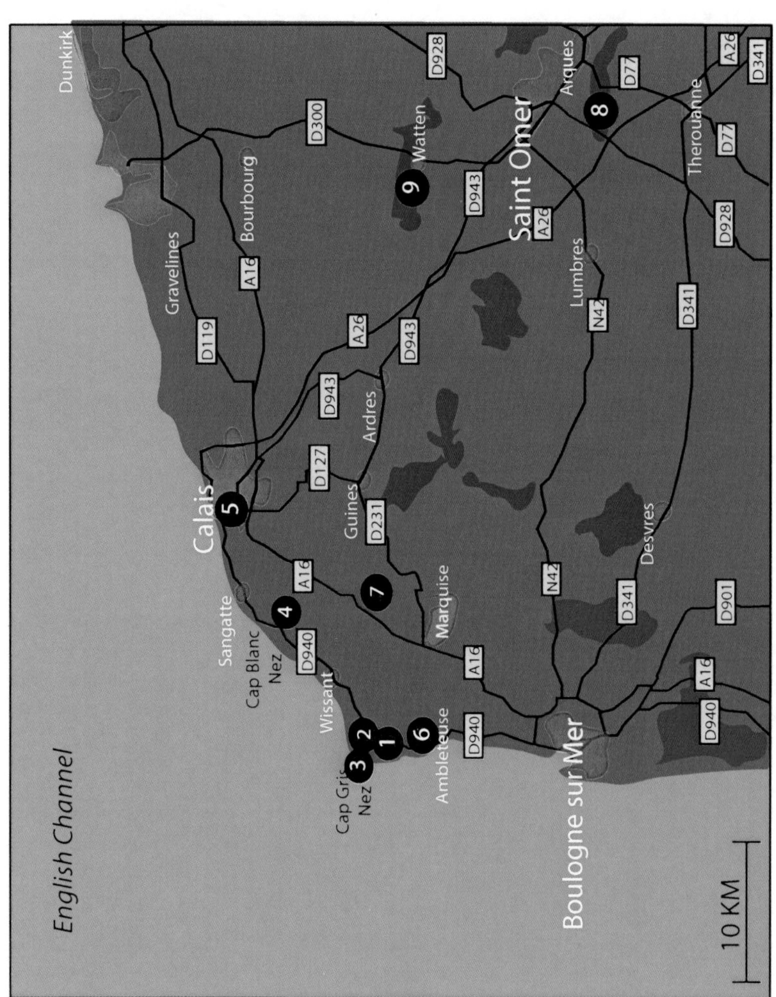
English Channel
Dunkirk
Gravelines
Bourbourg
Calais
Sangatte
Cap Blanc Nez
Wissant
Cap Gris Nez
Ambleteuse
Boulogne sur Mer
Guines
Ardres
Marquise
Desvres
Lumbres
Saint Omer
Watten
Arques
Therouanne
10 KM
Atlantic Wall 1942-1944
Approximate Fortifications
NAZI GERMANY EMPIRE

Places to See:

1. Musee Atlantique, Battery Todt Casement 1
2. Grosser Kurfurst Battery (remains)
3. Cap Gris Nez, remains of bunkers
4. Battery Lindemann (remains)
5. Museum Calais, Musee Memoire
6. Historique de la Seconde Guerre Mondiale (Ambletuese)
7. V3 Site, Fortress of Mimoyecques
8. V2 Site, La Coupole/The Dome Wizernes (near St. Omar)
9. V2 Site, Le Blockhaus D'Eperlecques

There are many places to see and explore. Just going hiking around the area you will see many bunker remains.

MUSEE

Musee Atlantique, Battery Todt. One of four bunkers that housed a 380mm cannon which fired on Southern England. It is about 1 KM from the coast and the scenic overlook. From the overlook, on a clear day you can see the Cliffsof Dover. The photo above right is from the overlook, looking up the French coast.

Leffe

The above photos are of the coast and beach below the overlook. And a photo of a beer break, looking towards Battery Todt (I was waiting for it to open from their lunch break. The area has many hiking paths that you can explore the many bunkers and beautiful views.)

Above, a V1 rocket which were launched from big permanent concrete structures. The V2 rocket, photo right, could be launched from a temporary station and the rocket flew at 3,580 mph and at altitudes above 50 miles! Far right photo, the V3 was built in Poland and France. The "super cannons" were never fully operational. (Bundesarchive Photos)

OPERATION OVERLORD, NORMANDY,

June 6–August 30, 1944

"You are about to embark upon The Great Crusade..."
– Dwight Eisenhower

SUMMARY: Operation Overlord was an Allied operation to gain a foothold in France and to push the Germans back across the Seine River. It lasted from June 6 through August 30, 1944. There is so much to tell and see about this operation. What follows is only a summary of the many battle sites and places to visit.

1. D-DAY/OPERATION NEPTUNE/NORMANDY LANDINGS, JUNE 6, 1944

OVERALL OBJECTIVES: Starting from west to east, U.S. troops were to land at Utah and Omaha Beaches, with airborne paratroopers landing first behind the beachhead to stop German reinforcements from attacking Utah Beach. The Allies' next objective was to secure Cherbourg as soon as possible so that they would have a deep-water port to bring in supplies. Next to Omaha Beach was Port-en-Bessin, a small town and dock. Beyond that were the British Gold Beach, the Canadian Juno Beach and the British Sword Beach. In addition, the British staged an airborne and glider assault so that they could capture gun emplacements and bridges behind the beaches and to stop German reinforcements. After securing the beaches, the British objective was to capture the city of Caen. Finally, once the Americans had captured Cherbourg, the beachhead had been secured and Caen had been taken, the Allies would build up their forces and supplies and move inland. The Allies believed they would need approximately 90 days to complete the mission.

U.S. AIRBORNE ASSAULT: In the west, the "Great Crusade" started at approximately 0040 on June 6 when 6,928 "Screaming Eagles" from the 101st Airborne began their assault. Shortly after their arrival, the next wave, consisting of 6,420 82nd Airborne paratroopers, started its assault. More than 800 Dakota C47 transport aircraft, each carrying 15 to 18 men, had delivered the divisions. Each group of men on the plane was called a "stick." In addition, the C47s towed gliders with men, equipment and field guns. The aircraft departed England at approximately 2230 on June 5, flew at 500 feet below radar and maintained perfect formation over the channel. However, upon arriving over the French coast, the aircraft began to lose formation and many of the paratroopers missed their drop zones. The reasons for the scattered drops were many: German flak, bad weather, ground fog, defective pathfinder DZ beacons, navigation errors and the fact that the C47s were flying too fast and too low. The objective of the 101st was to land north of Carentan and near Sainte-Marie-du-Mont and Saint-Martin-de-Varreville. The objective of the 82nd was to land just west of Sainte-Mère-Église. From both positions, the troops were to capture beach exits, bridges over the Douve River, river locks and main roads, thereby preventing the Germans from sending reinforcements to Utah Beach. Paratroopers from the 101st were dropped as far as 22 kilometers away. Drops for the 82nd went more smoothly, and the 82nd captured Sainte-Mère-Église by 0400. However, both divisions suffered badly, as their men landed in swamps and flooded fields (leading to several drowning deaths). The following days saw intense fighting; D-Day alone inflicted 40-percent casualties on the 101st Airborne Division.

BRITISH AIRBORNE AND GLIDER ASSAULT, Operation Tonga: In the east, the British airborne assault began at 2300 when six Horsa gliders towed by British bombers departed England. Their objective was to capture the bridges over the Caen Canal (Pegasus Bridge) and Orne River. Shortly after the first four gliders left, the rest of the British 6th Airborne departed. Their objectives were to capture bridges, protect against German reinforcements and take out the Merville Battery. The attempt to take the Caen Canal Bridge was a stunning success; all three gliders landed close to their target at 0020, collected themselves (with minimal injuries after hard landings) and took the bridge in 20 minutes. At the same time, the other three gliders landed near their Orne River Bridge objective and captured it within 20 minutes, also after a short fire fight. Next, the large force of more than 700 aircraft and gliders began its assault, carrying the remaining 8,000 paratroopers. Almost all of the units captured their objectives. One of the most famous objectives was the Merville Battery. It had been designated an objective because it was positioned to fire on Sword Beach and was believed to hold high-caliber cannons. The British were scattered throughout the area and Colonel Terence Otway, commander of the 9th Battalion, could gather only 150 of his men for the attack on their objective. Shortly before they assaulted the battery, as planned, Lancaster bombers began their run on it, but all the bombs fell short. By 0430, the commander did not want to delay the raid any longer. His 150-man force attacked the battery, which held 130 Germans. By 0500 the battery had been captured; only six Germans were uninjured, while the British suffered 65 casualties. The battery was silenced for 48 hours, the most critical time, but then reoccupied by the Germans.

BOMBING AND NAVAL BOMBARDMENT: At dawn, 0530, hundreds of heavy and medium Allied bombers dropped their ordnance on the beaches, rocket barges began to fire and battleships began blasting the shoreline. Their goals were to create craters where the ground forces could find protection and to decimate the defenses. The B17s totally missed their targets at Omaha Beach and the Navy's rockets all fell short. This would pose grave problems for the landing parties at Omaha Beach.

BEACH LANDINGS: The landings were scheduled to start after the bombardments, at 0630. To achieve that goal, many of the men boarded their landing crafts at 0330 for the two- to three-hour ride to shore, which was 16-19 kilometers away. Many of the soldiers suffered from seasickness, for which they had been issued dopamine. The landing crafts fought strong currents and the men were soaked with seawater and weighed down by heavy equipment. Within 600 yards of the beaches, the landing crafts received shell fire from mortars, cannons and machine guns. Upon landing in waist-deep water, the soldiers waded in 100 yards before hitting the actual beach, which was full of obstacles such as machine gun fire, mortars, mines and barbed wire. Then they had to travel 500 yards before they reached the German sea wall and bunkers. The soldiers' targets or beach exits were natural "causeways," small valleys between positions that the Allies had given the code names "Dog One exit" and the like. Following is a breakdown of the events at each beach, from west to east.

A. **UTAH BEACH:** Utah Beach was the Allied code name for the 5-kilometer strip of beach on the right flank of the Allied landings; the German designation of this sector of Normandy was W5. The landings came in four waves. During the first wave, 20 Higgins landing crafts arrived, each carrying 30 men. The next waves landed within 30 minutes of each other and included a mix of infantry, engineers and tanks. During the landings, some of the Higgins boats landed 1.5 kilometers off course. The only general to land in the first waves, not to mention the oldest soldier, 57-year-old Brigadier General Theodore Roosevelt, Jr., took command of the beach while under fire and directed the incoming soldiers to objectives and causeways. For his actions he received the Medal of Honor. The resistance at Utah Beach was not as intense due to many factors: fewer bunkers, the fact that the forces defending the beach were primarily "conscripts" from the Russian front, the bombing runs were successful, the terrain was flat, the majority of the "swimming" Duplex Drive tanks made it to shore, and the paratroopers had been fighting inland for several hours behind Utah Beach. By the end of the day, more than 23,000 troops had landed on Utah Beach, along with more than 1,500 vehicles. The Americans attacking Utah suffered only 200 casualties.

B. **POINTE DU HOC:** This was a high cliff between Utah Beach and Omaha Beach that maintained several gun emplacements. It was thought to contain 155mm cannons that could decimate the landings at Utah and Omaha. As a result, the Americans bombed Pointe du Hoc and sent the 2nd Ranger Battalion to take the gun emplacements. They landed around 0600 and climbed the cliffs with ropes, ladders and grappling hooks. They had the support of two offshore destroyers that kept the Germans from killing the Rangers while they scaled the cliff. Upon reaching the top of Pointe du Hoc, the troops found that all the guns had been withdrawn farther inland. They formed a patrol, found the guns in a field and destroyed them. For the rest of the day they fought off German counterattacks. By June 7, the Rangers had suffered 135 casualties out of the 225 men who landed.

C. **OMAHA BEACH:** The deadliest beach on D-Day was Omaha Beach. On a 6-kilometer front the Americans suffered 3,000 casualties in one day. The German defense consisted of 14 "resistance nests" (Widerstandnestern) or strong points guarding the causeways WN 60 through WN 74. The strong points contained 75mm cannons, MG42 machine guns and mortars that faced the length of the beaches. Many of the defenses could not be seen offshore, and they created deadly interlocking fire. The defenses included 7,800 infantry, eight artillery bunkers, 35 pillboxes, four artillery pieces, six mortar pits, 18 anti-tank guns, rocket launcher sites, 85 machine gun sites and six tank turrets. Not all the WNs were strong, either because construction was still underway or because they were "observation posts" with a gun emplacement. The strongest WN on Omaha was WN 62; that section had 35 men manning it, two each 75mm cannons, two each 50mm cannons, three each MGs, one each MG in a "tobruk"(concrete emplacement), two each 5cm mortars, one each double MG anti-aircraft site and trenches for small arms (rifles). In addition, they were manned by the 352nd Division, many of whose members were hardened Eastern Front veterans. Enhancing the German defense was the terrain, which included steep escarpments across the beach, whose crescent shape was ideal for heavy crossfire. At dawn, the Allies sent dozens of bombers overhead to flatten the defenses and create "craters of protection" where landing soldiers could jump to avoid enemy fire. In addition, naval ships bombarded the emplacements. However, unknown to the Allies, the German defenses went largely undamaged from the naval and aerial bombardment. The bombers dropped their bombs just past the defenses, where they fell harmlessly into marshes and fields. The naval bombardment was minimal and scored no direct hits. Unlike on the other beachheads, Omaha's defense was completely intact and ready to slaughter the landing parties. The 29th Infantry Division landed on the right flank of the beach, while the Big Red One, the 1st Infantry Division, landed on the left. At 0636, the first landing craft landed, containing men of Company A, 116th Regional Combat Team of the 29th Infantry Division. Within 10 minutes, they had suffered 75 percent casualties. Included among those were the "Bedford Boys," a group of 30 young men from Bedford, Virginia, 19 of whom died that morning. The landing crafts dropped off the men in waist-deep or deeper water. As soon as some of the landing crafts dropped their ramps, machine gun fire slaughtered all the men the crafts had carried. Soldiers drowned under the weight of their gear, never getting a chance to fight. The men who did wade through the water were met by barriers, mines, mortar rounds and artillery. Then they had 250 to 500 yards to travel before they made it to the cliff face. Ten landing crafts sank due to the swells, while more sank after taking on direct fire from the Germans. Of the 32 Duel Drive tanks scheduled to support the 116th Regimental Combat Team, only five made it to shore and gave direct fire support to the soldiers. The men hesitated to move on from the obstacles, which provided cover, but those areas were predetermined kill zones for the mortar, artillery and machine guns. Of the beach's five exits, D1 (Dog One) in the Dog Green Section on the western edge near Vierville took the most casualties and saw the least progress. In comparison, E1 near Saint-Laurent suffered minimal casualties. At 0700 the second wave landed. They advanced to the wall and quickly created six gaps in the eastern sector by Saint-Laurent. Next, General Norman Cota landed at 0730, organized the men and pushed them off the shore. On the western end, General Maxwell D. Taylor landed and said, "There are two kinds of people staying on the beach, the dead and those who are going to die; now let's get the hell out of here." By 1130, the Americans had taken Saint-Laurent. However, on the western edge, naval destroyers ran aground to provide direct fire support for the landing soldiers. The German positions at D1 were not silenced until nightfall. At the end of the day, one German machine gunner admitted to firing 12,000 rounds and even catching the grass on fire in front of his MG42 because the barrel(s) became so hot. At Omaha, the Germans suffered 1,200 casualties. The 1st Division suffered 1,036, the 29th Division suffered 743 and the Engineer Corps suffered 441.

D. **GOLD BEACH:** Next to Omaha was Port-en-Bessin. Just east of Port-en-Bessin was the beach that had received the code name "Gold Beach." At 0725, the British 50th Infantry Division began to land. Their main objectives were to capture Port-en-Bessin and secure a beachhead that would enable them to build one of the important Mulberry Docks. They landed slightly after the American forces to compensate for the different tidal flow. Overall, the German resistance was not very intense. The aerial and naval bombardments had significant impact, the forces had many Russian conscripts, the terrain was flatter and the German reserves attacked the 101st Airborne instead of counterattacking at Gold Beach. The British adapted to the situation by placing tanks directly on the beach, consequently bringing more firepower to the fight. Also, their tanks, "Hobart's Funnies," were equipped to move obstacles. Within one hour, three exits were open. By 1000, the entire 9-kilometer beachhead had been secured. Then the British began their attack on the inland German gun positions, such as Arromanches and Longues-sur-Mer, and set up attacks on Port-en-Bessin, which didn't fall until June 8. By the end of D-Day, the British had landed 24,970 men on Gold Beach and suffered only 400 casualties.

E. **JUNO BEACH:** Juno Beach was next to Gold Beach and considered the "Canadian Beach." The Canadian 3rd Infantry Division landed at approximately 0745 following a very effective aerial and naval bombardment. Juno Beach was considered the second most heavily fortified beach. The defenses centered around Courseulles and included 11 heavy batteries with 155mm cannons, nine each medium batteries with 75mm cannons and seven each fortified "nests" (WN 26, 27, 28, 28a, 29, 30, 31). Fortunately, the aerial and naval bombardments badly shook the defenses, which included Russian "volunteers." However, many of the guns were still operational and the soldiers, upon landing, faced a 200-yard dash to the sea wall. Despite the German defense, the Canadians fought hard and cleared the sea wall within one hour of landing. By 1200, most of the Canadian forces had landed. The Canadians fought their way 10 kilometers inland, the farthest of all the Allied shore parties on D-Day. By the end of the day, the Canadians had landed 21,400 men and suffered approximately 1,000 casualties.

F. **SWORD BEACH:** The easternmost beach of the Normandy landings, Sword Beach, was between Juno Beach and the Orne River. The 3rd British Infantry Division was the main force to take the beach, along with a detachment of Free French soldiers. Their objectives were to secure a beachhead, link up with the British paratroopers at the Orne and Caen Canal bridges, and capture the city of Caen. The Germans offered relatively weak resistance; the British were inland by 0800. By 1300, the British had linked up with the paratroopers at the Orne River and were on their way to Caen. Suddenly, at 1600, the 21st Panzer Division counterattacked with approximately 100 tanks, mostly Panzer IVs. By 2100, the British armor and infantry had pushed the Germans back and knocked out more than 50 of their Panzers. After that battle, the British landed 28,800 men on the beachhead, suffering only 683 casualties. Next, Bernard Montgomery prepared for the Battle for Caen.

June 10, 1944, Massacre of Oradour Sur Glane: On this day, near Poitiers six hundred and forty-two villagers, including women and children, were massacred by a platoon of German 2nd SS Panzer Division Das Reich on their march to Normandy.

2. BATTLE FOR THE COTENTIN PENINSULA, JUNE 6-30

The American objective after the D-Day landings was to wheel to the right (west) and capture the Cotentin Peninsula, which contained the vital deep-sea port of Cherbourg. Cherbourg was a necessary conquest if the Allies wanted to bring in large amounts of materiel, food, munitions, medicine and fuel directly from America.

A. BATTLE OF CARENTAN, JUNE 10-14: The port town of Carentan was a crossroads vital to linking the beaches of Utah and Omaha. The 101st Airborne Division received the task of capturing the town. Once captured, the Allies could cut off the Cotentin Peninsula and move in to capture Cherbourg. On June 10, after an artillery bombardment, the U.S. forces attacked with two airborne battalions (approximately 800 men) against four battalions of Germans who were defending the town and waiting for reinforcements. On Highway N13 between the Douve River and Carentan, the 3rd Battalion/502nd Regiment took heavy casualties as they advanced under mortar, artillery and machine gun fire. The N13 road became known as "Purple Heart Lane" because the Americans suffered 67 percent casualties on it. They had to advance down this narrow causeway because the terrain on either side was flooded. In addition, they had four bridges to cross as choke points. Upon reaching the edge of town, Lieutenant Colonel Robert G. Cole of the 502nd called in artillery to silence the German fire. The artillery bombardment did not silence the Germans. At 0615, still under intense fire, Cole called his men to fix bayonets and 70 men charged the German lines in an action later called "Cole's Charge." Fierce hand-to-hand fighting ensued and the Americans pushed the Germans out of their defensive positions. Cole would receive the Medal of Honor for leading the charge and displacing the Germans. After additional fighting the next day (June 12), Carentan was captured. The 501st and 506th Battalions were assigned to capture and defend the high ground, Hill 30, south of Carentan. There, on June 13, they defended against newly arrived German reinforcements. Easy Company of the 506th Division (known as the "Band of Brothers") held its ground against the fierce attack for over four hours of fighting until 60 Sherman tanks from the 2nd Armored Division were re-directed to the battle and crushed the German thrust. This action became known as the Battle of the Bloody Gulch. At Sainte-Mère-Église, the 82nd Airborne held out against fierce German counterattacks (for example, at La Fière Bridge over the Merderet River, where they had been outgunned and outnumbered). As a result of their heroism, the Americans stopped the German attacks and created a defensive line from the 101st in Carentan to the 82nd at Sainte-Mère-Église. The Americans' next mission was to capture the Cotentin Peninsula, where German forces continued to hold out. In particular, the Americans wanted to capture the batteries at Azeville and Crisbeque. The Germans held out for six days, sinking three destroyers and firing on Utah Beach.

June 15, Hitler believed the "real" invasion had not started.

B. BATTLE OF CHERBOURG, JUNE 15-30: After the Battle of Carentan, the U.S. forces, VII Corps, under the command of Lt. General J. Lawton Collins, drove west to cut off the peninsula from German reinforcements. The Germans under Field Marshal Erwin Rommel were commanded to withdraw to the defenses of Cherbourg. On June 18, after the Americans crossed the peninsula, Collins sent three divisions north (the 4th Infantry Division on the right, the 79th Infantry Division in the middle and the 9th Infantry Division on the left). They were reinforced by artillery and tank battalions, and their goal was to capture Cherbourg. There the Germans fought a fierce delaying defense while simultaneously destroying the port facilities. The city's 21,000 defenders refused to surrender. Then, on June 22, Collins ordered an all-out assault of Cherbourg. By June 26, the main fortress, Fort du Roule, was captured. The entire city was captured by July 1. During the Peninsula operations, the Americans suffered 22,000 casualties. The Germans suffered 8,000 casualties, plus 30,000 captured. The Germans had effectively destroyed the port facilities; as a result, the port would not be usable for another four weeks.

3. BATTLES FOR A BREAKOUT – CAEN AND OPERATION COBRA (ST. LO FRONT)

After the landings, the British and Canadian objective was to capture the city of Caen and the vital Carpiquet airfield, as well as to stop German attacks in Normandy. The 21st Panzer Division had stopped its initial attack on D-Day. Even after several large operations over the course of 40 days, the city would not fall. The battle lasted much longer than anticipated and Montgomery received criticism for his lack of aggression and overall success.

A. OPERATION PERCH, JUNE 7-14: After the D-Day attempt on Caen, a second attempt to take Caen, called Operation Perch, was staged. Its objective was to capture Hill 112, located southwest of Caen, and the high point overlooking the city and Normandy. Montgomery's plan was to implement a large "pincher movement" using two armored divisions and two infantry divisions on either side of Caen. They were up against three Panzer divisions and one infantry division. The Germans immediately shut down the attack in the east.

The pincher in the west took advantage of a gap the Americans had created to force German withdrawal in the area of Caumont. On June 13, the British 7th Armoured Division poured into that gap on the edge of Villers-Bocage, where a famous tank battle took place (see below). The result was a damaging defeat of the British. Also at the town of Le Mesnil-Patry, on June 11, the Germans defeated the Canadians, who lost more than 50 tanks and 200 men in a single afternoon.

VILLERS-BOCAGE, JUNE 13: During Operation Perch, the British attempted to flank the city of Caen and improve their position of attack so that they could take the city from the west. This led them into Villers-Bocage—and into the sights of the SS's deadliest tank commander. Lieutenant Michael Wittman was commanding officer of a heavy tank company consisting of 20 Tiger tanks (only five of which were in Villers) and was a legend among the Germans. He had killed 117 Russian tanks in the Eastern Front, then had been transferred to France. On June 13, Wittman was resting and completing maintenance tasks on his six Tigers in Villers-Bocage. That morning, a column of 7th Armoured British tanks, Bren gun carriers and halftracks advanced into the town and stopped along the main road. Wittman, only 200 meters away, charged the column on the main road (Hill 213) and started taking out the British tanks and armored carriers that had lined up. He went down the main road, blasting the British point blank while his other four tanks (the engines in one of his Tigers were not working) engaged the tanks on Hill 213. After blasting his way into town, Wittman's tank was damaged by a Sherman Firefly shooting from the far end of town. He turned to retreat to Hill 213 but was hit again, this time by a 6-pounder anti-tank gun crew that damaged one of his drive sprockets. He and his crew abandoned the tank and escaped on foot. In total, Wittman's company had stopped and eliminated the British brigade's advance by knocking out 27 tanks, 14 halftracks and numerous other transport vehicles, all within the space of one hour. Operation Perch ceased and the British retreated after the Germans occupied the town. Wittman was promoted to colonel a week later and was invited to teach at the armor training grounds, but he wanted to stay in the fight. He was killed on August 8 by a Sherman Firefly tank that attacked his flank during Operation Totalize. In the end, Wittman was credited with 138 tank kills and 132 anti-tank gun kills.

B. **OPERATION EPSOM, JUNE 26-30:** On June 26, after additional men, tanks and materiel arrived in Normandy, Montgomery launched Operation Epsom with the entire VII Corps. His goal was to capture the high ground south of Caen (Hill 112). The British and Canadians attacked with 60,244 men, 736 artillery pieces and air support. They initially gained 9 kilometers and a foothold on Hill 112, but were stopped by the German 1st and 2nd SS Panzer Corps. Once they realized that the Germans had surrounded them on three sides, the British withdrew from the hill. They suffered 4,000 casualties, while the Germans lost 3,000 men. Montgomery called off the attack on June 30.

C. **OPERATION WINDSOR, JULY 4-5:** The Canadians were assigned the task of taking the town of Carpiquet and the Carpiquet Airfield, located just west of Caen. Germans defended the airfield with pillboxes, 88mm battery, mines, 10 tanks and barbed wire. At 0515, the 8th Canadian Infantry Brigade, supported by two armored tank regiments, attacked the town and airfield. They were met by deadly rocket, mortar and artillery fire. At day's end, the Canadians were holding the town and repulsing German counterattacks. However, they weren't able to take the airfield. Only after Operation Charnwood would the Allies take the airfield. The Germans still held Hill 112 overlooking Caen and the airfield.

D. **OPERATION CHARNWOOD, JULY 7-9:** Montgomery launched the next attack on July 7. It was a frontal assault on Caen and its objective was to capture the northern half of the city. Operation Charnwood began when more than 300 Allied bombers destroyed the city, in theory because they wanted to kill the Germans and eliminate their bunkers. Next, three infantry divisions and three armored divisions fought their way into the rubble of Caen. On July 9, the operation ceased after the Allies reached the center of the city and the river crossings. The bombing of the city is considered one of the most futile and destructive Allied bombings of the war. It hadn't killed any Germans or destroyed any of their equipment because the Germans were primarily outside the southern part of the city. The rubble remaining after the bombing slowed the Allied offense, while the attack left more than 30,000 people homeless and killed 1,000 civilians. However, the operation was considered a partial success, though also an example of "too little, too late." The British suffered 3,800 casualties and 80 tanks destroyed. The Germans suffered approximately 2,000 casualties and 20 tanks destroyed.

E. **OPERATION JUPITER, JULY 10-12:** On July 12, the Allies suffered another setback. Operation Jupiter called for the 43rd Wessex Infantry Division to attack Hill 112 upon a bombardment by 100 artillery pieces. After two days of fighting, the attack failed. The infantry division suffered more than 2,000 casualties.

F. **OPERATION GOODWOOD, JULY 18-20:** On July 18, the British and Canadians finally captured the city of Caen, but fell short of the "breakthrough" that Montgomery had promised. The attack started with 700 artillery pieces firing more than 250,000 rounds and 942 Allied bombers leveling five villages to the southeast of Caen, where German forces had accumulated. Next, the Canadian ground forces attacked from the west with the objective of Verrières Ridge. The British objective was originally Falaise, but Montgomery "limited the thrust" to Bourguebus Ridge. The Allies committed three armored divisions, two infantry divisions and a total of 1,100 tanks. The Germans defended and counterattacked with the remnants of three armored divisions, two heavy tank battalions, four infantry divisions which included 370 tanks and more than 300 artillery pieces, including 78 each 88mm cannons on Bourguebus Ridge alone. The initial bombardments were very effective, but the Germans were able to regroup for defense and counterattacks. Montgomery couldn't provide his "breakthrough," but the Allies did capture the city of Caen. In addition, they expanded the front by 11 kilometers and pushed the Germans off Bourguebus Ridge. Citing bad weather, Montgomery ended the operation on July 20. The Allies suffered a total of 4,837 casualties and lost more than 469 tanks in just three days. The Germans suffered 2,000 casualties and lost 80 tanks. Because Operation Goodwood had not led to a breakthrough in the German line, the Americans would implement Operation Cobra as an attempt to achieve a breakout in the west.

July 17, Rommel was hospitalized after being strafed and wounded in his vehicle by a British aircraft patrol near Falaise.

July 20, Operation Valkyrie, an assassination attempt on Hitler implemented by German officers, took place.

OPERATION COBRA, JULY 24-30: By July 24, the Allies had been fighting for eight weeks and had advanced only about 32 kilometers. St. Lo had just been captured at the cost of 5,000 casualties. Bradley needed a "breakout" plan, so he created "Operation Cobra," which called for saturation bombing in a small 6,000-yard by 2,200-yard belt, followed by a concentrated attack on a 7,000-yard front to break through the German resistance. On July 24, more than 2,000 aircraft began to bomb the target area, but dropped their bombs short, causing more than 200 American casualties. As a result, the operation was postponed until July 25. Again, at 0930 on July 25, more than 1,000 cannon opened up and more than 2,000 bombers began their run. In a very costly mistake, the bombers made their run from north to south, ignoring orders to bomb from east to west parallel to the lines. As a result, more than 500 U.S. soldiers were wounded or killed. Many, including Lieutenant General Lesley J. McNair, were never found. However, the U.S. forces regrouped and attacked through the gap. Initially, the Panzer Lehr Division offered little resistance, as it had taken the brunt of the bombing. To their west, a Fallschimjager Division went untouched. The German forces regrouped and put up a stiff resistance, allowing the Americans to gain only 2,200 yards. Next, three more American divisions poured into the Germans and decimated the Panzer Lehr Division. On July 27, Coutances was captured, followed by Avranches on July 30. Operation Cobra had worked; it smashed a hole through the German forces. The Allies were out of the bocage and into better terrain. The Americans raced forward and began to outflank the Germans.

OPERATION BLUECOAT, JULY 30–AUGUST 7: In an effort to help the Americans exploit their western gains from Operation Cobra, Montgomery attacked from Caumont between the Vire River and the Orne River to capture the crossroads at the town of Vire and the high ground at Mont Pinçon. The British XXX Corps led the attack with the British VIII Corps on their right flank. The operation began with an artillery preparation and a 1,000-aircraft bombing run. Next, the ground forces attacked under cover of thick fog. The Germans were under strength and the British quickly exploited a breakthrough until the XXX Corps advance was slowed due to the terrain and land mines. On August 2, the advance had stalled and the British commander was relieved of command for inaction. By August 6, the force had captured Vire; by August 8, it had captured Mont Pinçon. However, the Germans had been given additional time to reorganize. Like similar

British attacks, Operation Bluecoat achieved no major breakthrough, though it did wear down the Germans further.

BATTLE OF MORTAIN, AUGUST 7-13: After the American breakout, instead of allowing his forces to retreat, regroup and create a better defense, Hitler commanded Günther von Kluge (the supreme German commander in the west) to counterattack at Mortain in an effort to split the American forces at Avranches. Against their wills, the German commanders gathered up the remains of four divisions (the 116th Panzer Division, the 2nd Panzer Division, the 1st SS Panzer Division and the 2nd SS Panzer Division, as well as the regiment remains of the 17th SS Panzer). In total, they had approximately 300 armored vehicles on hand for Operation Luttich. On August 7, the Germans began their attack and took the American defenders by surprise. The Germans initially took the town of Mortain, but couldn't dislodge the 30th Infantry Division, 120th Infantry Regiment, which held the high ground, Hill 314 (some sources say Hill 317), L'Abbaye Blanche and Hill 285. After air resupply, the Americans held out against the 2nd SS Panzer Division for six days, but at a high cost: 300 out of approximately 950 men were killed. In all, the Americans suffered more than 6,000 casualties during the counterattack. The Germans suffered greatly due to Allied air support and artillery, losing more than 150 tanks and many men. By August 13, the Germans received commands to go on the defensive and were pushed out of Mortain. At the same time, General George S. Patton's newly established 3rd Army was quickly moving southeast, capturing Le Mans on August 8. The combination of Patton's southeast drive and Kluge's thrust west created a pocket around the German Seventh and Fifth Armies. The Allies saw the opportunity to surround and destroy the remaining German forces of Normandy and attacked toward Falaise, creating the "Falaise Pocket."

4. **FALAISE POCKET, AUGUST 8-21:** After seeing the German counterattack at Mortain, the Allies took note of Germany's precarious position and saw the opportunity to crush the Seventh and Fifth Armies. The following are battles related to the Falaise Pocket.

A. **OPERATION TOTALIZE, AUGUST 8-11:** On August 8, the British and Canadians initiated "Operation Totalize." Its objective was to capture the town of Falaise (32 kilometers south) and trap the German armies. Blocking the Allies' advance was Verrières Ridge, a dominating ridge 5 kilometers south of Caen at which the British and Canadians had suffered severe losses when they had tried to take it throughout July. At 2330 on August 7, five British and Canadian divisions attacked using a rolling barrage and converted tanks for armored personnel carriers. By noon on the following day, August 8, they had captured the ridge. Next, the Polish, British and Canadian forces pushed south to Falaise. During the advance, the Allies suffered heavy damage in the initial attack on Hill 195 south of Grainville, where 50 German tanks held off 600 Allied tanks. On August 9, the Canadian Armored Division lost most of its tanks while attacking Hill 195. On August 10, the hill was finally taken and the Germans withdrew to another line of defense. Although the Allies had made advances, the encirclement had failed. Therefore, Operation Totalize was halted on August 11. Again, Montgomery had come up well short of his objective.

August 15, Operation Dragoon, Allied landings began in Southern France.

B. OPERATION TRACTABLE, AUGUST 14-20: Operation Tractable was initiated as another attempt to close the Falaise Pocket and trap the German Fifth and Seventh Armies in two pinchers. The objective was to capture Hill 159 overlooking Falaise. Then, the Allies would capture Falaise and link up with the Americans, who had captured Argentan on August 12. On August 14, the Canadians attacked south with the Polish 1st Armor Division on their left. The Canadians struggled to capture their objectives because of the fierce defense of the 12th SS Panzer Division and other units. Not until August 16 did the Canadians capture Hill 159, and it wasn't until August 18 that they finally cleared Falaise. In the meantime, Patton, without orders, began driving east to the Seine River for a larger envelopment. On August 16, the commanders changed the Allied meeting point to Chambois, a little farther east than Argentan. On August 16, Kluge was relieved of command; he committed suicide shortly afterward. Hitler assigned Field Marshal Walter Model to save the situation. The same day, Hitler finally called for an all-out withdrawal to the Seine River. By August 18, the Germans were fighting for their lives, trying to keep an exit open so they could escape to the Seine. They maintained organization by setting up bridge "commanders" and specific routes for all forces. However, their detailed plan quickly fell apart as the Falaise Pocket shrank and they were hit by artillery and strafed by aircraft. The Germans had to retreat northeast over the Dives River, which was really just a small canal. They had only three crossing points left over the Dives. In the north, the bridge at Saint-Lambert (as well as a foot bridge) was under attack by the Canadians, who had just taken the town of Trun. In the middle was the "Ford at Moissy," and in the south was the bridge over the Dives at Chambois, which the Polish 1st Armored and American 90th were attacking in an attempt to close the gap. On August 18 at 1240, the Polish 1st Armored Division, 1st Tank Regiment, reached the high ground (called Hill 262 North) overlooking all three crossings, next to the towns of Mont Ormel and Coudehard. The Poles had approximately 87 tanks and 2,000 men to hold the hill, while other elements fought toward Chambois to meet up with the Americans and capture Hill 262 South. The Poles had attempted to capture the hill, but did not have the numbers and strength to do so. The German route—left and right of the dominating Hill 262 North—became known as the "Corridor of Death" because the Germans found themselves shelled and strafed while stuck on small roads. On the night of August 19, the Poles and the American 90th linked up to "close the gap," but did not have sufficient strength to hold back the swarms of Germans. Also on August 19, Model ordered elements that had already crossed into safety to hit the Polish on their eastern flank so that the escape route would remain open. Several elements of German paratroopers attacked the Poles from the south. On August 20, the Germans were still well organized and able to commit several tanks, approximately 800 well-equipped men and artillery to keep the roads open for several hours. The Polish fought gallantly, suffered numerous losses and eventually ran out of ammunition. They continued holding Hill 262 North and calling in artillery on the fleeing Germans, who retreated via the narrow roads that ran directly around Hill 262 North.

> The fighting continued throughout the day. The Polish defended against more than eight concentrated attacks that came from all sides. They were very low on ammunition and, in many cases, were forced to use bayonet charges as a means of dislodging German pockets. Luckily, the Polish had a Canadian artillery liaison officer who helped them direct defensive fire. At 0400 on August 21, the Germans attacked again in force, but the Canadian 4th Armoured Division finally broke through. The Poles held on, surrounded for three days. In all, they suffered 1,600 casualties, of which 325 had been killed in action, 1,002 had been wounded in action and 114 were missing in action.

On August 22, the gap was finally closed. The Germans were devastated; as they would never recover the men and equipment they had lost. The 12th SS Division had lost 95 percent of its armor, and now maintained only 10 tanks and 300 men. In total, the Germans lost approximately 500 tanks, more than 2,500 trucks and vehicles, 300 pieces of artillery, 15,000 soldiers who had been killed in action, 20,000 soldiers who had been wounded in action and 50,000 soldiers who had been captured. The Allies also suffered greatly, with approximately 5,000 casualties.

In the south, the Americans could have pushed harder, but Montgomery, commander of the Allied Ground Forces, ordered Patton to halt on August 13. Again, Montgomery would receive criticism for his lack of aggression and his decision to halt the Americans. He would also be blamed for relying on the Polish and Canadians to close the gap. Nearly 50,000 Germans escaped, including some of the diehard SS divisions that the Allies should have crushed. As a result, these divisions would go on to kill more Allies in Operation Market Garden and the Battle of the Bulge.

OUTCOME: As a result of Operation Overlord, Paris was liberated on August 25. The combination of Operation Overlord and Operation Dragoon in southern France led the Germans to withdraw from France by mid-September. Sometimes overlooked in summaries of this time period is the capture of Rome on June 4, right before D-Day. The Germans would hold out until May 1945 in some locations, such as the Channel Islands and Saint-Nazaire, which the Allies left the Germans to defend so that they (the Allies) wouldn't expend lives on tactically undesirable locations. Overall, the operation was a success, but certainly fell short of its goals. After 90 days, the Allies had predicted they would be at the Loire River, near Orléans, approximately 322 kilometers inland. Consider the actual results: after 90 days, they were only about 161 kilometers inland and had achieved gains of less than 3 kilometers a day with more than 2,400 casualties for each 1.5 kilometer gained!

WHAT WAS IT OVER? Freedom

WHO?

ALLIES: America, the United Kingdom, Canada, Poland, France, Greece, Czechoslovakia, the Netherlands, Australia, New Zealand, Belgium and Norway. The attacking force contained 1,000,000 troops organized into 47 divisions (21 American, 19 British, five Canadian, one Polish and one French). By the end of the day on D-Day, 75,250 British and Canadian troops, 57,500 U.S. troops, 15,500 American paratroopers and 7,900 British paratroopers were on the shores of France. By the end of August, the number of Allied forces was more than 2,000,000.

ALLIED Casualties: 240,000 men, 4,000 aircraft and 4,000 tanks (America: 31,000 killed in action and 95,000 wounded; the United Kingdom and Canada: 25,200 killed in action and 58,600 wounded; aircrew casualties: 28,000 in only 90 days!)

AXIS Powers: Germany. The defending forces initially numbered 450,000. By July 25 that number had dropped to 380,000.

AXIS Casualties: 210,000 men, 2,200 tanks and 2,100 aircraft

WHEN? June 6–August 21, 1944

WHY AT NORMANDY? The British Prime Minister, Winston Churchill, wanted to attack the "soft underbelly of the Continent" through the Balkans and into Vienna so as to not only invade Germany but also stop the Russians. The Americans refused and wanted to land in France so that they would be closer to supply lines in England. Both nations had learned from Dieppe that a port should not be a landing site. Instead, they needed a landing site that would facilitate aircraft support. Pas de Calais was the shortest distance from England to France, but was heavily defended and contained difficult terrain past its shore. The Allies chose Normandy for its better geography, weaker defenses and space for inland operations. However, in choosing Normandy, the Allies would need to capture a deep sea port for logistics. Therefore, Cherbourg became the Allies' major objective. The U.S. forces landed in the west and turned to capture Cherbourg; the British and Canadians captured Caen. The landings were planned and scheduled for May 1, but delayed to await the arrival of additional landing craft.

TECHNOLOGY: Following is a short list of "new technologies" that each side used. Some were successful, some weren't.

A. ALLIES:

MULBERRIES: For vital logistics support, the Allies created portable prefabricated concrete harbors called Mulberries. Two were built secretly in England, then towed to Normandy. Once the first was operational, on D+10, it facilitated the offloading of 78 vehicles every 38 minutes. A fierce Channel storm in mid-June destroyed one of the anchored Mulberries off Omaha Beach. Remains of the second are still visible at Gold Beach.

FUEL, PLUTO: To obtain the vast amounts of fuel they required, the Allies came up with PLUTO (Pipeline Under The Ocean). This was another secret operation and marked the first-ever use of an underwater fuel pipeline.

HOBART'S FUNNIES: From lessons learned at Dieppe, the British developed specialized tanks named after the British military engineer Percy Hobart. These creatively designed tanks were very successful. They used the chasses of Sherman and Churchill tanks to overcome obstacles. For example, the "flail tank" used rotating chains to smash the ground in search of mines. Hobart also designed mobile bridges, trench crossers, flamethrowers and much more. The Americans opted not to use the Hobart's Funnies in Normandy, which proved to be a fatal mistake. Instead, the Americans used the rather unsuccessful Dual Drive (DD) Sherman, which had a propeller and snorkel that enabled it to swim ashore. Unfortunately, many DD tanks didn't make it that far.

HIGGINS BOATS: Very effective flat-bottom boats for landing troops. Each held approximately 30 men. The design was eventually upgraded to facilitate the moving of large groups of men and vehicles.

TANKS USED: The Americans used the M4 Sherman tank with a 75mm main gun, the M10 tank destroyer with a 76mm high-velocity gun, the M5 Stuart tank with a 37mm cannon, and bulldozer and hedgehog tanks to help plow through the French bocage. The British used M4 Sherman variants, the Churchill tank and the Cromwell tank. The British also designed the Sherman "Firefly," which featured a 17-pound, high-velocity 76mm cannon that could knock out the Tiger tanks. They assigned one Firefly to each platoon.

WEAPONS: The Americans used the very successful M1 Garand semi-automatic rifle, which brought more firepower to the fight as compared to the British and German bolt-action rifles. The Americans also used the Browning Automatic Rifle (BAR) a the full auto squad gun, which had a 20-round magazine as compared to the British Bren Gun, which had a 30-round magazine. In addition, the Americans used the very reliable and effective .30-calibre Browning machine gun and the "Ma-Deuce," M2 .50-caliber heavy machine gun. For close-quarter combat, the Americans had the .45-caliber Thompson, the .45-caliber "Grease Gun," and British had the 9mm Sten gun.

ALLIED NAVY: Used 6,950 vessels throughout the invasion, approximately 1,200 warships and 4,000 transports.

AIRCRAFT: The C-47 Dakota transport aircraft was very effective; more than 800 were used to drop Allied paratroopers on D-Day and to continue moving cargo and providing air resupplies. Also, the Allies had the fighter and bomber support of B17s, Lancasters, B25s, P-47s, P51s, P38s, Spitfires, Typhoons and Tempests.

GLIDERS: In addition to the C-47, the Allies developed gliders that were towed by Dakotas or bombers. They were cheap but risky methods of moving paratroopers and equipment. The British built the "Horsa" and the Americans built the "Waco" (constructed in Waco, Texas).

B. GERMANS:

ATLANTIC WALL: Still mostly intact, the wall stretched from the French/Spanish border to the Norwegian/Finnish border. It bristled with hardened defenses, pillboxes, bunkers, trenches and tunnels. Early in 1944, Rommel was assigned to the defenses; he saw that the defenses were woefully inadequate and began immediate upgrades. By D-Day, more than six million mines were in place in Northern France alone. On D-Day, the Allied ships had to survive large naval mines, large-caliber artillery, U-boats and torpedo boat attacks. When the landing boats disembarked, the troops faced the tide, artillery fire, mortar rounds, posts with mines attached, hedgehogs (angled "x" iron), Belgian gates (7-foot by 9-foot iron tank defenses taken from Belgium), more posts with mines, and ramp posts with mines. Next, the soldiers ran out of the landing craft in waist-deep water, 500 yards from the Atlantic wall and cliffs. At low tide they were dropped at the Belgian gates, where they moved forward past the poles with mines. Then, the pre-ranged machine gun and mortar fire started. Still moving forward, the soldiers and tanks hit a small wall, rocky shingles and sand dunes. Next, they ran into barbed wire, with still another 200 yards to go before they reached the cliffs. The Germans poured down artillery, mortars and machine gun fire. Still visible at the defenses are round "Tobruks" (concrete pits) for the machine guns. Octagonal Tobruks were used for mortars. Inland, the Germans had defense in depth, with additional pillboxes and cannons guarding the natural valleys and exits from the beaches. Also, Rommel ordered that the fields be flooded so that the paratroopers faced a disadvantage. In addition, he placed steel spikes known as "Rommel's Asparagus" in the open fields to destroy landing gliders.

GERMAN NAVY: The German Navy was virtually non-existent on D-Day. A couple of torpedo boats made attack attempts, but were repelled rather quickly. In addition, few U-boats were spotted during D-Day. On June 4, four German destroyers were sunk in the Channel, but otherwise few attacks occurred.

LUFTWAFFE: The German Air Force had two FW190s in action on D-Day. In total, the Germans had approximately 150 fighter aircraft available for use in Northern France and Belgium. Following D-Day, Allied air power overwhelmed these aircraft. Aircraft such as Stukas, BF 109s and JU-88s provided infantry support, but only after nightfall.

WEAPONS: The Germans had the much-feared MG 42 "Burp gun," which was developed as a less-expensive (i.e., less manpower and less steel) replacement for the MG 34. It was also lighter and could fire 1,800 rounds per minute. (The MG 42 served as an inspiration for the American M60). A version of the MG 42 is still in use today. German soldiers also carried the MP40 submachine gun and the newly arrived MP44 "Sturmgewehr," considered the first-ever "assault rifle." Historians debate whether the Russians stole the MP44's design to create the AK-47. The main soldier's weapon was the K98 Mauser bolt action rifle; it was an excellent rifle, but offered much less firepower than the American M1 Garand semi-automatic rifle. In addition, the Germans had the feared Panzerfaust (Armor Fist), which was a throw-away tank killer (in essence, an early rocket-propelled grenade).

TANKS AND ARTILLERY: The Germans maintained a range of excellent armor, but never had enough in terms of quantity. Their tanks boasted a five-to-one kill ratio against the Allied tanks because they (the German tanks) maintained superior armor, optics and high-velocity cannons. However, because the Allies could bring more tanks and crews to a fight, the Germans never recovered. In addition, Allied air superiority destroyed the German armor, especially the much-feared Typhoon (tank killer). The Germans' King Tiger (Tiger II), which premiered in the west, was considered the best tank of the war (and of the years following the war). Its predecessor, the Tiger I heavy tank, was very effective because of its 88mm cannon and heavy armor. The Germans used the Panther (Panzer V) with a 75mm high-velocity cannon, and the Jadgpanther with an 88mm cannon. The Sturmgeschutz "assault gun" had a very low profile, was easy to build and boasted an effective 75mm high-velocity cannon. The Nebelwerfer (Fog Thrower) was a very effective and mobile rocket launcher used by the Germans; the Americans called it the "Screaming Mimi" because of the screech it made. In addition, the Germans used French and Czech tanks, Panzer IVs and various anti-tank cannons and artillery. The 88mm Flak cannon was notorious for its long-range ability, but in many cases it was the 105mm German artillery pieces that proved just as devastating. Ultimately, the Germans' logistics suffered due to the fact that they required a variety of weapons, vehicles and ammunition. The act of resupplying the correct parts and ammunition for a variety of tanks and artillery proved to be a nightmare.

V1 ROCKETS: The Germans began using the V1 (Vergaltungwaffe 1, "retaliation weapon one") flying bomb on June 13, 1944, against London. At the weapon's peak, the Germans fired more than 100 per day against Allied targets. By mid-October 1944, Germany had fired more than 9,000. The V1 was successful, but it used an immobile ski launcher, which gave it little flexibility. Also, in retaliation for the bombing of German cities, Hitler wasted the V1 on primarily civilian targets instead of using it against military targets. The V1 could fly over 400 miles per hour at a height of about 3,000 feet. The Germans launched the last V1 in late March 1945. They didn't use the V2 until early September 1944. The V2 could fly over 1,700 miles per hour with a 2,200-pound warhead. Its advantage was its incredible speed, altitude and mobile launcher.

TACTICS: Deception. The Allies convinced the Germans that they (the Allies) would land in either Norway or Pas de Calais. They placed Patton in charge of a fake First Army Group, with fake tanks and radio traffic. In addition, they bombed Pas de Calais, spread metal strips to fool radar signals and sent fake paratroopers into Le Harve and Isigny. The Allies also maintained a significant advantage in terms of intelligence because, unbeknownst to the Germans, they had broken the Enigma code. The Germans' tactic was simple: to stop the Allies at the beach. As they had during World War I, they maintained mobile reserves and defense in depth. However, due to Hitler's control of the reserves and ignorance of the real situation, counterattacks materialized too late to have the necessary impact.

QUOTES: "You are about to embark upon the great crusade toward which we have striven these many months. The eyes of the world are upon you...I have full confidence in your courage, devotion to duty and skill in battle." – Dwight Eisenhower

"So sobbing the violin song of the autumn drags out,

I am dully and sorely before pain." – Paul Verlaine poem, used as the code for the attack

"John has a long moustache." – Code to the French Resistance that the invasion was starting

"Make peace you fools, what else?" – Field Marshal Gerd von Rundstedt when asked during a meeting what should be done about the Allied landings

"We'll start the war from here!" – Brigadier General Theodore Roosevelt, Jr., 57 years old, upon reorganizing the troops on Utah Beach

"Rangers, lead the way!" – Colonel Francis W. Dawson

"We want to get the hell over there. The quicker we clean up this goddamned mess, the quicker we can take a little jaunt against the purple pissing Japs and clean out their nest, too. Before the goddamned Marines get all of the credit." – General George S. Patton, who gave this politically incorrect speech to his troops on June 5, 1944

About Omaha Beach: "I was the first one out. The seventh man was the next one to get across the beach without being hit. All the ones in between were hit. Two were killed; three were injured. That's how lucky you had to be." – Captain Richard Merrill, 2nd Ranger Battalion

"The Capital of Ruins" – Samuel Beckett, describing St. Lo

AN ENTERTAINING NOTE:
During the Northern African campaign, Ernest Hemingway named a martini "The Montgomery." When asked why he had given the cocktail this name, Hemingway said, "Because it is 15 gin to 1 vermouth, like Montgomery; he doesn't attack unless he has 15-to-1 odds."

Franklin Roosevelt's D-Day Prayer, June 6, 1944

> *My fellow Americans: Last night, when I spoke with you about the fall of Rome, I knew at that moment that troops of the United States and our allies were crossing the Channel in another and greater operation. It has come to pass with success thus far.*
>
> *And so, in this poignant hour, I ask you to join with me in prayer:*
>
> *Almighty God: Our sons, pride of our Nation, this day have set upon a mighty endeavor, a struggle to preserve our Republic, our religion, and our civilization, and to set free a suffering humanity.*
>
> *Lead them straight and true; give strength to their arms, stoutness to their hearts, steadfastness in their faith.*

They will need Thy blessings. Their road will be long and hard. For the enemy is strong. He may hurl back our forces. Success may not come with rushing speed, but we shall return again and again; and we know that by Thy grace, and by the righteousness of our cause, our sons will triumph.

They will be sore tried, by night and by day, without rest – until the victory is won. The darkness will be rent by noise and flame. Men's souls will be shaken with the violence of war.

For these men are lately drawn from the ways of peace. They fight not for the lust of conquest. They fight to end conquest. They fight to liberate. They fight to let justice arise, and tolerance and good will among all Thy people. They yearn but for the end of battle, for their return to the haven of home.

Some will never return. Embrace these, Father, and receive them, Thy heroic servants, into Thy kingdom.

And for us at home – fathers, mothers, children, wives, sisters, and brothers of brave men overseas – whose thoughts and prayers are ever with them – help us, Almighty God, to rededicate ourselves in renewed faith in Thee in this hour of great sacrifice.

Many people have urged that I call the Nation into a single day of special prayer. But because the road is long and the desire is great, I ask that our people devote themselves in a continuance of prayer. As we rise to each new day, and again when each day is spent, let words of prayer be on our lips, invoking Thy help to our efforts.

Give us strength, too – strength in our daily tasks, to redouble the contributions we make in the physical and the material support of our armed forces.

And let our hearts be stout, to wait out the long travail, to bear sorrows that may come, to impart our courage unto our sons wheresoever they may be.

And, O Lord, give us Faith. Give us Faith in Thee; Faith in our sons; Faith in each other; Faith in our united crusade. Let not the keenness of our spirit ever be dulled. Let not the impacts of temporary events, of temporal matters of but fleeting moment let not these deter us in our unconquerable purpose.

With Thy blessing, we shall prevail over the unholy forces of our enemy. Help us to conquer the apostles of greed and racial arrogances. Lead us to the saving of our country, and with our sister Nations into a world unity that will spell a sure peace a peace invulnerable to the scheming of unworthy men. And a peace that will let all of men live in freedom, reaping the just rewards of their honest toil.

Thy will be done, Almighty God. Amen.

PLACES TO SEE, GROUPED BY BATTLES AND AREA (WEST TO EAST) (REFERENCE MAPS 41-49):

CHERBOURG, BATTLE OF CONTENTIN PENINSULA:

1a. LIBERATION MUSEUM CHERBOURG, FORT DU ROULE: It is dedicated to the liberation of Cherbourg, offers excellent views and is located downtown near restaurants. It was the main fort and southern gateway to the city and overlooks the harbor where the German commander, Karl-Wilhelm von Schlieben, surrendered on June 26 with his remaining garrison of 850 men. However, he refused to order the remaining forces to surrender.
N 49 37.884 W 1 36.956 (49.6314, -1.615933)

1b. FORT DES COUPLETS EQUEURDREVILLE: The western edge of Cherbourg fell to the 9th Division after it had captured Fort des Couplets (and 1,100 soldiers) on June 25. Now the site contains a newly renovated park, though it still houses the remains of German-built bunkers.
N 49 39.050 W 1 39.832 (49.650828, -1.663862)

1c. FORT DE L'OUEST: The remainder of the Cherbourg German garrison surrendered on June 29. The garrison's 30 men were in this small harbor fort. You will need a boat to get out there, but there's not really anything to see.
N 49 40.461 W 1 38.849 (49.674349, -1.647481)

1d. CAP LEVI: East of Cherbourg, the 4th Infantry Division, 22nd Regiment, captured the batteries near Cap Levi. The Cap has a beautiful setting as well as a lighthouse.
Main coastal battery: N 49 40.661 W 1 27.711 (49.677682, -1.461848)
Lighthouse: N 49 41.802 W 1 28.367 (49.696704, -1.472788)

1e. CAP DE LA HAGUE: Elements of the 9th Infantry Division captured approximately 6,000 Germans in Cap de la Hague, which is on the peninsula's western point. The area contains the remains of various bunkers.
N 49 43.514 W 1 56.493 (49.725235, -1.941545)

2. BATTERY AT CRISBECQ (BATTERIE DE CRISBECQ): This contains the 210mm cannons that stayed active during the invasion, taking on the U.S. Navy and knocking a destroyer out of action.
N 49 28.763 W 1 17.739 (49.479383, -1.29565)

3. BATTERY AT AZEVILLE (LA BATTERIE D'AZEVILLE): Close to Crisbecq, this is another impressive fortification to explore.
N 49 27.652 W 1 18.404 (49.460867, -1.306733)

4. **PATTON'S HEADQUARTERS, MONUMENT AND SHERMAN TANK, NEAR NEHOU:** This is where the Third Army commander, General George S. Patton, kept his headquarters.
   N 49 25.612 W 1 34.771 (49.426867, -1.579517)

UTAH BEACH, 101ST AND 82ND ACTION:

5. **UTAH BEACH MUSEUM (MUSÉE DU DÉBARQUEMENT UTAH BEACH):** A well-done museum that also offers a great spot to park, see Utah Beach, and compare the beach's geography to that of Omaha Beach.
   N 49 24.913 W 1 10.508 (49.415217, -1.175133)

6. **SAINTE-MÈRE-ÉGLISE MUSEUM:** Just inland from Utah Beach, this is famous for the "paratrooper" hanging from the church steeple (a feature based on a true event). The museum is outstanding and includes a glider display and C47.
   N 49 24.505 W 1 18.916 (49.408417, -1.315267)

7. **LA FIERE BRIDGE, MERDERET RIVER, "IRON MIKE" 507TH MEMORIAL, FOXHOLE OF GENERAL JAMES M. GAVIN, COMMANDER OF THE 82ND AIRBORNE:** This location offers a great example of the paratroopers' mission: to hold a small bridge and canal as a means of stopping German reinforcements. You'll get a great view of the terrain as well.
   N 49 24.061 W 1 21.833 (49.401017, -1.363883)

8. **BRECOURT MANOR:** This is the location where Lieutenant Dick Winters and paratroopers of the 101st Airborne took out four each 105mm cannons on the morning of D-Day, as portrayed in the mini-series Band of Brothers. The guns were positioned in the field across the road from the farmhouse.
   N 49 23.356 W 1 13.608 (49.389267, -1.2268)

9. **CHURCH AT ANGOVILLE AU PLAIN:** A very special location, the church was converted into a "hospital" where two 101st medics took care of 80 soldiers, including some Germans. A mortar round landed in the church floor, yet didn't go off. Take note of the stained-glass windows.
   N 49 20.952 W 1 15.177 (49.3492, -1.25295)

CARENTAN:

10. **DEAD MAN'S CORNER MUSEUM:** A small museum that offers a great collection of artifacts related to — and information about — the bitter fighting by the 101st in this small town. The 101st Airborne attacked down the road on D974 and had to cross four bridges as they slugged it out down the road.
    N 49 19.696 W 1 16.141 (49.328267, -1.269017)

11. **BLOODY GULCH:** At this location, against superior numbers and firepower, Easy Company of the 101st Airborne Division defended against the 12th SS west of Carentan until American armor arrived to defeat the Germans. No memorial or marker exists; this is simply the location of the American defensive line.
    N 49 17.965 W 1 16.370 (49.299417, -1.272833)

12. **GERMAN CEMETERY, CIMETIÈRE MILITAIRE ALLEMAND, LA CAMBE:** At this location, more than 21,000 Germans are buried, the largest number in Normandy.
N 49 20.470 W 1 01.600 (49.341167, -1.026667)

13. **GRAIGNES MEMORIAL:** On June 6, approximately 150 scattered paratroopers gathered at Graignes, just south of Carentan. Graignes was a small crossroad town surrounded by swampy land. The paratroopers decided, by vote of the villagers, to set up a defense that would stop German reinforcements from advancing onto Carentan. On June 10, the 17th SS Panzer Division began to attack the town on its way to reinforce Carentan. The paratroopers and villagers held out against the Germans until June 12. On June 12, the paratroopers retreated due to mounting casualties and increased artillery fire. With the help of the French, they made it to Carentan. The Germans severely punished the French because they (the Germans) had suffered more than 500 killed in action and 700 wounded in action. The Germans killed the town priests, the doctor and two old women who had helped the American wounded. They also beat and tortured the residents and killed wounded American soldiers. The Germans then burned down the town, leaving only two out of 200 homes standing. Now, a beautiful memorial in this town represents the sacrifice the villagers and the soldiers made against overwhelming odds.
N 49 14.654 W 1 12.358 (49.244233, -1.205967)

OMAHA BEACH:

14. **PONT DU HOC:** This land, like the cemeteries, is sovereign American land. The French gave it to America as a means of thanking the nation for its sacrifice. This is a top-ten site to visit, right next to Omaha Beach. The remains of bunkers and the devastation the bombers wreaked are still visible.
N 49 23.788 W 0 59.327 (49.396467, -0.988783)

15a. **DOG GREEN VIERVILLE EXIT AND WN72:** This is the landing area and exit on Omaha Beach that saw the most casualties on D-Day. The Dog Green area was a significant obstacle for the Americans. The natural terrain provided an advantage and the Germans had well-armed bunkers (WN70, WN72 and WN73). Soldiers from the 116th Regimental Combat Team and the 5th Rangers Battalion reached the east side of the Vierville exit, but were pinned down most of the morning. Thanks to assistance from destroyers, tanks and the battleship USS Texas, the exit was breached at 1700. The following coordinate is at WN72, which is now a memorial to the American National Guard that served in the battle.
N 49 22.752 W 0 54.183 (49.3792, -0.90305)

15b. **MUSÉE D-DAY OMAHA, VIERVILLE-SUR-MER:** This museum is on D514, just down the road from the Dog Green Exit. It's located in a former army hospital that was on the beach as part of the Mulberry destroyed during the June storm off Omaha. It contains a private collection with a great number of specialized weapons and equipment from the battle.
N 49 22.510 W 0 54.502 (49.375167, -0.908367)

16. **USÉE MEMORIAL OMAHA BEACH, "LES MOULINS":** This well-done museum is located on Omaha, right next to the beach at the exit of Easy Red. It contains large equipment such as a Sherman tank, 250mm cannon and landing craft.
N 49 22.027 W 0 52.930 (49.367117, -0.882167)

17. **AMERICAN CEMETERY, CIMETIÈRE AMÉRICAIN DE COLLEVILLE-SUR-MER:** Located between WN62 and WN65, this cemetery is a must see during any visit to Normandy. It's an amazing place from which to give thanks for the sacrifices the American servicemen made. It overlooks Omaha Beach and holds the graves of more than 9,500 men.
N 49 21.590 W 0 51.411 (49.359833, -0.85685)

18a. **WN62 (WIDERSTANDNEST), GERMAN BUNKER AT OMAHA:** Considered the strongest WN on Omaha, this German bunker is a great example of the type of fortifications the Germans made. It wasn't disabled until 1500 on D-Day, when Sherman tanks arrived. The bunker was well fortified and made to fire down the beach while remaining invisible to ships. It contained 35 men manning two each 75mm cannons, two each 50mm cannons, three each machine guns, one each machine gun in a "Tobruk"(concrete emplacement), two each 5cm mortars, one each double machine gun anti-aircraft site and trenches for small arms (rifles). Above the emplacement is one of the best views of Omaha Beach. At the top sits a monument to the 5th Special Engineer Brigade, which landed first to destroy obstacles. A little farther up the hill is a monument to the U.S. 1st Infantry Division, whose men landed here. The coordinates take you to the parking area for the monuments and WN.
N 49 21.668 W 0 50.818 (49.361133, -0.846967)

18b. **WN65 GERMAN BUNKER AT OMAHA:** This bunker retains one of its guns. It defended this exit and held up the American advance until mid-afternoon, at which point a halftrack with a 75mm artillery piece took out the firing position.
N 49 21.901 W 0 51.816 (49.36502, -0.863596)

BAYEUX:

19. **BAYEUX COMMONWEALTH CEMETERY, MÉMORIAL ET CIMETIÈRE DU COMMONWEALTH:** More than 3,900 British soldiers are buried here, as well as more than 400 Germans.
N 49 16.425 W 0 42.868 (49.27375, -0.714467)

20. **MUSÉE DE LA BATAILLE DE NORMANDIE, BAYEUX:** This museum contains one of the largest collections in Normandy, including a Churchill tank and M10!
N 49 16.407 W 0 42.739 (49.27345, -0.712317)

21. **BAYEUX TAPESTRY:** I strongly suggest that you see the cathedral in Bayeux, as well as the Bayeux Tapestry Museum. Give yourself a break from World War II machine guns.
N 49 16.453 W 0 42.041 (49.274217, -0.700683)

GOLD BEACH:

22. **LONGUES SUR MER BATTERY AND COMMAND POST:** This is one of the best intact batteries, and offers a beautiful view of Normandy. Note that these are naval cannons the Germans used to arm their guns. The command post is within walking distance and was used in the movie The Longest Day.
N 49 20.607 W 0 41.676 (49.34345, -0.6946)

23. **MUSÉE DU DEBARQUE ARROMANCHES, 360-DEGREE CINEMA AND VIEWPOINT:** This is another great museum about Gold Beach. It overlooks the remaining Mulberry dock. (The second Mulberry was destroyed during a large sea storm.)
Museum: N 49 20.406 W 0 37.301 (49.3401, -0.621683)

    VIEWPOINT AND CINEMA: Above the museum is a viewpoint and memorial that overlook the harbor. The area contained several bunkers that the naval bombardment destroyed, as well as a Wurzburg radar that an air raid took out the week before. The cinema offers an approximately 20-minute film about the June 6 actions that took place in this area.
N 49 20.352 W 0 36.879 (49.3392, -0.61465)

24. **LA RIVERIA/MONT FLUERY, TANK MONUMENT, SEXTON SELF-PROPELLED HOWITZER:** Just one of the many tanks and self-propelleds used in the area. The site also contains a memorial to the units that advanced and fought at this location.
N 49 20.607 W 0 30.993 (49.34345, -0.51655)

JUNO BEACH:

25a. **CHURCHILL TANK MONUMENT AND CROSS THAT MARKS WHERE DE GAULLE CAME ASHORE:** This Churchill tank was recently found buried at the beach exit. It had been disabled during fighting on D-Day and was buried rather than towed away. Nearby is a monument marking the site where de Gaulle came ashore.
N 49 20.230 W 0 28.142 (49.337167, -0.469033)

25b. **JUNO BEACH CENTER (THE ONLY CANADIAN MUSEUM IN NORMANDY):** A new and very well-done museum, plus the remains of the German bunker system.
N 49 20.165 W 0 27.673 (49.336076 -0.461216)

25c. **DUEL DRIVE SHERMAN TANK MONUMENT TO THE CANADIANS AND 50MM GERMAN ANTI-TANK CANNON:** At this location, in Courselles-sur-Mer, is a DD Sherman that was found underwater 27 years after the war. It has since been painted, and plaques were added to commemorate the sacrifice of the soldiers who landed at Juno Beach.
N 49 20.138 W 0 27.478 (49.335633, -0.457967)

26. **WN28 ON SWORD BEACH, PLACE DU CANADA:** The Canadians landed directly in front of this WN, which provided significant resistance throughout

the morning.
N 49 20.140 W 0 25.200 (49.335667, -0.42)

27. **WN27 ON SWORD BEACH, SAINT-AUBIN-SUR-MER:** At this bunker is a memorial and a 50mm cannon. It was knocked out by tanks early in the battle.
N 49 19.939 W 0 23.655 (49.332317, -0.39425)

28. **CANADIAN MILITARY CEMETERY AT BÉNY-SUR-MER REVIERS:** One of the many Allied cemeteries and one of the largest Canadian cemeteries.
N 49 18.150 W 0 27.017 (49.3025, -0.450283)

SWORD BEACH:

29. **CHURCHILL TANK MEMORIAL:** A tank marking the spot where the German 21st Panzer Division counterattacked the British and Canadians on D-Day, trying to push them into the sea.
N 49 18.361 W 0 19.475 (49.306017, -0.324583)

30. **CROMWELL TANK MONUMENT:**
N 49 17.786W 0 17.988 (49.296433, -0.2998)

31. **MUSÉE DU DÉBARQUEMENT NO. 4 COMMANDO:** A decent museum to the British commandos who landed at Normandy.
N 49 17.319 W 0 15.563 (49.28865, -0.259383)

32. **GRAND BUNKER MUSEUM:** Le Grand Bunker, Musée du Mur de l'Atlantique: A really well done and unique museum. The well-camouflaged bunker actually held out past D-Day as a German artillery observation post. It's worth the visit and contains one of the Higgins boats used in the filming of Saving Private Ryan.
N 49 17.229 W 0 15.164 (49.28715, -0.252733)

33. **MERVILLE BATTERY/MUSÉE DE LA BATTERIE DE MERVILLE:** This is a unique site to visit; it has a C47 and the artillery battery that was located here.
N 49 16.176W 0 11.797 (49.2696, -0.196617)

BATTLE FOR CAEN SITES:

34. **PEGASUS BRIDGE, MÉMORIAL PEGASUS:** Another very well done "park and museum." The original bridge is set to the side, while the park offers aircraft and equipment.
N 49 14.523 W 0 16.384 (49.24205, -0.273067)

35. **MEMORIAL DE CAEN/CAEN MUSEUM FOR PEACE:** A new museum focused on peace, then and now. It has a very well done short summary movie and a great collection of artifacts. It also has a modern focus for contemplation on peace today, and on other issues such as the Cold War, living in a nuclear world, etc.
N 49 11.852 W 0 22.997 (49.197533, -0.383283)

OPERATION PERCH (JUNE 7-14):

36a. VILLERS BOCAGE, HILL 213: Wittman's first kills were at this location just northeast of town. The street named "June 13, 1944" marks the road where many of the vehicles were destroyed. There is not much here, but you can see the terrain because the roads haven't changed much throughout the years.
N 49 05.579 W 0 37.474 (49.092983, -0.624567)

36b. LOCATION OF WITTMAN'S TANKS BEFORE BATTLE: This is the geo coordinate where Wittman and his five Tiger Tanks were performing maintenance prior to their attack. No monuments here, just the terrain.
N 49 05.388 W 0 37.568 (49.0898, -0.626133)

37. MONUMENT TO THE 7TH ARMORED DIVISION, DESERT RATS, WHO DIED AT VILLERS BOCAGE FOR FREEDOM: This is a small stone monument with a bronze plaque. At this location, a British six-pounder anti-tank gun crew damaged the drive sprocket and track of Wittman's Tiger Tank, forcing him and his crew to abandon the tank and escape by foot.
N 49 04.978 W 0 38.758 (49.082967, -0.645967)

OPERATION EPSOM (JUNE 26-30) AND OPERATION JUPITER (JULY 10-12):

38. HILL 112: "He who controls Hill 112 controls Normandy." In the open fields and scattered trees to the east of Caen is a Churchill tank marking the location of Hill 112. Hill 112 exchanged hands several times and was the site of bitter fighting. At one point, a Heavy Tiger Battalion smashed into the British and Canadians fighting for control of the hill.
The coordinates for the tank are: N 49 07.390 W 0 27.607 (49.123167, -0.460117)

In the woods just past the tank is a stele, Bois de Calloué; these coordinates mark the center of the hill.

N 49 07.239 W 0 27.427 (49.12065, -0.457117)

OPERATION WINDSOR (JULY 4-5):

39. CARPIQUET AIRFIELD: The battle for Carpiquet was a bloody fight that took place during Operation Windsor, July 4-5. The airfield was a D-Day+1 objective the Allies wanted to capture so that they could start flying in supplies. However, the Germans maintained a strong defense and held the high ground south of Caen, Hill 112 overlooking the airfield. The airfield was finally taken during Operation Charnwood, July 8-9, but was unusable because Hill 112 was still in the Germans' possession.
N 49 11.024 W 0 27.635 (49.183733, -0.460583)

OPERATION GOODWOOD (JULY 18-20):

40a. BOURGUEBUS RIDGE: A small memorial consisting of a stone marker, plaque and flagpoles sits in this town, part of Operation Goodwood. During the battle, the British fell victim to 78 each 88mm guns on the ridge and lost

more than 400 tanks in a few days!
N 49 07.288 W 0 17.813 (49.121467, -0.296883)

40b. IRISH GUARD MEMORIAL: In the field to the north of Cagny sits a memorial to the Irish Guards, who crossed the field during Operation Goodwood.
N 49 09.037 W 0 14.347 (49.150617, -0.239117)

40c. BANNEVILLE LA CAMPAIGN WAR CEMETERY: Near Sannerville, this cemetery contains the graves of 2,170 soldiers, many of whom died in Operation Goodwood. At this location, on July 18, the Allies were counterattacked from the south by six King Tiger tanks, which were stopped by anti-tank guns positioned nearby.
N 49 10.581 W 0 13.790 (49.17635, -0.229833)

OPERATION ATLANTIC AND OPERATION SPRING (JULY 18-20):

41a. VERRIÈRES RIDGE MEMORIAL: This is a small Canadian memorial plaque commemorating Operation Atlantic and Operation Spring, which were part of the southern fighting to capture Falaise.
N 49 06.612 W 0 19.946 (49.1102, -0.332433)

OPERATION BLUECOAT (JULY 30–AUGUST 7):

41b. MONT PINÇON, HILL 365 MEMORIAL: At dawn on August 8, the 43rd Wessex Division took Mont Pinçon after a platoon of Sherman tanks from the 18th Royal Hussars found an unguarded path to the summit. Quickly, the infantry supported the tanks and took the hill, but with great casualties after three days of battle. At the top of the hill you can see why the Germans fought so fiercely to maintain possession; it's an incredible view. Also on top of the hill is a memorial to the Allies who fought for it.
N 48 58.275 W 0 37.795 (48.97125, -0.629917)

BATTLE FOR ST. LO AND OPERATION COBRA:

42. MEMORIAL CHAPEL OF LA MADELEINE: This chapel is dedicated to the sacrifice the Americans made when capturing St. Lo.
N 49 07.033 W 1 03.666 (49.117217, -1.0611)

43. PLACE OF MAJOR HOWIE: Known as the Major of St. Lo, Thomas D Howie commanded the 3rd Battalion of the 116th Regiment, 29th Infantry Division. After landing on D-Day, he was killed a month later during an attack at St. Lo on July 17. The day before, his battalion had broken through German lines with bayonets to save the trapped 2nd Battalion.
N 49 06.927 W 1 04.962 (49.11545, -1.0827)

44. GERMAN CEMETERY MARIGNY: In terms of remains from or evidence of Operation Cobra, you'll encounter difficulty finding any bomb craters. However, this cemetery testifies to the number of Germans killed at that location, where the saturation bombing took place.
N 49 06.784 W 1 14.123 (49.113067, -1.235383)

BATTLE OF MORTAIN (OPERATION LUTTICH) AND AVRANCHES:

45. PATTON MEMORIAL AND TANK, AVRANCHES: This is a memorial to the Third Army, which passed through Avranches to break through the German lines. Avranches was the German Army's objective for Operation Luttich and the Battle of Mortain.
N 48 40.909 W 1 21.307 (48.681817, -1.355117)

46a.HILL 314 (SOME SOURCES CALL IT HILL 317), 30TH INFANTRY MEMORIAL, MORTAIN: At this location, the 2nd Battalion of the 120th Regiment, 30th Infantry Division, held out against numerically superior German forces in the 2nd SS Panzer Division. Out of 950 men, more than 300 were killed; only 376 left the hill fit for combat. This hill is not often visited, but is a worthy spot for seeing terrain and paying your respects. Hill 314 contains a monument to the 30th Division, as well as a small chapel. You can still see the trench lines and foxholes in the surrounding woods on the west and east sides of the hill.
N 48 38.809 W 0 55.980 (48.646817 -0.933)

46b.ABBAYE BLANCHE: At this location, men of the 30th Infantry Division took the initial brunt of the 2nd SS Panzer Division's attack into Mortain, yet were able to deal a serious blow to the attackers. The Germans had to take out this resistance before they could commit more forces to the attack on Hill 314. On August 8, the Germans unsuccessfully attacked with two halftracks armed with 75mm cannons; both were quickly knocked out. This area saw intense fighting throughout the battle, including on August 9, when the Americans lost nine tanks in front of the Abbey. Also worth a visit, just south of the Abbey, is the "Grande Cascade," the largest waterfall in western France.
N 48 39.439 W 0 56.724 (48.657318, -0.945406))

46c.HILL 285: To the west of Mortain, a company from the 120th defended this hill with anti-tank guns and mortars against several German assaults from the east. The Germans unsuccessfully attacked in force with artillery at 0030 on August 8, using captured Sherman tanks and flamethrowers. For the remainder of the battle the Americans held their ground. From this coordinate you can see the terrain and visualize the approach of the Germans from the east.
N 48 39.461 W 0 57.855 (48.657683, -0.96425)

46d.ST. BARTHELEMY ANTI-TANK GUN POSITION: At this approximate location, men of the 1st Battalion of the 117th Regiment, 30th Division set up one of their anti-tank guns (57mm). Across the street in the field they set up another to stop the initial attack of the 1st SS Panzer Division. The Americans knocked out the lead Panther tank by hitting its hull machine gun enclosure.

The Germans were delayed by an hour as they removed the tank from the road. Next, the Americans waited for the advance, trying to see through the thick fog. Suddenly, another Panther appeared; only 35 yards away the anti-tank crew knocked out that tank. This is only a quick pull-off spot where you can see the terrain and appreciate the size of the area.
N 48 40.769 W 0 57.082 (48.679483, -0.951367)

46e.ST. BARTHELEMY MEMORIAL: This site offers a memorial and explanation of the fighting that took place there. The 117th fought courageously throughout the daylight hours of August 7, knocking out several tanks via bazookas and anti-tank guns. They caused the Germans several hours of delay and lost momentum.
N 48 40.891 W 0 57.235 (48.681517, -0.953917)

47. BRITTANY AMERICAN CEMETERY AND MEMORIAL, ST. JAMES: Another beautiful monument to American sacrifices, holding more than 4,400 heroes.
N 48 31.199 W 1 18.067 (48.519983, -1.301117)

OPERATION TOTALIZE (AUGUST 8-11), OPERATION TRACTABLE (AUGUST 14-20) AND THE FALAISE POCKET:

48a.CANADIAN CEMETERY, BRETTEVILLE: More than 2,900 Canadians are buried in this cemetery off the main highway. Most of them were killed during the fight for Falaise.
N 49 03.600 W 0 17.502 (49.06, -0.2917)

48b.AMBUSH OF TIGER PLATOON, APPROXIMATE LOCATION WHERE TIGER TANK COMMANDER MICHAEL WITTMAN WAS KILLED: On August 8, the Canadians captured the town of Saint-Aignan during Operation Totalize. The 12th SS Panzer Division commander ordered a counterattack. Wittman led seven Tiger tanks of the 101st Heavy SS Panzer Battalion in the attack. They were ambushed by British and Canadian tanks. A Sherman Firefly shot penetrated Wittman's number 007 tank and ignited the ammunition rack, blowing the top off the tank. This is the approximate location of the field where the tank was destroyed (across the highway from the Canadian Cemetery).
N 49 04.017 W 0 17.595 (49.06695, -0.29325)

49. POLISH CEMETERY, URVILLE: The Polish heroes buried here number 696. They fell during the advance to close the Falaise Pocket.
N 49 01.384 W 0 16.194 (49.023067, -0.2699)

50. HILL 140 MONUMENT, PART OF OPERATION TOTALIZE: This is a memorial close to the summit of Hill 140, just northeast of Hill 195. It commemorates the Canadian British Columbia and Algonquin Regiments that were destroyed by Panther tanks of the 12th SS during Operation Totalize.
N 49 01.046 W 0 11.954 (49.017433, -0.199233)

51. HILL 195 MONUMENT, PART OF OPERATION TOTALIZE: A little-known location with a new monument to the battle for Hill 195. This was another vicious battle, which took place at night in early August as the Allies fought south to trap the Germans.
N 48 58.678 W 0 16.305 (48.977967, -0.27175)

52a. HILL 159, OBJECTIVE OF OPERATION TRACTABLE: One of the first objectives of Operation Tractable was for the Canadians to capture Hill 159, which overlooked Falaise and the route farther south. From there, they were to capture Falaise, then move swiftly to Chambois to link up with the Americans. However, the Canadians struggled to capture the hill. Not until August 16 did the 3rd Canadian Infantry Division take the hill. There is no known monument, but this is the approximate location.
N 48 55.013 W 0 11.480 (48.916883, -0.191333)

52b. FALAISE MUSEUM, MUSÉE AOUT 1944, LA BATAILLE DE LA POCHE DE FALAISE: In the town of Falaise is this older museum with some equipment outside. I believe there are plans to refurbish it. Also nearby is the beautiful downtown and an awesome castle that was the birthplace of William the Conquer. Falaise was cleared of Germans by August 18.
N 48 53.554 W 0 12.718 (48.892567, -0.211967)

53a. TRUN GAP CANADIAN MEMORIAL ON THE D13 OVERLOOKING SAINT-LAMBERT: Just past Trun is this memorial, located where the Canadians captured the high ground, Hill 117, overlooking Saint-Lambert. Here they underwent several attacks from escaping Germans.
N 48 49.478 E 0 04.152 (48.824633, 0.0692)

53b. MEMORIAL TO MAJOR DAVID CURRIE: This memorial commemorates the heroic actions of Major David Currie, who commanded elements of the Canadian forces. The troops first captured Hill 117 overlooking Saint-Lambert, then, eventually, Saint-Lambert itself. Currie received the Victoria Cross for his bravery and leadership throughout three days of intense battle.
N 48 49.352 E 0 04.318 (48.822533, 0.071967)

53c. TOURNAI SUR DIVES, HALFTRACK AND MEMORIAL: This small town was one of the main gathering points of the Germans prior to the push over the Dives. On August 21, the priests of Abbey Launay negotiated the surrender of 800 Germans to avoid further bloodshed. At this location is a memorial and an M3 halftrack.
N 48 48.725 E 0 02.644 (48.812083, 0.044067)

54. **CROSSINGS OVER THE DIVES "RIVER":** By August 18, the Germans had only three road crossings over the River Dives that they could use to escape. It is amazing that the Dives is so small, but was still a major obstacle for the Germans. At these locations were the most death and destruction as the Germans fought to escape. The foot bridge is included because many Germans used it to escape.

    A. **SAINT-LAMBERT FOOT BRIDGE OVER THE DIVES (APPROXIMATE LOCATION)**:
    N 48 49.189 E 0 04.170 (48.819817, 0.0695)

    B. **SAINT-LAMBERT ROAD CROSSING OVER THE DIVES:**
    N 48 48.891 E 0 04.470 (48.81485, 0.0745)

    C. **MOISSY FORD:**
    N 48 48.700 E 0 05.448 (48.811667, 0.0908)

    D. **CHAMBOIS BRIDGE OVER THE DIVES:**
    N 48 48.235 E 0 06.303 (48.803917, 0.10505)

55a.CHAMBOIS MEMORIAL TO ALLIED FORCES: A stone monument in the small but beautiful downtown of Chambois, next to the castle.
N 48 48.316 E 0 06.367 (48.805267, 0.106117)

55b.MEMORIAL WHERE THE POLISH AND AMERICANS MET IN CLOSING THE FALAISE GAP, CHAMBOIS: Another location only minutes from the museum. At this site, on August 19 at 1900, elements of the American 90th Infantry Division and the Polish 1st Division met to complete their mission. Still, the struggle for Chambois and the effort to stop the German retreat continued fiercely for the next two days.
N 48 48.181 E 0 06.763 (48.803017, 0.112717)

56a.HILL 262 NORTH, MONT ORMEL MEMORIAL AND MUSEUM: A must-see, this location marks the spot where the Germans counterattacked the Polish who were on top of the hill, surrounded for three days and taking the brunt of German attacks while trying to escape. The Germans were forced to flee over and around this hill.
N 48 50.285 E 0 08.516 (48.838083, 0.141933)

56b.HILL 262 SOUTH, MONT ORMEL LOCATION: Across D16 to the south is Hill 262. It was also a high point overlooking the fighting. The Poles maintained it as an objective but were never able to capture it.
N 48 49.395 E 0 08.791 (48.823254, 0.146513)

57. **POLISH MONUMENT ON ORMEL:** At this precise place, the Poles experienced a powerful blow in the form of a German counterattack carried out by a single Panther tank of the 2nd SS Panzerkorps. As a result of the assault, in just a few minutes the Poles lost as many as five Sherman tanks and sought refuge in the nearby woods.
N 48 50.912 E 0 08.433 (48.848533, 0.14055)

58a. MANOR AT BOISJOS: This is the spot where the Polish held out using the house for a hospital and blocking the Germans from escaping (still in private ownership). Throughout the retreat, the Germans tried several times to dislodge the Polish from the strong position. The Polish succeeded in repulsing all attacks, including a determined August 20 attack with several Panther tanks.
N 48 51.250 E 0 08.120 (48.854167, 0.135333)

58b. CHURCH OF COUDEHARD: From the museum, you can hike to this church, which the Poles used as shelter and which was in an area of intense fighting. From here you'll have a beautiful view of the landscape.
N 48 50.466 E 0 08.354 (48.8411, 0.139233)

59. TIGER TANK, VIMITOURS: One of the tanks that the Germans abandoned while escaping the Gap. It's on the outskirts of Vimitour and was one of five tanks that delayed the pursuing Allies until it ran out of fuel.
N 48 55.416 E 0 12.887 (48.9236, 0.214783)

60. MASSACRE OF ORADOUR-SUR-GLANE, JUNE 10, 1944: Six hundred and forty-two villagers, including women and children, were massacred by a platoon of the German 2nd SS Panzer Division Das Reich. The Germans attacked the town in retaliation of the French Resistance attacking their forces while they advanced to Normandy. They believed some of the French fighters were from the town. The town has been left as it was in 1944; cars are burnt out and sewing machines are still in homes. It's a very impressive exhibit and the experience of walking around the vacant memorial town is very moving.
N 45 55.729 E 1 02.013 (45.928817, 1.03355)

OPERATION OVERLORD OVERVIEW, JUNE 6 - AUGUST 15, 1944 MAP 41

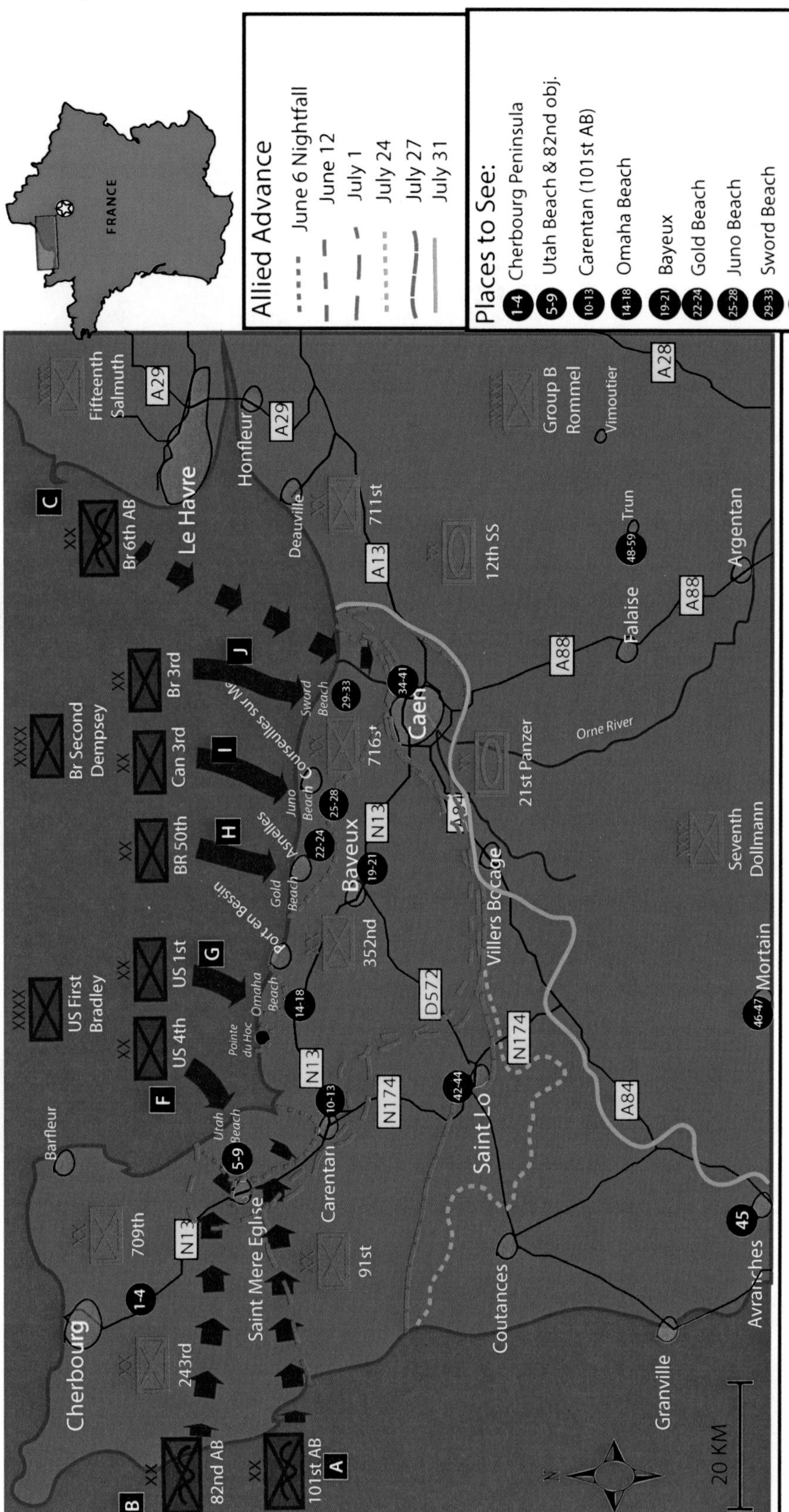
Allied Advance
June 6 Nightfall
June 12
July 1
July 24
July 27
July 31
FRANCE
Cherbourg
Barfleur
Saint Mere Eglise
Carentan
Utah Beach
Pointe du Hoc
Omaha Beach
Port en Bessin
Gold Beach
Asnelles
Juno Beach
Courseulles sur Mer
Sword Beach
Baveux
Caen
Le Havre
Honfleur
Deauville
Orne River
Villers Bocage
Saint Lo
Coutances
Granville
Avranches
Mortain
Falaise
Trun
Argentan
Vimoutier
82nd AB
101st AB
243rd
709th
91st
US 4th
US First Bradley
US 1st
352nd
BR 50th
Can 3rd
Br Second Dempsey
Br 3rd
716th
Br 6th AB
711st
12th SS
21st Panzer
Seventh Dollmann
Group B Rommel
Fifteenth Salmuth
N13
N174
D572
A84
A13
A88
A29
A28
20 KM

Places to See:

- 1-4 Cherbourg Peninsula
- 5-9 Utah Beach & 82nd obj.
- 10-13 Carentan (101st AB)
- 14-18 Omaha Beach
- 19-21 Bayeux
- 22-24 Gold Beach
- 25-28 Juno Beach
- 29-33 Sword Beach
- 34-41 Caen Battles
- 42-44 St. Lo (Op Cobra)
- 45 Avaranches (Patton landing)
- 46-47 Battle of Mortain
- 48-59 Battle of Falaise Gap
- 60 Massacre at Oradour Sur Glane (south of Poitiers) not shown.

June 6 MOVEMENTS:

A. At 0040 on June 6, the 101st paratroopers began to land around Carentan.
B. At the same time, the 82nd Airborne began landing around St. Mere Eglise.
C. 0020 the British Airborne began landing at the Caen Canal.
D. 0530, 100s of bombers began bombing the beach fronts, the navy ships bombarded the coast and rocket ships began firing onto the beachheads.
E. 0330 the soldiers began loading into the landing craft.
F. 0630 the first Americans landed at Utah Beach.
G. 0636 the first Americans landed at Omaha Beach, the 2nd wave at 0700 and finally at 0730 they broke out of the beachhead, capturing St. Laurant by 1130.
H. 0725 the British landed at Gold beach, opened up by 10am.
I. The Canadians landed at Juno beach at 0745 and made headway of 10 km by the end of the day.
J. At 0715, the British 3rd Division landed on Sword Beach against little resistance.

US LANDINGS AT UTAH BEACH AND PARATROOPERS, JUNE 6-13, 1944 MAP 42

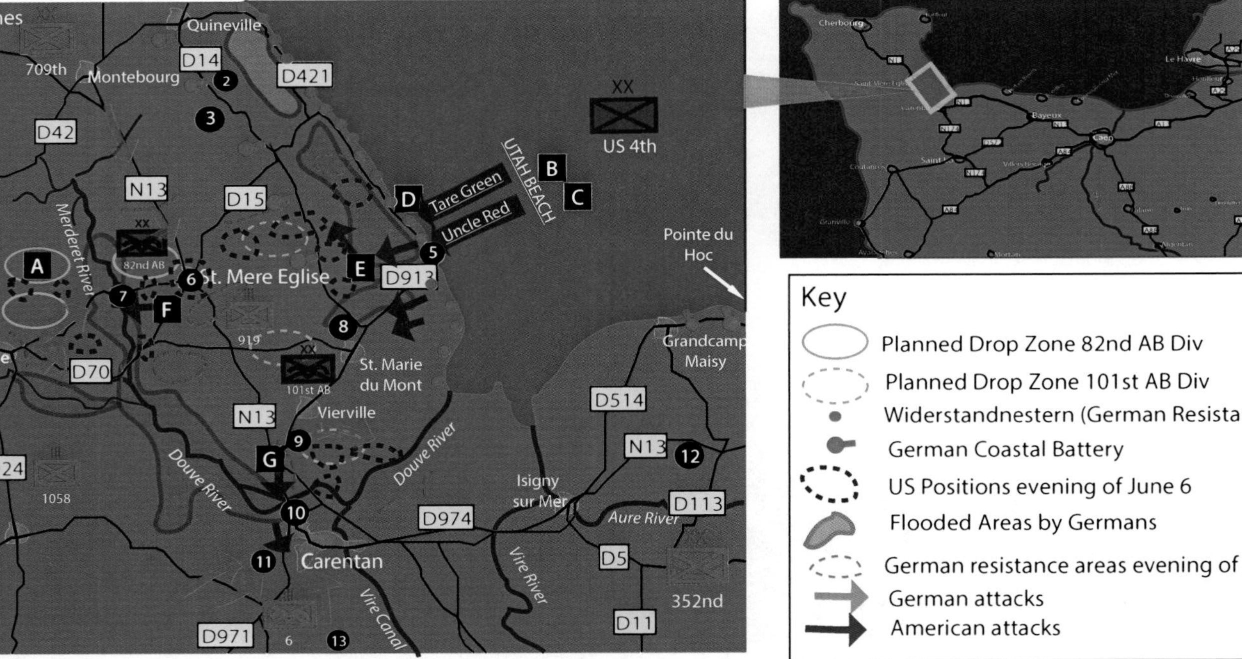
Valognes
Quineville
709th
Montebourg
N13
D14
D421
D146
D2
D24
D42
D15
XX
US 4th
UTAH BEACH
Tare Green
Uncle Red
B
C
D
A
E
F
G
St. Mere Eglise
82nd AB
101st AB
Merderet River
1057
Etienville
D70
D913
Pointe du Hoc
Grandcamp Maisy
St. Marie du Mont
Vierville
91st
1058
St. Jores
D903
Douve River
Carentan
Isigny sur Mer
Aure River
D514
D974
D113
D5
D11
352nd
Vire River
Vire Canal
D971
5KM

Key

- Planned Drop Zone 82nd AB Div
- Planned Drop Zone 101st AB Div
- Widerstandnestern (German Resistance Nests)
- German Coastal Battery
- US Positions evening of June 6
- Flooded Areas by Germans
- German resistance areas evening of June 6
- German attacks
- American attacks

Places to See:

**Please note, locations 1 and 4 are not on this map.

2 Battery Crisbecq
3 Azeville Battery
5 Utah Beach Museum
6 St. Mere Eglise Museum
7 La Fiere Bridge, Iron Mike Memorial
8 Brecourt Manor
9 Church at Angoville au Plain
10 Carentan, Dead Man's Corner Museum
11 Bloody Gulch Location (line of 101st)
12 German Cemetery La Cambe
13 Graingnes Memorial

MOVEMENTS:

A. At approximately 0040 the US paratroopers began to land to secure the approaches to the beaches. Many were scattered miles away from their intended targets. They engaged in combat where they could, such as St. Mere Eglise and La Fiere.
B. After bombing and naval bombardments, the 1st wave of the landing crafts landed 2,000 yards south of their intended area at 0630. Next 32 Sherman DD tanks arrived at 0640, then 0645 the 2nd wave of troops and dozer tanks arrived.
C. At 0647 the 4th wave arrived with the engineers that began blowing up obstacles.
D. The major German defenses began to crumble, such as WN5, WN4 and the HQ at WN7.
E. After suffering light casualties and some resistance, the Americans were inland by 0900.
F. **Battle at LaFiere** - At dawn the 82nd attacked the Germans at La Fiere Bridge over the Merderet River.
The battle continued for 3 days, the paratroopers, stopped the German armor attacks. On June 9, General Gavin ordered a frontal assault, they crossed the causeway and opened up the road for the Americans to advance further inland.
G. **Battle of Carentan** - After consolidating forces, the 101st attacked Carentan with 2 battalions on June 10 down D974. The battle continued for two days until the Americans were able to push the Germans out. On June 13, additional German forces counterattacked in strength. At the battle known as the Bloody Gulch, the 101st airborne held their ground and stopped the German armor. After securing Carentan, it allowed the Americans to continue south and west to begin capturing Cherbourg.

US LANDINGS AT OMAHA BEACH, JUNE 6, 1944 — MAP 43

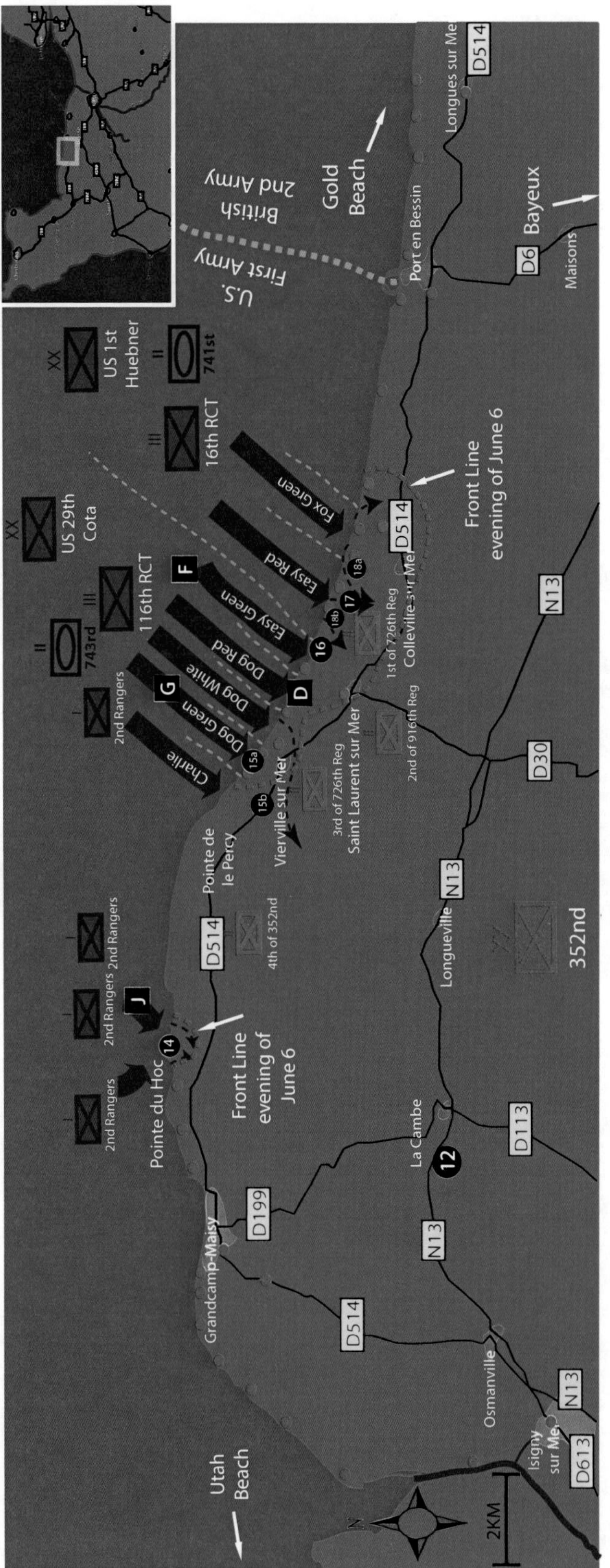
2nd Rangers
2nd Rangers
2nd Rangers
J
Pointe du Hoc
14
Utah Beach
Grandcamp-Maisy
D514
Pointe de le Percy
Front Line evening of June 6
D199
4th of 352nd
D514
Vierville sur Mer
15b
15a
2nd Rangers
743rd
116th RCT
US 29th Cota
Charlie
Dog Green
G
Dog White
Dog Red
D
Easy Green
F
Easy Red
Fox Green
16
18b
17
18a
3rd of 726th Reg
Saint Laurent sur Mer
2nd of 916th Reg
1st of 726th Reg
Colleville-sur-Mer
D514
16th RCT
741st
US 1st Huebner
U.S. First Army
British 2nd Army
Gold Beach
Port en Bessin
Longues sur Mer
D514
Front Line evening of June 6
D6
Bayeux
Maisons
N13
La Cambe
12
Longueville
N13
D113
D30
N13
352nd
2KM
Osmanville
Isigny sur Mer
D613
N13
N

Places to See:

- **14** Pointe du Hoc
- **15a** Dog Green Vierville Exit & WN72
- **15b** Musee DDAY Omaha (Vierville sur Mer)
- **16** Musee Memorial Omaha (Les Moulins)
- **17** American Cemetery Colleville-sur-Mer
- **18a** WN 62, German Defensive position
- **18b** WN 65, German Defensive position
- • German Resistance Nest
- **12** German Cemetery La Cambe

MOVEMENTS: (**Note:** Most of these I did not place markers above b/c they are all in the same vicinity)

A. 0200 the 1st wave of 1500 soldiers and 64 tanks began to load into the landing craft, 10 miles out from shore.(2-3 hr ride)
B. 0530, 40 each B17 bombers bombed Omaha Beach but released their bombs too early and missed the entire beach.
C. 0540 the Navy bombarded the shoreline with battery fire and rockets but with little effect on the Omaha defenses.
D. 0636 the first wave arrived on Omaha Beach, they were devasted with over 70% casualties within minutes.
E. 0640 the first wave of armor began to arrive, only 5 of the 32 designated to 116th RCT made it ashore.
F. 0700 the second wave began to arrive while the tide was coming in, with additional support they made some headway off the beach and began fighting for an exit.
G. 0730 at Dog Green near Vierville, General Cota arrived and with the help of the 2nd Rangers began to create an exit.
H. 0800 Navy Destroyers began pulling in close to shore to provide direct fire support.
I. 1130 St. Laurent was captured and by 1300 they began to secure most of the beach.
J. **Pointe du Hoc:** At 0600 the men landed at Point du Hoc and began to scale the cliffs with covering fire from 2 destroyers. By 0900 the Rangers captured Pointe du Hoc but found that the cannons were fake. They formed a patrol and found the real cannons in a farm field less than a mile away and destroyed them. Then they returned and fought off several attacks.

BATTLE OF MORTAIN, AUGUST 7-13, 1944

MAP 44

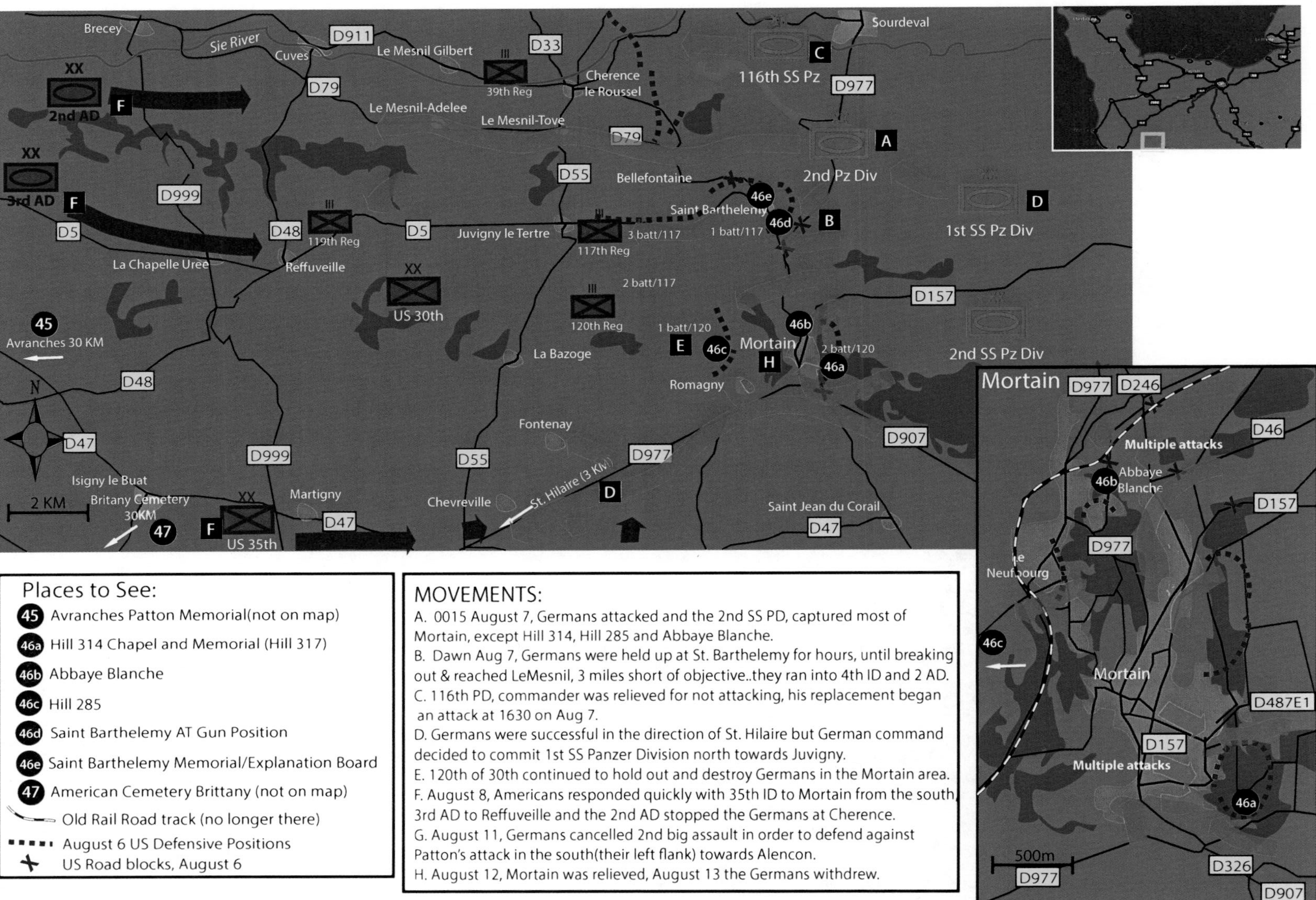
Brecey
Sie River
Cuves
D911
Le Mesnil Gilbert
D33
39th Reg
Cherence
le Roussel
Sourdeval
C
116th SS Pz
D977
D79
Le Mesnil-Adelee
Le Mesnil-Tove
A
2nd AD
3rd AD
F
D999
D5
D48
119th Reg
Reffuveille
La Chapelle Uree
D55
Bellefontaine
46e
Saint Barthelemy
46d
B
2nd Pz Div
D
1st SS Pz Div
Juvigny le Tertre
117th Reg
3 batt/117
1 batt/117
2 batt/117
US 30th
120th Reg
1 batt/120
E
46c
Mortain
46b
2 batt/120
46a
H
D157
2nd SS Pz Div
La Bazoge
Romagny
45
Avranches 30 KM
D48
N
D47
Isigny le Buat
Britany Cemetery 30KM
47
2 KM
US 35th
Martigny
D47
D999
D55
Chevreville
St. Hilaire (3 KM)
D977
Fontenay
D907
Saint Jean du Corail
Mortain
D977
D246
D46
Multiple attacks
Abbaye Blanche
D157
le Neufbourg
D487E1
Multiple attacks
500m
D326
D907
Places to See:
45 Avranches Patton Memorial(not on map)
46a Hill 314 Chapel and Memorial (Hill 317)
46b Abbaye Blanche
46c Hill 285
46d Saint Barthelemy AT Gun Position
46e Saint Barthelemy Memorial/Explanation Board
47 American Cemetery Brittany (not on map)
Old Rail Road track (no longer there)
August 6 US Defensive Positions
US Road blocks, August 6
MOVEMENTS:
A. 0015 August 7, Germans attacked and the 2nd SS PD, captured most of Mortain, except Hill 314, Hill 285 and Abbaye Blanche.
B. Dawn Aug 7, Germans were held up at St. Barthelemy for hours, until breaking out & reached LeMesnil, 3 miles short of objective..they ran into 4th ID and 2 AD.
C. 116th PD, commander was relieved for not attacking, his replacement began an attack at 1630 on Aug 7.
D. Germans were successful in the direction of St. Hilaire but German command decided to commit 1st SS Panzer Division north towards Juvigny.
E. 120th of 30th continued to hold out and destroy Germans in the Mortain area.
F. August 8, Americans responded quickly with 35th ID to Mortain from the south, 3rd AD to Reffuveille and the 2nd AD stopped the Germans at Cherence.
G. August 11, Germans cancelled 2nd big assault in order to defend against Patton's attack in the south(their left flank) towards Alencon.
H. August 12, Mortain was relieved, August 13 the Germans withdrew.

BRITISH AND CANADIAN LANDINGS, JUNE 6, 1944 — MAP 45

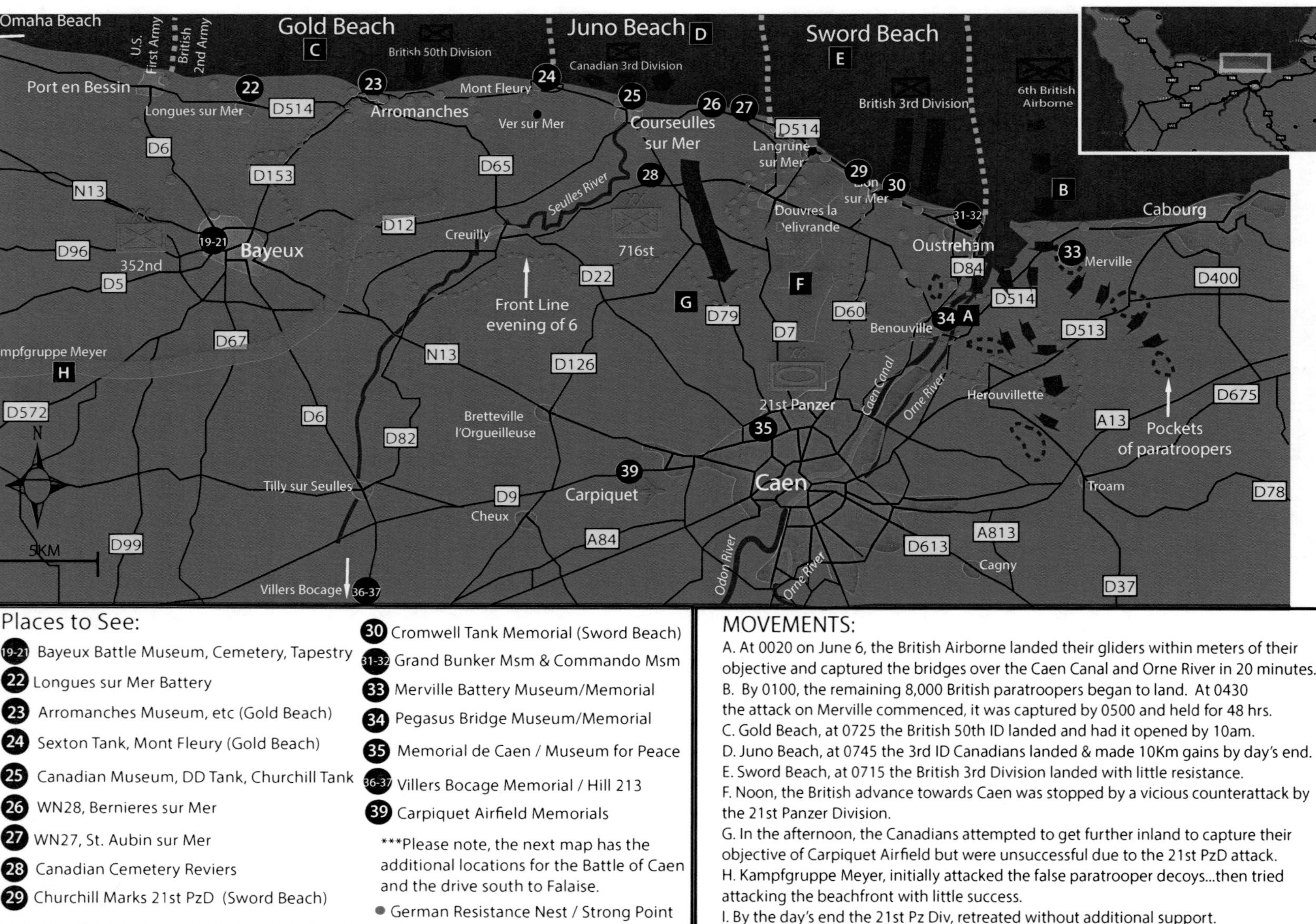
Omaha Beach
U.S. First Army
British 2nd Army
Gold Beach
C
British 50th Division
Juno Beach
D
Canadian 3rd Division
Sword Beach
E
British 3rd Division
6th British Airborne
B
Port en Bessin
Longues sur Mer
Arromanches
Mont Fleury
Ver sur Mer
Courseulles sur Mer
Langrune sur Mer
Douvres la Delivrande
Oustreham
Cabourg
Merville
Benouville
Herouvillette
Pockets of paratroopers
Bayeux
352nd
716st
Creuilly
Seulles River
Front Line evening of 6
F
G
21st Panzer
Caen Canal
Orne River
Caen
Odon River
Carpiquet
Cheux
Bretteville l'Orgueilleuse
Tilly sur Seulles
Villers Bocage
Kampfgruppe Meyer
H
Troam
Cagny
5KM
N
D514
D6
D153
N13
D96
D5
D67
D572
D99
D12
D65
D22
D79
D7
D60
D84
D513
D400
D675
A13
D78
D37
A813
D613
A84
D9
D82
D126
Places to See:
19-21 Bayeux Battle Museum, Cemetery, Tapestry
22 Longues sur Mer Battery
23 Arromanches Museum, etc (Gold Beach)
24 Sexton Tank, Mont Fleury (Gold Beach)
25 Canadian Museum, DD Tank, Churchill Tank
26 WN28, Bernieres sur Mer
27 WN27, St. Aubin sur Mer
28 Canadian Cemetery Reviers
29 Churchill Marks 21st PzD (Sword Beach)
30 Cromwell Tank Memorial (Sword Beach)
31-32 Grand Bunker Msm & Commando Msm
33 Merville Battery Museum/Memorial
34 Pegasus Bridge Museum/Memorial
35 Memorial de Caen / Museum for Peace
36-37 Villers Bocage Memorial / Hill 213
39 Carpiquet Airfield Memorials
***Please note, the next map has the additional locations for the Battle of Caen and the drive south to Falaise.
● German Resistance Nest / Strong Point
MOVEMENTS:
A. At 0020 on June 6, the British Airborne landed their gliders within meters of their objective and captured the bridges over the Caen Canal and Orne River in 20 minutes.
B. By 0100, the remaining 8,000 British paratroopers began to land. At 0430 the attack on Merville commenced, it was captured by 0500 and held for 48 hrs.
C. Gold Beach, at 0725 the British 50th ID landed and had it opened by 10am.
D. Juno Beach, at 0745 the 3rd ID Canadians landed & made 10Km gains by day's end.
E. Sword Beach, at 0715 the British 3rd Division landed with little resistance.
F. Noon, the British advance towards Caen was stopped by a vicious counterattack by the 21st Panzer Division.
G. In the afternoon, the Canadians attempted to get further inland to capture their objective of Carpiquet Airfield but were unsuccessful due to the 21st PzD attack.
H. Kampfgruppe Meyer, initially attacked the false paratrooper decoys...then tried attacking the beachfront with little success.
I. By the day's end the 21st Pz Div, retreated without additional support.

BATTLES FOR A BREAKOUT, JUNE 7 - AUGUST 16 1944

MAP 46

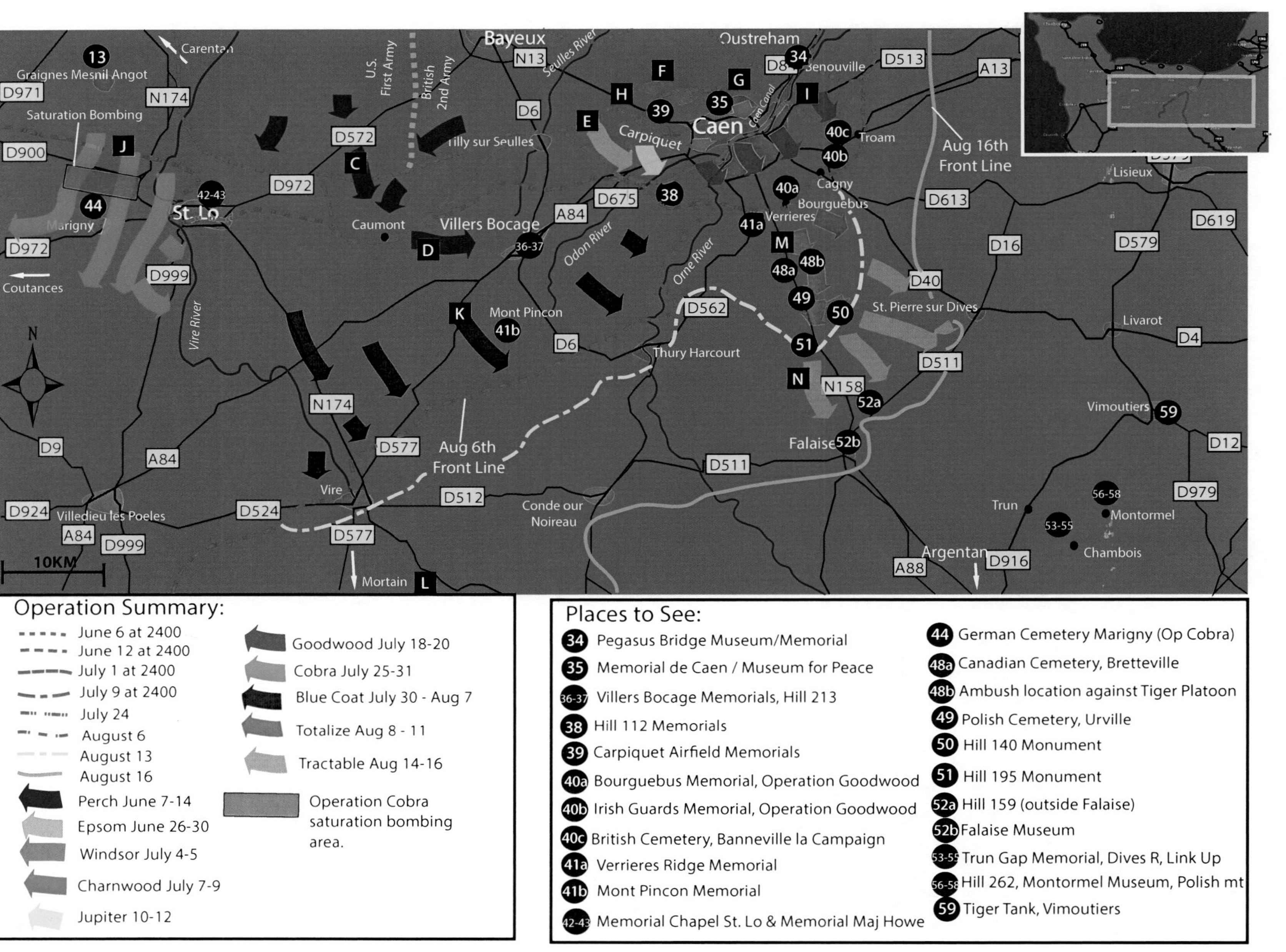
Bayeux
Oustreham
Caen
Carentan
Graignes Mesnil Angot
Saturation Bombing
St. Lo
Marigny
Coutances
U.S. First Army
British 2nd Army
Tilly sur Seulles
Caumont
Villers Bocage
Carpiquet
Seulles River
Odon River
Orne River
Vire River
Caen Canal
Benouville
Troam
Cagny
Bourguebus
Verrieres
Mont Pincon
Thury Harcourt
St. Pierre sur Dives
Falaise
Livarot
Lisieux
Vimoutiers
Trun
Montormel
Chambois
Argentan
Conde our Noireau
Vire
Mortain
Villedieu les Poeles
Aug 6th Front Line
Aug 16th Front Line
10KM
N
Operation Summary:
June 6 at 2400
June 12 at 2400
July 1 at 2400
July 9 at 2400
July 24
August 6
August 13
August 16
Perch June 7-14
Epsom June 26-30
Windsor July 4-5
Charnwood July 7-9
Jupiter 10-12
Goodwood July 18-20
Cobra July 25-31
Blue Coat July 30 - Aug 7
Totalize Aug 8 - 11
Tractable Aug 14-16
Operation Cobra saturation bombing area.
Places to See:
34 Pegasus Bridge Museum/Memorial
35 Memorial de Caen / Museum for Peace
36-37 Villers Bocage Memorials, Hill 213
38 Hill 112 Memorials
39 Carpiquet Airfield Memorials
40a Bourguebus Memorial, Operation Goodwood
40b Irish Guards Memorial, Operation Goodwood
40c British Cemetery, Banneville la Campaign
41a Verrieres Ridge Memorial
41b Mont Pincon Memorial
42-43 Memorial Chapel St. Lo & Memorial Maj Howe
44 German Cemetery Marigny (Op Cobra)
48a Canadian Cemetery, Bretteville
48b Ambush location against Tiger Platoon
49 Polish Cemetery, Urville
50 Hill 140 Monument
51 Hill 195 Monument
52a Hill 159 (outside Falaise)
52b Falaise Museum
53-55 Trun Gap Memorial, Dives R, Link Up
56-58 Hill 262, Montormel Museum, Polish mt
59 Tiger Tank, Vimoutiers

BATTLES FOR A BREAKOUT, CONTINUED

MAP 46

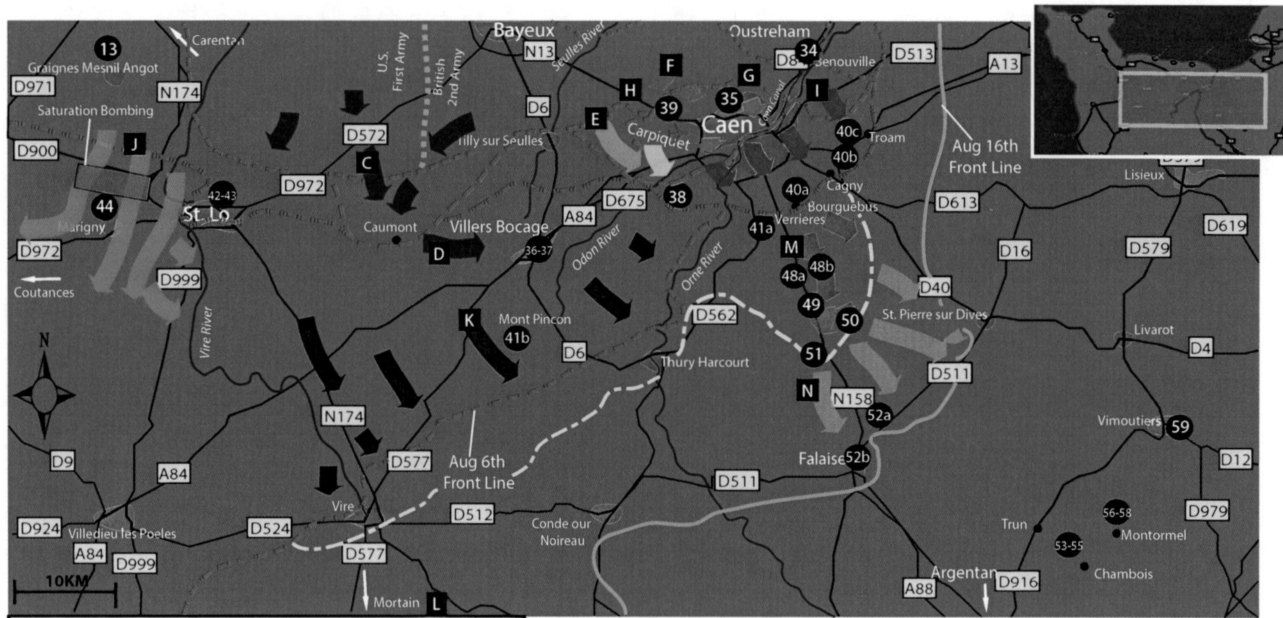
Bayeux
Oustreham
Carentan
Graignes Mesnil Angot
Saturation Bombing
U.S. First Army
British 2nd Army
Seulles River
Benouville
Tilly sur Seulles
Carpiquet
Caen
Troam
Aug 16th Front Line
Lisieux
Cagny
Bourguebus
Verrieres
St. Lo
Marigny
Caumont
Villers Bocage
Odon River
Orne River
Coutances
Vire River
Mont Pincon
Thury Harcourt
St. Pierre sur Dives
Livarot
Vimoutiers
Aug 6th Front Line
Vire
Falaise
Conde sur Noireau
Villedieu les Poeles
Trun
Montormel
Chambois
Argentan
Mortain
10KM
D971
N174
D900
D972
D999
D9
A84
D924
D524
D577
D512
D511
D562
D6
D572
N13
D8
D513
A13
D675
D613
D16
D40
D579
D619
D4
N158
D12
D979
A88
D916
13
44
42-43
39
35
34
40a
40b
40c
41a
41b
38
36-37
48a
48b
49
50
51
52a
52b
53-55
56-58
59
A
B
C
D
E
F
G
H
I
J
K
L
M
N

Movements:

A. June 7, Montgomery's primary objective was to capture Caen and allow the Allies to pivot to the east towards the Seine.

B. The German resistance was tough, top Panzer Armies were being sent in to reinforce the defense.

C. On June 13, after the US 1st Division broke through the German's 352nd defense, it created a gap for the British to exploit at Caumont.

D. Operation Perch drove into the gap but was stopped cold at Villers Bocage.

E. On June 26, after obtaining more supplies, Montgomery attemped Operation Epsom. Its goal was to capture Hill 112 with the entire VII Corps but they were stopped by the German I and II SS Panzer Corps.

F. On July 4 the Canadians made an ernest attempt to capture Carpiquet airfield. But they were replused after 2 days of bitter fighting.

G. Next on July 7, Operation Charnwood was initiated with a devasting bombing of Caen. It was followed by a frontal assault and new attack on Carpiquet. Carpiquet was captured and half of the city of Caen.

H. Operation Jupiter, July 10-12, was an attempt by the 43rd Wessex to capture Hill 112 to allow the Allies to use Carpiquet but they were repulsed again.

I. July 18, Operation Goodwood commenced with a massive attack east of Caen to break the stalemate. They finaly captured Caen but fell short of breaking through to Falaise and arrived only at Bourgeubus Ridge.

J. In the West, July 25-31, the Americans commenced Operation Cobra to try breaking through there. It resulted in a major breakthrough to the south.

K. Operation Bluecoat, July 30 - August 7 was another attempt to breakthrough south to Falaise but first capture the highground of Mont Pincon. After extreme losses the British took the high point but had no major breakthrough.

L. August 7 (not shown) the Germans attacked Mortain to try and split the American forces in the west. But this created a German pocket for Allied exploitation.

M. August 8, Operation Totalize commenced with the objective to breakthrough to Falaise but the Germans again resisted and forced great losses on the Allies.

N. August 14, after Bradley and Montogemery realized the opportunity to capture the Germans, operation Tractable was launched with furver to cut off the Germans and meet the Americans in Chambois.

BATTLE OF VILLERS BOCAGE, JUNE 13, 1944

MAP 47

Tilly sur Seulles
Caen
A
36a
A84
D675
D
D6
36b
C
Wittman and crew escape on foot.
British Advance Operation Perch
D33
E
F
J
37
I
G
H
D67
St. Lo
Villers Bocage
N
Vire
D675
A84
D6
Thury
500m
Mont Pincon

MOVEMENTS - in 1 hour of combat:

A. 22nd Armored Brigade Element, in the early morning of June 13 entered Villers Bocage from the west as part of Operation Perch, their attack path was to the east to out flank the defenses of Caen. The lead units stopped at the high ground of Hill 213 and deployed in a weak defensive pattern.
B. Unseen to their south, only 200 meters away were 6 each Tiger I tanks of the 101st Heavy SS Panzer Battalion, under the command of the Tank Ace Michael Wittman.
C. At 0900 Wittman broke out of his cover to attack the column. Four of his other tanks attacked Hill 213 (the 6th Tiger was stuck with engine problems).
D. Wittman knocked out a Firefly and a Cromwell then turned left towards Villers.
E. Next Wittman moved down the road & destroyed eight halftracks, four bren gun carriers and two each 6pdrs!
F. Then at the crossroads, three Stuarts were destroyed.
G. Next in the town, another halftrack was knocked out & four more Cromwell tanks!
H. Wittman then took out a Sherman command tank and another Cromwell. Next he was fired upon and damaged by a Sherman Firefly tank at the edge of town and Wittman retreated back to Hill 213.
I. On the way back, another Cromwell accidentally ran into the fray and was destroyed by Wittman.
J. Finally, Wittman's Tiger tank was stopped by a 6pdr gun crew that damaged his drive sprocket. He and his crew abandoned the tank and escaped on foot.
K. After Wittman's withdrawal, the British set up an ambush and took out 2 each Panzer IVs and 5 each Tiger Tanks when the Germans approached the town that afternoon. But soon after the British had to retreat that early evening. The village was leveled on June 30 by British bombers and not taken until August 4.

Total British losses: 27 tanks, 28 halftracks/bren gun carriers and 378 men that day.

Places to See:

- 36a Hill 213
- 36b Location of Wittman's Tanks prior to battle
- 37 Monument to the 7th Armored Division

- German Tiger I Tank
- British Cromwell, Sherman or Stuart Tank
- British Bren Gun Carrier or halftrack

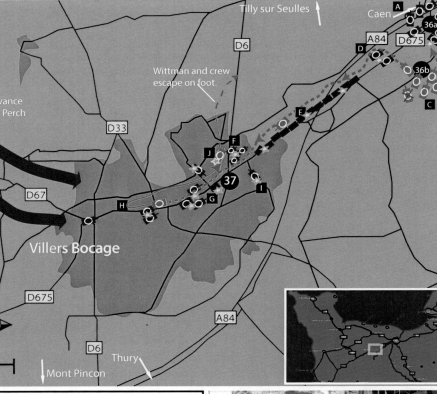

Wittman's disabled Tiger in Villers Bocage. Bundesarchive

FALAISE POCKET OVERVIEW AUGUST 16-21, 1944

MAP 48

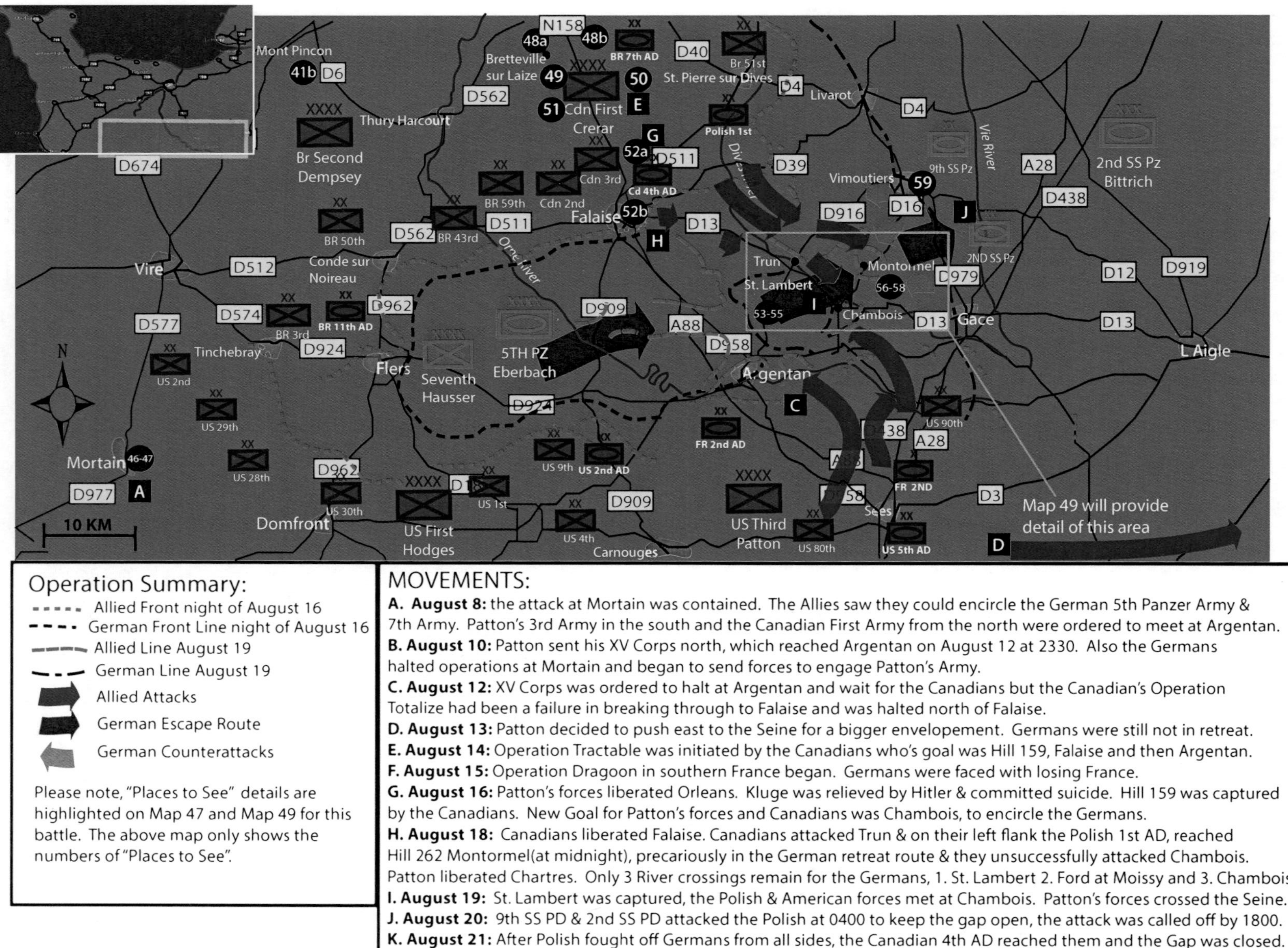
Mont Pincon
41b D6
XXXX
Br Second
Dempsey
Thury Harcourt
N158
48a
48b
Bretteville
sur Laize
49
D562
51 Cdn First
Crerar
50
E
BR 7th AD
D40
Br 51st
St. Pierre sur Dives
D4
Livarot
Polish 1st
G
52a
D511
Cdn 3rd
Cd 4th AD
BR 59th
Cdn 2nd
Falaise
52b
D13
H
D39
Vimoutiers
59
9th SS Pz
D916
D16
J
Vie River
A28
D438
2nd SS Pz
Bittrich
2ND SS Pz
D12
D919
D13
L Aigle
Trun
St. Lambert
Montormel
56-58
53-55
I
Chambois
D979
Gace
Orne River
D674
D512
Vire
D577
D574
BR 3rd
Tinchebray
Conde sur
Noireau
BR 50th
D562
BR 43rd
D511
D962
BR 11th AD
D924
Flers
Seventh
Hausser
5TH PZ
Eberbach
D909
A88
Argentan
C
FR 2nd AD
US 90th
A28
FR 2ND
D3
Sees
US 5th AD
US Third
Patton
US 80th
Map 49 will provide
detail of this area
D
US 2nd
US 29th
US 28th
Mortain
46-47
D977
A
10 KM
N
D962
US 30th
Domfront
US First
Hodges
US 1st
US 9th
US 2nd AD
D909
US 4th
Carnouges
Operation Summary:
Allied Front night of August 16
German Front Line night of August 16
Allied Line August 19
German Line August 19
Allied Attacks
German Escape Route
German Counterattacks
Please note, "Places to See" details are highlighted on Map 47 and Map 49 for this battle. The above map only shows the numbers of "Places to See".
MOVEMENTS:
A. August 8: the attack at Mortain was contained. The Allies saw they could encircle the German 5th Panzer Army & 7th Army. Patton's 3rd Army in the south and the Canadian First Army from the north were ordered to meet at Argentan.
B. August 10: Patton sent his XV Corps north, which reached Argentan on August 12 at 2330. Also the Germans halted operations at Mortain and began to send forces to engage Patton's Army.
C. August 12: XV Corps was ordered to halt at Argentan and wait for the Canadians but the Canadian's Operation Totalize had been a failure in breaking through to Falaise and was halted north of Falaise.
D. August 13: Patton decided to push east to the Seine for a bigger envelopement. Germans were still not in retreat.
E. August 14: Operation Tractable was initiated by the Canadians who's goal was Hill 159, Falaise and then Argentan.
F. August 15: Operation Dragoon in southern France began. Germans were faced with losing France.
G. August 16: Patton's forces liberated Orleans. Kluge was relieved by Hitler & committed suicide. Hill 159 was captured by the Canadians. New Goal for Patton's forces and Canadians was Chambois, to encircle the Germans.
H. August 18: Canadians liberated Falaise. Canadians attacked Trun & on their left flank the Polish 1st AD, reached Hill 262 Montormel(at midnight), precariously in the German retreat route & they unsuccessfully attacked Chambois. Patton liberated Chartres. Only 3 River crossings remain for the Germans, 1. St. Lambert 2. Ford at Moissy and 3. Chambois.
I. August 19: St. Lambert was captured, the Polish & American forces met at Chambois. Patton's forces crossed the Seine.
J. August 20: 9th SS PD & 2nd SS PD attacked the Polish at 0400 to keep the gap open, the attack was called off by 1800.
K. August 21: After Polish fought off Germans from all sides, the Canadian 4th AD reached them and the Gap was closed.

FALAISE POCKET: CLOSING THE GAP, AUGUST 19-21, 1944 MAP 49

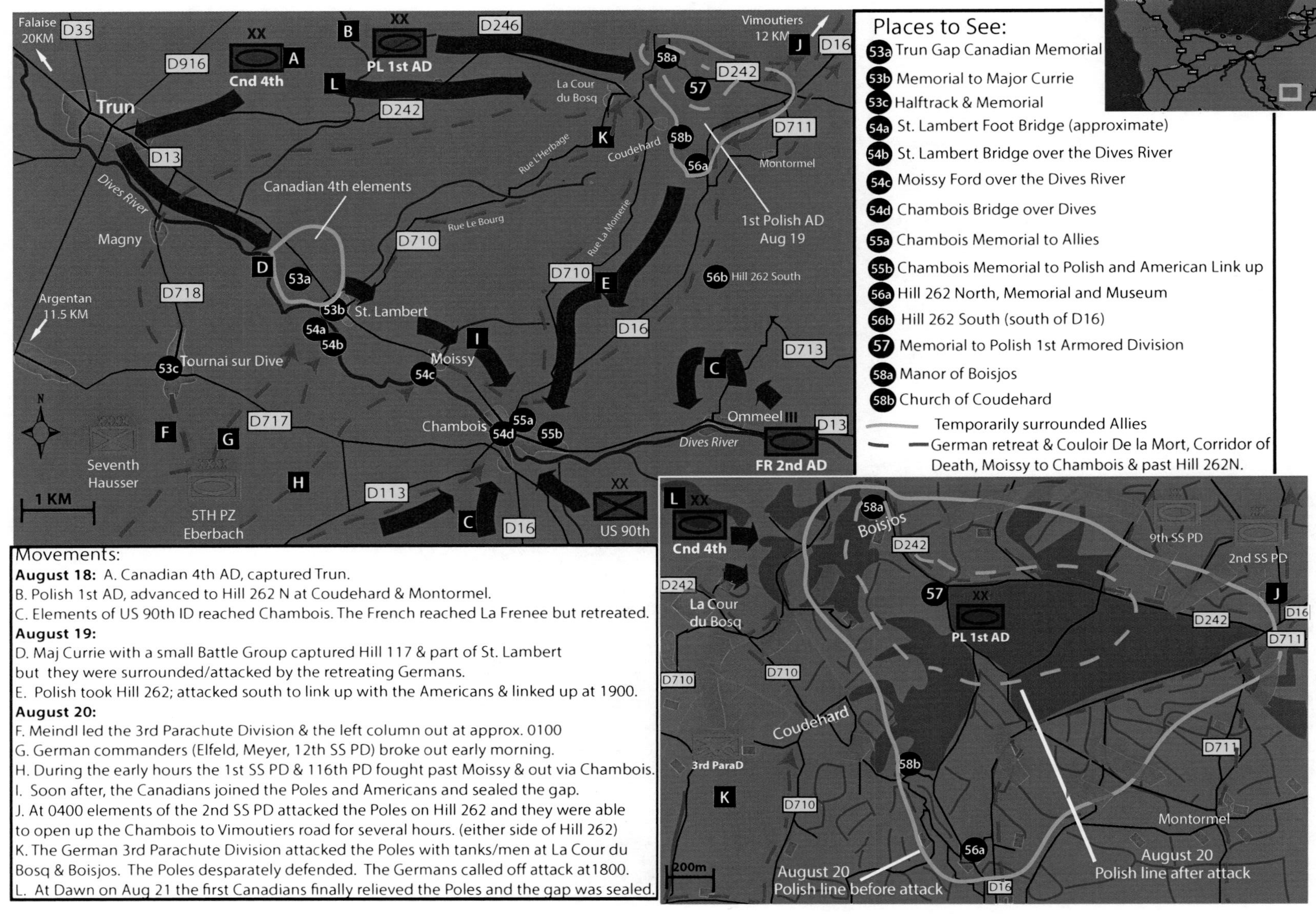
Places to See:
53a Trun Gap Canadian Memorial
53b Memorial to Major Currie
53c Halftrack & Memorial
54a St. Lambert Foot Bridge (approximate)
54b St. Lambert Bridge over the Dives River
54c Moissy Ford over the Dives River
54d Chambois Bridge over Dives
55a Chambois Memorial to Allies
55b Chambois Memorial to Polish and American Link up
56a Hill 262 North, Memorial and Museum
56b Hill 262 South (south of D16)
57 Memorial to Polish 1st Armored Division
58a Manor of Boisjos
58b Church of Coudehard
Temporarily surrounded Allies
German retreat & Couloir De la Mort, Corridor of Death, Moissy to Chambois & past Hill 262N.
Falaise 20KM
D35
D916
Cnd 4th
PL 1st AD
D246
D242
Vimoutiers 12 KM
D16
Trun
D13
Dives River
Magny
Canadian 4th elements
D710
Rue Le Bourg
Rue L'Herbage
La Cour du Bosq
Coudehard
Rue La Monerie
D711
Montormel
1st Polish AD Aug 19
Hill 262 South
Argentan 11.5 KM
D718
St. Lambert
Tournai sur Dive
Moissy
D713
Ommeel III
Chambois
D717
Seventh Hausser
5TH PZ Eberbach
D113
US 90th
FR 2nd AD
1 KM
Movements:
August 18: A. Canadian 4th AD, captured Trun.
B. Polish 1st AD, advanced to Hill 262 N at Coudehard & Montormel.
C. Elements of US 90th ID reached Chambois. The French reached La Frenee but retreated.
August 19:
D. Maj Currie with a small Battle Group captured Hill 117 & part of St. Lambert
but they were surrounded/attacked by the retreating Germans.
E. Polish took Hill 262; attacked south to link up with the Americans & linked up at 1900.
August 20:
F. Meindl led the 3rd Parachute Division & the left column out at approx. 0100
G. German commanders (Elfeld, Meyer, 12th SS PD) broke out early morning.
H. During the early hours the 1st SS PD & 116th PD fought past Moissy & out via Chambois.
I. Soon after, the Canadians joined the Poles and Americans and sealed the gap.
J. At 0400 elements of the 2nd SS PD attacked the Poles on Hill 262 and they were able
to open up the Chambois to Vimoutiers road for several hours. (either side of Hill 262)
K. The German 3rd Parachute Division attacked the Poles with tanks/men at La Cour du
Bosq & Boisjos. The Poles desparately defended. The Germans called off attack at1800.
L. At Dawn on Aug 21 the first Canadians finally relieved the Poles and the gap was sealed.
Boisjos
9th SS PD
2nd SS PD
3rd ParaD
200m
August 20 Polish line before attack
August 20 Polish line after attack

Far left, the approach to Omaha Beach. And left photo German defensive position, WN 62 on Omaha Beach. (NARA)

Far left: Omaha Beach, a stark contrast to decades ago. The photo to the left was taken from the view of the German crew in WN62 looking down Omaha Beach. They were protected from the naval shelling and had excellent fields of fire on the landing troops and vehicle.

Omaha Beach American Cemetery, far left photo located just west of WN62.

To left a sunset photo of Omaha Beach looking west. In distance you can see Pont du Hoc. It is also a great visual for the distance the soldiers had to cross with the tide out.

Far left is Pont du Hoc. The land was given to the US from DeGaulle in honor of their sacrifices. Today, you can still see the immense craters left by the US bombers on DDAY. It is definitely a top place to see and appreciate what the US Rangers scaled under fire and captured.

Photo inset and left are of the Longues sur Mer. The battery was in operation during DDAY. (NARA)

Le Merderet

Behind Utah Beach, is an important memorial to "Iron Mike"(left) at the La Fiere Bridge. The US paratroopers defended the river crossing and blocked the Germans, including some tanks from crossing. The center photo was taken looking from the position of the Americans facing south. The photo to the right shows the horses in the field across from Brecourt Manor where the 101st took out artillery pieces.

C-47

Left, is the inside of the Church at Angoville Plain. Center photo shows the church tower of St. Mere Eglise, that has a paratrooper mannequin hanging from it. And to the right is the outstanding St. Mere Eglise Museum.

Far left, at Utah Beach is another excellent museum. Outfront they have another Sherman and 88mm cannon. And very well done displays.

Left, on Utah Beach you can experience the drastic difference in terrain incomparison to Omaha Beach. Utah Beach does not have the same cliffs and defensive advantages that Omaha Beach had.

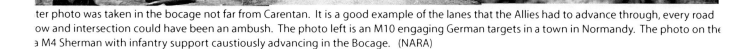

ter photo was taken in the bocage not far from Carentan. It is a good example of the lanes that the Allies had to advance through, every road ow and intersection could have been an ambush. The photo left is an M10 engaging German targets in a town in Normandy. The photo on the a M4 Sherman with infantry support caustiously advancing in the Bocage. (NARA)

Far left, Pont en Bessin memorial to soldiers that fought to liberate the port. It was the transition from American terroritory to the British beaches. Just a few miles inland is Bayeux with a beautiful Cathedral. Another must visit is the Bayeux Tapestry Museum, where the Tapestry depicting the story of the invasion of England in 1066 by William the Conquer is located.

Far Left: Gold Beach, just east of Port en Bessin has many memorials and an excellent museum. From this picture you can still see the remains of one of the Mulberry harbors. The other one was destroyed by a major storm off Omaha Beach. The tractor was on the shore for the fishermen to pull their boats in and out of the tide. It was resting amongst all the seaweed and shells.

Juno Beach, was the Canadian AOR. They have built a new museum and learning center just off the beach, shown far left. Outfront they still have remains of bunkers and beach obstacles.

Sword Beach, was similar to the Utah Beach terrain. But it did have some significant bunkers, to include what is now the Grand Bunker museum(far left). It was definitely one of my favorite museums in Normandy. Left middle is a photo of the Brits landing on Sword Beach and lower left inset, is a photo of another Churchill tank which was buried a few days into the war and rediscovered only a few years ago on Sword Beach.

Far left, Pegasus Bridge Memorial Park and Museum, a must see in Normandy. Left, is the Merville Battery Park, it surprisingly has a C47 which actually served also in the Balkans after the war.

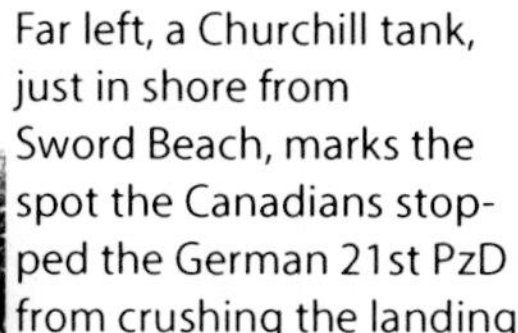

Far left, a Churchill tank, just in shore from Sword Beach, marks the spot the Canadians stopped the German 21st PzD from crushing the landing.

Left, a photo of another Churchill with a 57mm main gun on Hill 112. The Hill was won and lost several times. At this point you have a commanding view of Normandy and Carpiquet Airfield outside of Caen.

Far left, Villers Bocage Memorial to the the devasting battle that took place on June 13 as part of Operation Perch.

Left upper photo is of a destroyed Cromwell tank in Villers Bocage, one of many destroyed that day.

Left lower, is the main road with the destroyed bren gun carriers and halftracks.

Below left, is a photo of Wittman's tank. He was killed defending the route to Falaise Gap. It is believed he was killed by a Firefly Sherman like the one below.

In Western Normandy, Mont St. Michel is a great place to go visit. It sits out in the channel and is accessible from a small road.

Nearby is the Brittany American Cemetery, just outside the town of St. James and only a few miles from Mont St. Michel.

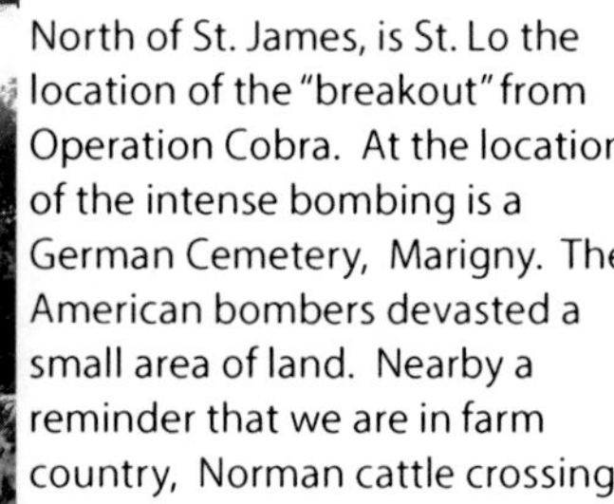

North of St. James, is St. Lo the location of the "breakout" from Operation Cobra. At the location of the intense bombing is a German Cemetery, Marigny. The American bombers devasted a small area of land. Nearby a reminder that we are in farm country, Norman cattle crossing.

VALOR
SACRIFICE
COURAGE

South from St. Lo and east of St. James is the town of Mortain. The photo to the far left is the memorial on top of Hill 314 recognizing the 30th ID and units that defended the town. You can still see traces of the the trenches and foxholes in the woods. The photo to the left is of destroyed German vehicles on the road to Mortain. (Bundesarchieve)

After defeating the Germans at Mortain the Americans rushed the southern route to encircle the Germans in the Falaise Gap. The photo on the far left is the memorial outside the town of Chambois to commemorate the link up between the Americans and Polish to close the gap.

The photo left, is the Falaise Museum in the town of Falaise with vehicles, equipment and displays to see from the battle of the Falaise Gap. Next to the museum is also the Castle in Falaise from the days of William the Conqueror.

Far left, is the memorial on Hill 195, one of the many ridges and hills the British and Canadian forces slugged their way through to Falaise Gap. The Imperial Museum photo to the left shows the innovation of using Sherman chasis to transport troops. These were first introduced in July to use to rush the ridge lines and hills, allowing the infantry to keep up with the armor formations in a night attack.

Far left, a photo of one of the few farm houses in the area of Montormel. Note the small roads that the Germans were retreating on. Up on Montormel Hill 262 is an excellent memorial & museum. You can hike along the path and explore the hill. The memorial includes the Sherman with the 76mm cannon and a M8 armored car.

Below Hill 262 are the small roads that became the "Corridor of Death" for the Germans in the Falaise Gap. Aircraft, artillery, tanks & infantry pounded the Germans as they escaped.

Far left, a great view from the memorial that shows the importance of Hill 262. Never thought roses and a Tiger I go together but in France they do. Just past Hill 262 in the town of Vimitours is one of the few remaing Tiger tanks.

OPERATION DRAGOON

(Operation Anvil)

August 15–September 14, 1944

"The Other D-Day"

SUMMARY: One of the most successful military operations in history commenced at 0430 on August 15, 1944 when more than 10,000 American, British and French paratroopers landed at their objective, Le Muy in Southern France. The airborne assault was one of the first elements in the "Other D-Day," Operation Dragoon (initially named Operation Anvil), the invasion of Southern France. Like Operation Overlord, Operation Dragoon involved deception, commando raids and an airborne assault. The French commandos attacked and sealed the flanks, while the airborne assault secured a main hub to the beachhead at Le Muy. In addition, more than 50 ships took part in a naval bombardment, while an aerial attack involved more than 1,300 aircraft. After the shelling and bombings, the Americans led an amphibious assault on beaches code named Alpha, Delta and Camel. The amphibious landing force consisted of three veteran American divisions. On Alpha, the western beach just west of Saint-Tropez, the 3rd Infantry Division landed. In the middle, on Delta, the 45th Infantry Division landed at Sainte-Maxime. Finally, on the right flank in the east, the 36th Infantry Division landed near Saint-Raphaël, just west of Cannes. The overall commander for the Allied forces was General Alexander Patch, whose main objectives to achieve in 120 days were as follows: establishing a beachhead, capturing the ports of Marseilles and Toulon, and driving north to link up with Patton's Third Army in Central France. The opposition was the solid Nineteenth Army under the command of Friedrich Wiese, stationed in Avignon west of the Rhone River. On this D-Day, as compared to Normandy, the bombardments were very effective and the deceptions worked very well. The Germans knew that a build-up was occurring, but did not know at which beaches the landing would occur. They had very little Luftwaffe support and even less naval support, and most of their reserves had been sent to Normandy. Based on the assumption that the Allied attack would occur near the major ports of Marseilles and Toulon, Wiese ordered on August 14 that the 11th Panzer Division and two infantry divisions cross the Rhone toward Marseilles. For additional preparation, Wiese had fortified the ports of Toulon and Marseilles because Hitler had issued the command to "stand and die." On August 15, the main attack commenced at 0800 just east of Toulon, where the first American soldiers and tanks rushed forward on the beaches, engaging and destroying German strongholds. By afternoon, the beaches had been secured and the Americans began moving inland. By the end of the first day, 94,000 men had landed, as had 11,000 vehicles.

On August 16, after the beachhead had been secured, the French First Army began to land. Patch did not want a repeat of Anzio, during which the Americans, despite having landed successfully with little to no resistance, waited out of fear of a German trap and, consequently, gave the Germans time to attack. Instead, Patch aggressively sent the 3rd and 45th Infantry Divisions west to engage the Germans. He also sent Task Force Butler and the 36th Infantry Division north to exploit openings. In addition, Patch sent the paratroopers east toward Nice to guard against any attack to the flanks from Albert Kesselring's forces in Italy. On August 17, the Germans received a message from Hitler calling for an all-out withdrawal from France because of the defeat in Normandy. At the same time, the ULTRA program intercepted and deciphered the message and the Allies became aware of German plans to withdraw.

By August 22, the 3rd Infantry Division had pushed the German lines back 96 kilometers to the west. The French attacked Toulon, which contained 18,000 German defenders, and Marseille, which contained 12,000 German defenders. By August 28, the French had captured the ports because the Germans didn't have enough time to set up their defenses. Approximately 17,000 Germans surrendered; the remaining Germans were casualties. At this point, Patch was well ahead of his objectives, but was running into logistical problems because he had not anticipated such a quick success.

While the French were capturing the ports, the 3rd Infantry Division was pursuing the retreating German Nineteenth Army. The army, partially broken except for the healthy 11th Panzer Division, was moving north along the Rhone River in a retreat toward Germany. However, they were trapped. Task Force Butler had moved 257 kilometers north, the 3rd Division was on its tail and the 36th Division had moved into Montelimar directly in the path of the fleeing Germans. Montelimar was a key city that contained bridges the Germans could cross over the Rhone River, after which they could head northeast to Germany. At Montelimar, the two forces clashed in brutal combat from August 21-28. Task Force Butler and elements of the 36th Infantry Division took up blocking positions on Hill 300 and Hill 430, which overlooked the main escape route, N7, on the east side of the river. Task Force Butler took a beating but held the ground by calling in artillery to thwart the Germans, who were trying to head east. On August 26, the Germans left an infantry division as a rear guard to hold the Americans at Montelimar. The rest of the German Army punched north toward Lyon, attempting to cut east from there. Because the Germans were pinned against the Rhone River and American-held hills, route N7 became the "Falaise Pocket" of the south, with destroyed German equipment and dead soldiers everywhere. In total, more than 2,500 Germans were killed, 3,500 vehicles destroyed and 500 horses killed.

On August 29, the German rear guard at Montelimar was eliminated. Next, the Allied forces continued the attack north in an attempt to stop the Germans from escaping. From west to east, the Allied formation was: the French 1st Armored Division on the left flank on the west bank of the Rhone River, the 3rd Infantry Division on the east bank, the 36th Infantry Division in the center and the 45th Infantry Division on the right flank. The Germans made it to Lyon first, but had no time to set up another defensive line and started to head east. The German commander sent the 11th Panzer Division to secure a route to the Belfort Gap across the Vosges Mountains into Germany.

On September 3, the 117th Cavalry Squadron of the 45th Infantry Division (a lighter unit made up of approximately 400 men with light tanks and armored cars) was sent to block the German escape in the town of Montreval en Bresse only 20 miles east of the Germans, directly in their escape route. Their plan was to threaten the German flank. However, at 1100 the Germans sent in the 11th Panzer Division's Reconnaissance Battalion reinforced with six medium tanks, a battery of self-propelleds and an engineer company. After hours of intense fighting, the 117th Cavalry Squadron was almost destroyed. In summary, the Americans lost the following: five soldiers killed, 126 captured, 31 wounded, 35 vehicles captured and two tanks destroyed.

By September 4, the Allies had to halt because of delays related to logistics. (Every division required 100,000 gallons of fuel a day!) After a 48-hour break on September 6, the Allies resumed their attack. By September 8 they were over the Doube River as the Germans fled northeast through the Belfort Gap. From September 10-12, elements of Patton's Third Army began to meet up with Patch's Seventh Army in and around Dijon. Patch halted his men on September 14 and transferred the Seventh Army command from the Mediterranean Command to the Supreme Headquarters Allied Expeditionary Force under Dwight Eisenhower. Operation Dragoon was a brilliant success in that it had defeated the enemy, but, unfortunately, is seldom discussed. The operation was supposed to take 120 days, but the Allies achieved all their objectives and more in only 30 days. The French and Americans had cut off large numbers of Germans trying to flee France; out of the 250,000 soldiers assigned to the Nineteenth Army, 7,000 were killed in action, 20,000 were wounded and 65,000 were taken prisoner. However, the Allies also paid a price in the form of 2,000 killed in action and more than 4,500 wounded. The Allies' relentless pursuit didn't let the Germans form a defense; they could only react to the Allies.

OUTCOME: On September 12, north of Dijon, the French 1st Armor linked up with Patton's Third Army at Autun. Also, the ports of Marseille and Toulon aided in logistics support, providing over one-third of the equipment and supplies the Allied forces used until Antwerp was opened in mid-November. In addition, all of the German forces were out of France except for small pockets of resistance that the Allies had bypassed, such as Saint-Nazaire on the Atlantic coast and the fortifications in Lorraine and Alsace.

WHAT WAS IT OVER? Freedom

WHO? Numbers and leaders? Initially, the forces consisted of approximately 200,000 Americans, followed by 200,000 French against 300,000 Germans. The Allies suffered approximately 6,000 casualties (2,000 killed in action). On D-Day of Operation Dragoon, the Allies suffered approximately 95 killed in action and 385 wounded in action. The Germans suffered more than 25,000 casualties (7,000 killed in action), while 65,000 were taken prisoner.

WHEN? August 15–September 14, 1944

WHY ON THE FRENCH RIVIERA? Churchill did not want the Allies to pull resources from the Italian peninsula and favored an Allied landing in the Balkans to drive north and capture Vienna. His strategy would cut off oil supplies from Romania and stop the Russians from capturing too much of Eastern Europe. However, fighting in the Balkans and even in Northern Italy would be deadly for any attacking forces because of the terrain. Eisenhower spearheaded the plan to attack in Southern France so that the Allies could gain a "broad front" in the west against the Germans. The Allies chose the French Riviera for the two main ports that sat nearby, its light defenses and its 30 miles of good beachhead for landings.

TECHNOLOGY/TACTICS: Both sides used technology similar to that of Operation Overlord, mentioned in the previous chapter. One item not mentioned was ULTRA, the secret program that deciphered the coded Enigma machine for German communications. ULTRA provided the Allies with the positions, numbers and plans of the German defenders. For example, when Hitler ordered the retreat, the Allies deciphered the message within one day. Tactically, the Allies used deception in the form of increased radio communication in non-important areas, bombardments farther east and fake landings closer to Italy. Also, the Americans set up a mobile exploitation force called Task Force Butler; it was an extremely successful, highly mobile force that exploited breakthroughs and reconnaissance to maintain contact with the enemy. The Germans were strung out all over France, reacting to the invasion of Normandy and their losses there. The Nineteenth Army had only one Panzer Division, the 11th, left. The 2nd SS Panzer, 9th Panzer, 17th Panzer Grenadiers and two battalions of the 11th Panzer Division were sent to Normandy. Due to the aggressive Allied assault, the Germans could never develop a second line of defense or counterattack. As a result, within two days the Germans were ordered to withdraw from France. Similar to the situation in Normandy, the Germans were plagued with logistical problems due to French Resistance activity and even the various weapon systems used in defense of the shore. At one location, the Germans may have deployed French, Italian, Czech and German cannons. Also, the units received small amounts of ammunition – only six units, or approximately 500 rounds, of fire. To note, the French Resistance was active and successful in this region. In just 1944, more than 1,400 special operations were conducted in the region. The Germans deployed their Kampfgeschwader 100 Wiking, which was a unit of Dornier 217s and a Heinkel He 177 that carried a guided missile for anti-ship and bridge missions. The unit had recently been removed from the Normandy operations, during which it lost more than 12 aircraft. In Operation Dragoon, the unit had 14 aircraft to deploy and succeeded only once in hitting a target. By mid-September, the unit had suffered 100 percent casualties and was disbanded.

QUOTE: "The characteristic which higher command always looks for in any officer is honesty. Honesty in thought, word, and deed. Second to honesty and courage of purpose, I would place an unselfish attitude as the greatest attribute of a leader. Place the care and protection of the men first; share their hardships without complaint and when the real test comes you will find that they possess a genuine respect and admiration for you. To do otherwise means failure at the crucial moment when the support of your men is essential to the success of the battle." – General Alexander M. Patch

PLACES TO SEE (SOUTH TO NORTH/THE INVASION ROUTE) (REFERENCE MAPS 50-55):

INITIAL LANDINGS AND COASTAL ADVANCES:

1. **NICE MONUMENT AUX MORTS, FRENCH MONUMENT TO FALLEN:** In Nice just off the coastal road is a memorial to the French fallen for both wars. Nice is beautiful, but was not technically part of the landing area during Operation Dragoon.
   N 43 41.608 E 7 16.875 (43.693467, 7.28125)

2. **CAMUEL BEACH, SAINT-RAPHAËL 36TH INFANTRY DIVISION MONUMENT AND HIGGINS BOAT:** Located just east of Saint-Raphaël is Eisenhower Square, which is off the main beach where the 36th Infantry Division landed. The beach is open to the public and is probably the invasion's biggest memorial. It includes a plaque, a Higgins boat and, just to the right of the boat, an information board on a path to the beach. From the beach you can get a great sense of the terrain and fields of fire.
   N 43 25.026 E 6 50.727 (43.4171, 6.84545)

3. **CAMUEL BEACH, GERMAN GUN EMPLACEMENT:** Along the shore you can see a machine gun post. This site was also the location of a major gun emplacement. The emplacement is blocked up, though you can easily tell that it was intended for a large-caliber cannon. About 200 yards off the shore, near the castle island, is a B17 that crash landed in the water during the invasion. Note that a great restaurant overlooks the main beach near the 36th Infantry Division monument.
   N 43 24.827 E 6 50.916 (43.413783, 6.8486)

4. **DELTA BEACH, SAINTE-MAXIME 45TH INFANTRY DIVISION MONUMENT:** In the middle of the invasion, the 45th Infantry Division landed at this location. Unfortunately, the monument is not much more than a three-foot by three-foot stone. At this location you can see the terrain and the beautiful beach.
   N 43 20.460 E 6 40.835 (43.341, 6.680583)

5. **ALPHA BEACH, MEMORIAL TO GENERAL PATCH:** At this location is a memorial stone to General Alexander Patch. Also here, elements of the 3rd Infantry Division landed along what is still a beautiful and popular beach.
   N 43 13.628 E 6 39.698 (43.227133, 6.661633)

6. **ALPHA BEACH, DEBARQMENT MEMORIAL:** At this location is the parking area for the beach and a memorial dedicated to the site where the 3rd Infantry Division landed. Between restaurants and the beach are flagpoles and an information board with a map and pictures of the landing. This is another

great spot to appreciate the landing and terrain…plus the food and the sun!
N 43 11.406 E 6 33.404 (43.1901, 6.556733)

7. **ALPHA BEACH/INLAND 3RD INFANTRY DIVISION MEMORIAL:** Just up the road from the Debarqment Memorial is another memorial for the 3rd Infantry Division and the French. It's located off D559.
N 43 11.639 E 6 33.641 (43.193983, 6.560683)

8. **ALPHA BEACH, LIBERATION MONUMENT FOR THE FRENCH AND 3RD INFANTRY DIVISION:** At this location next to the harbor is a monument to the liberation of the town and the coast. It was the location where the French and the U.S. 3rd Infantry Division landed, and features a large stone memorial. Just to the right is a dedication to the 3rd Infantry Division.
N 43 10.408 E 6 31.995 (43.173467, 6.53325)

9. **RAMATUELLE, AUDIE MURPHY LOCATION FOR DISTINGUISHED SERVICE CROSS:** Near this location, according to a map in Audie Murphy's award documentation is the site where Audie won his Distinguished Service Cross. During the heroic event, he took out four machine gun emplacements, inflicted more than 10 German casualties and captured half a dozen more. Part of his fearless action stemmed from the fact that his best friend, Lattie Tipton, had been killed when he stood up after a German position deceptively raised a white flag. At that instant, Audie killed the crew with grenades, then took the machine gun and shot it from his hip, taking out another two machine gun positions. Tipton is buried in the American Rhone Cemetery. The following geo coordinates will take you to the crossroads where the action related to Audie Murphy's Distinguished Service Cross took place. See Map 53 for more information.
N 43 13.199 E 6 38.884 (43.219983, 6.648067)

10a. **LE MUY LIBERATION MUSEUM:** Le Muy is the town where some sharp but short engagements took place between the Allied paratroopers and the defending Germans. Unfortunately, due to a flood in 2010, this museum has been closed and is not planning to reopen anytime soon.
N 43 28.315 E 6 34.188 (43.471917, 6.5698)

10b. **TRAFFIC CIRCLE FREDERICK MEMORIAL:** Nearby the museum is a traffic circle dedicated to General Robert T. Frederick, the commander of the 1st Airborne Taskforce that liberated Le Muy.
Traffic circle: N 43 28.290 E 6 34.360 (43.4715, 6.572667)

11. **DROP ZONES:** Along this road are the primary areas where the 1st Airborne Taskforce landed. These geo coordinates provide the location of the D1555 roadside. Just north of this is Drop Zone A.
N 43 28.754 E 6 31.400 (43.479233, 6.523333)

12. **FRENCH ARTILLERY MUSEUM, DRAGUIGNAN:** This museum, the National Artillery Museum, is situated on a French military base. It maintains an outstanding collection of recently updated displays, tanks and equipment.
N 43 31.609 E 6 29.795 (43.526817, 6.496583)

13. **AMERICAN CEMETERY RHONE:** In Draguignan, this beautiful cemetery and memorial holds the graves of 860 American heroes. The graves include that of Private Lattie Tipton, Audie Murphy's friend who was killed during the fighting around Ramatuelle.
N 43 32.169 E 6 28.390 (43.53615, 6.473167)

14. **AIX EN PROVENCE LIBERATION MEMORIAL, 3RD INFANTRY DIVISION:** In a pedestrian zone in the arch of the old tower in the town of Aix is a plaque that honors the 3rd Infantry Division for liberating the city.
N 43 31.799 E 5 26.863 (43.529983, 5.447717)

15. **CAMP DES MILLES, INTERNMENT, TRANSIT AND DEPORTATION CAMP:** Just southeast of Aix-en-Provence is a memorial to and museum about a concentration camp that held many writers, artists and political opponents. Today it houses new and permanent exhibits; the grounds are largely intact.
N 43 30.209 E 5 22.963 (43.503483, 5.382717)

TOULON:

16. **MAUVANNE BATTERY, CASEMENT AND COMMAND BUNKER:** At this location east of Toulon were four each 150mm cannons with a range of over 19 kilometers in type M272 casements. On August 19, French commandos attacked and captured the bunker as well as most of the Germans in it. The fortification's remains still exist and are worth a stop so that you can see the massive walls and field of fire.
N 43 07.952 E 6 11.490 (43.132533, 6.1915)

17. **D-DAY MUSEUM OF TOULON, MUSÉE MÉMORIAL DU DÉBARQUEMENT DE PROVENCE:** This is probably the "main" and best museum dedicated to Operation Dragoon. It is located on top of the high mountain overlooking Toulon. The road leading up to it is long and narrow, but well worth the views, the opportunities for hiking and the nice restaurant next to the museum. In front, the museum features a Sherman tank, 88mm anti-aircraft cannon and German 75mm PAK (Panzerabwehrkanone) cannon. The museum has unique artifacts and maps and is well worth the visit. The French attacked Toulon from the north and fought for these hills from August 22-23.
N 43 09.067 E 5 55.851 (43.151117, 5.93085)

18. **FORT DE LA CROIX FARON:** This fort is still a military base and closed to the public. It is located just down the road from the museum/fortification and overlooks the main Fort Faron.
N 43 08.697 E 5 57.621 (43.14495, 5.96035)

19. **FORT FARON:** Located below the museum are the actual remains of the fort that overlooks and protects the port and city. You can park here and explore the area.
N 43 08.433 E 5 57.473 (43.14055, 5.957883)

PUSH NORTH AND OFF THE COAST: The following are locations, starting at Montelimar, where deadly engagements took place as the Allies tried to cut off the Germans. It is a beautiful country and I recommend using highway N7 to drive along the Rhone River. N7 is the main road the Germans used to retreat on the east side of the Rhone. It's also the road the Americans used to pursue the Germans.

20. **MONTELIMAR MEMORIAL:** For several days at the end of August, intense conflict occurred as the trapped Germans fought viciously to escape. The Americans held the high ground north of the city, while the Germans tried to punch east and north. At this location is a monument dedicated to the French and Americans who fought from these hills to cut off the German retreat. It overlooks route N7.
N 44 41.023 E 4 48.826 (44.683717, 4.813767)

21. **LA COUCOURDE VILLAGE:** Located on N7 and under Hill 430 is the location of road blocks that Task Force Butler placed starting on August 23 to stop the German retreat. On August 25, the Germans attempted a breakthrough and failed. Later that night, the Germans, with tanks, finally broke through. On some of the older buildings you can still see bullet marks and patches. These geo coordinates mark a location on N7, just north of a small bridge, that's an ideal spot for a road block.
N 44 38.839 E 4 46.900 (44.647317, 4.781667)

22a. **HILL 430 CREST:** This hill and the area around it experienced sharp fighting between the escaping Germans and the Americans firing down on them. The hill exchanged hands several times. Limited access is available, but on either side are locations in which to park. A trail is also available for hiking throughout the area. The following coordinates are for the crest of the hill:
N 44 37.452 E 4 48.618 (44.6242, 4.8103)

22b. **HILL 430 PARKING LOCATION:** These coordinates direct you to a place where you can park in a town north of the hill. To get to the crest, walk south from this parking spot in a diagonal direction past a farm and onto a path to the hill.
N 44 38.259 E 4 48.765 (44.63765, 4.81275)

23. **HILL 300:** Overlooking the Battle for Montelimar is Hill 300, not too far from the memorial. At this location, Task Force Butler called in artillery and fought to keep the hill against the retreating Germans. These coordinates are for the top of the hill. The Germans were traveling on the hill's west side, along route N7. The hill offers parking and decent hiking paths at the top. It has a very impressive view and provides great insight into the terrain. Note that the

road leading up to the overlook is Chemin du Relais.
44 36.785 E 4 46.744 (44.613083, 4.779067)

24a.MARSANNE MEMORIAL AND BULLET HOLES: East of Hill 300 and Hill 430 is a plain with the towns of Sauzet and Marsanne at the foot of the hills. The Germans, desperate to prevent the Americans from blocking their retreat north, attacked Sauzet on August 23 but were defeated by a battalion from the 36th Infantry Division. The Germans tried to attack this area again on August 25 without success. In the town of Marsanne, the mayor's house still shows bullet holes from the fighting and also has a plaque dedicated to Task Force Butler, which liberated the town. These geo coordinates will take you directly in front of the mayor's house, where the plaque is.
N 44 38.626 E 4 52.398 (44.643767, 4.8733)

24b.PUY-SAINT-MARTIN: On August 21, Task Force Butler passed through this town on its way from Grenoble prior to taking up positions on Hill 300. On August 22, elements of the 11th Panzer Division captured the town, but were soon ousted as additional elements of Task Force Butler arrived in the battle area. This is the top of Cemetery Hill; it offers a pretty good view of the battle area from the eastern edge.
N 44 37.839 E 4 58.398 (44.63065, 4.9733)

25a.DROME RIVER BRIDGE AT LIVRON SUR DROME: At this location, the French Resistance and commandos fought fierce battles with the retreating Germans. The bridge is dedicated to commando Henri Faure and his men. On August 16, Faure and his troops destroyed a large section of the bridge, forcing the Germans to head east in search of another bridge they could cross or a place where they could ford the river. The bridge's destruction did not allow the Germans to retreat in good order or set up another defensive line near Lyon. Instead, it created a death trap along route N7 on the Rhone River, resulting in 2,500 Germans killed in action, 3,000 German prisoners of war and 3,500 destroyed vehicles.
N 44 45.973 E 4 50.407 (44.766217, 4.840117)

25b.FRENCH RESISTANCE MEMORIAL, ALLEX: This memorial commemorates the more than 20 resistance fighters who disrupted the German retreat over the Drome River.
N 44 47.366 E 4 53.839 (44.789433, 4.897317)

NORTH OF LYON: After the fighting in Montelimar, fierce engagements took place when the overstretched Americans tried cutting off the Germans north of Lyon.

26. MEXIMIEUX: On September 1, elements of the 45th Division arrived in Meximieux, just south of the crossroad town of Bourg, which was part of the German escape route. A Kampfgruppe from the 11th Panzer Division attacked Meximieux with a large tank force, inflicting casualties of 200 men, two M10s, two armored cars and several vehicles. However, the Germans lost

more than 150 men (80 killed in action) and 12 tanks, including nine Panthers. At this location is a French statue with a memorial plaque to the Americans who fought and died in the Meximieux Battle.
N 45 54.295 E 5 11.519 (45.904917, 5.191983)

Location of Hotel du Lion D'Or/photo of where a Panther tank was destroyed:
N 45 54.207 E 5 11.530 (45.90345, 5.192167)

Note: Next to Meximeux is an impressive walled medieval town called Perouges that is worth a stop. It has been in various movies, including The Three Musketeers (1961). The geo coordinates will take you to the main entrance and parking area.

N 45 54.354 E 5 10.507 (45.9059, 5.175117)

27. **MEMORIAL, BOURG-EN-BRESSE:** At this location is a memorial to the liberation of Bourg-en-Bresse in September 1944 by the French and the 45th Infantry Division.
N 46 12.189 E 5 13.250 (46.20315, 5.220833)

28. **MEMORIAL, MONTREVAL-EN-BRESSE:** In this town, the 117th Cavalry Squadron of the 45th Infantry Division was destroyed by units of the 11th Panzer Division. On September 3, General Lucian Truscott sent his 117th Cavalry Reconnaissance Squadron out for one more blocking attempt on the Germans in this town. Unfortunately, they were outgunned and outnumbered by the retreating German forces. The squadron suffered five killed in action and 126 taken prisoner. It also lost 20 Jeeps, two light tanks and 15 armored cars. At this location, next to the post office, is a small park called "Place du 3 Septembre."
N 46 20.268 E 5 07.696

On the edge of the town's east side is a stele in memory of the 117th Cavalry Squadron; it includes the names of those who died in the battle.
N 46 20.218 E 5 07.971 (46.336967, 5.13285)

29. **FRENCH RESISTANCE MUSEUM AND MEMORIAL, VASSIEUX-EN-VERCORS:** The town of Vassieux-en-Vercors contains a museum dedicated to the French Resistance. Also, in the mountains is a memorial to French Resistance fighters. It is located east of Montelimar halfway to Grenoble.
N 44 54.417 E 5 21.617 (44.90695, 5.360283)

FOLLOWING THE NORTHERN ROUTE OF THE ALLIES:

30. **BEAUNE SHERMAN:** The retreating Germans took out a French tank just south of Dijon on the outskirts of the beautiful and historic Burgundy town of Beaune. Note that the Sherman is hidden from the road, with a significant amount of brush in front of the little park and the Sherman. I suggest traveling on route D974 to Dijon for the Burgundy wine trail.
    N 47 00.651 E4 49.689 (47.01085, 4.82815)

31. **LINK UP OF PATTON'S THIRD ARMY AND PATCH'S SEVENTH ARMY, AUTUN:** By September 12, units of the Third Army and the Seventh Army started to link up with each other. There was a re-enacted photo outside the mayor's hall in the town of Autun, just southwest of Dijon. The link up was established between the French 2nd Dragoons, the French 2nd Armored Division and the American 6th Armored Division. These geo coordinates provide the location where the staged photo took place in front of the mayor's hall.
    N 46 57.045 E 4 17.948 (46.95075, 4.299133)

32. **"THE REAL" LINK UP MONUMENT AND LOCATION, NORD-SUR-SEINE:** This location is the site of the "French Official" link up point, in a small town called Nord-sur-Seine. Here, a beautiful memorial with a Jeep and halftrack commemorates the September 10 link up of Patton's Third Army and Patch's Seventh Army (including the French First Army). It is located only 70 kilometers northwest of Dijon.
    N 47 46.059 E 4 34.227 (47.76765, 4.57045)

33. **DIJON SHERMAN:** This was a Sherman assigned to the French Army. It's dedicated to the liberation of the city. Dijon is beautiful and worth a stop to see the famous Église Notre Dame. Take time to purchase some mustard and more Burgundy wine!
    N 47 19.746 E 5 2.583 (47.3291, 5.04305)

CHAMPAGNE CAMPAIGN OVERVIEW, AUG 15-SEPT 12, 1944 MAP 50

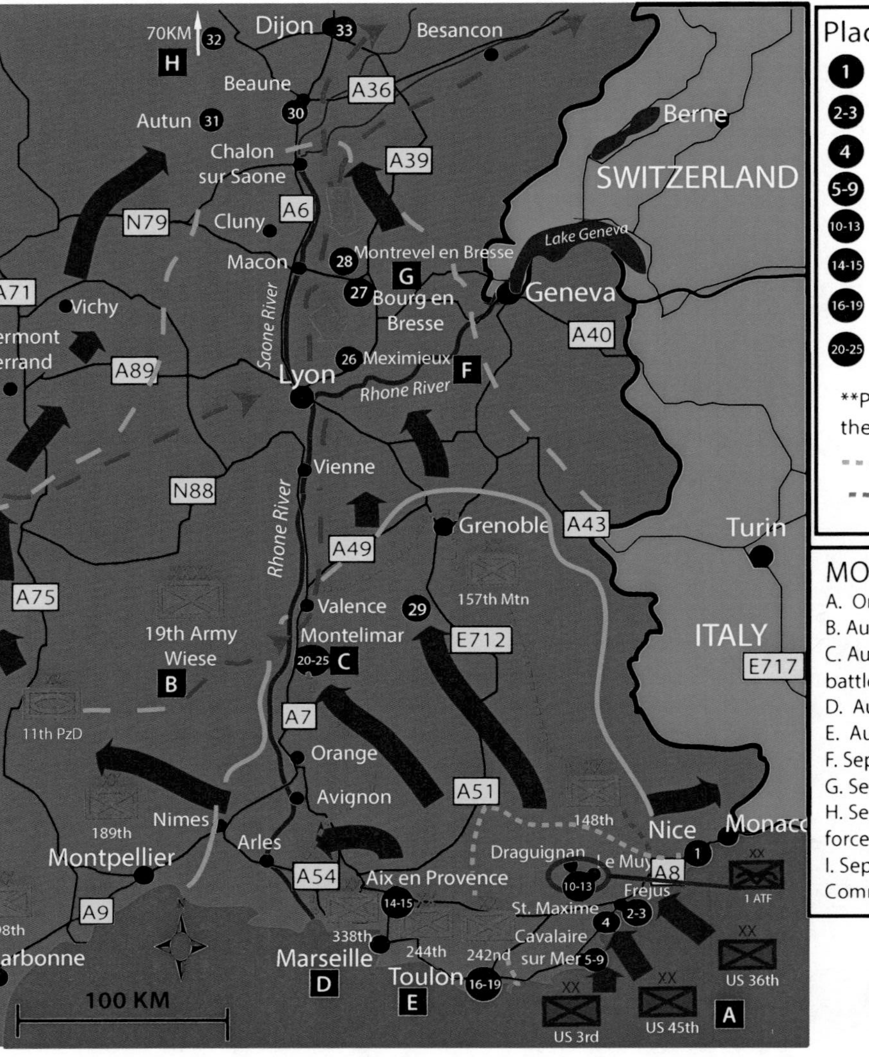
70KM
H
Dijon
33
Besancon
Beaune
A36
30
Autun
31
32
Chalon
sur Saone
A39
Berne
SWITZERLAND
N79
Cluny
A6
Lake Geneva
Macon
28
Montrevel en Bresse
G
27
Bourg en
Bresse
Geneva
A71
Vichy
Saone River
A40
Clermont
Ferrand
A89
Lyon
26
Meximieux
F
Rhone River
Vienne
N88
Grenoble
A43
Turin
Rhone River
A49
A75
Valence
29
157th Mtn
19th Army
Wiese
Montelimar
E712
ITALY
20-25
C
E717
B
A7
11th PzD
Orange
Avignon
A51
148th
Nice
Monaco
189th
Nimes
Arles
Draguignan
Le Muy
A8
1
Montpellier
A54
Aix en Provence
10-13
Frejus
1 ATF
A9
14-15
St. Maxime
2-3
4
198th
338th
244th
Cavalaire
Narbonne
Marseille
242nd
sur Mer
5-9
US 36th
D
Toulon
16-19
E
100 KM
US 3rd
US 45th
A

Places to See:

1 Nice Monument to Fallen
2-3 Camuel Beach, 36th ID
4 Delta Beach, 45th ID
5-9 Alpha Beach, 3rd ID
10-13 US Cemetery, Drop Zones, Le Muy, etc
14-15 Aix Memorial & Internment camp
16-19 Toulon Museum and Forts
20-25 Montelimar Battle
26 Meximieux Memorial
27 Bourg en Bresse Memorial
28 Montrevel en Bresse Memorial
29 Vassieux en Vercors, Resistance
30 Beaune Sherman
31 Autun Link Up
32 The Real Link Up, Nod sur Seine
33 Dijon Sherman Tank

**Please note, this area is beautiful...please look at the Roman section for France for the areas of Arles, Orange, Frejus, etc. Tons of wonderful places to see here!

August 18 Line
August 22 Line
August 28
September 3 Line

MOVEMENT HIGHLIGHTS:

A. On August 15, Operation Dragoon began with deceptions and paratroopers.
B. August 17, Hitler ordered the withdrawal of all forces from southern France.
C. August 21-28, after Task Force Butler captured the hills around Montelimar, a fierce battle lasted for 7 days between the escaping Germans and the American forces.
D. August 27, the French captured Marseille.
E. August 28, Toulon was liberated.
F. September 1, Recon force 117th was destroyed by the 11th PzD in Meximieux.
G. September 3, Lyon was captured and there was a deadly battle in Montreval en Bresse.
H. September 12, Patch's 7th Army forces officially linked up with Patton's 3rd Army forces, in Autun for the Press photos but the "real" link up was in Nord sur Seine.
I. September 14, Patch halted the VI Corps and passed command from the Mediterranean Command to Eisenhower's SHAEF.

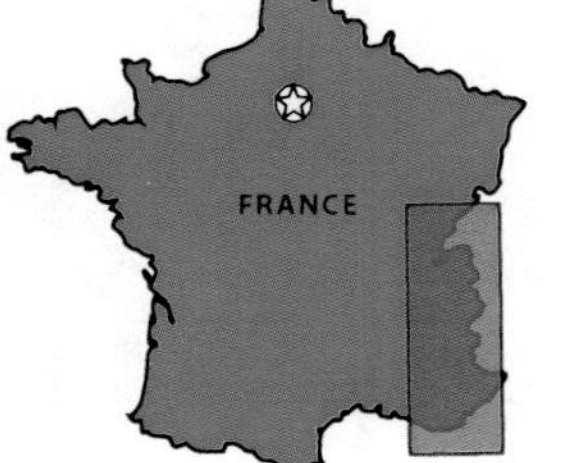
FRANCE

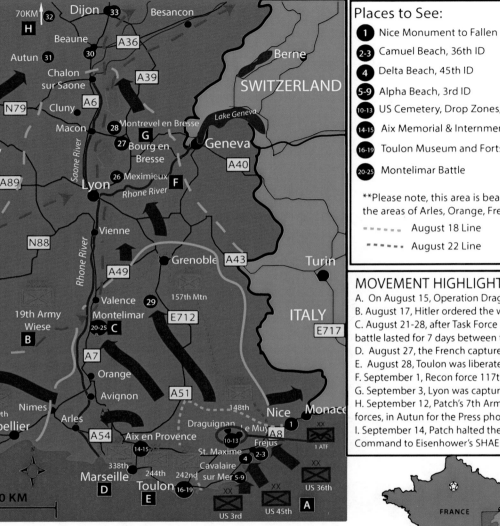

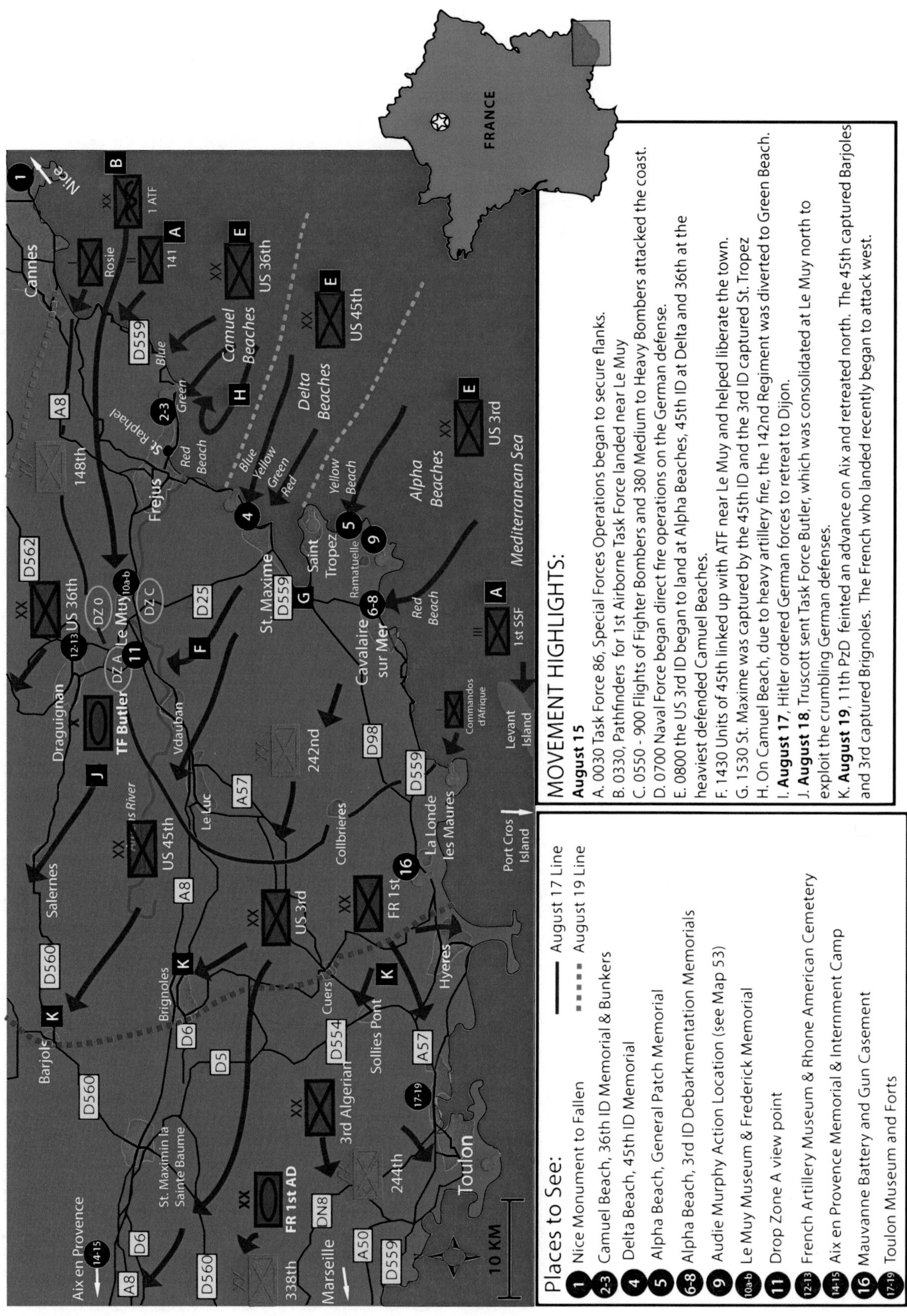
OPERATION DRAGOON, AUGUST 15, 1944
MAP 51
FRANCE
MOVEMENT HIGHLIGHTS:
August 15
A. 0030 Task Force 86, Special Forces Operations began to secure flanks.
B. 0330, Pathfinders for 1st Airborne Task Force landed near Le Muy
C. 0550 - 900 Flights of Fighter Bombers and 380 Medium to Heavy Bombers attacked the coast.
D. 0700 Naval Force began direct fire operations on the German defense.
E. 0800 the US 3rd ID began to land at Alpha Beaches, 45th ID at Delta and 36th at the heaviest defended Camuel Beaches.
F. 1430 Units of 45th linked up with ATF near Le Muy and helped liberate the town.
G. 1530 St. Maxime was captured by the 45th ID and the 3rd ID captured St. Tropez
H. On Camuel Beach, due to heavy artillery fire, the 142nd Regiment was diverted to Green Beach.
I. August 17, Hitler ordered German forces to retreat to Dijon.
J. August 18, Truscott sent Task Force Butler, which was consolidated at Le Muy north to exploit the crumbling German defenses.
K. August 19, 11th PzD feinted an advance on Aix and retreated north. The 45th captured Barjoles and 3rd captured Brignoles. The French who landed recently began to attack west.
Places to See:
1 Nice Monument to Fallen
2-3 Camuel Beach, 36th ID Memorial & Bunkers
4 Delta Beach, 45th ID Memorial
5 Alpha Beach, General Patch Memorial
6-8 Alpha Beach, 3rd ID Debarkmentation Memorials
9 Audie Murphy Action Location (see Map 53)
10a-b Le Muy Museum & Frederick Memorial
11 Drop Zone A view point
12-13 French Artillery Museum & Rhone American Cemetery
14-15 Aix en Provence Memorial & Internment Camp
16 Mauvanne Battery and Gun Casement
17-19 Toulon Museum and Forts
August 17 Line
August 19 Line
10 KM

BATTLE OF MONTELIMAR AUGUST 23-26, 1944

MAP 52

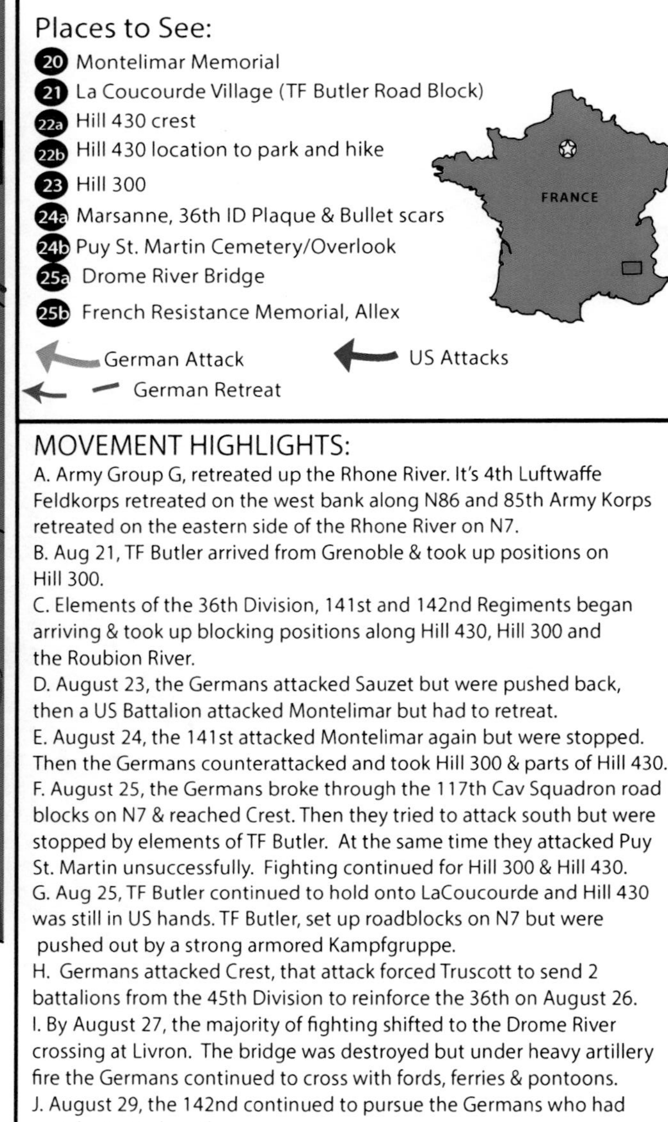
FRANCE

Places to See:

20 Montelimar Memorial
21 La Coucourde Village (TF Butler Road Block)
22a Hill 430 crest
22b Hill 430 location to park and hike
23 Hill 300
24a Marsanne, 36th ID Plaque & Bullet scars
24b Puy St. Martin Cemetery/Overlook
25a Drome River Bridge
25b French Resistance Memorial, Allex

German Attack
German Retreat
US Attacks

MOVEMENT HIGHLIGHTS:

A. Army Group G, retreated up the Rhone River. It's 4th Luftwaffe Feldkorps retreated on the west bank along N86 and 85th Army Korps retreated on the eastern side of the Rhone River on N7.

B. Aug 21, TF Butler arrived from Grenoble & took up positions on Hill 300.

C. Elements of the 36th Division, 141st and 142nd Regiments began arriving & took up blocking positions along Hill 430, Hill 300 and the Roubion River.

D. August 23, the Germans attacked Sauzet but were pushed back, then a US Battalion attacked Montelimar but had to retreat.

E. August 24, the 141st attacked Montelimar again but were stopped. Then the Germans counterattacked and took Hill 300 & parts of Hill 430.

F. August 25, the Germans broke through the 117th Cav Squadron road blocks on N7 & reached Crest. Then they tried to attack south but were stopped by elements of TF Butler. At the same time they attacked Puy St. Martin unsuccessfully. Fighting continued for Hill 300 & Hill 430.

G. Aug 25, TF Butler continued to hold onto LaCoucourde and Hill 430 was still in US hands. TF Butler, set up roadblocks on N7 but were pushed out by a strong armored Kampfgruppe.

H. Germans attacked Crest, that attack forced Truscott to send 2 battalions from the 45th Division to reinforce the 36th on August 26.

I. By August 27, the majority of fighting shifted to the Drome River crossing at Livron. The bridge was destroyed but under heavy artillery fire the Germans continued to cross with fords, ferries & pontoons.

J. August 29, the 142nd continued to pursue the Germans who had mostly crossed north.

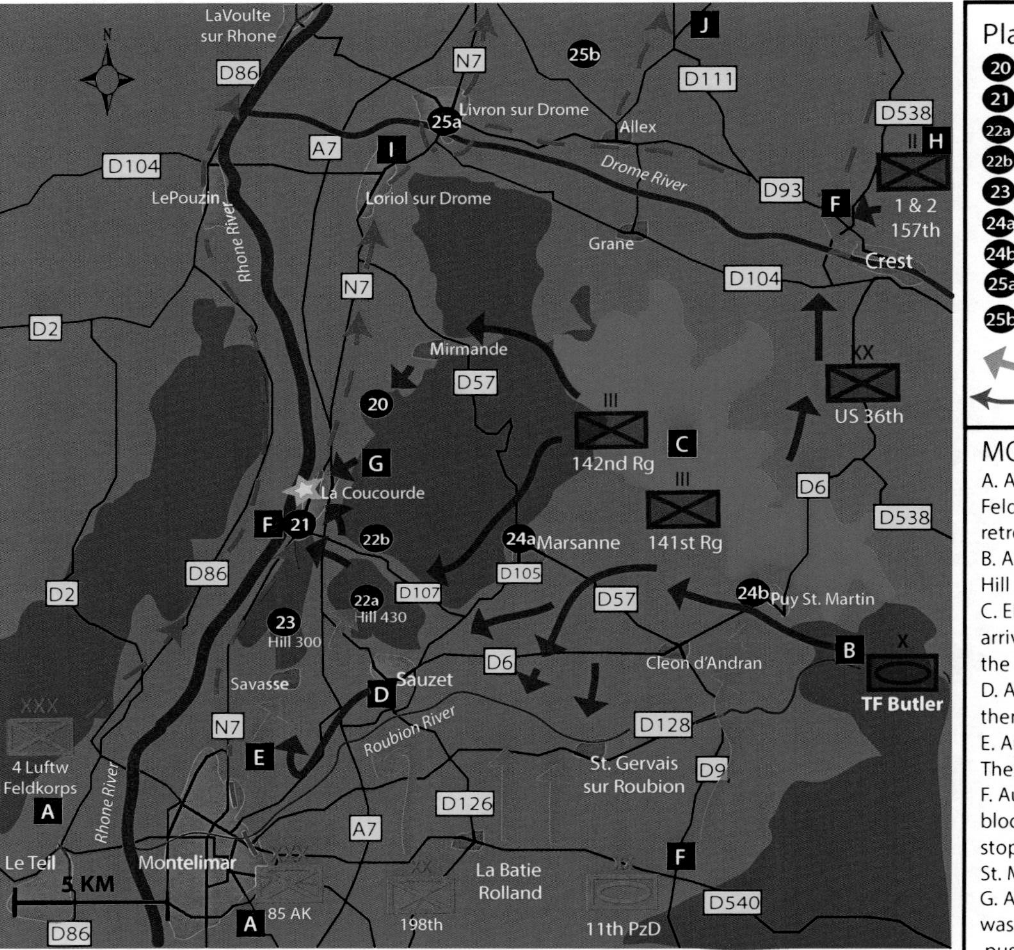
N
LaVoulte sur Rhone
D86
N7
25b
J
D111
D538
H
1 & 2 157th
25a Livron sur Drome
Allex
A7
I
D104
LePouzin
Rhone River
Loriol sur Drome
Drome River
D93
F
Grane
Crest
D104
N7
D2
Mirmande
D57
20
142nd Rg
C
141st Rg
US 36th
G
La Coucourde
F 21
22b
24a Marsanne
D6
D538
D86
D105
D107
22a Hill 430
D57
24b Puy St. Martin
D2
23 Hill 300
D6
Cleon d'Andran
B
TF Butler
Savasse
D Sauzet
D128
N7
E
Roubion River
St. Gervais sur Roubion
D9
4 Luftw Feldkorps
A
Rhone River
D126
A7
F
Le Teil
Montelimar
La Batie Rolland
5 KM
85 AK
A
198th
11th PzD
D540
D86

AUDIE MURPHY'S DSC ACTION, AUGUST 15, 1944 — MAP 53

Movements:

A. August 15, 3rd Platoon Company B, 15th Reg 3rd ID advanced off shore towards Ramatuelle.
B. Audie Murphy, after his platoon came under fire, took a .30 cal MG and went in a ditch to out flank the German position.
C. Next he surprised the Germans and killed 2 Germans and silenced the German position.
D. He returned to his line and advanced with his friend PFC Lattie Tipton. Two more Germans came out of the farm with a white flag. Lattie stood up to wave them back and he was shot by a sniper.
E. Murphy fired his rifle and killed the 2 Germans. Then went up the hill behind the German line.
F. In close combat he wounded two Germans, killed two more and captured five. Next more Germans ran out of the farm house, Murphy killed two of them and captured 6 more!

For these actions he was awarded the Distinguished Service Cross.

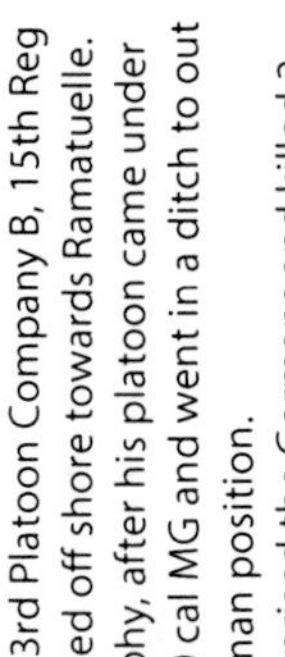
FRANCE
Shoreline
3rd Platoon
D93
Chemin des Barraques
Chemin de l'Oumede
A
B
C
D
E
F
9
50m
N

Places to See:

9 Crossroads of advance

These are all approximate locations, based on After the Battle Magazine Documentation & the Sketch that was sent in with the request for the DSC in December 1944.

BATTLE OF MEXIMIEUX, SEPTEMBER 1, 1944

MAP 54

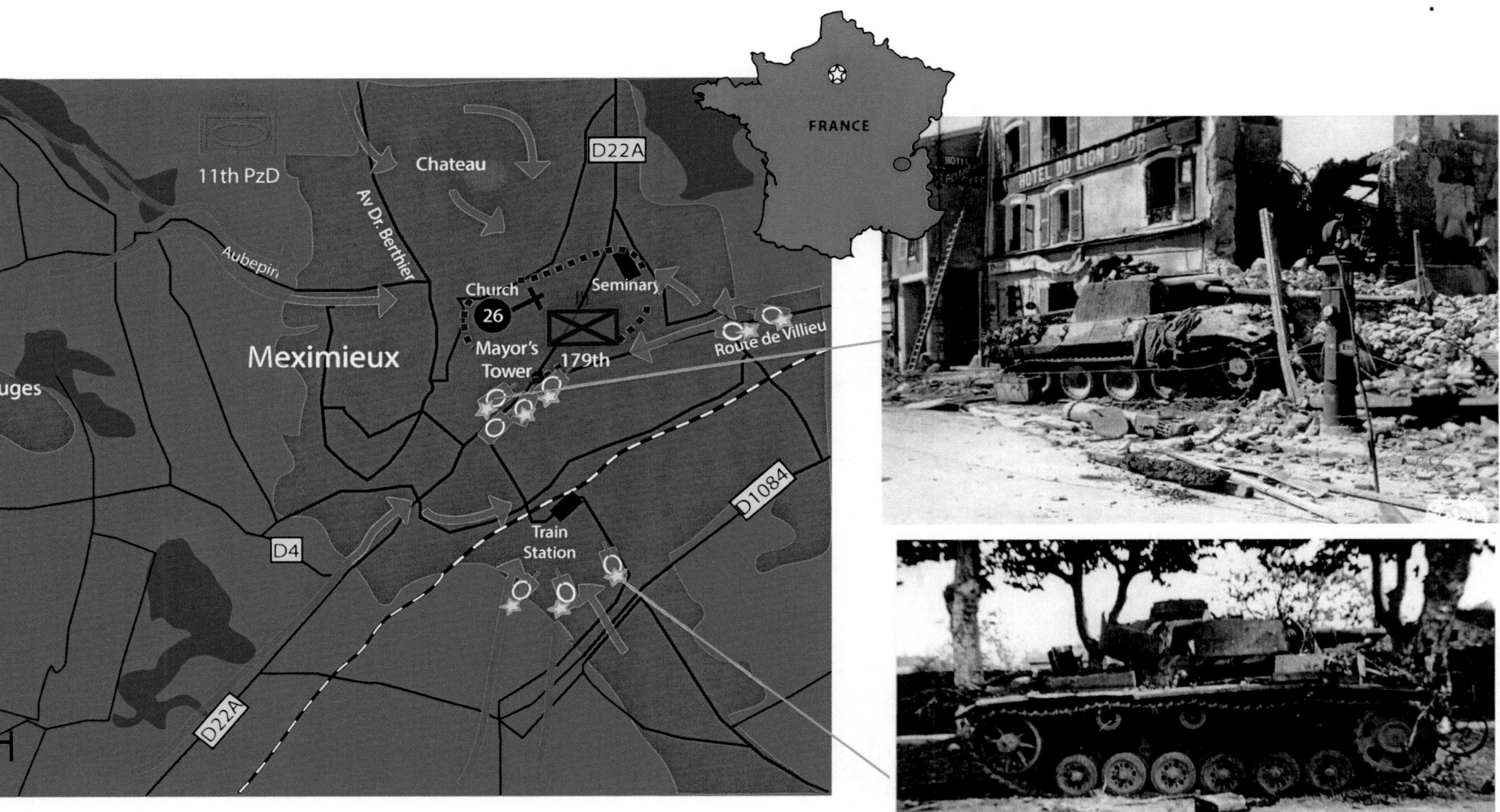
11th PzD
Chateau
D22A
FRANCE
Aubepin
Av Dr. Berthier
Church
26
Seminary
Mayor's Tower
179th
Route de Villieu
Meximieux
Perouges
D4
D4
D1084
Train Station
N
200M
D22A

Summary and Places to See:

On September 1, the 11th Panzer Division commander, Wietersheim, was ordered to attack the American forces on their eastern flank and rear, near Meximieux. Meanwhile, elements of the 45th ID were assembling north of Meximieux. On that day, the Germans fought into the town center of Meximieux, missing the forces located north of the town. A battle ensued, with 2 companies of the 179th Regiment, 45th Division. The Americans fought desepartely against well armed men and tanks. The fighting continued all day into early night, until American units north of the town began to arrive. This map highlights the direction of the German attack & where the 9 Panther tanks were destroyed.

26 Meximieux memorial plaque — Destroyed Panther — German attack

**Note, Perouges is an excellent place to visit. It is a walled medieval town.

Top: One of the 9 Panther tanks destroyed in the battle, in front of Hotel du Lion D'Or, (see Geo coords). Lower Photoe: Approximate location of destroyed Panzer IV, with 75mm cannon on Rue des Stades. (US Army)

BATTLE OF MONTREVAL EN BRESSE, SEPTEMBER 3, 1944 — MAP 55

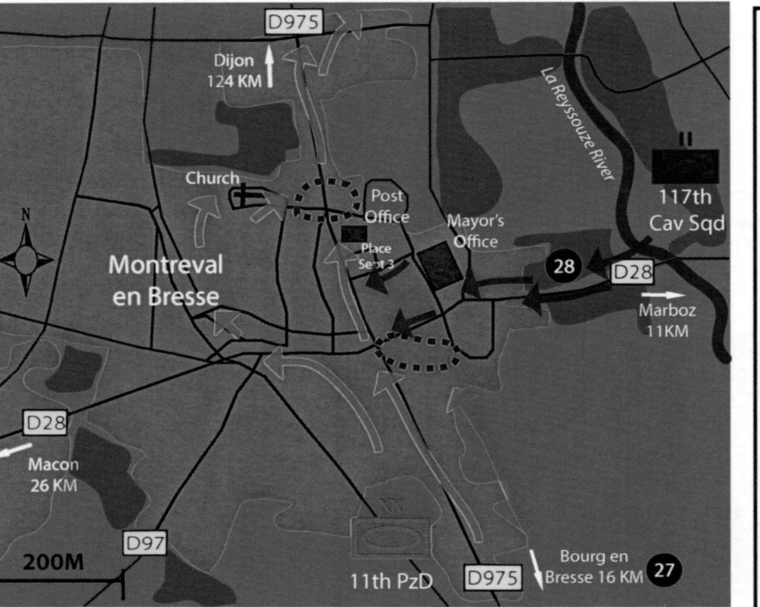
D975
Dijon
124 KM
Church
Post Office
Place Sept 3
Mayor's Office
La Reyssouze River
117th
Cav Sqd
28
D28
Marboz
11KM
N
Montreval
en Bresse
D28
Macon
26 KM
D97
200M
11th PzD
D975
Bourg en
Bresse 16 KM
27

Summary & Places to see:

On 2 September at 1730, Troop B of the 117th Cavalry Squadron entered Marboz 11 Km east of Montreval en Bresse. Next they were ordered to occupy Montreval en Bresse, directly in front of the retreating11th PzD, who had their HQ in Bourg. The 117th tried to take the town on September 2 but were pushed back. On September 3, the commander waited for his additional troops with light tanks & assault guns. But they failed to show, so he attacked anyways with only his two Recon Troops. At dawn on September 3, Troop B attacked the town then Troop A followed them, both units were able to seize the town by 0930 after ousting about 300 Germans. and taking 70 prisoners. The commander of the 11th PzD, in response sent, from Bourg the 11th Pz Recon Battalion, with a battery of SP Artillery, six tanks and an engineer company to recapture Montreval. The Germans arrived at 1100. The Americans only with light armored cars and light arms held the Germans back until encirclement at 1430. The other Troops tried to reach the town but were beaten back by the stronger Germans. By 1710, after several attempts to break out, Troop A and B had to surrender. In the end Troop A lost 12 men and only 8 from Troop B could be found. In total, the Germans captured 126 men, 20 Jeeps and 15 armored cars. They only lost 1 tank, 2 armored cars and 4 other types of vehicles.

2nd Lt. Lee of Troop B, was awarded the Medal of Honor for his actions on September 3. During the battle, he organized a patrol to dislodge a German mortar team causing casualties. On the patrol, his men provided covering fire while he attacked two mortar teams. Next he was wounded, then fired a panzerfaust knocking out a German armored car. He was found 2 days later, recovering from his wounds.He was back in action by January 1945. In total, the Americans were awarded 1 MOH, 3 DSC, several silver and bronze stars, and 150 purple hearts that day.

27 Bourg en Bresse Liberation Memorial (16 KM south)

28 Montrevel en Bresse Memorial to the 117th Cavalry Squadron

Locations of Troop A and B defenders

FRANCE

M8 armored car with a 37mm cannon. It looks like it belongs to the 45th division. The 117th Cavalry Squadron used M8s to quickly exploit the German retreat and it had "some" fire power but it was useless against heavy German armor. But on September 3 suprisingly an M8 did take out a light tank and then a medium German tank by hitting its track.

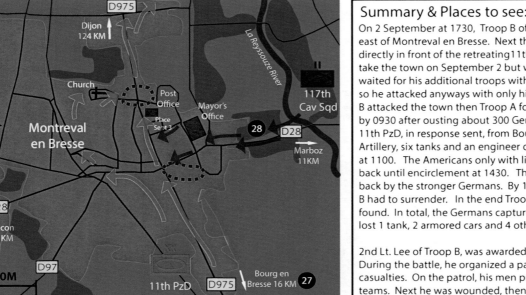

On the eastern edge of Operation Dragoon, on Camuel Beach is a memorial park called Eisenhower Square with an original LC. The beach which the 36th ID landed on you can see a difference in the terrain of rocky out crops and a rocky beach.

Far right, a proud French man taking his stroll along the beach. The photo to the right is of a bricked up German gun bunker on the shore of Camuel Beach. It is a great hike walk along the beach. Typically the beach is less crowded than the other sandy beaches.

On the center landing beach, Delta Beach, near St. Maxime, is a small memorial rock to the 45th ID who landed there.
It is a stark contrast to visiting Normandy which has memorials every 100 feet!
Note, the sand and the perimeter land with low terrain which did not provide the Germans much of a defensive edge.

On the western edge of the landing zone was Alpha Beach. At this location, to the west of St. Tropez is a memorial and a information board (far right picture). The photo right was taken facing east towards St. Tropez. The 3rd ID who landed in this zone had a challenging terrain inland to over-come.

US282
Square
Général
Dwight D. EISENHOWER

Left: A visit to the Riviera would not be complete without stopping in St. Tropez. Above is a photo of the armada off the coast of the Riviera during Operation Dragoon. (NARA)

Above, inset is a photo of the Liberation museum in Le Muy which has been closed due to a flood in 2011. The fields just north of the town were the target areas for the paratroopers who quickly secured Le Muy and awaited the advancing soliders from the beachheads. The left photo is of the Operation Dragoon air drop. Further up the road is the Rhone American Cemetery and Memorial. A very beautiful setting and incredible stories to hear from the caretaker and information in the welcome center. Uniquely, it has a large bronze 3D terrain map in front of the chapel that is very helpful to appreciate the battles. (NARA photo above left)

Not far from the the Rhone American Cemetery is the French National Artillery Museum, it has recently been updated. The photo to the right is of the sunset inland towards Aix en Provence. The terrain changes to canyons and rocky mountains as you move further inland.

Above the city of Toulon is "the" Operation Dragoon Museum. The drive up to the museum is a very narrow road skirting drop offs but well worth the trip for the view. Outside the museum is a German PAK 75mm cannon and a Sherman tank. Excellent artificats and photos are in the museum. Outside, there are hiking trails, more forts and of course 2-3 cafes for a refreshment.

A view of Toulon and its harbor. The Germans had many fortifications around the harbor but they were largely ineffective because the French attacked from behind. The harbor and some of the forts are still in use today by the French Military. Photo right is from the other side of the museum looking north west into the mountain range.

LIBEREE LE 21 AOUT 1944
PAR LA 3EME DIVISION D'INFANTERIE U.S.
AVEC LA PARTICIPATION
DES FORCES FRANCAISES DE L' INTERIEUR
DEPUIS LEUR DEBARQUEMENT
SUR LES COTES DE LA PROVENCE
ACCOMPAGNEE DES RESISTANTS AIXOIS
DEPUIS LES PORTES DE LA CITE
VILLE D'AIX-EN-PROVENCE REND HOMMAGE
COMBATTANTS DE CETTE GLORIEUSE UNITE
19 JUILLET 2004

Northwest of Toulon is the ancient town of Aix en Provence. It is a bustling college town with a beautiful oldtown area. Underneath a tower gate is the above plaque in honor of the liberators August 21, 1944.

Far left: The memorial overlooking the Rhone River and N7, the main German retreat route. The memorial is near the beautiful town of Mirmande.

Left: One of the hills overlooking the retreat route of the Germans. The hills were fought over throughout the 9 days of battle.

Far left: The photo was taken on top of Hill 300 facing south-east. The Rhone River is just below and the retreat route N7. The foliage is an almost impenetrable brush.

Left: Route N7, the road of death for many Germans near Hill 300 and Hill 430. (NARA)

LA COUCOURDE

Far left and left: A comparison of then and now. The town of La Coucourde is on N7 and below Hill 430 and Hill 300.

Far left: The photo was taken above the town of Marsanne looking south towards the German lines. In the distance is the backside of Hill 430 and the Rhone River. The Germans tried to push their way thru the town. Bullet impacts are still easily found on the town hall. (photo left) Also on the town hall is a plaque in honor of TF Butler.

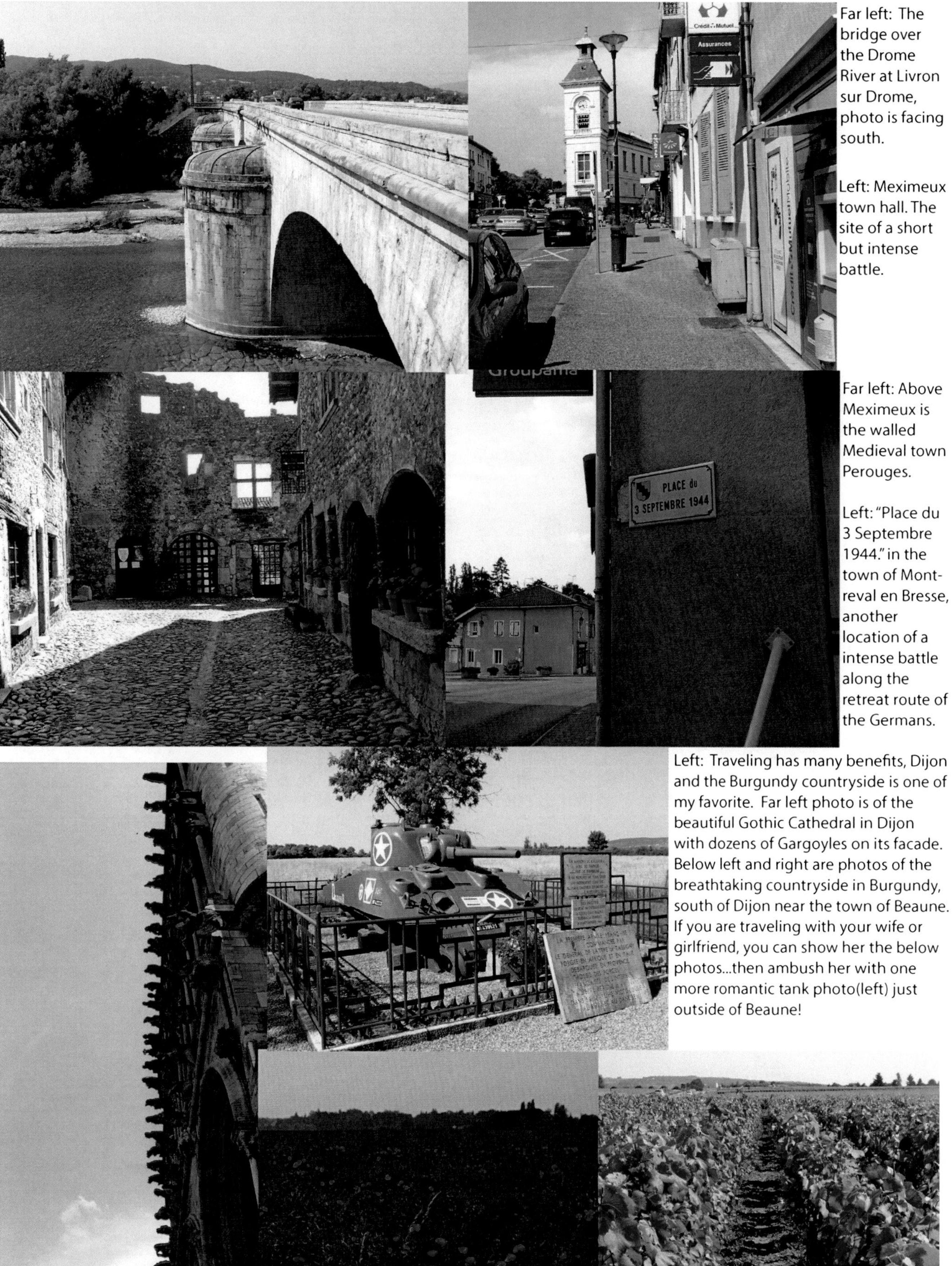
Crédit Mutuel
Assurances
Groupama
PLACE du
3 SEPTEMBRE 1944

Far left: The bridge over the Drome River at Livron sur Drome, photo is facing south.

Left: Meximeux town hall. The site of a short but intense battle.

Far left: Above Meximeux is the walled Medieval town Perouges.

Left: "Place du 3 Septembre 1944." in the town of Mont-reval en Bresse, another location of a intense battle along the retreat route of the Germans.

Left: Traveling has many benefits, Dijon and the Burgundy countryside is one of my favorite. Far left photo is of the beautiful Gothic Cathedral in Dijon with dozens of Gargoyles on its facade. Below left and right are photos of the breathtaking countryside in Burgundy, south of Dijon near the town of Beaune. If you are traveling with your wife or girlfriend, you can show her the below photos...then ambush her with one more romantic tank photo(left) just outside of Beaune!

LORRAINE CAMPAIGN

September 1–December 18, 1944

"I am a soldier, I fight where I am told, and I win where I fight." – General George S. Patton

---

SUMMARY: By September 1, 1944, there was talk that the Allies would defeat the Germans by Christmas. The Germans were in full retreat out of France and at this point had lost about 3.6 million men and officers. On paper the Germans still had seven million soldiers, but in reality they had approximately 700,000 available for combat in the west and 1.5 million in the east. An example of their poor condition was the fact that the German First Army had only nine infantry battalions, 20 tanks and two batteries of artillery left. The Allies had approximately 38 divisions committed in the west and outnumbered the Germans two to one in artillery and 20 to 1 in tanks. In addition, the Allies maintained total air superiority. Supreme Commander Dwight Eisenhower employed the strategy of a broad front to stretch the German defense and prevent it from concentrating forces.

The Allied front-line situation, from north to south, started with the Canadian First Army, which was pushing into Holland to capture the port of Antwerp. On the right flank of the Canadians was the British Second Army, which was fighting into Holland so that it could get around the German west wall from the north. On the right shoulder of the British was the American First Army, attacking Aachen and heading into the Hürtgen Forest to cross the Rhine and capture the Ruhr industrial area. On the flank of the First Army was the Ninth Army, pushing through Luxembourg and the Ardennes. On their flank to the south was the Third Army under Patton, with a large front from Luxembourg to the top of the Vosges Mountains. Finally, in the south was the U.S. Seventh Army and the French First Army, which attacked into the Vosges Mountains. The only problem with the broad front strategy was logistics. There simply was not enough fuel, ammo, trucks or planes to support more than one major attack at a time. Unfortunately for Patton, Montgomery had gained priority in the north for Operation Market Garden, a major thrust into Holland intended to capture a bridge over the Rhine at Arnhem. Supplies were redirected and caused fateful delays for the Third Army. For example, on September 2 the Third Army, which required 400,000 gallons of fuel every day, received only 25,000 gallons. Patton's army traveled 400 kilometers in the last few weeks, keeping the Germans off balance and preventing them from organizing, setting up defenses and counterattacking. Patton's aggressive "a pint of sweat today saves a gallon of blood tomorrow" was true. However, with the halt in supplies and attack, the Germans had time to organize and set up kill zones and defensive perimeters. Thus, the Lorraine

Campaign began on September 1. The campaign featured three main phases. (These phases were not necessarily "official," but they make the process of writing about the campaign easier) General Patton's objective was to cross the Rhine into Germany. His obstacles included fuel shortages, bad weather, difficult terrain, 19th-century German forts, the Moselle River, the Saar River, the Maginot Line, the West Wall (Siegfried Line), the German First Army and the German Fifth Army.

FIRST PHASE – CROSSING OF THE MOSELLE RIVER, SEPTEMBER 1944

After a crucial week of delay, the Third Army received enough fuel to make attempts at crossing the Moselle River. Initially, the 5th Infantry Division had experienced limited success fighting the fierce German counterattacks at Arnaville. The 5th Infantry Division was forced to withdraw from the bridgehead on September 22 due to materiel shortages. On September 5, the 317th Regiment (800 men) of the 80th Infantry Division attempted a boat crossing just south of Pont-à-Mousson, north of Nancy. The German defense was well prepared and held the high ground. After the first crossings at 0930, intense fighting began. Two companies of the 317th made it across but were wiped out by 1100 after elements of the 3rd Panzer Grenadiers Division charged with fixed bayonets and machine guns. The remaining crossings for the operation were cancelled.

ATTACK ON MAIRY, PANZER BRIGADE 106, SEPTEMBER 8: On September 7, the German First Army Commander General Otto von Knobelsdorff obtained permission to counterattack the Americans on the western side of the Moselle River. The high command approved the use of the newly formed Panzer Brigade 106 for no more than 48 hours. The Panzer brigades had been formed in the summer of 1944 for use on the Eastern Front. Each brigade had approximately 90 tanks, one regiment with 40 Panthers, another with 40 Panzer IVs and four Flak Panzers. For the attack, the Germans committed Panzer Brigade 106, which had 36 Panthers, 11 Panzer IVs and 119 halftracks. In addition, the 59th Infantry Regiment was attached to the brigade to provide infantry support. The German objective was to attack the 90th Infantry Division, which was on the exposed left flank of the XX Corps near Thionville. On the night of September 7, the Germans attacked south in two columns from Audun-le-Roman toward Briey. That night, the Germans began to roll past the 90th Division headquarters in the woods southeast of Landres. At daylight, the Americans reorganized to meet the threat. The Germans attacked the town of Mairy, surrounded by hills and occupied by the 1st Battalion of the 358th Infantry, which was armed with 76mm anti-tank guns. The Americans used the anti-tank guns to stop an attack by Panther tanks. At 0800, the Americans stopped a column of Panzer Grenadiers in 11 halftracks with a mix of artillery, anti-tank fire and bazookas. That attack was followed at approximately 0900 by another Panther tank attack, which was also stopped by artillery fire. The attack on Mairy cost the Germans 48 halftracks and seven Panther tanks. In the meantime, elements of the 90th Infantry Division fought to cut off escape routes for the first column of Germans. The column asked for permission to retreat and for immediate assistance from the second column. Permission to retreat was granted, but the second German column couldn't reach the first column in time.

The German column was decimated. By the end of the day, it had lost 21 tanks and 60 halftracks and suffered more than 1,000 casualties.

ATTACK ON DOMPAIRE, PANZER BRIGADE 112, SEPTEMBER 13: After the link up of the Sixth Army Group and the Third Army on September 10, the Allies had a united front to begin an advance over the Moselle River. As at Mairy, the Germans wanted to pierce through the loose American line and hit the Third Army hard. As a result of the Americans' attack on Nancy and the American link up, Johannes Blaskowitz, commander of Army Group G, needed to keep the defensive line intact. Therefore, he ordered Hasso von Manteuffel to use Panzer Brigade 112 to stabilize the line and attack the southern/right flank of the Third Army near Dompaire. The right flank was currently held by elements of the French 2nd Armored Division. On September 12, the German forces departed Épinal and split into two regiments: Regiment 29 with approximately 42 Panther tanks and Regiment 2112 with 45 Panzer IV tanks. On the evening of September 12, Regiment 29 bivouacked in the small towns of Dompaire and Lamerey. Regiment 2112 stopped in the town of Darmey. The French, thanks to good intelligence, knew of the German force enroute. They quickly formed a task force, "Combat Team Langlade." Colonel Paul Girot de Langlade positioned his forces on the high ground, looking down at the largely inexperienced German tank crews resting in the towns below. Langlade's forces consisted of three groups, each with 15 Shermans, one Sherman with a 76mm, four M10s and one or two companies of infantry. He was outnumbered but had the element of surprise, artillery support, air support and experienced crews. On the evening of September 12, a short fire fight ensued and both sides lost a tank. On September 13, at daylight, the Germans realized their situation and attempted to break out. The French engaged them from outside of town, calling in artillery and air strikes on Regiment 29. Regiment 29 called for assistance from Regiment 2112 just south of it. Regiment 2112 was slow to respond, but pulled together a small force to attack the French perimeter at Ville-sur-Illon. The regiment's Panzer IV infantry escort left the tanks vulnerable because the soldiers had found a local liquor stash on the way to battle! The French quickly dispatched Regiment 2112's counterattack, which came from the south and west. By day's end, the German Panzer Brigade was destroyed. Regiment 29 escaped with only four operational Panthers out of 42, and Regiment 2112 had only 17 operational Panzer IVs. In addition, throughout the one-and-a-half days of fighting, the Germans suffered 350 killed in action and 1,000 wounded in action. The French lost four Shermans, two Stuarts, two halftracks and two Jeeps. One American P-47 was shot down. The French suffered 44 killed in action and 100 wounded in action.

CROSSING ATTEMPTED AGAIN: Still with the order to cross the Moselle and capture Nancy, the Americans adjusted their strategy for an encirclement of Nancy. Tactically, they decided to encircle Nancy because this maneuver would split the German defensive response, create success at two crossings and avoid a frontal assault on the city. After initial artillery preparations, the attack began on September 11 at 0500. The 35th Infantry Division attacked from the south of Nancy and crossed at Flavigny, while the 4th Armored Division provided an added punch to the attack and established a bridgehead at Bayon, just south of the 35th. The Germans engaged in intense fighting and counterattacks, and the Allies faced difficult terrain. The German 15th Panzer Grenadier Division crushed another American bridgehead on September 11. However the Germans were eventually pushed back after additional American armor crossed to support the infantry. After better preparations, scouting and feint attacks, the 80th Infantry Division attacked north of Nancy at Dieulouard, just south of Pont-à-Mousson, the place from which they had withdrawn earlier that month. Two battalions of the 80th Division captured the high ground. On September 13 at 0100, the Germans counterattacked again with 10 Stug IIIs and a battalion of 3rd Panzer Grenadiers. The Germans pushed back the Americans to within 100 yards of the river until a company of Sherman tanks arrived to help defend the bridgehead. As a result, the Americans succeeded in crossing the Moselle River and began encircling Nancy.

The German command was furious at the reports of American armor crossing the bridges. On September 16, after two days of continuous counterattacks, the 3rd and 15th Panzer Grenadier Divisions were withdrawn from Nancy. Hitler himself demanded a major counterattack within the week to stop the Third Army's progress. (He initially wanted the attack to occur on September 3 to stop the Dijon link up.) Hitler wanted his German forces to thrust northwest toward the Marne River and wipe out the American forces in Luneville, restoring the defensive lines along the Moselle. The German commander of the Fifth Army, Manteuffel, protested because the effort would be a waste of men and equipment. Hitler was asking for the impossible; he wanted the attack to consist of seven divisions that were still recovering from their defeats in France and Italy. In reality, to keep his defensive lines intact, Manteuffel could commit only shadows of these divisions.

GERMAN COUNTERATTACKS, SEPTEMBER 18-30: Despite the lack of materiel and men, Hitler insisted that the Fifth Panzer Army should destroy the American Moselle bridgehead at Nancy. For the attack, Manteuffel had three Panzer grenadier divisions, three Panzer brigades, another three Panzer brigades in reserve and three Panzer divisions. In total, he had 262 tanks (75 Panzer IVs, 107 Panthers and 80 assault guns). The original start date was September 15, but the attack was delayed due to equipment arrival delays.

FIRST ATTACK, SEPTEMBER 18: On September 18, the Germans attacked the American 4th Armor Division at Luneville. The Germans attacked in two thrusts. During the first, the 58th Panzer Corps (Panzer Brigade 113 and the 15th Panzer Grenadier Division) attacked west along the Marne-Rhine canal. During the second thrust, Panzer Brigades 111 and 112 and the 21st Panzer Division attacked toward Luneville. The tanks and men quickly brushed aside the American light line of defense. The Germans thought Luneville was in German hands and advanced to the town. However, the brave American soldiers with small arms and bazookas delayed the German advance just enough to enable M18 Hellcat tank destroyers with 76mm cannons to arrive and stop the German Panther tanks. By the end of the day, the Germans had withdrawn to regroup in the protection of Parroy Forest. A little farther north, on September 19, the Germans launched a major attack out of the Parroy Forest toward Arracourt. In a four-to-one advantage, Panzer Brigade 113 attacked Lezey, the eastern flank of Combat Command A, and Panzer Brigade 111 attacked Arracourt, the center of Combat Command A. In the early-morning fog, 42 Panther tanks and the Panzer grenadiers advanced. It was a surprise to the Americans, but they knew the terrain and the 37th Tank Battalion (commanded by Lieutenant Colonel Creighton Abrams) was bivouacked in Arracourt. In the fog, the Americans maneuvered for flanking shots on the Panthers and quickly decimated Panzer Brigade 113. (Panzer Brigade 111 had gotten lost.) The American tanks had advantages in the form of hills and terrain that mitigated the German tank advantages of long-range, high-velocity cannons. As a result, by the end of the day the Americans had knocked out 42 Panther tanks and lost only two M18 tank destroyers and four Sherman medium tanks. However, the Germans were not finished! On September 20, Panzer Brigade 111 attacked Arracourt again, but had to retreat after an artillery barrage. Next, Abrams sent his tanks to Lezey to clear out the Germans, but the tanks were ambushed. The battalion lost six Shermans in one minute but regrouped and destroyed 16 German Panzers. On September 21, Hitler fired Blaskowitz and replaced him with General Hermann Balck. The Germans then chose the town of Moyenvic, located just northeast of Arracourt and on the flank of the 4th Armored Division, as their target. The Germans attacked in the morning and overran the 25th Cavalry Squadron, which was screening the 4th Armored Division flank. Then, 704th M18 tank destroyers, P-47s and artillery blunted the German attack. The fierce fighting destroyed Panzer Brigade 111, leaving it with only seven tanks and 80 men out of an initial 90 tanks and 2,500 men. However, this engagement also took a toll on the American 4th Armored Division, which lost 14 Shermans and seven Stuarts, and suffered 25 killed in action and 88 wounded in action. On September 23, Patton went on the defensive because supplies were being pulled for Montgomery's Operation Market Garden. Manteuffel attacked again on September 24 with the 559th Volksgrenadier Division and the 106th Panzer Brigade near Château Salins. The attack started with an artillery barrage at 0830. Then the Panthers advanced on the right flank, while the infantry advanced primarily on the left. There was low cloud cover, but brave P-47s dove in and, at just 15 feet above the ground, attacked the Germans. The attack was over in just 15 minutes, resulting in 300 Germans killed in action and 11 German tanks lost. Next, believe it or not, Manteuffel attacked again. On September 24, he finally captured the unoccupied town of Moyenvic. On September 27, Manteuffel wanted to capture, on the flank of the 4th Armored Division, Hill 318 and Hill 293, which overlooked the 5th Panzer Army positions. The Germans created two Kampfgruppes. In a divisionary attack, they seized Lezey and Ley. Then, Panzer Grenadier Regiment 111 captured Bezange-la-Petite next to Hill 265. Fierce fighting continued in the night. Throughout the next four days, the Germans attacked the hills, capturing only parts of them until being forced to withdraw after air and artillery attacks. During these last days, the Fifth Panzer Army suffered 700 killed in action and 300 wounded in action, and lost 14 Panzer IVs and 22 Panthers. The 4th Armored Division lost 41 Shermans and seven Stuarts, and suffered 228 killed in action and 645 wounded in action.

From September 18-30, the German Fifth Army suffered thousands of casualties and lost more than 285 tanks and armored vehicles. However, the Germans believed their counterattack had worked because Patton's major push had been halted. They didn't realize the halt was because of the major shift of resources to Operation Market Garden. The first phase of the Lorraine Campaign was over. Next the "October Pause" would begin, but with Eisenhower's approval, the American XX Corps still made attempts to capture Fort Driant in Metz.

SECOND PHASE – BATTLE FOR METZ:

OPERATION THUNDERBOLT: North of Nancy sits the historic fortress city of Metz. Since Roman times it has guarded the route to the heart of France. During the modern era, the Germans built massive fortifications around Metz after the Franco-Prussian War. After World War I, the French took over the forts and incorporated them into the Maginot Line. In 1944, the Germans, in their retreat, occupied the Maginot Line forts around Metz to guard the Moselle River crossing. On September 27, the 5th Division attacked, without air support, the most modern and strongest position in Metz, Fort Driant. Driant was at an elevation of 360 meters and sat west of the Moselle, commanding all of Metz. At 1415, a battalion of men attacked from the southwest but was immediately blocked by pillboxes, mines and barbed wire. Artillery and P-47s with napalm were called in, but created no significant damage. Next, the battalion brought up five tank destroyers to shoot point-blank into the pillboxes, but most of tanks were destroyed or unable to pass the obstacles. At 1830, the battalion withdrew. During the next attempt, on October 3, the battalion attacked again from the southwest with two companies of infantry and combat engineers. It also attacked from the northwest with a company of men and 12 tanks outfitted like bulldozers. The attackers had some initial success from the southwest when Company B was able to enter the fort, but the northwest advance was stopped because the tank dozers broke down and the demolition charges didn't work. By October 5, the Americans had suffered 200 casualties out of 300 men committed. Next, on October 7 at 1000, Task Force Warnock attacked and gained 200 yards. On October 8, the task force breached the tunnel system using torches, shaped charges and TNT. However, on October 9, General Patton cancelled Operation Thunderbolt and they withdrew from the hill from October 12-13. Patton had to wait for more supplies before he could commit additional men. The 5th Infantry Division suffered 798 casualties, consisting of 64 killed in action, 187 missing in action and 547 wounded in action. The division had also lost 10 tanks.

OPERATION MADISON: In October, Eisenhower continued to divert supplies and focus on the battles north of the Third Army. At that time the British ended their push of Market Garden, but the U.S. First Army was attacking Aachen and the Hürtgen Forest. Therefore, for the remainder of October the Third Army rested, refitted and trained for the upcoming attack toward the Rhine, which would occur "when logistics permit." On October 21, after bitter fighting, the Americans captured Aachen, the first German city to fall into Allied hands. Eisenhower wanted to resume a thrust north with the British, but the British said they were not ready! Instead, Eisenhower asked Patton, and Patton said yes. He had replenished his strength to the extent that he now had approximately 250,000 men (six infantry divisions and three armored divisions), 567 medium tanks and 273 light tanks (M5 Stuarts). Even though the Third Army had not been involved in a major operation, it still had suffered about 14,000 casualties (including those not related to combat) throughout October.

Patton was only "132 miles from the Rhine" and wanted to attack quickly before the Germans adjusted their defenses. On November 8, Patton sounded the code "play ball" and Operation Madison began with an artillery barrage at 0600. At Metz, 30 infantry battalions, 500 tanks and 700 guns were committed. Their objective was to destroy the Germans in Metz, then shift the advance to the northeast to obtain a bridgehead over the Saare River. The Germans had approximately 14,000 men committed to Metz's defense. Hitler commanded that the city should be held to the last man and that the troops should let themselves be surrounded as a means of delaying the Americans and providing more time for the West Wall preparations. The defense included the 19th Volksgrenadier Division, 1215th Regiment, 101st Security Regiment, 1217th Regiment and 22nd Fortress Regiment; the 17th SS Panzer Grenadier Division; and the hardened 462nd Fusiliers. They concentrated their defense on the main forts of Jeanne d'Arc and Driant. Both were in need of repair, but maintained approximately 14 main cannons as well as several machine guns. However, the forts' water systems would not work and supplies were low. On the attack side, elements of the 3rd Cavalry struck northeast to block German reinforcements from that direction. After the 90th Infantry Division obtained a bridgehead, the 10th Armored Division pushed northeast, then swung south to stop any escaping Germans. The 5th Infantry Division attacked from the south and the 95th Infantry Division attacked from the west towards Metz. The river was turbulent and 1,000 yards wide at some points. The Germans had the high ground and fired on the Americans while they advanced and built bridges. In the north, the 90th Infantry Division crossed near Cattenam and fought to take the forts of Metich and Koenigsmacker, which lay along a ridge covering roads leading out of Metz. On November 9, the Eighth Air Force committed 1,299 planes to the region. Of them, 689 bombed Metz and missed all their targets. The remaining attacked the German reserve areas and also missed. By November 10, the American battalions were at 50 percent strength and in dire need of supplies because the Germans had prevented supplies from crossing the river. The troops were cold, wet, hungry and out of explosives with which to attack the forts. However, on November 11, Koenigsmacker surrendered after a loss of 301 German casualties and 111 U.S. casualties. Also on November 11, the German commander, General Vollrath Lübbe, had a stroke and the German First Army was evacuated to refit and avoid capture, leaving German defenses with minimal fortress garrisons. General Luebbe was replaced by the reluctant General Friedrich Kittel, who had achieved success in the east with fortress defenses.

On November 12 at 0300, the Germans counterattacked in the north at Kerrling against the 90th Infantry Division. They used 10 tanks and a regiment of men in an attempt to destroy the bridgehead at Malling. The Americans, including Sergeant Forrest Everhart fought bravely against the strong German attack; Everhart was awarded the Medal of Honor for his actions. Before being overrun and killed, Private Earl Oliver continued to man his machine gun. After the battle, 22 dead Germans were found within 15 feet of Oliver, who received the Distinguished Service Cross for his actions. The heroic infantry delayed the German counterattack, while artillery support from across the river stopped it altogether. On November 15, in the midst of snow and sleet, supplies began crossing at Malling; the troops finally received dry socks, overcoats and blankets. Progress increased after the

306th Engineers, while under fire, built the largest Bailey Bridge at Thionville. The 95th Division pushed in and met the 90th at Thionville, where they used shaped charges and 10-pound blocks of TNT to take out the Maginot Line fort. In the northeast, the 10th Armored Division protected the left flank and took Bounzonville to stop German reinforcements from reaching Metz. The division also positioned for the Saare River crossing. Meanwhile, in the south, the 5th Infantry Division was enveloping Metz with the objective of meeting the 90th and closing the exits across the Nied River. After fierce fighting, the 5th Infantry Division successfully beat back the 17th SS Division across the Nied River. (The 17th SS was pulling back to refit for the German winter offensive.)

On November 14, General Kittel arrived in Metz. The situation was dire and supplies were very low, but Kittel had achieved success in the east against Russia under difficult circumstances. That same day, the 90th and 5th Infantry Divisions had almost completed their encirclement of Metz and the U.S. was about to make a big push into the community. Amazingly for the Germans, on November 14, a train full of provisions made it into Metz, providing another three weeks of supplies and 48 cannons for defense. Also, in typical German fashion, Kittel, upon his arrival, immediately called for a counterattack.

On November 15, Kittel assembled a Kampfgruppe and counterattacked at Distroff. The 90th Division wrote that it was "the most violent counter blow of the campaign." The Germans were repulsed after four hours and left behind 200 killed in action, eight destroyed tanks and 16 destroyed halftracks. On November 16, one of the largest northern Maginot Line forts—Fort Hackenburg—was taken through the use of 155mm howitzers from within 2,000 yards. Also close to this time, the big push into Metz proper began. The 95th pressed from west into Metz, while Task Force Bacon arrived from the north and the 5th Infantry Division came from the south and east. Task Force Bacon's mission was to clear the east bank of the Moselle and drive straight into Metz. The task force contained two battalions of infantry, two companies of tank destroyers, one 95th Infantry Division reconnaissance troop and a company of Shermans. Task Force Bacon faced several German counterattacks and "88 Alley," a reference to the German defenses along the main road. The 95th also faced fierce opposition in the town of Woippy, where the Germans counterattacked three times. Even through the tough defense, the Americans advanced. On November 18, encirclement was completed when the 90th Infantry Division and the 5th Infantry Division met north of Retonfey. By November 19, the Americans were fighting inside Metz city. Shortly afterward, on November 21, General Kittel was found in a basement, wounded. On November 22, Metz city surrendered except for its forts. At the same time, General Walker forbade direct assaults on the holdout forts in an effort to minimize needless casualties. The forts were isolated and began to run out of ammunition and food. On November 26, Fort Verdun surrendered. Fort St. Privat followed on November 29, then Fort Quentin on December 6, Fort Plappeville on December 7 and Fort Driant on December 8. On December 13, Fort Jeanne d' Arc finally surrendered. The Germans had lost, but had also done their job and held up the American advance for over a month, permitting an organized withdrawal to the Saare River.

THIRD PHASE – ADVANCE OVER THE SAAR RIVER TO THE WEST WALL (SIEGFRIED LINE):

While some U.S. forces contained the German holdout forts in Metz, Patton pushed on to cross the Saar River, begin engaging the West Wall (Siegfried Line) and get into German territory. Hard fighting took place near Farebersviller, but the Third Army pushed on into Saarlautern (Saarlouis), where, on December 3, the 95th Infantry Division captured an intact bridge just north of the city center. A small unit crossed the 125 feet in boats at 0545, surprising a lone tank guarding the bridge and holding off multiple counterattacks. The 90th Infantry Division also captured a bridgehead near Pachten on December 7. Soon after, the Americans began pouring over the bridge and expanding their gains as much as possible. However, due to a lack of manpower, the advance died out. At this time, the 90th Infantry Division was at 43 percent capacity and the 95th at 61 percent. On December 17, Patton had to cancel the drive through the West Wall because of reports describing a major German breakthrough in the Ardennes Forest. The Battle of the Bulge had begun.

OUTCOME: As a result of the fighting, the Americans had inflicted great losses on the Germans and gained substantial ground, but not as quickly or decisively as planned due to supply shortages. However, Patton's forces pulled the German armor reserves to Lorraine, preventing their use in the Aachen and Arnhem sectors. It was a small gain, only 48 kilometers during the battle of Metz in exchange for 30,000 casualties. After the campaign, the German Fifth Panzer Army was decimated and the German First Army shattered. On December 16, the Battle of the Bulge stopped the entire offensive action for almost two months, forcing a pullback over the Saar River and resulting in the loss of captured territory. General Patton had already prepared for an event like the German offensive in the Ardennes and was able to mobilize forces within three days to rescue the men trapped in Bastogne.

WHO? Numbers and leaders? It was General Patton's Third Army against the German First Army under Knobelsdorff and the German Fifth Army under Manteuffel. The Third Army was well equipped in terms of men, armor, artillery and aircraft support. The Third Army had almost 600 tanks as compared to the Germans, who had only 300. However, the Germans balanced their forces through the use of similar amounts of artillery and fairly strong defensive positions. It's hard to say what the German casualties and equipment losses were, but they certainly numbered more than the Americans'. During this campaign, the Germans had lost 75,000 men alone as prisoners (25,600 in the Battle for Metz). The Americans also suffered greatly with 55,182 casualties (6,657 killed in action, 36,406 wounded in action and 12,119 missing in action). These numbers don't include the more than 42,000 non-battle casualties due to combat fatigue, frostbite and trench foot. By early December, the Third Army began having a hard time filling its rosters; it had experienced 38,510 casualties in November and could provide only 26,000 replacements. It also suffered greatly in terms of equipment, losing more than 400 tanks in the Lorraine battles, as well as more than 1,000 vehicles.

WHEN? September 1–December 18, 1944

WHY IN LORRAINE? This was the sector assigned to the Third Army. It was a historical route in and out of France via Germany.

TECHNOLOGY/TACTICS: The Third Army was particularly successful because it attacked aggressively. The army was able to keep the Germans from setting up solid defenses or counterattacks. Its drives depended on the XIX Tactical Air Command, which maintained 600 aircraft, medium bombers (B-26s) and P-47s to protect the Third Army's flanks while the army drove forward. Once inclement weather arrived in September, the army received much less assistance from the Air Force. Their success depended on thorough training and planning, as well as effective execution. As the weather changed, the army charged from hill to hill, town to town. In the towns they used direct artillery and tank fire to destroy pillboxes and shape charges that would break through the forts. The soldiers tried getting their hands on the Browning Automatic Rifle as a means of providing faster firepower than the Garand. The Americans used 155mm and 240mm howitzers as supporting artillery to stop German counterattacks, but they also used these for direct fire at pillboxes. The Americans also relied heavily on combat engineers to prepare bridges using boats and portable Bailey Bridges. In addition, the Americans maintained a significant advantage in combine arms and communications. The communication/radios in tanks, artillery stations (forward observers) and tactical air command gave the Americans the ability to accurately call for artillery fire and/or aircraft support when needed. The U.S. aircraft used napalm against the forts which was first used in March 1944 against the Germans.

QUOTES: by Patton:

"Prepare for the unknown by studying how others in the past have coped with the unforeseeable and the unpredictable."

"It is foolish and wrong to mourn the men who died. Rather we should thank God that such men lived."

"No bastard ever won a war by dying for his country. He won it by making the other poor dumb bastard die for his country."

"Nobody ever defended anything successfully, there is only attack and attack and attack some more. "

"A good plan, violently executed now, is better than a perfect plan next week."

"Fixed fortifications are monuments to man's stupidity."

"In case of doubt, attack."

"Live for something rather than die for nothing."

"May God have mercy upon my enemies, because I won't."

"Wars may be fought with weapons, but they are won by men."

PLACES TO SEE (REFERENCE MAPS 56-60):

FIRST PHASE, MOSELLE CROSSING AND GERMAN COUNTERATTACKS, SEPTEMBER 5-30:
MOSELLE CROSSING:

1. **5TH INFANTRY DIVISION STONE MEMORIAL, DORNOT:** Located on the eastern side of the river is a stone memorial to the 5th Infantry Division, which crossed at this location on September 5 only to be forced back by the Germans after fierce fighting. Their efforts were severely hampered by Fort Blaise, which was directly across from the landing site and one of the 5th Infantry Division's first objectives to capture.
   N 49 02.823 E 6 03.787 (49.04705, 6.063117)

2. **5TH INFANTRY DIVISION STONE MEMORIAL, ARNAVILLE:** On September 5, the 5th Infantry Division crossed the Moselle River south of Metz at Dornot and Arnaville. Due to attacks from the 17th SS Panzer Division and shellfire from Fort Blaise, Fort Driant and Fort Verdun, the division couldn't hold a bridgehead at Dornot, but was able to build up a bridgehead at Arnaville after several days of fierce fighting. On September 22, due to lack of supplies they pulled back across the river after suffering many casualties.
   N 49 0.664 E 6 2.638 (49.011067, 6.043967)

3. **SHERMAN MEMORIAL TANK AND RESISTANCE MEMORIAL, NANCY:** Located on the western edge of Nancy is a small memorial park that holds an M4 Sherman with 4th Armored Division markings. It serves as a memorial to the American sacrifices that helped liberate Nancy.
   N 48 41.703 E 6 7.536 (48.69505, 6.1256)

4. **BRIDGEHEAD, SEPTEMBER 5 AND BATTLE OF MOUSSON HILL (HILL 382), MEMORIAL TO BRIGADIER GENERAL EDMUND SEARBY, PONT-À-MOUSSON:** On September 5, elements of the 80th Infantry Division crossed the river at Pont-à-Mousson. Soon after establishing a bridgehead, elements of the 3rd Panzer Grenadiers counterattacked and crushed the bridgehead. One of the obstacles was Mousson Hill, which overlooked the town and river. After the crossings cited below at Dieulouard on September 11, the Americans expanded the bridgehead and took control of Mousson Hill. On September 12, an infantry company attacked the hill and the 80th Division Artillery commander, Brigadier General Edmund Searby, and Lieutenant David Hindlemann decided to go along. Upon reaching the crest, they could see the entire battlefield. The unit's artillery observer was not there, so Searby and Hindlemann began calling in the artillery. Several counterattacks of tanks and infantry were stopped due to their heroism. On the second day, a tank made it through the lines but was disabled by an artillery round. The tank continued to sweep their position with machine gun fire. Per Hindle-

mann, Brigadier General Searby said, "I'm gonna get that son of a bitch!" and he took a rifle....we were down behind the wall.....and he stands up like he was shootin' targets and he aims at the guy and a machine gun just literally cut him in half." Hindlemann continued calling in artillery throughout the next two days (for a total of three days). Because of his efforts, the hill remained in American control. At the top of the hill is a road named after Searby and a small memorial. Also at the top are castle ruins and a fantastic view. The geo coordinates are for a parking spot about 50 yards from Searby Road.
N 48 54.388 E 6 04.753 (48.906467, 6.079217)

5. **MEMORIAL TO THE MOSELLE CROSSING, 35TH INFANTRY BRIDGEHEAD, FLAVIGNY BRIDGE, SEPTEMBER 10:** At this location, the Americans discovered that a bridge was still intact. At 1900 on September 10, the 2nd Battalion of the 134th Regiment rushed the bridge. After three hours of fighting against dug-in Germans and armored cars, they secured a bridgehead on the east. However, the Germans bombed the location and used artillery to destroy the bridge. Then they pounded the soldiers. Next, elements of the 15th Panzer Grenadier Division swept the remaining soldiers into the river. Casualties were very high. Those who could swim made it back to the other side. At this location is a memorial to the 35th Infantry Division, which crossed here.
N 48 34.633 E 6 10.777 (48.577217, 6.179617)

6. **MOSELLE CROSSING, 35TH INFANTRY DIVISION BRIDGEHEAD, SEPTEMBER 11, LOREY:** On the morning of September 11, as planned, two battalions of the 137th Regiment crossed the Moselle after an artillery barrage. They dug in between the villages of Crevechamps and Lorey until armor crossed a little farther south. This was the successful crossing of the Moselle, which the division held against several German attacks. These geo coordinates are for a parking area next to the Moselle, on the eastern bank near Lorey. You can hike and explore along the Moselle, approximately from this location to three kilometers north.
N 48 29.908 E 6 18.086 (48.498467, 6.301433)

7. **80TH INFANTRY MOSELLE CROSSING AT DIEULOUARD, SEPTEMBER 12:** At this approximate location, north of Nancy, two battalions of the 317th Regiment crossed the river and canals at 0400 on September 12. This is a good place to park, see the river and appreciate the high hills where the German positions were situated across the river.
N 48 50.855 E 6 04.607 (48.847583, 6.076783)

8. **HILL 382:** This hill was one of the first objectives for September 12. After taking the hill, two battalions of the 317th Regiment defended against several fierce counterattacks by elements of the 3rd Panzer Grenadier Division; the counterattacks lasted from early September 13 until nightfall on September 15. On Hill 382, the village of Sainte-Geneviève is nestled on the top, with hiking trails linking it to the crest and other hills.
N 48 51.815 E 6 07.232 (48.863583, 6.120533)

9. **BATTLE AT MAIRY, SEPTEMBER 8:** Mairy is located northwest of Metz. In this town and surrounding towns, elements of the 90th Infantry Division defended against and outright destroyed the Panzer Brigade 106. At this geo coordinate is a street named "September 8, 1944" in memory of the battle. Mairy was the cornerstone of the defense. It was here at 0700 that German Panzers attacking from the west were stopped by towed 57mm anti-tank guns. Then, at 0800, halftracks with Panzer grenadiers approaching from the west and southwest were shot up by U.S. anti-tank guns, artillery and bazookas.
N 49 18.230 E 5 51.609 (49.303833, 5.86015)

BATTLE AT DOMPAIRE, SEPTEMBER 13:

10. **VILLE-SUR-ILLON SHERMAN MEMORIAL:** During the September 13 battle with Panzer Brigade 112, French commander Langlade established his headquarters in town. The Germans attempted a counterattack from the west and south to break through to the trapped German Panther Regiment 29. At this location is a Sherman tank and a memorial to the French.
N 48 10.552 E 6 12.380 (48.175867, 6.206333)

11. **DOMPAIRE SHERMAN MEMORIAL:** At this location is a memorial and Sherman tank dedicated to the French who fought and died here during the destruction of Panzer Brigade 112.
N48 13.228 E6 14.673 (48.220467, 6.24455)

12. **M8 HOWITZER MOTOR CARRIAGE, ANDELOT-BLANCHEVILLE:** In Andelot, west of Dompaire, is a memorial with an M8 Howitzer motor carriage for the French 2nd Armored Division. This tank was lost during the battle from September 10-11.
N 48 14.657 E 5 18.414 (48.244283, 5.3069)

GERMAN COUNTERATTACKS, BATTLE OF ARRACOURT, SEPTEMBER 18-30:

13. **LUNEVILLE (SOUTH OF TOWN):** This site contains a memorial to the 704th Tank Destroyer Battalion. Luneville was the German objective on September 18.
N 48 33.214 E 6 33.535 (48.553567, 6.558917)

14a. **MOYENVIC CENTER:** On September 24, Moyenvic became a target of Manteuffel as part of his attempt to push back the 4th Armored Division and other American units. The German 559th Volksgrenadier Division and 106th Panzer Brigade attacked from Château Salins, but were stopped by American artillery and tanks. The geo coordinates for Moyenvic follow.
N 48 46.715 E 6 33.709 (48.778583, 6.561817)

14b. **HILL 310, MOYENVIC:** The 26th Infantry Division waged a significant three-day battle over Hill 310 just north of the town on November 10 during the battle for Metz.
N 48 47.580 E 6 32.624 (48.793, 6.543733)

15a. BATTLE OF ARRACOURT HISTORICAL CIRCUIT, SHERMAN TANK: In this area is a circuit that starts in Arracourt at the site of the Sherman tank located at this grid. About two minutes east in the town of Réchicourt-la- Petite is a second board showing the circuit and the follow-on towns.
N 48 43.376 E 6 31.831 (48.722933, 6.530517)

15b. ARRACOURT MONUMENT TO THE 704TH TANK DESTROYER BATTALION, 4TH ARMORED DIVISION (IN FRONT OF CHURCH):
N 48 43.471 E 6 32.170 (48.724517, 6.536167)

16. HILLS 318 AND 295: These hills are in the shape of a camel back. They were fiercely fought over during the Battle of Arracourt, especially from September 27-30 when the Germans threw everything they had against these hills to capture them from the Americans. The 51st Armored Infantry Battalion stoutly defended it, and the hill exchanged hands several times. This geo coordinate will take you to the eastern edge of the ridge, where you can park and hike into the woods. The Germans attacked from the south and east.
N 48 42.357 E 6 32.127 (48.70595, 6.53545)

17. RÉCHICOURT-LA-PETITE INFORMATION BOARD: The town located just east of Arracourt saw a significant amount of action. On September 19 it was at the center of the tank battle. Use this information board ro learn about the actual battle.
N 48 43.144 E 6 34.898 (48.719067, 6.581633)

18a. LE PETITE PLAQUE TO U.S. ARMOR, BEZANGE: On the church is a plaque to the 37th Tank Battalion that commemorates its actions in area battles.
N 48 43.826 E 6 36.794 (48.730433, 6.613233)

18b. HILL 265: This is not much of a hill, but on September 27 it was fiercely fought over for three days and ultimately held onto by the Americans. During the fight, Lieutenant James Field of the 10th Armored Infantry Battalion engaged in heroics that he was awarded the Medal of Honor. The following geo coordinates will take you up a small road and almost to the top of the hill. If you pull over here and look south, you will have the crest of the hill to your left. With discretion, you can walk into the field to look over the site where Lt. Field watched the Germans advance.
N 48 43.785 E 6 36.171 (48.72975, 6.60285)

19. INFORMATION BOARD, LEZEY: On September 22, the German 111th Panzer Brigade attacked American positions in Lezey and Juvelize.
N 48 45.162 E 6 37.772 (48.7527, 6.629533)

20a. INFORMATION BOARD, JUVELIZE: On September 22, the German Panzer Brigade 111 captured Juvelize, which offers a commanding view of the battle area. In response, the 37th Tank Battalion occupied Trois Crois, which looked over the German assemblage at Juvelize. The Americans engaged them with artillery, tanks and aircraft.
N 48 45.744 E 6 38.927 (48.7624, 6.648783)

20b. TROIS CROIS (HILL 257): The Americans held this position on September 22 to engage and stop the advancing Germans. From this site they could watch the German Panzer Brigade 111 advancing from the east and into Juvelize. After Panzer Brigade 111's attack failed, Manteuffal committed his last reserves, the remaining tanks of the Panzer Brigade 113. They were also decimated and their commander killed when his halftrack was destroyed.
N 48 46.215 E 6 37.465 (48.770248, 6.624413)

21. **INFORMATION BOARD, LEY:** Ley was another little village that saw fierce battle in the surrounding hills. On the other side of the church is a memorial stone to a bomber crew that perished during World War II.
N 48 44.135 E 6 39.299 (48.735583, 6.654983)

22. **INFORMATION BOARD, MONCOURT:** The Germans attacked the Americans through Moncourt, an assembly area that saw significant amounts of fighting.
N 48 43.079 E 6 38.200 (48.717983, 6.636667)

23. **COINCOURT CENTER:** Coincourt was on the route of German attacks from Parroy Forest. It saw intense action throughout the battle as the Germans shifted their angles of attack. I believe the information board is at this location, though I didn't get to this particular spot.
N 48 41.983 E 6 36.707 (48.699717, 6.611783)

24. **INFORMATION BOARD, PARROY:** This site provides information about the German main assault route throughout the battle. Parroy was the Germans' jumping-off point and retreat route into the Parroy Forest.
N 48 40.949 E 6 36.040 (48.682483, 6.600667)

25. **PARROY FOREST (FORÊT DE PAROY):** Still a forest today, this was used by the Germans as a launching point for the attack on September 18 and throughout the remainder of September. Specifically, it was used by Panzer Brigade 111. The geo coordinates are for a parking area from which you can hike into the woods on the northern side, south of the town of Parroy. The 79th Infantry Division was assigned the task of clearing the forest; a gritty battle ensued from September 25–October 21, 1944. The assignment to Parroy Forest was under the XV Corps, which included the French 2nd Armored Division. In total, the Americans suffered 365 killed in action, 2,310 wounded in action, 165 missing in action and 2,410 non-battle casualties.
N 48 40.038 E 6 36.458 (48.6673, 6.607633)

26. **INFORMATION BOARD, BURES:** The small town of Bures was directly in the Germans' route of attack to capture Hills 318 and 295. It was devastated during the battle, especially by the P-47 Thunderbirds that completed more than 100 sorties during the first day of the German attack.
N 48 41.636 E 6 34.544 (48.693933, 6.575733)

27. **MEMORIAL TO THE 37TH TANK BATTALION AND INFORMATION BOARD, VALHEY:** Valhey is at the westernmost edge of the battlefield route. At this location is a memorial to a tank crew from the 37th Tank Battalion. If you face the memorial, directly to your left is an information board about the battle that took place in this area.
N 48 40.750 E 6 29.466 (48.679167, 6.4911)

SECOND PHASE, BATTLE OF METZ, OCTOBER–DECEMBER:

28. **FORTRESS METZ:** Metz had more than 46 forts built in two rings. Before the Franco-Prussian War of 1870, the French had built a belt to protect themselves from the Germans. Then the Germans built a belt to protect Metz from the French from 1899–1912. The French took possession of these forts after World War I and incorporated them into the Maginot Line. In 1944, only 10 percent of the forts were armed. The Germans incorporated them into their defensive line as well as they could. By November, the Germans were able to scrap together a defense that included cannons they had pulled from the Metz museum. (Several forts had been stripped for the Atlantic Wall.) Following are the highlights directly around Metz. Fort Driant experienced the most action, but all are great to see. (Just be careful, as they're located in hiking areas that likely contain unexploded ordnance, barbed wire, spikes, etc.) The following are directly around Metz, starting with Fort Verdun at the "7 o'clock" position, then going clockwise.
    - A. **VERDUN FORTS (ST. BLAISE):**
    N 49 03.096 E 6 05.512 (49.0516, 6.091867)
    - B. **FORT DRIANT (LOCATION TO PARK, SEE MAP 60):**
    N 49 04.714 E 6 03.399 (49.078567, 6.05665)
    - C. **FORT JEANNE D' ARC:**
    N 49 07.007 E 6 04.042 (49.116783, 6.067367)
    - D. **FORT KELLERMAN:**
    N 49 09.918 E 6 03.777 (49.1653, 6.06295)
    - E. **FORT PLAPPEVILLE:**
    N 49 07.644 E 6 06.792 (49.1274, 6.1132)
    - F. **FORT QUENTIN:**
    N 49 07.271 E 6 07.650 (49.121183, 6.1275)

G. **FORT DE LAUVALLIERE/DE BELLCROIX AND MONUMENT TO THE 95TH INFANTRY DIVISION:** On November 18, the fort surrendered, but the Germans had set a delayed demolition charge. As the Americans advanced past the fort, the charge blew one of the buildings apart, killing 42 Americans and wounding many more.

N 49 07.489 E 6 11.270 (49.124817, 6.187833)

H. **FORT QUEULEU:**
N 49 05.797 E 6 12.243 (49.096617, 6.20405)

29. **MEMORIAL TO THE LIBERATION OF METZ:** Next to the beautiful Cathedral of Metz is a stone monument commemorating, in French, the liberation of Metz. "On November 22, 1944 on this spot General Walker commanding the XX Corps of the Third Army, handed over the French the city of Metz, liberated by his troops."
N 49 07.192 E 6 10.562 (49.119867, 6.176033)

NORTHERN FORTS: During the Battle of Metz, the attack included a wide encirclement from the north and south. The following are some highlights in the north.

30. **MEMORIAL TO THE 377TH INFANTRY REGIMENT OF THE 95TH INFANTRY DIVISION, PARC DE BRIEUX, MAIZIÈRES-LÈS-METZ:** I Company of the 377th Infantry Regiment fought here and liberated the well-defended Château de Brieux in November 1944. Now the site contains a small plaque and stone. The company crossed the Moselle near this location to take Fort Illange and also to secure a road for Task Force Bacon (95th Infantry Division with tank battalions) to drive south into Metz.
N 49 12.336 E 6 09.954 (49.2056, 6.1659)

31. **OCTOBER PAUSE, CAPTURE OF MAIZIÈRES-LÈS-METZ, HOTEL DE VILLE (MAYOR'S HOUSE):** Eight kilometers north of Metz, able to use limited amounts of men and materiel the 90th Infantry Division captured and held this town throughout October. The Germans resisted until October 30, after which the 90th Infantry Division used 155mm, M12 and 240mm cannon on the hold outs. Maizières-lès-Metz was an important gain that gave the 90th Infantry Division a proper launching point for Operation Madison. The geo coordinates will take you in front of the newly built mayor's house. There's nothing in particular to see in town, only the terrain and the river.
N 49 12.625 E 6 09.629 (49.210417, 6.160483)

32. **FORT DE GUENTRANGE:** The Germans built this fort before World War I and used it to defend Thionville from the French. The Germans occupied it briefly from August–September 1944, but the 90th Infantry Division took it without a fight in November 1944. There is a museum here with information about the Battle of Metz.
N 49 22.554 E 6 07.988 (49.3759, 6.133133)

33. **FORT ILLANGE:** Fort Illange consisted of four small forts. It was held by a small garrison force from Grenadier Regiment 74. The fort threatened the successful crossings of the 90th Infantry Division and Task Force Bacon (which contained elements of the 95th Infantry Division), but on November 14, a company from the 378th infiltrated the defenses. By November 15, the Americans had cleared the fort with the help of TNT.
N 49 20.244 E 6 10.789 (49.3374, 6.179817)

34. **FORT KOENIGSMACKER:** This fort posed a significant threat to the crossings and mission of the 90th Infantry Division. Under cover of darkness on November 9, two companies of the 358th Infantry Division managed to quickly get into the fort's defensive belt without being noticed. As the Americans used demolition charges to fight through the fort's defenses, the fort garrison fired its artillery on the river landings. By November 11, the garrison had surrendered, resulting in a total of 372 prisoners of war.
N 49 22.673 E 6 15.050 (49.377883, 6.250833)

35. **FORT METRICH:** In part of a very large park is one of the three largest forts of the Maginot Line. It was occupied by elements of the 19th Volksgrenadier Division. On November 10, the 90th Infantry Division attacked it, but was repulsed. Eventually, on November 12, the Germans in the fort surrendered. The following geo coordinates are for the southeastern edge of the fort, which runs almost to the river.
N 49 21.595 E 6 19.404 (49.359917, 6.3234)

36. **MALLING CROSSING:** At this small, scenic parking area you can see the site where the Americans crossed the Moselle north of Metz. The 359th Infantry Regiment crossed on November 9 at 0330 and landed at Malling, capturing most of the German defenders. This site is also near the location where the Combat Engineer Battalions struggled under fire to build bridges and footways across the swollen river. In addition, Malling was the target of German counterattacks.
N 49 25.423 E 6 17.590 (49.423717, 6.293167)

37. **GERMAN COUNTERATTACK AT KERLING, LES SIERCK TOWARD PETITE HETTANGE:** These geo coordinates will take you in front of the church, where there is a small memorial. On November 9, the American 359th Infantry Regiment attacked and occupied Kerling. At 0300 on November 12, a Kampfgruppe of Panzergrenadiers with 10 tanks attacked the town in an attempt to knock back the bridgehead. The Germans captured the town but were later pushed out. The Germans suffered greatly for the attack – 400 killed in action, 150 prisoners of war and nine lost tanks. On November 12, Sgt. Forrest Everhart bravely defended his position during the German counterattack. He was awarded the Medal of Honor for his actions, the citation reads: "He commanded a platoon that bore the brunt of a desperate enemy counterattack near Kerling, France, before dawn on 12 November 1944. When German tanks and self-propelled guns penetrated his left flank and overwhelming infantry forces threatened to overrun the 1 remaining machinegun in that

section, he ran 400 yards through woods churned by artillery and mortar concentrations to strengthen the defense. With the 1 remaining gunner, he directed furious fire into the advancing hordes until they swarmed close to the position. He left the gun, boldly charged the attackers and, after a 15-minute exchange of hand grenades, forced them to withdraw leaving 30 dead behind. He re-crossed the fire-swept terrain to his then threatened right flank, exhorted his men and directed murderous fire from the single machinegun at that position. There, in the light of bursting mortar shells, he again closed with the enemy in a hand grenade duel and, after a fierce 30-minute battle, forced the Germans to withdraw leaving another 20 dead. The gallantry and intrepidity of T/Sgt. Everhart in rallying his men and refusing to fall back in the face of terrible odds were highly instrumental in repelling the fanatical enemy counterattack directed at the American bridgehead across the Moselle River."

N 49 23.840 E 6 21.001 (49.397333, 6.350017)

38. **90TH INFANTRY DIVISION MEMORIAL, DISTROFF:** At dawn on November 15, a Kampfgruppe from Panzergrenadier Regiments 35 and 74 smashed into the 2nd Battalion, 358th Infantry Regiment, in Distroff. After a four-hour battle, the Germans withdrew. As they had in Kerling, the Germans suffered heavily; they lost four tanks, four Stug IIIs and 16 halftracks, and suffered 150 killed in action.

    N 49 19.918 E 6 15.803 (49.331967, 6.263383)

39. **M10 TANK AT THE BASE OF HACKENBURG:** M10 tank destroyers were used throughout the battle to provide infantry support and to fire directly on the forts. This tank with U.S. markings is at the foot of the hill to the museum/fort.

    N 49 20.123 E 6 21.763 (49.335383, 6.362717)

40. **MUSEUM FOR THE MAGINOT LINE AND THE METZ BATTLE, HACKENBURG:** Hackenburg was a Maginot Line fort occupied by the Germans as a means of shelling the American crossings. The 90th Infantry Division had to use M12 155mm Gun Motor Carriages for close direct fire to silence the fort. Be aware that it's operated by volunteers, so the fort has very limited hours; one can explore it only during a tour.

    N 49 20.478 E 6 21.931 (49.3413, 6.365517)

41. **NIED RIVER AND CLOSING OF THE ENCIRCLEMENT, COURCELLES-SUR-NIED:** On November 18, the 2nd Infantry of the 5th infantry Division closed one of the Germans' main escape routes near this geo coordinate. Courcelles-sur-Nied maintained an important road and rail junction. The Americans went on to close additional escape routes. On November 19, around 1030, they linked up with the 90th Infantry Division from the north at the town of Retonfey.

    N 49 03.971 E 6 18.801 (49.066183, 6.31335)

42. LORRAINE LIBERATION CROSS AND MEMORIAL: On top of Mont-Saint-Pierre is a cross dedicated to the French, Americans and Allies who liberated Lorraine.
N 49 03.472 E 6 26.562 (49.057867, 6.4427)

THIRD PHASE, ADVANCE OVER THE SAAR RIVER, DECEMBER:

43a. LORRAINE AMERICAN CEMETERY AND MEMORIAL NEAR SAINT-AVOLD: Another very impressive American cemetery. It's always shocking to see the number of crosses and Stars of David. The cemetery contains the graves of more than 10,400 men.
N 49 07.302 E 6 42.872 (49.1217, 6.714533)

43b. HALFTRACK MEMORIAL TO LIBERATION: At this location, on Avenue General Patton, is a halftrack that serves as a monument to the liberation of Saint-Avold.
N 49 06.623 E 6 42.317 (49.110383, 6.705283)

44. CHAFFEE TANK OF THE 70TH INFANTRY DIVISION AND MARBLE MONUMENT, SPICHEREN: At this location outside of Spicheren, overlooking the Saar River, a great battle was waged during the Franco-Prussian War of 1870. At the same location is a Chaffee tank, the remains of the German West Wall and a marble monument to the U.S. 70th Infantry Division, which fought to capture this area.
N 49 12.158 E 6 58.135 (49.202633, 6.968917)

45. SAARLAUTERN (SAARLOUIS)/SAAR RIVER CROSSING, DECEMBER 3, 1944: At this location, the American 379th Regiment crossed the Saar River and snuck up behind the tank guarding the bridge. The regiment crossed the bridge and a furious German commander ordered several counterattacks that the Americans rebuffed. The Americans crossed the Saar with little loss. Today, the Saar River has been "straightened"; the old river bends around an island that has been created. In this area you'll find many old bunkers and pillboxes. The following coordinates are for the rebuilt bridge that was captured about 500 meters to the northwest, "up the river" from where the troops crossed the Saar. Today there is another bridge to the island where the troops crossed in boats to capture the bridge.
N 49 19.021 E 6 44.913 (49.317017, 6.74855)

SITUATION NW EUROPE SEPTEMBER 15 - DECEMBER 15 1944 MAP 56

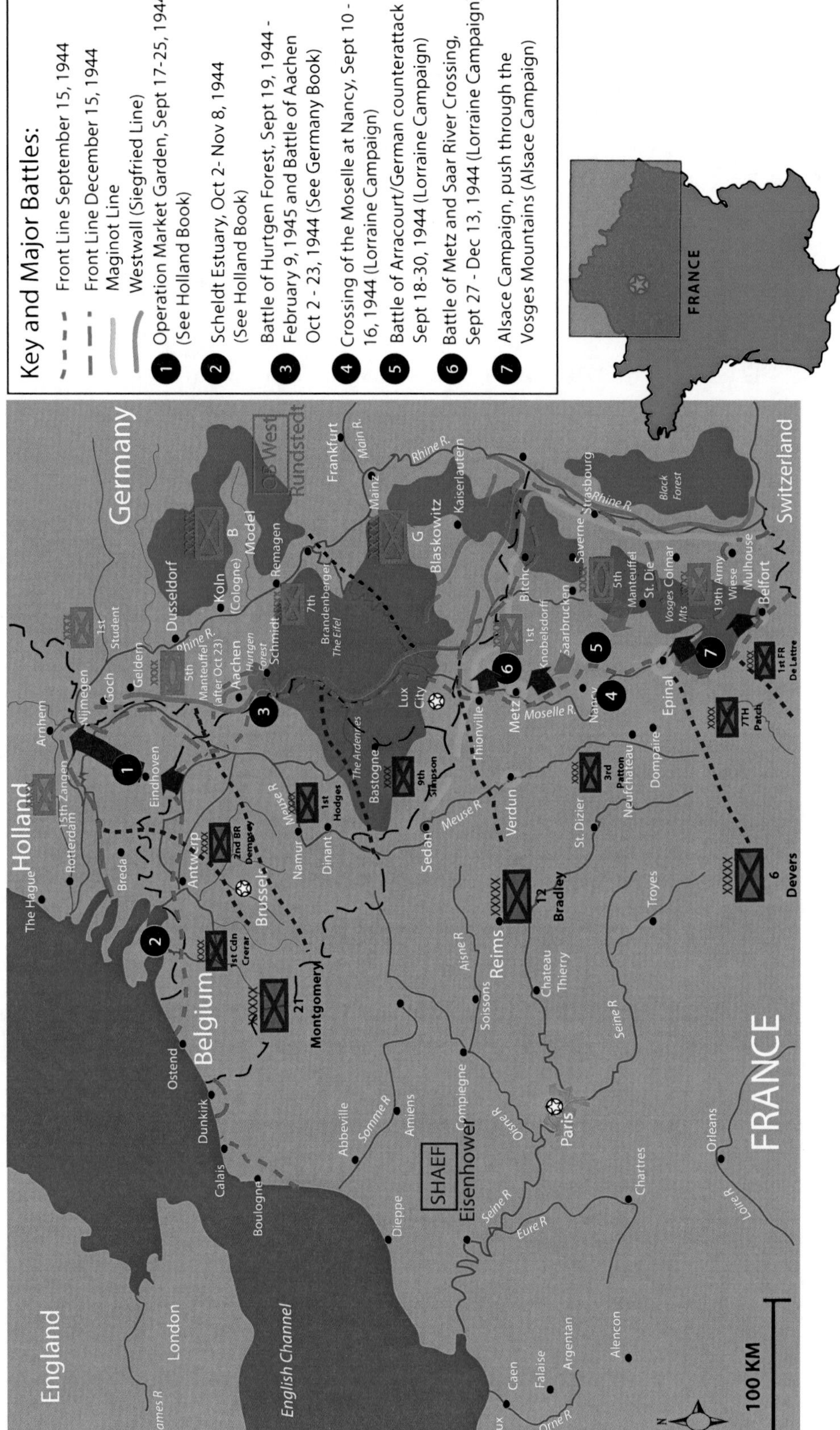
Key and Major Battles:
Front Line September 15, 1944
Front Line December 15, 1944
Maginot Line
Westwall (Siegfried Line)
1 Operation Market Garden, Sept 17-25, 1944 (See Holland Book)
2 Scheldt Estuary, Oct 2- Nov 8, 1944 (See Holland Book)
3 Battle of Hurtgen Forest, Sept 19, 1944 - February 9, 1945 and Battle of Aachen Oct 2 - 23, 1944 (See Germany Book)
4 Crossing of the Moselle at Nancy, Sept 10 - 16, 1944 (Lorraine Campaign)
5 Battle of Arracourt/German counterattack Sept 18-30, 1944 (Lorraine Campaign)
6 Battle of Metz and Saar River Crossing, Sept 27 - Dec 13, 1944 (Lorraine Campaign)
7 Alsace Campaign, push through the Vosges Mountains (Alsace Campaign)
FRANCE
England
London
Thames R
English Channel
Holland
Belgium
Germany
Switzerland
FRANCE
The Hague
Rotterdam
Breda
Antwerp
Brussels
Ostend
Dunkirk
Calais
Boulogne
Arnhem
Nijmegen
Eindhoven
Goch
Geldern
Dusseldorf
Koln (Cologne)
Remagen
Aachen
Hurtgen Forest
Schmidt
Namur
Dinant
Meuse R
Sedan
Bastogne
The Ardennes
The Eifel
Lux City
Thionville
Metz
Moselle R.
Nancy
Epinal
Verdun
St. Dizier
Neufchateau
Dompaire
Saarbrucken
Bitche
Saverne
Strasbourg
St. Die
Colmar
Vosges Mts
Mulhouse
Belfort
Kaiserlautern
Mainz
Main R.
Frankfurt
Rhine R.
Black Forest
Abbeville
Somme R
Amiens
Dieppe
Compiegne
Soissons
Aisne R
Reims
Chateau Thierry
Paris
Oise R
Seine R
Eure R
Troyes
Chartres
Orleans
Loire R
Caen
Falaise
Argentan
Alencon
Orne R
SHAEF
Eisenhower
21 Montgomery
1st Cdn Crerar
2nd BR Dempsey
1st Hodges
9th Simpson
12 Bradley
3rd Patton
6 Devers
7TH Patch
1st FR De Lattre
15th Zangen
1st Student
5th Manteuffel (after Oct 23)
7th Brandenberger
B Model
OB West Rundstedt
G Blaskowitz
1st Knobelsdorff
5th Manteuffel
19th Army Wiese
100 KM

LORRAINE CAMPAIGN SUMMARY, SEPTEMBER 5-DECEMBER 15, 1944 MAP 57

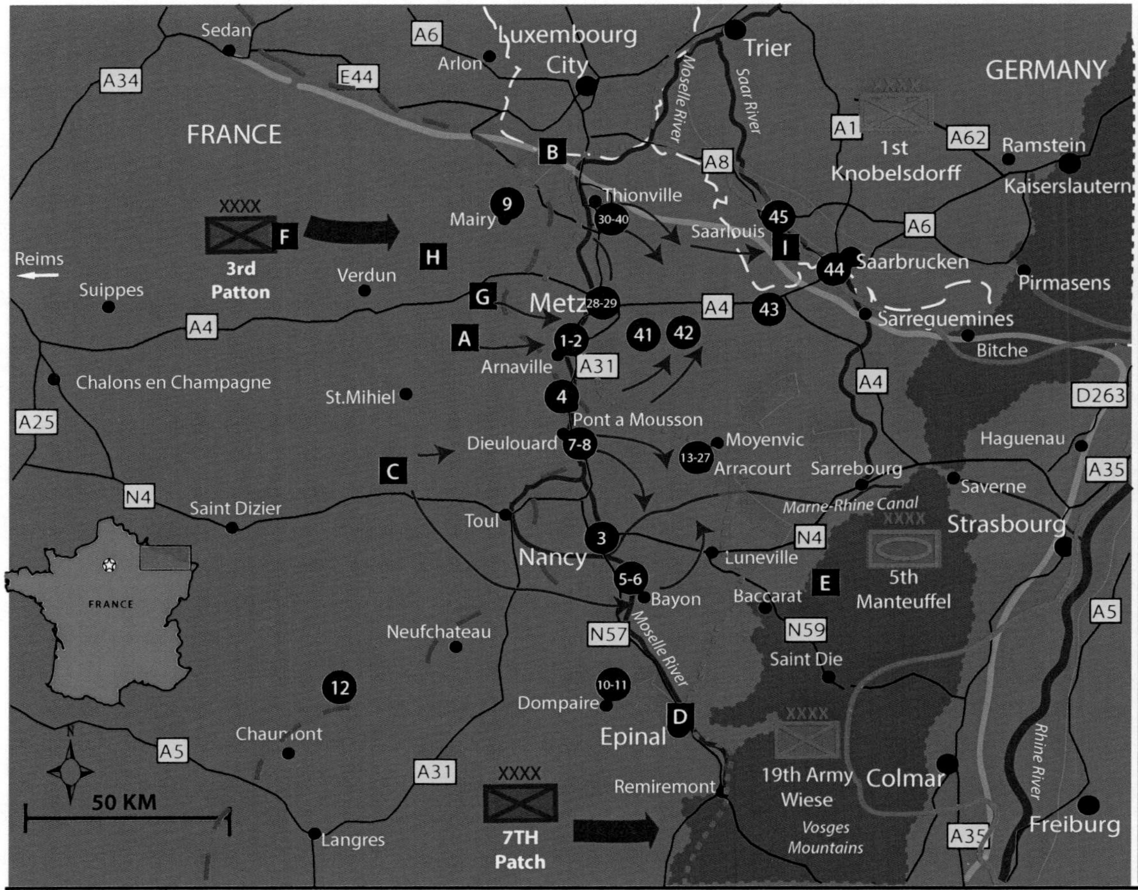

Places to See:

Moselle Crossings & German Counterattacks

- 1-2 5th ID Crossings, Dornot & Arnaville Memorials
- 3 Nancy Sherman and Memorial
- 4 Pont a Mousson Crossing, Mousson Hill 382
- 5-6 35th ID Crossing locations (and Memorial)
- 7-8 80th ID Crossings, Dieulouard, Hill 382
- 9 Battle of Mairy, September 8
- 10-11 Battle of Dompaire, Shermans, September 13
- 12 Andalot, M8 HMC & Memorial

Battle of Arracourt, September 18-30

- 13-27 Sherman Memorial, Hills & info boards

Battle for Metz, September 27 - December 13

- 28-29 Metz Forts and Memorials
- 30-40 Northern encirclement, memorials & forts.
- 41 Nied River Crossing (approximate)
- 42 Lorraine Cross Memorial, Mont St. Pierre
- 43 American Cemetery, St. Avold
- 44 Chaffee Tank & Memorial to 70th ID
- 45 Saar River, first Crossing Location (Germany)

***See next Chapter for Vosges Campaign locations

Front Line September 5, 1944
Front Line September 25, 1944
Front Line December 15, 1944

Movements:

A. September 5, American 3rd Army drove towards Metz. The 5th ID crossed at Dornots & Arnaville but with limited success due to fierce German oposition.
B. September 8, Germans counterattacked the Americans at Mairy, with the new Panzer Brigade 106, in an unsuccessful attempt to separate the 3rd Army from the US 1st Army.
C. September 10-16, the 35th ID, 80th ID and 4th AD defeated sharp German counterattacks and successfully encircled Nancy.
D. September 13, the Germans committed two more Panzer Brigades in another unsuccessful attempt to crush the Third Army from its southern right flank at Dompaire.
E. September 18-30, Manteuffel attempted several armor heavy counterattacks to push the Americans back over the Moselle. Considered the largest tank battle in the west.
F. September 22, Patton halted all major operations due to supply shortages.(Operation Market Garden began in the north)
G. September 27 - October 9, Operation Thunderbolt, elements of the Third Army attempted the capture of Fort Driant on the outskirts of Metz.
H. November 8 - December 13, after the "October pause" Operation Madison began, the Third Army captured Metz and its surrounding forts.
I. December 3, elements of the 3rd Army captured a bridge across the Saar River. But on December 17, Patton recalled his forces from the bridgehead b/c the Battle of the Bulge.

BATTLE OF ARRACOURT, SEPTEMBER 18 -30, 1944

MAP 58

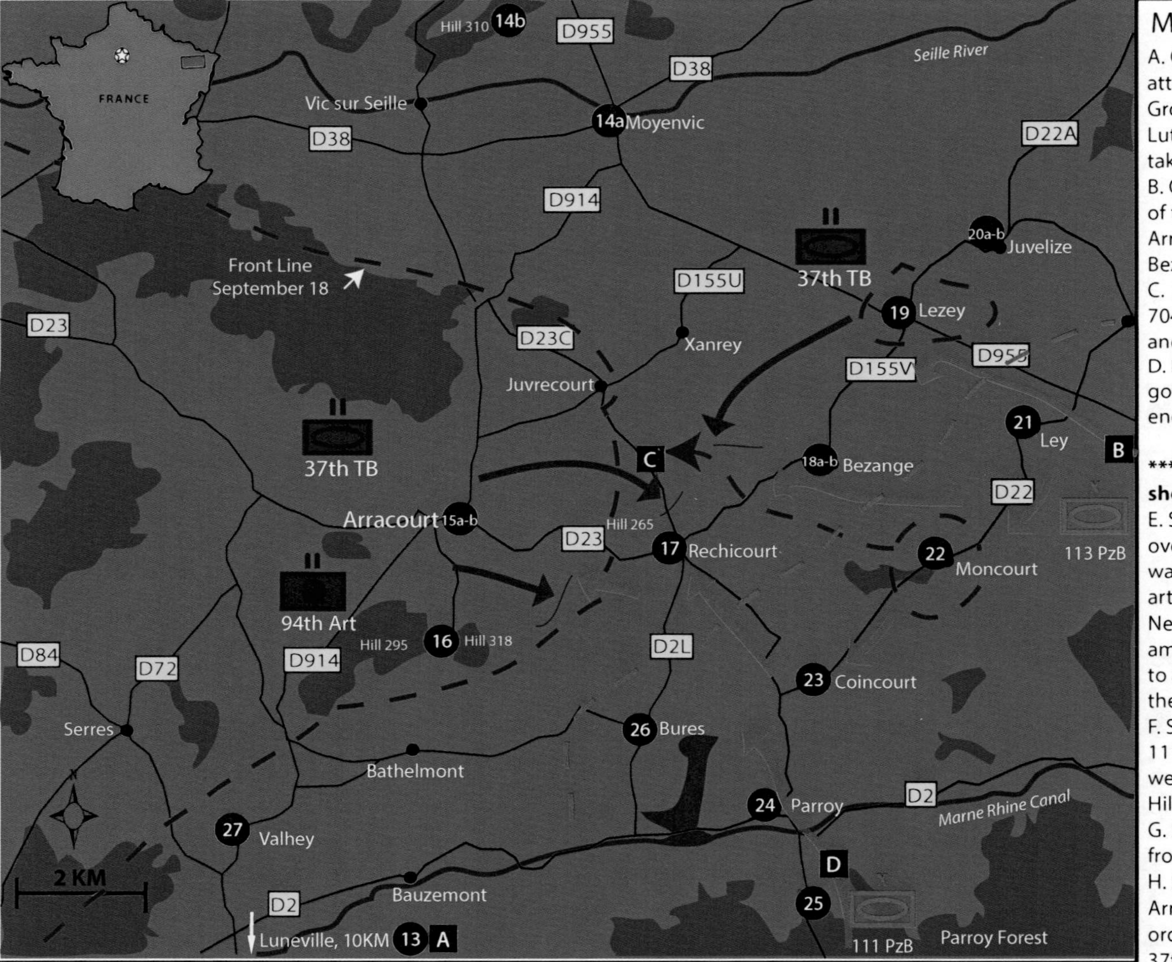
Hill 310
14b
D955
D38
Seille River
FRANCE
Vic sur Seille
14a Moyenvic
D38
D22A
D914
20a-b
Juvelize
Front Line
September 18
37th TB
D155U
D23
D23C
Xanrey
19 Lezey
D155V
D955
Juvrecourt
37th TB
21
Ley
B
C
18a-b Bezange
D22
Arracourt 15a-b
Hill 265
D23
17 Rechicourt
22
Moncourt
113 PzB
94th Art
D84
D72
D914
Hill 295
16
Hill 318
D2L
23 Coincourt
Serres
26 Bures
Bathelmont
24 Parroy
D2
Marne Rhine Canal
27 Valhey
D
2 KM
D2
Bauzemont
25
Luneville, 10KM 13 A
111 PzB
Parroy Forest

Places to See:

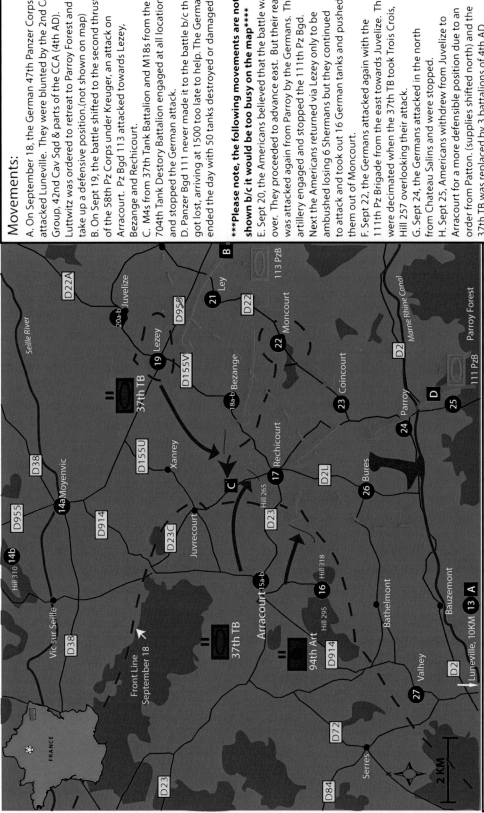

- 13 Luneville Memorial (off map)
- 14a Moyenvic Center of Town
- 14b Moyenvic , Hill 310
- 15a-b Arracourt Sherman & 704th Memorial
- 16 Hill 318 and Hill 295
- 17 Rechicourt and Hill 265
- 18a-b Bezange, Plaque to US AD
- 19 Lezey Info Board
- 20a-b Juvelize Info Bd & Hill 257
- 21 Ley Info Board
- 22 Moncourt Info Board
- 23 Coincourt Center
- 24 Parroy Info Board
- 25 Parroy Forest
- 26 Bures Info Board
- 27 Valhey Memorial and Info Board

Movements:

A. On September 18, the German 47th Panzer Corps attacked Luneville. They were blunted by the 2nd Cav Group, 42nd Cav Sqd & parts of the CCA (4th AD). Luttwitz was ordered to retreat to Parroy Forest and take up a defensive position.(not shown on map)

B. On Sept 19, the battle shifted to the second thrust of the 58th Pz Corps under Kreuger, an attack on Arracourt. Pz Bgd 113 attacked towards Lezey, Bezange and Rechicourt.

C. M4s from 37th Tank Battalion and M18s from the 704th Tank Destory Battalion engaged at all locations and stopped the German attack.

D. Panzer Bgd 111 never made it to the battle b/c they got lost, arriving at 1500 too late to help. The Germans ended the day with 50 tanks destroyed or damaged.

*****Please note, the following movements are not shown b/c it would be too busy on the map******

E. Sept 20, the Americans believed that the battle was over. They proceeded to advance east. But their rear was attacked again from Parroy by the Germans. The artillery engaged and stopped the 111th Pz Bgd. Next the Americans returned via Lezey only to be ambushed losing 6 Shermans but they continued to attack and took out 16 German tanks and pushed them out of Moncourt.

F. Sept 22, the Germans attacked again with the 111th Pz Brigade from the east towards Juvelize. They were decimated when the 37th TB took Trois Crois, Hill 257 overlooking their attack.

G. Sept 24, the Germans attacked in the north from Chateau Salins and were stopped.

H. Sept 25, Americans withdrew from Juvelize to Arracourt for a more defensible position due to an order from Patton. (supplies shifted north) and the 37th TB was replaced by 3 battalions of 4th AD.

I. Sept 27-30, Manteuffal shifted the attack to capture Hill 318 and 295. They occupied Juvelize, Coincourt, Lezey, Ley and Bezange. Fierce attacks were repulsed by the Americans, over the hills that exchanged hands several times. On Sept 29 at 2330 Balck ordered Manteuffal to call off the attack - the battle was over.

BATTLE FOR METZ, SEPT 27 - DEC 13, 1944

MAP 59

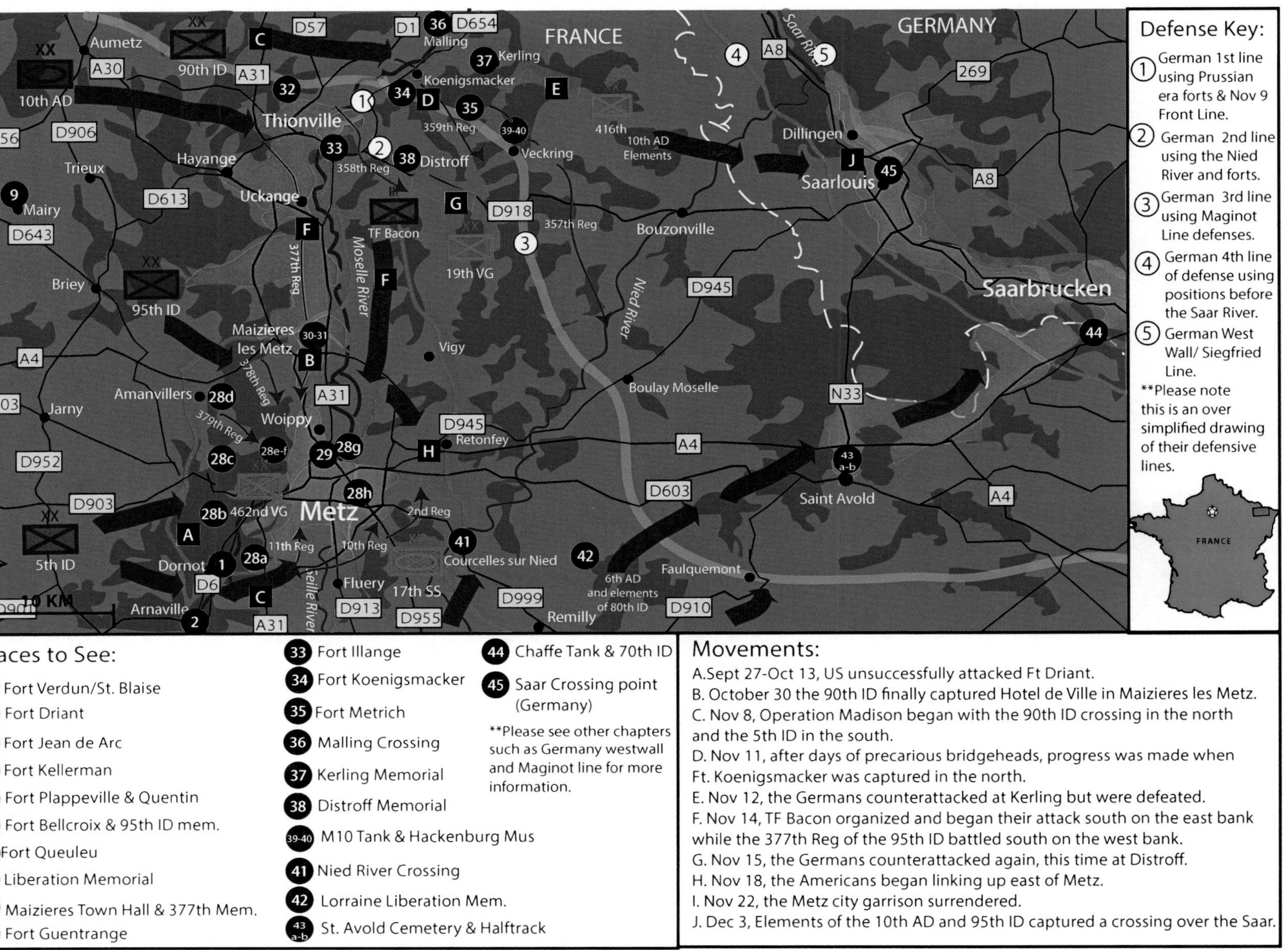
Defense Key:
1 German 1st line using Prussian era forts & Nov 9 Front Line.
2 German 2nd line using the Nied River and forts.
3 German 3rd line using Maginot Line defenses.
4 German 4th line of defense using positions before the Saar River.
5 German West Wall/ Siegfried Line.
**Please note this is an over simplified drawing of their defensive lines.
FRANCE
GERMANY
Saarbrucken
Saarlouis
Dillingen
Thionville
Metz
Saint Avold
Bouzonville
Boulay Moselle
Faulquemont
Remilly
Courcelles sur Nied
Retonfey
Vigy
Woippy
Maizieres les Metz
Amanvillers
Uckange
Hayange
Trieux
Mairy
Briey
Jarny
Aumetz
Dornot
Arnaville
Fluery
Distroff
Veckring
Kerling
Koenigsmacker
Malling
Moselle River
Nied River
Seille River
Saar River
10th AD
90th ID
95th ID
5th ID
19th VG
462nd VG
17th SS
TF Bacon
416th
10th AD Elements
6th AD and elements of 80th ID
357th Reg
358th Reg
359th Reg
377th Reg
378th Reg
379th Reg
2nd Reg
10th Reg
11th Reg
10 KM
Places to See:
28a Fort Verdun/St. Blaise
28b Fort Driant
28c Fort Jean de Arc
28d Fort Kellerman
28e-f Fort Plappeville & Quentin
28g Fort Bellcroix & 95th ID mem.
28h Fort Queuleu
29 Liberation Memorial
30-31 Maizieres Town Hall & 377th Mem.
32 Fort Guentrange
33 Fort Illange
34 Fort Koenigsmacker
35 Fort Metrich
36 Malling Crossing
37 Kerling Memorial
38 Distroff Memorial
39-40 M10 Tank & Hackenburg Mus
41 Nied River Crossing
42 Lorraine Liberation Mem.
43 a-b St. Avold Cemetery & Halftrack
44 Chaffe Tank & 70th ID
45 Saar Crossing point (Germany)
**Please see other chapters such as Germany westwall and Maginot line for more information.
Movements:
A.Sept 27-Oct 13, US unsuccessfully attacked Ft Driant.
B. October 30 the 90th ID finally captured Hotel de Ville in Maizieres les Metz.
C. Nov 8, Operation Madison began with the 90th ID crossing in the north and the 5th ID in the south.
D. Nov 11, after days of precarious bridgeheads, progress was made when Ft. Koenigsmacker was captured in the north.
E. Nov 12, the Germans counterattacked at Kerling but were defeated.
F. Nov 14, TF Bacon organized and began their attack south on the east bank while the 377th Reg of the 95th ID battled south on the west bank.
G. Nov 15, the Germans counterattacked again, this time at Distroff.
H. Nov 18, the Americans began linking up east of Metz.
I. Nov 22, the Metz city garrison surrendered.
J. Dec 3, Elements of the 10th AD and 95th ID captured a crossing over the Saar.

BATTLE OF FORT DRIANT, SEPT 27 - OCT 13, 1944

MAP 60

D11
Ars sur Moselle
D11
Lehrgang 3
Rue du Fort
28b
A
E
VII
VI
H
K
Fort Driant
V.
IV
I
II.
L
III
G
J
I. Moselle Battery
Moselle River 500m
K
B
F
11th Reg
N
200 m

Movements:

Sept 24, P47s attacked and bombed Ft. Driant.
Sept 26, 35 aircraft attacked Ft. Driant again.
Sept 27, 0930 two squandrons of P47s attacked again using napalm. Next 11-1400, American Artillery pounded the fort.
A. At 1400 on Sept 27, company E of the 2nd Batt/11th Reg of 5th ID attacked the fort but were stopped by machine gun fire and barbed wire, they retreated at dark.
B. 5th ID refited, trained & obtained additional equipment to attack the fort. (flamethrowers, dozer tanks, snake bombs)
C. Germans received reinforcements, for a total force of about 5 infantry companies.
D. Oct 2, 23 field artillery battalions concentrated an artillery barrage on the fort. (no impact)
E. Oct 3, Company E and G attacked the NW corner again. And Company B attacked the SW corner at approx. noon with tank support. (by Oct 4, 9 of 12 tanks were out of op)
F. Oct 3, Company B obtained a toehold in the fort after breaching an airshaft in Caserne 5. Company E - no gains.
G. Oct 3, Company G was sent to reinforce Company E at 1730 which allowed them to advance to Casement O & P.
H. Oct 3, the German garrison counterattacked and stopped additional American gains. Next they called in artillery from surrounding forts onto the Americans.
I. Oct 4, Germans pushed the Americans out of casements O & P.
J. Oct 4-5, Company K tried to push SE but was stopped.
K. Oct 6, two Jagdpanzer IV tanks entered the fort with a company of Germans to attack the Americans, after 2 hours the attack was repulsed by American artillery fire.
L. Oct 7-12, US continued to try to clear the SE corner of the fort with little success and the Germans attacked outside of the fort with little progress.
M. Oct 13, after limited gains, the attack was called off.

Places to see and Key:

28b Parking Spot for Fort Driant on "Rue du Fort"
I. Moselle Battery, three each 100mm cannons
II. Barracks
III. Casement P, 3 x 150mm cannons
IV. Casement O, 3 x 100mm cannons
V. Central Fort
VI. Casement M, 3 x 100mm cannons
VII. Casement L, 3 x 150mm cannons

Barb-wire fields
Deep Ditches
Infantry Trenches
Caserne, concrete bunker
Casement, heavy artillery
Armored outpost/fighting position

***The terrain is very steep and dangerous with barb wire stakes, barb wire, unexploded ordnance. Stick to the paths if you go to explore.

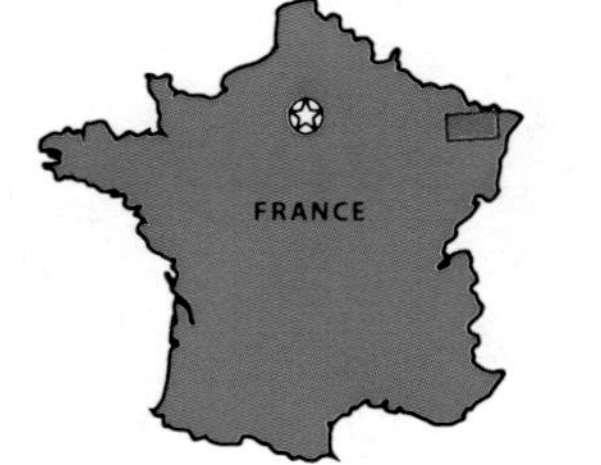
FRANCE

Above Fort Driant under attack by a P47 during the September and October attack. (NARA) Above center is the gate of Fort Driant(NARA) with a German PAK 40 75mm facing out, photo right is the same view today.

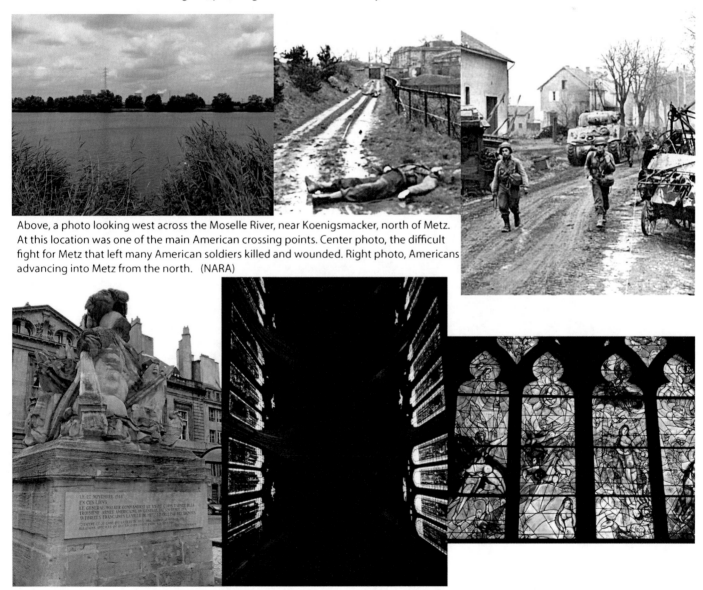

Above, a photo looking west across the Moselle River, near Koenigsmacker, north of Metz. At this location was one of the main American crossing points. Center photo, the difficult fight for Metz that left many American soldiers killed and wounded. Right photo, Americans advancing into Metz from the north. (NARA)

In the square in front of the Metz Cathedral and Mayor's house is a stone plaque to the November 22, 1944 liberation of Metz. The Metz Cathedral is an amazing site to see. It is enormous, inside one of the apses are beautiful and colorful stainglass windows by the French artist Marc Chagall. The cathderal and his art remind us what the Allies were fighting for.

Sentier de Mémoire
L'évasion des trois résistants de Coincourt
ARRACOURT

Far left: Parroy Forest is still a thick forest and a place to explore.

Left: An example of the information boards in the battle area of Arracourt.

Far left: Sherman M4A3 with a 75mm main gun & a welded hull. Note the extra plating on the sides and front, located in Arracourt.

Left: The fields in the battlefield area, only tractors now, no tanks!

Far left: Germans outside Arracourt mount up for an attack on the US Forces. (NARA)

Left: Memorial in Arracourt.

Far left: Shermans on the move near Arracourt. (NARA)

Left: Sherman outside Nancy. I believe a M4A1E6, it had a 76mm gun and a cast hull. Like the photo, the US would try to place a 76mm version in a platoon of 75mm tanks.

Above left: The bridge in the background is the approximate crossing point of the Americans over the Saar River on Dec 3, 1944. The above photo is of a Chaffee tank memorial to the 70th ID, outside of Spichern on heights overlooking the Saar River. The Chaffee tank was built as the replacement to the Stuart tank for a light recon vehicle.

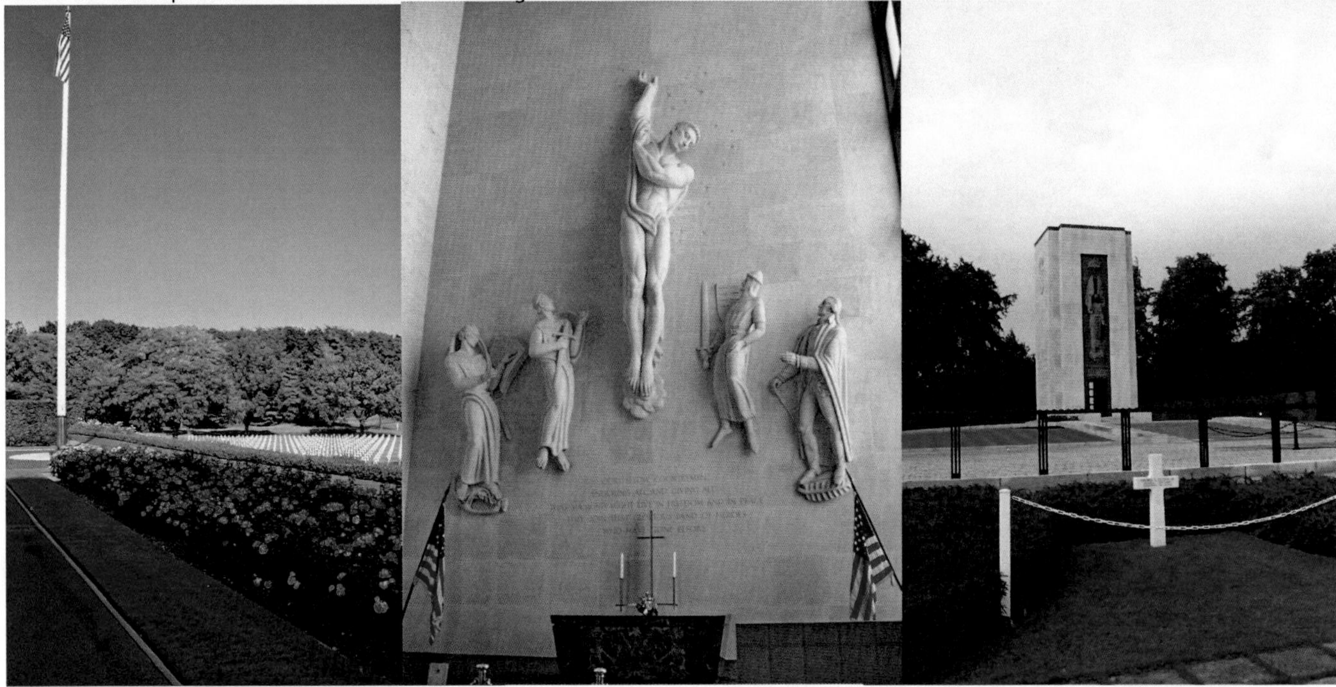

Above left, is another shocking testimony to see; the American St. Avold Cemetery just east of Metz. Above is the beautiful altar inside the chapel with sculpted images admiring and revering the sacrificed soldier. Above right is the grave of General Patton, actually located in the American Luxembourg Cemetery.

70TH DIVISION US
TRAILBLAZERS

Left, a German Officer's face says it all, in Saarlautern. Above center, soldiers from the 70th ID take a break from the fighting. (NARA) Right, on Spichern near Saarlautern is a monument to the 70th ID who liberated the area which also contains memorials to the Franco-Prussian battle of Spichern.

ALSACE CAMPAIGN, VOSGES MOUNTAINS

September 15, 1944–February 9, 1945

"Mountains are greater obstacles than rivers. One can always cross a river, but never a mountain." – Napoleon Bonaparte

---

SUMMARY: The Battle of the Vosges is a much-forgotten theater of war but saw some of the fiercest fighting. It experienced the last major German western offensive of World War II and marked the first time the Allies reached the Rhine River. After the stunning success of Operation Dragoon, the Seventh Army and French First Army continued their drive north on the tail of the German Nineteenth Army. By September 15, the Allies had traveled 643 kilometers, taken 100,000 prisoners, created a solid front with Patton's Third Army and pushed the retreating Germans through the Belfort Gap and into the Vosges Mountains. The Vosges are a range of mountains just west of the Rhine that run from southern Lorraine all the way to the Swiss border. Only two major gaps existed in the range – the Saverne Gap in the north and the Belfort Gap in the south. In modern times, an invading army had never been able to cross it.

OPERATION DOGFACE, OCTOBER 20–NOVEMBER 3, 1944: As the Allies advanced in mid-September, the Germans fought intense delaying actions to give themselves additional time to set up defenses in the Vosges Mountains. Fierce fights took place at locations such as Raddon – where Sergeant Harold Messerschmidt received the Medal of Honor for fighting against 200 SS – and the Cleurie Quarry, which ended up being a six-day battle. The 36th Infantry Division crossed the Moselle River south of Epinal on September 21. The 45th Infantry Division crossed north of Epinal at Châtel and soon after attacked Epinal city on September 22. On September 24, after a brutal fight, the 45th Infantry Division captured Epinal. Similar to the Third Army, the Seventh Army had to slow down in late September to wait for supplies. In October, the army resumed its attack. On the Seventh Army's northern flank, the XV Corps (79th Infantry Division, 44th Infantry Division and French 2nd Armored Division) fought through the Parroy Forest. On the southern flank, the French fought toward Belfort with limited success. In the center, in mid-October, the Seventh Army VI Corps began Operation Dogface to attack through the Vosges Mountains. Their objective was first to capture the towns of Bruyères and Brouvelieures. Then they would drive farther east and capture Saint-Dié, the main road and rail junction in the Vosges on the Meurthe River. Facing the divisions were the 21st Panzer Division, the 16th Infantry Division and the 716th Infantry Division. In addition to the German defenses (mines, road blocks, artillery) the Allies faced extremely difficult terrain and poor weather.

The Vosges evened the odds because of the very thick forests and steep hills, which reduced the effectiveness of American artillery, tanks and air cover. During Operation Dogface, the 45th Infantry Division was on the north/left flank, the 36th Infantry Division was in the center and the 3rd Infantry Division's 30th Regiment was on the south/right flank. (The 3rd Infantry Division's 7th and 15th Regiments served as an exploitation force in reserve.)

Since October 1, on the northern/left flank, the 180th Regiment 45th Infantry Division had been fighting to liberate Fremifontaine and to secure a crossing over the Mortagne River. On October 6, the Germans counterattacked with the help of a tank company and surrounded the regiment. The 180th finally defeated the Germans in the heavily mined and defended woods of Fremifontaine on October 23, but the 45th suffered badly, with 119 killed in action, 554 wounded in action and 86 missing in action. On October 23, the 45th Infantry Division crossed the Mortagne River and quickly continued east. The 45th was redirected from the center toward a northeast attack past Rambervillers and into the Rambervillers forest toward the Meurthe River and Raon L'Étape. By October 30, the 45th had arrived at N59, which runs along the Meurthe River, and stopped to hold the line. On their northern/left flank, the 117th Cavalry Squadron continued to provide protection and contact for the 2nd French Armored Division. On the squadron's right flank was the center advance element, the 3rd Infantry Division.

In the center, on October 20, the 3rd Division's 7th and 15th Regiments effectually replaced the 45th Division's Dogface center mission because of the 45th Infantry Division's slow initial advance and inability to muster an advance past Brouvelieures. The 3rd Infantry Division attacked east toward Saint-Dié and moved rather rapidly along N420, but eventually ran into some stiff resistance as the Germans responded to the penetration. Just north of Brouvelieures, the 3rd Battalion of the 15th Regiment captured a crossing over the Mortagne River, which allowed them to turn the flank of some of the surrounding German defenses. After Brouvelieures had been fully secured, the 7th Regiment continued directly east. They faced brutal artillery barrages, minefields and counterattacks on their predictable path toward Saint-Dié. The division commander sent in the 30th Regiment to continue the push north of N420. The regiment encountered new resistance in its efforts to capture Hill 616, which dominated the route to Saint-Dié. In fact, the road junction of Les Jueaux and Le Haut Jacques became known as the "Crossroads of Hell" where Private Wilburn Ross received the Medal of Honor because of his heroic actions defending against eight counterattacks during a fierce five-hour fire fight. On November 4, after five days of fighting, the 3rd Division finally captured Haut Jacques Pass, but only after suffering 148 killed in action and 822 wounded in action.

On the southern flank, the 36th Division attacked toward Bruyeres southwest of Saint-Dié. The 36th Infantry Division had only the 143rd Infantry Regiment and the newly arrived Japanese-American 442nd Combat Regiment available for the operation. Their objectives were to first capture the four hills that surrounded Bruyeres and then the town, all heavily defended by the Germans. On October 15 at 0800, the 143rd attacked Bruyeres from the south and the 442nd attacked through the heavy woods from the west. The 442nd contained three battalions, the 100th, the 2nd and the 3rd. (The 100th was the original battalion until more volunteers were added.) Among the three, the goal was to capture Hill 555, then Hills A and B. After fighting all day on October 15, the troops were able to advance only 500 yards. Due to German mortar fire, artillery, mines, roadblocks, stone houses and dominating positions, progress was deadly and slow. Not until October 18 did the battalions capture Hills A and B and, then, the town. On October 19, just east of the town, they captured Hill C, then Hill D. (Hill D was recaptured at night by a German counterattack.) During the fighting on October 19, the American forces tried to rescue the wounded, but the Germans shot down the medics. After seeing this, a company of the 3rd Battalion fixed bayonets and charged the German positions, killing more than 50 Germans. The event was later remembered as the famous "Banzai Charge."

After the dogged fighting for Bruyeres, the 100th Battalion/442nd Regiment was sent to hold a ridge overlooking the town of Biffontaine on October 21. They were attacked from three sides and in desperate need of supplies. After an initial failed resupply attempt, men were able to sneak through the German lines with water, food and ammunition on their backs. On October 23, the 100th Battalion was ordered to take the town. Initially, the plan went well, but soon the battalion was surrounded by the Germans, who shot at the troops with anti-aircraft cannons, small arms and artillery. After holding out for over 24 hours, the 3rd Battalion/442nd Regiment broke through. In this battle, the 100th Battalion suffered 21 killed in action, 122 wounded in action and 18 prisoners of war, all to take a town that was home to no more than 300 people.

THE STORY OF WORLD WAR II, THE 36TH DIVISION LOST BATTALION:

At Biffontaine, one of the most amazing stories of World War II took place. It involved bravery and sacrifice. On October 26, as part of Operation Dogface, the 1st Battalion/141st Regiment/36th Infantry Division advanced on its objective – the heights (Hills 624 and 645) overlooking La Houssière in the Forêt Dominale de Champ. On October 24, the American unit's supply route was overrun by German units from Grenadier Regiment 933, and the unit was cut off from the other Americans. The Germans quickly felled trees and set up mines and booby traps to stop any relief or escape attempts. Ironically, the surrounded men of the 36th from Texas maintained the motto "Remember the Alamo," while the 442nd Regiment that was sent to rescue the surrounded men maintained the motto "Go for Broke." The battalion consisted of only 270 men who had a day's worth of rations, ammunition and medicine. They quickly set up a perimeter defense with what little they had and made a few unsuccessful patrols and attempts to break out. For four days they went without food and were down to three rounds per man when air resupply efforts finally succeeded. On October 30, after fierce fighting for five days, the 442nd Regiment finally broke through the German lines thanks to a bayonet charge up the mountain by two companies (I and K). The regiment suffered more than 800 casualties. Company I had gone in with 185 men; only eight walked out unwounded. After the war, the 442nd Regiment became the most highly decorated regiment in the history the United States Army, as 21 members received the Medal of Honor. Of the 36th Infantry Division's battalion, only 211 of 270 returned from the battle.

By late October, Operation Dogface was at a standstill and all three divisions needed rest, as they had taken part in continuous fighting since Operation Dragoon over 70 days earlier. However, General Jacob Devers needed one more push to complete the Dogface objectives and get the units in position for the November Offensive. To secure a better position for the November attack, the 2nd French Armored Division was committed to capture Baccarat, which it did on November 1, surprising the battered 21st Panzer Division. The capture of Baccarat ended Dogface operations for the left/northern flank forces, XV Corps. In response, on November 1, the German commander, Hermann Balck, pulled his men back to their Vosges defensive foothill positions/Winter Line. Balck also ordered a scorched earth policy and the removal of all French men from the ages of 16 to 60 across the Rhine for forced labor. Balck's "retreat" allowed the VI Corps to advance a little closer to their Dogface objectives. The 45th Infantry Division reached Saint-Benoît on November 3 and relieved the 2nd French Armored Division in Baccarat. On their southern flank, the 3rd Infantry Division finally broke through Le Haut Pass and captured Hill 616 overlooking Saint-Dié and D420, which ended its Dogface objectives. To the division's right, the battered 36th Infantry Division could make it only to road D31 by November 7. Operation Dogface was over for the 36th Infantry Division, but it was about 4 kilometers short of its objective to capture the high ground overlooking Saint-Léonard.

NOVEMBER OFFENSIVE, NOV 13-26:

The November Offensive was set to take place in coordination across the western front and to include the First Army in the Ardennes/Hürtgen region as well as Patton's Third Army. Unfortunately, Devers' Sixth Army (the Seventh Army plus the French First Army) was more or less on a mission to support Patton's attack. His attack was to begin two days after Patton's Army began its offensive because, typically, the Germans shifted reserves within two days. His objective was to capture Saverne Gap in the north, fight into the Alsatian Plain on the Rhine and capture the Belfort Gap in the south. However, his forces were battered from the October fighting. At this time, the 100th and 103rd Infantry Divisions arrived from America to bolster Patch's Seventh Army and to allow some units (including the 45th Division and the 3rd Division) to go into reserve. The next objective was to break the German Winter Line located along the Meurthe River. The U.S. forces aimed to cross at Raon-l'Étape in the north and Saint-Dié in the middle of the front. On November 5, the 100th Division relieved the 45th Division, while the 103rd Division replaced only two regiments of the 3rd Infantry Division for the attack on Saint-Dié. (The 15th Regiment did not get a break!) The 36th Infantry Division received even less; they didn't get any rest and continued holding their positions south of Saint-Dié.

For the offensive, Devers assigned the XV Corps to attack on November 15 along N4 to Sarrebourg and into the Saverne Gap. South of the XV Corps, the VI Corps' mission was to attack on November 17 northeast along N420 and N392 to the Alsatian Plains and to capture Strasbourg. In the south, the French Second Army was assigned to attack for a limit of three days, while the French First Army was to attack on November 15 toward Belfort. In total, the Americans were attacking with 14 divisions: the XV Corps (44th Infantry Division, 79th Infantry Division and French 2nd Armored Division), the VI Corps (117th Recon, 14th Armored Division, 100th Infantry Division, 3rd Infantry Division, 103rd Infantry Division and 36th Infantry Division), the French Second Army (3rd Algerian Infantry Division, 1st Infantry Division) and the French First Army (2nd Infantry Division, 9th Infantry Division, 1st Armored Division). Facing the Americans was the battered German Nineteenth Army with a total of 10 divisions: the LXIV Corps (553rd Volksgrenadier Division, 951st Volksgrenadier Division, 708th Volksgrenadier Division, 716th Infantry Division and 16th Volksgrenadier Division), the IV Luftwaffe Field Corps (198th Infantry Division and 269th Volksgrenadier Division) and the LXXXV Corps (159th Volksgrenadier Division, 189th Volksgrenadier Division, and 338th Volksgrenadier Division). They were only skeletons of divisions; for example, the LXIV Corps' 708th Volksgrenadier Division had 3,500 men, while the 16th had only 1,000, the 716th 1,500 and the 198th 2,500. However, the Germans did have terrain, weather, artillery and close supply lines to their advantage. The German defensive line at the Meurthe River was rather weakly built and was intended for use only as a delay that would give the Germans time to occupy the Vosges Ridge defensive, which had much better defenses.

On November 6, Devers learned that the American First and Ninth Armies were delaying their attack until November 16. Devers assumed that Patton would delay as well. However, on November 8 Patton initiated his attack; Devers called on his commanders to move the XV Corps attack start date to November 13, the VI Corps start date to November 15 and the French Army start date to November 13.

On November 13, despite freezing rain and flooding, the XV Corps attack began. It began with the 79th Infantry Division assault on Montigny and the 44th Infantry Division attack to the Rhine Canal. After some stiff resistance, on November 18 the divisions broke through the German 708th and 553rd Division defenses. The 553rd defense unraveled and opened the gate to Sarrebourg. On November 19, the exploitation force, the 2nd French Armored Division, was committed to Badonviller along N392 and bypassed Sarrebourg as the 44th Infantry Division was mopping up the German resistance. Shortly after Sarrebourg, the city of Saverne fell to the Americans. The next objective was Strasbourg, the famous French city on the Rhine. The 45th Division was sent back into battle and pushed farther northeast of Strasbourg. On November 23, Strasbourg fell after an attack by the 45th, 44th and 79th Infantry Divisions and the 2nd French Armor. The 2nd French Armor was given the "honor" of capturing the city, which it did except for a German bridgehead across from the German city of Kehl on the Rhine. Shortly after, the Americans celebrated the first Holy Mass in the famous cathedral since the Germans had taken the city in 1940. On the same day, November 23, Hitler released the Panzer Lehr Division (rebuilt from Normandy) to counterattack with units of the 361st Volksgrenadier Division at Phalsbourg to cut the Allied supply route on N4 and stop the Americans from completing the capture of Strasbourg. The Americans were aware of the buildup and positioned the 44th Infantry Division, a regiment of the 45th Infantry Division and the 106th Cavalry Group to block the attack. The Panzer Lehr Division attacked from Sarre-Union south in two columns – one on the west with 12 Panzer IVs down route D8 into D90 and one on the east with 25 Panther tanks that attacked south on D340 toward Eywiller. The Germans made initial gains of about eight kilometers, but were still well short of their objective, N4. The Americans held their ground at Baerendorf and Weyer, eventually pushing back the Germans with help from elements of the 4th Armored Division. On November 25, the German command withdrew the Panzer Lehr Division to save it from destruction and to let it refit for the upcoming Ardennes offensive.

On November 10, in the VI Corps sector, the 398th Regiment of the 100th Infantry Division feigned a frontal assault on the Vosges town of Raon-L'Étape, which was well fortified by approximately 1,750 soldiers of the 708th Volksgrenadier Division, both in the town and the surrounding mountains. The feint was effective and surprised two regiments (the 399th and the 397th) that crossed the river north of Raon-L'Étape at Baccarat, outflanking the German defenses. The 397th attacked south along the river to capture Bertichamps and Hill 443. On the left flank of the 397th, the 339th attacked south toward Hill 539 to cut off the supply route to Raon-l'Étape. The Americans fought hard for the high ground behind Raon-l'Étape. The mountainous battle area contains sites named "Purple Heart Lane" and "Bloody Knob" (Hill 462.8), where three platoons of the 399th Regiment fought off counterattacks and forced German withdrawal. As a result, a deep bridgehead was established and threatened the German defense, forcing it to withdraw further east. Raon-l'Étape was liberated on November 20. To the south of the 100th Infantry Division, on November 10, the Germans burned the major junction town in the North Vosges, Saint-Dié. Across from Saint-Dié was the 3rd Infantry Division and the inexperienced 103rd Infantry Division, holding for a November 20 crossing. On November 19, elements of the 3rd Infantry Division crossed just 1.5 kilometers north of Saint-Michel without incident. The Americans exploited this route and, on November 20 and 21, the 103rd Infantry Division crossed. On November 22, the troops entered Saint-Dié unopposed. The biggest problems were the weather, traffic jams, felled trees, mines and craters. On November 22, the 100th and 3rd Divisions raced toward Strasbourg, covering the right flank of the XV Corps. On November 23, the 3rd Division liberated Natzweiler-Struthof, the only Nazi concentration camp in France; 46,000 prisoners were liberated. Just east of Natzweiler, the 3rd and 14th Armored Divisions attacked Fort Mutzig, a formidable old Prussian fortress that did not fall until December 5, when the Americans used a captured German halftrack stuffed with TNT to smash into a wall of the fortress. On November 25, the VI Corps had attained its objectives (except for the tired 36th Infantry Division, which had yet to reach Selestat on the Alsace Plains). At that point, the 103rd was shifted to attack Selestat, the 36th toward Colmar and the 100th to assist the northern flank with the XV Corps.

The French First Army began its attack on November 13 with a two-hour artillery barrage. The French First Army's Corps were deployed with two infantry divisions each; the two armored divisions were held in reserve as exploitation forces. They were successful in their main attack route because, unknowingly, the Germans had placed their weakest division, the 338th in France's path. The German command believed that the French would attack through the high Vosges rather than through the open fields toward Belfort. As it was, the French were able to exploit a breakthrough south of Belfort and, on November 19, actually reach the Rhine River at Rosenau with a platoon of Shermans and halftracks. The Germans immediately counterattacked with limited forces of the 198th, 30th SS Infantry, to cut off the French supply line, route N463. Their November 21-23 attack from Dannemarie was successful but untenable due to mounting casualties. On November 28, after much debate, Hitler consented to the retreat of the German divisions to a line closer to Colmar, forming a very large bridgehead that would be called the Colmar Pocket. As a result, the French completed the capture of Mulhouse and Belfort and tallied approximately 15,000 prisoners of war captured. The French had succeeded, but their situation was precarious and their gains came at a great loss. The French suffered 1,300 killed in action, 4,500 wounded in action and approximately 4,500 non-battle casualties. In terms of equipment they lost 55 Shermans, 15 Stuarts, 15 M10s and about 50 halftracks.

The November Offensive was an incredible success. Devers' Sixth Army was at the Rhine River and the German 19th Army had only two divisions in marginal fighting condition. As a result, Devers developed plans to cross the Rhine River in the north at Ratstatt, where patrols discovered that the German defensive positions were unoccupied. However, Eisenhower ordered Devers not to cross the Rhine, but, instead to shift forces north to assist Patton's Third Army and clear the German West Wall using Patch's Seventh Army. In addition, Devers was to attach the 36th Infantry Division and the 2nd French Armored Division to the French First Army to close the Colmar Pocket. Eisenhower's decision stopped all momentum, allowed the German 19th Army to regroup and the Ardennes Offensive to continue.

DECEMBER OFFENSIVE:

As a result of the reorganization and new mission, the Seventh Army positioned itself to attack north toward Bitche, cross the Lauter River and enter Germany's West Wall. On November 30, the 103rd and 36th Infantry Divisions combined forces and attacked Selestat, but did not clear the town of Germans until four days later. Although typically less experienced fighters as compared to regular Wehrmacht and SS divisions, the German Volksgrenadiers resistance was formidable and ferocious. For example, during the attack on Selestat on December 2, four battalions of the 409th Regiment, 103rd Infantry Division, crossed the Giessen River. The Germans quickly counterattacked. Only 15 of 158 men in the 1st Battalion of Company D survived.

In the north, on December 5, the American Seventh Army began its offensive to clear the Germans west of the Rhine and to support Patton's army. The Americans slugged it out with the Germans across significant Maginot Line defenses centered on the town of Bitche. As of December 20, the Germans still retained control of Bitche, Fort Otterbiel and Fort Grand Hoehkirkel. The Americans continued north and bypassed much of Bitche, hoping the Germans would eventually surrender. On the right flank, the Americans had made it across the Lauter River into Germany and had begun to engage the West Wall. However, the Ardennes Offensive was in effect and Eisenhower ordered Devers to halt all offensive operations. As a result, the Seventh Army pulled most of its forces back across the river and planned to resume the offensive by January 5.

In the south, after the capture of Selestat, the exhausted 36th Infantry Division and French 2nd Armored Division were reassigned to the French First Army. They began the attack from the north, planning to crush the Colmar Pocket. On the southern end of the Colmar Pocket, the French First Army was in a holding pattern because its forces needed trained replacements as well as materiel. In addition, the 1st French Infantry Division was pulled out of line to assist in the capture of German holdout positions in Bordeaux, a plan called Operation Independence. Luckily, they eventually turned back to Colmar, but not in time to help with the December operations. Therefore, the brunt of the attack was the responsibility of the French 2nd Armored Division and the American 36th Infantry Division. In the meantime, the German 19th Army was pulling together reinforcements for its decimated 10 divisions located in the Colmar Pocket and east of the Rhine. On December 10, Hitler created Army Group Oberrhein under the command of Heinrich Himmler. This was a very unique entity that complicated the chain of command because now Himmler commanded Friedrich Wiese's Nineteenth Army and other elements, and reported directly to Hitler, not to Heersgruppe G Commander Johannes Blaskowitz.

OPERATION HABICHT, DECEMBER 12-19 AND THE DECEMBER PUSH:

On December 5, elements of the 36th Infantry Division arrived in Sigolsheim to begin their attack on the Colmar Pocket. On December 7, the Germans began shelling the town in preparation for their counterattack, Operation Habicht (Hawk), whose objective was to capture the hills/fingers of the Vosges overlooking the plains and Sigolsheim. Those fingers were Hills 351, 393, 621, 666 and 672. In addition, the Germans wanted to capture Riquewihr and Sigolsheim. The Germans committed some 6,800 men to the attack, which was launched from the towns of Kaysersberg and Kientzheim. Under the command of Himmler, Operation Habicht was fought from December 12-19. Initially, the Germans achieved some success, such as the capture of Sigolsheim and Hills 666, 672 and 393. However, they were unable to push the Americans off Hills 621 and 351, which overlooked Sigolsheim. On December 17, after four assaults on Hill 351, the Germans finally captured the hill and held it until December 26. Only after heroic Medal of Honor action by Colonel Keith Ware of the 3rd Infantry Division (see "Places to See") did the Americans recapture it. The Germans were never able to capture Hill 621 due to additional stalwart American defense. By December 19, the German attack had faded and losses were significant: 600 killed in action, 1,000 wounded in action and 1,316 prisoners of war. Also note that the Germans fiercely attacked Selestat with the 198th Infantry Division, but were repulsed after a couple of days of fighting.

In the meantime, on December 15, the exhausted 36th Infantry Division was replaced by the rested 3rd Infantry Division, which promptly resumed the attack to the Ill River towards Colmar. On December 16, the German Ardennes Offensive "Watch on the Rhine" began – the great Battle of the Bulge in the north. As a result of the Battle of the Bulge, Patton moved a corps of his forces north to liberate Bastogne. The Seventh Army was spread to cover Patton's reduced defenses. Like the Seventh Army, the French First Army was ordered to halt any major operations and to consolidate defenses. Devers cancelled the major attack at Colmar, but still formed Task Force McGarr to assault Kayserberg and Sigolsheim and keep some pressure on the Germans. On December 20, after five days of fighting, Kayserburg fell. Then, on December 26, Sigolsheim was recaptured. At that point, the lines had stabilized. However, the Americans became aware of a German build up across the Rhine and north of Bitche. Although the Germans were still fighting in the Bulge, Hitler wanted an attack to split the Seventh and Third Armies because he knew that Patton had moved forces to the north. The stage was set for the last German Western Front offensive of World War II: Operation Nordwind.

GERMAN SYLWESTER OFFENSES:

OPERATION NORDWIND, DECEMBER 31, 1944–JANUARY 8, 1945:

Hitler wanted an offensive to take pressure off the Ardennes Offensive. On December 23, he approved Blaskowitz's plan to attack from Bitche into the Saverne Gap, split the Seventh Army's XV and VI Corps and link up with the Colmar Pocket. The attack was organized into two thrusts: Sturmgruppe 1 and Sturmgruppe 2, with a total of nine divisions and two in reserve. The terrain and weather was very poor for the Germans, who lacked equipment and full units. For example, the 17th Panzer Grenadier Division had only 45 Stug IIIs, 10 Flakpanzers and three Panzer IIIs. (They really should have had at least twice those amounts.) The 21st Panzer Division was in better shape; its Regiment 22 had 38 Panthers, 34 Panzer IVs and four Jadgpanzer IVs. Facing the Germans were the experienced but tired troops from the following (from Sarreguemines in the west to Philippsbourg in the east): 103rd Infantry Division, 44th Infantry Division, 100th Infantry Division, 36th Infantry Division and 45th Infantry Division. In many cases, these units received replacements from the United States who had been pulled out of training eight months early. As far as we know, the Americans did not receive any ULTRA intercepts about the attack, but Devers' intelligence units did notice a build up near Bitche and stiff resistance during patrols. They concluded that a major attack was imminent and expected that it would come down the Savarene Gap. The Americans were ready.

At 2330 on New Year's Eve, Sturmgruppe 1 on the western flank began its attack. In the lead was the 17th SS Panzergrenadier Division, supported by the 36th Volksgrenadier Division. Down the Saar Valley, the Germans poured west of Rimling and reached Singling, but were quickly slowed by artillery and anti-tank fire from units of the 44th and 100th. The German armored attack of Nordwind had failed. In the eastern thrust, Sturmgruppe 2 attacked on January 2 with four infantry divisions, the 559th Volksgrenadier Division, the 257th, the 361st and the 256th. Their attack was through even more difficult terrain. Also due to the terrain, the Americans had a thin defensive screen set up with Task Force Hudelson. The Germans made some gains, but because of a lack of experience and scouting, they encountered difficulty making headway. On the night of January 3, Blaskowitz released his best unit, the 6th SS Gebirgsdivision, which had just arrived from Finland. The troops were well equipped, rested and experienced. Regiment 12 quickly attacked through 257th positions over the hills and into the town of Wingen-sur-Moder via Fischback Creek. The Germans overwhelmed the headquarters of the First Battalion, 179th Regiment, 45th Infantry Division. Elements of the 45th Infantry Division and the 70th Infantry Division reacted quickly, but their counterattacks failed to regain the town. The Germans fiercely defended the surrounded town until casualties began to mount. After failed attempts to break the encirclement, the Germans were authorized to escape on January 7. Of the 800 who attacked the town, only 205 left. The recapture of Wingen on January 8 marked the end of Nordwind.

OPERATION SONNENWENDE, JANUARY 5-12:

Because no breakthrough had been achieved, Operation Zahnartz, the planned exploitation by the reserve elements, the 21st Panzer Division and the 25th Panzergrenadier Division, was cancelled. However, the Germans, ever resilient, wished to redirect their resources. The Nineteenth Army (Group Oberrhein) commanded by Himmler wanted to attack and recapture Strasbourg. As Nordwind faded into failure, Himmler initiated Operation Sonnenwende. The Germans knew that the American units north of Strasbourg were weak. The operation called for a river crossing attack just north of Strasbourg, then an attack from the northern edge of the Colmar Pocket to surround Strasbourg and link up with the river crossing units. Instead of waiting for Sonnenwende to begin, Berlin ordered the river crossing to commence at once. On January 5, the beat-up 553rd Volksgrenadier Division, supplemented with two regiments and Panzer Battalion Luttichau (containing approximately 15 Panzer IVs, 30 Nashorns and 40 Hetzers) crossed the Rhine at Gambsheim. The Germans quickly captured Gambsheim and moved on to Herrlisheim and Offendorf. At that time, the Americans mistakenly saw the Germans as a minor threat and believed that the German troops numbered only about 500. On January 8, the rest of Sonnenwende began when the 198th Infantry Division and the Panzer Brigade 106 attacked north from Colmar toward Strasbourg to link up with the Gambsheim units. Panzer Brigade 106 and the 198th were quickly stopped and made very little progress, reaching only Erstein. In the meantime, Himmler "convinced" Blaskowitz to shift his cancelled Zahnartz units to attack from Lauterbourg along the Rhine so that they would link up with the Gambsheim success. The German command was very hesitant to pursue this effort due to the fact that the Americans held Maginot Line forts, not to mention the dangers posed by mines, terrain and artillery. Undeterred, on January 6 at 0200, the German 21st Panzer Division, 245th Volksgrenadier Division and 25th Panzergrenadier Division attacked south toward Hatten and into Hagenau in an attempt to recapture the Maginot Line forts. After slowly working their way through the forts with flamethrowers and Flammpanzer Hetzers, the Germans began their attack on the towns of Hatten and Rittershoffen on January 9. From January 9-20, a brutal infantry and tank battle clashed over these two small towns. The German

Panzergrenadiers quickly overran the Americans, but were stopped by a platoon of Shermans from the 14th Armored Division. The result was a terrible stalemate. After the fierce fighting in Hatten, only five out of 365 homes were left standing. The Americans lost 31 Shermans, five Stuarts and eight halftracks. The Germans lost 51 Panzers and 12 halftracks. Brutal fighting occurred across the entire Seventh Army front. On January 16, west of Hatten and north of Reipertswiller, the 3rd battalion (companies L, I, C, K and G), 157th Regiment of the 45th, was destroyed by the 6th SS Mountain Division. Only two men out of 500 escaped after holding out for a week north of Reipertswiller (Hill 420).

While the other battles raged, on January 6 the rookie 12th Armored Division was ordered to clear the Gambsheim bridgehead, which contained approximately 3,300 Germans, not the estimated 500. On January 8, a combat command from the 12th Armored Division attacked Herrl esheim from the north and west. It did not go well. The command was quickly stalled by well-placed German anti-tank guns and the Americans lacked infantry support to assist the armor. On January 13, the Americans committed the entire 12th Armored Division to the operation. The Americans tried several attacks, but German reserves had been committed on January 16. The 10th SS Panzer Division and the 7th Parachute Division began arriving into the bridgehead with 50 Panzer IVs and 40 Panthers. On January 19, after additional failed attacks, the 12th Armored Division pulled back; it had lost 38 Shermans in just three days of fighting. On January 20, the majority of the American VI Corps pulled back to the Moder River and south of Hagenau to consolidate, save lives and regroup. The Germans were slow to regain the vacated ground, but then pushed south on January 22 to link up with Gambsheim. On the night of January 24, in a driving snowstorm, the Germans attacked once more with five divisions from Rothbach to Kaltenhouse. Their units penetrated the new American line for a short while until the American forces counterattacked. The Americans counterattacked the next day, putting the Germans on the defensive and forcing them to halt all offensive operations. At that point, the 21st Panzer Division and the 25th Panzergrenadier Division were ordered east to meet the Russian threat. Also at this time, Himmler left and Group Obberrhein disappeared. The Sylwester Offenses had proven to be a waste of German resources and lives. They gained little and resulted in 23,000 casualties (17,000 wounded in action or killed in action and 6,000 prisoners of war) in just over 20 days. The Americans suffered greatly as well, with 14,000 casualties. For its January casualties, the VI Corps reported 773 killed in action, 4,838 wounded in action, 3,657 missing in action and 5,448 non-battle casualties. In addition, most of the land lost to the Germans was not recovered until early March. With the northern threat contained/burned out, the Americans and the French turned their attention to the Colmar Pocket.

COLMAR POCKET ATTACK, OPERATION CHEERFUL, JANUARY 20–FEBRUARY 9:

On January 20, Operation Cheerful, the attack to clear the Colmar Pocket, began. The operation was under the command of Jean de Lattre's First French Army with the 1st and 2nd Corps. To assist, Devers attached the American XXI Corps because the French forces lacked the materiel, men and experience to complete the mission. The plan was for an initial diversionary attack by the French 1st Corps out of Mulhouse in the south to draw out the German reserves. Then the American XXI Corps would attack toward Colmar and Neuf Brisach, while the French 2nd Corps attacked to clear the Erstein Bulge, which had been created by Operation Sonnenwende. Facing the Allies were about 22,000 Germans with approximately 189 tanks, including Panzerjager 654 with 44 Jagdpanthers and 22 Nashorns. They were divided into two corps, the 63rd and the 64th. The 63rd defended the southern and western zones, while the 64th defended the northern flank. The Germans' best unit was the newly arrived 2nd Mountain Division, which was held in reserve.

On January 20, Operation Cheerful began on schedule in a driving snowstorm. The German command immediately sent its reserves to meet the threat and the French attack stalled. Although the Germans did not believe it to be the main effort, the French feint still worked as planned. The main attack began on January 22 with the attached American XXI Corps, with the 3rd Infantry Division in the vanguard. Their objective was to capture Neuf-Briesach and cut off a German retreat. The advance was very difficult. The Americans had trouble getting past Hill 216 south of Bennwihr as well as the towns of Jebsheim and Ostheim. In addition, the Germans counterattacked. On January 23 at Holtzwihr, Audie Murphy fired a .50-caliber machine gun from a burning M10 and stopped a German advance, later receiving the Medal of Honor for his actions. The French 2nd Armored Division advanced against some stiff German resistance to clear the Erstein Bulge from Rhinau down to Jebsheim.

On January 27, Himmler left his post and the German command was reunited once again, this time with Siegfried Rasp in command of the Nineteenth Army. On February 1, Rasp began to withdraw troops without Hitler's approval. On January 29, the Americans reached their first objective, the Colmar Canal. On February 2, the 28th Infantry Division began clearing the suburbs of Colmar with the assistance of the French 5th Armored Division. The 3rd Infantry Division captured Neuf Briesach on February 5, cutting off the primary German retreat route. That same day, the Americans and French linked up in Rouflach, cutting off four German divisions in the western portion of the pocket. Without withdrawal permission, Rasp continued to pull out as many troops as he could. Finally, on February 8, Hitler approved a withdrawal! On February 9, the Germans blew up the Chalampe Bridge, marking the end of the Battle for Colmar. In this fighting alone, the Germans suffered 16,438 prisoners of war and 7,500 additional casualties (wounded in action or killed in action). The Allies suffered a total of 13,380 casualties. Of that total, the French suffered 1,595 killed in action and 8,583 wounded in action. The Americans fared a little better, with 722 killed in action and 4,807 wounded in action. The Allies also suffered tremendous non-combat casualties from frostbite and the cold – more than 7,000 in just three weeks.

OUTCOME: As a result of the Alsace campaign, all German resistance south of Lorraine was beaten across the Rhine and the campaign had destroyed the German Nineteenth Army. The stage was now set for an attack over the Rhine River into the heartland of Germany. Eisenhower had received criticism for favoring the northern push with Montgomery. Then, after the Bulge, Eisenhower favored the attempts Patton's Third Army made to push through the West Wall. Meanwhile, General Devers' Sixth Army Group had reached the Rhine at Strasbourg on November 23, ahead of schedule and ready to cross, turn the German flank and roll up the German West Wall from the south. In theory, the war could have been over much sooner had Eisenhower poured resources into the southern (right) flank. Instead, the Allies would attack head-on through the Ardennes and wouldn't cross the Rhine (at Ludendorff Bridge at Remagen) until March 7, 1945. However, in Eisenhower's defense, had Devers crossed the Rhine at Rastatt, with, say, three divisions, Hitler probably would have brought several well equipped units south from the planned Ardennes Offensive to crush them.

WHAT WAS IT OVER? The Alsace Campaign's objective was part of Eisenhower's broad-front plan to push the Germans out of France. The Seventh Army's mission was to destroy the German Nineteenth Army, which protected the southern (left) flank of Germany.

WHO? Numbers and leaders?

AMERICANS AND FRENCH: The Sixth Army Group, commanded by General Devers, was made up of the Seventh Army and the French First Army. The Seventh Army was commanded by General Patch, who had approximately 12 divisions (200,000 men) at his disposal. In addition, the French First Army, with approximate 150,000 men, was holding the line south of Strasbourg with American equipment and vehicles. Through this campaign, the Allied soldier suffered greatly from non-combat casualties like trench foot and frostbite. The constant fighting in the mud, rain, sleet and snow led to non-combat casualty rates as high as 10 percent. There were also increases in the number of psychiatric casualties from the incessant combat and miserable conditions. In terms of combat casualties during Operation Nordwind, the Americans suffered 29,000, including those not related to combat. During the fight to reduce the Colmar Pocket, the Americans suffered 8,000 casualties (500 killed in action) and the French suffered 13,300 (1,800 killed in action). Note that, including Mediterranean operations, three of the Seventh Army's divisions suffered some of the highest rates in terms of casualties and days in combat throughout the war. The 3rd Infantry Division suffered a total of 25,977 casualties with 531 days of combat. The 45th Infantry Division suffered 20,993 casualties with 511 days of combat, and the 36th Infantry Division suffered 19,466 casualties in 400 days of combat. Keep in mind, the authorized size of each division was 15,000 which included support units, not all 15,000 were in combat, these numbers signify a great deal of replacement soldiers and casualties among those replacements.

GERMANS: The German First and Nineteenth Armies defended this territory. The First Army was commanded by Hans von Obstfelder and committed a minimal amount of troops to the northern edge of the line. The majority of the fighting was done by the Nineteenth Army, commanded by Friedrich Wiese until mid-December. In December, Wiese was removed and Group Oberrhein created with Himmler as commander. In this area, the Germans were able to commit about 15 damaged divisions. In Operation Nordwind, they committed nine divisions, including their last reserves. Their casualties were very high and they suffered greatly from constant combat with the Seventh Army. During Nordwind, the Germans suffered 23,000 casualties. During the Colmar Pocket fighting, the Germans suffered 22,000 casualties (killed in action and missing in action) and 16,000 captured. There are no accurate records relating the number of German soldiers and equipment lost in this stage.

WHEN? September 15, 1944–February 9, 1945

WHY IN ALSACE? The Allied Sixth Army Group's objective was to maintain a broad front and push the Germans across the Rhine. Then, ideally, they would cross the Rhine at Strasbourg and drive northeast to roll up the German defenses. The Vosges Mountains and weather were defensive equalizers for the Germans against the Allies' soldiers, air power and equipment. The Vosges run from Belfort in the south to just beyond Saverne in the north. The Upper Vosges is considered the southern part, closer to Switzerland. The Lower Vosges is the area in the north. The terrain played a major role, as the Allies had only a few routes to take. For example, at Belfort is a big gap between the Vosges and the Alps. In the north, at Saverne, is another gap to exploit. Between them is Saint-Dié, an important road junction in the mountains.

TECHNOLOGY/TACTICS: Tactically, the Americans maintained continual contact with the Germans, preventing them from significantly building up troops. On the northern flank, the Americans (the 44th and the French 2nd Armored Division) attacked Sarrebourg, then the Saverne Gap to move onto Strasbourg. Covering their right flank was the 3rd Infantry Division and the 45th Infantry Division with the mission of capturing Saint-Dié. On the right flank, the Allies continued to advance with the 36th Infantry Division and then with the French First Army. Very successfully, the Americans used the French 2nd Armored Division as an exploitation force for their left flank. On the southern flank, the French attacked through the Belfort Gap toward Mulhouse, then swung up to Colmar. The Germans initially held the western Vosges foothills before trying to retreat to the more-prepared Vosges ridgeline. Throughout the fighting, they used anti-tank guns, old World War I forts, Panzerfausts, wooden bunkers and thousands of mines (including wood, glass and plastic). The Americans used strong small unit tactics to move, outflank and overwhelm the German defenses. Because of the speed at which the Americans attacked, the Germans never had a chance to fully occupy the Vosges ridgeline defenses. The Allied tanks and artillery were effective only in the towns and had much less effect in the rugged, icy mountain terrain. Even in the towns, the tanks began taking heavy casualties due to the German Panzerfausts. In terms of aircraft, the American and German aircraft were much less effective because of the weather and the terrain. However, the Germans did use the Me262 during the battles of the Alsace plains, to limited effect. The Americans were able to send sorties for only approximately half the month of January, though to greater effect because they targeted supply centers in the German rear areas. Overall, it's pretty surprising that the Germans were able to continue their counterattack and deploy significant amounts of armor. However, the German's poor training and reliance on Volksgrenadier units undermined any possible success.

QUOTES: "Devers has made a monkey of me." – General George S. Patton in a letter to his wife, referring to the fact that Devers and the Seventh Army reached the Rhine before he did

"Go for Broke" – 442nd Regiment Motto

"Remember the Alamo" – Motto of the Lost Battalion of the 36th Division

"Always Forward" – 45th Division motto (Firebirds)

"Century Soldiers" – 100th Division motto

PLACES TO SEE (REFERENCE MAPS 61-66):

PLACES FROM EPINAL TO SAINT-DIÉ AND THE MEURTHE RIVER (WEST TO EAST), BATTLE OF BRUYERES:

1. **WORLD WAR II AMERICAN EPINAL CEMETERY:** The 45th Division captured Epinal on September 24 after fierce house-to-house fighting. The cemetery contains the graves of 5,255 U.S. military dead, including four Medal of Honor recipients.
   N 48 08.617 E 6 29.481 (48.143617, 6.49135)

2. **MOSELLE CROSSING MONUMENT:** At this location, On September 21, the 36th Division secured a crossing over the Moselle River. The division crossed with virtually no casualties, surprising the Germans south of Epinal. Today the site holds a beautiful park with a stone sculpture dedicated to the American soldier.
   N 48 03.927 E 6 36.516 (48.06545, 6.6086)
   From here, the division advanced toward Tendon at N 48 7.185 E 6 40.723 (48.11975, 6.678717)

3. **MEMORIAL STONE TO THE 45TH DIVISION, FREMIFONTAINE:** This is a very special monument placed in the woods by Jean-Marie Siret, a member of the Firebird Society and a retired French major. On his initiative, Siret created the memorial to recognize the fierce fighting that took place to liberate the village from September 30–October 24.
   N 48 16.155 E 6 41.786 (48.26925, 6.696433)

4a. **SAWMILL MONUMENT TO 3RD INFANTRY DIVISION SOLDIERS AND FRENCH CIVILIANS, MONPLAISIR:** At this location on N420 toward Saint-Dié is a memorial to five 3rd Infantry Division soldiers and French civilians who were killed in a tremendous explosion at the sawmill on October 25, 1944.
   N 48 15.726 E 6 48.701 (48.2621, 6.811683)

4b. **"CROSSROADS OF HELL MEMORIAL," HAUT-JACQUES MOUNTAIN PASS:** Departing Bruyeres and traveling east toward Saint-Dié on N420, you'll see the attack route of the 3rd Infantry Division. The 3rd Division's

7th Regiment engaged in hand-to-hand combat for this high mountain pass starting on October 29 until the regiment finally captured it on November 4. At this location is a nature park and stone monument to the 3rd Division. Across the road sits a monument to the Free French. It was also near here where Private Wilburn Ross earned his Medal of Honor. His citation follows:

"For conspicuous gallantry and intrepidity at risk of life above and beyond the call of duty near St. Jacques, France. At 11:30 a.m. on 30 October 1944, after his company had lost 55 out of 88 men in an attack on an entrenched, full-strength German company of elite mountain troops, Pvt. Ross placed his light machinegun 10 yards in advance of the foremost supporting riflemen in order to absorb the initial impact of an enemy counterattack. With machinegun and small-arms fire striking the earth near him, he fired with deadly effect on the assaulting force and repelled it. Despite the hail of automatic fire and the explosion of rifle grenades within a stone's throw of his position, he continued to man his machinegun alone, holding off 6 more German attacks. When the eighth assault was launched, most of his supporting riflemen were out of ammunition. They took positions in echelon behind Pvt. Ross and crawled up, during the attack, to extract a few rounds of ammunition from his machinegun ammunition belt. Pvt. Ross fought on virtually without assistance and, despite the fact that enemy grenadiers crawled to within 4 yards of his position in an effort to kill him with hand grenades, he again directed accurate and deadly fire on the hostile force and hurled it back. After expending his last rounds, Pvt. Ross was advised to withdraw to the company command post, together with 8 surviving riflemen, but, as more ammunition was expected, he declined to do so. The Germans launched their last all-out attack, converging their fire on Pvt. Ross in a desperate attempt to destroy the machinegun which stood between them and a decisive breakthrough. As his supporting riflemen fixed bayonets for a last-ditch stand, fresh ammunition arrived and was brought to Pvt. Ross just as the advance assault elements were about to swarm over his position. He opened murderous fire on the oncoming enemy; killed 40 and wounded 10 of the attacking force; broke the assault single-handedly, and forced the Germans to withdraw. Having killed or wounded at least 58 Germans in more than 5 hours of continuous combat and saved the remnants of his company from destruction, Pvt. Ross remained at his post that night and the following day for a total of 36 hours. His actions throughout this engagement were an inspiration to his comrades and maintained the high traditions of the military service."

N 48 16.467 E 6 51.748 (48.27445, 6.862467)

4c. HILL 616: This was the high point along N420 that overlooked the road and Saint-Dié. The Germans fiercely defended this hill. After suffering dozens of casualties in a battle of attrition, the 3rd Infantry Division captured it on November 5.
N 48 17.180 E 6 53.743 (48.286333, 6.895717)

5. **BROUVELIEURES PLAQUE TO THE 179TH REGIMENT, 45TH DIVISION:** On the Mayor's Building is a stone plaque dedicated to the men of the 179th Regiment, who fought to liberate the town on October 21, 1944. It was fully liberated by the 7th Regiment of the 3rd Division after it relieved the 45th Infantry Division.
   N 48 14.213 E 6 43.865 (48.236879, 6.731089)

6. **MEMORIAL TO THE 442ND REGIMENT OF JAPANESE-AMERICANS, BRUYERES.** The battle for bruyeres began on october 15. The 442nd regiment began its attack from this memorial's location. The regiment's objectives initially were hill 555, hill a and hill b. Nearby you can see foxholes and really appreciate the terrain. Warning: The road is very rugged, it is a lumber road. A car parking area offers space where you can park and hike up instead.
   N 48 13.052 E 6 41.614 (48.217533, 6.693567)

   BRUYERES HILLS (WHERE THE GERMANS SET UP THEIR DEFENSES):
   HILL 555: **N 48 12.789 E 6 42.073 (48.21315, 6.701217)** (near memorial – the geo coordinates are on Rue du 442nd Regiment)

   HILL A: **N 48 13.090 E 6 42.756 (48.218167, 6.71260)** (the 100th Battalion's objective for October 15), Buemont

   HILL B: **N 48 12.794 E 6 43.075 (48.213233, 6.717917)** (old castle remains)

   HILL C: **N 48 13.202 E 6 43.527 (48.220033, 6.72545)**

   HILL D: **N 48 12.580 E 6 43.780 (48.209667, 6.729667)** (location of the Banzia Charge of October 19)

7a. **BIFFONTAINE CHURCH PLAQUE AND MEMORIAL:** At this location, at the front of the church, is a small plaque that commemorates the 100th Battalion of the 442nd Regiment, which liberated the town on October 23, 1944. The 100th Regiment was initially surrounded on the ridges overlooking the town and then in the town until the troops were finally broken free of German attacks on October 23 by the 3rd Battalion/442nd Infantry Regiment. The 100th Battalion suffered 21 killed in action, 122 wounded in action and 18 prisoners of war. Only 50 feet away is a small memorial area to those lost in World War I and World War II.
   N 48 12.710 E 6 48.308 (48.211833, 6.805133)

7b. **BORNE 6 (HILL 645), LOST BATTALION LOCATION:** 36th Infantry Division and 442nd Regiment Memorial, Biffontaine: On this mountaintop is a memorial to the 442nd Regiment, which rescued the 1st Battalion, 141st Regiment, 36th Infantry Division at that spot. This location is even more dangerous to drive up. It's another old logging road, but drivable; just be extremely careful. There the 442nd Regiment had another Banzai charge at this location to break the German encirclement. The regiment took the main road to break

through to the 36th Infantry Division. Just a little farther up on either side you'll find foxholes and trenches used by the 36th Infantry Division.
N 48 12.850 E 6 51.068 (48.214167, 6.851133)

7c. HILL 624: On Hill 624, the 2nd Battalion/141st Regiment was cut off for a day.
N 48 13.305 E 6 48.881 (48.22175, 6.814683)

8. PARK MEMORIAL, 103RD INFANTRY DIVISION, SAINT-DIÉ: In Saint-Dié is a monument to the 103rd Infantry Division, which liberated the community on November 22, 1944.
N 48 16.677 E 6 57.187 (48.27795, 6.953117)

PLACES RELATED TO THE 100TH INFANTRY DIVISION ATTACK ON THE WINTER LINE AND CROSSING OF THE MEURTHE RIVER:

On November 9, the 100th Infantry Division completed its rotation with the 45th to continue an advance in the Northern Vosges and to cross the Meurthe River. Its goal was to break the German Winter Line defense and capture the important crossroad town of Raon-l'Étape. This is a small "micro" tour of the action of the 399th Regiment, 100th Infantry Division, during the fighting from November 10-18, 1944. Much of this was inspired by Franklin Gurley's book, Into the Mountains Dark. The area has many hiking trails; north of this location is a beautiful lake, which sits next to the town. (called "Lac de Pierre Percée".) To note, a small discrepancy exists between Gurley's book and the Army's official history book. The U.S. Army book states that it captured Hill 539, which seems more logical, but Gurley is pretty clear – and the President's Unit Citation states – that it was Hill 462.8. (The hills are very close to each other.)

9a. BACCARAT BRIDGE: Here you can see the bridge and location where the 100th Regiment crossed over to outflank the Germans and then to follow their route into the mountains. There are no plaques or memorials; this is just the location of the town. (It's a beautiful little community famous for its Baccarat Crystal.) It was captured by the French 2nd Armored Division on its exploitation mission in early November. Then the positions were held by units of the 45th Infantry Division until the 100th Infantry Division began to arrive as replacements for the 45th Infantry Division. On November 10, the 100th Infantry Division began to cross the bridge in trucks for the jumping-off point and attack to outflank the Winter Line.
N 48 26.846 E 6 44.351 (48.447433, 6.739183)

9b. HILL 372, OVERLOOKING NEUFMAISONS, 1ST OBJECTIVE, 399TH REGIMENT: This location was the first objective of the 399th Regiment after it crossed at Baccarat. On November 12, the regiment met stiff German resistance, but forced the Germans to abandon their machine gun positions. The Germans retreated to Neufmaisons. Shortly afterward, the Americans began receiving artillery fire.
N 48 27.370 E 6 49.875 (48.456167, 6.83125)

9c. PURPLE HEART LANE, LE ROUGE VETU: The 399th advanced to this area on the way to its objective, Hill 409.9. It became known as "Purple Heart Lane" because it was here that a German ambush occurred, with crossing fields of machine gun fire. At this point in the battle, the lines were shifting so quickly that the Americans had a difficult time ensuring the woods remained clear to their flanks and rear. Now the site is just a small dirt intersection; you can still see foxholes off the roadside.
N 48 26.774 E 6 50.596 (48.446233, 6.843267)

9d. HILL 409.9, SECOND OBJECTIVE OF THE 399TH REGIMENT: The next objective was to capture Hill 409.9, which dominated the highway (D8) from Neufmaisons to Raon-l'Étape. The Germans at this location also had barbed wire, trenches, snipers and log emplacements with machine guns. After several attempts, the men of the 100th finally captured the hill on November 14.
N 48 26.772 E 6 49.981 (48.4462, 6.833017)

10. HILL 431: Across the highway from Hill 409.9 was Hill 431, which was also part of the German Winter Line, the first line of defense in the Vosges. (It had been built by forced labor.) On November 15, companies I, K and L charged the hill following a rolling artillery barrage and "officially" broke through the Winter Line.
N 48 26.405 E 6 50.985 (48.440083, 6.84975)

11a. ATTACK ROUTE TO HILL 462.8, BLOODY KNOB: At this location, on November 16, 1944, Company A of the 1st Battalion, 399th Regiment, attacked the fortified hill that was part of the Winter Line position. The attack started with the aid of a 45-minute artillery barrage and the minor support of three Shermans that avoided going up the dangerous paths. By mid-afternoon, after hand-to-hand combat and the taking out of several log bunkers and machine gun nests, Company A captured the hill. However, shortly after doing this, the company had to defend against a company-size German counterattack, then a platoon-size attack later in the day. Because the Americans held the hill, the Germans were forced to retreat from Raon-l'Étape. The American 1st Battalion suffered many casualties in its advance. By the end of the day, the battalion's strength had been depleted. Company A was left with only 60 men fit for combat out of 190. In total, to take the hill, the Americans suffered 22 killed in action, while the Germans suffered 35 killed in action. Note that Company B, 1st Battalion, 399th Regiment, captured Hill 468 on November 17 just east of here. At these geo coordinates is an area where you can park and see the trench at the intersection in the woods. Next, follow the trail southwest and the logging trail (blue diamond) toward Raon-l'Étape. This was the path of the American attack up to Hill 462.8 (later called Bloody Knob).
N 48 26.750 E 6 52.472 (48.445833, 6.874533)

11b. HILL 462.8, BLOODY KNOB: This is the approximate location of the top of Hill 462.8. The men of the 100th defended the hill against two major German counterattacks through mortar and artillery barrages. Company A set up its two .30-caliber machine guns facing the route that the troops had just

ascended earlier that day in preparation for a German counterattack. (That section was covered by the 2nd and 3rd Platoons. The 1st Platoon was on the southeast edge of the Knob.) The Germans, as expected, counterattacked from the north into the .30-caliber machine gun fire, managing to push back the Americans. Eventually, the Americans regained their positions after brutal fighting. You can find remains of foxholes throughout the area.
N 48 26.234 E 6 52.657 (48.437233, 6.877617)

11c. HILL 539: The Germans also held Hill 539, which, on November 17, elements of the 397th Regiment captured against little resistance, as the capture of Hill 462.8 had forced the Germans to begin withdrawing.
N 48 25.486 E 6 53.165 (48.424762, 6.886078)

12. 100TH INFANTRY DIVISION PLAQUE ON THE CITY HALL, RAON-L'ÉTAPE: This is a plaque honoring the 100th Infantry Division, which liberated Raon-l'Étape on November 20.
N 48 24.429 E 6 50.637 (48.40715, 6.84395)

LOCATIONS EN ROUTE TO STRASBOURG (WEST TO EAST):

13. BADONVILLER SHERMAN, "MORT HOMME": A Sherman tank of the French 2nd Armored participating in the November Offensive was knocked out here on November 17, 1944, just north of Raon-l'Étape. The crew had circled Badonviller to clear it of Germans when the tank was hit by a shell and caught on fire.
N 48 30.178 E 6 53.674 (48.502967, 6.894567)

14. STRUTHOF CAMP, NATZWILLER: Located on top of a mountain, this was the largest concentration camp in France. It was liberated by the 3rd Infantry Division during its attack toward Strasbourg in November 1944. The 3rd Infantry Division freed 46,000 people. The Nazis opened the camp on May 1, 1941. During the war, more than 80,000 people were deported from there. More than 22,000 never returned.
N 48 27.246 E 7 15.015 (48.4541, 7.25025)

15. ALSACE MOSELLE MEMORIAL, SCHIRMECK (BAS RHIN): This is a resistance museum and victims' memorial; it's new, but focused not just on World War II.
N 48 29.226 E 7 13.310 (48.4871, 7.221833)

16. FORT MUTZIG: The German Kaiser built this fort in 1895 to house 8,000 men and to stop a French southern attack into Germany (while the Germans attacked from the north). Significant volunteer effort has gone into making it a very impressive fort again. The French copied it 40 years after its original construction to build the Maginot Line. During World War II, the Germans occupied the fort while the Americans advanced. The Americans took the fort by using a captured German halftrack, loading it

with TNT and driving it into one of the walls. Currently, the fort is open for tours on Saturdays, and shares some land with the French military.
N 48 33.491 E 7 27.454 (48.558183, 7.457567)

17. **SHERMAN TANK, "CHERBOURG," STRASBOURG:** In Strasbourg not far from the Rhine River is this Free French Sherman tank of the 2nd Armored Division. Named "Cherbourg," it was lost in fighting on November 23, 1944 near where it now rests.
N 48 34.363 E 7 47.784 (48.572717, 7.7964)

LOCATIONS RELATED TO THE DECEMBER OFFENSIVE AND THE NORDWIND OFFENSIVE (NORTH OF STRASBOURG):

18. **"BOURG LA REINE," M4 SHERMAN TANK NEAR PHALSBOURG:** On November 21, 1944, while on approach to liberate Phalsbourg, this French armor Sherman was hit by an 88mm cannon that killed the driver. As the tank caught fire, the rest of it crew escaped. At that point, it was hit again, first at the turret ring and then at the fuel tank. The crew was rescued by a halftrack that was also hit by a shell and caught fire, injuring all the crew.
N 48 46.133 E 7 14.466 (48.768883, 7.2411)

19. **SIMSERHOF, BITCHE MAGINOT LINE, NORDWIND:** This site was occupied by the Germans, then taken in late November by the 44th Division. The Germans retook it during Nordwind in January. The Americans finally re-occupied it on March 16, 1945.
N 49 03.438 E 7 22.519 (49.0573, 7.375317)

20a. **100TH INFANTRY DIVISION PLAQUE IN CITADEL, BITCHE:** A plaque in honor of the 100th Infantry Division, the "Sons of Bitche" who liberated Bitche. Bitche is dominated by the very impressive Citadel, which is a great place to visit.
N 49 3.123 E 7 25.747 (49.05205, 7.429117)

20b. **WINGEN SUR MODER 70TH ID PLAQUE:** From January 4-8, 1944, during the opening days of Nordwind, Regiment 12 of the 6th SS Gebirgsjager Division stormed the small town of Wingen sur Moder from the northeast. At this location is Saint-Felix Church, which the Germans used as their headquarters during the fighting. From the southwest, the two battalions of the 274th regiment, 70th Infantry Division, fought their way back into the town at this location. Now, a plaque memorializes their sacrifices.
N 48 55.106 E 7 22.845 (48.918433, 7.38075)

21a. **100TH INFANTRY DIVISION PLAQUE ON THE TOWN HALL, RIMLING:** A plaque rests here in honor of the 100th Infantry Division, which liberated Rimling in January 1945.
N 49 05.693 E 7 15.853 (49.094883, 7.264217)

21b. **FORT CASSO:** Just south of Rimling is a Maginot Line fort, well preserved.

A Char B1 tank turret is part of the fortification, as is an American halftrack with anti-aircraft guns. The fort saw fighting during the German invasion, again during the German retreat and again during the German Nordwind Offensive.
N 49 03.518 E 7 16.001 (49.058633, 7.266683)

21c. SINGLING PLAQUE: On the church in Singling is a plaque honoring the American units that fought for the liberation of Singling on December 6, 1944 and defended it again against the initial Nordwind attack by the 17th SS Panzer grenadiers and the 36th Infantry. Singling is the farthest the Germans reached in their Sturmgruppe 1 attack on New Year's Eve/Day. A few Maginot Line blockhouses and pillboxes rest along the D84.
N 49 02.813 E 7 13.366 (49.046883, 7.222767)

22. CASEMATE D'INFANTERIE ESCH A HATTEN: This museum costs only 2 euros, is well preserved, short and sweet. It is two minutes from the Fort Hatten Museum. It has a Sherman on top, offers great photos and maintains a unique collection of materiel. During the battle of Nordwind in January 1945, it was in the middle of fierce fighting around Hatten-Rittershoffen.
N 48 53.546 E 7 59.417 (48.892433, 7.990283)

23a. MUSÉE DE L'ABRI A HATTEN, MAGINOT LINE AND HATTEN MUSEUM, NORDWIND: This site has a great museum within the Maginot Line casement, with unique photos and materiel. It also displays dozens of tanks, artillery and aircraft. (Plan ahead and you can ride in or drive a tank.) Just across the fields to the south is Hagenau Forest, where fierce fighting took place in January 1945.
N 48 53.959 E 7 58.036 (48.899317, 7.967267)

23b. HATTEN MEMORIAL, RITTERSDORF: At this location is a stone memorial to remember the fierce tank battles that took place in this area in January 1945.
N 48 54.150 E 7 57.861 (48.9025, 7.96435)

24. FORT SCHOENENBURG: Close to Hatten is a very popular gros ouvrage (www.lignemaginot.com). This is one of the best forts to visit and one of the largest in the Maginot Line.
N 48 57.982 E 7 54.733 (48.966367, 7.912217)

25a. 45TH DIVISION BATTLE REIPERTSWILLER, HILL 420: On January 12, the Germans attacked again from the north and Hitler released his last reserves. The 45th Division, 3rd Battalion, 157th Regiment was simultaneously advancing to take recently lost hills north of the town of Reipertswiller on the far western edge of the Hagenau Forest. The troops were overrun and surrounded for three days by the 6th SS Gebirgs Division (Mountain Division). Several attempts were made from January 16-20 to break them out. They fought off Germans who were attacking with mortar, artillery and flamethrowers, but to no avail. The battalion was lost; the result after eight days of

fighting (for the battalion plus reinforcements) was 158 killed, 350 evacuated for wounds and 426 captured (many of them wounded). Only two men made it out of the woods on the final attempt for a breakout.
Hill 420: N 48 57.216 E 7 28.778 (48.9536, 7.479633)

25b."SPIELBACH DRAW" TRAILHEAD FOR THE PATH UP TO HILL 420: At this location is a parking area from which you can hike up to Hill 420. It is also one of the routes along which the Americans tried to supply the trapped units. Their efforts included sending up Stuart tanks to break through.
N 48 56.071 E 7 29.246 (48.934517, 7.487433)

26a.M24 CHAFFEE TANK (WITH A FRENCH FLAG), SANDFELD: This is located at an intersection close to a French military base, Just be careful, as there is nowhere to park!
N 48 47.549 E 7 50.794 (48.792483, 7.846567)

26b.HERRLISHEIM PLAQUE TO THE 12TH ARMORED DIVISION: Next to the church is a garden with a memorial to the war's fallen. On the memorial is a small plaque to the 12th Armored Division, which fought the Germans here in an attempt to reduce the German bridgehead on January 16. The armor battle raged for several days and the 12th Armored Division had two battalions totally wiped out on January 17 when the 10th Panzer Division entered the battle.
N 48 43.749 E 7 54.452 (48.72915, 7.907533)

27a.MUSEUM PAYS DE LA ZORN, "THE SUSSEX PLAN 1944" AND WANTZENAU VEHICLE AND EQUIPMENT MUSEUM: The Sussex Plan Museum, which focused on spy operations by the Americans and French during World War II, has combined forces with a Vehicle and Equipment Museum in Wantzenau.
N 48 39.928 E 7 48.658 (48.665467, 7.810967)

27b.KILSTETT MEMORIAL: At the edge of town, in Kilstett, is a memorial to the fighting that took place in January 1945 when the Germans held a bridgehead here after their daring Rhine River crossing. Note that Gambsheim also contains a memorial, outside the main church off D468.
N 48 40.774 E 7 51.644 (48.679567, 7.860733)

OPERATION HABICHT AND THE BATTLE OF THE COLMAR POCKET:

OPERATION HABICHT, DECEMBER 12-14 AND OTHER DECEMBER FIGHTING LOCATIONS:

****Riquewihr: This was the objective of the Germans during Operation Habicht. It is a very beautiful town, a must stay/visit when on this route.*

28. GERMAN CEMETERY, BERGHEIM: Situated on the slopes overlooking the small winemaker's town of Bergheim is a German cemetery holding more than 5,300 Germans killed in action, most from the battles around Colmar and from Nordwind. From December 2-4, the American 36th Infantry Division fought to liberate the town.
N 48 12.727 E 7 21.397 (48.21212, 7.35662)

29a.BENNWIHR MEMORIAL: At this location is a bullet-riddled statue, a memorial to the fallen of the town of Bennwihr. This town was fiercely fought over from December 22-24, 1944. During the battle, Sergeant Gus Kefurt of the 15th Regiment, 3rd Infantry Division earned the Medal of Honor for his heroism, which included killing 15 Germans and clearing several houses. He died of his wounds later that day. The memorial is also part of the walking trail around Bennwihr and Mittelwihr, called "Sentier des Grands Crus."
N 48 08.690 E 7 19.470 (48.144833, 7.3245)

29b.MITTELWIHR PLAQUE: On the church wall is a plaque commemorating the liberation of Mittelwihr. It is also part of the walking trail around Bennwihr and Mittelwihr, called "Sentier des Grands Crus."
N 48 09.067 E 7 19.316 (48.151117, 7.32193)

30a.HILL 351/BLOODY HILL/MEMORIAL TO AMERICAN DIVISIONS AND FRENCH CEMETERY, SIGOLSHEIM: At this location, some of the fiercest and bloodiest fighting of the Alsace Campaign took place. The Americans held against several German attacks during Operation Habicht until they finally lost it on December 17. The hill was then occupied by 200 fanatical SS soldiers. Starting on December 22, the Americans made several attempts to take back the hill. All were unsuccessful until Colonel Ware, on the fourth assault, led two officers, nine men and one tank up the hill to clear the machine gun nests. He used his Browning Automatic Rifle and tracer rounds to define targets for the tank and systematically took out the German defenders. For his heroism and bravery, he was awarded the Medal of Honor. After capturing the hill, the Americans were able to recapture Sigolsheim on December 28. During the liberation of Sigolsheim, another soldier, First Lieutenant Eli Whiteley, was awarded the Medal of Honor. During the fighting, Whiteley was wounded twice (including an injury to his eye), killed nine Germans, captured 23 Germans and, at one point, to clear a building, fired a bazooka at the wall to make a hole that he then jumped through while holding his submachine gun with one hand. This is Eli Whiteley's citation:

"While leading his platoon on December 27, 1944, in savage house-to-house fighting through the fortress town of Sigolsheim, France, he attacked a building through a street swept by withering mortar and automatic weapons fire. He was hit and severely wounded in the arm and shoulder; but he charged into the house alone and killed its 2 defenders. Hurling smoke and fragmentation grenades before him, he reached the next house and stormed inside, killing 2 and capturing 11 of the enemy. He continued leading his platoon in the extremely dangerous task of clearing hostile troops from strong points along the street until he reached a building held by fanatical Nazi troops. Although suffering from wounds which had rendered his left arm useless, he advanced on this strongly defended house, and after blasting out a wall with bazooka fire, charged through a hail of bullets. Wedging his submachinegun under his uninjured arm, he rushed into the house through the hole torn by his rockets, killed 5 of the enemy and forced the remaining 12 to surrender. As he emerged to continue his fearless attack, he was again hit and critically wounded. In agony and with 1 eye pierced by a shell fragment, he shouted for his men to follow him to the next house. He was determined to stay in the fighting, and remained at the head of his platoon until forcibly evacuated. By his disregard for personal safety, his aggressiveness while suffering from severe wounds, his determined leadership and superb courage, 1st Lt. Whiteley killed 9 Germans, captured 23 more and spearheaded an attack which cracked the core of enemy resistance in a vital area."

At the location is a memorial to the Americans who fought here. Just up the hill from the memorial is a French cemetery with 1,684 graves. It is at the pinnacle of Hill 351.
N 48 08.366 E 7 18.688 (48.139433, 7.311467)

30b.HILL 393: Hill 393 was also a target of the Germans, who captured it during Operation Habicht. It has some forest trails and very beautiful views of surrounding towns and vineyards. You can hike from Hill 351 through vineyards to Hill 393. The following geo coordinates are for the far side of Hill 393.
N 48 08.838 E 7 17.241 (48.1473, 7.28735)

TRAILS FOR HILL 621, HILL 666 AND HILL 672: If you start from the Kaysersberg, like the Germans did, follow the Blue Cross Trail north. You can start with this trail at the château ruins, which are located up the hill behind the church. On this trail you will pass to Hill 621, then Hill 666 and at the fork of the Red Triangle Trail to the right toward Riquewihr and the Blue Cross Trail to the left. Go left about 100 meters to see Hill 672. (I highly suggest getting a map from one of the tourist shops).

Trail head/château: N 48 08.429 E 7 15.752 (48.140491, 7.262532)

31a.HILL 621, HOCH SCHWAERTZ: Hill 621 was one of the Germans' targets during Operation Habicht. The Germans attacked from Kientzheim in the south and captured Hills 666 and 672 just north of Hill 621. Throughout the fierce shelling and hand-to-hand combat, the American soldiers held onto

this hill. The German attack succeeded in capturing some of the surrounding towns, but the Germans suffered greatly: 1,316 prisoners of war and more than 1,000 wounded in action and 500 killed in action. At this location, you'll find bunkers built by the Germans during World War I in 1915; the Americans used these bunkers to their advantage. Trails throughout the hills connect Kaysersberg and Riquewihr.
N 48 09.079 E 7 16.248 (48.151317, 7.2708)

31b. HILL 666: Hill 666 was lightly held by the Americans, who inflicted heavy casualties on the German initial assault. On December 13, the Germans took the hill as part of their attack on Hill 621.
N 48 09.478 E 7 16.499 (48.157967, 7.274983)

31c. HILL 672: Hill 672 was captured by the Germans on December 12 and used as a launching point to attack Riquewihr.
N 48 09.893 E 7 16.262 (48.164883, 7.271033)

32a. KIENTZHEIM SHERMAN AND MEMORIAL: On December 17, as part of the attack on the Colmar Pocket, the 36th Infantry Division attacked with a French company of Shermans from the 5th French Armored Division. They rushed the town and captured it, surprisingly within one hour. This tank was knocked out of action on December 18 after it disabled a Panther.
N 48 08.172 E 7 16.925 (48.1362, 7.282083)

32b. 3RD INFANTRY DIVISION STONE/PLAQUE FOR THE LIBERATION OF AMMERSCHWIHR: At this location is a small stone and plaque laid as a memorial to the 3rd Infantry Division, which liberated Ammerschwihr in December 1944.
N 48 07.659 E 7 16.921 (48.12765, 7.282017)

32c. 3RD INFANTRY DIVISION PLAQUE FOR THE LIBERATION OF KAYSERSBERG: In this beautiful little town, on the south side of the church, is a plaque commemorating the 3rd Infantry Division's liberation of Kaysersberg on December 18, 1944. On the other side of the church sits a small grave for French soldiers, as well as a plaque to the French 5th Armored Division, which was involved in the fighting.
N 48 08.328 E 7 15.806 (48.1388, 7.263433)

JANUARY PUSH TO DESTROY THE COLMAR POCKET, JANUARY 20–FEBRUARY 9:

33. HILL 216, BENNWIHR: As a means of highlighting the strength of the resistance in the Colmar Pocket, consider this: the Americans did not attack Hill 216 until January 23 even though they held Bennwihr since late December. The Germans were in place on Hill 216 because it provided visibility of the fields north of Colmar. On January 23, at 0700, elements of the 3rd Infantry Division attacked, but were shortly caught in a German minefield. The explosions alerted the Germans to the attack. After an all-day firefight, the Ameri-

cans took command of the hill by 2100. These geo coordinates are for the crest of Hill 216, currently in the middle of a vineyard.
N 48 08.154 E 7 19.856 (48.1359, 7.330933)

34. **3RD INFANTRY DIVISION PLAQUE, OSTHEIM:** On January 23, 1945, on a 14-degree-Fahrenheit day, elements of the 3rd Infantry Division liberated this town after fierce fighting against SS and Gestapo troops. At this location is a memorial to the dead and a small plaque dedicated to the 3rd Infantry Division.
N 48 09.576 E 7 22.242 (48.1596, 7.3707)

35. **FRENCH M10 TANK DESTROYER, "PORC EPIC," ILLHAEUSERN:** Located north of the Colmar Pocket, this tank was attached to the forces that attacked to reduce the pocket in late January 1945. It was destroyed and three of its crew killed on January 26, 1945 during fierce fighting against the German Kampfgruppe Blasius. The tank was most likely knocked out by a Nashorn tank destroyer, which was attached to the Kampfgruppe.
N 48 10.478 E 7 27.029 (48.174633, 7.450483)

36. **M4A2 SHERMAN "CHEMIN DES DAMES," GRUSSENHEIM:** This Sherman belonged to the French 2nd Armored Division. On January 26, 1945, it – like the M10 – was taken out by a Nashorn tank destroyer while fighting to block a German breakout from the pocket.
N 48 09.304 E 7 28.531 (48.155067, 7.475517)

37. **MARCKOLSHEIM MUSEUM, SHERMAN AND HALFTRACK:** This third-line casement of the Maginot Line saw intense fighting in mid-June 1940. The inside has been refurbished and contains many exhibits of equipment and militaria. Also, on the outside, is a halftrack, armored car, cannons and a Sherman tank!
N 48 09.507 E 7 33.354 (48.15845, 7.5559)

38. **JEBSHEIM MEMORIAL:** From January 24-29, 1945, Jebsheim was bitterly fought over and exchanged hands three times. The attackers were the American 3rd Infantry Division, supported by French tanks of the 5th Armored Division, against German defenders composed of a tank hunter battalion (Jagdpanthers) and a lethal regiment of the 2nd Mountain Division. The memorial is located north of the town where a mill stood during the battle. By January 29, the Americans had captured the town and 600 Germans; 500 Germans had been killed in action. The Allies suffered approximately 400 killed in action (French and American).
N 48 08.365 E 7 27.799 (48.139417, 7.463317)

39. **JEBSHEIM PILLBOX:** Just past the memorial is a small bunker that pinned down a company of the 254th Regiment. Not until a M36 Jackson tank destroyer arrived with its 90mm cannon was the company able to advance.
N 48 07.925 E 7 28.146 (48.132083, 7.4691)

40. **AUDIE MURPHY MEMORIAL, HOLTZWIHR:** At this location on January

26, 1945, Audie Murphy shot the .50-caliber marchine gun on the back of a burning M10 tank against a German attack. He received the Medal of Honor for his heroism. The memorial is a cut-out of an M10 tank with Murphy on the back. The citation reads:

"2d Lt. Murphy commanded Company B, which was attacked by 6 tanks and waves of infantry. 2d Lt. Murphy ordered his men to withdraw to prepared positions in a woods, while he remained forward at his command post and continued to give fire directions to the artillery by telephone. Behind him, to his right, 1 of our tank destroyers received a direct hit and began to burn. Its crew withdrew to the woods. 2d Lt. Murphy continued to direct artillery fire which killed large numbers of the advancing enemy infantry. With the enemy tanks abreast of his position, 2d Lt. Murphy climbed on the burning tank destroyer, which was in danger of blowing up at any moment, and employed its .50 caliber machine gun against the enemy. He was alone and exposed to German fire from 3 sides, but his deadly fire killed dozens of Germans and caused their infantry attack to waver. The enemy tanks, losing infantry support, began to fall back. For an hour the Germans tried every available weapon to eliminate 2d Lt. Murphy, but he continued to hold his position and wiped out a squad which was trying to creep up unnoticed on his right flank. Germans reached as close as 10 yards, only to be mowed down by his fire. He received a leg wound, but ignored it and continued the single-handed fight until his ammunition was exhausted. He then made his way to his company, refused medical attention, and organized the company in a counterattack which forced the Germans to withdraw. His directing of artillery fire wiped out many of the enemy; he killed or wounded about 50. 2d Lt. Murphy's indomitable courage and his refusal to give an inch of ground saved his company from possible encirclement and destruction, and enabled it to hold the woods which had been the enemy's objective."

N 48 07.368 E 7 25.256 (48.1228, 7.420933)

41. COLMAR LIBERATION MEMORIAL, SHERMAN AND GERMAN CANNON: This is a Free French Sherman tank memorial that contains a German 105mm cannon dedicated to the liberation of Colmar.
N 48 04.984 E 7 21.368 (48.083067, 7.356133)

42a.COLMAR POCKET MUSEUM, TURCKHEIM: This is located in the cool little town of Turckheim. It's a small but well done museum and worth a visit. Turckheim was liberated by the 112th Infantry Regiment of the 28th Infantry Division on February 4, 1945.
N 48 05.304 E 7 16.612 (48.0884, 7.276867)

42b.GERMAN CEMETERY, CERNAY: In the southern area of the Colmar Pocket is the town of Cernay. Here a cemetery contains the graves of 1,479 men involved in that battle. It also contains more than 7,400 graves from World War I.
N 47 48.015 E 7 10.171 (47.80025, 7.169517)

FRENCH ZONE, BELFORT GAP (WEST TO EAST):

43. FORT DU SALBERT: French commandos took this fort, which guarded the approach to the Belfort Gap. It is part of an open park and offers a great view of the gap. Belfort itself is an excellent place to visit, and maintains an old citadel.
N 47 39.602 E 6 48.865 (47.660033, 6.814417)

44. BELFORT MUSEUM, FORT AND SHERMAN: Belfort was in the French offensive sector and was a major retreat route for the Germans. Traditionally, Belfort had been a fortress city for hundreds of years because of its location in a natural break between the Swiss Alps and the Vosges Mountains. At this location is the Citadel museum. Just above the museum is a Sherman tank!
N 47 38.269 E 6 51.973 (47.637817, 6.866217)

45. MULHOUSE TRAIN MUSEUM (AND EQUIPMENT): Located in the southern city of Mulhouse is an excellent train and equipment museum. The displays include military trains and materiel. (Note that somewhere in Mulhouse is the Sherman "Austerlitz"; I couldn't locate it when I visited the city!)
N 47 44.996 E 7 17.674 (47.749933, 7.294567)

46. M4 A1 SHERMAN, ROSENAU, NEAR BASEL: This is where Lieutenant Jean de Loisy and his Sherman reached the Rhine River. Loisy and his comrades were first French – and the first Allies – to do so!
N 47 38.402 E 7 32.160 (47.640033, 7.536)

ALSACE CAMPAIGN / VOSGES MOUNTAINS - SEPT 15, 1944 - FEB 9, 1945 MAP 61

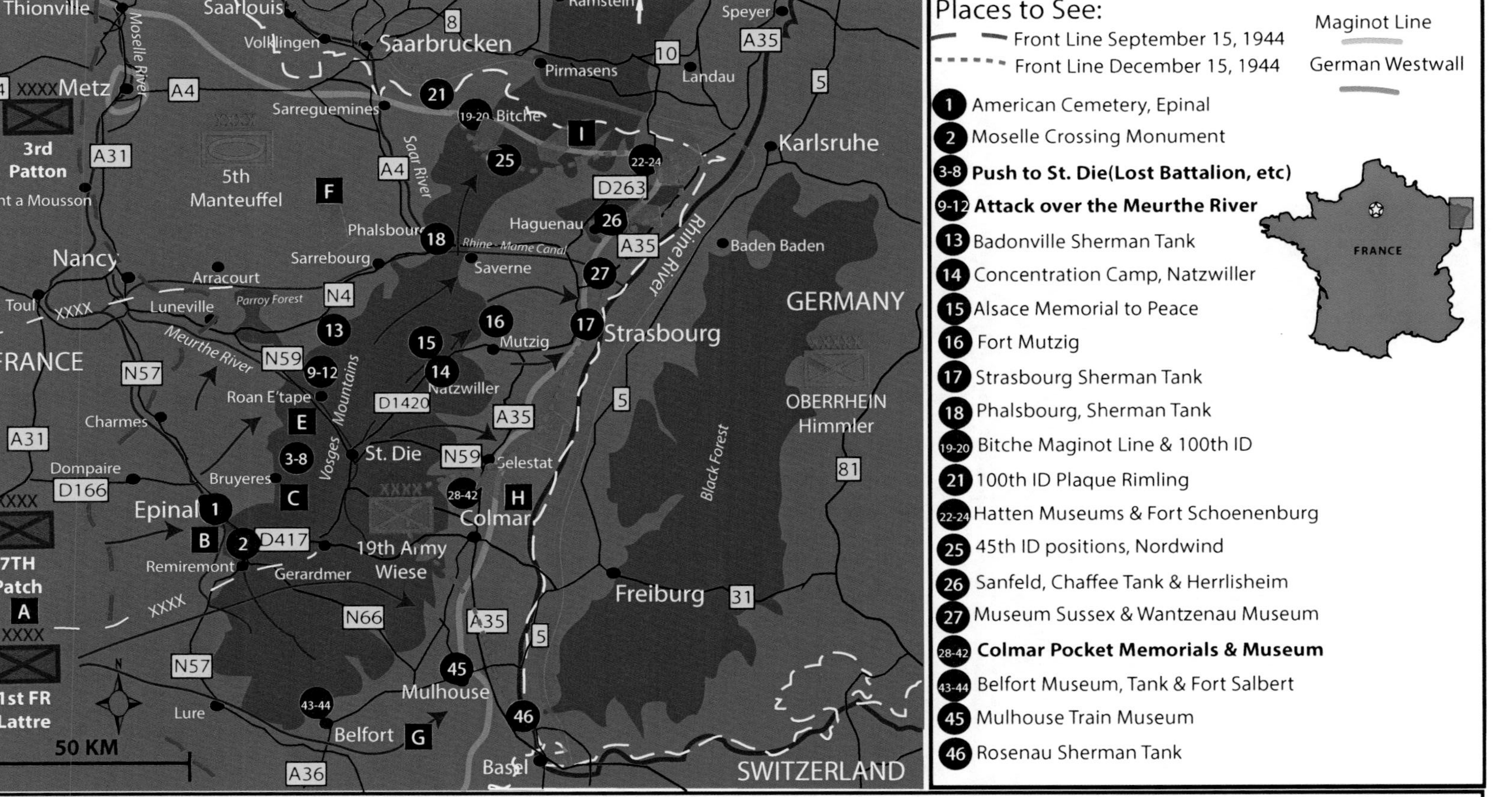
Thionville
Saarlouis
Volklingen
Saarbrucken
Ramstein
Speyer
Pirmasens
Landau
Karlsruhe
Metz
Moselle River
Sarreguemines
Bitche
3rd
Patton
Pont a Mousson
5th
Manteuffel
Saar River
Phalsbourg
Haguenau
Rhine - Marne Canal
Saverne
Sarrebourg
Baden Baden
Rhine River
Nancy
Arracourt
Toul
Luneville
Parroy Forest
GERMANY
Meurthe River
Mutzig
Strasbourg
FRANCE
Vosges Mountains
Natzwiller
Roan E'tape
OBERRHEIN
Himmler
Charmes
St. Die
Selestat
Dompaire
Bruyeres
Black Forest
Epinal
Colmar
19th Army
Wiese
7TH
Patch
Remiremont
Gerardmer
Freiburg
1st FR
Lattre
Lure
Mulhouse
Belfort
50 KM
Basel
SWITZERLAND
A4
A31
A35
A36
N4
N57
N59
N66
D166
D417
D1420
D263

Places to See:

- Front Line September 15, 1944
- Front Line December 15, 1944
- Maginot Line
- German Westwall

FRANCE

1. American Cemetery, Epinal
2. Moselle Crossing Monument

3-8 **Push to St. Die(Lost Battalion, etc)**

9-12 **Attack over the Meurthe River**

13 Badonville Sherman Tank

14 Concentration Camp, Natzwiller

15 Alsace Memorial to Peace

16 Fort Mutzig

17 Strasbourg Sherman Tank

18 Phalsbourg, Sherman Tank

19-20 Bitche Maginot Line & 100th ID

21 100th ID Plaque Rimling

22-24 Hatten Museums & Fort Schoenenburg

25 45th ID positions, Nordwind

26 Sanfeld, Chaffee Tank & Herrlisheim

27 Museum Sussex & Wantzenau Museum

28-42 **Colmar Pocket Memorials & Museum**

43-44 Belfort Museum, Tank & Fort Salbert

45 Mulhouse Train Museum

46 Rosenau Sherman Tank

Movements: (please note that some letters are not shown because it is too busy.)

A. Sept 15, Dever's 6th Army Group which contained Patch's 7th Army & Lattre's 1st French Army, formed the southern front and began plans to advance east.
B. Sept 24, the 45th ID captured Epinal and Sept 26, the 36th ID crossed the Moselle River.
C. Oct 6, Operation Dogface began, the push into the Vosges. 79th ID attacked through Parroy, 45th ID to Saverne, 3rd ID to St. Die, 36th ID towards Colmar & French attacked through to Belfort.
D. After rather unsuccessful attacks through the Vosges, the Allies refitted & replaced units. Nov 13 they began a much stronger attack through the Vosges & to Belfort.
E. Nov 9, the Meurthe River was crossed by the 100th ID, Nov 19 the French reached the Rhine, Nov 20 103rd liberated St. Die, Nov 23 the 2nd FR AD liberated Strasbourg.
F. Nov 25, the Germans counterattacked south with the Panzer Lehr Division in a failed attempt to recapture Strasbourg.
G. Nov 28, the French captured Belfort & Mulhouse but struggled to push further north against stiff German defenses. Dec 4, Americans arrived at Selestat, past Vosges.
H. Dec 9-18, the Germans counterattacked the Americans in Operation Habicht to push them out of the high hills just north of Colmar.
I. Dec 30 - Jan 25, Operation Nordwind, the Germans attacked from Bitche and then across the Rhine at Gamsheim, overall a total failure but it inflicted heavy losses.
J. Jan 20-Feb 9, reduction of the Colmar pocket, the the French First Army, with an attached American Corps destroyed the Colmar Pocket.

OPERATION DOGFACE, LOST BATTALION, OCT 15 - NOV 10, 1944 MAP 62

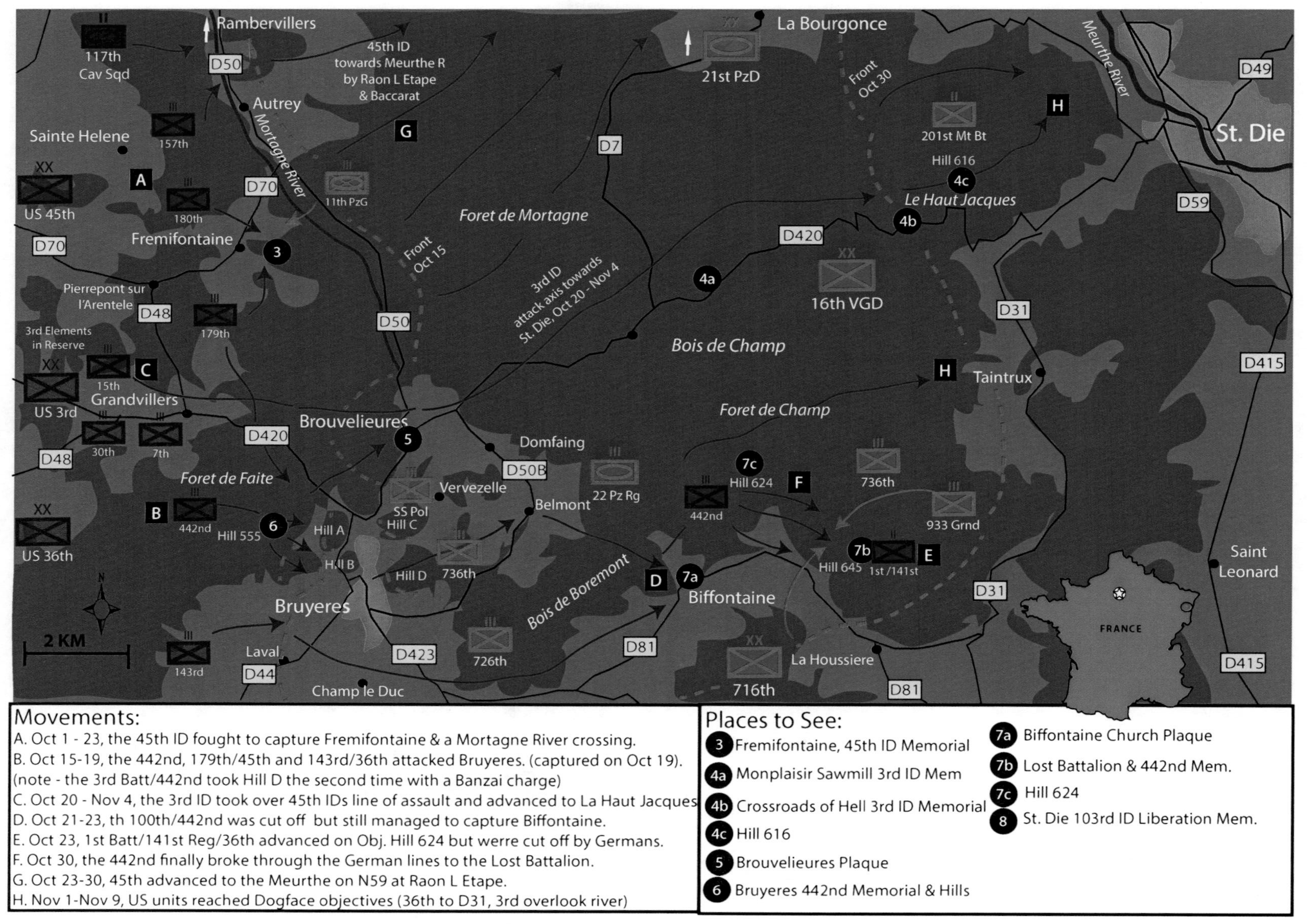
Rambervillers
117th Cav Sqd
45th ID towards Meurthe R by Raon L Etape & Baccarat
La Bourgonce
21st PzD
Front Oct 30
Meurthe River
St. Die
Autrey
Mortagne River
Sainte Helene
157th
201st Mt Bt
Hill 616
Le Haut Jacques
US 45th
180th
11th PzG
Foret de Mortagne
Fremifontaine
Front Oct 15
3rd ID attack axis towards St. Die, Oct 20 - Nov 4
16th VGD
Pierrepont sur l'Arentele
179th
3rd Elements in Reserve
Bois de Champ
Taintrux
15th
Grandvillers
US 3rd
Brouvelieures
Foret de Champ
30th
7th
Domfaing
Foret de Faite
Vervezelle
22 Pz Rg
Hill 624
736th
442nd
Hill 555
SS Pol
Hill C
Belmont
933 Grnd
Hill A
Hill B
Hill D
Hill 645
1st /141st
US 36th
Bois de Boremont
Biffontaine
Saint Leonard
Bruyeres
FRANCE
2 KM
143rd
Laval
726th
La Houssiere
Champ le Duc
716th
Movements:
A. Oct 1 - 23, the 45th ID fought to capture Fremifontaine & a Mortagne River crossing.
B. Oct 15-19, the 442nd, 179th/45th and 143rd/36th attacked Bruyeres. (captured on Oct 19).
(note - the 3rd Batt/442nd took Hill D the second time with a Banzai charge)
C. Oct 20 - Nov 4, the 3rd ID took over 45th IDs line of assault and advanced to La Haut Jacques
D. Oct 21-23, th 100th/442nd was cut off but still managed to capture Biffontaine.
E. Oct 23, 1st Batt/141st Reg/36th advanced on Obj. Hill 624 but werre cut off by Germans.
F. Oct 30, the 442nd finally broke through the German lines to the Lost Battalion.
G. Oct 23-30, 45th advanced to the Meurthe on N59 at Raon L Etape.
H. Nov 1-Nov 9, US units reached Dogface objectives (36th to D31, 3rd overlook river)
Places to See:
3 Fremifontaine, 45th ID Memorial
4a Monplaisir Sawmill 3rd ID Mem
4b Crossroads of Hell 3rd ID Memorial
4c Hill 616
5 Brouvelieures Plaque
6 Bruyeres 442nd Memorial & Hills
7a Biffontaine Church Plaque
7b Lost Battalion & 442nd Mem.
7c Hill 624
8 St. Die 103rd ID Liberation Mem.

100TH ID ATTACK ON RAON L'ETAPE, NOVEMBER 10-18, 1944 MAP 63

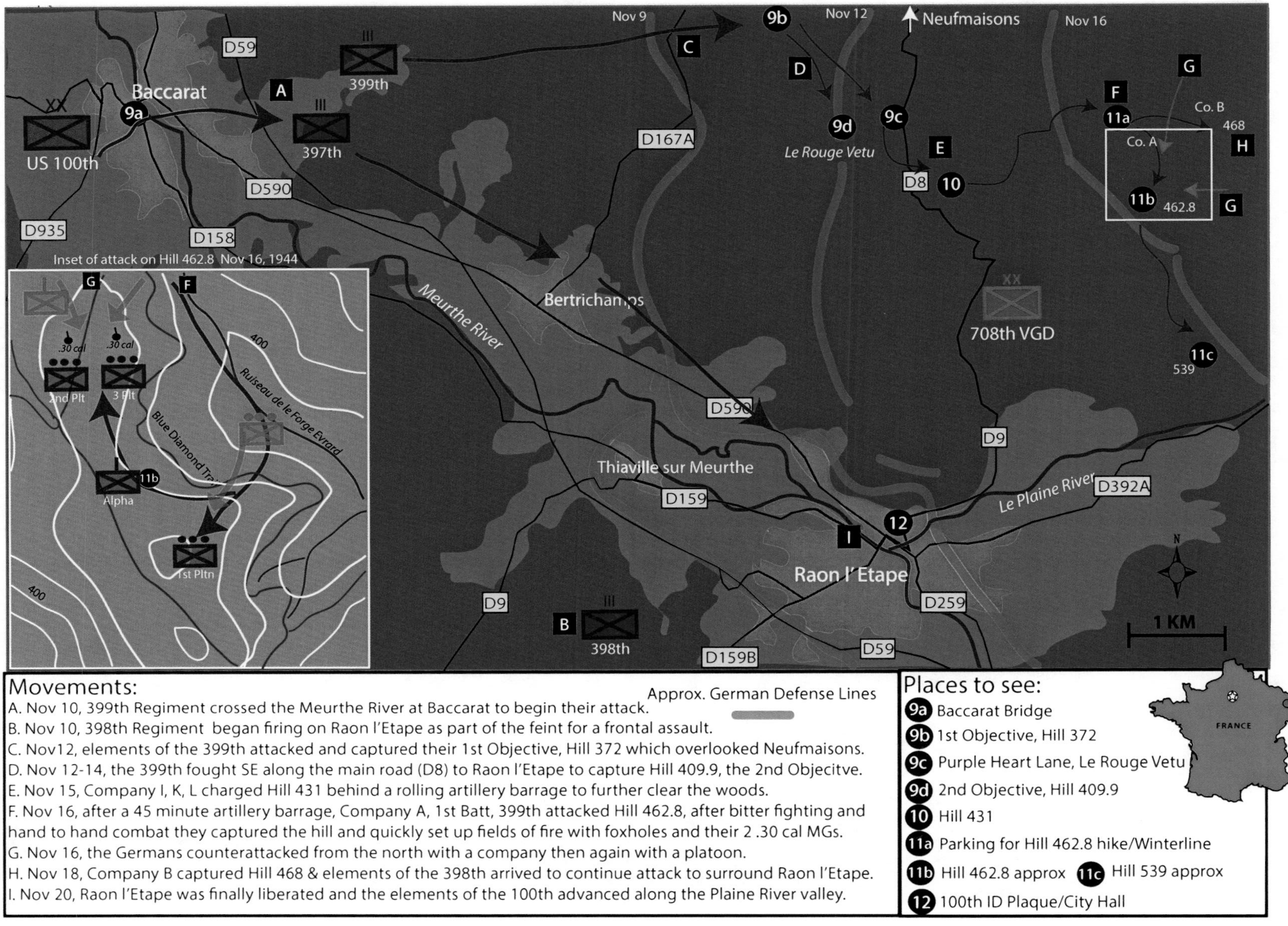
Neufmaisons
708th VGD
Le Rouge Vetu
Nov 9
Nov 12
Nov 16
Co. A
Co. B
468
462.8
539
D8
D9
D59
D158
D159
D159B
D167A
D259
D392A
D590
D935
Le Plaine River
Meurthe River
Bertrichamps
Thiaville sur Meurthe
Raon l'Etape
Baccarat
US 100th
397th
398th
399th
1 KM
FRANCE
Inset of attack on Hill 462.8 Nov 16, 1944
Ruiseau de le Forge Evrard
Blue Diamond Trail
Alpha
1st Pltn
2nd Plt
3 Plt
.30 cal
400
Approx. German Defense Lines
Places to see:
9a Baccarat Bridge
9b 1st Objective, Hill 372
9c Purple Heart Lane, Le Rouge Vetu
9d 2nd Objective, Hill 409.9
10 Hill 431
11a Parking for Hill 462.8 hike/Winterline
11b Hill 462.8 approx 11c Hill 539 approx
12 100th ID Plaque/City Hall
Movements:
A. Nov 10, 399th Regiment crossed the Meurthe River at Baccarat to begin their attack.
B. Nov 10, 398th Regiment began firing on Raon l'Etape as part of the feint for a frontal assault.
C. Nov12, elements of the 399th attacked and captured their 1st Objective, Hill 372 which overlooked Neufmaisons.
D. Nov 12-14, the 399th fought SE along the main road (D8) to Raon l'Etape to capture Hill 409.9, the 2nd Objecitve.
E. Nov 15, Company I, K, L charged Hill 431 behind a rolling artillery barrage to further clear the woods.
F. Nov 16, after a 45 minute artillery barrage, Company A, 1st Batt, 399th attacked Hill 462.8, after bitter fighting and hand to hand combat they captured the hill and quickly set up fields of fire with foxholes and their 2 .30 cal MGs.
G. Nov 16, the Germans counterattacked from the north with a company then again with a platoon.
H. Nov 18, Company B captured Hill 468 & elements of the 398th arrived to continue attack to surround Raon l'Etape.
I. Nov 20, Raon l'Etape was finally liberated and the elements of the 100th advanced along the Plaine River valley.

OPERATION HABICHT, DECEMBER 12-14, 1944 (& US ADVANCE) MAP 64

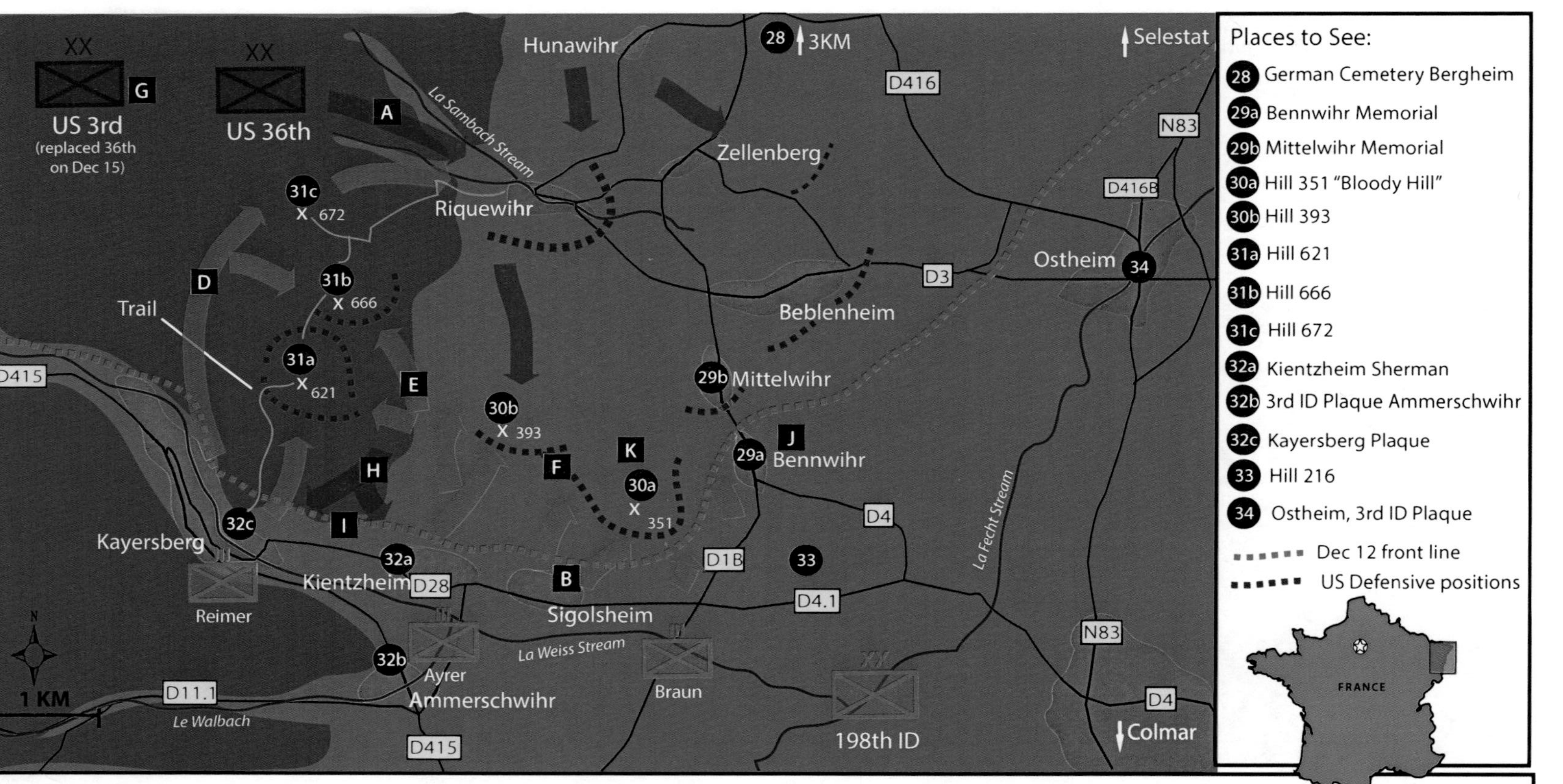
Places to See:
28 German Cemetery Bergheim
29a Bennwihr Memorial
29b Mittelwihr Memorial
30a Hill 351 "Bloody Hill"
30b Hill 393
31a Hill 621
31b Hill 666
31c Hill 672
32a Kientzheim Sherman
32b 3rd ID Plaque Ammerschwihr
32c Kayersberg Plaque
33 Hill 216
34 Ostheim, 3rd ID Plaque
Dec 12 front line
US Defensive positions
FRANCE
US 3rd
(replaced 36th on Dec 15)
US 36th
Hunawihr
3KM
Selestat
La Sambach Stream
Riquewihr
Zellenberg
Beblenheim
Ostheim
Mittelwihr
Bennwihr
Trail
Kayersberg
Kientzheim
Sigolsheim
La Weiss Stream
Ayrer
Ammerschwihr
Braun
Reimer
198th ID
La Fecht Stream
Le Walbach
Colmar
1 KM
D415
D416
N83
D416B
D3
D4
D1B
D4.1
D28
D11.1
X 672
X 666
X 621
X 393
X 351

Movements:

A. Dec 5, elements of the 36th ID liberated Riquewihr.

B. Dec 9, US forces held Sigolsheim for a few hours until they were pushed out.

C. Dec 11-12, the Germans pounded the American positions and towns. Next the 198th VGD attacked Selestat.

D. Dec 12, the German attack began at 0700, on the west flank, Regiment Reimer attacked Hill 672 to position for an attack on Riquewihr. They attacked the town from 0840 to 1130 but had to pull back.

E. In the middle, Regiment Ayrer could not advance due to heavy fire from Hill 666 and Hill 621. With the aid of units from Reimer they took Hill 666 but were unable to dislodge the Americans from Hill 621.

F. Dec 12-14, Hill 351 and Hill 393 held their ground until the third attack, the Germans from Regiment Braun captured the Hills after bitter hand to hand fighting on December 14. The Germans also captured Sigolsheim and still held Bennwihr.

G. Dec 14, Operation Habicht was ended with major casualties and little gains. Dec 15, the 3rd ID replaced the tired 36th ID.

H. Dec 16, the 3rd ID went on the offensive.

I. Dec 18, Kayersberg and Kintzheim were liberated.

J. Dec 22-24, Bennwihr was attacked and liberated.

K. Dec 22-28, Sigolsheim & Hill 351 were retaken.
(not shown on map, too busy)

Note: Ostheim & Hill 216 were not taken until late January when the Colmar Pocket attack began. See map 66 for that battle.

OPERATION NORDWIND & SONNEWENDE, DEC 31 - JAN 27, 1945 MAP 65A

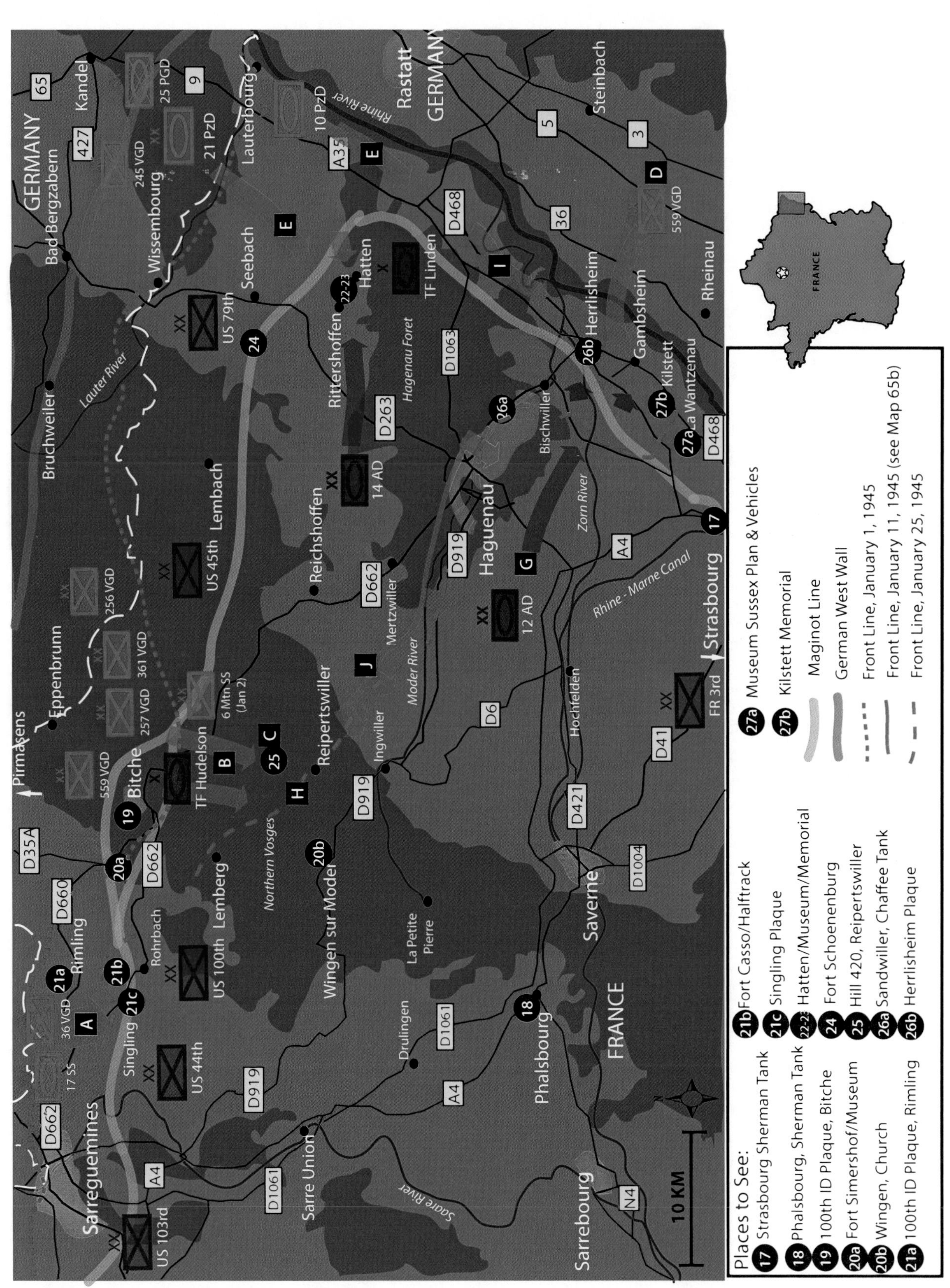

Places to See:
17 Strasbourg Sherman Tank
18 Phalsbourg, Sherman Tank
19 100th ID Plaque, Bitche
20a Fort Simershof/Museum
20b Wingen, Church
21a 100th ID Plaque, Rimling
21b Fort Casso/Halftrack
21c Singling Plaque
22-23 Hatten/Museum/Memorial
24 Fort Schoenenburg
25 Hill 420, Reipertswiller
26a Sandwiller, Chaffee Tank
26b Herrlisheim Plaque
27a Museum Sussex Plan & Vehicles
27b Kilstett Memorial
Maginot Line
German West Wall
Front Line, January 1, 1945
Front Line, January 11, 1945 (see Map 65b)
Front Line, January 25, 1945
10 KM
GERMANY
FRANCE
Bad Bergzabern
Kandel
Wissembourg
Lauterbourg
Seebach
Rastatt
Steinbach
Rhine River
Lauter River
Bruchweiler
Lembach
Reichshoffen
Rittershoffen
Hatten
Hagenau Foret
TF Linden
Herrlisheim
Gambsheim
Kilstett
La Wantzenau
Rheinau
Bischwiller
Haguenau
Zorn River
Mertzwiller
Moder River
Strasbourg
Rhine - Marne Canal
Hochfelden
Ingwiller
Reipertswiller
Eppenbrunn
Pirmasens
Bitche
TF Hudelson
6 Mtn SS (Jan 2)
Northern Vosges
Lemberg
Wingen sur Moder
La Petite Pierre
Rohrbach
Rimling
Singling
Drulingen
Phalsbourg
Saverne
Sarre Union
Saare River
Sarreguemines
Sarrebourg
US 103rd
US 44th
US 100th
US 45th
US 79th
14 AD
12 AD
FR 3rd
17 SS
36 VGD
559 VGD
257 VGD
361 VGD
256 VGD
245 VGD
25 PGD
21 PzD
10 PzD

OPERATION NORDWIND & SONNEWENDE, CONTINUED

MAP 65B

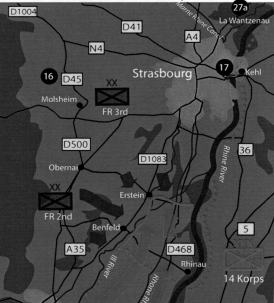

Sonnewende Attack from South, Jan 7-11:
D1004
D41
A4
N4
D45
D500
D1083
36
5
A35
D468
3
27a
16
17
37
28-42
La Wantzenau
Marne Rhine Canal
Strasbourg
Kehl
Molsheim
XX
FR 3rd
Obernai
FR 2nd
Erstein
Benfeld
Rhine River
Rhinau
Ill River
Rhone Rhine Canal
14 Korps
Selestat
F
Ettenheim
106 Bgd
198th ID
10 KM
Marckolsheim

Movements:

Nordwind

A. Dec 31 at 2330, Sturmgruppe 1 attacked with the 17th SS Panzer Grenadiers & 36th VGD but were stopped by the 44th ID and 100th ID.

B. January 1, Sturmgruppe 2 attacked with 4 Divisions with some success. With little options, Germans committed their reserve, the 6th SS Mountain Division Regiment which broke through and captured Wingen sur Moder, over running elements of the 70th ID.

C. January 6, the US forces redeployed the 103rd, 36th, 14th AD and 12th AD to bolster defenses and on January 8, the Americans recaptured Wingen, marking the end of Nordwind.

Sonnenwende

D. January 5, the 553rd VGD and armor units crossed the Rhine, captured Gambsheim and created a bridgehead.

E. January 6, Blaskowitz's Army Group G forces, 21st PzD, 245th VGD, 25th PGD attacked south along the Rhine River to link up with Gamsheim. From January 6 to 20, bitter fighting ensued around Hatten. The Germans pushed through the stubborn defenses of the 79th ID; in response Americans committed the 14th AD.

F. January 7, the 198th VGD and 106th PzB attacked from the Colmar pocket to link up with Gambsheim but this attack was called off on January 11 after very little success.

G. January 8, the 12th AD failed in an attack on Gamsheim. Then on January 12-19, the 12th AD attacked in force with additional set backs until the attack was called off.

H. January 20, the Americans pulled back their line of defense to the Moder River and dug in. But in the south the Allies began Operation Cheerful to reduce the Colmar Pocket. (see Map 66)

I. January 22, the Germans finally linked up with their Gambsheim forces.

J. January 24-25, the Germans attacked with 5 divisions with little success. The Americans counterattacked and pushed the Germans back to their defensive lines.

K. January 27, Germans called off all offensive operations, transfered forces to Russian Front and dug in.

OPERATION NORDWIND & SONNEWENDE, CONTINUED

MAP 65C

Encirclement of elements of 157th Regiment, January 15-20, 1945

Movements

A. Jan 13, 2nd Battalion, 157th Regiment, 45th ID took up positions on Hill 415.
B. Jan 14, F, K, L, I Companies of 3rd Battalion attacked north to take Hill 420 and 410. Meanwhile, on the right flank 1st Battalion attacked Hill 363 & 390 but failed.
C. Jan 15, K Company reached Hill 420 with little German resistance. L Company took up Hill 410, I Co held up in the saddle. They repulsed 3 fierce German attacks.

D. Jan 16, C Company in an attempt to take Hill 390, went around Hill 363 up into Hill 410 area and was stuck in a German attack on the forward companies.
E. Jan 16, B Company tried to reach the units but only reached the forward slope of Hill 341.
F. Battalion Command created a composite company (CC) to secure a supply route to the forward units which was successful in evacuating wounded & bringing in supplies by using M8 Armored Cars, trucks and Stuart Tanks until midnight.
G. After midnight the Germans encircled the forward units.

H. Jan17, Battalion request for withdrawl was denied.
I. Composite Company & 2 tanks failed to clear path to units, until midnight a Stuart reached the unit. It was ambushed the next morning and destroyed.
J. Jan 18, Germans attacked & overran Company G's line.
K. 2nd & non-trapped 3rd Battalion units attacked. 3rd Battalion used 3 armored cars with no success. 2nd Battalion used 2 Shermans and rescued a platoon.
L. Jan 19, 2nd Battalion attacked again to rescue and 1st Battalion attacked Hill 363 & 390 with 4 Shermans via the Fliesshal Draw. Both attacks failed.
M. Jan 20, 2nd Battalion, 411st Reg, 103rd ID attacked 3 times and failed to breakthrough over Hill 415 to Hill 363.
N. Battalion Command tried once more to link up with surrounded units at 1530, only 2 men escaped. (158 KIA, 350 WIA and 426 POWs(many WIA).

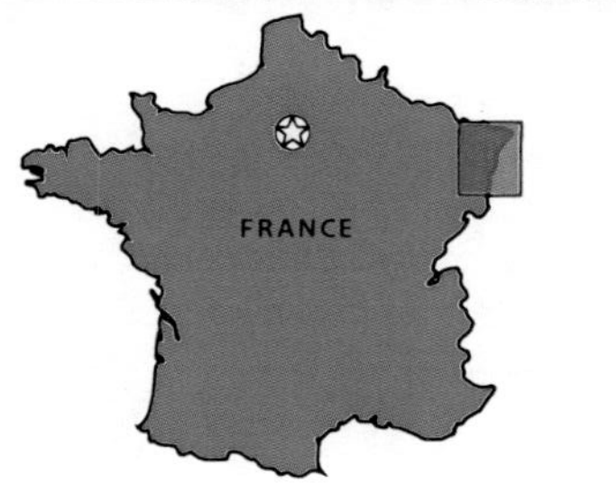
FRANCE

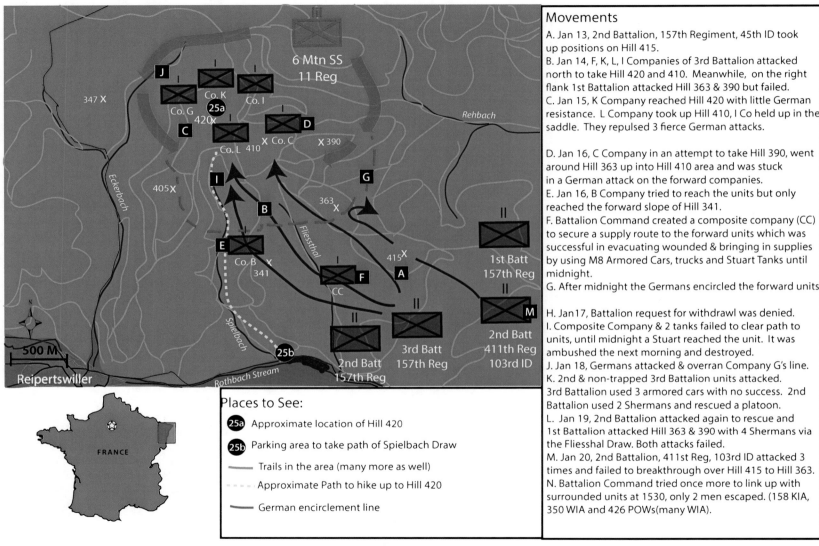

Places to See:

- 25a Approximate location of Hill 420
- 25b Parking area to take path of Spielbach Draw
- Trails in the area (many more as well)
- Approximate Path to hike up to Hill 420
- German encirclement line

OPERATION CHEERFUL, COLMAR POCKET JANUARY 19 - FEBRUARY 9, 1945 MAP 66

Movements:

A. Jan 20,the French attacked from Mulhouse and drew out the German reserves but stalled in gaining ground.
B. Jan 21, the main attack began with the US 3rd ID driving east over the Ill River then south towards Neuf Breisach
C. Jan 22, the French 1st ID began to grind down the Erstein Bulge.
D. Jan 23, elements of the 708th VGD overran 3rd ID near the Ill River, past the bridge at Maison Rouge. (just east of Ostheim on D3)
E. Jan 26, Audie Murphy stopped a German attack near Holtzwihr, resulting in him being awarded the Medal of Honor. (#40)
F. Jan 27, Himmler departed theatre.
G Jan 29-30, the US reached the Colmar Canal and the 3rd ID attack was reinforced with the arrival of the 28th ID, 12th AD and 75th ID.
H. Feb 1, Rasp the German commander began to withdraw men.
I. Feb 2, the 28th ID started clearing the suburbs of Colmar. (S of #40)
J. Feb 3, the French 5th AD entered Colmar central with tanks.
K. Feb 5, the 75th ID & 3rd ID captured Neuf Breisach & cutoff the major German escape routes. (bridge & barges)
L. Feb 5, the French Morrocan 2nd ID & US 12th AD linked up at Rouffach, which trapped 4 German Divisions.
M. Feb 5, Rasp ordered all out withdrawl via Chalampe.
N. Feb 8, Hitler finally "approved" a withdrawl from the pocket. (too late)
O. Feb 9, the French 2nd AD from the north linked up with the French 9th Colonial Division at Chalampe and pushed the last Germans across the Rhine River. This forced the Germans to blow the bridge the same day.
**A few letters are not shown because it would be too crowded!

Allied Exploitation/Attack Routes
German Front Line January 19
Allied gains January 20-31

Places to See:

- 3-8 **Push to St. Die(Lost Battalion, etc)**
- 9-12 **Attack over the Meurthe River**
- 13 Badonville Sherman Tank
- 14-15 Natzwiller & Alsace Peace
- 16 Fort Mutzig
- 28-32 Op Habicht & Dec Battles
- 33 Hill 216
- 34 Ostheim, 3rd ID Plaque
- 35 M10 Tank Destroyer, Illhaeusern
- 36 M4 Sherman Grussenheim
- 37 Marckolsheim Museum
- 38-39 Jebsheim Memorial & Pillbox
- 40 Audie Murphy Memorial
- 41 Colmar Liberation Memorial
- 42a Colmar Museum (Turckheim)
- 42b German Cemetery Cernay
- 43 Fort Du Salbert
- 44 Belfort Museum, Fort & Sherman
- 45 Mulhouse Train Museum
- 46 Rosenau Sherman Tank

Other great places to see, not directly related to this battle:

- # Memorial Du Linge (See WW1 Period)
- Veil Armand Battle Memorial (See WW1 Period)
- Haut Koenigsbourg Castle (See Crusader Period)
- Vauban Museum, Neuf Briesach

Above, is the location where the 36th ID crossed the Moselle against little to no resistance. Our guide and local expert, Herve Claudon, was extremely helpful. He & his wife Sylvie provide tours and they have a B&B in the area. They specialize in tours for the battles of Bruyeres, Operation Dogface. Above right is the memorial the local French built to commemorate the crossing and US sacrifices.

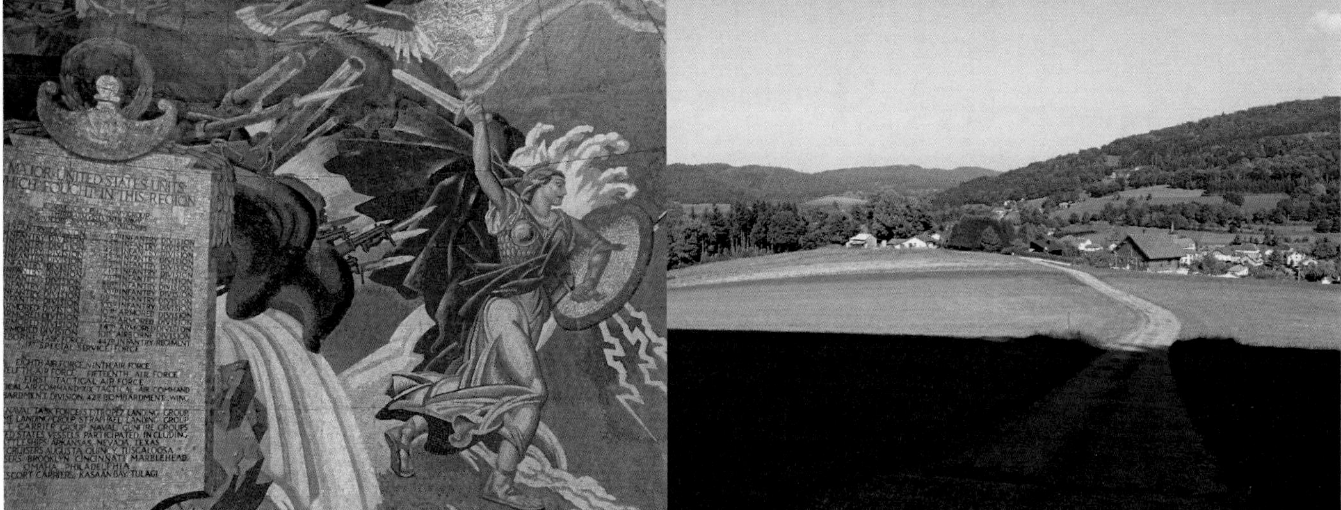

Above left is a beautiful and moving mosaic in the chapel of the American Epinal Cemetery. After the Americans crossed the Moselle and captured Epinal they faced the Vosges Mountains, this photo was taken looking east towards Tendon, just beyond Tendon is Bruyeres.

BRUYÈRES

Above left, the entrance into Bruyeres, the town surrounded by the Hills which were heavily fortified by the Germans. Lower left is the memorial to the Japanese American unit on Hill A, west of Bruyeres. The center photo is the logging trail that you can hike or drive up to see the memorial and explore the hills, the trails are certainly something you want to drive on slowly and carefully. Above right, a photo of US soldiers marching through the dark and thick Vosges Mountains. (NARA)

Far left, Hill 645 36th ID l ost battalion memorial and 442nd Regiment memorial.

Center photo, all through the woods are foxhole remains and craters.

Right photo, looking out from the logging trail on the way up Hill 645 overlooking the town of Bruyeres below.

Left: Memorial to the Thunderbird Division in Fremifontaine. Built by local French to honor the American sacrifices.

Center photo, the memorial to the 3rd ID at the Crossroads of Hell on route N420.

Photo right, captures the dangerous terrain the soliders had to fight through in the Vosges. (NARA)

Left photo is the town of Baccarat and the bridge over the Meurthe River.

Right photo: After crossing the Meurthe River, the 100th ID attacked through the trails and woods shown.

HOTEL
PIZZERIA
100
103 RD
INFANTRY DIVISION

Left photo, is Raon l'Etape, it is overlooked by hills the 100th fought for. In the photo inset is the plaque on the townhall dedicated to the 100th ID.

Photo right, is the memorial in St. Die to the 103rd ID.

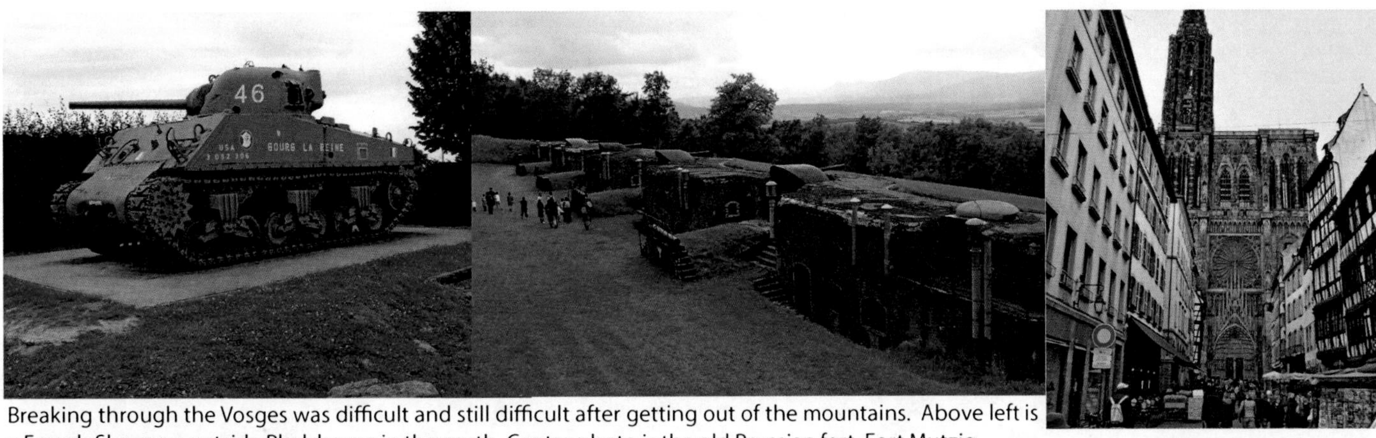
46
BOURG LA REINE

Breaking through the Vosges was difficult and still difficult after getting out of the mountains. Above left is a French Sherman outside Phalsbourg in the north. Center photo is the old Prussian fort, Fort Mutzig. And rightis the Cathedral of Strasbourg, the city was liberated on November 23, 1944.

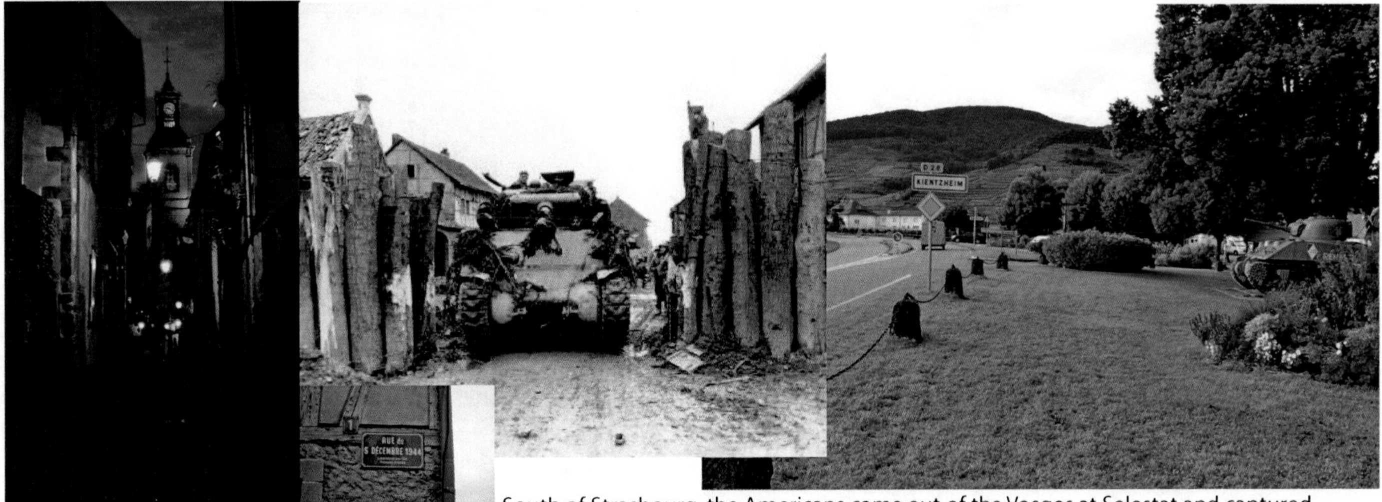
KIENTZHEIM

South of Strasbourg, the Americans came out of the Vosges at Selestat and captured other picturesque towns such as Riquewihr(left). The town's liberation is marked only with a street named, December 5, 1944. Center is an example of the unique roadblocks the Germans created. Photo right is a Sherman outside the walled village of Kientzheim, overlooked by Hill 621.

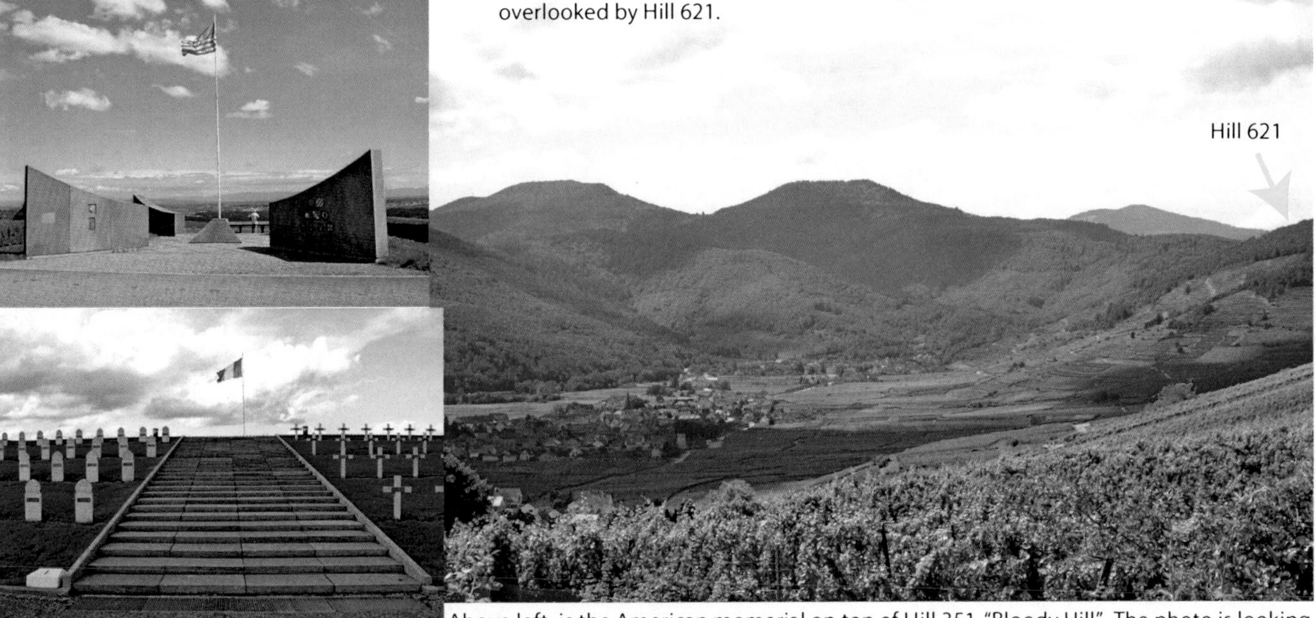
Hill 621

Above left, is the American memorial on top of Hill 351, "Bloody Hill". The photo is looking east towards Germany and the Alsace Plain. The lower photo, walking distance from the American memorial is the top of Hill 351, a French cemetery. The right photo is from the French cemetery looking west, below left is Sigolsheim, the center village is Kientzheim and the far town is Kayersberg. The hill to the right is Hill 621 which the Germans attacked up.

PLAINFAING
The sun setting and the moon rising over the Vosges.

American soldiers marching over the snow covered mountains.

Wingen, cleaning up the town from German occupation, it was one of the hotly contested towns during Operation Nordwind. (NARA) The above right photo is of Wingen today, where the plaque to honor the defense and liberation by the 70th ID is located.

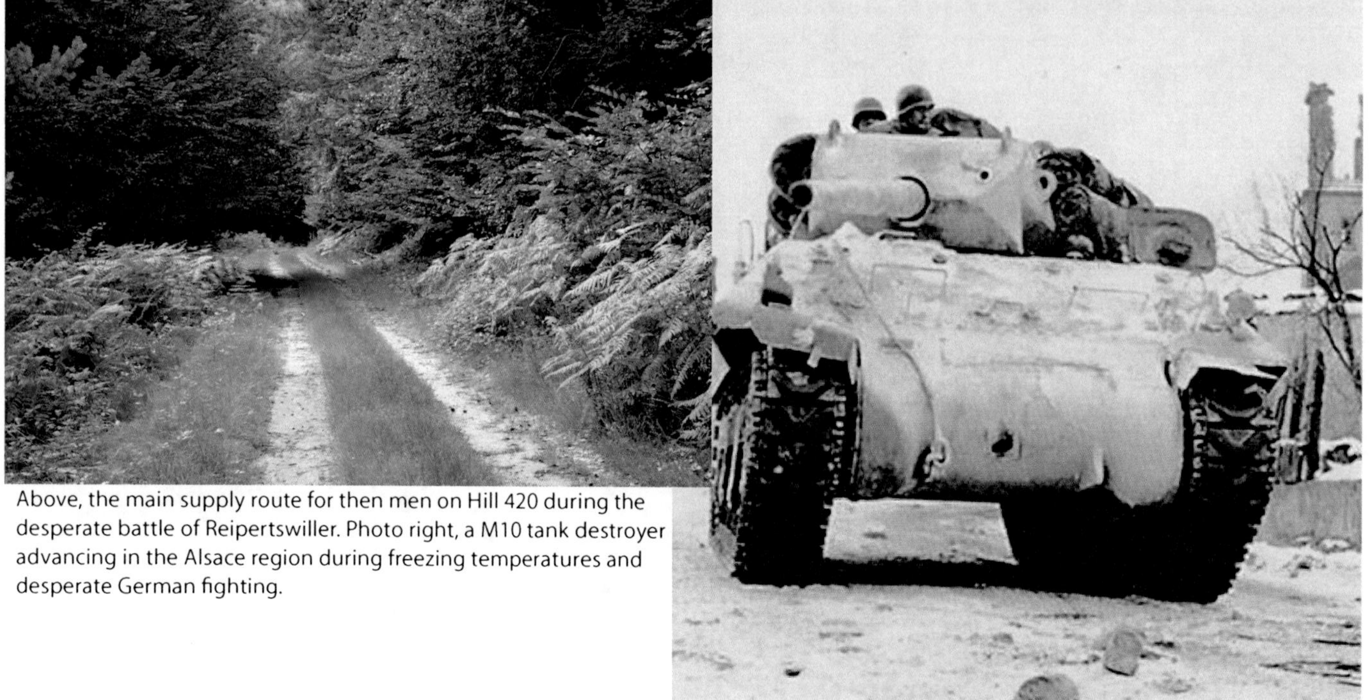
Above, the main supply route for then men on Hill 420 during the desperate battle of Reipertswiller. Photo right, a M10 tank destroyer advancing in the Alsace region during freezing temperatures and desperate German fighting.

2573 R

Far Left, Illhaeusern, M10 TD memorial park.

Left, Holtzwihr memorial to Audie Murphy. The painted steel memorial is an image of Murphy on top of an M10.

The above left M10 was destroyed by the far left Nashorn or one out of that battalion. (NARA)

As well as destroying the M10, the Nashorn unit destroyed the Sherman, photo left located outside of Grussenheim.

Far left, in the beautiful town of Turckheim is the museum dedicated to specifically the Colmar Pocket.

Center photo is of the remains of a building in Ostheim and the plaque to the 3rd ID. Photo left is a memorial in the town of Bennwihr.

Left, the stork is one of the symbols of Alsace. Many of the towns have nests for the migration of the birds to the south. Left photo is an attempt to capture the beauty of Alsace.

One of the Jagdpanthers with the deadly 88mm cannon located in Jebsheim. They reeked havoc on the US forces. Left, Jebsheim Memorial outside of the town.

Far left: Belfort the French fort and objective in the south. Left is looking at the "gap" / valley that is on the approach to Belfort. On the horizon is Switzerland.

Far left, another photo of Belfort from Fort Salbert.

Left, the map for the town of Neuf-Brisach. It was a Vauban masterpiece. It was captured by the 3rd ID to cut off the German retreat across the Rhine.

Far left, a photo of the beautiful town of Ribeauville. Just behind it you can see the hills and vineyards.

Slightly north outside of Bergheim is the German Cemetery up on the hills overlooking the Alsace plains and Rhine River.

NAZI OCCUPATION, FRANCE,

June 1940–December 1944

SUMMARY: After the invasion of France, the Germans occupied the country's northern zone and allowed the elected Vichy government to administer southern France. During this time, the Vichy French cooperated with the Germans to hunt down rebels, Jews, Communists, resistance fighters, Gypsies and other "undesirables." Of the approximately 350,000 French and foreign Jews in France, it is believed 76,000 were deported and died in extermination camps. Many others, including French soldiers, were used as forced labor to build the Atlantic Wall, maintain weapons factories, etc. Following are memorials and museums dedicated to record the history of concentration camps located in France.

1. **STRUTHOF CONCENTRATION CAMP, NATZWILLER:** Located on top of a mountain, this was the only "concentration" (as compared to "internment") camp in France. Toward the end of the war, a gas chamber was installed; in it, more than 80 people were killed. In total, approximately 5,000 were killed from overwork, medical experiments, poor nutrition, executions (in the case of Special Operations Executive agents) and beatings. It is a generally well-preserved location and offers a very well done memorial and museum.
   N 48 27.241 E 7 14.996 (48.454012, 7.249938)

2. **DRANCY:** Located outside Paris, this camp was used to intern French Jews. Starting in 1942, more than 65,000 French Jews were deported from this location to the Polish death camps. At the site is a small park that stands where the building once stood. It includes a monument and deportation rail car.
   N 48 55.122 E 2 27.245 (48.9187, 2.454083)

3. **CAMP ROYALLIEU INTERNMENT CAMP, COMPIEGNE:** Located here are the remaining buildings of a 25- barrack camp used to deport more than 45,000 people, including prisoners of war and political internees, to concentration camps outside of France. The memorial and museum contain artifacts, documentation and stories about the people who suffered in the camp.
   N 49 24.170 E 2 48.486 (49.402833, 2.8081)

4. **INTERNMENT CAMP, GURS:** Located near the Pyrenees, this camp was originally built for refugees from the Spanish Civil War. When the "phony war" began, the camp was used to intern people of German descent, including German Jews fleeing from Germany. It was under Vichy government control and, in 1942, at the government's command, handed over 5,500 Jews to the Nazis for deportation to extermination camps. The location contains a newly built memorial, information center and walking path.
   N 43 16.412 W 0 44.335 (43.273533, -0.738917)

5. **INTERNMENT, TRANSIT AND DEPORTATION CAMP, CAMP DES MILLES:** Just southeast of Aix-en-Provence is a memorial/museum and grounds to explore. This concentration camp held many writers, artists and political opponents. Today it houses new and permanent exhibits. Its grounds are largely intact.
   N 43 30.209 E 5 22.963 (43.503483, 5.38271)

Chapter 9

ALL THE YEARS, MUSEUMS AND MONUMENTS

Following are locations that do not pertain to a specific battle or era but rather maintain military artifacts related to a range of conflicts.

1. **MUSÉE DE L'ARMÉE, PARIS:** This museum contains the tomb of Emperor Napoleon and also many pieces of history, from a great collection of medieval knight armor to World War II artifacts. I can't say enough how well done this museum is, and how complete. It's a must see if you are in Paris.
   N 48 51.487 E 2 18.706 (48.858117, 2.311767)

2. **MUSÉE DES BLINDES SAUMUR TANK MUSEUM:** Probably the best tank museum in the world. It offers a large range of tanks; perhaps the only close comparison is the tank museum in Russia. Almost all the tanks you can think of are in working order; check out the museum's website (www.museedes-blindes.fr) to learn when it holds its tank parade.
   N 47 14.631 W0 4.284 (47.24385, -0.0714)

3. **BAYEUX TAPESTRY MUSEUM (MUSÉE DE LA TAPISSERIE DE BAYEUX) :** This is a newly renovated museum located in Bayeux, near Normandy. It contains the famous Bayeux Tapestry, which depicts the invasion of England by William the Conqueror in 1066. It is certainly a very important piece of history and well worth a visit.
   N 49 16.448 W 0 42.030 (49.274133, -0.7005)

4. **SAINT REMI MUSEUM, REIMS:** This museum has a room dedicated to local military history, but the majority of it is dedicated to St. Remi, the founder of Reims, who converted the king of the Franks, Clovis, to Christianity.
   N 49 14.590 E 4 02.422 (49.243162, 4.040362)

5. **SURRENDER MUSEUM, REIMS:** In this small museum is a memorial, displays and information about the unconditional surrender of Nazi Germany, which took place on May 7, 1945 at 0241.
   N 49 15.727 E 4 01.572 (49.262117, 4.0262)

6. **MUSÉE GUERRE ET PAIX:** Located between Reims and Sedan, this museum covers all the wars, specifically, the Franco-Prussian War, World War I and World War II. It has an excellent collection of tanks and materiel.
   N 49 36.035 E 4 25.067 (49.600589, 4.417784)

7. **MUSÉE DE L'ARTILLERIE DE DRAGUIGNAN (FRENCH ARTILLERY MUSEUM):** This is located in southern France near the American Cemetery of Dragunian and maintains a collection of various artillery pieces from throughout the ages.
   N 43 31.609 E 6 29.795 (43.526817, 6.496583)

8. **RETHONDES CLAIRIERE DE L' ARMISTICE, WORLD WAR I AND WORLD WAR II, COMPIEGNE:** This is where the Allies signed the World War I armistice. It contains a monument and small museum with a replica of the rail car where the armistice was signed. At this location, Hitler had the French sign their surrender agreement in the same rail car. At the end of the war, Hitler took the rail car; it was blown up by the Germans in 1945 to avoid another surrender signing!
   N 49 25.633 E 2 54.383 (49.427217, 2.906383)

9. **THE FREEDOM TRAIL:** There were several escape routes that downed pilots could take from occupied Europe. This is just one location with a memorial to those who helped these men escape into Spain. More than 33,000 French and 6,000 servicemen escaped over the Pyrenees. The Le Chemin de la Liberté is a four-day hike that retraces the dangerous path to Spain for the escapees and their resistance fighter escorts. It starts in Saint-Girons and ends over the Pyrenees.
   Saint-Girons Bridge: N 42 59.038 E 1 08.658 (42.983967, 1.1443)
   One memorial on the path is located near Bagnères-de-Luchon:
   N 42 43.245 E 0 39.298 (42.72075, 0.654967)

10. **NOSTRADAMUS MUSEUM, SALON DE PROVENCE:** Stated to be Nostradamus's residence, this museum in Provence between Orange and Aix-en-Provence has just been renovated and includes seven rooms of well-done wax figures and information about Nostradamus's life and prophecies.
    N 43 38.443 E 5 05.856 (43.640709, 5.097605)

IV. REFERENCE SECTION

A. WORLD WAR II APPROXIMATE UNIT BREAKDOWNS:

The following is a guide to the "approximate" breakdown and quantity of units during World War II. The numbers change when one looks at the German, American, Russian and British forces. The Germans, for example, had more firepower in their Armor Divisions and their Panzer Grenadier Divisions. Also, down to the platoon, the Germans had more squad machine guns per platoon as compared to the Americans; thus, the Germans maintained more firepower to overcome the same number of troops. Firepower and maneuver were two key aspects. Also, the Russian divisions maintained only about 8,000 men per division.

TASK FORCE AND KAMPFGRUPPE: You will hear these terms (for example, "Kampfgruppe Peiper" or "Task Force Cherry") a lot. "Task force" was a term used by the Americans and named after their commander. The same goes for a Kampfgruppe, which was named after a German commander. Task forces and Kampfgruppes were units pulled together, sometimes hastily, to bring a lot of firepower and maneuverability to a fight. They consisted of a mix of medium tanks, tank destroyers, halftracks, artillery and infantry. They were set up for a specific goal; for example, Task Force Cherry was quickly set up as a means of stopping/delaying the German advance on Bastogne. On the German side, Kampfgruppe Peiper was set up as the "hard point" of the German thrust on the northern shoulder during the Battle of the Bulge.

U.S. GROUND FORCES

Name	Quantity Of Men	What?	Map Symbol	Commander Rank
Army	200,000	2 or more Corps	XXXXX	4 star Colonel General
Corps	30,000	2 or more Divisions	XXX	3 star or Lt. General
Division	15,000	2-4 Brigades/Reg	XX	2 star or Major Gen
Brigade	3,000	2-4 Regiments/ Brig	X	1 star or Brgd Gen
Regiment	1500-3000	2-4 Battalions	III	Colonel
Battalion	500	2-4 Companies	II	Lt. Colonel
Company	150	3 Platoons	I	Captain or Major
Platoon	40	3-4 Squads	...	Lieutenant
Squad	5-12	1-3 Fire Teams	..	Corporal/Sgt
Fire Team	4		0	Lance Corporal/Sgt

ARMOR FORMATIONS

The use of armor varied greatly among the combatants due to differing capabilities and theories. For example, the Americans built tank destroyers – such as the M10 Wolverine and the M18 Hellcat – that, while maintaining less armor, were faster than medium or heavy tanks and maintained higher-caliber cannon. Their purpose was to remain in the rear until the German armor showed up; then the tank destroyers would rush into battle.

AMERICAN ARMOR

The American armor divisions varied in terms of organization throughout the war. Initially, they maintained brigades, which ultimately became too large to move and support. By the end of the war, the divisions had developed combat commands, of which there were typically two or three per division. This setup allowed for more flexibility and combined warfare. The combat commands contained armor battalions, infantry battalions and artillery. In total, a U.S. armored division had approximately 180 medium tanks, 80 light tanks, 54 self-propelled howitzers and 500 halftracks.

U.S. ARMOR DIVISION
(DOES NOT INCLUDE NUMBERS FOR ARTILLERY AND INFANTRY)

Name	Quantity of Tanks	What?
Division	216+	3 Combat Commands*
Combat Command	108+	3 Battalions
Battalion	36+	3-4 Companies
Company	12	3 Platoons
Platoon	4-5	

***In addition to the combat commands, the Americans had divisional artillery, support elements and reconnaissance squads. In some cases, there were no combat commands, but simply battalions.*

GERMAN PANZER DIVISION

The Germans experimented with various sizes of armor formations. Initially, they had two regiments of tanks in each division; however, this proved to be too much. After the invasion of France, the Germans reduced their Panzer divisions to one Panzer regiment of approximately 150 tanks, two Panzergrenadier regiments with halftracks, a self-propelled Panzerjager battalion with 20 or more tank destroyers and PAK 75mm cannons, an artillery regiment with three battalions and a recon battalion with light tanks and armored cars. In all, a pretty formidable force, similar to the American makeup.

Name	Quantity of Tanks	What?
Panzer Army	600+	2-3 Korps
Panzer Korps	300+	2-3 Divisions
Division	200+	4 Regiments*
Regiment	150	2 Battalions
Battalion (Abteilung)	36	3 Companies
Company (Kompanie)	12	3 Platoons
Platoon (Zug)	4-5	

**1 Panzer regiment, 1 Panzerjager battalion, 2 Panzergrenadier regiments, 1 armored recon battalion, 1 artillery regiment*

RUSSIAN ARMOR

At the highest level, the Russians maintained tank corps that contained three each brigades with 93 tanks each. Therefore, approximately 200 tanks were in a tank corps. A tank corps also had a motorized rifle brigade and supporting artillery. Therefore a Russian Corps was really equal to a German Division.

BRITISH ARMOR

The later-war British armor divisions had one tank brigade, one motorized battalion of infantry and one infantry brigade. They could typically deploy 200 to 300 tanks per division.

U.S. ARMY AIR FORCE

Name	Quantity of Aircraft	What?
Command	576	3-4 Wings
Wing	192	4-5 Groups
Group	48	3 Squadrons
Squadron	16	4 Flights
Flight	4	2 Wingmen, 2 Leaders

BRITISH AIR FORCE

Name	Quantity of Aircraft	What?
Command	576	3-4 Groups
Group	192	4-5 Wings
Wing	48	3 Squadrons
Squadron	16	4 Flights
Flight	4	2 Wingmen, 2 Leaders

RUSSIAN AIR FORCE

Name	Quantity of Aircraft	What?
Army Corps	324	3-4 Divisions
Division	108	3 Regiments
Regiment	36	3 Squadrons
Squadron	12	3 Sections
Section	4	2 Wingmen, 2 Leaders

GERMAN AIR FORCE (LUFTWAFFE)

Name	Quantity of Aircraft	What?
Luftflotten (Air Fleet)	1250	3-4 Korps
FliegerKorps	324	3-4 Geschwader
Geschwader (Group)	108	3 each Gruppen
Gruppen	36	3-4 Staffeln
Staffeln	12	3 Schwarm
Schwarm	4	2 Wingmen, 2 Leaders

B. BIBLIOGRAPHY

Amt, Emilie. (2001) Medieval England 1000–1500. Ontario: Broadview Press, p. 335

Bartlett, W.B. (1999) The Crusades an Illustrated History. Gloucestershire: Sutton Publishing

Bishop, Chris and Rosado, Jorge. (2005) Wehrmacht Panzer Divisions 1939-1945. London: Amber Books

Blumberg, Arnold. (2014) "The Fall of Cherbourg" Strategy & Tactics Edition 289

Blumenson, Martin. (1961) Breakout and Pursuit. Washington, D.C.: U.S. Government Printing Press

Chandler, David G. (1994) On the Napoleonic Wars. Mechanicsburg: Greenhill Books

Chevallier, Gabriel. (2011) Fear. London: Serpeant's Tale

Clarke, Jeffery and Smith, Robert Ross. (1995) Riviera to the the Rhine. Minnetonka: National Historical Society

Featherston, Alwyn. (1993) Battle for Mortain. Novato: Presidio Press

Ford, Ken. (2005) Falaise 1944 Death of an Army. Oxford: Osprey Publishing

Griess, Thomas (2003) Atlas for The First World War. New York: Square One Publishers

Griess, Thomas (2002) Atlas for The Second World War. New York: Square One Publishers

Gurley, Franklin L. (2000) Into the Mountains Dark. Bedford, PA: The Aberjona Press

Harpur, James. (2005) The Crusades an Illustrated History. New York: Thunder's Mouth Press

Harrison, Gordon. (1951) Cross Channel Attack. Washington, DC: U.S. Government Printing Press

Holt, Tonie and Valmai. (2004) The Western Front – North. Barnsley: Pen & Sword Military

Holt, Tonie and Valmai. (2005) The Western Front – South. Barnsley: Pen & Sword Military

How, Major J.J. (2004) Hill 112 Cornerstone of the Normandy Campaign. London: J.J. Fedorowicz Publishing, Inc.

Hucht, Patrick. (2011) The Knights Templar. Rennes: Ouest-France

Jorgensen, Christer. (2007) Great Battles. Bath: Parragon

Junger, Ernst (2003) Storm of Steel. New York: Penguin Books

Kebric, Robert B. (1996) Roman People. Mountain View: Mayfield Publishing Company

Keegan, John. (1976) The Face of Battle. New York: Penguin Books

Keegan, John. (1998) The First World War. New York: Vintage Books

McGilvray, Evan. (2010) The Black Devils' March. West Midlands: Helion & Company

McMeekin, Sean. (2010) The Berlin Baghdad Express. New York: Penguin Books

Merriman, John. (2014) Massacre. New York: Basic Books

Moczar, Diane. (2005) Ten Dates Every Catholic Should Know. Manchester: Sophia Institute Press

Mueller, Robert. (2009) Fields of War. Buffalo Grove: French Battlefields

Munoz, Antonio J. (1999) Iron Fist: A Combat History of the 17 SS Panzergrenadier Division. New York: Axis Europa Books

Nicolle, David. (2004) Poitiers 1356. Oxford: Osprey Publishing

Nicolle, David. (2008) Poitiers AD 732. Oxford: Osprey Publishing

Nightingale, Keith. (June 2013) "The Battle of Graignes." The American Legion June 2013, 30-36

Pallud, Jean Paul. (2013) "The Battle of Metz." After the Battle, Number 161
Pallud, Jean Paul. (2007) "The Riviera Landings." After the Battle, Number 110
Reardon, Mark J. (2002) Victory at Mortain. Lawrence: University Press of Kansas
Roberts, Andrew. (2009) The Storm of War. New York: Penguin Group
Rudigoz, Rene-Charles. (1979) La Bataille de Meximieux. Trevoux: Acheve D'Imprimer
Stars and Stripes. (2010) The Story of the 45th Infantry Division. Whitefish: Kessinger Publishing
Strachan, Hew. (2003) The First World War. New York: Penguin Books
Wedgewood, C.V. (2005) The Thirty Years War. New York: The New York Review Book
Wilson, Derek (2006) Charlemagne. New York: Doubleday
Zaloga, Steven. (2000) Lorraine 1944. Oxford: Osprey Publishing
Zaloga, Steven. (2009) Operation Dragoon 1944. Oxford: Osprey Publishing
Zaloga, Steven. (2010) Operation Nordwind 1945. Oxford: Osprey Publishing
Excellent Websites for reference and information:
www.45thdivision.org
www.audiemurphy.com
www.tracesofwar.com
www.uswarmemorials.org
www.liberationroute.com
www.home.eckerd.edu
www.ibiblio.org/hyperwar/USA/USA-E-Breakout/USA-E-Breakout-24.html
www.aerosteles.net
www.standwheretheyfought.jimdo.com
www.abmc.gov (American Battle Monuments Commission

C. ACKNOWLEDGEMENTS

This book was only possible from the support of many friends, family and history enthusiasts. The book was written over a period of 4 years as a hobby as time permitted. I was extremely lucky to have the opportunity to travel overseas for work and be in close proximity of many of the locations.

During this time, my family was always supportive in providing feedback and ideas for the book. I dedicated the book to my mother who always provided us the unconditional love and encouragement to believe that we can achieve anything. My words and this book would never be enough to express how much she did for us. My father has always shown us through example the importance of military history and even more so the importance of meeting, recognizing and honoring our veterans. His example inspired me to write this book to encourage others to embrace the history and honor our veterans. I greatly appreciate all my family and friends who have helped and encouraged me. Many thanks to friends in Germany and those who visited me in Germany who were always helpful, patient and open to seeing just one more Sherman tank, "Tanks for the memories!" Also many thanks to those that kept me on pace to stop procrastinating!

Big thank you to those that contributed with technical and professional expertise such as Laura and Tammy for their valuable artistic skills in the early stages of making maps, Anita helping design the cover, Tonya for the multiple edits and Matthew for professionally preparing the book for publishing.

I would not have traveled to many of the places without the inspiration and help of many friends I met along the way such as: the wild Dutchman Ron von Rijt, Jean Siret in Fremifontaine and Herve and Sylvia Claudon in the Vosges. In addition many thanks to all the caretakers from the American Battle Monuments Commission, the patriots, the historians and museum caretakers that I met along the way. I greatly appreciate everyone's assistance and support!

Made in United States
North Haven, CT
11 December 2022

28462954R00215